*John Wilkes: The Scandalous Father
of Civil Liberty*

ARTHUR H. CASH

John Wilkes

THE SCANDALOUS FATHER
OF CIVIL LIBERTY

Yale University Press
New Haven
& London

Published with assistance from the Annie Burr Lewis Fund and from the
foundation established in memory of Philip Hamilton McMillan of the Class of
1894, Yale College.

Set in Sabon type by Keystone Typesetting, Inc.
Printed in the United States of America.

Library of Congress Cataloging-in-Publication Data
Cash, Arthur H. (Arthur Hill), 1922–
John Wilkes : the scandalous father of civil liberty / Arthur H. Cash.
p. cm.
Includes bibliographical references (p.) and index.
ISBN-13: 978-0-300-10871-2 (alk. paper)
ISBN-10: 0-300-10871-0 (alk. paper)
1. Wilkes, John, 1727–1797. 2. Great Britain—Politics and government—1760–
1789. 3. Freedom of the press—Great Britain—History—18th century. 4. Civil
rights—Great Britain—History—18th century. 5. Politicians—Great Britain—
Biography. 6. Journalists—Great Britain—Biography. I. Title.
DA512.W6C37 2006
941.07′3′092—dc22
2005016633
A catalogue record for this book is available from the British Library.

10 9 8 7 6 5 4 3 2 1

For Hilarie, Anna, and David

If you know why you should read about John Wilkes, you may skip this paragraph. If you think that John Wilkes shot Abraham Lincoln, you may not. If you think voters have always been represented by people whom they have elected, read on. If you think a violent street mob cannot contribute to civil liberty or that a nobleman in a carriage drawn by four horses cannot be part of a protest march this story may surprise you. If you think that sexual politics is a modern invention, you may learn something here. If you think newspapers always have been free to report what goes on in government, you need this book. If you think the founding fathers of America had no support from England, this is required reading. If you believe dirty books should be burned, pause to think before you continue. If you think that blue-collar workers should not be allowed to vote, this book is not for you. If you think the police have the right to arrest forty-nine people when they are looking for three, shut it now. If you think that people should be imprisoned for writing essays against the government, I have nothing to say to you.

There are no imaginary characters, events, or conversations in this book. The story is based upon primary materials, letters, newspapers, legal documents, parliamentary records, and the work of qualified biographers and historians.

A Greek chorus to this drama will be provided by James Boswell, the biographer of Dr. Samuel Johnson, who adored Wilkes but disapproved of his politics, and Horace Walpole, son of a prime minister, member of Parliament, scholar, memorialist, novelist, voluminous letter writer, and wit, who did not like Wilkes but liked what he stood for. The spelling and punctuation of quotations have been modernized, and sometimes quotations have been slightly modified to make them fit the narrative.

Contents

A Preemptive Glossary

The following glossary includes words and terms whose meanings have changed since the eighteenth century or whose British meaning may be misunderstood by Americans.

Bill of Rights   A particular set of laws limiting the powers and prerogatives of the monarchy, agreed to by William and Mary in the Revolution of 1688 (which had deposed James II). The Bill of Rights effectively ended absolute monarchy.

Constitution   In Great Britain, the body of laws, not a particular set of fundamental laws against which other lesser laws are to be measured, but all the laws together.

First minister   What we would call the prime minister, a term which in the middle years of the eighteenth century was used derisively or as a joke.

First Lord of the Treasury   The position usually held by the first minister, though not always. The name for the department of the Treasury was a misnomer, a hangover from ancient times, for the department no longer handled state monies; that was done by the chancellor of the exchequer. See "Ministry, government," below.

Jacobite   One who supports the return of James II or his male descendants to the throne of Great Britain. The name was taken from *Jacobus*, the Latin form of *James*. James II, a Catholic, was forced from the throne in the Revolution of 1688 and fled to France. His Protestant daughter, Mary II, and her husband, William III, Prince of Orange, were brought to the throne. They were succeeded by James II's second daughter, Anne, who died child-less, ending the recognized Stuart line. George I, great-grandson of James I and elector of the German state of Hanover, who could not speak English, was brought to the throne in 1714. The exiled James II died in France in 1701, but his son, the "old pretender" to the throne, fomented three re-bellions in Scotland early in the eighteenth century, all of which failed. The next in line, Charles Edward Stuart, the "young pretender" (in Scottish myth, "Bonnie Prince Charlie") led a major rebellion in 1745–46, con-quered Scotland, and came close to conquering England. In Wilkes's time, *Jacobite* usually meant a participant in or supporter of "the '45."

Lord, as an honorary title   Americans can be confused by the honorary uses of the title *Lord*. It is given to the mayors of London, "My Lord Mayor," to the dignitaries of the civil courts, "Lord Chief Justice Mansfield," and to bishops of the Church of England. Most confusing is its use for the sons of noblemen, even though they themselves are not noblemen. Thus, "Lord North" and "Lord Strange" sat in the House of Commons.

Ministry, government   A British king in the eighteenth century appointed his own ministers and advisors without having to seek the approval of Parlia-ment. He appointed the members of a large advisory group called the Privy Council. From these he selected a much smaller group as his cabinet, which established policies and made plans. It was unusual, but a man without a place in the ministry could be seated in the cabinet. The cabinet was pre-sided over by the first minister, who usually, but not always, held the office of First Lord of the Treasury. He was the general administrator of the gov-ernment, carrying out the wishes of the king and the policies of the cabinet, and the ministry was designated by the first minister's name, the Pelham ministry or the Newcastle ministry. Typically the first minister was the leader of a faction that had control of the House of Commons. Other ap-pointments in the ministry, made by the king upon the recommendation of the cabinet and the first minister, went to members of the faction. A secre-tary of state for the north handled domestic matters, and a secretary of state for the south, called the principal secretary, handled foreign affairs. The chancellor of the exchequer handled finances, the attorney general legal matters, and the lord chancellor headed the judiciary. There were numerous lesser offices. Combined, they were called the *ministry* or the *government*, interchangeable terms. When a first minister was dismissed or resigned, his entire ministry usually left office with him, though often in piecemeal fashion. The professional servants who did the drudgery of departments usually kept their jobs with a change of ministries but had no guarantee of security.

Money values and wealth   There were twenty shillings in a pound, twenty-one in a guinea. A hired curate in a country parish, if he had a kitchen garden and a few farm animals, could live on £30 a year. The rector of the parish might live comfortably on £120 a year. The squire would be well off with an income of £800. In London, £30 could barely keep one from starvation. A gentleman might maintain his status in the city at £300 but would not think of himself as comfortable until his income reached something like £600. The least wealthy gentleman living in Grosvenor Square would have an income of some £1200, the most wealthy, impossible to say. The distribution of wealth was shockingly uneven.

Place, as a political or governmental term   The popular word for an appointment or position in the government.

Radical, radicalism   Radicalism was a movement among politicians, political theorists, printers, publicists, and voters that advocated reform of the judiciary to allow equality before the law and regularity in criminal proceedings, reform of Parliament to extend the franchise, and curtailment of the influence of Crown and ministry upon the House of Commons. After his return from exile in 1768, Wilkes was a radical. He is sometimes said to have started the movement. Radicals had nothing to do with socialism or communism, the modern versions of which were not yet known, nor did they seek to do away with the limited monarchy of Great Britain or its parliamentary system. They were reformers, not revolutionaries.

To stand, as in an election   Equivalent to American "to run" for an office.

Prologue

This book is about an audacious journalist and politician who was born in the City of London in 1726 and died in the City of Westminster in 1797, his life spanning a time that included the American Revolution, which he admired, the French Revolution, which he hated, and the industrial revolution, which he did not know was happening. In his writing, he excoriated the ministers of King George III, and he fought duels to defend what he was doing. He had a strong, lithe body, but a distorted face. Of his eyes, brown and therefore particularly noticeable in that society, the right was severely cast inward — crossed eyes, we Americans would say. He had a prognathous jaw that exposed his lower teeth when he spoke. The teeth began to fall out before he reached the age of thirty. He was told in print that his face was "an indication of a very bad soul within" and should not be exposed to pregnant women.[1] Though the face jolted whoever looked at it for the first time, it became a symbol of Liberty and as such was drawn and sketched and etched many hundreds, perhaps thousands, of times. About his addresses to women, he liked to say he needed only "twenty minutes to talk away my face." He never hid his libertine indulgences and went to prison for printing the dirtiest poem in the English language. He was not a gambler, but an impulsive borrower. He ran up mountains of debt, from which he was rescued again and again by people who would rather see him fighting for their cause than languishing in a debtors' prison. His wit was proverbial. When Lord Sandwich said to him, using a word that then meant *syphilis,* "Wilkes, you will die either by hanging or the pox," he replied, "That depends, my Lord, on whether I embrace your lordship's principles or your mistress."[2] His manly bearing and refined manners charmed all of his enemies. His fiery writing and his daring taunts to people in power galvanized the cockneys of London, whose threats of riot provided his power base. With their help he won for Great Britain and its American colonies the liberty to use rights that Thomas Jefferson said were inalienable, but the people knew were suppressible.

Wilkes was arrested by the government on the authority of a general warrant, an order for arrest that named the crime—in this case the writing and printing of *North Briton* No. 45—but not the criminal, that allowed the king's messengers to take up anyone they deemed suspicious and to seize any private papers that might contain evidence. The messengers arrested forty-nine people and seized the papers of four. Wilkes's aggressive response, his suing of the king's ministers and messengers for false arrest and illegal seizure of private papers, and his leading other of the victims in similar suits resulted in the nullification of that terrible instrument, the general warrant. At another time, Wilkes played the key role in a dramatic showdown between the houses of Parliament and the City of London that removed the prohibition against newspaper reporting of the debates and activities of Parliament, resulting in a new freedom of the press that made possible the modern newspaper. He advocated unconditional religious tolerance and the separation of church and state. He made the first-ever motion in the House of Commons to extend the franchise to all adult males, but a Parliament made up of landowners, noblemen, judges, and bishops would not accept such a change, and Great Britain would have to wait another century for an equivalent law.

Wilkes's every move was followed in the American press, and his victories over government celebrated in the colonies. He corresponded with Samuel Adams, John Hancock, and other of the founding fathers and was among the foremost supporters of American causes through essays, petitions, and speeches in Parliament. The Commons House of South Carolina sent him fifteen hundred pounds and closed down the provincial government rather than obey the royal governor's demand to rescind the gift. He might have been tried for treason if the king had learned he was secretly sending money to America during the war. Wilkes's steadfast support led to his being honored by the naming of Wilkes County, North Carolina, and its seat, Wilkesboro, and along with his fellow supporter of the American cause, Isaac Barré, the naming of Wilkes-Barre, Pennsylvania and eventually Wilkes University, located in that town.

While Wilkes was an outlaw, he was elected to the House of Commons to represent the county of Middlesex. The House refused to seat him. He was arrested but was reelected from prison — three times. An exasperated majority in the House voted to declare him incapable of election and seated his opponent, who had far fewer votes. Four years later Wilkes won his seat in a general election and, after many years of trying, in 1782 pushed through a motion to expunge from the record of the House of Commons the resolution whereby he had been declared incapable of running for election. His purpose was to make certain that the resolution would not become a precedent in law. To allow the House of Commons to declare this candidate or that incapable of election for this reason or that would allow the majority party to exclude the minority and establish a one-party oligarchy. In America the impact of his action was felt at the Constitutional Convention at Philadelphia in 1787. James Madison, using the very argument Wilkes had used, convinced the Convention to fix in law the requirements for candidacy in an election to Congress. In 1969, in a case famous among lawyers, the United States Supreme Court decided in favor of Adam Clayton Powell in his suit against the Speaker and the House of Representatives, who had excluded him. The majority opinion, written by Chief Justice Earl Warren, gives to Wilkes the credit for having seen the danger in allowing the legislature an unlimited right to exclude any individual from election and the credit for expunging the resolution that had allowed such abuse.[3] John Wilkes had established for Great Britain and subsequently the United States two closely related principles: within the simple limits of constitutional law, the people can elect as their representative whomever they please regardless of the approval or disapproval of the legislature; and they have a right to be represented by someone they have elected, and not by someone appointed to represent them. Moreover, the first ten amendments to the American Constitution, the Bill of Rights, were written by men to whom *Wilkes* was a household word. There can be no doubt, Wilkes's history lay behind the guarantees of a free press, the right to privacy, the freedom from unreasonable searches and seizures, and the prohibition of nonspecific arrest warrants.

His daring and impetuosity cost Wilkes his comfortable life as the squire of Aylesbury and sent him into banishment for four years and into prison for two. But in France he was cheered on by Diderot and the philosophes. In London he was adored by the working classes as the man who stood up for them, and while he was still a prisoner they made him an alderman of the City. When he was released, he was elected to be sheriff. Within four years he was lord mayor of London and sitting in Parliament as representative for Middlesex. He fought two duels, suffered an unhappy marriage and sundry happy affairs, begat a daughter who became his lifelong companion, an illegitimate son whom he cared for and educated, and a second daughter, illegitimate but acknowledged, who became the pet of his old age.

For a few years John Wilkes was the talk of England, America, and western Europe. Revolutionaries and sovereigns watched with keen interest his outlandish demands for liberty, his skill in marshaling popular support, his success in changing laws, and, to be sure, the flamboyance with which he moved through the world and the scandals that trailed along after him. Voltaire told him, "You set me in flames with your courage, and you charm me with your wit," and King George III called him "that devil Wilkes."[4]

I

The Making of a Gentleman

Jack, as his family and friends called him, must have been an appealing child despite the severe inward cast of his right eye and his forward-jutting jaw. There is a sketch portrait of him at about the age of twenty (illustration 1) that makes it easy to imagine the child with a twisted face smoothed over by a healthy skin, surprising, ironic in its forecast, cute. He was touching to older folk, the favorite of his father and his schoolmaster, and in his teens of the Scottish philosopher Andrew Baxter.

Jack came from a wealthy family that, to use our modern terms, was middle class but upwardly mobile. He once described himself as "a private gentleman ... of inferior, but independent condition," and he said candidly that his father was "in trade," that tag which for centuries has limited the ambitions of what then was called "the middling sort."[1]

His mother, née Sarah Heaton, was the daughter and heiress of such a middle-class man, the successful proprietor of a tannery. Her fortune enabled her husband to buy Hoxton Square on the north edge of the City of London, an area inhabited largely by Presbyterians. She had been reared a Presbyterian and would remain so all of her life. Presbyterians and Quakers and other Protestant sects outside the Church of England were recognized in English law as Dissenters, deprived of the right to hold most public offices but free to worship in their own chapels, to labor, to engage in business, and, if they had the qualification, to vote. The tastes of Sarah Heaton Wilkes were cultivated, and she owned bronze and marble statues of Greek mythical figures as well as religious and decorative paintings. It was risky to cross her. She once took her daughter to Bow Church, perhaps for a wedding or baptism, for she did not normally go there. Unable to find a seat in the crowded church, she asked a lady of higher social rank than she if she would mind sharing her box, for there were no pews at that time, only boxes containing seats assigned to particular families. When the lady refused, she went home and wrote her an excoriating letter: "I was astonished at so unpolite a refusal! But why should I soften the expression? . . . No! it will bear a more severe reflection . . . that all haughty and assuming airs is most repugnant to the mild and benevolent genius of our religion."[2] But this earliest of her few surviving letters is no key to her personality. She was a woman of cardinal virtues, loyal to her family and protective of them without dominating them. But she was strong. Her usual place of worship was a little Presbyterian chapel in Carter Lane within the shadow of the great dome of St. Paul's Cathedral.

Jack's mother was content with the social status into which she had been born, but his father was not. Israel Wilkes worshiped in the established Church of England, though he had been reared a Presbyterian. He was well educated by the standards of a day when university degrees were required of no one except clerics and professionals, but looked to a mastery of liberal arts and classical languages acquired at secondary schools or at the hands of private tutors. Israel was wealthy, having inherited from his father and uncle a prosperous distillery that stood behind the Church of St. John of the Cross and fronted on James Street. In time, he bought or built the house at the other end of the distillery, fronting on St. John's Square. He did not grow rich by selling gin to the poor, for that dangerous drink was made in the back rooms of almost every tavern. But he was a little ashamed of his business and sometimes gave it out that he was a brewer of beer. He kept a coach and four and paid a coachman, a groom, and three or four other servants. He has been said to have opened his house to bon vivants and artists and literary people, though their identities have not been established.[3]

The eldest son, also named Israel, turned out to be a restless youth of mediocre talents who squandered his father's fortune in failed trading ventures.[4] The third son, named Heaton for his mother's family, was to take over the family business. But Jack, who came between these middle-class siblings, was singled out by his father to be a gentleman, to speak the English of a gentleman, to be a scholar and a man of leisure, to wear a wig and to carry a sword. Accordingly, on Sundays his father took him to the Anglican church of St. John of the Cross, which stood in the angle between Israel's house and his distillery.

There were three daughters. Sarah, the eldest child, turned out to be a disgruntled spinster who played little part in Jack's later life. Ann, the youngest, died in her teens of smallpox. Mary, the middle girl, a tomboy, would prove a bright, eccentric woman and outlive three husbands, heiress to the first two, cheated of her inheritance by the last.[5]

Oddly, we cannot be certain in which year John Wilkes was born, for no birth record has been found for him or any of his siblings. They may have been baptized in Carter Lane chapel, but the registers for those years are lost. More likely the children were baptized at a home service, a common practice among dissenters. Very probably Jack was born on 17 October 1726, though in his maturity he habitually gave out that it was 1727.[6] October the seventeenth is an Old Style date. When New Style became official in 1752 with the dropping of eleven days from the calendar so as to give Great Britain the same calendar as that used on the Continent, Jack's birthday became 28 October, the date on which his birth was always celebrated. He was christened John for the great uncle who had been his grandfather's partner in the family distillery.

Israel Wilkes's house was located in the part of London called Clerkenwell, the largest house in a new residential development, Jerusalem Court, soon to be renamed St. John's Square. It was a handsome brick house surrounded by a fence of iron palings standing next to St. John's church and looking southward across a grassy common to an ancient Gothic arch, St. John's Gate. The cloister of the priory of St. John had once stood here, but the stones had been cleared away to prepare the space for houses. Three medieval structures remained, the arch, the gatehouse next to it, and the church. They still may be seen, but the houses around the square are gone, and noisy Clerkenwell Road now cuts through the middle of an ugly space that had once been the fashionable, grassy Jerusalem Court. Jerusalem passage at the north end of the court led to Clerkenwell Green, where children might play under the supervision of a servant, but to the south all was the bustle and hurry of the City of London. St. John's Gate itself was a beehive of activity. Edward Cave had a printing press in the gatehouse, where he published the celebrated *Gentleman's Magazine* with an image of the gate on its masthead. There Samuel Johnson turned in his essays and his reports on the debates in the parliament of Lilliput. William Hogarth, the great painter and caricaturist, grew up there, for his father had a coffee shop in the gatehouse where the customers pored over the latest issues of the *Gentleman's Magazine* and other publications. There young David Garrick, who would become the greatest actor of his age, put on his first London performance, playing the lead in Henry Fielding's *Mock Doctor* on a contrived stage in Cave's printing shop, with printers and apprentices dragooned into reading the other parts.[7] Might a boy with a cast eye have been in the audience?

Southward from the Gate all was commotion, the City of London, not greater London, but the ancient City, roughly defined by what remained of the medieval walls — the City distinct from Holborn and Westminster, the chartered "City of London," with its own laws and courts and rights, jealously guarded. Here was the world of manufacture and the Spitalfields weavers, the world of finance and the Royal Exchange, the world of business and the Guildhall, the Inns of Court (as the law colleges were called), the Old Bailey criminal court, the booksellers and printers in Fleet Street, the ships tied up at Wapping, the Protestant meetinghouses, and the magnificent Cathedral of St. Paul. Four hundred thousand persons were packed into the City, the area of which was equivalent to a single square mile, and in time most of them would become aware of John Wilkes, in time come to admire, even adore him, and in time to reward him for his sufferings. The word *sufferings* was widely used to describe Wilkes's four-year exile and two years in prison, but it must be said that he had a pretty good time during both.

Sarah Wilkes was determined not to have her sons educated in the decadent institutions of the rich. Israel was bent upon classical languages and literature. They reached a compromise: Jack and his two brothers were sent to a boarding school in Hertford run by a Presbyterian, John Worsley, who was also a classical scholar. Off the boys were packed, each as he reached the age of eight, to Hertford, to the castle at the top of the town, through a dry moat, up a set of stairs, into Tower House, an ancient fortification rising from the castle wall that had been revamped to make a residence and school for Mr. Worsley. Jack would live there for five years, not a lonely life, for he had his brothers and Worsley's boy, who was his friend. Mr. Worsley laid for Jack a foundation in Latin and Greek that would serve him well for the rest of his life. Days after he left the school, the master, brokenhearted to have lost such a pupil, wrote him a letter praising his "generous sentiments and that love of letters which I myself beheld the first dawnings of." For the rest of his life, Wilkes would regard himself as a man of letters and would attain no mean reputation as such. "Go on, dear youth," Mr. Worsley continued, "and prosper in your noble pursuits: and I pray that the giver of every good and perfect gift may not only succeed your endeavors after human knowledge and sound learning, but also enrich your mind with that heavenly wisdom which is still more excellent and valuable." Mr. Worsley was a clergyman as well as a classicist.[8]

Jack's father, delighted with his progress and promise, decided to continue his education beyond that which he would give the other boys. He sent him to Thame, Oxfordshire, to be tutored by a friend, Matthew Leeson, preacher to a Presbyterian congregation. Israel was convinced that Mr. Leeson was a first-rate classical scholar, which he may well have been, but he was no typical

Presbyterian. Late in life, he had taken up theology and was in revolt against
the doctrines of the church. "He was continually poaching in dull volumes . . .
for some new heresy," Wilkes would later write.[9] About a year after Jack
joined Leeson's family, Leeson announced to his congregation that he had
become an Arian, that is, he did not believe in the divinity of Jesus or in the
doctrines of original sin and redemption. His flock, as might be expected,
turned him out.

Sarah and Israel Wilkes, wanting to be of help, introduced Mr. Leeson to a
new convert to Presbyterianism whom Sarah had met at chapel, Mrs. Mary
Mead, née Sherbrooke, the widow of a wealthy grocer whose shop had been
on London Bridge. Mrs. Mead lived in Red Lyon Square behind the church of
St. Sepulchre in the old City. Moved by the "warmth" of her conversion, said
Wilkes, Mrs. Mead set about rescuing the wayward Leeson. She invited him to
take over an empty parsonage house that she owned at Aylesbury in Buckinghamshire. Her uncle had been the leading resident at Aylesbury and had
built Prebendal House, the largest house in that town, now Mrs. Mead's
summer residence. Leeson and two or three pupils moved into the old parsonage, a timber house fronting on the street called Parson's Fee. Jack commenced the study of French, in which language he would quickly develop a
proficiency.[10]

There is an amusing letter from the seventeen-year-old Jack to his father
when he was returning to Mr. Leeson's school after the Christmas holidays.
He describes the other passengers in the stagecoach, including a woman big-
oted against dissenters, and how he turned the laugh against her and made her
look ridiculous.[11] Though he would never leave the Church of England, Jack
would be a friend to dissenting religions for the rest of his life and a believer in
the separation of church and state.

Mrs. Mead asked no rent of Mr. Leeson. It seems odd that an enthusiastic
convert to Presbyterianism should go to such trouble for a preacher who had
been drummed out of chapel for becoming an Arian. One wonders whether
Mrs. Mead had other interests in Mr. Leeson and his pupil. It happened that
she had a daughter, also named Mary, a silent, withdrawn, unmarried woman.
In her portrait by Sir Joshua Reynolds, Mary appears to be far from ugly,
though not a beauty (illustration 2). Looks such as hers in a wealthy heiress
would seem to be good enough to attract a husband. She, not her mother,
owned Prebendal House and the estate that went with it, and she had been
named heiress to even greater riches in the wills of her mother and her rich,
unmarried uncle, Richard Sherbrook, who lived with them. Rumor said she
had rejected three suitors that the family had found acceptable.[12] The difficulty was that Mary Mead was deeply neurotic, almost catatonic, and proba-

bly unable to take the final steps toward marriage. As she grew older, her mother must have become desperate to find a husband for her odd daughter. And then she met Mrs. Wilkes, who had an odd son. Sarah Wilkes must have thought that a boy with Jack's face would never make a marriage of love, so why not one of convenience? What difference if Mary Mead was ten years older than Jack so long as she came from a good Presbyterian family and was an heiress? The mothers, it seems, decided to foster a match, but they would have to be patient. Jack was only fourteen years old when he moved to Aylesbury with Mr. Leeson. Mrs. Mead often invited him to dine.

Israel Wilkes, bent upon making his son a gentleman, fetched him one autumn day when he was fifteen or sixteen and took him to Lincoln's Inn, one of the four Inns of Court, the venerable law colleges of London. Israel had wanted his oldest son, Israel, to be a lawyer, but the young man declined to pursue that profession; and so "John Wilkes, 2nd son of Israel W., the younger, of the Parish of St James, Clerkenwell, Middlx, malt distiller," was enrolled on 17 November 1742.[13] Also enrolling at that time was Charles Townshend, son of Viscount Townshend, who would reappear at the University of Leiden in Holland when Wilkes would go there. But then, Wilkes may never have met him or any other student at Lincoln's Inn and may never have attended a lecture. Youths were often enrolled in the Inns of Court for reasons other than the study of law. Some came because membership gave them social status: it admitted them to the court of St. James. Israel more probably enrolled his son because it would make it easier for him to be accepted at the University of Leiden, which was attended by many young Englishmen of dissenting families.

In 1744, Mr. Leeson worked out a plan with the families of Jack and another pupil, Hungerford Bland, son of a Yorkshire baronet, to continue their education at Leiden. He would be their tutor at the university. English dissenters were especially attracted to Leiden because they were denied access to Oxford or Cambridge. The stones of Leiden were not as ancient, but the education was superior to that at the English universities, which were at their nadir as institutions of learning. Professorships at Oxford and Cambridge had become political appointments and were sometimes given to men who knew nothing about the subject they were to teach. Professional education in law and medicine was a little better, but by and large the only education in the arts to be had at Oxford and Cambridge was that afforded by the college tutors. At Leiden the lectures had a better reputation, but the tutoring of the young men from England was out of the hands of the university. The tutors were provided by the students' families. They would guide the young men in their studies and, their parents hoped, supervise their social lives.

In early September 1744, Mr. Leeson and his two pupils reached the lovely

1. John Wilkes at about the age of twenty, artist unknown. National Portrait Gallery, London.

old town of Leiden, with its tenth-century castle, its ancient churches and tree-shaded streets and seventeenth-century houses. On 8 September, shortly before his eighteenth birthday, Wilkes was enrolled as a student of law.[14] He and Mr. Leeson settled into a boardinghouse close to one of the oldest churches, the Pieterskerk. Wilkes's brother Israel wrote, expressing the hope of a middle-class family, that Jack would acquire "a stock of useful knowledge" and "such generous and virtuous and heroic principles as will render you useful to the world, and an honor to your friends at least, perhaps to your country and the age you live in," and warning him against "idle sophistry, effeminate pleasure, and a degenerate race of men who laugh at . . . virtue."[15] Wilkes did not much like this brother with a Puritan streak, pompously anticipating the role of family head, and had no intention of submitting to his authority.

Alexander Carlyle, a Scottish student of theology at Leiden, was startled at the first sight of Wilkes's face. "The son of a London distiller or brewer," he was told, "who wanted to be a fine gentleman and man of taste, which he could never be, for God and nature had been against him." But the students found Jack Wilkes "a sprightly, entertaining fellow" and soon got used to his face, which, for all its distortions, was a "cheerful countenance," said Dr. Samuel Johnson.[16]

Carlyle in his *Autobiography* left a lively account of his student years at Leiden, especially of the gatherings at the boardinghouse of Madam Van der Tasse. "In the evenings about a dozen of us met at one another's rooms in turn three times a week and drank coffee and smoked tobacco, and chatted about politicks, and drank claret, and supped on bukkam [Dutch red herrings] and eggs and salad, and never sat later than twelve o'clock."[17]

Though the young scholars hardly knew it themselves as yet, they formed a brilliant coterie. Carlyle would one day make a mark as the leader of the Broad Church Presbyterians of Scotland; John Gregory was destined for the professorship of philosophy at Aberdeen and then of medicine at Edinburgh; Mark Akenside was already recognized as an important poet for his *Pleasures of the Imagination;* and both William Dowdeswell and Charles Townshend would one day be chancellors of the exchequer, the treasurers of England.

"Though Jack was but eighteen," said Carlyle, he was "passionately desirous of being thought something extraordinary" and "fond of shining in conversation — very prematurely, for at that time he had but little knowledge." In shining he was outdone by Charles Townshend, though Townshend had even "less furniture in his head." Townshend would one day prove himself such a brilliant speaker in the House of Commons that no ministry seemed able to do without him. Though he was slippery in his loyalties and far to the right of Wilkes in politics, he and Wilkes remained secret friends and protected one another.[18] They are both remembered today, Wilkes for his reforms of legal and electoral systems and Townshend for the Townshend Duties imposed upon the American colonies with disastrous results.

No records were kept of the students' academic programs or performances, but Wilkes, said Carlyle, had a thirst for learning. Before that, there were other thirsts to be satisfied, as Wilkes was later to explain: "I was always among women at Leiden. My father gave me as much money as I pleased, so I had three or four whores and got drunk every night. I woke up with a sore head in the morning, and then I read."[19] Little wonder that Carlyle should report, "Even then," in his teens, "he showed something of the daring profligacy, for which he was afterwards notorious." Mr. Leeson must have known what was going on and blinked at it, probably because he had been told by Israel Wilkes that young gentlemen abroad were supposed to be initiated into the mysteries of love.

Only a few weeks after he arrived in Holland, Wilkes met an older man whom he greatly admired and who admired him in turn. Andrew Baxter was a respected Scottish theologian who was tutoring two students at the University of Utrecht, thirty miles to the east of Leiden. A gifted teacher, Baxter had declined holy orders to take up the life of a tutor, though at the moment he was bored, having lived for five long years in inns with two dull pupils who were more interested in hunting the boar than hunting knowledge. In the autumn of 1744 before lectures commenced, he was taking his tutees for a brief holiday at Spa, that famous watering place in western Germany, when by chance he met Leeson and his two charges, who it happened were also going to Spa. Enjoying each other's company, they decided to make one party and travel together. Baxter soon fell under the spell of young Jack. Wilkes, with his keen intelligence, his mastery of Latin and French, his lively way of talking, his hunger for learning, was the most interesting young man Baxter had met in many years. They began to have philosophical talks and, as eighteenth-century gentlemen seem always to do, went for long walks as they talked. There was a lovely garden at Spa built among the ruins of a monastery, and Mr. Baxter in later years remembered with particular pleasure the talk he and Jack had while walking about the Capuchin Gardens.[20]

Baxter was a deeply religious man, but an intellectual trained in theological controversy. His fundamental postulate was that all matter was inert, by which he meant at rest. Because matter changes, he argued, it must be constantly acted upon by some immaterial principle, a view that earned him the popular sobriquet Immateriality Baxter. His ideas were anathema to the scientists of the day, caught up in Newtonian physics, but they appealed to many men of religion. His *Enquiry into the Nature of the Human Soul* (1733) and his dialogue *Matho* (1740) had been well received, but recently he had fallen out of favor because of his theory that dreams were caused by divine spirits.[21]

Baxter's ideas excited young Wilkes, who was seeking a way to maintain his religion in an intellectual world that threatened it. Leeson was no help, constantly teasing John about his orthodoxy and trying to make an Arian of him, even to the point of declaring that he did not believe the Bible, "which produced a quarrel between them," said Carlyle, "and Wilkes for refuge went frequently to Utrecht, where he met with Immateriality Baxter. . . . This gentleman was more to Wilkes's taste than his own tutor for though he was a profound philosopher and a hard student, he was at the same time a man of the world, and of such pleasing conversation as attracted the young."

Baxter was hardly back at Utrecht before he began writing a new dialogue, which he called "Histor," the central character of which was based upon Wilkes, and the topics discussed were taken from Wilkes's and Baxter's conversation walking through the Capuchin Gardens. Baxter and Wilkes began a correspondence which went on for some years. Baxter's letters to Wilkes survive, though unfortunately Wilkes's letters to Baxter are lost. Baxter had a son in whom he was deeply disappointed — "a thoughtless fellow, and fit only to be a soldier." So, in Baxter's mind at least, Jack became his surrogate son. The poor man was not well, and in 1747 he would return to his wife in Scotland. His final philosophical work was to be "Histor," and in his last years it became powerfully important to him to publish the book and thereby to honor the young man he so admired. "You are the Hero of my Dialogue. I would do Justice to your character: If I succeed in that, I am not so diffident of the rest. If I do not succeed, I shall burn my Papers, which is the next best thing I can do." To his great disappointment his bookseller finally turned down "Histor." "I wrote too much in passion which should be avoided in these matters."

Andrew Baxter never saw Wilkes after he left Leiden, and three years later he died. His last letter, dictated from his death bed, was addressed to Wilkes. When the *Introduction* to part 2 of the *Enquiry into the Nature of the Human Soul* appeared posthumously in 1750, it included a dedication to Baxter's favorite person in all the world, John Wilkes. Wilkes, some years later, for no discernable reason except to pay tribute to him, privately published his friend's penultimate letter under the title, *A Letter from Andrew Baxter*.[22]

Wilkes made another lasting friendship at Leiden, this one with someone his own age, the only youth in Madam Van der Tasse's smoke-filled rooms who was not from Britain, Paul-Henri Thiry d'Holbach, later called the Baron d'Holbach and famous as a philosophe, atheist, and host to the intellectuals of Paris. D'Holbach was a German, born with the surname Thiry at Edesheim in the Rhineland. Orphaned, he was adopted by a wealthy uncle who gave him his own surname, d'Holbach, and made him and his sister heirs to the vast fortune he had made in Paris. When Wilkes met d'Holbach, he was living as the squire of the uncle's estate at Héese, though he would soon become a naturalized citizen of France and move to Paris. Being intensely intellectual, he spent the academic terms at Leiden studying the physical sciences. Falling in with the circle of English and Scottish students, he singled out Wilkes and made him his friend. He later wrote about the memory he treasured of their conversations as they strode along the Cingle, "a fine walk" along the Rhine, sometimes talking until morning. It was the closest friendship that either made at the university. When Wilkes would flee to France in 1763, he would be welcomed by d'Holbach and petted by his friends, the philosophes. When Wilkes's daughter Polly was abroad, d'Holbach and his wife would look out for her. It was a life-long friendship between youths who would become in time two of the most interesting and influential men in Europe.[23]

What were they talking about on those midnight walks? Perhaps Baxter's philosophy. We know that Wilkes read Baxter's book and thereafter gave up theology. We know that d'Holbach was still outwardly a Roman Catholic but moving toward deism, a faith in God but not in the church. A few years hence Denis Diderot would convince him to give up *any* belief in God; but at the time when d'Holbach met Wilkes, he had not yet embraced the materialism for which he and Diderot are now famous. Today we usually think of d'Holbach as the materialist and atheist who coedited with Diderot the famous *Encyclopédie*, wrote numerous articles for it, and sat at the head of the most brilliant table of intellectuals in the history of France. What had this great man learned from the English friend of his youth? What did Wilkes learn from him? We do not know, but one is left pondering the possibility that ours might be a different world had not these young men walked along the Cingle and talked until morning.[24]

In one of his letters, d'Holbach tells about going home to find his uncle's house taken over by the Austrian army.[25] The War of the Austrian Succession was the general European war fought here and there throughout Europe from 1740 to 1748. France, Spain, Prussia, and other German states were ostensibly contesting the rights of Maria Theresa and the Hapsburg dynasty to Austria but actually were engaged in a landgrab. Britain supported Maria Theresa.

The Jacobite Rebellion of 1745, led by Charles Edward Stuart ("Bonnie Prince Charlie"), son and heir of the pretender to the throne of England and Scotland, was actually a part of this war, a halfhearted attempt by France to invade Great Britain. In August, Prince Charles Edward set sail from France with a tiny force of expatriots in cast-off French ships, landed in Scotland, rallied the Scottish clans (who, being Catholic, had been loyal to the prince's grandfather), marched to Edinburgh, took control of Scotland, and began a bold march into England. All Scotsmen abroad fell under suspicion, and Baxter and his tutees were spied upon and had their mail searched. Wilkes hastened to London, where he joined the Loyal Association, men preparing to meet this threat.[26] But before he was called upon to take up arms, the rebellion collapsed, and he returned to Leiden.

Wilkes left the university in June or July 1746. By this time, said John Almon, his early chronicler, "his manners were elegant and polite, and his conversation gay and entertaining."[27] He left without a degree, but gentlemen of leisure seldom took degrees, which by and large were for professional men. But he had learned much about law at Leiden. He never sought admission to the bar, but he would serve many years as a judge, first as a justice of the peace in Buckinghamshire, then as an alderman of the City of London; and history records no fault in these services. But most of his accomplishments in law would come from the position of the man accused. In his contests with the government, his weapon would be law, and his successful reforms would be reforms of law.

As to Wilkes's liberal education, one can see the effects in James Boswell's record of a conversation in Italy in 1764. Boswell had sought out the by-then famous Wilkes, who was living in Naples with his mistress, and the two had become friends. One afternoon Wilkes found Boswell dispirited. "What shall I do to get life over?" he asked. Wilkes replied cheerfully, "While there's all ancient and modern learning and all arts and sciences, enough for life of three thousand years." "Yes," said Boswell, "but what about fate and free will?" Wilkes would have none of such worries: "I talked to Baxter of the immateriality of the soul and read his two quarto volumes, and have never thought of the matter since." Then he added, "But I always take the sacrament." And then he added further, "Dissipation and profligacy . . . renew the mind. I wrote my best *North Briton* in bed with Betsy Green."[28]

2

The Squire of Aylesbury

"Jack, have you got a purse?" Israel Wilkes asked his son when the boy was yet a small child. "No, sir." "I am sorry for that, Jack. If you had, I should have given you some money to put in it." Some days later, "Jack," asked his father, "have you got a purse?" "Yes, sir." "I am glad of it. If you had not had a purse I would have given you one."[1] In those days fathers paid so little attention to small children, I am sure Jack took it as a compliment that his father teased him. Still, the story makes one uncomfortable because it reveals a father's indifference to his son's feelings. The same indifference was to have serious consequences.

When Wilkes was yet underage, Israel arranged his marriage with the pitifully neurotic Mary Mead. He was twenty, she thirty. One of Wilkes's friends described her as a woman who "had lived a recluse, under the roof and subjected to the restraint of her mother; and she was now advanced too far in life to alter habits which had been so long contracted under the esteem and affection of a parent whom she dutifully loved, and almost adored."[2] Chronically beset with fears, Mary would not leave her mother's side, would not appear in public without her, would not appear in public *at all* except at Presbyterian chapel.

Wilkes, home from Leiden for a few weeks in the summer of 1746, went for a visit to the Mead-Sherbrooke family at Aylesbury. The evening before he took his leave, he wrote to his mother, "I am infinitely obliged to this excellent family for their exceeding kind treatment. I must own to you I shall part from them with great regret." He had known Mary since he was a boy, and they had grown to like each other. Probably he could make her laugh. Within the protection of her house, she seems to have mustered charm enough to allow Jack to trick himself. He wrote the news of his engagement to d'Holbach and Baxter: she was lovely, charming, he was in love. John Wilkes and Mary Mead were married on 23 May 1747 in the Church of St. John of the Cross.[3]

The marriage was doomed from the start: "In my *non-age* to please an indulgent father I married a woman half as old again as myself. . . . It was a sacrifice to Plutus, not to Venus. . . . Are such ties at such a time of life, binding? — and are school-boys to be dragged to the altar?"[4]

Jack now found himself an outsider in an established extended family consisting of his wife, his mother-in-law, and her widowed brother, Richard Sherbrooke. They were, each in his or her own right, rich. Jack's income was modest: at his marriage his father had given him lands that yielded £450 per annum, enough for a gentleman, but a no-frills gentility. The Mead-Sherbrooke-Wilkes family spent the colder months in London, as did most gentle families, not in a brick house in the fashionable West End, but in a gloomy old timber house in Red Lyon Court, a passage that connected Cock Lane to the backyard of St. Sepulchre's Church. John Almon, who sometimes dined with them, described Wilkes as a husband who patiently tolerated his wife, "the woman in the world most unfit for him . . . an extremely civil and complaisant husband, rather cold, but exactly well-bred." His mother-in-law's friends saw another sort of husband. A certain Mrs. Fleming, a guest for dinner, was shocked at his grumbling at the table about the meal: "There are many ways to dress a calf's head, but plain boiling is the very worst." She told how Wilkes one day happened upon a gathering of Presbyterian ladies who had just returned from listening to a particular preacher and were chatting about him. He wanted to know what they were talking about, and when they told him, he burst out, "I hate your damned Gospel gossips."[5] Marriage was expected to have a public face, and even husbands who did not love their wives took them to the theater, to balls, to court, to Ranelagh Gardens or Vauxhall. But this couple would never appear in public together after their wedding day — except in a court of law.

Aylesbury, to which the family moved in the summer, was a day's coach drive westward from London. An old town with timber houses crowded around two cores, a green in which stood the parish church and a market square. A regular stop on the road linking London and Oxford, it was the economic center of Buckinghamshire. It had many inns and taverns, and to the market the farmers and cottage industrialists brought their produce and

2. Mary, wife of John Wilkes, nèe Mary Mead, by Sir Joshua Reynolds, 1755. Courtesy of Sotheby's.

goods. It was a lively town compared to Buckingham, further to the west, which was the political center of the county, a pocket borough in control of the powerful Grenville family. The Mead house, Prebendal House, faced the green surrounding the church. It had once been part of a prebend, an estate that in the Middle Ages had provided income to a particular church officer, a preben-

dary or canon of a cathedral. That office having been abandoned in the Refor-
mation, the new Church of England had sold or given away the estate. One
small wing of the house was old, but the main house was one of the newer
buildings of the town and its largest residence. It is still there, now occupied by
the publisher Ginn and Co., a handsome house in the Queen Anne style, not
sprawling, but tall, gathered, dignified. The front overlooks the churchyard;
the vista from the back at that time took in broad gardens, fields, and woods,
all belonging to the prebendal estate.

But the house was not John's. His wife's great uncle had built it, his wife
owned it, and the Sherbrookes had been established in Aylesbury for generations. Having no confidence in this young husband, they had talked Wilkes's
parents into a marriage settlement that placed the Aylesbury estates in the
hands of trustees, a device commonly used to keep the wealth that a woman
brought to her marriage out of the hands of her husband. A mature man
would have said no, but Wilkes had submitted to the wishes of his elders. After
all, the trustees would see that the profits would be used for the benefit of the
couple and any offspring they might have.[6] Of course. How could he, not yet
twenty-one, take charge of this house or this family, especially since they were
Puritans in spirit, and he fancied himself a cavalier?

Yet from this unpromising marriage arose the happiest and most enduring
relationship of Wilkes's life. On 24 August 1750, a daughter was baptized at
Carter Lane Chapel. She was named Mary after her mother, but would be
called Polly. Like her father, Polly had brown eyes, unusual in that world. Alas,
she also had something of her father's prognathous jaw.[7] She and her Papa
adored one another.

In 1752, five years after the marriage and two after the baby, the Mead-
Sherbrookes decided to abolish the marriage agreement and allow Wilkes the
husband's right to ownership of the property the wife had brought into the
marriage. The lease of Prebendal House and the ownership of various farmlands, some as distant as Lincolnshire, passed to Wilkes's sole ownership.[8]
Possession devolved upon him the title of Squire of Aylesbury, an honor
granted originally to Mrs. Mead's uncle when he was made high sheriff of
Buckinghamshire.

Since in that world property qualified the owner for public office, almost
overnight Wilkes became a public man. He was made a churchwarden, a
feoffee of the Free Grammar School, and a trustee of the turnpike. These
offices demanded considerable time, but they rewarded the holder with honor
in the community.

In our age, when people are compensated with money for virtually every
public service, it is hard to imagine how in the eighteenth century men of every

class except the indigent poor took part in government and contributed a considerable portion of their time and money to it with no reward but honor. In the parish, which was the smallest unit of government, the demanding offices of constable, beadle, overseer of the poor, or overseer of the highways were taken in turns by local people who not only served, but also met whatever expenses the job entailed. County and borough governments depended upon boards of governors and appointed officers, such as the returning officers responsible for counting and reporting the votes in elections. It was considered shameful for a squire or a City trader not to contribute generously to the campaign fund of his party, and members of Parliament served without salaries. It was by the unrecorded efforts of individuals, as much as by the historical monarchs and generals, that the English political system had been moved out of the chaos of the Elizabethan age toward the relatively ordered system of the eighteenth century. We who think of Shakespeare and Donne when we think of Elizabeth I and James I are usually unaware of the overwhelming arbitrary and cruel power exercised by these monarchs, the contingency of office, the uncertainty of ownership of land, and the near slavery of peasants and soldiers and sailors. We forget that Sir Walter Raleigh financed the Jamestown colony by piracy, by taking everything of value from four Spanish galleons and murdering the sailors, that he himself was ordered to the block by his king on the flimsiest excuse.[9] Yet a century and a half later, the problems of organizing society and government had been solved, though imperfectly. The constitutional historian Sir David Lindsay Keir wrote, "In no European country save Holland were freedom of discussion and intellectual liberty more complete or individual rights so adequately protected."[10] Such vast and rapid changes in the political institutions and practices could not have been made without the concerted efforts and sacrifices of ordinary people.

Israel Wilkes must have felt that his son's credentials as a gentleman were complete when at the age of twenty-eight he was sworn in as a justice of the peace. Wilkes was unusually well qualified to be a justice because of his training in law. In the system of the day, justices were the main extension of the law into rural communities.[11] At Aylesbury the men and women who had been arrested for misdemeanors were tried without a jury before Justice Wilkes in the County Hall, a handsome new building on the south corner of the market square. The punishments that Squire Wilkes meted out for those he had found guilty were fines or the stocks or the whipping post. Cases of felony, which by definition were punishable by transportation or hanging, he remanded to the summer assize courts for a trial by jury presided over by the king's judges.

We get a glimpse of Justice Wilkes in letters his sister Sarah wrote while she was visiting at Aylesbury in the summer of 1755. Little Polly, she reported, "is the present tyrant; and the grave justice; my brother, is not half so absolute in this place as she . . . he writes nothing but warrants for noisy, quarrelsome fellows." Her little brother Jack, whom she called "his worship," was "as solemn all the morning as a City alderman and as upright, I assure you, as a candle in a socket." "My little niece is the prettiest play-thing in the world," Sarah Wilkes continued; "she diverts me ten times more than my squirrels or door mouse." Sarah was in mourning for the door mouse, for it had died when she failed to cover it one chilly night. Wilkes could not have enjoyed a visit from this older sister, who suffered a depression almost as deep as that of his wife. Still unmarried at thirty-four, Sarah wrote about the name Wilkes, "Alas! I fear I shall carry the odious name to the grave with me." Ten years later she would die, still unmarried.[12] No doubt she had the cursèd Wilkes jaw.

Wilkes had little interest in the typical squirearchical sports of hunting and shooting. He was interested in the house itself and made extensive repairs and changes. He purchased several pieces of property into which he extended the garden. An enthusiastic gardener, he was pleased that it would cost only eighty pounds a year to maintain it, a sum that would have comfortably maintained a farmer's family. Perhaps it did, for most of it went to pay Thorpe, his gardener. His democratic ideals somewhere in the future, Wilkes ordered the servants to deny access to riffraff, but to open the gates to any gentlefolk who might wish to see the garden.[13] He much admired the gardener, and when Thorpe died in 1751, Wilkes had a monument to his memory prepared with an inscription from Virgil's *Eclogues,* "The laurel and myrtle wept for him," which he planned to mount on the wall of the churchyard. The parson when he heard of the plan objected to having a heathen poet cited in a churchyard, but Wilkes explained that Virgil was the prophet of Christ, and that calmed him — or so Wilkes said. The monument is still there, looking over the gravestones.

Wilkes spent much of his time reading. His habit was to rise early and to study before breakfast. With eyes focusing two inches in front of his face, he must have held the book up to his nose or covered one eye. He built a library at Prebendal House of nearly 1,000 volumes. Roughly 175 of these were in French, around 275 in Latin, and some 20 in Greek. Alas, he had to sell the library in 1764 when he was forced to flee the country, but did that stop his collecting? For his second library, sold after his death, the auction house printed a sale catalogue for 1500 books. The collections included works of philosophy, science, fiction, law, and parliamentary history. His mastery of Latin was admired, his French was fluent. Late in his life he would publish editions of Catullus and Theophrastus. Wilkes was one of the few people of his time who could still read the black letter, or Gothic, type that had predominated before the Restoration period. He persisted in reading it even though it made his damaged eyes ache.[14]

Wilkes had friends at Aylesbury from the time when he had lived in Parson's Fee with Mr. Leeson. Leeson himself was there, in the old parsonage; but he was old and would not live long.[15] A neighbor, John Dell, whose family operated a brewery at Aylesbury, had been a fellow student of Mr. Leeson's. Few people in the town had a university education, but an exception was the Rev. Mr. John Stephens, vicar of the church and headmaster of the local grammar school, who had been a fellow of Exeter College, Oxford, and would be granted a doctor of divinity degree in the near future. He lived in the new parsonage next door to Prebendal House and was courting Dell's sister. Both Dell and Stephens admired Wilkes and would work hard for him in his future political campaigns.

No doubt Wilkes followed protocol and called upon and was called upon by the squires whose houses were within a one- or two-hour ride, among them Sir William Stanhope of Eythorpe, Sir Francis Dashwood of West Wycombe, Thomas Edwards of Turrick, and Dr. Thomas Brewster of Burton-court.

Edwards was old enough to be Wilkes's father, but he and Wilkes had a lively friendship. They talked about Homer and Cervantes and Shakespeare, they exchanged books, and they were forever sending back and forth game and fish. They or their friends or their servants were hunters and fishermen, and dead animals must soon be eaten. But a barrel of oysters?[16] Wilkes idealized Edwards, comparing him to Addison and Steele's famous fictional squire of the *Spectator Papers,* Sir Roger de Coverley. But Edwards was a writer, which de Coverley was not, and Wilkes may have learned from him that a pompous clergyman who busies himself in literature is fair game. Edwards had written the *Canons of Criticism,* a stinging satire of the Rev. Mr. William Warburton's edition of Shakespeare, though considerably more polite than Wilkes's later satire of Warburton in the Essay on Woman.[17]

Wilkes had a friend in John Willes, the filazar of Middlesex. If you have never heard of a filazar, be not embarrassed. The filazar was an officer who issued writs and other papers of the Court of Common Pleas in London. The presiding judge of the court was John's father. The filazarship was not precisely a sinecure, but young Willes did not spend a lot of time at Common Pleas. Wilkes saw him mostly in London, but the family had extensive landholdings at Aylesbury. The younger son, Edward, was one of the two parliamentary representatives for the town.[18]

Wilkes seemed to have a knack for friendships with medical men. Dr. Thomas Brewster practiced at Bath and introduced Wilkes to that most popular watering place for the gentry and literati of England. Bath would color Wilkes's life, for there he would meet some of the most vivid of his friends and lovers. Dr. Brewster was a bibliophile, a student of the classics, and a man of taste, but something of a roué.[19]

John Armstrong, a Scottish physician who had migrated to London, had a considerable reputation as a poet. His *Art of Preserving Health,* a poem that ran to eight hundred or so couplets, was one of the more successful books of the time. He also wrote literary criticism and published in 1753 a thin quarto entitled *Taste: An Epistle to a Young Critic.* He frequently offered guidance to Wilkes in his book buying and reading. He did not recommend *Tristram Shandy:* "Such a pert insipid crazy, conceited, pedantic, impertinent piece of Buffoonery never had the impertinence to show its posteriors in broad daylight before." Wilkes paid no attention: *Tristram Shandy* was his favorite novel.[20] Armstrong, who had been reared a poor Scotsman, was enchanted with Wilkes's life as a squire, about which he wrote a sort of pastoral poem called *Day: An Epistle to John Wilkes of Aylesbury, Esq.* Like many of Wilkes's friends, he was something of a libertine, having published in 1763 a humorless erotic piece, *The Oeconomy of Love.* Finding that the piece was damaging his reputation as a physician, he tried to disown it.[21]

Armstrong introduced Wilkes to his Scottish countryman, Dr. Tobias Smollett, the celebrated novelist. Smollett was a close friend to a cousin of Wilkes's, Robert Nesbitt, son of Wilkes's paternal aunt Deborah. This was a literary circle. Cousin Nesbitt was a lawyer and the author of *An Essay on the Necessity and Form of a Royal Academy for Painting, Sculpture and Architecture.* Smollett's novel *Roderick Random* had been the hit of 1748 and *Peregrine Pickle* in 1751. When Wilkes met him, he was preparing to open his great *Critical Review,* sort of the *New York Review of Books* of that time. Armstrong was one of its four anonymous reviewers. Though Dr. Johnson was the leading literary figure of the midcentury, Smollett was on his way to becoming the second. Neither Smollett nor Armstrong was in love with his work as physician, and both strove to make their livings as men of letters. Armstrong never attained that goal, but Smollett made money as well as a reputation by his written work. Smollett admired Wilkes the squire and once declined an invitation to Aylesbury, explaining, "I am sure I should there find much more agreeable company, and much better cheer than ever Plato, or at least than ever his master Socrates, knew; nor at your table should I have any reason to complain that the *sal atticum* was wanting." "Attic salt" was a common metaphor for wit.[22]

Jack Wilkes, the youngest among these friends, delighted them with his generosity, his liveliness, his wit, and, yes, his naughtiness. "I hope I shall live to see you as good as you are agreeable," wrote Willes, "as religious as you are sincere, and as much inclined to serve the public as you are capable of."[23] "My heart is with you wherever you go," wrote Armstrong, "whether you ramble around the cheerful country, or indulge the genial hours with the jovial Bucks [a nickname for men of Buckinghamshire], or sport rompingly with the wild panting does."[24] True, romping with the does went with the role of squire, even with the straight Thomas Edwards. Wilkes described Edwards's festival for his tenants and neighbors in his hall, enjoying "the long loud laugh sincere" and "the kiss, snatched hastily from the sidelong maid on purpose guardless, or pretending sleep. The leap, the slap, the haul, and, shook to notes of native music, the respondent dance." One understands why Wilkes was anxious to get out of London to visit Edwards, and why his wife "moved heaven and earth" to prevent him.[25]

These gentlemen had normal heterosexual drives, but for libertinism, Wilkes outdid the others. He sometimes entertained them in the company of Peggy, his mistress of the day, "dear coy wanton Peggy," Armstrong called her. Smollett, too, enjoyed the company of Wilkes when he was with his Peggy and once collaborated with him on a "translation" of an epitaph Armstrong had written for a certain Mr. Arnold, coauthoring a bawdy poem they thought would delight Peggy.[26]

Loving books, Wilkes was drawn toward booksellers and printers. He knew Andrew Millar, who had published Andrew Baxter, and he had a friendship with Dryden Leach, today considered the finest printer of eighteenth-century England. A highly intelligent man who wrote at least one review for the *Gazette littèraire de l'Europe*,[27] Leach worked quietly for radical causes and may have helped to turn Wilkes's mind in that direction.

Millar was a friend of Dr. Johnson and one of the proprietors of Johnson's *Dictionary,* but Wilkes did not yet know many people in Johnson's circle. In fact, to a young left-leaning intellectual reared in the age of satire, Johnson looked like fair game. When the *Dictionary* appeared in 1755 to great and deserved acclaim, Wilkes, in a mischievous mood, wrote a satirical piece about it. He sent a "Letter to the Printer" of the *Public Advertiser,* drawing attention to Johnson's comments upon the placing of the letter *H* in orthography. In the "Grammar of the English Tongue," prefixed to the *Dictionary,* Johnson had explained an orthographic principle concerning the letter *H*: "It seldom, perhaps never," said Johnson, "begins any but the first syllable." About this Wilkes commented, "The author of this remark must be a man of quick *apprehension,* and *compre-hensive* genius; but I can never forgive his *un-handsome be-havior* to the poor *knight-hood, priest-hood,* and *widow-hood,* nor his *inhumanity* to all *man-hood* and *woman-hood.* I do not indeed wonder at so great a Scholar's disregarding a *maiden-head,* but should he dare to treat the *God-head* with neglect?"

Before he was done, Wilkes had used twenty-six words in which *H* begins an internal syllable. In the fourth edition of the *Dictionary* (1773), Johnson finally expunged the embarrassing "perhaps never" and added a statement about *H* that included a dig at Wilkes: "It sometimes begins middle or final syllables in words compounded; or derived from the Latin, as *comprehended, blockhead.*"[28]

On 12 January 1748/9, Wilkes was proposed for membership in the Royal Society. It would be hard to overemphasize the importance of the Society. It had been founded in 1662 and had numbered among its members Robert Boyle, Isaac Newton, Samuel Pepys, Christopher Wren, and John Dryden, though it had slipped from its heyday into something like a debating society. The emphasis was on the physical sciences, but it was also the gathering place of biologists, antiquarians, physicians, and anatomists. Their publication, the *Philosophical Transactions,* included the papers of continental scientists and scholars, who had no other outlet. Wilkes was admitted to this illustrious society upon a petition signed by Dr. Richard Brocklesby, whom Wilkes had known at Leiden, Thomas Birch, the well-known antiquarian, and Dr. Richard Mead, possibly the most famous physician of the day. Dr. Mead was first cousin to Wilkes's wife's late father and the most illustrious member of the Mead family. He and his colleagues described Squire Wilkes as "a gentleman of distinction, merit, and learning, well qualified for the honour he desires and likely to be a useful member of our body." The record does not reveal what accomplishments of the candidate were discussed. In that period candidates were not required to submit anything in writing so long as they paid the fees. That Wilkes qualified as a scholar no one doubted.[29]

Wilkes must have been pleased to discover Mead among his in-laws, for the doctor was a libertine. Laurence Sterne would get into hot water when in *Tristram Shandy* he would allude to the doctor's geriatric sexual activities in the satirical sketch of "Dr. Kunastrokius," who took "the greatest delight imaginable in combing of asses tails, and plucking the dead hairs out with his teeth." Dr. Mead was rumored to have become impotent when he was at or close to the age of seventy-five but, it was said, kept in his house a young woman for the pleasures of dalliance, about which the woman's husband was perfectly complacent, knowing that the foreplay could lead nowhere.[30]

On 19 January 1754, Wilkes was initiated into the Sublime Society of Beef Steaks, a men's club notorious for indecent conversation that met above the Covent Garden Theatre. William Hogarth, the painter, Theophilus Cibber, the leading comic actor of the age, and John Beard, a great singer and the manager of the theater, were members. "Chaffing" or teasing of one another was a large part of the program, as was singing. If anyone offended, he was stripped of his coat and waistcoat and wrapped in the tablecloth to be chastised. When James Boswell was taken there as a guest in November of 1762, he found Lord

Sandwich as president sitting under a canopy, above which in golden letters were the words "Beef and Liberty." At the table political enemies and literary enemies sat side by side talking and laughing together. Wilkes was among them, laughing with his political opponent, Lord Eglinton. Dinner consisted of nothing but beefsteaks and wine.[31]

In 1758, Wilkes became a governor of the celebrated Foundling Hospital. This admirable institution had been established by Thomas Coram, a retired sea captain who had struggled many years to establish a hospital in London for abandoned or desperate children. In 1759, the hospital opened a branch at Aylesbury with a board of governors that included John Dell, the Rev. Dr. John Stephens, and Jack Wilkes, serving as treasurer.[32]

In the archives of the Coram Foundation — as the institution is now called — may be found a description of Wilkes's first attendance at a meeting of the Court of Governors in London:

> The celebrated Mr. Wilkes was elected a governor when very young and attending on a court day in a gay and rather fantastic dress attended by a couple of dogs he sat much observed although no one knew his name indeed at the time he had not taken up the trade of patriotism. The court was engaged in a knotty discussion and could not arrive at an issue when Mr Wilkes rising said "I see no difficulty in the matter before you — forget all the arguments which have been used — the question is this "Are the benefits of this charity to be limited to children exposed and deserted, that is left naked on Salisbury Plain or a dunghill. I maintain that a mother dying from want with her infant at her breast is an exposed and deserted case, and that her child is exposed and deserted too — Are we living under the dispensations of Christianity and yet cripple our notions of charity?" Then turning to Hogarth's picture of Moses and Pharaoh's daughter, "if so," continued he, "let us fall back upon ancient times and take a lesson from the heathen maid."[33]

The dogs were named Dido and Pompey.

The Foundling Hospital had flourished in large part through the unstinting support of artists. George Frideric Handel trained the children in music and gave the chapel an organ. Vast numbers of gentlemen and ladies came to hear Handel lead the children in singing the *Messiah*. Laurence Sterne preached a charity sermon there. Hogarth gave numerous paintings to the institution. In 1759, there was a meeting of artists who had given paintings to the hospital to discuss the possibility of their setting up their own exhibition, a radically new notion. The meeting led eventually to the formation of the Society of Artists, which in May 1761 opened the first exhibition in history organized exclusively by professional artists for their own benefit.[34] The initial meeting was chaired by John Wilkes.

By the age of thirty Wilkes had the acquaintance or friendship of virtually all the men of distinction in Buckinghamshire and at least half of those in London. He was an admired squire, a scholar, and a wit. James Harris, the member of Parliament for Christchurch, who was a "respectable" man, conceded that Wilkes had "a constant flow of mirth and humor," though his sentiments and morals tended "to the profligate and debauched." For all that, lively Jack Wilkes brought out the good humor in those around him. "It is impossible," said a contemporary, "to be dull in his company."[35]

Wilkes was careless, however, of his debts, which were beginning to be the subject of gossip — lies, he called them. Stories were circulated that linked him to his neighbor Sir William Stanhope, the wealthy brother of Lord Chesterfield. Taking his cue from Stanhope, who laughed at small debts, Wilkes told Dell, "These things hurt Merchants, not gentlemen, at least those like me, who do not, to my knowledge, owe sixpence at Aylesbury or elsewhere."[36] If he paid his bills in the village, not those in London. He thought his position entitled him to purchase whatever he wanted, and in eighteenth-century England, credit was all too easy. Tradesmen gave credit to attract business in a competitive market and to manage sales in a world where specie was in short supply. Tailors, apothecaries, vintners readily sold their goods and services on credit to gentlemen; and moneylenders, counting on the value of gentlemen's estates, put up cash for larger endeavors. But the value of farmlands was seldom realized until a lease was sold or renewed, at great cost to the lessor. These windfalls being far apart, and the year-by-year income from farmland being low, landed gentlemen were often behind in paying their bills.

Wilkes was not dishonest, but he was irresponsible. As treasurer of the Aylesbury branch of the Foundling Hospital, he made use of money that was entrusted to him, but when the branch was abandoned, he was unable to pay it back. "Much obloquy," said his friend John Almon, "was cast on Mr. Wilkes" for this debt. One twentieth-century historian calls it an embezzlement, but this is too harsh a term. According to the common practices of the day, when the money belonging to an institution was placed in the hands of its treasurer, he was free to invest it and to keep whatever it earned. Money for government departments, for instance, instead of being placed in the Bank of England, was given to the departments and kept in chests. It could be invested and the interest kept by the minister. The practice was legal, but not admired.[37] William Pitt had won popularity for not doing it when he was paymaster of the armed forces, while Henry Fox, who followed him in that office, made himself enormously wealthy by the practice and came to be detested by the common man.

Wilkes had not gambled the money away, for that was not his vice. In his youth he had once lost five hundred guineas at play. His father had paid the debt, but told him, "Jack, mind, I do so no more," and he never gambled again.[38]

There is no knowing what Wilkes did with the Foundling Hospital money. His fellow governors at Aylesbury must have known; but they did not think him morally at fault, for they colluded to protect him in 1764 when the London governors demanded an audit. By that time, Wilkes was no longer the squire, having sold Prebendal House to meet other debt, and was in exile in France. The task of doing the audit was assigned to two seemingly impeccable auditors, the Rev. Dr. Stephens and the Rev. Mr. William Pugh, who taught in the grammar school and served as Dr. Stephens's curate. But these two parsons managed to do some arithmetical magic and reported that the Foundling Hospital owed the money to Wilkes. It is unthinkable that they would have behaved in this manner had Wilkes's financial management or mismangement been hurtful to the children. Again in 1768, when the Aylesbury governors were threatened by the London governors (who had been sued for one of Wilkes's debts), his Aylesbury friends would not give him up. By then, he had returned from his exile, and, though an outlaw, he was standing as a candidate for Parliament. To the people of Buckinghamshire, he had become a hero who defied a despotic government and was made to suffer for it. Nowhere did Wilkes have more admirers. At one point, the county voters submitted to the House of Commons a petition in support of Wilkes signed by eighteen hundred freeholders. Nevertheless, there was still the debt to the Foundling Hospital, unmet until 1769, when two unidentified supporters who regarded Wilkes as the champion of liberty came to Aylesbury to investigate the matter and then paid what was owing.[39]

Wilkes never did learn to be responsible about his personal finances, spending lavishly what he did not have and expecting his family and friends to bail him out. They always did. He never saw the inside of a debtors' prison, which is one of the strongest evidences of how charismatic was John Wilkes. The Foundling Hospital fiasco, however, taught him to be careful of public funds. During the last two decades of his life, he did impeccable service as the treasurer of the City of London, and so far was he from making himself rich off of this public money, he would die poor.

At Bath, Wilkes met Thomas Potter, a gentleman born to a higher station than was Wilkes, a man of fashion, exceedingly handsome, a wit, an orator, and a notorious libertine. Within months the two had become the closest of friends. "The highest pleasure that can be afforded me next to the company of a woman," Potter wrote, "is that of my dear Wilkes." During the autumn of 1752, he sent a servant to Prebendal House with a note for Jack: "If you have either religion or morality, if you have but a pretense to one single social virtue, if you prefer young women and whores to old women and wives, if you prefer the toying away hours with little satin-back to the evening conferences of your mother-in-law . . . if life and spirit and wit and humour and gaiety, but above all if the heavenly inspired passion called LUST have not . . . deserted you and left you a prey to dullness and imbecility, hasten to town that you may take a place in my post chaise for Bath next Thursday morning." Potter was in a hurry to get to Bath to escape the birth scenes at his town house and "the odious yell of a young female yahoo that thrust herself into the world yesterday."[40]

Potter was the second son and heir of the late Thomas Potter, archbishop of Canterbury. The archbishop, having made himself wealthy from the proceeds of his office, had intended to pass his fortune to his eldest son, John, who was in holy orders, but the young man had married a servant! Infuriated, the archbishop disinherited him and rewrote his will in favor of his second son, Thomas. Before this event, Thomas, thinking he must make a living, had taken a law degree. His father had made things easy for him, presenting him to the post of principal registrar for the Province of Canterbury, the most lucrative position in the spiritual courts of England, for which he was qualified by training if not by spirit. Most of the work was done by surrogates and scribes, who were compensated with a small portion of the income.

After his father's death in 1747, Thomas Potter was wealthy, but in poor health. He frequently carried his "rotten carcass," as he called it, to Bath to take the waters. There he became a friend of the most influential man in town, Ralph Allen, the celebrated quarry owner and innovator of postal services, the patron of Alexander Pope and friend of Henry Fielding, who was often called the "benevolent man." With Allen's help and his own law degree, Potter fell into the position of recorder of Bath, another responsibility that usually could be met by hirelings. His passions were politics and women, and when Wilkes first got to know him, he was member of Parliament for Cornish borough of St. Germans. There was no need in that age for a member of Parliament to be a resident of the town or district he represented. In 1754, he was elected to one of the two seats for Aylesbury and would soon become Wilkes's political mentor.

According to Almon, Potter was "the ruin of Mr. Wilkes, who was not a bad man early, or naturally, but Potter poisoned his morals." Almon seems not to have known about "coy wanton Peggy" or the whores at Leiden. But it is true, Potter's friendship intensified Wilkes's libertinism. "You have done every thing in your power," Potter wrote him, "to ruin and destroy my body by strong soups, filthy claret, rakish hours and bad example. Avant Satan with all thy temptations." Having surfeit of the bed of a certain youthful Mrs. M., Wilkes offered the bed to Potter. Not to be behindhand, Potter was soon writing, "May Venus and every other deity of pleasure be propitious to you at Tunbridge. Should you meet there a goddess under the vulgar appellation of Miss Betty Spooner, offer incense to her for my sake. . . . You will find in her liveliness and lechery. The latter quality usual enough both to mortals and divinities, but the first confined to the sacred few."[41]

Wilkes would not have qualified for the label of *rake* as the word was used then. He did not go gambling, get drunk, stagger about the street singing bawdy songs, bully the night watch, and end up in a whorehouse. He was a gentleman libertine. Potter, despite his good breeding, was the more rakish of the two. When writing to Wilkes about how he might be remembered after he was gone, he speculated that it would be for the time when he was seen copulating with a cow on Wingrove Common. He was right. Potter died in 1759, and we are still talking about the cow.[42]

In the midfifties Potter had an affair with Gertrude Warburton, the wife of the Rev. Dr. William Warburton, the literary churchman of the time, soon to be elevated as bishop of Gloucester. Gertrude was the niece and heiress of Ralph Allen, Potter's powerful friend at Bath, and Potter had gotten to know her when he was a guest at Allen's house, Prior Park, close to Bath. Potter loved Allen as a father figure, but his love for the beautiful niece was not familial. And how he hated Warburton, who came into Prior Park acting like its master. Warburton had married Gertrude when she was eighteen and he forty-eight.[43]

Potter seems to have deflected his seething detestation of Warburton into a bawdy hobby. He began writing an obscene parody of Alexander Pope's long poem, *An Essay on Man,* the most popular poem of the age. Pope was dead, but he had left the rights to the poem to his friend Warburton, who proceeded to bring out editions of it every year. Potter's parody, which he called "An Essay on Woman," satirized both Pope's *Essay on Man,* which Potter found pretentious, and Warburton's notes, which he found pompous. "An Essay on Woman" has been called the dirtiest poem in the English language, but it is not pornographic in the modern sense; rather, it reaches the extreme of indecorum, boundlessly bawdy, using every indecent word, yet in couplets that are astonishingly close to those of Pope. The mock footnotes imitate the turgid notes of Warburton.

As Potter wrote these bawdy couplets, he showed them to Wilkes, who made suggestions and annotations. Wilkes, whose commitment to religion was tenuous, could readily join in his friend's laughter at Pope's piety. Though he had no personal quarrel with Warburton, like most young men of the time, Wilkes loved satire. And Warburton, unlovable and a bully in literary controversy, was the perfect game. He joined in the chase the more willingly because Potter and Edwards, two older men he enormously admired, had gone after Warburton.

If we may take a "peep into futurity," as Wilkes called it, we will see that the "Essay on Woman" would one day give Wilkes a great deal of trouble. Potter would leave the manuscript with Wilkes when he would die. Wilkes would modify it, augment it with his own bawdy poems, complete the introductory material and footnotes, and print twelve copies. He would never publish it, that is, he would never make it public; and the public of the Georgian era would never see it. It was a private printing for the members of Wilkes's men's club. Nevertheless, Wilkes would be sent to prison for "publishing" the Essay on Woman. But this is a story to which we shall return.

At some point in the 1750s, Potter began taking Wilkes to the now-famous, but then little-known, hellfire club called the Order of the Knights of St. Francis of Wycombe. Sir Francis Dashwood, later Lord le Despenser, the founder and chief mover of the club, lived at West Wycombe Park, which Wilkes passed on his trips to and from London. Dashwood extensively re-modeled the plain house he had inherited, turning it into one of the most beautiful houses in England, with classical porticos on three fronts. Scattered through the extensive gardens and park were various temples to Greek or Roman deities, one of which bespeaks his sense of comedy. He built two dikes of some 250 feet in length that came together in a V. Where they met, he made a low mound on which he placed a Temple to Venus, cylindrical, with columns all around, no more than 10 or 12 feet in diameter. Beneath, in the crotch of the V formed by the two dikes, he made a shallow cave with an oval entrance —"an erotic design representing the female anatomy," said Dashwood's twentieth-century heir, the late Sir Francis Dashwood.[44]

An ardent student of art, architecture, and revelry, Sir Francis had founded in London the Dilettanti Society, which encouraged publications and exhibitions of antique art. "The nominal qualification" for membership, said Horace Walpole, "is having been in Italy, and the real one being drunk."[45] At their feasts, the archmaster of ceremonies, wearing a crimson robe, Hungarian cap, and Spanish toledo, was accompanied by the Imp, in red robe with a tail fastened to his behind. Dashwood also had founded the Divan Club, whose members had visited the Ottoman empire. They met in the Thatched Tavern in St. James's Street, wearing turbans and robes and carrying daggers. The standing toast was "The Harem."

These men were libertines, and a libertine was a gentleman and a scholar. The phrase, now so trite, was meaningful then. The libertine was polite in his behavior and stylish in his dress; he kept company with men of refinement and intellect, with whom he discussed books and paintings as well as pornography and sex. He eschewed streetwalkers and common whores, finding his pleasure with ladies, perhaps courtesans, but always ladies. A libertine was skeptical of Christianity and put his faith in "the religion of nature." In 1760 Dr. John Armstrong sent Wilkes a rambling meditation on religion in which he concluded about the Knights of St. Francis, "Such a retreat in such company I should think sufficient to correct the most hardened and obstinate atheist and soften his mind to receive impressions of the universal religion—the religion of nature which I believe is better delineated by your holy orders than by any metaphysical philosopher that ever wrote a dry unreadable quarto." It was different on the Continent, where libertines defiantly made fun of the powerful Roman Catholic Church, but in Buckinghamshire, the protest against organized religion was confined to harmless mockery of what they called priestcraft. English libertines were more philosophical than rebellious. The freedom in sexual matters they allowed themselves was, they believed, morally and intellectually healthful. Like Claude Lévi-Strauss, they thought sex was good for thinking.[46]

To accommodate the Knights of St. Francis, Dashwood and two or three other members leased Medmenham Abbey, an ivy-covered ruin of a thirteenth-century Cistercian abbey that stood some six miles to the south of West Wycome, on the banks of the upper Thames near Marlowe. They rebuilt this ancient pile as a "Gothic" clubhouse. The abbey house was made habitable but purposely kept gloomy by stained-glass windows. The ceilings were decorated with indecent fresco paintings. They added a "ruined" cloister with five or six arches and a "ruinous" tower to give it a more romantic look. Prints of the kings of England were hung in the chapter room, with a piece of paper stuck over the face of Henry VIII because he was no friend to monasteries.

Conspicuous among the members was John Montagu, fourth earl of Sandwich, who was to play a major role in Wilkes's life. This is the very man who, not wanting to rise from the gambling table, used to order a lunch of bread with something between the slices. He was a duke, the highest of the noble ranks other than those of royalty, but his family fortune had been squandered away by generations of playboys, leaving him dependent upon government for an income. He had served in the Admiralty, and as a surprisingly young plenipotentiary to the French royal court at the close of the previous war with France. He had no place when Wilkes came to the hellfire club, but he would again be brought into government and prove to be Wilkes's bête noire. In later years he was made first lord of the admiralty, and a worse lord of the admiralty can hardly be imagined. He "employed the vast patronage of the office as an engine for bribery and political jobbery," he sold public offices, and committed "wholesale robbery" of those who did business with the navy. He allowed the navy to sink into such decrepitude that he can easily be seen as one of the major reasons England lost the American colonies. Wilkes knew none of this, of course, when he first got to know Sandwich. What Wilkes knew was a tall man with an unattractive face and a nervous defect that gave him a strange gait. Somebody, perhaps it was Wilkes, said that Sandwich walked down both sides of the street at once. His bawdy-wit was famous. Lord Auckland once sent him a letter critical of his politics, to which Sandwich returned a short note: "Sir, your letter is before me, and it will presently be behind me. I remain, sir, your most humble servant."[47] Wilkes delighted in him.

Most of the members of the Medmenham club were local squires, but some came from London to join their festivities, politicos such as George Bubb-Dodington and Lord Sandwich, poets such as Dashwood's sidekick Paul Whitehead and Laurence Sterne's friend John Hall-Stevenson. Membership changed as the years passed, but at any one time the number was limited to twelve, called the apostles. They could bring one guest each, who made up an inferior order without the privilege of participating in the secret rites carried on in the old chapel. Wilkes would eventually be moved from the inferior to the superior order, but not until Potter's death.

During the morning hours, the club members and guests played chess or backgammon, boated in their handsome pleasure boat, or fished. In the afternoon they dined, and the drinking began. In a letter to Lord Temple, Wilkes spoke of coming from Medmenham "where the jovial monks of St Francis kept me up till four in the morning." In the evening, they got themselves up in the habits of monks for their mock religious ceremony. No fewer than four times, Sir Francis had himself painted in a monk's habit toasting with a communion cup the backsides of a statue of Venus.[48] In the portrait done by Hogarth, the halo surrounding Sir Francis's head contains the face of Lord Sandwich.

Rumors went round that the Monks of St. Francis did the black rite, which may have been the case. In their letters to each other, they often used images of the mass. Hall-Stevenson, writing that he is too ill to attend, "desires thee prayers of thee congregation and hopes their Devotions may be attended with the choicest blessings . . . Health, Wealth, and never failing vigor." Sir William Stanhope, when he could not attend, sent his compliments to the "Brethren," assuring them that "they may have my prayers, particularly in that part of the Litany when I pray the Lord to strengthen them that do stand."[49]

Stories began to circulate about sexual orgies at Medmenham. Horace Walpole, on a tour of ancient buildings, was shown around the abbey. After talking to the servants and steward, he wrote, "Each member has his cell, in which indeed is little more than a bed. They meet to drink, though the rule is pleasure, and each is to do whatever he pleases in his own cell, into which they may carry women." According to other reports, ladies, possibly high-class prostitutes or adventurous lady friends, were admitted to the table and showed every politeness. The women, not the men, would chose a paramour, and the couple would retire to his cell. If children were born out of such unions, they were called Sons or Daughters of St. Francis and reared up to become officers or domestics to the club. Dashwood himself had several illegitimate children, the boys among whom were invariably named Francis.[50]

When Wilkes fell out with Dashwood and Sandwich, he wrote about the club. Since he was under a vow of secrecy that prohibited his divulging their rituals and sexual frolics, he used the device of talking about the garden at Medmenham.[51] Here and there, he said, were Latin inscriptions, which Wilkes translated. One read, "Here the happiest of mortals died of joy." The ancient metaphor of orgasm as a death was still very much alive. Another: "Here the vanquished naiad overcame the conquering satyr." On the back of a stone couch was the injunction, "Go to it, you youngsters, put everything you have into it, both of you; let not doves outdo your cooings, nor ivy your embraces, nor oysters your kisses."

The younger men in the garden, said Wilkes in his comments, "sinned naturally." Wilkes thought it particularly important to give out that his own libertinism was of the heterosexual variety and to imply that this was not necessarily true of the older members. The older members had all become his enemies when he wrote these remarks. In Wilkes's generation, heterosexuality had become the mark of a true gentleman, and the bisexuality that had been practiced by men of rank from the Elizabethan age was scorned as effeminate.[52] According to Wilkes, buggery, even heterosexual buggery was warned against at Medmenham. On the buttocks of a statue of Venus in a bent position, appeared a quotation from Virgil: "Here is the place where the way divided into two: this on the right is our route to Heaven; but the left-hand path exacts punishment from the wicked, and sends them to pitiless Hell." By way of contrast, the older members who had restored the buildings had carved over the main entrance a motto from Rabelais' fictional Abbey de Thélème, "Fay ce que voudras," "Do what you will."

Wilkes is never known to have felt any guilt for his libertine life. On the contrary, he regarded his sexuality as a talent, and it was his privilege as a gentleman to exercise it: "A man who has not money to gratify passions does right to govern them," he explained; "but he who can indulge them, is better off."[53]

Wilkes, like many young men of his age, had an admiration for Archbishop Thomas Herring of Canterbury because of his vigorous leadership in organizing defenses during the Jacobite Rebellion of 1745. When someone slandered his hero, Wilkes responded by writing a sonnet:

To His Grace Thomas Herring, Archbishop of Canterbury:

Prelate, whose steady hand, and watchful eye,
   The sacred vessel of religion guide,
   Secure from superstition's dangerous tide,
And fateful rocks of infidelity;

Think not, in this bad age of obloquy,
   (When Christian virtues Christians dare deride,
   And worth by party-zeal alone is tried)
To 'scape the poison'd shafts of calumny;

No, though the tenor of thy blameless life,
Like His, whose flock is to thy care consign'd,
Be spent in teaching truth and doing good;
  Yet, 'mongst the sons of bigotry and strife,
   Thou too, like Him, must hear thy good malign'd,
   Thy person slander'd, and thy truths withstood.

He sent the poem to the archbishop in December 1753. The prelate replied, thanking him "not for the panegyric part, to which I lay no claim in the least degree, but for that which better becomes an honest man and friend, its grave and good instruction. . . . You have long had my esteem, this instance of the integrity of your mind has raised it to something higher." Integrity Wilkes had, at least in the original sense of the word, for theism and animal desire were seamlessly integrated in him. As he explained to Boswell, "Thank heaven for having given me the love of women. To many she gives not the noble passion of lust."[54]

3

Into Parliament

As the general election of 1754 approached, "Mr. Wilkes's friends strongly urged him to come into parliament," wrote John Almon; "Potter pressed him very much: it was the only place, he said, in which a young man of Mr. Wilkes's talents could commence the world with éclat."[1] Member of Parliament. For a gentleman of modest fortune, the title was the ultimate status symbol. Members were not paid for their services, but Wilkes had, or thought he had, enough money to afford the honor. He wanted to represent Aylesbury. The town had been without a squire for years, and here came young Wilkes, playing the part well, respected by the village fathers, liked by the common folk. It was only reasonable he should represent the town, or borough, for that was the legal name of a community that sent one or more members to the House. Aylesbury sent two. But what was Wilkes to do? One of the Aylesbury seats was occupied by Potter, and the other by Edward Willes, who was resigning it in favor of his older brother, John, who was Wilkes's good friend. Wilkes could not compete with friends. To stand for another borough was a possibility, for there were no residential requirements. If a candidate showed up to make one speech at a nomination meeting, that was thought sufficient to launch his candidacy. Openings for candidates were kept track of in Westminster by the first minister, Henry Pelham, and his brother, the Duke of Newcastle, so they could send their own people to stand; but at this election, they had nothing for Wilkes. Unhappy, but not complaining, he pitched in and helped Potter with his campaign. In the end, no one else entered the contest for Aylesbury, and Potter and Willes were elected without opposition.

Wilkes's disappointment and subsequent work for the candidates did not go unnoticed. One January morning in 1754, he broke open the seals of a letter from the Marquis of Buckingham, lord lieutenant of Buckinghamshire. Wilkes had been chosen to be high sheriff of the county. The term was only for a year, but it was a great honor. Most of the high sheriff's duties had been relegated in Wilkes's time to under-sheriffs and bailiffs. There were ceremonial duties, the most showy of which was attendance upon the judges at the assize, that annual court presided over by the king's judges who came to try the felony cases which local justices were forbidden to adjudicate. The cases were presented at the assize court by justices of the peace, who came from all over the county, so that the assize had a festival air, old friendships renewed, elaborate dinners, and horse racing. Wilkes had the duty of riding with assorted justices to the border of the county to meet the judges as they entered, to escort them to Buckingham and the courthouse, and in the court to attend to their wishes. With few exceptions, the punishments for felonies were deportation or death by hanging. The hangings were carried out promptly on the fields where the horse racing was done. The high sheriff, whose attendance was required, traditionally rode to the gallows on horseback behind the cart that carried the condemned. He was dressed in black and carried a white wand.

Lord Buckingham had preferred Wilkes to the high shrivality upon the solicitation of Potter, who spoke for the powerful politicians under whom he labored, William Pitt and his brother-in-law, Richard Grenville, Lord Temple. Potter had asked them to repay Wilkes for his labors and to assuage his disappointment at not being able to stand for Aylesbury. To Wilkes he wrote, "You have supported me in every way, and I now return the favor." Potter spoke in a spirit of genuine affection, but to men of their class and time, friendship was almost indistinguishable from political affiliation. Potter, fully aware of the irony that dirty politics were inseparable from noble friendship, warned Wilkes: "A true political scoundrel maxim is, that the friendship which one does not use is worth nothing."[2]

The leader of Potter's faction was the celebrated William Pitt, a political giant who would loom over Wilkes's career for years to come. At the moment he was member of Parliament for Seaford and paymaster general. The greatest orator of his time, he was and still is spoken of as "the Great Commoner" for his sway over the House of Commons. He would eventually be elevated to the earldom of Chatham. Pitt was enormously popular with the lower and middle classes because he had brought prosperity to the City and, unlike most politicians, he was free from corruption. He did not need the money, for his grandfather had made a vast fortune in India. It was the grandfather who brought to England the Pitt diamond, one of the largest and most famous diamonds in lapidarian history. Potter, who had been a follower of Pitt for years, had an unbounded admiration for him, and Pitt in turn called Potter, "one of the best friends I have in the world."[3]

Pitt's political partner was Richard Grenville, Earl Temple, master of the magnificent estate called Stowe, some twenty miles north of Aylesbury. For reasons yet unrevealed, Potter hated Lord Temple's sister, Lady Hester Grenville. When his lordship announced the engagement of Lady Hester to Pitt, Potter was furious. How could his brilliant hero debase himself by marrying such a woman? "All that wit and fire and spirit," he wrote to Wilkes, "is to be matrimonially soaked in the cold, slimy, aquatic cunt of Lady H. Grenville. What can so unnatural a mixture produce? The seed of heaven will congeal into frog spawn."[4] He could hardly have been more wrong: the offspring of this couple would be the great prime minister of the next generation, William Pitt the younger, who saw England through the terrible days of the French Revolution. It would have been beyond Wilkes's powers of imagination to think that he would end his political career as the follower of the baby boy born to William and Hester Pitt.

Earl Temple had no interest in dominating the faction. Though the leader of a great Whig family, he had come to accept Pitt's view of politics. Pitt had convinced him of the inadequacy of a government run by an oligarchy of great families and to the needs and political potential of the lower and middle classes, especially those of London. Temple looked forward to playing a new political game, for, as he once declared, he "loved faction, and had a great deal of spare money." He had no office in the ministry, which was how he liked it. Lord Temple had no charisma. He had a "huge ungainly figure" and the unwelcome nickname of Lord Gawky.[5] He was active in the House of Lords but preferred to stand aside from other fields of political battle. He would devote his energy and keen intelligence to the management of Pitt's publicity and, not to mince words, propaganda. Better than any political figure of the day, he understood how to use the power of the pen, sometimes his own pen, but more often the pens of talented writers.

In the early years of the eighteenth century the Whigs and Tories had been national parties competing against one another — in-group against out-group, the sort of political struggle that we in the United States are used to. But party politics on a national scale had disappeared when George I had come to the throne. In Wilkes's day, most members of Parliament and most ministers called themselves Whigs. There were a few Tories in the landscape, fiercely

independent squires who detested government, and in London a few independent thinkers, such as Samuel Johnson, who called himself a Tory. (The colonial American use of the word *Tory* for loyalists and *Whig* for revolutionaries
was unknown in England.) Neither the Tories nor the Whigs at this time were
political parties in the modern sense of the word. Government was in control
of a few families, the Whig Oligarchy historians call it. Some of the families
had control of a "faction" made up of local political leaders, friends, elected
officials, members of Parliament, and, if the families' wishes had come true,
ministers and their subordinates. Members of a faction were expected to stick
together on issues, elections, and appointments, though in fact they were
constantly unraveling and being rewoven. *Faction* had recently become a
nasty word. A kinder term was *party*, or more euphemistically, *friends*. There
were smaller factions, too, men loyal to a particular leader who gained power
by the deftness with which he could ally his friends with a larger group.
Politics consisted largely of the jockeying for power and office of various Whig
factions. A pattern of in-group, out-group, however, was beginning to appear
in the banding together in the House of Commons of out-factions called "the
opposition." Yet many individuals who opposed the current ministry would
not join the opposition, but remained "independents." The talents of individuals were always prized in England, and a few independents rose to greatness
without party affiliation. The younger William Pitt held the highest office for
many years without belonging to a faction.

The senior William Pitt was the star and leader of the Pitt-Grenville faction,
sometimes called the Pittites and sometimes the Cousinhood. They had originally been organized by Temple's late uncle, the childless Richard Temple,
Lord Cobham, who had enlisted his ten nephews, young men of the Grenville
and Lyttelton families. Lord Temple, the oldest of the cousins, had been heir to
his uncle and now headed the family, but Pitt, a brilliant politician, had taken
over the leadership. The Lyttleton brothers had gradually withdrawn, leaving
the faction to the Grenvilles. Their headquarters was Lord Temple's house at
Stowe. Three younger Grenville brothers belonged, one of whom, George
Grenville, next in age to Lord Temple, was destined to play a large part in
Wilkes's story.[6] Potter was chief among the non-family members. The Pittites
were supporters of the current Pelham-Newcastle ministry.

Potter's bringing Wilkes in as high sheriff had the effect of binding him to the
Cousinhood, and Wilkes was happy to be so bound. He quickly charmed the
circle at Stowe, once again playing the role of the brilliant young man amusing
his older friends with his audacity and naughty wit. Pitt had no problem with
the bawdy talk of his young friend.[7] Once when Potter called at Stowe, he
showed Pitt an indecent parody written by Wilkes, no doubt one of the lesser

poetical bawdries that eventually would appear in the Essay on Woman. Pitt laughed, Potter reported to Wilkes, and "bid me to tell you that he found with great concern you was as wicked and agreeable as ever."[8]

Lord Temple, who would soon take Wilkes as a sort of protégé and underwrite his journalistic and political endeavors, developed a great affection for Jack Wilkes, "with all your faults and all your good qualities too which blot out the former." A sign of his admiration can be found in the beautiful west pavilion that he added to Stowe. One of the statues along the roof is a representation of Lady Liberty, a traditional figure of a woman in the cap of Liberty, but this lady has crossed eyes.[9]

Unexpectedly an opportunity arose for Wilkes to try for Parliament. The Duke of Newcastle wanted one of his people at Berwick-on-Tweed. Would Wilkes stand? Temple approved and Potter urged, but Wilkes needed little urging. Berwick was on the River Tweed at the Scottish border, which must have seemed like the end of the world. Nevertheless, young Mr. Wilkes, confident and in high spirits, trotted off with nothing to recommend him but a letter from George Grenville describing him as a traditional Whig and supporter of Newcastle.[10]

At Berwick he was greeted and entertained by Newcastle's friends and engaged in a brief campaign, talking to the leading men of the town. As expected, he appeared with the other men who were announcing their interest at a nomination meeting, a raucous affair held in a tavern, to which came the "principal gentlemen" of the community and as many independent voters as could crowd in. There were speeches full of platitudes, cheers and boos, and much drinking. Newcastle's political machinery had been grinding away, and a local printer named Robert Taylor had written Wilkes a speech, which Wilkes delivered on 16 April 1754. Wilkes was pleased by "the assurances I had received of your steady attachment to the cause of liberty. I early embarked on the same generous cause, and have always had it nearest to my heart." What could the freemen of Berwick have thought of this lisping stranger holding the paper he was reading up to his nose and talking about his dedication to the cause of liberty? They were astonished when he declared, "As I never will take a bribe, so I never will offer one."[11] Buying votes, though illegal, was countenanced, even expected, in a great many boroughs. The small landowners counted on the money.

On election day, Wilkes mounted the "hustings," the temporary platform built in the town square from which speeches were made and upon which the voting took place. There he bowed and bowed to queue of freemen waiting to sign the election books. He did not have a chance. Two well-established, adept Berwick politicians, Thomas Watson and John Delaval, who understood the itch of the voters, walked away with the election.[12] Wilkes was angry and after his return to London submitted a formal petition to the House of Commons charging that Watson and Dulaval had won by bribery.

Determined to make the charges stick, he returned to Berwick to gather evidence. When his work was done, Wilkes rode into Scotland to have a look. Passing through Edinburgh, he called upon David Hume. One would wish to have seen skinny, cross-eyed Jack Wilkes shaking the hand of fat David Hume with his cherubic face. Hume had published his great philosophical work, the *Treatise of Human Nature,* but as he said, "it fell dead-born from the press." His inquiries and discourses had been better received and had gained him a reputation abroad. He had just finished writing the first volume of his *History of Great Britain,* which would make him famous in England, but the volume was not yet in print. Hume and Wilkes got on very well, and Wilkes asked if he could borrow the manuscript of the history to read while traveling, but it was already at the printer's, and the printer would not relinquish it. Wilkes set off for the west on horseback, traveling with a friend by the name of Stone. Upon his return to Edinburgh, he tried to see Hume again but, missing him, went on to England. Shortly thereafter Hume wrote to say how sorry he was that they had not met a second time: "I shall be proud to cultivate a friendship and acquaintance with you, if ever an opportunity offers." A week later he wrote to Wilkes again. His *History* had just come off the press, and he was sending Wilkes one of the few large-paper issues. "I was desirous you should read it with as little disadvantage as possible." He was thinking, of course, of Wilkes's eyes.[13] "Le bon David" deserves the reputation for kindness which has been preserved through two centuries.

Hume in his letter went on to ask Wilkes to send him any suggestions he might have about his use of English. He had spent years in the study of that language, he said, but still felt uncertain. He did not mean that he grew up speaking Erse, the language of the Highlands; his first language was English, but his use of it contained many Scotticisms that were considered substandard south of the Tweed. Whether or not Wilkes sent any suggestions is not known, but in later years when they were opposed politically, Wilkes made fun of Hume's writing, saying it was a shame it had never been translated into English.[14]

Wilkes's petition alleging corruption in the Berwick election was read in House of Commons on 25 November 1754, discussed on 11 February 1755, read again on 17 November, delayed again until 17 February 1756. Wilkes was called to testify at the November session and soberly presented his facts and figures. Delaval, speaking from the floor as a member, tried to gain support by poking fun at Wilkes, whom at one point he called "the knight of the sorrowful countenance," a label usually reserved for Don Quixote. This got

Pitt's dander up, and the great man hurried onto the floor to commence a speech in support of the youngest member of his faction. Pitt was inspired, rising to greater and greater heights, "the finest speech that was ever made." He passed beyond the topic of Wilkes's petition and began to attack the minions of the Duke of Newcastle, who had been made first minister upon the death of his brother, Henry Pelham. The house was riveted, for they were learning for the first time that Pitt was breaking from Newcastle, his ally of many years, and the long hold on government of the Pelham brothers might be coming to an end. The speech "brought the House to a silence and attention that you might have heard a pin drop." Wilkes himself felt the terror he used to feel when his master Mr. Worsley threatened him with his birch rod, until he recalled that the great speaker was defending *him*.[15]

The speech crushed Delaval and changed Pitt's career, but it did nothing for Wilkes's petition. His futile efforts, however, made him a wiser politician. He learned that challenges to elections were always decided by the House along party lines. He went home and wrote a satire of the Berwick contest called the "Battle of the Tweed," but Potter told him, "It may do very well upon the banks of the river, but the rest of the world will not feel the wit of it."[16] So he gave up the protest and with it the high idealism. If he were going to enter politics, he had better get used to buying votes.

Not caring to join the Mead-Sherbrooke clan in Red Lyon Square behind St. Sepulcher's, where his wife had gone with five-year-old Polly, Wilkes went to Potter's house in Bedfordshire for the Christmas holiday. He then rode to London and withdrew his petition. Preparing to returned to Aylesbury, he wrote to John Dell, who now seemed to be acting as his steward as well as his political agent: "I wish you would order in a fillet of veal, a sirloin of beef, four fowls, and a couple of rabbits, besides all sorts of game, for I do not choose to be starved among you."[17]

In 1756 the Mead-Sherbrookes, tired of worrying about their daredevil, profligate, playboy son-in-law, decided to get rid of him. Divorces were rare and hard to obtain, but agreements to live apart could be managed if one had good lawyers. Her lawyers would have advised Mary Wilkes that a separation would mean she would lose her child, for in eighteenth-century England, custody in such cases was always given to the father. Yet the loss of this bright six-year-old girl did not deter Mary Wilkes or Mrs. Mead from proffering a separation agreement. Wilkes's lawyers, seeing how anxious the family was to be quit of Jack, drove a hard bargain. In the end, his ownership of the Aylesbury house and estates, as well as lands scattered here and there in Bucks and neighboring counties, was confirmed absolutely. In exchange, he was to pay his wife an annuity of two hundred pounds a year.[18]

Father and daughter now withdrew and moved into "elegant lodgings" in the house of a certain Mrs. Murry in St. James's Place, Westminster, leaving Mary Wilkes with her mother and uncle in Red Lion Court. With the help of Tobias Smollett, who lived in Chelsea and had a daughter not much older than Polly, Wilkes found a suitable school in that town. The mistresses were Mrs. Aylesworth and Mme Beete. Polly flourished, writing her father in French at the age of nine.[19] Since Wilkes had no intention of keeping her from her mother, Polly returned to the house behind St. Sepulchre's for most holidays. Eventually she would inherit her mother's and grandmother's considerable fortunes as well as that of her uncle.

John Armstrong now became Polly's doctor and, in April of 1757, at Wilkes's insistence, inoculated the little girl for smallpox. This risky preventive measure, only recently brought to England, consisted of taking pus from a sore of someone suffering a mild case of the disease and introducing it under the skin of the receiver's arm or leg. Polly underwent the ordeal at Dr. Armstrong's house. The live bacteria raced through her system, bringing her down with the disease, but in a less dangerous case than she might have contracted naturally. The child submitted patiently and kept in good humor. "She is pretty full," wrote her anxious father, "but not above a dozen in her face." To a friend he wrote, "I had desired her Mother to attend her before and after the inoculation was performed; I wrote to Mrs Wilkes, recommending Miss Wilkes to her Mother's care; but she has never once come near her." It was, in fact, Wilkes's mother who showed up to help nurse the child. Within a week, Polly was out of danger, and in May, Wilkes brought her home, having engaged two women servants whose entire duty was to care for Miss Wilkes. "She will not have a single scar," he wrote. Three months later she returned to school. Dr. Armstrong reported to her father, "I went to make Miss Wilkes a visit on Sunday last. She is very well and as killing as ever." It seems that the doctor had suffered some sort of accident because "she laughs at my wounds and says we must all die one time or other but that I always come alive again."[20]

In the spring of 1757, an opportunity opened for Wilkes to stand for Aylesbury. A vacancy had occurred at Bath, and Pitt decided he would like to represent that town. He resigned Oakhampton, a pocket borough he controlled, and offered it to Potter. A pocket borough was one in which there were only a handful of voters, all of whom were dependent upon one landlord and voted as the landlord requested. Potter had been offered a lucrative place as vice treasurer to Ireland. If he were to accept, he would be required by law to relinquish his seat in the House of Commons. He could then run in the by-election to fill the seat. The law permitted the voters to elect a placeman if they wished, but if they had elected someone without a place, a place could not be given to him without their approval. Potter knew that if he accepted the place and resigned his chair in the House, he would never be reelected at Aylesbury, where there was a strong animus against placemen. The slavish voters of Oakhampton, however, were in no position to object. He resigned the Aylesbury seat in June, kissed the king's hand to signify his acceptance of the Irish position, and went through the charade of an election for Oakhampton.[21]

Wilkes began preparing a campaign to be elected for Aylesbury. Dell now took over as his election manager, or agent, to use the language of that day, and proved himself indefatigable, a "prince of agents," as Potter had called him. Dell was also one of four returning officers, the officials who counted and reported the vote. He had been appointed by Wilkes, who as owner of Prebendal House had the right to appoint two returning officers. One would think that someone might have called, conflict of interest, but that issue seems never to have been raised. Wilkes and Dell went to work, Parson Stephens and a few others helping.[22]

Only one of the two Aylesbury seats was in contest in this by-election, and only two candidates had announced their intentions to vie for it, Wilkes and Edward Willes, the younger of the Willes brothers. Edward's brother John, Wilkes's friend, held the other seat, which was not under contest. Their powerful father, Sir John Willes, lord chief justice of the Court of Common Pleas in London, hoped to see both sons in the Aylesbury seats. The lord chief justice would have been forgotten long ago had he not attained an unenviable immortality as the sleeping judge in Hogarth's satirical print "The Bench."

The first election business of Wilkes and his friends was to do a canvas. They called upon each of the four hundred or so voters to ask his intentions. The right to vote was limited to owners of property that, in the judgment of the tax assessor, returned at least forty pounds a year. But many who owned enough land to vote also leased or worked fields belonging to large landholders, and so were dependent upon them. Usually they voted as their landlords wished out of courtesy, rather than fear. But voting was not secret, and to vote against one's landlord was to risk one's livelihood. In his canvas, Wilkes would pass over Sir John's people and concentrate on the independents. He was pleased to find that some were willing to promise him their votes without asking anything in return. He and Willes would have to bid for the others.

In all of the constituencies of England, votes were exchanged for favors; in some, for hard cash. Aylesbury was a notorious "venal constituency," where votes were sold to the candidate who would pay the most.[23] The price during Wilkes's time varied between one and five pounds. As Wilkes well knew, to a man with an annual income of *sixty or seventy pounds,* the bribes represented a lot of money. Determined to get this seat in the House of Commons, he wrote to Dell from London, "Depend upon it, I will sink Willes by the weight of metal." Soon after, he wrote, "If Mr. Willes comes sooner than me, and lends five to the poor, I will lend six, he does six, I will lend seven, if he seven, I eight, and so on." This talk of lending was nonsense, a euphemism for bribing. It had been a mere three years since he had told the Berwick voters that he would never offer a bribe. Jack Wilkes had become a politician.

How was he to get the money? He asked Potter, who had in previous years gone heavily into debt to buy Aylesbury votes. Potter gave him, Wilkes later said, "the worst advice." Wilkes gave his bond for five hundred pounds to a Mr. Thomson, careless of the mathematics of interest: in the next twelve years, the debt would increase fourfold.[24]

And then, Edward Willes withdrew from the contest. He had been given a place in the ministry. About a quarter of the voters had promised to vote for Wilkes without asking for money, but he already had doled out a guinea apiece to some 250 "mercenaries"![25]

For all that, Wilkes's dream came true, and on 6 July 1757 the returning officers announced that he was elected for Aylesbury without opposition. Wilkes hurried to the White Hart tavern, where he had ordered a feast for the independents. George Grenville wrote to congratulate him, and Wilkes rushed off to London to call upon Pitt. Not finding him in, Wilkes wrote him a letter: "My ambition will ever be to have my parliamentary conduct approved by the ablest minister, as well as the first character, of the age. I live in the hope of doing my country some small services at least, and I am sure the only way of doing so is by a steady support of your measures. I beg leave to assure you that I shall never depart from these sentiments." Pitt replied, thanking him for the compliment. He was "mortified" to lose the pleasure of seeing him and congratulated him on "being placed in a public situation of displaying more generally to the world the great and shining talents which your friends have the pleasure to be so well acquainted with."[26]

Wilkes was now heavily in debt. Besides the new bond, he had accrued many smaller debts — for Polly's care and education, improvements at Aylesbury, high living in London, and his debaucheries. But this spendthrift had a sense of entitlement unusual in a gentleman so recently risen from a Presbyterian family with its traditions of the Puritan work ethic. He thought it quite acceptable that other people should make good on his debts. Why not his wife? She was wealthy. Jack Wilkes had the temerity to ask his separated wife to quit her claim upon the two-hundred-pound annual alimony. Of course she refused. Astonishingly, he proceeded to sue her in the Court of the King's Bench. Poor torpid woman that she was, she would not come to the court, and the case threatened to die. So Wilkes moved for a writ of habeas corpus to bring her there. Her mother brought her in, but the whole thing backfired. On the bench was Pitt's oldest enemy, William Murray, Lord Chief Justice Mansfield. Mary Wilkes's testimony, and no doubt her pitiful looks, put Wilkes in a light that Mansfield was ready to see as vicious. He promptly ordered Wilkes not to attempt to seize his wife or molest her in any way. It was an outlandish order. Rape her pocketbook, Wilkes might, but seize or molest his wife? Unthinkable. Wilkes, seeing that his suit was hopeless, dropped it. He would continue to pay the alimony, but he and his wife would never see one another again.[27]

Lord Chief Justice Mansfield would be Wilkes's enemy for years to come. A handsome man who looked every inch the wise judge, he rose to great prominence and is remembered as the judge who outlawed slavery in Great Britain. Some call him "the father of modern Toryism." He was a Scot, and his enemies repeatedly suggested he was a Jacobite. It was impossible for him to get entirely clear of the suspicion because some of his family had supported the revolution of 1745. Wilkes would come to see Mansfield's Scottishness as the soft underbelly of his enemy. As a student at Oxford, Mansfield had begun his lifelong rivalry with Pitt by defeating him in a poetry contest. He had been a friend of Pope and was close to Bishop Warburton. Fortunately for Jack Wilkes, he did not know about the Essay on Woman. Unfortunately for Jack, he would one day find out about it.

Mary Mead Wilkes, or more likely her mother, confident now that Wilkes had no claims upon them, sold all the art objects that Wilkes had left in the house in Red Lyon Court behind St. Sepulchre's—thirty-seven paintings, twenty-five sculptures, fifty-six porcelains, eleven tapestries, and ten bronzes.[28] But the court case had a benefit for Wilkes: the separation and his custody of Polly now had the sanction of the highest of English courts. He now had no fear that they would try to take back his beloved daughter. For the next few years, Wilkes spent most of his time in London so he could attend Parliament and be close to Polly at her school in Chelsea with Mrs. Aylesworth and Mme Beete.

It must have been a heady experience the first day Wilkes walked into the House of Commons. Both houses of Parliament met in buildings that originally had belonged to Whitehall Palace but stood adjacent to the main structure. The palace, no longer a royal residence, was used for government offices. The House of Lords convened in an ancient Gothic building, once a dining hall. Close by, the House of Commons met in a revamped chapel that everyone continued to speak of as St. Stephen's Chapel. Tiers of benches were ranged on either side, with the speaker's elaborate throne centered at one end. At the other end was the bar, a paneled fence that separated the seated members from nonmembers who had been called to speak to them. Only members could pass

3. William Murray, first earl Mansfield, Lord Chief Justice of the Court of King's Bench, by John Singleton Copley. National Portrait Gallery, London.

beyond the bar, going through a sort of gate in the center guarded by an officer called a tipstaff. In recent years members had begun to seat themselves so that supporters of the ministry were to the right of the speaker, opponents to the left, a practice that gave rise to our terms, the political right and left. The buildings are gone now, razed in the nineteenth century to make way for the present houses of Parliament.

Early on the morning of 1 December 1757, the members of both houses began to arrive. To the House of Lords, the great nobles came in carriages drawn by four or even six horses with two or more footmen clinging to the back; others were brought in sedan chairs carried by husky chairmen by means of poles fixed to the bottom of the sedan, a tall box with a door and windows that contained the seat. At the House of Commons, more often than not, men arrived on horseback accompanied by mounted grooms who would care for the horses until they were called for. No doubt Wilkes walked, for he was known to prefer that form of travel, and no doubt he was dressed in the fashion of the day, a brocaded coat over a waistcoat, sword at the side, a short, white wig, and a tricornered hat.

Wilkes came into Parliament at a time when his faction was enjoying great success. Britain was in the midst of the Seven Years War, the great war for empire, and the Pittites were the hawks. The war was highly popular because it was profitable for business and commercial interests; and because it stimulated manufacture, it profited workers too. But it was draining the national treasury, and the question of whether England could afford to continue it would be the paramount question in Parliament for the next five years. The war had begun in America with the French and Indian Wars. Then Prussia had invaded Saxony, precipitating the Seven Years War, which could be described as two wars being fought simultaneously. The continental battle between Prussia and Hanover, on one side, and Austria and Russia, on the other, was primarily a struggle for territorial control. Although a sizable British force fought with Prussia, the continental struggle had little relationship to the naval war. The war at sea between Britain and France was fought to gain control of India, the West Indies, and North America.

In times of crisis, English kings have tended to seek the services of new ministers who they thought could handle the new situations. When France had declared war against England in 1756, George II had formed a coalition ministry. Henry Pelham being dead, the king retained his brother, the aging Duke of Newcastle, as first lord of the treasury and nominal first minister, but he was to share the power with Pitt. The sharing was reluctant, for Pitt had distanced himself from the duke, and it was unequal. Pitt was named secretary of state for the south, actually for foreign affairs, and it was he who had the most power.

Pitt was the actual first minister, though Newcastle had the title. Many historians speak of this government as Pitt's first ministry. Pitt also continued to hold his seat in the House of Commons, where he had great influence. Temple, who wanted to keep a low profile, was named the privy seal. The official responsibility of this officer was to seal state papers, to drop hot wax upon the envelope, and to press upon the wax the royal seal. The work was done by one faithful employee. It was the unofficial responsibility that counted — membership in the cabinet, that body of ministers that really ran the government.

Pitt now transformed the government into a war ministry with himself as commanding officer who issued orders directly to generals and admirals. He was a brilliant strategist, and under him the British and allied forces had victory after victory. The public was delighted, especially in London, for the riches that poured into the harbors were obvious. Pitt was adored by the public.

Among the few voices raised in opposition to the war was that of Dr. Samuel Johnson, who decried it as a war of aggression that served only the interests of a greedy, materialistic society: "The American dispute between the French and us," he said, "is . . . the quarrel of two robbers for the spoils of a passenger."[29] Such moral considerations were little heeded, certainly not by Wilkes, who cheered on a war which would give, and indeed did give, to Great Britain an empire.

Only days after he took his seat, the obscure Mr. Wilkes was given the chair of a committee to consider a bill that had already been passed in the House of Lords, "An Act to enable John, Earl of Sandwich, Welbore Ellis, Esq., and Thomas Potter, Esq. to take in Great Britain the Oath of office as Vice Treasurer and Receiver General and Paymaster General of all His Majesty's Revenues in the Kingdom of Ireland." The bill was designed to allow Ellis, Wilkes's fellow member for Aylesbury, and Sandwich and Potter, his two friends and fellow libertines, to be absentee ministers of Ireland. We can hardly doubt that the nobleman and two gentlemen so favorably treated had manipulated Wilkes into the chair of the committee. He had his work cut out for him, but he did it well. It took only one meeting of the committee to recommend passing the bill, though the committee consisted of forty-four members of the House! After receiving the committee report, the House immediately moved and passed the bill. John Wilkes, Esq., was ordered to carry the bill to the House of Lords to acquaint them of the action. It received royal ascent on 23 December, a sort of Christmas present for these outstanding leaders of Ireland.[30]

In this exciting Parliament, Wilkes did not shine. Of course, he always voted with his leader, but what made a member's reputation was the ability to speak well. Pitt, the greatest speaker of the age, used his stentorian voice, long, expressive face, and frail body in dramatic monologues that hypnotized the House. Wilkes had no such talent. A few of his colleagues admired the wit of his speeches and discovered a "classic fire" in them, but his articulation was poor because he spoke through uneven teeth. In the years to follow he began to lose teeth, and his lisp grew worse.[31] He began to write out his speeches in advance, and probably he memorized them; otherwise he would have to read them with a hand covering one eye or with the paper at his nose.

Wilkes presented a new bill in 1762, but it attracted no attention. It was for the naturalization of four persons, none of whom had any known connection with Wilkes, no doubt a routine matter undertaken at the behest of Pitt. Wilkes did make one mark in his first year, but only one. His motion to provide a financial grant to the Foundling Hospital was passed by a voice vote.[32]

Being in favor with ministers gave Wilkes some influence that he did not hesitate to use. There was no impropriety attached to the use of influence, which was an integral part of the system, though a century later it had come to be called "corruption." He got an appointment as an army physician for his old friend Armstrong. Smollett did not hesitate to ask his influence in obtaining a commission in the navy for the son of a friend. He once tried to get a small place for his brother Heaton when the family business was doing badly, but he did not succeed. In March 1759, he tried to get some help for Dr. Johnson. Johnson's servant, Francis Barber, had been pressed into the navy, a kind of involuntary recruiting practiced by the navy, more like a legalized kidnapping than a signing-on. Johnson, who was devoted to this former slave and eventually would make him his heir, was trying to get him released. At first, he turned to Smollett for help, thinking Smollett had maintained some navy connections from his days as a naval surgeon. Unable to help, Smollett turned to Wilkes: "You know," he wrote, "what matter of animosity the said Johnson has against you, and I dare say you desire no other opportunity of resenting it than that of laying him under an obligation. He was humble enough to desire my assistance on this occasion, though he and I were never cater-cousins." Wilkes succeeded in getting a release order, and Johnson made a second application, and one or the other of these actions got the young man his freedom, but not until a year later. It appears that Johnson never thanked Wilkes for his efforts.[33]

In 1759 we catch a glimpse of Wilkes the emerging reformist arguing the rights of a free press in yet another situation in which Smollett asked for his help. Smollett had been accused of libeling Admiral Sir Charles Knowles in the *Critical Review*. The shockingly ill-defined crime of seditious libel amounted to the crime of criticizing the government, in this case, the military. He wrote to ask if Wilkes and his political allies could persuade the admiral to withdraw the prosecution. Admiral Knowles could not be moved, and Smollett was fined one hundred pounds and spent three months in the King's Bench Prison. In the course of the letter Smollett declared, "I shall be very proud to find myself comprehended in your league offensive and defensive; nay, I consider myself already as a contracting party and have recourse to the assistance of my allies." Though we do not know exactly what the "league offensive and defensive" amounted to, we see from the letter that the league was attempting to defend the freedom of the press and doing so through public statements — a foreshadowing of the champion of the press Wilkes would become, though not before he too would feel the lash of libel law.[34]

Wilkes had written to Dell in January 1754 repeating what he had said to the Berwick voters: "You see I declare myself throughout a friend to liberty, and will act up to it."[35] Such a sentiment accompanied by the "league offensive and defensive" bespeaks what we, and sometimes eighteenth-century writers, call a liberal. His position was compatible with his membership in the Pittite party, for Pitt himself was a liberal and the champion of the common man. Before long, however, Wilkes would move to the vanguard of liberal politics and far outdo his master, Pitt.

Wilkes was fond of the phrase "a friend to liberty" and would one day direct that it should mark his grave. It appears on the memorial plaque in the gallery of the Grosvenor Chapel, in the crypt of which, beneath South Audley Street, lie his worldly remains.

The word *liberty* is elusive. Today it is synonymous with the word *freedom*. In eighteenth-century England, *freedom* meant a condition without restraints, whereas *liberty* suggested breaking away from restraint, usually breaking free of oppression by the Crown or the judiciary. And in America? The Liberty Bell was cracked in celebration, not of general freedom, but of liberty from the oppressions of Great Britain.

Like the other Pittites, Wilkes sought to serve "the people," a category that did not include the impoverished masses. Edmund Burke defined *the people* as the adults above menial dependency, who took an interest in politics, who had the means to acquire knowledge of it, and who had "tolerable leisure for such discussions." Burke estimated their numbers at four hundred thousand, less than 5 percent of the population Those who actually had a vote were even fewer.[36] When Wilkes entered Parliament, he was a friend to the people so defined, and he may have foreseen the possibility of becoming their champion. What he could not have foreseen was that one day he would become the champion of the disfranchised poor. A quarter of a century in the future, he would offer in Parliament the first-ever bill to extend the franchise to every adult male.

Wilkes's talents as a propagandist were beginning to appear. When Dr. Armstrong was in Germany with the army, he sent Wilkes a poem, a romantic reverie of the times he had spent at Prebendal House. He called the poem "A Day: An Epistle to John Wilkes of Aylesbury, Esq." He hoped Wilkes would print it and gave him permission to revise it. Wilkes, seeing that the poem might enhance his public image, revised it accordingly. Armstrong did not see the printed version until his return to England, but he was upset with the alterations. The episode augured the propagandist who would make of himself a symbol that appealed to the deepest wishes of the people.[37]

For one reason or another, Wilkes in 1758 made a second trip to Scotland, this time into the western isles. It took some courage for an Englishman to venture into the remote highlands, where only twelve years before the English had quelled the Jacobite Rebellion of 1745 and had broken the power of the rebels by the terrible slaughter of the highland clans after the battle of Culloden. At Inverary he found himself in a courtyard of the great castle of the Duke of Argyll, chief of the Campbell clan, surrounded by kilted highlanders with their broadswords and staves talking to each other in Erse. One of them who spoke English congratulated Wilkes upon his winning the friendship of the duke. Wilkes replied with a double-edged compliment: "It is then, gentlemen, truly lucky for me; for if I had displeased the duke, and he had wished it, there is not a Campbell among you but would have been ready to bring John Wilkes's head to him on a charger."[38]

"I was never happier then when in Scotland," Wilkes wrote, yet he was not above making a joke at the expense of Scottish dignity. He began a letter to Dell written from Edinburgh on 26 September 1758, "I hope before you have opened this letter, you took the necessary precaution of airing it, drying it by the fire, etc., and washing your own hands in vinegar, for fear of a propagation of some Scotch animals in our own good County town." Scottish lack of cleanliness was a common joke in England. In a letter to Armstrong, now lost, he made such fun of Scottish women that Armstrong was constrained to defend his countrywomen: "I have known many of them very clean and sweet as to their persons — not so much as one ringlet to be seen or felt but what you might have kissed with rapture." But in 1758 Wilkes's jokes against Scotland were only jokes. "I love the people for their hospitality and friendship," he wrote, "as much as I admire them for their strong manly sense, erudition, and excellent taste." The words would come back to haunt him when, as writer of the *North Briton,* he made political capital out of English fear and dislike of the Scots.[39]

Toward the end of 1758, Wilkes gave up his lodgings in St. James's Place and moved closer to the scenes of power. He purchased a newly built house at No. 13 Great George Street, Westminster, only a few yards from the houses of

4. This house in Great George Street, London, stood next to Wilkes's house, which was of a similar size and style.

Parliament. The house is no longer there, but the house that stood next door to it, of similar size and style, has been preserved by the Royal Institute of Surveyors, who have connected it to their twentieth-century building. The homes of the politically great clustered in this area. Lord Coke lived at No. 14, and Lord Halifax two doors away.

The parish church for the area was the beautiful Church of St. Margaret, which stands next to Westminster Abbey and also serves as the parliamentary church. The vestry promptly elected Wilkes a member, perhaps encouraged by the rector, the Rev. Dr. Thomas Wilson, who, unlike most clergy, was a declared liberal. The trouble was that Wilkes never attended a vestry meeting.[40]

Wilkes may have thought he had now accomplished what Potter had predicted and entered the world "with éclat." But James Harris, a colleague in the House of Commons, was not so sure: "He has great vivacity, but in sentiment and morals rather tending to be profligate and debauched. His constant flow of mirth and humors gives him an opportunity of saying almost what he pleases of all men to all men." Horace Walpole summed up what he had heard and observed of Wilkes's reputation: "Abominable in private life, dull in Parliament, but, they say, very entertaining in a room."[41]

Wilkes lost his mentor in the spring of 1759, for Potter's "rotten carcass" finally gave out, and he died at Bath. One supposes that Wilkes and members of the Medmenham club went to the funeral, but no record survives. The death of this once brilliant speaker and politician was noticed in the London papers by no more than a bare two-line announcement in the *Gentleman's Magazine.*

The club honored Potter's memory by electing his protégé to fill his place. Wilkes began to go regularly to the meetings and clowned about in a monk's costume and did the satirical rites and joined the sexual antics. He once wrote a letter to Dashwood in Latin hexameters expressing his regret at not being able to attend the prayers and the drinking of consecrated wine "with greedy gulps." Always the scholar, he took over as club librarian and historian. He drew up a list of their books, and in the back of a great King James Bible that belonged to the club left a detailed history of the abbey, including an impressive list of his sources.[42]

Wilkes also had a social life in London. Lord Temple wrote on 27 December 1761, "you are attending my dear Senator to all the humors of St. Stephen's Chapel or amusing yourself with those of Mrs. Cornelys in Soho." Theresa Cornelys had taken over the great Carlisle House in Soho Square, turned it into an assembly room, and was putting on concerts, balls, and sometimes masked balls, admission by subscription only. At his new house, Wilkes entertained respectable gentry, no doubt in part for Polly. Once Mrs. Cibber, the celebrated actress, came and sang for the company the plaintive ballad "Henry and Catherine."[43]

Because the war had raised anxieties that France might invade England, a militia act had been passed in 1757, creating a citizens' army, for which able-bodied men under fifty were to be drafted. In September 1759, Earl Temple, who was now serving as lord lieutenant of Buckinghamshire, announced that the Bucks Militia would be formed ("Bucks" was the common nickname for the county), ten companies, with Sir Francis Dashwood (the St. Francis of the Medmenham monks) to be colonel, and John Wilkes, the captain of a company. They would not be mustered until 1762. Meanwhile, Wilkes could be addressed as captain and wear a red uniform if he chose. He did so choose, and the uniform became his favorite outfit. Though he would never be called to a battlefield, he would prove to be an energetic and enthusiastic soldier who loved the military life.[44]

In the warm months he went frequently to Aylesbury. He had worked out a special arrangement with a new housekeeper named Catherine. Presumably it was Catherine's father who threatened trouble after Wilkes took her into his house. Wanting to avoid an action, Wilkes turned for advice to a lawyer, who told him, "Take the girl as an upper servant, and give her double wages — extra wages denoting that something more than common services were expected to be performed by her." Wilkes did so and enjoyed a mistress at the bargain rate of twenty pounds per annum.[45]

On 10 December 1762, Catherine bore Wilkes a son. Some two years later, when he was in exile in France, Wilkes wrote to his friend Cotes, "I have a boy, about two years old at nurse near Hounslow; a lively little rogue. . . . His mother was my house-keeper, and when she went to see her friends in the country, or to lie-in . . . she went by the name of *Smith* — I believe there is about 5 or 6 pounds due to the nurse." Would Cotes look after them? The child had been christened John, but Wilkes would always call him Jack or Jacky. As Wilkes later told his friend Suard, smallpox innoculation in England was more necessary than baptism; and so Jacky was innoculated. "I love Jack Smith well," wrote Wilkes. "I would give him a finished education." And indeed he saw to it that Jacky was cared for in his childhood and given the education of a young gentleman. But to the boy, Wilkes was always Uncle John, for Wilkes never formally acknowledged the relationship. One wonders how long it took Jacky to figure it out.[46]

George II died on 25 October 1760 and was succeeded by his grandson, George III. The youthful king did not hesitate to bring into the Privy Council his former tutor and father figure, John Stuart, third earl of Bute. The king's father had died when he was thirteen, and George had been reared by his mother and Lord Bute. His emotional dependency upon Bute was obvious, even to the yeomen of the guard, one of whom reported, "The King cannot live without my Lord Bute" and told how when the king went out, upon his return he would always stop his cortege, to their annoyance, and ask if Lord Bute had yet arrived. Bute was exceptionally handsome, and there was a widespread rumor that he and the princess mother were having an affair, something that scholars today tend to think untrue, but masses of people then believed. Bute and the princess mother had brought up the prince to be proud of his responsibilities. "George," his mother is supposed to have said, "be a king!" To that charge he brought a generous and courageous heart, a mediocre education, a limited intelligence, and a determination that often seemed like stubbornness. He was honest and idealistic and wanted the best for his subjects; but he did not know his subjects, for he had passed a childhood in isolation. The so-called madness for which he is remembered today did not begin until 1788, when Wilkes's political career was over. The king who figures in Wilkes's story was a powerful monarch who tried to return Great Britain to a benevolent "personal government," to use the term of the great historian George Otto Trevelyan. When young George first took the throne, he was a romantic figure. Laurence Sterne wrote to John Hall-Stevenson, "He rises every morning at six to do business — rides out at eight to a minute, returns at nine to give himself up to his people . . . the system being to remove that Phalanx of great people which stood betwixt the throne and the subjects." He blamed the troubles of the people upon faction and the Whig oligarchy, and he believed he had the wisdom to appoint ministers who would act in behalf of the people. What he got was the cold, vain, imperious, jealous Lord Bute. "To the pride of birth and rank," wrote John Brooke in his biography of George III, "Bute added a soul-destroying pride in his own intellectual powers and an undue contempt for those who disagreed with him."[47] Lord Bute would prove the catalyst to Wilkes's fame.

The young king had hardly buried his grandfather before he loosed a major controversy. With the encouragement of Bute, he announced he would seek to end the war. Pitt would not hear of it. Bute argued the high costs and diminishing benefits; Pitt, the great advantage to trade and wealth. At the opening of Parliament on 12 November, the king, addressing the assembled Houses, announced his determined goal, to seek a peace. Changes in the government were certain to follow.

Wilkes began to think he had better look for a place for himself. In February 1761, he asked Pitt to use his influence to get him a place on the Board of Trade, a committee answerable to the cabinet that controlled shipping, the protection of ships and colonies, and the administration of colonies. Members usually made themselves rich. He was disappointed. Then he learned there was a vacancy in the Embassy to Constantinople and hastened to apply for it. This time, he could not ask Pitt's help, for Pitt was advancing his brother-in-law, Henry Grenville. So Wilkes asked Henry Legge, the chancellor of the exchequer, to intercede in his behalf, but that was a bad move because Legge, an old stalwart of Newcastle, had fallen out of favor with Bute. Wilkes was passed over again.[48] Though he was to prove himself a genius in elective politics, he had no talent at all for hierarchical politics, that is, for the manipulations and contests among those already in office.

There was a general election in March 1761, and Wilkes, determined to remain in Parliament, announced his intention to stand again for Aylesbury. Once more, the Willes brothers were eyeing the two Aylesbury seats, but when they told the Grenvilles of their ambition, Lord Temple gave them to know that he supported Wilkes. "He has declared," Wilkes wrote to Dell, "for me alone in terms which do me the highest honor." Wilkes now made clear to the voters that he would outbid the Willeses. He was not going to stake the outcome on local support from the independents, no more than "if my squinting phyz had never been seen at Aylesbury." Then unexpectedly another knight rode into the lists. The son-in-law of Wilkes's neighbor and friend Sir William Stanhope, who bore the name of Welbore Ellis, announced he was coming in and would pay five pounds per vote. The canvas and the buying of votes began at once. The price finally rose so high that the Willes brothers withdrew, but not until the polling was under way. That meant that Wilkes and Ellis would be elected unopposed. But the voting had commenced and must be continued. Since the contest was over, Wilkes took himself to Medmenham, where he spent the night. The next morning he made a dramatic reentry into Aylesbury, escorted by a group of horsemen who had ridden out to meet him. That afternoon, he gave a feast for the independents at the White Hart Inn, and a "rout" for the rest of the town "in the usual manner."[49]

Wilkes fared better than Ellis because some of the independents had come through for him after all. He had kept an up-to-date record of everyone who had voted for him and knew it so well that he could address a voter he had never seen before as a friend. He initiated into British politics a new device. Within hours of the close of the polls, he would send a card of thanks to every man who had voted for him, flattering the voter's vanity and disposing him to work for Wilkes in future elections. Still, he called this a "damned election" because it was so costly. His father had recently died, and some assumed that Wilkes used money he had inherited for bribes, but not so. In his will, Israel Wilkes said explicitly, "On the marriage of my son John Wilkes I conveyed to him Lands and Tenements value £330 yearly, which with the presents I have made him I declare to be the whole to be given to him." No doubt Wilkes again borrowed the money.[50]

While the elections were going forward, the king was shifting a few of his ministers. He elevated Lord Bute to secretary of state for the northern department, which dealt with domestic matters, but at the moment the king was afraid to remove Pitt as secretary of state for the south. Pitt's genius for military and naval strategy had given Britain control of ports and lands around the globe. He was cheered everywhere he went, honored by city corporations, adored by the freemen of Westminster and the City. Nevertheless, the king was steadily moving toward a peace.

Wilkes became aware that Great Britain would end up with control of Canada. Could he be made the first governor? His French was excellent, and he hoped, he said, "to reconcile the new subjects to the English; and to show the French the advantages of the mild rule of laws, over that of lawless power and despotism." So carried away with the thought did he become that he went one day to Bute's levee at Whitehall intending to ask for Canada, but his lordship did not appear that day. As it turned out, Wilkes's disappointment was his good luck, for asking a favor of Bute would have been seen as a betrayal of his friends. Thinking better of it, he never went back. When questioned about this in later years, he was able to respond truthfully that "he never did apply for Canada or anything else from Lord Bute."[51] He never did apply, but he had thought about it.

On 8 September 1761, the king married Princess Charlotte of Mecklenburg-Strelitz six hours after he had met her for the first time. He had sent ambassadors on a long search for a princess among the German states, and he did not think there was any point in questioning their choice. Besides, he was in haste because the coronation was scheduled for 22 September.[52] As things worked out this was the happiest marriage of a British king for centuries. Wilkes went to court: "I kissed the queen's fair hand on Thursday."

Coronation day approached. The crowning of the king took place in Westminster Abbey, but then the party moved to Westminster Hall, which stood close by, and there the king and queen would be seated on thrones and honored with elaborate ceremony. From St. Margaret's church one could see both the Abbey and the Hall, so the vestry had a scaffold built from which people could watch and sold places on it for nine or ten pounds. Wilkes wrote to Dell's sister and her fiancée, who was Wilkes's friend the vicar John Stephens, inviting them to visit and join him and Polly on the scaffold and to bring Dell and his wife: "Your tickets are ready." It would not be long before Wilkes and Polly would return to Aylesbury for the wedding, and Wilkes would sign the register as a witness. But why, on coronation day, was John Wilkes, member of Parliament, outside on a scaffold when Pitt and Temple and many other members were entering Westminster Hall? The answer is, he had neither their power nor their money. Inside seats were too dear for a rural squire with guests.[53]

One event in that Gothic hall that day would set off a chain of events that would bring Wilkes into the national limelight. William, first earl Talbot, though handsome and dashing, had cut a foolish figure in his capacity as steward of the royal household. "He had some wit and a little tincture of a disordered understanding," said Horace Walpole, "but was better known as a boxer and a man of pleasure, than in the light of a statesman." But King George or Bute or somebody was besotted with him, and he had been given the honor of participating in the coronation. There was an office called the champion of England, which entailed none but ceremonial duties. The champion was to enter Westminster Hall on horseback, armed cap-à-pie, to challenge anyone disputing the king's rights and to throw down a glove for any challenger to pick up. Three horsemen who represented the knighthood of Britain, one of whom was Talbot, were to ride in after the champion, salute the king, and withdraw. They were to enter by what was then the great main door, on the west end of the Hall where one today sees a set of stairs. The champion and the other two knights had an uncomplicated notion of their duties and supposed that when it was time to leave the Hall, they would simply turn their mounts and ride out. Not Talbot. Since no one was supposed to turn his back to the king, he would not let his horse turn its rump to him. He would *back* his horse out of the Hall. For days he went to Westminster Hall to train the animal, riding him up the stone steps, over the stone flags to the dais. Stop. Salute. Back out. Over and over until the horse was perfect. On the day of the coronation, gaily dressed, noisy people were everywhere, lining the streets outside, arrayed around the walls inside, and laughing and chatting in the gallery which then ran round the Hall. The horse was nervous. He followed the other horses up the steps all right, but as soon as he was ridden into the Hall itself, the animal turned himself around and backed up to the king. The crowd roared with laughter and broke into applause, which was not supposed to be done in the presence of royalty. The king's military uncle, the fat Duke of Cumberland, laughed, said Walpole, till his whole huge body shook.[54] Lord Talbot was mortified and in no mood to tolerate any teasing — as Wilkes would discover when he made fun of the incident in print.

Shortly before this ceremony, in August 1761, rumors had flown across the channel that Spain was secretly joining France in its war against Great Britain and that the two nations had signed a "family compact," so called because both monarchs were Bourbons. A fierce debate was going on among the ministers. Bute wanted to make peace with France at once before Spain got involved, and he was willing to make concessions. Pitt and Temple conceded that a peace treaty was inevitable, but they were the only members of the cabinet who insisted that the treaty should reserve all of the gains bought by the lives of sailors and soldiers.

Then in October, Pitt was brought a letter that had been intercepted at sea, written by the Spanish minister of foreign affairs, the Marquis Grimaldi, that spoke explicitly about a family compact secretly signed in August. Pitt demanded that Great Britain declare war against Spain at once. Unable to move Bute or Newcastle, who was still the nominal chief, Pitt resigned on 5 October 1761. The public was shocked. Then, as the newspapers revealed the terms of his resignation, the shock was doubled. Pitt had accepted a pension of three thousand pounds per annum for himself and a peerage as Baroness Chatham for his wife. Richard Rigby wrote to the Duke of Bedford, "The city and people are outrageous about Lady Cheat'em, as they call her, and her husband's pension." Lord Temple was at pains to write a long letter to Wilkes, trying to explain away Pitt's conduct. Pitt would have been, he said, "the most insolent, factious, and ungrateful man . . . had he waived an offer of this sort, which binds him to nothing, but to love and honor His Majesty." Pitt lost many followers. He managed to keep in politics by publishing a well-crafted letter to his henchman in the City, Lord Mayor William Beckford, explaining his position, but he never would regain fully the control of the City of London he had enjoyed.

Four days after Pitt resigned, Lord Temple returned the seals of his office to the king and retired from his majesty's service. Then Pitt and Temple learned that Temple's younger brother, George Grenville, who had been Wilkes's friend and adviser, had broken from them and gone over to Bute. The king at once invited Grenville into the cabinet, though he had no place in the ministry, and asked him to take the management of the king's friends in the House of Commons. Flattered, he accepted. Furious, Temple threatened to cut his brother out of his paternal estate and give it to their younger brother, James.[55] But the principle of tolerance was strong in Temple, and he had not the heart to punish a brother for his political position.

On 6 November 1761, Parliament opened, and again the king addressed a joint meeting of Commons and Lords. It was the practice in the House of Commons to respond to the king's speech in a letter called "the address," which was usually a political football, hotly debated from the floor. A draft had been prepared the evening before by a caucus of ministers and their supporters in the House of Commons. Grenville moved the acceptance of this draft. Wilkes was among those who opposed. "Mr. Wilkes," reported Walpole, "passed some censures on the King's speech, which, in the language of Parliament, he said he was authorized to call the speech of the minister; though of what minister he could not tell." He said that in reality England was in an unacknowledged state of war with Spain, yet no notice was taken in the king's address of the insults offered by Spain. "He himself had seen a Spanish memorial," continued Walpole, "that had been delivered by a French agent." Pitt next made a long, "guarded, artful, and inflammatory speech" on the ministers' unwillingness to be candid about Spain's hostilities. The proposed address was then passed and, out of honor to the Crown, declared to have been approved unanimously. But there was no real unanimity.

A motion was promptly made by the opposition and quickly passed, demanding that the government put before the House all papers sent to and received from the Spanish embassy. Then the House adjourned for Christmas.

On 10 December 1761, the Spanish government sent orders to all their ports to detain every English ship in them. By the time Parliament was convened after the recess, England had been forced to go to war against Spain, as Pitt and Temple had advocated. War was declared on 4 January 1762. Three weeks later George Grenville laid before the House the papers relative to the declaration of war.[56]

The so-called Spanish papers were not in order, but jumbled together; and it was soon discovered that some documents were missing.[57] On 9 March an anonymous pamphlet appeared under the title *Observations on the Papers relative to the Rupture with Spain, laid before both Houses of Parliament on Friday, Jan 29th, 1762.* The writer defended Pitt against charges of hawkishness and made a masterly, sometimes amusing, critique of the bumbling of the administration in regard to Spain. Pitt was represented as open and candid, Bute as devious. The paper accused the ministry of suppressing documents and castigated them for losing the opportunity of reducing the power of Spain before a war broke out. The writer did not mince words. Bute's new ministry was a ministry of "folly, cowardice and imbecility." The pamphlet caused a considerable stir, and there was much speculation about who had written it. No one suspected the squinting Mr. Wilkes, member for Aylesbury, who in his obscurity had discovered a talent for acerbic writing that would make him famous.

Another wave of panic about a French invasion brought the muster of the Bucks militia. In April 1762, Captain Wilkes returned to Aylesbury, assembled his company, distributed uniforms and supplies, and shortly thereafter marched with them to Winchester or, rather, rode: the officers of foot soldiers were mounted.[58] No doubt he made a dashing figure in his tricornered hat, red coat, sword at side, unforgettable to the troops once they had caught sight of his ugly face.

The militia of several counties came together at a large camp outside the town of Winchester under the command of Deputy Earl Marshall Lord Effingham. In the months that followed, Captain Wilkes led his company through the drills and parades that soldiers being held in readiness seem always to perform. The only action the company saw was the pursuit and apprehension of a small group of French prisoners who had escaped. Two of these poor creatures were shot. For such heroism, Wilkes rewarded the sentries with three weeks' leave, and Colonel Dashwood sent a guinea to the man who had pulled the trigger.[59]

Wilkes's duties were not onerous, he was liked by his men, and he loved the companionship of his fellow officers. Edward Gibbon, who would one day write *The Decline and Fall of the Roman Empire,* was at Winchester as a captain in the South Hampshire Regiment. He had met Wilkes once before when they served on a panel of judges at a courts-martial and found him entertaining "to a very high degree." That autumn, 23 September 1762, Gibbon wrote in his journal,

> Colonel Wilkes, of the Buckinghamshire militia, dined with us, and renewed the acquaintance that Sir Thomas Worsley and myself had begun with him at Reading. I scarcely ever met with a better companion; he has inexhaustible spirits, infinite wit, and humour, and a great deal of knowledge; but a thorough profligate in principle as in practice; his character is infamous, his life stained with every vice, and his conversation full of blasphemy and bawdy. These morals he glories in — for shame is a weakness he has long since surmounted. . . . This proved a very debauched day: we drank a good deal both after dinner and supper and when at last Wilkes was retired, Sir Thomas and some others (of whom I was not one) broke in to his room, and made him drink a bottle of claret in bed.[60]

Wilkes had brought to the camp the manuscript of Potter's "Essay on Woman" and to amuse himself began preparing it for the press. He made a design for an illustrated title page and sent it to a London bookseller, George Kearsley, instructing him to have it engraved and to send him a proof. Kearsley engaged two engravers, William Tringham and William Sherwin.[61] In due time, Wilkes received the proof of this title page, which featured an erect penis beside a ten-inch ruler under which was a Greek motto that can be translated as either "preserver" or "savior of the universe." According to the title page, the work was written by Pego Borewell. *Pego* was an old cant term for penis; the pornographicity of *Borewell* speaks for itself. Less obviously, the name Borewell suggests the name of the other member of Parliament for Aylesbury, Welbore Ellis, who had become a follower of Lord Bute. A Latin note at the bottom of the page referring to the erect penis can be translated, "From the original frequently in the crotch of the Most Reverend George Stone, Primate of Ireland, more frequently in the anus of the intrepid hero George Sackville." George Sackville, later to be called Lord George Germaine, a younger son of the lord lieutenant of Ireland, had been court-martialed for cowardice at the battle of Minden but had been brought into the court of George III by Lord Bute. Sackville's friendship with Archbishop Stone had been the subject of much gossip. Wilkes, not yet entirely satisfied with the page, wrote to Kearsley, "I wish the engraver to make the trifling alterations I have marked, and be so good as to send me a proof here worked off in red ink, and another in black. Keep the plate till I see you." The change was duly made and second-state proofs in red and black were returned to Wilkes. Now completely happy with the title page, he sent one of the proofs to his new friend, the poet Charles

Churchill, who replied, "I have just received Mr. Borewell's favour. I long for the essay." But the essay was not forthcoming. Wilkes could not find a printer willing to do the job. For the time being he gave up the project, though he would eventually return to it and would make use of the copperplate now bearing the change he had ordered. The Latin motto newly appearing under the erect penis and ten-inch scale was, "In recto decus." This was a pun. It could mean either "In uprightness is beauty" or "In the rectum is beauty."[62]

4

The North Briton

We turn now to the story of John Wilkes's daring attacks upon Lord Bute and his ministers in the weekly paper Wilkes began while still stationed at Winchester, the *North Briton*. About Lord Bute and the effect of these polemical essays on his ministry, Horace Walpole had this to say:

> The tide of power swelled the weak bladder of the Favorite's [Bute's] mind to the highest pitch. His own style was haughty and distant; that of his creatures insolent. Many persons who had absented themselves from his levée were threatened with the loss of their own, or the places of their relations, and were obliged to bow the knee. But this sunshine drew up very malignant vapors. Scarce was the earl seated but one step below the throne, when a most virulent weekly paper appeared, called the *North Briton*. Unawed by the prosecution of the *Monitor* (another opponent periodic satire, the author of which had been taken up for abusing favorites), and though combated by two Court papers called the *Briton* and the *Auditor* (the former written by Smollet, and the latter by Murphy, and both of which the new champion fairly silenced in a few weeks), the *North Briton* proceeded with an acrimony, a spirit, and a licentiousness unheared of before even in this country. The highest names, whether of statesmen or magistrates, were printed at length, and the insinuations went still higher. In general, favoritism was the topic, and the partiality of the Court to the Scots. Every obsolete anecdote, every illiberal invective, was raked up and set fourth in strong and witty colors against Scotland.[1]

Thomas Potter's death in 1759 had left a void in Wilkes's life that remained unfilled until the spring of 1762, when Wilkes met the Rev. Mr. Charles Churchill, the most heteroclite parson and most celebrated poet of the time. A few months before, Churchill had published a long poetic satire on actors and theater people that had become the rage of London. This unlikely literary lion was really a bear. He weighed something like three hundred pounds and was nicknamed the Bruiser. Churchill had been born, as they say, with a pewter spoon in his mouth, the son of a struggling parson whose footsteps he was supposed to follow, but a few years of service to the church had left him hating preaching and hating teaching and hating parish life and hating family life. What he had chosen was a libertine life. This was not a man difficult for John Wilkes to understand.

Wilkes took Churchill to the Beef Steaks and the hellfire club. They talked about their current mistresses and sometimes shared them. Wilkes sent a note summoning Churchill to the rooms of an unidentified young woman: "You shall kiss the lips . . . you shall suck the sweetest bubbies of this hemisphere." From Paris, where Wilkes had gone for a holiday, he wrote to Churchill, "I long to introduce you here to the prettiest bubbies, and most pouting xxxx I ever kissed or made a libation to." In an extravagant signature to one of his letters to Churchill, Wilkes declined to write the traditional "I am yours" and wrote instead, "I am — heart, head, soul, and body — except prick, that is not yours but — it *concenters in the center of all virtues* — in Miss — H — ." Unfortunately, Churchill often was careless about the women into whose beds he heaved his large bulk. He repeatedly suffered from clap or pox and was forever undergoing the dread mercury cure.[2] Wilkes was more cautious and has no known history of venereal disease.

Churchill had a sidekick, Robert Lloyd, a poet who came from a Welsh family. He too had a father who was trying to thrust a church career on him, and he too had revolted by embracing a libertine life. By the time Wilkes met them, Churchill and Lloyd had a history of carelessly throwing around borrowed money and rakishly celebrating, as Wilkes said, "the rites of Eros." As a poet, Lloyd left no mark on the history of literature. "He was," Wilkes would write after his death, "content to scamper around the foot of Parnassus on his Welsh pony, which seems never to have tired"[3]

Churchill, a highly intelligent man, recognized more clearly than anyone else Wilkes's talents and so took him to Bonnell Thornton and George Coleman, his and Lloyd's friends from their days at Westminster School. Thornton, an established political writer with financial interests in newspapers, was a faithful supporter of Pitt. Coleman was a lawyer who coedited a periodical with Thornton, but he had begun writing plays and would later become the manager of the

Covent Garden Theatre. Today he is called George Coleman the elder, to distinguish him from his son, who also was a celebrated playwright. Churchill, Lloyd, Thornton, Coleman, and Wilkes soon made a circle of friends that an admiring youthful James Boswell called the "London Geniuses."[4] Together, they would provide encouragement and support for Wilkes's political writing. Wilkes's career from this point forward would prove so spectacular that it would become the subject of Churchill's verse, almost the *only* subject for the rest of his tragically short life.

Wilkes, still on duty in Winchester, decided to test the waters by writing an essay for the London paper the *Monitor*. The editors and writers were champions of Pitt, and one of them, Arthur Beardmore, was Lord Temple's lawyer. The *Monitor* and the other periodicals that Wilkes wrote for, or against, appeared weekly. They were different from the dailies or the three-a-week papers, which had some resemblance to modern newspapers in that they carried accounts (very brief) of political or other events and letters about foreign events from readers or from "correspondants" abroad. The weeklies were not newspapers in any present-day sense, but rather essays along the lines of a modern editorial, though considerably longer. Their circulation was not large, but individual copies were read over and over. Rural squires would share them with their households and neighbors. City people read them in coffeehouses and taverns. Some coffeehouses built up their business by laying out the current papers on tables to be pored over and discussed at length by their customers as they sipped coffee — apprentices and journeymen, small businesspeople, the urban middle and lower middle classes. Both weeklies and dailies were thought to have a great impact upon politics, and some of them certainly did. So politicians financed the papers that supported them and sometimes launched new ones. "The broadening of English political consciousness," wrote the historian Robert Rea, "and the deepening of the roots of political activity was the work of the press."[5]

Monitor No. 357, which appeared on 22 May 1762, was an essay on royal "favorites," anonymous, as were all such political essays, but certainly by Wilkes.[6] A favorite, he wrote, generally begins by getting close to the monarch as a child, discovers his weakness and ingratiates himself "till he gains an entire ascendant over his will; and governs him." As the monarch matures, the favorite "attempts to maintain his own influence and power, by destroying and preventing the growth of great and royal sentiments in his mind; and to usurp the whole authority and management of the state." The implications were crystal clear, for Lord Bute had been the tutor to George III during his late teens. Moreover, Wilkes's essay was a coup, for he had the jump on the big developing political story. Bute and the king had dumped the nominal first minister, the Duke of Newcastle, by dismissing his followers from numerous offices so as to make clear that the old man had lost what was left of his power. Newcastle, after devoting forty years and an enormous fortune to keeping the Whig oligarchy stable, declined a pension the king offered and resigned. Four days after Wilkes's essay appeared, Bute was elevated to first minister as first lord of the treasury. As soon as Bute had kissed hands, he began secret negotiations for a peace treaty with his counterpart in France, the duc de Choiseul, not the official public negotiation, which would come later, but the real one.

On 5 June 1762, there appeared a new paper, the *Briton,* the first issue of which was an answer to Wilkes's essay in the *Monitor.* Lord Bute had been urged by his chief adviser, Henry Fox, to seize the day and establish a newspaper to make fun of "Pensioner Pitt and Lady Cheat'em" and to support the peace negotiations. Bute had dawdled, but, stung by Wilkes's satire, he finally set to work on a propaganda program. Bute hated newspapers, hacks, and controversy. He had no notion of how to choose a writer or how to instruct him. *The Briton* was the result. The writer set about his work with clumsy vigor, attacking the *Monitor* essay as "the vilest work of the worst incendiary; he has scattered his fire-arrows with a rash and desperate hand; he has not only directed them at the bosom of a M[inistr]y without blame, but even dared to aim them at the bosom of a sovereign that never knew dishonor." The effect was to clarify Wilkes's implications to any readers who had been in doubt. The inept writer was none other than Wilkes's friend Tobias Smollett. It is a puzzle how Smollett, a brilliant writer, a novelist, poet, historian, and critic, should have let himself be drawn into political writing, for which he had no talent. Bute wanted a proven writer to work for him, and no doubt he appealed to their common Scottishness. But Smollett disliked politics and was too high-minded for the rough play of political journalism. He was embarrassed because three years before he had dedicated his *Complete History of England* to Pitt. Worse still, he was unable to disguise the contempt he felt for the audience to whom he was supposed to appeal.[7]

On Saturday, 5 June 1762, appeared in London another paper, the *North Briton,* Wilkes's own paper. Wilkes was both chief writer and chief editor, but his name did not appear on it. Issue No. 1 opened with a thoughtful defense of a free press, "the firmest bulwark of the liberties of this country . . . the terror of all bad ministers." A free press throws light upon the "dark and dangerous designs" and the "weakness, inability, and duplicity" of ministers. Wicked governments then use every means "to blunt the edge, of this most sacred weapon, given for the defence of truth and liberty." But most of the paper was less serious, and many of the early issues were given over to making fun of the author of the *Briton,* who was, said Wilkes, bold because he knows he is safe.

He "declares his design to be to detect the *falsehood of malice:* mine shall be to detect the *malice of falsehood.*"

Wilkes certainly knew the identity of the Briton, as he called him. It was not very punctilious to attack a friend with whom he had been exchanging warm letters only two months before. At that time, Wilkes had entrusted Smollett with a secret (about what, we do not know), and Smollett, acknowledging their growing political distance, had said in his letter, "When I presume to differ from you in any point of opinion, I shall always do it with diffidence and deference."[8] Wilkes in other instances took the position that political differences should not interfere with friendship, but not here. It was Wilkes, not Smollett, who began the barrage of insults that Mr. Briton and Mr. North Briton would soon be firing at each other.

Wilkes wrote anonymously, holding that anonymity was one of his rights. But the press was not free, and if he had published the essays under his name, he would have been arrested after the second issue. Yet it was no deep secret who wrote the *North Briton*. Authorship was hard to hide from the spies that watched the presses, and Wilkes's was known to the ministry within days. Wilkes enjoyed being given the credit by hearsay so long as his enemies could not come up with actual proof. During the rest of his life, he admitted to writing only three issues, but only to his opponents in the two duels he was to fight to protect his anonymity. His enemies were not so scrupulous, and in 1764 the House of Commons would vote to declare him the author of *North Briton* No. 45 even though they had no legal evidence.[9]

Lord Temple was the principal backer of the *North Briton* and made no bones about it, while the dukes of Devonshire, Newcastle, and Portland also contributed, but secretly.[10] The publisher, the entrepreneur who received the money from Temple and his friends and established the periodical, was George Kearsley, an obscure bookseller with a shop in Ludgate Hill in the old City. He organized the production and sold and distributed the paper. He hired the printer, William Richardson, who had a printing shop in Salisbury Court.

Richardson, using the standard equipment of the day, printed the paper on a large wood-frame press that supported a steel screw device, the handle of which was tugged by a boy called the printer's devil, forcing down a plate that pressed a sheet of paper against a tray of inked type to stamp two pages onto one sheet, which later would be turned over to print two pages on the other side and then folded once to make four pages. A second printed and folded sheet was inserted into the first, both went into a cover, and all were sewn together at the seam to make an eight-page "folio." By this laborious process, a thousand or so folio copies were turned out on strong paper with large, easily read type.[11]

In his attacks upon Lord Bute and the new ministry, Wilkes's most telling method was to state as forcibly as he could the damaging facts for which he had evidence and then to hold the perpetrator up to moral judgment or ridicule. Never purposely untruthful, he was a master of what in present-day political lingo is called spin. But it was an eighteenth-century spin, making extensive use of sarcasm. Week after week, Wilkes risked arrest for libel, that vaguely defined crime of criticizing the government. He attacked ministers, ministry, and even the courts of law, pointing out gleefully how often Lord Chief Justice Mansfield had put writers like himself in the stocks.

Although he had each issue vetted by a legal expert, he put his confidence in an interpretation of the libel law that by no means was held universally. In his view, to prove a libel one would have to show two things, who wrote the piece and what untruth had been stated. In both points he thought himself safe. He could not be charged with libel if his authorship could not be demonstrated. As to truth or untruth, again and again he challenged anyone to find an untruth in the *North Briton*.[12] Lord Mansfield, on the other hand, whose opinion was certain to be followed, held to the doctrine of his predecessor, Chief Justice Holt: "It is very necessary for all governments that the people should have a good opinion of it."[13] In a libel trial before Mansfield, the jury would be allowed to determine only whether or not the accused had written the passage. The judges would determine whether or not the damage done to the king or minister or judge or member of Parliament or general or admiral was permissible. The permissible was not fixed by statute. Presumably judges reviewed precedents, but in practice they were allowed virtually unlimited discretion. For Mansfield, the essential matter was damage, and truth or falsehood of the statements had nothing to do with the matter.

Wilkes the cool propagandist had also appeared in the *North Briton*. In paper after paper he attacked the Scots for their encroachments upon English society and government. For a while he used the comic narrative device of pretending to be a "north Briton," that is, a Scotsman, although Mr. North Briton was a perfected Scotsman who had rid himself of Scottish chauvinism and the atrocious Scottish dialect. This Scottish persona could speak of his "countrymen" with great freedom. But the device grew stale, and after a few issues he dropped the sham and spoke in his own English voice, though he never let up on the Scots. Making fun of Scotsmen had enormous appeal in England, especially among the Cockneys, the people who lived in the old City of London. Wilkes deplored the great influx of Scots into England and especially their being given places in the very government that a Scottish army had tried to capture only twenty years before. Actually most Scots had opposed the Jacobite Rebellion of 1745, but Wilkes simply ignored that fact. He was playing to the English, who usually regarded "the '45" as a Scottish rebellion to support the claims of the Scottish Stuart line to the throne occupied by an English king. Bute's name was John Stuart, and he was closely related to the pretender, who lived in the Papal State of Rome and was still claiming the throne of England. When Wilkes implied that Bute's ministry might provoke another Jacobite rebellion, he was playing upon a widespread English fear.[14]

Most Scotsmen never forgave Wilkes. So hated was he in that nation that all facts were lost in a new myth of Jack Wilkes. He became in Scotland as much a bogey as Bute was in England. Numerous times he was burned in effigy by mobs of Edinburgh apprentices. Small boys began to observe the king's birthday by burning effigies of Wilkes, much as English children burned effigies of Guy Fawkes. The custom is gone now, but well into the age of Victoria, children in Edinburgh were burning up John Wilkes.[15]

To avoid the charge of libel, political writers regularly hid names behind asterisks or dashes. Not Wilkes. He usually wrote in terms that were just general enough to make the use of individual names unnecessary, though, to the astonishment of the public, he spelled out the names of the most powerful people: Nathan Carrington, the chief of the crown messengers, as the king's police were called; Lord Chief Justice Mansfield, the highest ranking judge in England; Lord Bute, the first minister; and Bute's friend, the powerful Henry Fox, the most crafty and dangerous politician of the time. Smollett in the *Briton* had been afraid even to use the innocuous word *ministry,* rendering it *m — t — ry.* "I despise so pitiful an evasion," Wilkes wrote. "The laws of my country are my protection; my only patron is the PUBLIC, to which I will ever make my appeal, and hold it sacred. I would not use any *stars,* though I could dispose them as judiciously, and in as proper numbers, as that amazing *comic* genius *Tristram Shandy;* unless indeed I meant them to the same *comic* purpose."[16] Never once did Wilkes disguise a name. His protection was that the paper did not have *his* name on it. But the protection was not strong enough. Eventually he would be arrested by this same Nathan Carrington of the crown messengers, but not until the *North Briton* had reached the number of forty-five. Ultimately, he would be condemned to prison by this same Lord Mansfield of the Court of the King's Bench, though not until the *North Briton* had reached the number of forty-six.

Lord Temple was alarmed at the way his protégé was going about his task. After the appearance of the third issue, he had been approached by the ministers and asked to dismiss Wilkes from the militia. He protested; and because they had no actual proof of Wilkes's authorship, they let the matter drop. What was Wilkes doing? "Attacking at once the whole nation of Scotland, by wholesale and retail in so very invidious a manner," Temple wrote, and "Lord

B's name at full length, may be attended with unhappy consequences." Pitt began to have cold feet and spoke to Temple. Wilkes replied to Temple, asking what qualifications Pitt had to evaluate the paper? "Mr. Pitt ought to fear the shadow of a pen," for though he was undoubtedly the best speaker of the age, he was the worst writer: "He would do well to harangue the 500 deputies of the people in the cause of liberty, and the *North Briton* would endeavor to animate the nation at large."[17] Wilkes had the bit in his teeth, and Temple's attempt to check him did no good. He had found his place in the political world, and he was very excited.

Though initially Wilkes had not expected the *North Briton* to last long, when it became apparent that he was making a powerful political impact, he invited Churchill to be his editor. Together, they reorganized the paper. Wilkes would send the manuscripts of his essays from Winchester. Churchill, using Wilkes's house as an office, would edit them, not for content, but for style, and then take them to William Johnston, a bookseller, who would advise whether the writing was libelous, "for fear," said Wilkes, "I have got too near the pillory." Churchill would then deliver them to Kearsley, the publisher, who would have them printed and distributed. Churchill would see to it that Kearsley had done a satisfactory job, and he would provide essays of his own when and if Wilkes could not. Churchill wrote at least five, possibly seven, of the forty-six issues.[18]

The *North Briton* appeared regularly every Saturday. On June 10, a few days after the first issue, yet another essay-sheet made an appearance, the *Auditor,* written by Arthur Murphy, an actor and writer of considerable accomplishment. The *Auditor* was the second paper financed by Lord Bute. Now there were four cudgellers in two teams. On one side was Smollett at the *Briton* with Murphy at the *Auditor* as his partner; the opposing team consisted of Wilkes at the *North Briton* and Beardmore and others at the *Monitor.* So interesting did the public find this play that a thieving printer proceeded to pirate all four periodicals and reissue them under one cover as *Political Controversy.* This pirate publisher outrageously adopted the name of John Caesar Wilkes, but he was certainly not John Wilkes. His name was Brookes, and Wilkes was contemptuous of him.[19]

Smollett proved himself so inept that he never developed a following of more than 250 buyers. After a few months, Wilkes and the others simply ignored him. Years later Smollett lamented "the absurd stoicism of Lord Bute, who had set himself up as a pillory to be pelted by all the blackguards of England."[20] The *Auditor* had a following almost as thin, but Murphy scored two hits in the names he gave to Temple and Wilkes. Calling attention to Lord Temple's tall, awkward person, he named him Lord Gawky. Wilkes he named

Colonel Cataline, likening him to the disreputable and impoverished politician of ancient Rome who attempted to regain power by fomenting a rebellion. But Murphy was careless about facts and handicapped by having to
write nothing but defenses of Lord Bute, a man so unpopular that he was
stoned in the streets. Though the *Monitor* was the most scholarly paper of the
four and would outlast the others by years, the star of the day was Jack Wilkes.

It was Wilkes's treatment of the Scots that most worried his friends and
infuriated his enemies. No. 2 was devoted to an ironic celebration of Bute's
attaining an office that would benefit his countrymen. Mr. North Briton reviewed the history of the payments made to the Scottish chiefs after the rebellion of 1712, which assured their peacefulness, and expressed confidence
that Lord Bute would now dip into the national treasury to make a second set
of payments due to them for ceasing the rebellion of 1745. In No. 3, Mr.
North Briton celebrated Scottish clannishness and their loyalties to one another. "The time is at length arrived, when the being born in Scotland shall be
found to be the best and most effectual recommendation to preferment in
England." When Temple again protested, Wilkes replied that the facts justified
him. He described the massive displacement of English by Scotsmen in the
government bureaus, the clannishness of the Scots, and their zeal to help each
other. Nothing like this happens, he argued, among the Irish. "No Scot ever
exerted himself but for a Scot. This was an odious, and a national character."
The accuracy of Wilkes's view was corroborated by Bute's confederate, Henry
Fox: the press, said Fox, meaning the *North Briton,* set a fire of hatred of Bute
that spread quickly because "blown by a national prejudice which is inveterate
and universal. Every man has at some time or other found a Scotsman in his
way, and everybody has therefore damned the Scotch: and this hatred their
excessive nationality has continually inflamed."[21]

Wilkes's treatment of the Scots was nothing but a blatant propaganda device. He made fun of Lord Mansfield as the successful Scotsman, though
Mansfield had been born and reared in England and was an Englishman at
every point except his family history. Wilkes had no personal hatred of Scotsmen. Baxter, Carlyle, Smollett, Armstrong, and Hume had been his friends,
and he would soon make a friend of James Boswell. Smollett, Armstrong, and
Hume broke with Wilkes over the paper, and Baxter was dead. But Boswell
remained a friend for life. "Wilkes is a most agreeable companion," Boswell
mused. "He is good-humored and vivacious, and likes the Scots as well as
anybody; only he considers the abusing that nation as a political device, which
he must make use of. Whether or not this can be esteemed fair, I am really at a
loss to say." Wilkes had, said John Brooke, "the knack which marks the good
journalist of being able to put into words what is in the minds of his readers —

and was bold enough to do so. Whether he believed what he wrote is immaterial — the point is, his readers did."[22]

The issue of the *North Briton* that most delighted the nation of England was
the audacious No. 5. The entire paper was taken up by an anonymous letter
sent to the editor, a common and quite transparent device of essay-papers such
as this. The "letter writer" told the story of the boy king, Edward III (born in
1312), his mother, Isabella, and her lover, Roger de Mortimer, the first Earl of
March. When Edward came to the throne as a small child, a regency of twelve
nobles was established. It was dominated by Mortimer, who manipulated the
court to keep the young king away from anyone not a member of Mortimer's
crew. When the king was in his teens, the Scots invaded England under their
king, Robert Bruce. Edward personally marched out at the head of his army to
meet the invaders, driving them back over the border. The Scots then agreed to
a peace treaty drafted by Mortimer remarkable for the benefits it gave to
himself. Then someone told the young king that Mortimer had been a spy for
the Scots and was having an affair with the queen mother. Edward had the
man arrested before his mother's eyes and sent to the Tower. He called a
Parliament and talked them into an act that abolished the regency and left him
in control of the nation, though still a minor. He promptly had Mortimer
hanged at Tyburn. The parallels to King George in his youth, his mother the
Dowager Princess of Wales, and Lord Bute the tutor of the boy king and lover
of his mother (in the popular view) were obvious to all.[23]

Churchill was worried. "The paper of the third will never be forgotten," he
wrote, "and you will never be forgiven, as it is universally ascribed to you. It
has opened the eyes of many. . . . I desire you to take great care of your health,
and still more of your life."[24] Churchill's fears were not realized, and Wilkes
was neither arrested nor assassinated.

A contemporary broadside, "Malice and Fortitude," depicts an innocent,
unarmed Wilkes standing within a low picket fence called "the Pale of English
Liberty," that inadequately protects him from a group of attackers, including
Lord Mansfield, Fletcher Norton, Lord Bute with a drawn sword, and the
Dowager Princess of Wales with a raised dagger! In the clouds above, an
angelic figure holds over Wilkes's head a laurel wreath (illustration 5).

Though Wilkes had been careful to base his story upon recognized histories,
duly cited, many people found it the most libelous thing he had written. At a
later date, when a friend advised him to tone down his essays, he replied that
"he had tried the temper of the court by the paper on Mortimer, and found
they did not dare to touch him."[25] Subsequent events would prove that he was
overconfident, for the story raised in King George III a passionate hatred. "I
hear from all hands," Wilkes wrote, "that the King is enraged at my insolence,

5. "Malice and Fortitude." Lord Mansfield, Lord Bute, the Princess Mother, and others attack Wilkes within the Pale of Liberty. Courtesy of Gerald M. Goldberg.

as he terms it. I regard not his frowns nor his smiles. I will ever be his faithful subject, never his servant." Loyalty to the crown meant for him loyalty to Great Britain, but not to the king as a person, whom he despised. "Hypocrisy, meanness, ignorance, and insolence, characterize the king I obey."[26]

Then it came to Wilkes's attention that the story of Mortimer had been dramatized in an old play of William Montfort (1664?–92) recently adapted for the current public by William Hutchett. Wilkes hastened to publish an edition of the Hutchett version, the real purpose of which was to provide a vehicle for a dedication. "Wormwood," said Horace Walpole. The drama, wrote Wilkes in the dedication, shows how one "bad Man" came close to sacrificing the constitution and liberties of the nation, but how they were rescued by the king's friend, Montacute, "aided by a Patriot Band." The followers of Pitt were often called patriots. Wilkes wrote to Kearsley asking him to send a gilt-edged copy to Bute and to include a card with the following message: "The Author of the dedication presents his compliments to Lord Bute, and desires his Lordship would do him the Honour of adding this Volume to the Argyle Library." A few days later, Wilkes happened to meet Jeremiah Dyson, who worked under Bute, and asked if he were going to the Treasury, "because," said he, "a friend of mine has dedicated a play to Lord Bute, and it is usual to give dedicators something. I wish you would put his Lordship in mind of it."[27]

On 30 September 1762, Murphy published in the *Auditor* a story about Wilkes with the intention of blackening his name. Bute had a twelve-year-old son who was at school in Winchester. According to Murphy, Wilkes, when he was on duty with the militia close to that town, happened to meet the lad in a bookseller's shop. Wilkes was supposed to have accosted him and said, "Young gentleman, your father will have his head cut off." The boy was said to have attempted some defense, but Wilkes insisted, "Your father will lose his head, or the mob shall tear him to pieces," whereupon the boy, bursting into tears, called him a "squinting scoundrel" and ran out of the shop. Dr. Brocklesby, the physician and friend of Wilkes from his Leiden years who had sponsored his admission to the Royal Society, came forward with another account. He had been in the bookseller's shop and had overheard a conversation between the boy and a gentleman, not Wilkes, but someone else. The boy, reading John Caesar Wilkes's *Political Controversy,* began uttering curses against the "goggle eyed son of a bitch who by his writings approved himself more his father's enemy than any other person besides Mr. Pitt." The gentleman then spoke up in favor of Wilkes as a "good natured man" who "would not hurt a worm" but declined to comfort the boy's fears that his father might be mobbed. Someone in the shop had talked about what happened, but the

facts had gotten twisted. Wilkes hastened to deny he had ever had a confrontation with the young man and called upon the *Auditor* to produce some evidence. Murphy did not. Wilkes asked the headmaster of the Winchester school
to arrange an interview with the boy, but the headmaster did not feel he could
do that, though he said he believed Wilkes. The bookseller too defended him.
No one could believe Wilkes would have been cruel to this boy, for it was well
known how much he enjoyed children. The matter was soon forgotten.[28]

But Wilkes had his revenge against Murphy. The debates about the peace
had raised questions about the value of Florida, a far-off land about which
Englishmen knew almost nothing. What use could be made of it? How valuable was it as a bargaining chip in the peace negotiations? Wilkes and Churchill wrote an anonymous letter to the *the Auditor* which they signed "Viator."
Viator told about traveling the length of Florida, where he visited numerous
small, but prosperous, well-run towns and neat, comfortable plantation
houses. One outstanding resource of the territory was the peat that could be
taken from its many bogs. Since fuel for domestic use was scarce in the West
Indies, there was a ready market there for the peat. Murphy bit. "The Auditor," he wrote "will continue to throw all the lights in his power upon the solid
value of the advantages procured for us by the late negotiation, and he thinks
he cannot better answer this laudable end at present than by inserting the
following letter exactly in the form, which he received it." Then, on 24 December 1762, Bonnell Thornton's paper, the *St. James's Chronicle,* printed a letter
signed "Observator," which roasted Murphy. Who would want "comfortable" peat fires in a place "where every art is tried to moderate the perpetual,
unremitting, and almost intolerable heat?" The next thing to expect will be
Murphy's suggesting that the Canadians sell ice to Greenland.[29] The blow was
fatal. Two weeks later, the *Auditor* collapsed. A few days after that the *Briton*
ceased, though Smollett had stuck it out until Parliament approved the peace
treaty.

Neither Smollett nor Wilkes was paid for writing his paper. Murphy had a
pension. Smollett expected to have a pension or a place in the foreign service,
though neither was ever granted.[30] Wilkes expected a place when Pitt came
back into office, but none was ever given him.

Wilkes did not expect the *North Briton* itself to make much money and
soon signed over his share of the profits to Churchill. Wilkes had no monetary
benefit from the *North Briton,* notwithstanding a comment by Edward Gibbon that seemed to say otherwise. Gibbon's description in his diary of that
rowdy evening with the officers of the Bucks militia included this: "He told us
himself, that in this time of public dissension he was resolved to make his
fortune. Upon this noble principle he has connected himself closely with Lord

Temple and Mr Pitt, commenced a public adversary to Lord Bute, whom he abuses weekly in the *North Briton* and other political papers in which he is concerned." Wilkes did not mean to say that the paper would be profitable as a business venture. He meant that when and if Pitt were returned to office, he would reward Wilkes for his writing by finding him a place in the service of the king. This was only reasonable; it was the system. Men of little power attached themselves to greater men and served them through thick and thin in the expectation that the great, when they came into power, would reward their services. That is how men rose in the bureaus of government and in politics. It was this dynamic that made factions cohere and ministries stable. It was the way impoverished clergymen rose in the church.[31] Gibbon put a negative spin on Wilkes's remark, not because he did not understand the way of the world, but because he did not like Wilkes's treatment of Lord Bute.

Let us look at the principal themes and devices of the *North Briton*.

Wilkes's primary purpose was to bring down Bute and restore Pitt to the ministry, but he could not say so directly. Rather, he found fault with Bute's intentions and the practices of his ministers, setting them in contrast to the wise conduct of Pitt when he had been the minister. He said repeatedly that Pitt wanted to win the peace as well as the war, to maintain the advantages won by the military at great cost, whereas Bute would settle for terms favorable to France because he was a Jacobite at heart.

Another major theme was the cruelty of excise taxes. Though money must be raised to pay the national debt, the proposed excise tax on cider and perry (a drink like cider, but made from pears) was odious because it would legitimate forced entries and searches of houses and barns, putting into the hands of politicians the means to harass and even destroy their opponents. It was Wilkes's first expression of the right to privacy that he would later champion in the courts.

The relationship of ministers to monarch was a more abstract theme. If ministers are corrupt, as Wilkes so often asserted, the system breaks down. If they encroach upon the rights of Parliament, they cannot be excused upon a plea of "royal prerogative." Wilkes took some risk in speaking so, for in the assumed journalistic ethic of the day, criticizing the policies of a government was permitted, but if a writer criticized the king for choosing his ministers badly or criticized the ministers when they spoke in the name of the king, he was subject to the accusation of libel.[32]

Ignoring such traditions, Wilkes based his criticisms on commonsense ethics. Smollett in the *Briton* had defended the impending peace treaty by arguing that a state is not bound to keep a treaty if it turns out to be "manifestly prejudicial to its interest." Wilkes replied in No. 14, "Is this the good faith for which England has ever been celebrated?" And then he attacked Smollett for having advanced a wicked doctrine.

The rule of law was a principle Wilkes held up to his readers over and over again, and for good reason. In France, law was the word of the monarch, no more. As Louis XV famously said, "L'état, c'est moi." Great Britain was a constitutional monarchy, and the king could not act against or countermand any part of the constitution, the established body of law. The Tories and Jacobites, Wilkes maintained, embrace "the infernal doctrine of arbitrary power and indefeasible right on the part of the sovereign, and of passive obedience and non-resistance on the part of the subject . . . that the people were made entirely for the sovereign and that he had a right to dispose of their fortunes, lives and liberties, in defiance of his coronation oath, and the eternal laws of reason."[33]

Wilkes believed in "the law of reason," or "natural law," as it was often called, and he had faith in "common sense," a term that meant the sense of something shared by most or all people. But he did not write treatises on such subjects. He was a practicing politician and journalist, not a systematic philosopher.

Wilkes interlarded his respectable commonsense ethics with much less respectable appeals to prejudice and invitations to ridicule. "No political paper," he told Lord Temple, "would be relished by the public, unless well seasoned with personal satire."[34] About the ten-year-old son of Gilbert Elliot, a Scottish member of the Privy Council, Mr. North Briton begged in No. 43 to know how long the boy had held a commission of captain in the army. Having hooked his readers by a laugh at the thought of a ten-year-old army captain, Wilkes slipped into the serious accusation. An army list that included the boy's name actually had been published, but the secretary at war had bought up the entire impression in order to destroy the evidence. The secretary at war was none other than Wilkes's fellow member for Aylesbury, Welbore Ellis.

In No. 12, Wilkes spoofed Dr. Samuel Johnson for accepting a pension from the Bute ministry, gleefully quoting from Johnson's *Dictionary: Pensioner,* "a slave of state, hired by a stipend to obey his master"; and *pension,* an allowance "generally understood to mean pay given to a state hireling for treason to his country." Thereafter, whenever Wilkes had occasion to refer to Johnson in the paper, he called him Pensioner Johnson.

More damning of the administration was the exposé in No. 40 of an embezzlement in the army. An inspector of supplies in Germany by the name of Ghest had discovered that the government had been shipping spoiled oats to the army and had reported it to the officer in charge, Lieutenant Colonel Pownal, but Pownal took no notice, continued the shipments, and succeeded in having Ghest dismissed from his job. Though the ministers had learned of these developments, they neither changed the practice nor removed Pownal from his command. At the end of the paper in which all of this was revealed, Wilkes printed the entire correspondence, thereby pinpointing the minister who had been responsible, the secretary of the treasury, Samuel Martin, whom Wilkes proceeded to characterizes as "the most treacherous, base, selfish, mean, abject, low-lived and dirty fellow that ever *wriggled* himself into a secretaryship."[35] No one had ever seen such a string of epithets in print. Martin would eventually challenge Wilkes to a duel.

How did Wilkes get inside information about the spoiled oats? How did he get the letters? One cannot but wonder if the story were not leaked to him by Charles Townshend, Wilkes's friend and competitor from their days at Leiden. Townshend had replaced Welbore Ellis as secretary at war in March 1761. Who better to know the facts than a secretary at war who had come into office shortly after the discovery of this corrupt trade? When Wilkes was going abroad, he wrote to Churchill telling him that in no circumstance was he to write against Townshend, "for reasons too long to give you." This was code, meaning he could not explain in a letter because his letters were being read. Wilkes complimented Townshend in the *North Briton* at least three times, in Nos. 17, 20, and 30. In No. 20 Wilkes praised him at length as the only honorable man in the ministry. Churchill, seeking a place for his brother as an army physician, felt free to ask Townshend for help. All told, it is likely that Townshend was Wilkes's Deep Throat. But they had a falling out when Townshend gave up the ministry of war in December 1762 in order to take a place on the Board of Trade, the lucrative position Wilkes had coveted two years before and had asked Pitt to get for him. Townshend had the reputation of being a "splendid shuttlecock" for shifting sides so often. Wilkes used a harsher image in the satire he called "A Peep into Futurity," discussed below, which was published in February or March 1763. He called him a "hermaphrodite, heterogeneous, amphibious animal."[36]

Wilkes was in constant danger of having his ironies taken literally by humorless or stupid men. The first earl Talbot was both. This was the athletic earl who at the coronation had been humiliated when his horse presented his rump to the king. Almost a year later, in *North Briton* No. 12, the issue devoted to pensioners, Wilkes wrote,

> Every species of elegance and refinement in the polite arts may, I think, without censure, be rewarded with a *pension*. A politeness equal to that of lord Talbot's *horse* ought not to pass unnoticed. At the coronation he paid a new, and, for a *horse*, singular respect to his sovereign. I appeal to applauding

multitudes, who were so charmed as to forget every rule of decency, and to *clap* even in the *Royal* presence, whether *his,* or his *lord's* dexterity on that day did not surpass any courtier's. . . . What the exact proportion of merit was between his *lordship* and his *horse,* and how far the pension should be divided between them, I will not take upon me to determine. . . . In my private opinion, however, the merit of *both* was very great, and neither ought to pass unnoticed. The impartial, and inimitable pen of *Cervantes* has made *Rozinante* immortal as well as *Don Quixote.* Lord Talbot's horse, like the great planet in Milton, *danc'd about in various rounds his wandering course.* At different times, he was *progressive, retrograde, or standing still.* The *progressive* motion I should rather incline to think the merit of the *horse,* the *retrograde* motion, the merit of the *Lord.*

On 10 September, Talbot sent Wilkes an angry letter, demanding to know whether or not he had written the passage. Wilkes replied, "My answer is, that I must first insist on knowing your Lordship's right to catechise me about an anonymous paper. If your Lordship is not satisfied with this, I shall ever be ready to give your Lordship any other satisfaction becoming me as a gentleman." Talbot replied, "Every man's sense of honour ought to direct his conduct; if you prefer a personal engagement to the denying being the author of a paper that has been so free with my name; I, who am publicly affronted by that paper, cannot, in honour, avoid requiring the satisfaction you seem most desirous to give." Wilkes did not answer. Talbot wrote again, and again Wilkes refused to answer. Talbot then became specific: "If you do not deny the paper, I must and will conclude you wrote it." Wilkes: "Your Lordship has my free consent to make any conclusions you think proper, whether they are well or ill grounded; and I feel the most perfect indifference about what they are, or the consequences of them."

Wilkes showed the letters to Sir Francis Dashwood, at that time his commanding officer, and to Lord Temple. Temple, without faulting Wilkes's conduct, went to Talbot and tried to reason with him. He got nowhere. A few days later, Talbot's appointed second, Colonel Norborne Berkeley, member for Gloucestershire, came to the Winchester camp and talked with Wilkes. They came to an agreement, and Wilkes, to make all clear, wrote it out thus: "Be assured that if I am between heaven and earth, I will be on Tuesday evening at Tilbury's, the Red Lyon at Bagshot, and on Wednesday morning will play this duet with his Lordship." His own second was to be his adjutant, one Harris. He would bring no servant for fear of the parties being known. "My pistols only, or his Lordship's, at his option, shall decide this point." As the challenged person, Wilkes could choose the form of combat: he chose pistols. He also was to have the choice of the specific weapons, but he gave it to Talbot.[37]

We who are not familiar with the traditions of dueling, might ask, what was going on here? Why were these men ready to kill one another? Wilkes was ready to put his life on the line to defend his right and, through him, the right of the press in general to publish anonymous pieces. Lacking that right, in Wilkes's view, the press would not be free. Talbot thought a free press was a danger to society, and noblemen had every right to demand its secrets and control its product. When Wilkes asked what "right" Talbot had to question him, he was asking if Talbot, who represented both administration and nobility, was threatening to break the anonymity of the *North Briton*. Wilkes would fight to prove that he had no such right. To be sure, Talbot was thinking less of principle than of the dishonor Wilkes's satire had cast upon him, and Wilkes might have been thinking of how his image would be enhanced if he survived. Talbot was an athlete, and both his eyes were good. But formally, personal motives were not part of the challenge or acceptance, which were made in terms of civil rights.

The duel was fought with pistols on the evening of 5 October 1762 outside an inn on the remote Bagshot heath, famous for its robberies and duels. We know the details of the story through a letter Wilkes wrote to Lord Temple immediately after the event and from other accounts based on what the seconds had told their friends.[38]

Let us begin at the beginning. Wilkes and Harris, dressed in their red officers' coats, had arrived on horseback in the afternoon, horse pistols in their saddle holsters. They alighted at the Red Lyon, an old coaching inn at Bagshot, and sent for Colonel Berkeley, who came down to them. After the soldierly greetings, Colonel Berkeley told them that Talbot wished to get the matter over with at once. Such haste was contrary to what Wilkes had understood. He expected, he explained, that all four men would sup together that evening and meet in the morning, and on that expectation he had passed a drunken night at Medmenham Abbey and had been up until four a.m. He was in no condition to fight today. "Their parti quarrée that night would not spoil the duet which was to be the entertainment of the following day." Colonel Berkeley agreed that this was reasonable. Wilkes and Harris went in to Talbot, whom they found in "an agony of passion." Again he insisted upon knowing if Wilkes wrote the essay or not. As Wilkes told the story to Lord Temple, "I observed, that I was a private English gentleman, perfectly free and independent, which I held to be a character of the highest dignity; that I obeyed with pleasure a gracious Sovereign, but would never submit to the arbitrary dictates of a fellow subject, a Lord Steward of his Household; my superior indeed in rank, fortune, and abilities, but my equal only, in honour, courage, and liberty."

Talbot wanted to fight that very night. Wilkes repeated his reasons for wanting to wait until morning, but Talbot was insistent. So Wilkes gave up the point. He called for pen and paper to write a letter to Temple and another to Lady Temple, asking her to look after Polly's education.[39] Talbot grew restive, then frantic and abusive, saying Wilkes would be hanged and damned, and the like. "I said I was not to be frightened, nor in the least affected by such violence; that God had given me a firmness and spirit, equal to his Lordship's." Talbot again demanded that he own or deny the paper. Wilkes would not. If he survived he would then declare it, but not before. Talbot then allowed that he admired Wilkes exceedingly, really loved him, "an unaccountable animal — such parts! but would I kill him who had never offended me? &c. &c. &c." Then Talbot wheeled about again and accused Wilkes of trying to murder him: "If you will fight, if you kill me, I hope you will be hanged; I know you will." Wilkes, amused, asked whether he was first to be killed and afterward hanged? "I knew his Lordship fought me with the King's pardon in his pocket, and I fought him with a halter about my neck; that I would fight him for all that." If Talbot should fall, said Wilkes, "I should not tarry here a moment for the tender mercies of such a ministry, but . . . make the best of my way to France, as men of honour were sure of protection in that kingdom. He seemed much affected by this."

Wilkes then entrusted his letters to Colonel Berkeley and rose from the table. As they walked out the door Lord Talbot asked how many rounds they should fire; Wilkes answered, "Just as many as your lordship pleases." The seconds paid no attention to this, but taking one large horse pistol from the saddle of each of the combatants, they charged them. They tossed a coin to see which second was to give the command to fire. It fell to Harris. They went into the garden at some distance from the house. It was seven in the evening and the moon very bright. Wilkes then asked his opponent to declare in front of the seconds that it was he who had desired this meeting. Talbot could not refuse. They stood about eight yards apart, not facing, but had agreed to turn about and fire on command and to continue facing. Harris gave the word. Both whirled about and fired at the same time; both missed. The seconds, thinking enough had been done, stepped in to prevent any reloading of the pistols. "I walked up immediately to his lordship," wrote Wilkes, "and told him that now I avowed the paper. . . . His lordship paid me the highest encomiums on my courage, and said he would declare everywhere that I was the noblest fellow God had ever made." As William Rough, Wilkes's son-in-law, pointed out many years later, it is unlikely Talbot would have said such a thing had Wilkes not fired into the air. Probably they both did.[40] Then Talbot, said Wilkes, "desired, that we might now be good friends and retire to the inn to drink a bottle of claret together, which we did with great good humour and much laughter."

Many of the details of the affair were talked about by the seconds and soon were spread over the town. The public, said Edmund Burke, "think this Business ended to the advantage of Wilkes, who they think behaved more firmly, consistently, and coolly than Lord Talbot." Wilkes was well known before this event, but after it he was famous. The image of the duelist, with all its suggestions of high class and manly courtesy, of valor and soldierly conduct, was affixed to Jack Wilkes from then on. Lord Temple wrote to him, "I think you could act no otherwise than you have done, like a man and a gentleman in every part of it." Churchill, in a letter written three weeks later, told his friend, "The affair of Lord Talbot still lives in conversation, and you are spoken of by all with the highest respect. Lord Weymouth gives you the greatest encomiums. Your friends at the Beef Steak enquired after you last Saturday with the greatest zeal." A year later Lady Temple told her husband, "Wilkes is raised very high in people's opinion, and my Lord Talbot as low, and feels it so much he has never lifted up his head since." Wilkes's mother took another view, talked gravely, and asked, "Why rush into presence of your Maker?" "I've been always in it." "And into eternity?" "Where have I been all this time?" One may doubt that Wilkes told his mother of the ultimate ephemeral reward awaiting him, but he told Churchill, "A sweet girl, whom I have sighed for unsuccessfully these four months, now tells me she will trust her *honor* to a man who takes so much care of his own. Is not that prettily said? Pray look me out *honor* in the dictionary, as I have none here, that I may understand the dear creature."[41]

It is likely that this dear creature was the new mistress Wilkes acquired about this time. Her maiden name is not known, but she survives in record by the name she aquired later when she married John Barnard, a City merchant. There is no proof that the sweet girl was the woman who would marry Barnard, but the identification is suggested by their cleverness with words, their interest in sex, and the charm by which they expressed it. Blackheath, where Wilkes first met the future Mrs. Barnard, was not far from Winchester. They met in the house of a certain Grace Ozier and first went to bed under Mrs. Ozier's roof. Soon after, Wilkes carried her to an elegant dinner at Greenwich. They continued to meet, ostensibly to have tea, either at Grace Ozier's or at a love nest Wilkes established in Marlebone. She had the cool head of an adventuresome woman, but that did not stop her from falling in love with Wilkes, the "reigning sovereign" of her being. It is doubtful Wilkes told her about Catherine at Aylesbury, much less about Mrs. Grosvenor, another woman who came into his life in the spring of the next year about whom we know nothing but the name. Wilkes would hardly have been candid with these women and may well have made love to all three during the spring of 1763. But the future Mrs. Barnard was a survivor on the model of DeFoe's Moll Flanders. Knowing her situation to be precarious, she asked Wilkes to give her a settlement, that is, to endow her with the means to sustain herself. Wilkes declined, no doubt saying, as he was to say to his Italian mistress two years hence, that settlements were made after years of a shared love life, not months. She went to a lawyer, but he was unable to bring about an agreement. When the lawyer sent her a bill, she asked Wilkes to pay it. He refused, and the ensuing quarrel led to a breakup.[42] But she was not bitter, and when by accident she would reappear in Wilkes's life, she would be his lover again, this time while he was a prisoner of the Crown.

Wilkes's admission to Lord Talbot that he was the author of No. 12 had annoying consequences. Lord Litchfield, who was treated roughly in No. 29, a not-very-successful satiric allegory of the internal politics at the University of Oxford, told his lawyers to commence a prosecution. Wilkes responded with a letter to his lordship: he had not thought that admitting his authorship of No. 12 to Talbot would lead to "wrangling litigations." "The morning after his lordship commenced any kind of proceeding in Westminster Hall, Mr Wilkes would oblige him to decide the affair by the laws of honor or to drop it." Lord Litchfield chose to drop it.[43]

Part of Wilkes's success in the *North Briton* arose from an appearance of complete candor, which in actuality was skillfully crafted. At the time he was preparing No. 6, he wrote to Churchill that he was sending "good combustible matter . . . that will vex where you and I wish to vex: mentioning the late king with honour, the battle of Culloden, &c., &c. is to plant daggers in certain breasts." And far from being ashamed of what he did, Wilkes was proud of it. When Boswell met him in Italy in 1765, they fell into this conversation: "I make it a rule," said Wilkes, "to abuse him who is against me or any of my friends point-blank." "But Dr. Johnson," protested Boswell, "he is such a respectable character in the world of literature." Wilkes shrugged: he treated Dr. Johnson as "an impudent pretender to literature, which I don't think, but 'tis all one. So is my plan."[44]

Wilkes could see the ridiculous side of all this and once wrote a playful satire of political writing directed at Murphy, the writer of the *Auditor,* and at himself as the writer of the *North Briton.* In "A Peep into Futurity" he explained that every political writer "sits down with encomiums on the right and obloquy on the left, . . . with whitewash in one hand, and black-ball in the other, like Jupiter between the tubs of good and evil." The *Auditor,* he went on, "is by far the most respectable character, and most polite writer of the two.

The *North Briton* sounded the *nether trump of fame* at the very first onset, and furiously charged the Scots and the ministry at once. The *Auditor* set out with professions of moderation and impartiality." He had intended, the peeper into futurity continued, to provide a list of both the blackened enemies and whitened friends of the two papers but can save himself the trouble by a general rule: "Such as are blackened in the *North Briton,* are by act of grace, whitewashed in the *Auditor,* and so *vice versâ.*" Having thus set aside the need to list the friends of the *North Briton,* he presented two lists of the people blackened, one for each paper. Each list is arranged by rank, like a dramatis personae. The list of people blackened in the *North Briton* begins daringly, "P.D.of W." — that is, the Princess Dowager of Wales. Then come the nobles one might expect, "the Duke of Bedford, Earl of Bute, Earl of Louden, Earl of Litchfield, Earl of Talbot, Earl of Talbot's Horse."[45]

Sir Francis Dashwood, commander of both the Bucks militia and the Medmenham knights, having been called by his king to take a place in the ministry, resigned his colonelcy of the militia in favor of Wilkes. In a letter to the officers, he praised Wilkes as "a man of spirit, good sense and civil deportment."[46] Wilkes responded from Winchester, "It shall be always my endeavor to merit the obliging things you are so kind to say of me, and I shall esteem myself particularly happy, if I can in any manner alleviate the loss which the whole corps must easily feel. . . . I feast my mind with the joy of Medmenham on Monday, and hope to indemnify myself there for the noise and nonsense here." On 25 October 1762, Jack Wilkes was duly elevated to the colonelcy, the chief officer of the regiment, and promoted to the rank of lieutenant colonel.[47]

Wilkes was now in command of the entire camp at Winchester with responsibility for the militia of five counties as well as the 34th Foot, a regiment of regulars; but the command was the least glamorous of such honors. The newly signed preliminary peace treaty ended the need for the militia, and Wilkes's major duty was to oversee the breakup of the camp and the return of the various regiments to their several counties. He set to work.

The commander of the regulars, the 34th Foot, was a colleague in the House of Commons, Colonel Isaac Barré. Wilkes feared he would have trouble from this bellicose one-eyed soldier who had fought with Wolfe and Amherst in America, but no trouble arose.[48] Wilkes and Barré in time would become fellows in the support of America, but never friends. It is unlikely they would have been glad to see their names joined in the name of Wilkes-Barre, Pennsylvania.

When the last of the troops had marched off, Colonel Wilkes took horse and rode to Oxford for a visit with his friend the Rev. Dr. Thomas Frye, president of St. John's College. Frye, a subversive in the heavily Tory university, had supplied him with information for the attack he had made on the Oxford

Tories in *North Briton* No. 26.[49] From Oxford, Wilkes set off for London, making a short stop at Aylesbury. Thereafter we find him at his house in Great George Street, Westminster — or do not find him because he is in bed somewhere else with Mrs. Grosvenor. In December he made a trip to Reading to meet the officers who had been under his command and to give them "a farewell drink."[50] We can guess how that day ended.

William Hogarth, the painter and print satirist, had for some years been a friend of Wilkes's, meeting him at the Beefsteaks and Foundling Hospital, but had avoided talking politics. It mattered not at all to Wilkes that Hogarth was a Tory, at least by temperament, or that his liking of the ministry had led Bute to obtain for him the position of Sergeant Painter to the King. Wilkes seldom let politics interfere with his social life. Besides, Hogarth was old and sickly. Grateful to the ministry, Hogarth decided to make a political print, something he had never done before. *The Times* depicted a house with a globe hanging at the door, marking it as a symbol of the world. The house is on fire, and Pitt is fanning the flames while Bute is pumping water from a small fire engine trying to put them out. Before Hogarth had finished the print, someone saw the plate and tipped Wilkes off about it. He wrote to Hogarth, telling him it was an unfriendly act and advising him to keep clear of political prints. Hogarth replied that Wilkes need not be concerned since neither he nor Churchill were attacked in the picture, although Pitt and Temple were. Wilkes wrote again, explaining that he did not care if he were satirized, but if his friends were attacked, he should then think he "was wounded in the most sensible part, and would, as well as he was able, revenge their cause." This only angered Hogarth, who promptly changed the print and in the three upper windows of the "Temple Coffee House," drew Wilkes, Churchill, and Temple squirting water at Bute the firefighter. Hogarth printed four thousand copies of *The Times,* an exceptionally large run, and they sold well. Wilkes's response appeared in North Briton No. 17: "I am grieved to see the genius of Hogarth, which should take in all ages and countries, sunk to a level with the miserable tribe of party etchers, and now, in his rapid decline, entering into the poor politics of the faction of the day." Wilkes went on to denigrate Hogarth as a writer, to imply that his great book, *The Analysis of Beauty,* was ghostwritten, and to make fun of his title of Sergeant Painter to the King. He spoke of "the rancor and malevolence of his mind," his "unabating zeal, and unrelenting gall." No sooner was this published than Wilkes had qualms of conscience for treating an old man so roughly. He wrote to Temple on 23 November 1762 , "Mr. Hogarth is said to be dying, and of a broken heart. It grieves me much. He says that he believes I wrote that paper, but he forgives me, for he must own I am a thorough good-humored fellow, only Pitt-bitten." Hogarth did not die for another two years. He never forgave Wilkes, and he would, as we shall see, have his own revenge.[51]

Meanwhile, there was an ominous governmental ploy. On 6 November 1762, Lord Halifax, secretary of state for the south, handed chief messenger Carrington warrants for the arrest of Arthur Beardmore and John Entick as authors of the *Monitor*. The two were arrested on 11 November. Beardmore, being a well-established lawyer close to Lord Temple, was let off easy, but Entick, a Grub Street writer, was punished. His house was broken into, and for four hours the messengers ransacked it, breaking locks and doors, searching boxes, carrying off letters and printed pamphlets, doing damage that cost two thousand pounds to repair. Beardmore was imprisoned in a messenger's house, where Wilkes found him and sat with him for a day. Wilkes was worried that he might be next since he had written at least one, probably two, of the papers named in the warrant, but neither Beardmore nor Entick spilled the beans, and Wilkes was not arrested. Temple wrote to him from Stowe, "With what face can the patrons of the Auditor and of the Briton seize and confine the Monitors? Monitoribus asper! . . . I beg you to weigh your own conduct very maturely. You have to deal with a very strange world."[52]

Beardmore and Entick were soon released, and after all the fuss, no indictments were made against either. None had been intended. The arrests had been made to put the paper out of commission temporarily while the preliminary peace treaty was discussed in Parliament. The ploy was not a complete success: although no issues appeared for two weeks, the *Monitor* was soon back in business and managed to get out two issues criticizing the peace negotiations before the preliminaries were presented to Parliament. Wilkes tried to persuade Beardmore to bring an action for false arrest against Lord Halifax, but he declined. Entick was more plucky and sued the messengers. It took eight years to settle the suit! but Entick won. Moreover, his cause proved to be critical in the development of privacy law, for the court declared the search warrant to be illegal.[53]

From that point on, the people at the *North Briton* and the *Monitor* were engaged in a sort of running battle with the ministry over freedom of the press. Wilkes warned Kearsley, "Be cautious as to your remarks, for be assured that all my letters will be opened." Lord Temple nicknamed the postal service Argus, after the Greek mythical monster with eyes all over his body. "I . . . am so sure that every line I write must be seen, that I never put anything in black and white which might not be read at Charing Cross, for all I care." They began sending their substantive messages by courier. One wonders if they knew that the opening of their letters was done with King George's specific approval.[54]

Wilkes had long believed that a free press was worth fighting for, as we

know from his "league offensive and defensive" and the opening issue of the
North Briton. Now the arrests of Beardmore and Entick intensified his commitment to the principle. Freedom of the press would be Wilkes's ruling passion in politics for the next decade. This is not to say that he cooled in his
support of Pitt or gave up his hope that Pitt might reward him when he
returned to the ministry. But Wilkes was finding that a fight for a principle of
liberty was more important to him than a contest for a place in government.

Twelve days after the *Monitor* arrests, on 18 November 1762, Lord Halifax
signed two warrants for the arrest of the "Authors, Printers, and Publishers"
of the *North Briton*. The warrants were never served and never intended to be.
The first specified Nos. 1–25, but *North Briton* No. 25 was published two
days after the date on the warrant. The second specified Nos. 1–26, but No.
26 was not published until nine days later. Obviously, warrants would not
have stood up in court, but they were not intended for court; they were intended to frighten. One was shown to William Johnston, the bookseller who
had been vetting the *North Britons* for passages that might lead to charges of
libel, and he quit.[55] One was shown to the printer, William Richardson, and he
quit. Churchill rushed off a letter to Kearsley, the publisher, to see if he were
willing to continue. Kearsley said he would. Churchill found a lawyer, Charles
Sayer, who agreed to take over the advising about the risk of libel charges.
Wilkes, who was still on duty in Winchester, learning that neither Churchill
nor Kearsley had been able to find another printer, dashed off a plea to his
friend Dryden Leach. Leach agreed to take over and managed to get *North
Briton* No. 26 out on time, but only barely. Most of the content was mere filler,
some verses by Robert Lloyd. It was prefaced, however, by a brave defiance:
"The public may rest assured, that whilst the *North Briton* is actuated with
affection and fidelity to his KING, with love for his country, and is directed by
those principles which naturally fall in with our excellent constitution, he will
never tamely give up the glorious cause in which he is engaged . . . and,
according to the old *English* plan of liberty, will praise or censure any minister,
according to their behavior."[56]

Then the king's messengers got to Leach's men. His journeyman Peter Cock
"had the terrors of the Lord, of the Isle of Bute, so strong before him," Wilkes
wrote to Churchill, that he has fallen ill to avoid printing the paper. Leach said
it was too risky, and he would not print another issue. Kearsley saved the day:
he found Richard Balfe, "a very poor printer who worked up two pair of stairs
in an alehouse in the Old Bailey."[57] His poverty and isolation would make it
hard for the government spies to find him. Balfe printed No. 27 and would
print all the subsequent issues of the *North Briton* up to and including the
fateful No. 45.

Pitt, obviously worried, asked Wilkes to come to see him at his house in Kent. Wilkes found him in pain from the gout, his legs wrapped in bandages. They talked for three hours. There is no record of what was said, but Wilkes came away convinced that Pitt would support him in his battle with the government over freedom of the press. Churchill, who had been left in charge, wrote *North Briton* No. 27, including a description of what it is like to live under a tyrannical government:

> Almost every man I meet looks strangely on me — some industriously avoid me — others pass me silent — stare — and shake their heads. — Those few, those very few, who are not afraid to take a lover of his country by the hand, congratulate me on my being alive and at liberty — They advise circumspection — for, they do not know — they cannot tell — but — the times — Liberty is precious — fines — imprisonment — pillory —— not indeed that they themselves — but — then in truth — God only knows. . . . letters which used to breathe the genuine spirit of *old English liberty,* are become insipid, tame, and languid. Caution hath got the better of public virtue, and discretion is substituted in the place of true wisdom.

The king and Lord Bute were now moving rapidly to put an end to the war. The preliminary treaty would be presented to Parliament for approval when it opened in November, but Bute was worried. He thought he had the House of Lords under control, but he was uncertain of the House of Commons. He had failed to check the opposition newspapers, and he feared their influence upon the members. Something bold was needed. Bute turned to the cleverest and most corrupt of his friends, Henry Fox, the paymaster of the armed forces, who agreed to take charge.

Wilkes had Fox's number. In *North Briton* No. 23 he had spoken of "his breaches of private faith, and his abuses of public trust." There was no question that his abilities were great, wrote Wilkes, "but will his warmest friends say that he ever employed them to any good purpose? The greatness of his understanding serves only to make the badness of his heart more formidable, and to render our apprehensions of him more terrible." Fox might well have charged libel, but that was not his style. He preferred "to nip an opponent in the bud by providing for him." He now offered Wilkes what Wilkes had often asked for, the governorship of Canada.[58] Wilkes did not give in. So passed the first of several bribes with which the ministry would try to end the opposition of John Wilkes.

Word of this proffered bribe was soon out and so agitated Lord Devonshire that he came to Lord Temple in great distress, crying, if Wilkes were to give in "the opposition would be undone, for Wilkes was the life and soul of it." A broadside print appeared in which Bute, with a devil's wings and tail and a handful of coins, is offering to feed Wilkes, who is almost in his lap, with a wooden spoon upon which is written, "Kaw, Jack, have Canada or to the Tower" (illustration 6). Kaw or Caw, the cry of the crow, was sometimes used to cry down repeated gross lies. A worried Lord Temple (if it is he) looks on in the background. Beneath is a doggerel rhyme,

> "B**t humbly entreats you will now condescend
> to tell at what price he can make you his friend.
> He only implores you will lay down your pen,
> And say on your honor you will not write again.
> The empire of Canada lies at your feet,
> To plunder and fleece — what a delicate treat.
> But if a round sum in the dark you should like,
> Not offensible now; that bargain I'll strike."
> Ashamed of such meanness, disdaining their gold,
> Wilkes answered thus, as I'm credibly told,
> "Avaunt, vile corrupter, I'll take no such thing.
> I'll be true to Old England, the Whigs, and the King![59]

Bute now asked the king to grant Fox the power to gain control of the House of Commons. The king responded by giving Fox the unofficial position of "cabinet councillor and his Majesty's minister in the House of Commons." His duty was to obtain a majority vote to approve the peace treaty. How he did it would be of no concern to the king, but he would have all the resources of the Crown at his disposal.

Fox vigorously attacked his new assignment, using the resources of the Crown to bribe the members of the House. He offered them places in the government, commissions in the military, or chairs in the universities. If such favors for themselves or their families failed, he offered money. John Almon wrote, "The royal household had been increased beyond all former example. The lords and grooms of the bedchamber were doubled. Pensions were thrown about indiscriminately. Five and twenty thousand pounds were issued in one day, in bank notes of one hundred pounds each. The only stipulation was, *Give us your vote.* A corruption of such notoriety and extent had never been seen before." According to Walpole, "A shop was publicly opened at the Pay Office, whither the members flocked, and received the wages of their venality in bank-bills, even to so low a sum as two hundred pounds for their votes on the treaty." Fox worked night and day with unrelenting energy, so that "in a single fortnight, a vast majority was purchased to approve the peace." Two men who would later prove themselves among Wilkes's most vicious enemies were deeply involved in this project: Lord Sandwich was Fox's

6. "Kaw, Jack, have Canada or to the Tower." Lord Bute (with devil wings and tail) offers Wilkes a choice between the governorship of Canada or imprisonment in the Tower of London. A worried Lord Temple looks on. Courtesy of Farley Library, Wilkes University.

second in command, and Samuel Martin, Secretary to the Treasury, was in charge of issuing those banknotes to members of Parliament.[60]

The night before Parliament was to be convened, Wilkes went to a meeting of members to discuss and modify the speech that the ministry had drafted for the king to read to the joint meeting of both Houses. They met in the Cockpit, a handsome auditorium used for unofficial meetings built on the site where cockfights used to be held. Some 240 members were there, of whom only five were not friends of the king. One of the five was Edmund Burke, but even he was shocked to find next to him Jack Wilkes, "a capital enemy. . . . It was rather impudent of him to appear there." No doubt Wilkes enjoyed crashing the enemy's party, but he had a good practical reason to come. It was against the law to take notes during a session of Parliament, but in the Cockpit pencils and paper were distributed to those in attendance.[61]

On 25 November 1762, Parliament met. Bute, as he alighted from his carriage, was hissed and stoned by a mob, and soldiers had to be called. Two weeks later the debate opened on the preliminary treaty. Bute, in an impassioned speech in the House of Lords, said he hoped it would be written on his tomb, "Here lies the Earl of Bute, who, in concert with the King's ministers, made the Peace." There was little debate in the House of Commons, where the majority vote had been bought and paid for. The only moment of doubt was the appearance of Pitt, wrapped in bandages, hobbling to his seat. He made a dramatic speech that lasted three and a half hours and followed it with a melodramatic exit, half carried across the floor. But he probably did not change a single vote. The peace preliminaries were approved on 14 December 1762 upon a vote of 227 to 63. The Princess Dowager of Wales upon hearing of the victory, said, "Now my son *is* King of England."[62]

Then began "the massacre of the innocents," as historians call it. Fox commenced to back up his bribes with punishments. Every member of Parliament who also held a place in government and who had voted against the preliminaries was instantly dismissed from his government post. Anyone who had been brought into the bureaus of government by the Duke of Newcastle or his brother Henry Pelham was dismissed. Old men who had been given insignificant places in the bureaucracy as a reward for their services were ferreted out and their livelihood taken away. The Duke of Newcastle himself, the Duke of Grafton, and the Marquis of Rockingham were removed from the lord lieutenancies of their counties. Lord Bute, hooted and pelted with mud whenever he went outside, hired a force of "butchers and bruisers" to run beside his carriage to protect him.[63]

The Peace of Paris was signed on 10 February 1763. Wilkes likened it to the peace of God, "which passeth all understanding."[64]

Wilkes's life was more dangerous now, for the wily Fox might come after him. Not a whit daunted, he charged back into the battle, writing more boldly than ever. No. 38, appearing on 19 February 1763, was a breathtaking satire of Bute. It purported to be a letter from the pretender, James Francis Edward Stuart, who lived in Rome, recognized by the pope as King James III of Great Britain, to his "Dear Cousin," whom everyone would immediately identify as John Stuart, Earl of Bute, who was indeed a cousin to the pretender. In Wilkes's fiction, King James writes to congratulate Bute upon reversing the years of misfortune for Jacobites. "Every thing, through your benign influence, now wears the most pleasing aspect. . . . The sons of *Scotland,* and the friends of that great line of the *Stuarts,* no longer mourn." He goes on to give Bute instructions on how to behave, how to deceive, how to prepare for the restoration of his throne. The letter is signed and dated in the fashion of a royal communication: "Given under our sign manual and privy signet, of the thistle, at our court at Rome, the second day of January, in the sixty-third year of our reign. J. R.," that is, James Regis, James the King. King George, upon reading the satire, was so furious he virtually ordered Bute to begin a prosecution of Wilkes. Were it not for Charles Yorke, the attorney general, who was jockeying for the support of Pitt in a bid to be chancellor, Wilkes would surely have been arrested on the spot.[65]

North Briton No. 42, which followed four weeks later, was "a masterpiece of mischief." The subject was the "New Loan," by which the government had borrowed £3.5 million from a handful of wealthy friends of the ministry and then repaid the debt in short order with enormous interest to the lenders. Peregrine Cust, the brother of the speaker of the House, one of the profiteers, started to bring an action against Kearsley as the publisher of the *North Briton,* but upon learning he would have to disclose his profit on the deal, which amounted to £20,000, he withdrew the prosecution.[66]

While all of this was going on, Lord Sandwich was appointed ambassador to Spain. Wilkes was not one to keep apart from old friends who happened to have joined his political opponents, and so he went to a farewell dinner for Sandwich at the Beef Steaks, prepared to tease Lord Sandwich in the manner much practiced by the club. Out of his pocket he drew a set of instructions for the ambassador from his friends at the club and proceeded to read it aloud: "Although we have the most entire confidence in the ability and integrity of the said John, Earl of Sandwich, yet it has been heretofore usual to instruct even the wisest of our councillors previous to their departure to foreign courts." His lordship may take as his secretary a gentleman that the club recommends as a man wise in all political matters, one Mr. Wilkes. "We did indeed design to have transported this gentleman to have polished and peopled the bleak and barren deserts of Canada, but we have dropped that purpose, because we are apprehensive of his turning out rather a missionary than a governor." The ambassador is advised that when approaching his embassy, he should not allow himself to be in the presence of women, to the following good effect: "By all the principles of hydrostatics the quantity as well as impetuosity of all fluids is much heightened by being for some time dammed up, and I hope, by a close adhering to my advice your lordship will prove if not a sweet yet a saline and pleasing jet d'eau to more than one Spanish lady." The Spaniards are "very bad fucksters," so "we therefore command your lordship to . . . make all your thrusts at the women with the little short rapier, which you always carry about you, and which is I fear not only your hanger on, but your eternal dangler."[67] The instructions to the ambassador give some sense of the juvenile bawdry which informs Wilkes's contributions to the Essay on

Woman. More to the point: it could not have been written by anyone who did not consider himself a personal friend of Lord Sandwich. As it turned out, Sandwich's embassy was withdrawn a few weeks later, the king and council having decided it had more important work for him at home, work which would mark him as the enemy of Jack Wilkes.

North Briton No. 43 was another daring exposé of the mismanagement of government monies that sometimes amounted to fraud. No. 44 blasted Bute's accomplishments and predicted his imminent resignation. Mr. North Briton deplored "the inglorious peace which he [Bute] hath infamously patched up, and whereby he hath sacrificed the glory and interests of this country to his own private ambition." The ministry, Wilkes went on, would like to silence Mr. North Briton, but "that impudent libeller, as they are pleased to call him . . . shall still pursue the path in which he hath hitherto trod."

Late in February 1763, Wilkes made a brief visit to Paris to arrange for Polly to be schooled there. Within a week he returned to find a letter, dated 8 March, from Lord Sandwich. Sandwich had written on behalf of the ministry offering another bribe to stop the *North Briton,* though he was too delicate to say so outright. "Allow us to find you a qualification," Sandwich had written, to become one of the directors of the East India Company.[68] This must have been even more tempting than the bribe of Canada that Fox had offered, for it was a post in which a man could easily and legally enrich himself. But the offer came too late. Having roused the nation against the ministry, Wilkes could not accept place in that ministry. It would undercut all his labors. He said no.

Anxious now to take Polly to Paris and get her settled with her new tutor, Mme Carpentier, he and Churchill worked out a plan for Churchill to take over the paper in Wilkes's absence. Having cleared his calendar for the next three weeks, on 26 March 1763 Wilkes again set off for France, this time with Polly.[69] They were accompanied by Mrs. Shepherd, the serving woman who regularly attended Polly, and Wilkes's man. According to Walpole, at Calais Wilkes chanced to meet an incredulous Duc de Croÿ, commandant of the port, who asked how far the liberty of the press extended in England. "I cannot tell," replied Wilkes, "but I am trying to find out."[70]

5

Number 45

Wilkes and Polly arrived in Paris, and Polly was soon settled in the house of Madame Carpentier and her husband. Seeing that Polly had no need of her own servant at the Carpentier house, Wilkes decided to take Mrs. Shepherd and his man Brown back with him. They set off on 7 April 1763, traveling by post chaise, one carriage for the entire trip, but changing horses every ten or twelve miles at a post, as the stations were called. Wilkes was restless and left the carriage to the servants, who were sweet on each other, and rode on one of the small horses that drew it, chatting with the postboy, who was astride another. Surprisingly, he had a fall from the horse and sprained his thumb. By the time they reached Calais, the thumb had turned black and stiff. It was difficult to write, but he managed a letter to Polly, advising her about money, asking her to attend the English ambassador's chapel, telling her how to find a dancing master and music master:

> You have as much sense as any body I know, and I am sure will conduct yourself in every thing so as to win the esteem and love of every one. Let me beg you freely to write your opinion to me on every thing. I have the highest opinion of you, and wish to make you happy. You have an excellent genius, given you from heaven, and it will be your own pleasure to cultivate it. Read the best books, and they will be your pleasure through life. Desire Monsieur Carpentier to buy for you Boileau, Racine, and Molière in small volumes, you

cannot read them, as well as Shakespeare, Pope, and Swift, too often: yet by no means tire yourself. God has give you excellent understanding, but the best land requires cultivation."[1]

Polly was thirteen years old.

Wilkes had hardly posted this letter when he had astonishing news from a gentleman who had just come over. Lord Bute had resigned! Elated, he caught the next boat and reached London on 11 April. Churchill had suppressed the forty-fifth issue — too long, too dull, and no longer needed. To be sure, on his last day in office, Bute had made eighteen appointments, sixteen of which had gone to Scotsmen, but that did not make enough copy to warrant an entire issue. The *North Briton* would seem to have come to an end, its purpose complete.[2]

Had the paper brought down the minister? Not by itself, certainly. Bute had resigned for a complex of reasons — lack of support from other ministers, "backstairs intrigues and cabals" in the young queen's apartments, the desertion of Lord Mansfield, his growing unpopularity and fear of the mob.[3] But the *North Briton* had been the major fomentor of the popular and widespread detestation of Lord Bute.

Wilkes had every expectation that Pitt now would be called by the king to take over as first minister and to form a new ministry, in which no doubt Wilkes would have a modest place. But Pitt was not called at all. The new first minister was to be George Grenville, Temple's brother, Pitt's brother-in-law, Wilkes's erstwhile friend, the Grenville who had betrayed his family to support Bute. Worse still: it was said that Bute would remain the king's adviser, though without any office. In the popular phrase of that day, he would direct the king and ministry "from behind the curtain."

Wilkes was no longer willing to close down the paper. On 13 April, he published a handbill, a letter from "the North Briton" to the public. He was holding back, he explained, because he did not yet have all the facts about the ministry. Yes, "the Scottish minister has indeed retired. Is his influence at an end? Or does he still govern by the three wretched tools of his power, who, to their indelible infamy, have supported the most odious of his measures."[4] The "wretched tools" were Grenville and the two secretaries of state, Lords Halifax and Egremont.

Lord Temple, at Stowe when he heard of the resignation, hurried to London. He was in his house in Pall Mall talking with Pitt when a letter arrived from his brother. The king, Grenville wrote, would not make him first lord of the treasury unless he could be assured he could keep his seat in the House of Commons. Heretofore, he had been a member of the cabinet and the chief

organizer of the king's party in the House, but neither was an official government position. As in the case of Thomas Potter's change of constituencies, if
Grenville were to accept a place, he would have to resign his seat; he could
then be reelected while holding the place. Grenville represented Buckingham,
a pocket borough belonging to Lord Temple: it had twelve voters, all depen-
dents of his lordship. So Grenville was in the ignominious position of having to
beg a leader of the opposition to allow him to return to the House of Commons after being preferred to the highest ministerial post in the land. A meaner
man might have said no, but Temple did not.

As a courtesy, Grenville had sent along a copy of the speech he and his
colleagues had drafted for the king to deliver at the close of the session of
Parliament. Temple and Pitt were reading and discussing this speech when
Wilkes knocked on the door. This chance event set the stage for the shocking
events to come: Wilkes left his lordship's house with a copy of the speech
before it was known to the public. He went to work at once on a new *North
Briton*, No. 45.[5]

On 19 April 1763, the king delivered the speech before the joint session and
dismissed the Parliament (illustration 7). His Majesty then retired to a ceremony to create new noblemen, among them Sir Francis Dashwood, whom he
created Baron le Despenser. The new baron had just been preferred (appointed, we would say) as chancellor of the exchequer. It was an astonishing
preferment, for Dashwood had no experience handling money. "His capacity," Wilkes said, "did not extend to the settling a tavern bill, yet the department of the finances was entrusted to him." He was known as a squire, an
antiquarian, a rake, and a cutup. He had never held an administrative position. "We must now . . . make room for a doughty hero of more comic cast,"
wrote Horace Walpole to a friend. Le Despenser's first budget was presented
to Parliament, said Walpole, "so awkwardly, with so little intelligence or clear-
ness, in so vulgar a tone, and in such mean language, that he, who had been
esteemed a plain country gentleman of good sense, said himself afterwards,
'People will point at me, and cry, There goes the worst Chancellor of the
Exchequer that ever appeared!' "[6]

An aging lawyer with poor eyesight and mean soul named Philip Carteret
Webb had been preferred to the solicitorship to the treasury, a place in the
second-level echelon, charged with handling legal matters for the department
— "a most villainous tool and agent in any iniquity," according to Walpole.
His spies having told Webb that Wilkes was preparing an essay on the king's
speech, Webb arranged to meet him the next day in Westminster Hall. One of
Wilkes's lawyers recorded the exchange: "Mr. Webb advised him to have the
name of his bail in readiness" because the secretaries of state were weighing

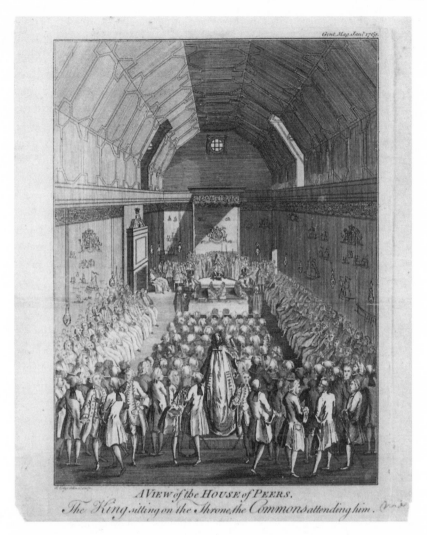

A VIEW of the HOUSE of PEERS.
The King sitting on the Throne, the Commons attending him.

7. The king on the throne in the House of Lords addresses a joint session of Parliament. Members of the House of Commons sit in the center on temporary chairs. Courtesy of the Lewis Walpole Library, Yale University.

the possibility of arresting him. "Mr Wilkes declared that he was determined to give no bail, to answer no questions, that the secretaries of state might commit him as they thought proper."[7]

The now famous *North Briton* No. 45 appeared on Saturday, 23 April 1763. It was a daring essay. Wilkes put up a guard of sorts by declaring that he was treating the king's speech, not as the king's speech at all, but as the speech written by the ministers. The accepted fiction that the king spoke in his own name had never been challenged, and Wilkes's assertion infuriated King George, who prided himself on his independence from ministers. When Wilkes asserted that the monarch has been brought "to give the sanction of his sacred name to the most odious measures, and to the most unjustifiable, public declarations," he put the responsibility back upon the king, and that infuriated the ministry. As a propaganda piece, No. 45 was outrageous — page after page of invectives and sarcasms against the ministers. Then at one point Wilkes came close to a call to rebellion. The king's speech had included a directive "to promote in your several counties that spirit of concord, and that obedience to the laws, which is essential to good order." Concord? Wilkes asked. How can concord be promoted in the cider-producing counties, where "private houses are now made liable to be entered and searched at pleasure? . . . A nation as sensible as the *English,* will see that a *spirit of concord,* when they are oppressed, means a tame submission to injury, and that a *spirit of liberty* ought then to arise, and I am sure ever will, in proportion to the weight of the grievance they feel. *Every* legal *attempt of a contrary tendency* to the *spirit of concord* will be deemed a justifiable resistance, warranted by the *spirit of the English constitution.*" No doubt King George thought this spoke treason. Wilkes closed his essay with a play on the word "prerogative," and not only the word, but the concept of royal prerogative which the current ministers had frequently offered as justification of their actions. "The prerogative of the crown," wrote Wilkes, "is to exert the constitutional powers entrusted to it in a way, not of blind favour and partiality, but of wisdom and judgment. This is the spirit of our constitution. The people too have their prerogative, and, I hope, the fine words of Dryden will be engraved on our hearts, 'Freedom is the English subject's prerogative.'"

The words of No. 45, wrote George Nobbe, "earned for Wilkes the enduring epithet of demagogue. But their ultimate effect was a much greater one than Wilkes could have foreseen, for they stimulated the imaginations of men all over the world."[8]

The king at once demanded that Wilkes be arrested, but the ministers, unwilling to move that fast, begged for time. This was England, and laws had to be obeyed. "Having given great offense," a court record reads, "Mr. Nathan Carrington (a person very conversant in affairs of that sort) was directed by the Secretaries of State to endeavor to discover who were the author, printer, and publisher." As we have seen, Wilkes had made fun of Carrington, the chief of the central government's constabulary force, such as it was. Carrington's forces consisted of numerous spies, hired ad hoc, and some fifty unarmed policemen called messengers, who were on government salaries.

While Carrington moved his forces into position, the attorney general, Charles Yorke, was examining No. 45. The barrier to the arrest of Wilkes that the government would have to overcome was parliamentary privilege. The ancient law that prohibited the arrest of a member of Parliament had evolved to protect members in situations exactly like that which Wilkes now faced. It protected them from arrest for political reasons, be it by the Crown or by other powerful enemies. It protected the right of the member to speak and act freely as an individual. Yorke was inclined to move against Wilkes by "information," that is, by a charge made in the courts of law, not by general warrant, which ordered the culprit to be brought before the secretaries of state for their disposal. He was ruled against. Uncertain what to do, Yorke sought the advice of his father, the great retired chancellor Lord Hardwicke. Hardwicke reminded his son that there were three exceptions to privilege: a member could be arrested for a felony, a breach of the peace (raising a riot), or treason. Hardwicke advised his son to issue a warrant that used the word "treasonable."[9]

On 26 April the arrest warrant was drawn up by Webb and his law clerk, Lovel Stanhope. It was addressed to Carrington and three other of "his majesty's messengers in ordinary," John Money, James Watson, and Robert Blackmore. Lord Halifax did not hesitate to sign it. His signature bore great authority, for Halifax was not only the principal secretary of state, but also a member of the Privy Council and a lieutenant general of the army.

> These are in his Majesty's name to authorize & require you (taking a Constable to your assistance) to make strict & diligent search for the Authors, Printers & Publishers of a seditious and treasonable paper intitled, the North Briton Number 45, Saturday Ap: 23: 1763, printed for G. Kearsley in Ludgate Street, London, & them, or any of them, having found, to apprehend & seize, together with their papers, & to bring in safe custody before me to be examined concerning the premises, & further dealt with according to Law. In the execution whereof all Mayors, Sheriffs, Justices of the Peace, Constables & others His Majesty's Officers civil & military, & loving subjects whom it may concern, are to be aiding & assisting to you, as there shall be occasion. And for your so doing this shall be your warrant.
>
> Given at St James's 26 Ap: 1768 in the 3rd year of his Majesty's Reign.
> Dunk Halifax[10]

Lord Halifax had been born George Dunk.

This was a "general warrant," one that named the offenses but not the offenders, leaving the messengers to decide whom to arrest. The part of the warrant that permitted the seizure of papers was clearly illegal. The law stated that papers could be seized only *after* the perpetrator of an alleged crime had been identified and arrested. Finally, the word "treasonable" notwithstanding, the warrant could not be executed against a member of Parliament who had done no more than to write or print or publish a libel, for libel was not treason.[11]

Because the case against Wilkes was not strong, the secretaries' plan was to arrest first the printer and publisher, to examine them, and to seize and examine their papers so as find evidence of Wilkes's authorship. Lord Egremont, the second secretary of state, who had not signed but had concurred in the warrant, was a Scot who harbored the Scottish hatred of Wilkes. He called the messengers before him and sternly admonished them to obey Carrington's orders in every detail.

Carrington went to work. He had just received a report from David Bell, a spy who had been watching the print shop of Dryden Leach. Mr. Wilkes, Bell reported, had gone in and out of Leach's shop numerous times in the past two weeks and sometimes had stayed there for two or three days. Moreover, a note had been passed to Bell by an old printer saying that Leach had been printing the *North Briton.* The old printer's note was literally true, for Leach had begun a second edition of the *North Briton;* but he had not gotten far into the project and was nowhere close to No. 45. The actual printer of No. 45 was Richard Balfe, up four flights above an alehouse in the Old Bailey.[12] As to Wilkes's visits, Bell was later to admit when put under oath that he had seen Wilkes go in once only; the rest had been told to him by Leach's servants.

Night had fallen by the time the messengers broke into Leach's house. They seized sheets of the new edition that were hanging up to dry. They pulled Leach out of bed, though his wife was also in it and their child lay ill in another bed in the room. They then arrested all the journeymen printers and servants they could find. They seized and bundled off masses of papers. They took the servants and journeymen, some twenty in number, to an alehouse named Huddle's, where they were held under guard for the next twelve hours.[13]

While this was going on, other messengers were breaking into the bookshop of George Kearsley. There could be no mistake who was the publisher of *North Briton* No. 45, for Kearsley's name was on the masthead. They arrested Kearsley with his servants and seized his papers, including many letters from Wilkes, and locked him up in a messenger's house.[14]

Though there were prisons in that age, there were no jails in the modern sense of the word. The need was supplied by the senior messengers, who fitted out their houses to hold prisoners temporarily. In the afternoon of Wednesday the twenty-seventh, Wilkes, hearing of the arrests, found out in which messenger's house Kearsley was being held and went to him. Kearsley told him that the warrant named only one issue, No. 45. Wilkes declared that he thought it "an innocent paper" and hurried off to the Court of Common Pleas to seek a writ of habeas corpus to spring Kearsley, but the court had closed for the day.[15]

Early the next morning, Thursday the twenty-eighth, Kearsley was taken to the secretaries. It did not take much urging for him to give up Balfe. With more browbeating, they wrung an admission that he thought Wilkes was the writer. He excused himself by stating that when he took over as publisher, he and Wilkes had agreed that "in case he should be called upon by authority for publishing the same, he should consider himself at liberty to give up or name the authors." But that was not Wilkes's understanding, and Wilkes never forgave him. "It would be difficult," he wrote, "to name a man for whom his friends so early and so warmly interested themselves, who so entirely lost sight of his honour and his interest."[16]

Meanwhile, Wilkes had found Dryden Leach in the house of Robert Black-more, one of the messengers. Blackmore, when Wilkes asked him, showed him his copy of the warrant, and Wilkes sat down and copied it. Leach, who had not been told about Kearsley's arrest, was under the impression that the messengers had no idea who the printer was. Good, thought Wilkes, we can get the next issue out. So he hurried off to Balfe's shop, gave Balfe the manuscript for No. 46, and ordered him to print it at once. Balfe was worried, but Wilkes assured him that the messengers "would not trouble themselves with him" and left.

On Friday midday, 29 April, Balfe was engaged in printing No. 46 when messengers appeared in the street and halooed to the windows of his shop two flights above the alehouse; he would not come down. So they pretended to be bringing him a printing job of handbills; he came down and they arrested him. They forced him to open the shop, arrested all of his men that they could find, took the copies of No. 46 that had been printed and other papers, but left the printing equipment alone. They then boarded up the door leading to the stairs, bundled the servants and printers off to one of the messengers' houses, and took Balfe to the secretaries of state.[17]

Balfe, when examined, admitted he had printed No. 45 from a manuscript brought to him by Wilkes. That confession, the ministers decided, was ground enough to arrest Wilkes. Balfe's testimony was, in fact, the only evidence they had for Wilkes's authorship of No. 45, and as time would show, it would not hold up in court because Balfe had not been put under oath when he gave it. But at the time Webb and Stanhope advised the secretaries of state to proceed with the arrest of Wilkes. Halifax was prepared to make out another warrant in which Wilkes would be named, which would have been the correct legal proceeding, but Webb said, "It was better not." So a copy of the same general warrant was given to messengers with verbal orders to arrest Wilkes. Lord Egremont, his Scottish heart bitter against Wilkes, told them they might enter Wilkes's house, even at midnight, seize his person, and seize his papers.[18] The messengers had the good sense not to obey. That afternoon, Friday, the twenty-ninth, they knocked on Wilkes's door, but being told he was not at home, posted themselves about the house and waited for him.

Blackmore, the messenger in whose house Leach was being held, may not have received the verbal order to arrest Wilkes, or he may not have wanted to obey it. In any event, when Wilkes arrived at Blackmore's house, the messanger allowed him to go up to the room that was serving as jail. There Wilkes and Leach and Leach's father, who had also been arrested, proceeded to celebrate the imminent publication of No. 46 — or so they presumed. They got so drunk and laughed so much and sang so loudly that Blackmore came up and asked them to hold down the noise as they were attracting the attention of passersby. This messenger, Robert Blackmore, had no stomach for his assignment. It seems obvious he was an admirer of Wilkes, as was his colleague, James Watson.[19]

About midnight of Friday, very drunk, Wilkes staggered out of Blackmore's house and toward his own. In Great George Street he was accosted by two or three messengers who tried to arrest him. "He swaggered," said Carrington, "and talked a great deal over his bottle how he would serve any messenger who offered to take him," and he was going into his house and to bed. The messengers, fully aware of Wilkes's sword, did not think it wise to make an issue of the matter and let him go in. Wilkes told a servant to wake him at dawn and fell into bed. The messengers, with Blackmore now among them, reassumed their strategic places in the street and waited. At dawn of Saturday, 30 April, John Money, the messenger in charge of this detail, who was positioned up the street from the house, "saw a little Gentleman come out of Mr Wilkes's house and walk very fast towards Parliament Street. When he came to the corner of the street, he saw Blackmore, and took him by the hand, and some words passed between them," and Wilkes hurried off. Money ran up the street toward them. Well, Blackmore explained lamely, Mr. Wilkes said he needed to see his lawyer, but he promised he would come to my house after and give himself up. Money bolted after Wilkes, but unable to find him and fearing he was about to make an escape from London, ran to Westminster Steps, where the small boats were tied up. Nothing. On he ran to the next set of steps, and the next.[20]

But Wilkes was no more seeking to escape than he was seeking his lawyer. He was on his way to the Old Bailey to pick up the copies of No. 46 from Balfe's shop. When he got there, his heart sank, for the door was boarded up. Wondering if the messengers might have left behind No. 46, he contemplated the window two flights up. He managed to rouse the landlady, who told him that Mr. Balfe's chief journeyman printer, John Williams, had not been arrested but was asleep in his room. Wilkes woke the man. Together they borrowed a tall ladder from some bricklayers down the street, put it against the house, and Williams went up and through the window into Balfe's shop. Wilkes, not wanting to be spied on the street, retired to the Bell Ale House. Williams could not find any copies of No. 46 but found the press undisturbed and in it the forms for the issue — the frames in which the type had been set to print the pages. He printed off a proof copy, came down, asked a bricklayer to deliver it to Mr. Wilkes and to tell him that the messengers had taken the printed copies of the issue. Wilkes sent back word that he needed the forms themselves. If he could find a printer who was willing to print the issue, the set forms would save time. It was already Saturday, the day the *North Briton* usually appeared. Williams went back up the ladder and tried to bring down the forms, but one of them fell and the type scattered about the street. Cast types were expensive little items, so he swept them up, wrapped them in an apron, and gave them to the landlady, who promised to hold them for Mr. Balfe. Wilkes, being told of the accident, waited no longer but went off to try to find a printer. His luck was running out. No. 46 would not be published for another month, but it did finally appear on 28 May, printed by E. Sumpter, bookseller in Fleet Street.[21]

Wilkes knew, of course, that he would be arrested if he went home, but he went anyway.

Many legal precedents would eventually be set as a result of these events. Following the public outcry over the messengers' arresting of forty-nine people when they were searching for only three, general warrants would be outlawed. Indignation over the seizure of papers would lead to suits that established the rights of privacy that have been treasured in American and English law — and in the past decade whittled away.[22] The right to sue the government for false arrest would be made far stronger and clearer than it had been.

It is doubtful that Wilkes, the gleeful fugitive walking through the streets of London, would have predicted these reforms. He was on this day driven by only one legal ideal, the freedom of the press, the ideal of his league offensive and defensive, the subject of the first paragraphs of the first issue of the *North Briton*. Now they were trying to shut down the *North Briton*. He had done what he could to keep it going under attack from the secretaries of state. That having failed, at least for the day, he would go to Great George Street and get arrested. Then he would fight for his rights and those of all printers, publishers, and writers in the courts of law. It would be another sort of adventure, and he was in high spirits.

In the street before his house, Wilkes was accosted by the four messengers, saying they had a warrant to take him up. He calmly announced he would put to death anyone who attempted violence in the street, but they might follow him into his house. They marched in. Wilkes politely walked up to Money, whom he knew, took his hand, and said, "Your servant, Mr. Money." He asked to see the warrant, read it, tossed it aside. Worthless, he said. Since there was no name on it, it might be used to arrest the lord chancellor or Lord Coke, who lived next door, or any one of the messengers who were standing there. The messengers said they had been told to arrest Mr. Wilkes. Wilkes asked Money to come upstairs, where he intended to explain to him that as a member of Parliament, he was immune from arrest. Halfway up the stairs, he noticed new messengers who had come in and were standing below. "I insist upon your going out of my house immediately, gentlemen," he said; "I do not mean you any harm, but you shall not stay a minute longer," whereupon he pulled out his watch. They went outside.[23]

At this juncture, Wilkes's young friend John Almon, the printer, came in. Wilkes took him aside, told him that the men were the king's messengers, and asked him to go to Lord Temple. Almon flew.[24]

Having listened to a lecture from Mr. Wilkes about parliamentary privilege, a puzzled Money came downstairs. He sent a messenger down the street to the corner of Great George and Parliament Streets, to Lord Halifax's house, where the two secretaries of state were waiting. What, asked the messenger, were the messengers to do? The secretaries sent him back with a polite note to Wilkes from Halifax requesting the honor of a visit. Wilkes dashed off a reply and sent the messenger back with it: he had never had the honor of being invited to Lord Halifax's house before, and he thought this way of inviting him "rather rude and ungentlemanlike." Then Charles Churchill strolled in. Before he could say a word Wilkes called out a greeting: "Good morning, *Mr. Thompson,* how does Mrs. Thompson do today? Does she dine in the country?" They chatted a few moments about insignificant matters, and "Mr. Thompson" took his leave and hurried into the country and into hiding. He was never arrested.[25]

Next Lord Temple appeared, decked out in the blue ribbon of the Order of the Garter, followed by an entourage of friends, Humphrey Cotes, Alexander Phillips the lawyer, Wilkes's brother Heaton, and ten or twelve others. They proceeded to expostulate with the messengers. The warrant was not legal; Mr. Wilkes was a member of Parliament. They were long-winded in their explanations because delaying for time. Temple had sent a message to Arthur Beardmore, his lawyer and the writer for the *Monitor,* directing him to get a writ of habeas corpus. Beardmore wisely decided not to seek the writ at the Court of the King's Bench presided over by Lord Mansfield. He went instead to the

Court of Common Pleas, though that court had not been applied to for a habeas corpus for a century. His first application was rejected as insufficient. Beardmore left, found Wilkes, took his copy of the warrant, and hurried back to the court. Charles Pratt, lord chief justice of the Court of Common Pleas, examined it and wrote on the back, "The Warrant, I think a very extraordinary one: I know no law that can authorize it, nor any practice, that it can be founded on." He would grant the habeas, but unfortunately the papers could not be issued until Monday.[26]

At Wilkes's house, Mr. Money, confused by the gentlemen who had crowded into the house and fearful of their swords, went himself to Halifax's and told the secretaries of state he and the messengers were being "intimidated." The secretaries of state told him they would send more messengers, but they *must* arrest Mr. Wilkes. The reinforcements did no good. Wilkes would not obey, and the messengers were afraid to lay a hand on him. In came a burly constable whom the messengers had summoned, accompanied by two husky young men. This was Robert Chisholme, constable of the City of Westminster, a man known to Wilkes. Wilkes asked why he was here. To arrest you. And the young men? To take you. By force? Yes. Did he know he was a member of Parliament? Yes. Very well, said Wilkes, dismiss the young men and I will go with you quietly, but it must be understood that I am taken under duress. Yes, sir. Chisholme then asked Wilkes to give him his sword. Wilkes turned his distorted face to the assembled gentlemen and messengers, drew himself up to a dignified stance, and declaimed as he handed over his sword: if the messengers or Chisholme had broken in during the night, as Lord Egremont had told them to do, he would have shot the first man, "and with this sword that I now give you, would I have spilled the last drop of your blood with this arm that well knows how to use it."[27]

Wilkes asked all the messengers and the constable and assistants to enter their names on a list, which he put into a drawer. He then announced he was ready to go to the secretaries of state, but he would go in a chair. Two chairmen were called. Wilkes climbed into the boxlike sedan, and the chairmen picked up the poles attached to it and carried Mr. Wilkes all of about a hundred yards to Lord Halifax's house at the corner, a crowd of cowardly messengers and cheering passersby following.[28]

At one o'clock on Saturday, 30 April, Wilkes, well escorted, entered into the presence of Lords Halifax and Egremont, their law clerk, Lovell Stanhope, and the treasury solicitor, Philip Carteret Webb. These gentlemen were seated at a large table covered with papers, pens, and ink. Lord Egremont had "a supercilious, insolent air," said Wilkes, but Lord Halifax was polite. He was sorry that a gentleman of Wilkes's rank and abilities should engage against the king. Wilkes interrupted: "Your lordship could not be more mistaken, for the king has not a subject more zealously attached to his person and government than myself." He then protested having been taken by force on a general warrant "which named nobody in violation of the laws of my country and of the privileges of parliament." Moreover, the messengers had orders to take him out of his bed at night. It was fortunate they had not attempted such a thing because he kept loaded pistols by his bed and it would have been the death of the first man who approached him, though he supposed he would have fallen by the second. He would rise in the next meeting of Parliament and impeach the secretaries of state. Halifax was patient and replied that he was acting under the advice of "the best lawyers" and that he had a list of questions. Wilkes interrupted his lordship again, explaining, "what they knew, it would be great impertinence in him to repeat; and of what they did not know, he should not inform them." Lord Halifax, thinking he could ease into the examination, began with the easy question, "Mr. Wilkes, do you know Mr. Kearsley?" Wilkes replied by repeating his position: as "laudable" as he found his lordship's curiosity, at the end of the interview, "all the quires of paper on your lordships' table shall be as milk-white as at the beginning." "Am I to understand, Mr. Wilkes, that you will answer no questions at all?" "Certainly, My Lord, and I thank God I am in a country where there is no torture, and if there was, I hope I have firmness enough to endure it."

They asked him whether he would prefer house arrest or Newgate prison or the Tower of London. Wilkes thanked them but declined to choose: "I demand my immediate delivery. I will go where I please, but if I am restrained by a superior force, I must yield to the violence, but I will never give color to it by a shameful compromise." They sent him to another room and made out a warrant of commitment to the Tower. When Wilkes was told of it, he asked that his servant, Matthew Brown, be allowed to attend him with linens, razor, etc. The secretaries agreed, though Brown was not allowed to see him until the next day.

The door burst open and two gentlemen rushed in, John Walsh, member for Worcester, and Richard Hopkins of Oving, Bucks, Esq. They had been present in the Court of Common Pleas when Beardmore had applied for the habeas corpus, and they could inform the secretaries that the writ had been granted, though it could not be issued until the next day. The effect of this information was to move the secretaries of state into an action not at all unusual for ministers, trying to defeat a habeas corpus by moving a prisoner about and issuing warrants that placed him in various hands so that it was difficult to serve the writ. The secretaries made out another warrant addressed to messengers George Collins and Thomas Ardan instructing them to deliver Wilkes to the Tower, and the messengers forthwith set off with Wilkes in a hackney coach.[29] The messengers did not bind their prisoner but trusted that as a gentleman he would not resist them. He did not.

Webb, Stanhope, and Robert Wood, undersecretary for the northern department of state, along with a crew of messengers, then returned to Wilkes's house to seize his papers. Lord Temple and Heaton Wilkes and other friends were still there. Wood invited them to witness the sealing up of the papers. His lordship replied, "What you are doing is too barbarous an act for any human eye to witness." The other gentlemen likewise refused. Stanhope went up to Wilkes's study with the men and proceeded to pull papers out of drawers, scatter them about the floor, then thrust them into sacks. They made off with Wilkes's private pocketbook and numerous maps and charts. They fetched a locksmith, one Fairbones, and paid him a shilling to pick the locks, but he was not very good at his job. So the messengers proceeded to break numerous locks and hinges of doors, desks, and chests.[30]

Wilkes, unaware of what was going on at his house and ignorant of the content of the warrant of commitment, arrived at the Tower of London in his usual gay mood and was met by Major Rainsford, the elderly, dignified lieutenant-governor of the Tower. The Tower of London is not a tower at all, but a fortified village with heavily armed walls. It was still functional, for it protected the east edge of the City from attack up the Thames. Wilkes, who still had a commission as lieutenant colonel in the militia, outranked the major, who saluted him in soldierly greeting. He was to be confined in one of the more modern houses. He hoped, Wilkes said, he would not be forced to stay in a room where a Scotsman had been imprisoned, though he might accept the room where Sir William Windham had been confined as a rebel in 1745. Sir William was Lord Egremont's father.[31]

Then Major Rainsford apologetically explained the orders he had received. The warrant specified that the prisoner was to be kept "close," never without the presence of one of the warders of the Tower, as the guards were called. The guards "shall not presume to leave him for a moment alone, either night or day. . . . They are to permit no person to have admittance into the room he is confined in, or to speak to him" without the permission of the secretaries of state. The major had also received these commands verbally. Commands from whom? Wilkes asked. Lord Egremont. Wilkes exploded with anger, vowing to Major Rainsford as his fellow officer that the moment that "Right Honorable Rascal" Egremont would give up his office as secretary of state, Wilkes would challenge him. Dueling was not a matter that military men took lightly, and as time would show, Wilkes considered himself bound by this vow and would call Major Rainsford as witness to it. Wilkes had reason to be upset, for the order was a gross insult. To keep a prisoner close, said Walpole, was "a severity rarely, and never fit to be, practiced but in cases of most dangerous treason." In fact, according to law, keeping a prisoner close was illegal unless the prisoner were charged with high treason. The warrant addressed to the major ordering the close confinement was illegal because the words *close, treason,* or *treasonable* did not appear in it.[32] Moreover, a commitment was supposed to be made only in consequence of previous information made on oath, but Balfe's information, Wilkes would soon discover, was not made on oath.

Wilkes was taken to his room. He asked for paper and pen to write a letter but was refused. Lord Temple, Lord Bolton, Mr. Beardmore, another lawyer for Wilkes named John Gardiner, and Wilkes's brother Heaton came to the Tower and, being refused admittance, confronted Webb. Webb protested lamely that the order to keep the prisoner close must be a mistake, but he would go to the secretaries of state.[33] The secretaries of state had gone to their country estates for the Easter Sunday.

The next morning, Easter morning, after repeated entreaties, pen and ink and paper were brought to him, but a warder stood by his chair while he wrote a letter to Polly: "Be assured that I have done nothing unworthy of a man of honour who has the happiness of being your father. . . . I have not yet seen my accusers, nor have I heard who they are. My friends are refused admittance to me. Lord Temple and my brother could not be allowed to see me yesterday. As an Englishman, I must lament that my liberty is thus wickedly taken away, yet I am not unhappy, for my honor is clear, and my health good, and my spirit unshaken, I believe indeed, invincible. The most pleasing thoughts I have are of you."[34]

Webb came into Wilkes's room, but Wilkes asked him to leave. As he later said, "If I was not allowed to see those whom I loved, I would not see those whom I despised."[35] But being assured his letter to Polly would be posted, Wilkes entrusted it to Webb. Webb did not post it but confiscated it as evidence. Months later, it was returned to Wilkes, and eventually he published it.

Wilkes asked if he might be allowed to copy the warrant of commitment, was given permission, made the copy, and set about preparing it for the press. The result was a three-page handbill entitled *Magna Charta, Cap. 29,* which would appear on 4 May, an account of the arrest that included the warrant. It is said to have sold five hundred copies in the space of half an hour.[36] Word of what was happening to Wilkes had spread rapidly. Numerous other broadsides appeared, deploring the treatment of the people's hero. Ballads were hawked about the street. One of them, "The Jewel in the Tower," treated Wilkes as more valuable than the crown jewels that were kept in the Tower. It was rumored to have been written by Countess Temple. Within days, his image appeared on dozens of tavern signs.

The Duke of Newcastle, usually the calm, quintessential Whig, was alarmed: "The city and suburbs are in the utmost alarm at these proceedings." Saturday evening, Newcastle invited Lords Temple and Bolton to come to him, and they with other of Wilkes's friends set about organizing what must be the most classy protest march in history. Word spread among the nobles. "Our friends are in the highest spirits upon this violent proceeding," Newcastle wrote to the Duke of Devonshire; "they say the whole city of London will attend Mr Wilkes to Westminster Hall when he comes up to be bailed or to be discharged." Lord Midleton wrote to Lord Hardwicke, "For God's sake, my Lord, consider well the point . . . and show Wilkes that we will not abandon him unconvicted to the fury of an insolent minister."[37]

The parade took place on Easter Sunday. On horseback were Wilkes's supporters in the House of Commons (though not Pitt), his lawyer friends, printers, and City businessmen. Riding in carriages were fifteen or sixteen nobles, including the Dukes of Newcastle, Grafton, and Bolton, the Earls Temple and Cornwallis, and the Viscounts Midleton and Villiers. One or two at a time the carriages rattled over the drawbridge only to be stopped in the courtyard, where the noblemen were told they could not see Mr. Wilkes. Yet the protest was to good effect: on Monday morning, Lord Halifax rescinded the order for close guard and ordered open access. So many rushed to see Wilkes that Major Rainsford sent a hurried note to Halifax: he could not be answerable for his prisoner unless permission was given for only a small number at a time. Halifax did nothing. Among the visitors was Wilkes's older brother, Israel, who fussed at him for his boldness and begged him to ease off. Wilkes never forgave "the narrowness of his views and the littleness of his ideas."[38]

Meanwhile, in the Court of Common Pleas, an involved legal debate was taking place between a Sergeant James Hewitt, for the government, and Sergeant John Glynn, for Wilkes. The ancient title of *sergeant* was the proudest that an eighteenth-century lawyer could have; it was given only to those who finished what we would call the postgraduate course of study at Sergeants Inn, a small law college that qualified its members for judgeships. Wilkes's friends had asked several lawyers to represent him, but Glynn, who had qualified as sergeant only months before, was the only one with the courage to undertake the task. He and Wilkes had known each other at Leiden, but they had not been close, Glynn being a rather proper man. And a brilliant one. He would make his reputation in this and Wilkes's legal battles to come, have a political career as a Wilkite, and be remembered as one of the greatest lawyers of the age, "the very spirit of the constitution itself," Pitt said of him.[39] The debate in the Court of Common Pleas ended with the court's ruling that a writ of habeas corpus was to be issued to bring Wilkes into court the next day.

Glynn then took himself to the Tower and told Wilkes he should be ready to name supporters who were willing to stand bail should that be asked. Wilkes wrote at once to Lord Temple, asking for his help and asking him to approach Lord Grafton about the bail. Grafton, though he had participated in the Easter protest, was a man of good heart and weak backbone. He declined to guarantee bail, as he explained in a letter to Temple, on the grounds that doing so might offend the king. Temple wrote a polite reply which hardly masked his contempt: "No man in the kingdom can bear a more dutiful regard than I do to the Crown, or is more full of veneration for His Majesty than myself. At the same time I hope there is not any man in the kingdom more ready to stand forth, as far as in me lies, as zealous protector of the liberty of the subject. . . . I hold it an honor to be his bail, and so does the Duke of Bolton, who on the same principle has voluntarily offered himself." Pitt finally broke silence and announced to friends that declaring No. 45 a libel was a threat to the liberty of the press, but he did not back up his liberal position by offering bail.[40]

On Tuesday morning, 3 May, Wilkes was transported to Westminster Hall, the ancient Gothic hall where the coronation had been held. It had been built as a royal throne room and had served that purpose at the coronation, but between coronations it served a number of less glamorous purposes. The Chancery of the Exchequer met in a room above the entrance hall. The Court of the King's Bench, presided over by Wilkes's enemy Lord Chief Justice Mansfield, met at the southeast corner of the great hall; the Court of Chancery at the southwest; and the Court of Common Pleas, presided over by Lord Chief Justice Pratt, at the middle of the south wall. Their spaces were marked off by flimsy temporary screens, and in the isle that connected them were chapmen in stalls selling books and clothes and hawking other goods. The courts had met so for centuries, and their rituals were nearly as old. The judges in black robes and long white wigs sat elevated on a dais without any table immediately before them. There was a long table below at which the clerks sat and a rail, the bar, behind which stood lawyers in their shorter white wigs, witnesses, and prisoners. Above was a gallery from which spectators looked down on the proceedings. The gallery was removed in the nineteenth century, drawing the eye to the magnificent hammer-beam roof that, unaided by a single column, covers this vast, noble space.

Wilkes was brought before the justices by Major Rainsford. The accusations having been read, Chief Justice Pratt asked Wilkes if he had anything to say. He had. He drew a paper from his pocket and holding a hand to one eye, lisped his way through it.

> My lord, I am happy to appear before your lordship and this Court, where liberty is so sure of finding protection and support, and where the law (the

principle and end of which is the preservation of liberty) is so perfectly understood. Liberty, my lord, hath been the governing principle of every action of my life; and actuated by it, I always have endeavored to serve my gracious sovereign and his family, knowing his government to be founded upon it; but as it has been his misfortune to have employed ministers who have endeavored to cast the odium and contempt arising from their own terrible and corrupt measures on the sacred person of their sovereign and benefactor, so mine has been the daring task to rescue the royal person from ill-placed imputations, and fix them on the ministers, who alone ought to bear the blame and the punishment due to their unconstitutional proceedings.

When he had finished, a great cheer went up from the gallery. Pratt banged upon his gavel and said with dignity that the spectators had forgotten this was a court of law and that no one should imagine that the justices would be led to do their duty "by the clamor of a mob." Wilkes, "with unparalleled effrontery," jumped to his feet and addressed the chief justice: "This is not the clamor of a rabble, my Lord, but the voice of liberty, which must and shall be heard."[41] One of the government lawyers objected that what Wilkes had said in his speech had nothing to do with the case. No, it had not, said Pratt, but it was the custom of this court to allow a prisoner to make his statement before proceedings begin, and he had heard nothing in his speech that hindered the business before the court.

The proceedings got under way. Sergeant Glynn raised several objections to the "general warrant" of arrest, which named no criminal but left the determination of who was a criminal to the messengers. Then he argued that Wilkes had been protected by parliamentary privilege, the only exceptions to which were felony, breach of the peace, and treason; the writing or publishing of a libelous paper was none of these. The prosecution lawyers answered that the paper was indeed a breach of the peace. The justices consulted one another, then Justice Pratt arose. They needed more time to consider the case. "I am sorry to be instrumental in keeping Mr. Wilkes a moment in prison," but "I dare say Mr Wilkes himself will think the time not misspent"; a case that concerned all of his majesty's subjects ought to be "settled and declared by a solemn determination." Wilkes stood up and said he believed the court had "the liberty of the subject at heart," and he submitted entirely. At Glynn's request, an order was issued to the warders that Wilkes's friends be allowed to see him. He was then remanded to the Tower until Friday next. As he and his guards rose, a great cheer went up from the spectators, and as he was escorted out, the cheer was picked up by the crowd in the street, clapping and calling encouragement as Wilkes was put into the warders' carriage.[42]

That evening Wilkes's room at the Tower was crowded with friends. The

8. John Wilkes, Esqr., Member of Parliament for Aylesbury, Bucks., by I. Miller. The caption from Alexander Pope's "First Epistle to the First Book of Horace" referred to Henry Saint John, Viscount Bolingbroke. Courtesy of Farley Library, Wilkes University.

next morning, the newspapers described it as a levee, a term usually reserved for the ceremonial morning audiences of royalty or the highest of noblemen. It happened to be the morning of the king's birthday, a holiday in eighteenth-century England; people dressed in their new "birthday suits" and "birthday gowns" and danced at balls and attended elaborate dinners. Gaily dressed men traipsed in and out of Wilkes's room all day, many bringing food and wine. Wilkes was careful to send Brown back to Great George Street to light up the house in honor of the king by putting candles in the windows when darkness came on. It cost something to use up forty or fifty candles in one evening; so it was with admiration, and a sly dig at Lord Halifax, that the *Public Advertiser* reported how no house in Great George Street was lighted up so early and so well as Mr. Wilkes's.

The next day a letter was brought from Lord Temple. As lord lieutenant of Buckinghamshire, he had been commanded by the secretaries of state to dismiss Wilkes from the Bucks militia. They had the authority to make the demand, and he was now obeying, though, he said, "I cannot at the same time help expressing the concern I feel at the loss of an officer by his deportment in command endeared to the whole corps." It was mean and devious of the secretaries of state to require Temple to dismiss his friend when the secretaries were planning to dismiss Temple himself from his lord lieutenancy, which they did the very next day. He was succeeded by Dashwood, or rather Lord Le Despenser, as he was now called.[43]

On Friday, 6 May, the warders drove their carriage over the bridge to take Wilkes back to court and were greeted by a crowd of cheering people who ran behind the carriage through the City and along The Strand and down Whitehall Street, "crowded into Westminster Hall and into every corner and balcony," and packed themselves into the streets in front of the Houses of Parliament and Westminster Abbey and Westminster Hall.

Among those in the gallery was old William Hogarth, with pad and pencil, making sketches of squinting Wilkes.[44]

Again Justice Pratt invited Wilkes to have his say.

> The liberty of all peers and gentlemen, — and (what touches me more sensibly) that of all the middling and inferior set of people, who stand most in need of protection, — is, in my case, this day to be finally decided upon; a question of such importance, as to determine at once whether English liberty be a reality or a shadow. Your own free-born hearts will feel with indignation and compassion all that load of oppression under which I have so long labored: close imprisonment, the effect of premeditated malice; all access to me for more than two days denied; my house ransacked and plundered; my most private and secret concerns divulged . . . together with all the various insolence of

office; — form but a part of my unexampled ill-treatment. Such inhuman principles of star-chamber tyranny, will, I trust, by this court, upon this solemn occasion, be finally extirpated; and that henceforth every innocent man, however poor and unsupported, may hope to sleep in peace and security in his own house, unviolated by king's messengers, and the arbitrary mandates of an overbearing secretary of state.

Silence. Then Pratt pronounced the decision of the court. Wilkes felt a deep disappointment as the justice read the first part, vindicating the secretaries of state: the court had found ample precedent for the warrant. Then the second part: writing or publishing a libel was not a breach of the peace. Mr. Wilkes was discharged on the ground of parliamentary privilege. Serjeant Nares, a government prosecutor jumped to his feet: "My Lord, I have just received a note from the attorney and solicitor general desiring they may be heard upon the point of privilege." Lord Chief Justice: "It is too late."[45]

Wilkes stood up, and Pratt acknowledged that he could have the floor: "Great as my joy must naturally be . . . allow me to assure you, that I feel far less sensibly on my account, than I do for the public. The sufferings of an individual are a trifling object when compared with the whole; and I should blush to feel for myself in comparison with considerations of a nature so transcendently superior."

He then "turned about and made a low bow" to the spectators. "This occasioned such a shout as reached the Exchequer," said Dr. Wray, "and called us all down from our seats." Chaos reigned in the old hall, with applause and cheers and shouts of joy that would not stop. His friends managed to get Wilkes out a private door, but he was recognized at once and "a prodigious multitude of people" pressed around him calling out, "Wilkes and Liberty." According to Newcastle's nephew George Onslow, "Amidst continual acclamations and loud huzzas," a crowd of many thousands followed to Great George Street, people "of a far higher rank than the common mob." Wilkes opened an upper window and stood bowing to them. "The evening concluded with bon-fires, illuminations, and other rejoicings."[46]

As the common folk were celebrating in the streets, Wilkes and his friends Lord Temple, Sergeant Glynn, Humphrey Cotes, and Heaton Wilkes were celebrating at Great George Street. They were shocked by the condition of the house after it had been ransacked by the messengers: broken doors, rifled desks, books on the floor. Wilkes decided then and there he would protest. He sat down and drafted a letter to the secretaries of state and showed it to the company, who, a bit in their cups, told him to send it. He made the final copy the next morning and dispatched it to Lords Egremont and Halifax:

Great George Street, May 6, 1763
My Lords,

On my return here from Westminster Hall, where I have been discharged from my commitment to the Tower under your lordships' warrant, I find that my house has been robbed, and am informed that the stolen goods are in the possession of one or both of your lordships. I therefore insist that you do forthwith return them to
your humble servant,
John Wilkes

The next day Wilkes received the following:

Great George Street, May 7, 1763
Sir,

In answer to your letter of yesterday in which you take it upon you to make use of the indecent and scurrilous expressions of having "found your house had been robbed, and that the stolen goods are in our possession," we acquaint you that your papers were seized in consequence of the heavy charge brought against you, for being the author of an infamous and seditious libel . . . for which libel, notwithstanding your discharge from commitment to the Tower, his majesty has ordered you to be prosecuted by his attorney-general.

We are at a loss to guess what you mean by *stolen goods:* but such of your papers as do not lead to a proof of your guilt, shall be restored to you; such as are necessary for that purpose, it was our duty to deliver over to those whose business it is to collect the evidence, and manage the prosecution against you. We are your humble servants,
Egremont,
Dunk Halifax

This did not satisfy Wilkes, who claimed an "absolute robbery" on the ground that a silver candlestick was missing from his house. Taking a lawyer, he proceeded to the Bow Street magistrate's court and confronted the sitting judge of that day, John Spinnage, Esq., demanding an injunction to force the secretaries of state to return his property. His request, of course, was denied. He returned home, sent an account of how he had been refused to the *Public Advertiser,* and sent off the letter he had addressed to the secretaries of state to be printed and distributed as a handbill. That done, he wrote again to the secretaries of state:

My Lords,

Little did I expect when I was requiring from your Lordships what an Englishman has a right to, his property, taken from him and said to be in your lordships' possession, that I should have received in answer from persons in your high station, the expressions of *indecent* and *scurrilous* applied to my legal demand. The respect I bear to His Majesty, whose servants it seems you still are, though you stand legally convicted of having in me violated, in the highest and most offensive manner, the liberties of all the commons of England, prevents me returning you an answer in the same Billings gate language. . . . I fear neither your prosecution nor your persecution, and I will assert the security of my own house, the liberty of my person, and every right of the people, not so much for my own sake, as for the sake of every one of my English fellow subjects.

I am,

My Lords,

your humble servant,

John Wilkes[47]

Later, when the excitement had quieted down, Wilkes came to regret these letters. When he was condemned in the press for writing such "ludicrous letters," he bristled. Later he admitted that he and Temple and Glynn had been "too much elated in the victory obtained in that moment," he said, by which he probably meant they were too drunk, to see that the letters really were "flippant" and "ludicrous." But the letters were prophetic: this was not the last time Wilkes would dare to attack the secretaries of state and their minions for violating his rights to privacy and personal property. In the end, he and his allies would establish far-reaching precedents whereby those rights could be protected. Still, he found the letters of the day "unbecoming the dignity of the cause."[48]

Wilkes was enlivened by risk, but his letters to the secretaries of state had done no honor to the grand vision of liberty that was taking shape in his imagination. After May of 1763, he would put his daring at the service not of a Pitt, not of Temple, not of a Whig faction; he would put it at the service of "the middling and inferior set of people, who stand most in need of protection." He was disappointed that the ground of his release had been parliamentary privilege instead of the illegality of the warrant. "He expressly states the case," he later wrote, referring to himself in the third person, "as the case of every subject. . . . He pleaded the cause of the nation, not of the House of Commons."[49] The cause of the nation. In May 1763, John Wilkes became what in English history is called a radical. He wanted radical change in the laws and institutions so that they would protect all people and give them a voice in government. When he asserted "the security of my own house" and "the liberty of my person," it was "not so much for my own sake, as for the sake of every one of my English fellow subjects."

Wilkes did not lose a minute in inducing the press to come to his support.

Copies of the speeches he had made that day in the Court of Common Pleas would be printed and reprinted over and over in newspapers and pamphlets and read by many thousands of people. His popularity skyrocketed and would soon reach a point beyond the imaginations of most politicians. His image could be found on tobacco papers, halfpenny ballads, porcelain dishes, punchbowls, teapots, prints, and broadsides. There was hardly a workingman who did not believe that Wilkes was the only man who would stand up for him; dissenters almost to a man were ready to serve him; small businessmen, farmers, lawyers, virtually all of the middle classes found hope in his audacious challenges to authority. Liberty for "every innocent man, however poor and unsupported" became for Wilkes a cause that was "transcendent."

With his keen sense of public desires, Wilkes understood that his power lay ultimately in offering purpose to the unorganized masses of people. His enemies thought in other terms. Lord Chief Justice Mansfield had listened to the proceedings of the court and the riotous behavior of the mob from behind the screen that separated the Court of Common Pleas from the Court of the King's Bench. He was furious. "No man every behaved so shamefully as Lord Chief Justice Pratt," he told the king; "he has denied to Your Majesty that justice which every petty justice of the peace would have granted to a highwayman."[50] Lord Mansfield's words would have dire consequences for John Wilkes.

The pursuit of a noble cause would change the practical terms of Wilkes's life, taking him farther and farther from the Squire of Aylesbury and farther and farther into debt. Forced to live by his wits, he would try to make money as a printer-publisher, one of those rare gainful occupations that a gentleman could engage in without losing his social status, but he would prove not very good at the business and would be forced to sell Prebendal House. He would discover in himself a genius for elective politics. As for hierarchical politics, the manipulating of the government system from within, he had no talent at all. He was never in his life to have a place in national government. He had wanted one, but when it was finally offered, it was offered as a bribe, and he would not take it. So there he was, a parliamentary politician, unpaid for his services. For the next decade he would depend heavily upon money provided by his family and friends for his personal debts. In political matters he would depend upon his fellow radicals to support him as their front man, the public figure who had the courage and skill to fight for the cause of liberty.[51]

In all matters, he would depend upon Lord Temple. "I am my own man, and Lord Temple's," he wrote to his patron. "If I have any talents which can please, they shall ever be dedicated to his service." He even asked Temple's permission to go abroad to see his daughter.[52] When Temple demurred, Wilkes went anyway. He was daring in the matter of patronage as in everything else, pliant in his letters to his patron, but repeatedly risking or ignoring his disapproval.

Would a dignified cause make of John Wilkes a dignified man? Hardly. At least not in the sense of Puritan dignity. He would continue to present himself to the world, a gentleman at all points, perfect in his manners and manly in his bearing, but openly a libertine. The libertinism was probably a political asset, but the ministers, supposing that the public would disapprove, leaked a story: by their account, when Webb and his crew returned such of Wilkes's papers as they did not want, among them was an envelope containing several condoms.[53]

6

The Great George Street Printing Shop

When Wilkes examined his house to see what the messengers had taken, he realized that the manuscript of An Essay on Woman was missing. He was not worried that the ministry would see it, for they already knew of its existence. When the messengers had raided George Kearsley's shop, they had seized three or four of Wilkes's letters that mentioned the satire, and they had taken one of the proofs of the indecent title page with the erect penis next to a ten-inch scale and the damning uses of the names of two prelates. But there was no law against owning a bawdy parody or an indecent title page that made fun of a bishop. It was against the law only to publish it. But a work like the Essay would always be in danger of pirating, and, knowing Philip Carteret Webb and Lovell Stanhope, Wilkes thought they would be capable of letting it be stolen and published and then foisting the authorship upon him. In the *Public Advertiser* of 10 May 1763 there appeared an advertisement in the style usual for a forthcoming book:

Speedily will be published,
by Philip Carteret Webb and Lovell Stanhope, Esqrs.
An Essay on Woman.

That, thought Wilkes, should keep the poem out of the press. Two days later, many bundles of Wilkes's papers were returned to the house in Great

George Street, and there was the manuscript.[1] But the game was not over: Webb had kept Wilkes's letters to Kearsley, including those mentioning the Essay, and he had kept the title page.

The secretaries of state and the attorney general, Charles Yorke, questioned Kearsley and Richard Balfe for several hours on 9 May 1763. Yorke took what he had learned to the king, and his majesty directed him to move ahead with charges against Kearsley as publisher and Wilkes as author of *North Briton* No. 45. Yorke did not much like the task, but he proceeded to the Court of the King's Bench and entered "informations" (that is, charges) against the two men. Summonses were dispatched. Kearsley came into court, pleaded not guilty, and was bailed. Wilkes ignored his summons, confident that he was protected by parliamentary privilege. It was a mistake for him not to appear and make his case before the judges. Before long, King George would use his failure to appear as a reason for the House of Commons to bring him to justice.

Then Yorke dropped the case against Wilkes. He gave out to the other ministers that he did so to avoid starting a battle between Lord Chief Justice Pratt of the Court of Common Pleas and Lord Chief Justice Mansfield of the King's Bench, but probably he had decided that his evidence for Wilkes's authorship would not hold up in court. He may also have wanted to make peace with Wilkes. If he dropped the charges, he hoped Wilkes, quid pro quo, would withdraw his suits against the ministers.[2]

But Wilkes did not think himself obliged to the attorney general for any favors and went ahead with his legal attacks. On 14 May he initiated actions for false arrest against Constable Chisholme and the three leading messengers, John Money, James Watson, and Robert Blackmore. The following February, when Wilkes was in France in virtual banishment and could not testify, the grand jury would dismiss these cases on grounds of insufficient evidence.[3]

But Wilkes was up to something of far greater importance to the history of law and to his image as champion. He brought actions of trespass against the secretaries of state, Egremont and Halifax, against the solicitor to the treasury, Philip Carteret Webb, and against the undersecretary of state, Robert Wood. He charged all and each of them with illegal invasions of his privacy and illegal damage to his property. He entered a claim of five thousand pounds damages each. Wilkes was represented by a lawyer named James Phillips, whose fees very nearly emptied Wilkes's pockets.[4]

Glynn did not represent Wilkes in this instance because he was engaged in another, even more important suit, one that everyone who watched these developments understood to be of major importance to the law. Twenty-five journeymen printers and apprentices entered suits against the messengers

Money, Watson, and Blackmore. Moreover, Dryden Leach brought suit for false arrest and trespass against the same messengers.[5] Suits such as these were unheard of. Working-class men — printers, even apprentice printers — were suing Great Britain in all her majesty. People of high station were shocked. People on the street were excited. Wilkes, who with Sergeant Glynn had worked up the printers to the point of action, was pleased: "Everything legal wears the most smiling aspect, and every mean art which has been used to protract justice has proved ineffectual, and I believe the trials will come on the end of next week." He was wrong about that: the printers' causes did not come to trial until July, and Wilkes's and Leach's causes much later.

Meanwhile, Wilkes went to work as propagandist for his causes and for himself. The causes and the man could hardly be separated, for Wilkes realized that his own image had come to stand for his ideals. He solicited the help of friends and printers who wrote for newspapers or owned interest in them, including John Almon, John Williams, Roger Thompson, who owned the *Gazetteer*, Cuthbert Shaw of the *Middlesex Journal*, and Henry Samson Woodfall, the owner and editor of the *Public Advertiser*. He sought the assistance of engravers and printers. The propaganda he turned out took every shape and form possible in that day, pamphlets, periodicals, newspaper letters, handbills, ballads, and verses. Wilkes was especially astute in recognizing that he should provide something for every sort of buyer. He produced or encouraged broadsides such as *Number Forty-Five, a New Ballad;* he sent the speeches he had made in court to newspapers; he sent letters under fictitious names to be inserted in magazines, printed handbills in a style that journals would pick up and reprint, and wrote newspaper stories about himself; he began to produce what eventually would become his book, *English Liberty*, a collection of letters, papers, and legal documents calculated to enhance his image and further his causes: it first appeared piecemeal, a few pages at a time that were put on sale for a halfpenny. Later he would produce for wealthy buyers a handsome, two-volume *English Liberty*, expensively printed by Dryden Leach.[6]

In these endeavors Wilkes was inadvertently helped by someone trying to hurt him. Wilkes had welcomed the many political cartoons in which he figured, but he was disappointed that no one had made a portrait engraving of him. A year before he had written to Kearsley, "Why do not the print shops take me? I am an incomparable subject for a print."[7] Ten days after his release from the Tower, his wish came true. William Hogarth, who had sketched Wilkes from the gallery during his second appearance in the Court of Common Pleas, put on sale his now-famous satire of Wilkes.

In Hogarth's symbol-rich engraving, Wilkes is shown seated in a posture commonly used for images of Lady Liberty. On the table next to him are *North Briton* No. 17, the issue in which Wilkes had attacked Hogarth, and No. 45. The staff traditionally held by Lady Liberty, resting in the right hand, supports a cap of liberty, a well-known emblem deriving from classical Rome, where such a cap was given to slaves when they were freed. In the mayoral processions of the City of London, the symbolic hat was carried on a pole. The cap in the print is stiffly domed so that it resembles a chamberpot. Its lower rim circles above the head of the subject like an ironic halo, ironic because the wig on the honored head is fashioned to look like the horns of the devil. Below it, the face, jut-jawed, gap-toothed, and cross-eyed, serves well enough to suggest "that devil Wilkes" (illustration 9).

"It must be allowed to be an excellent compound caricatura, or a caricature of what nature had already caricatured," Wilkes wrote, but he could hardly hide the hurt: "I know but one short apology can be made for . . . the person of Mr. Wilkes. It is, that he did not make himself, and that he never was solicitous about the *case* of his soul, as Shakespeare calls it, only so far as to keep it clean and in health. . . . I fancy he finds himself tolerably happy in the clay cottage to which he is tenant for life, because he has learned to keep it in good order. While the share of health and animal spirits which heaven has given him shall hold out, I can scarcely imagine he will be one moment peevish about the outside of so precarious, so temporary a habitation."[8]

Churchill was not so complacent. His cruel *Epistle to William Hogarth* appeared in the last days of June 1763. In the poem, Genius is personified as a woman grieving to see the decay which overtakes men like Swift whom she had inspired in their younger years. Now she is looking upon Hogarth "in second childhood's night":

> Are Men, indeed, such things, and are the best
> More subject to this evil, than the rest,
> To drivel out whole years of Idiot breath,
> And sit the Monuments of living Death?[9]

After that, it was the stylus against the quill. Hogarth responded on 3 August with a caricature of Churchill. To create this satire, Hogarth made use of a self-portrait done some years before. Hogarth had drawn an oval frame and then the image of himself within it; outside the frame sat his pug dog, Tramp. The joke had been that Tramp looked very like his master. A great many copies having been made of this print, Hogarth was ready to scrap it. But no, he could use it again. He erased the image of himself and substituted his caricature of Churchill. What now appeared within the oval frame was a bear dressed in clerical black with the collar bands that symbolized his priestly status, hugging

9. Hogarth's satiric portrait of Wilkes. Courtesy of Farley Library, Wilkes University.

in his left arm a huge club, the knots of which are labeled "Lie 1," "Lie 2," etc. His right arm awkwardly hugs a great mug of ale. Hogarth did not erase the image of the dog, which still sat outside the frame, but added a stream of urine emitting from between his legs in a watery arc that lands upon "An Epistle to Hogarth by C. Churchill." The title engraved across the bottom of the print reads, "The Bruiser, C. Churchill (once the Rev:d!) in the Character of a Russian Hercules, Regaling himself after having Kill'd the Monster Caricatura that so sorely gall'd his Virtuous friend, the Heaven born Wilkes."

Churchill, reluctant to let the quarrel drop, wrote to Wilkes, "I intend an elegy on him, supposing him dead." But Churchill's passion for satire was overwhelmed by another passion. His mistress was at his elbow: "I feel my spirit stir and my bowels yearn . . . she tells me with a kiss that I have killed him, and begs I will never be her enemy. How sweet is Flattery from the Woman we Love."[10] He never wrote the elegy.

Although Hogarth could not have predicted it, his print turned out to be a boon for Wilkes. There were many excellent engraved protraits, but political picture satires were crude, showing no attempt to make the figures look like the person they represented. The identification was spelled out in a balloon above the figure. Hogarth's print, halfway between portraiture and satire, suggested to the engravers that a physical feature could identify the figure, in the case of Wilkes, his squint. Suddenly the papers and broadsides were full of images of a figure with a cast eye, and before long the squint had come to stand for freedom from general warrants and other ideals of liberty Wilkes championed.[11]

In June, a scandal was spread that Wilkes had embezzled money from the militia by taking funds designated for uniforms and recruitment. Fortunately, he had the final account, correctly stated and approved by the major and adjutant of the regiment. It showed a small balance due *to* Wilkes, not *from* him. He had made copies and sent them to Lord le Despenser, Lord Temple, and all the officers.[12] Temple wrote angrily that the story was "an *infamous* falsehood," and he, who had been Wilkes's superior as lord lieutenant of the county, had the papers to prove it; it was another of the "scandalous calumnies which have been industriously circulated against your private character." He too had been the subject of malicious gossip, but he was "proud and happy in all the odium which I have drawn upon my poor head in consequence of the liberty I have taken of daring to avow the cause of freedom in opposition to that of tyranny and persecution. . . . I neither mind smiles nor frowns; I only am happy in doing what I think my duty and in supporting you."[13] But his lordship was mistaken about the uniforms. Some years hence Wilkes cleared up the matter by paying what the accountants claimed for the militia.

Wilkes's next enterprise was to publish a second edition of the *North Briton* or, more precisely, to return to his project of publishing a second edition that had been interrupted by his arrest. But Leach, who had been turning out the book when the messengers raided his shop, had had his fill of ministers and messengers. The seventy-two reams of paper in his shop that Wilkes had bought for the project Leach now sent to Wilkes's house.[14] Wilkes began to cast about for other booksellers or printers who might be willing to undertake the edition but could find none. He scaled down his project. He would print only issues 1–44. If he did not include No. 45, would not a willing publisher or printer come forward? He could not find a single one down the length of Fleet Street. But how could he waste seventy-two reams of printing paper sitting in his front parlor?

He would set up his own print shop and print and publish the edition himself. It would serve the cause of liberty and, he hoped, the relief of his pocketbook. He would publish by subscription, a widely used device whereby people agreed in advance to buy the book. He would omit No. 45 so that people would not be afraid to subscribe. The list of those who eventually subscribed includes virtually every gentleman whose name appears in these pages, be they friend or foe, but it is not a long list by eighteenth-century standards.

On 21 May 1763, a press carpenter named John Yallowby, assisted by his son, began setting up two press machines in the front parlor of Wilkes's Great George Street house, the two-pair-of-stairs room, the spies always called it. Though Leach would not undertake the printing of the book, he would help Wilkes to do the job himself. He lent the machines to Wilkes, recommended printers, and became Wilkes's consultant and sometime supervisor of his shop. To accommodate the machines, Wilkes had called in carpenters to enlarged the hall, paperers to paper the staircase, and painters to spruce up everything.[15]

Lord Temple, worried, begged Wilkes to desist, and when Wilkes refused, offered to pay him to dismantle the presses. Wilkes would not listen. He was determined to take his chances in court, where, if he were arrested, he would be protected, he was sure, by parliamentary privilege. His cause was freedom of the press, the courts were on his side, he was winning the fight, and he was not going to back away now. He was enjoying a new self-image, no longer the playboy, now the champion of liberty. It sat well with the Puritan heritage from his dissenting mother. "I lead a very philosophical life" he wrote to Temple; "I rise early, and pass the day alone, or only with one or two friends. I have never lost sight of the great object of the liberty of the subject at large. All my researches are directed to that great point; and if . . . your lordship cannot approve as much so I wish some particulars of my conduct, I trust that the dénouement will fully justify, not only to so great candor as your lordship possesses, but to the world, however artfully prejudiced against me, all points of real importance."[16]

Lord Temple's disapproval did not prevent Wilkes's asking his lordship for financial backing. On 25 May, he begged a loan of two hundred pounds because the two presses and the fees of his lawyer Phillips had "cost me so much more than I imagined." He said nothing about the remodeling of the room and papering of the stairway. On 5 June he was again begging from his patron.[17] Temple sent the money. Yallowby finished erecting the machines on 28 May: his bill came to twenty-eight pounds, but four months later he still had not been paid.[18]

Wilkes hired two printers, Michael Curry and George Savile Carey.[19] At that time printers had a relationship with their employers different from that of a modern workman to his employer. Printers were the servants of the owner of the shop in which they worked. They addressed their employer as master. The relationship was subject to the ethics of honesty, trust, and loyalty between master and servant that were assumed without question in that society. As time would show, most of the printers who would come into Wilkes's house would prove trustworthy servants, but not all.

Finally the press got started. Curry and Carey printed off a pamphlet on Wilkes's arrest, and Wilkes put it on sale for a guinea. They printed the suppressed *North Briton*, the one Wilkes and Williams had found at Balfe's shop when Williams had climbed the ladder to gain entrance. They printed an affidavit by Peregrine Cust that made outlandish charges against Kearsley, an open letter to Egremont and Halifax on the seizure of papers, and some of Wilkes's verses. A major undertaking was to reprint *Recherches sur l'origine du despotisme oriental,* a work in French by Nicholas Antoine Boulanger, a member of the d'Holbach set who had died. A friend and ally in the House of Commons, Joseph Mawbey, prevailed upon him to publish Mawbey's *The Battle of Epsom: A New Ballad,* a satirical account of a political meeting at Epsom. Mawbey was a handsome fellow, but no gentleman. He was a distiller and pig farmer who fed his pigs on the husks of the barley used in the distilling. He cracked so many bad jokes about the pigs that he acquired the nickname "Hog-sty" Mawbey and became himself the butt of many jokes. Wilkes called his poetic attempt "the dull Epsom ballad my press groaned under."[20]

Wilkes kept putting off the printing of the *North Briton*, even though it was his primary object in establishing the press. He was waiting to see how the suits by the printers, scheduled for trial in early July, would work out. The results might well determine whether he would include No. 45. His friends in the House of Commons were warning that there was a movement afoot to expel him, and the appearance of the edition, especially No. 45, might hurt him. Wilkes responded that he would wait.

In early June, Wilkes went to Aylesbury to look after political matters. He had "the honor of being escorted into the town by every man who had, or could hire, a horse, and if I have the honor of being expelled [from the House of Commons], the declaration is universal that I shall be re-chosen." At Prebendal House he found Churchill, who had been staying there since he had escaped arrest the month before. He and Dell and Dr. Stephens and other friends celebrated the king's birthday, "all of us in full chorus, to the liberties of our country and the virtues of our sovereign."[21]

On a Sunday Wilkes and Churchill rode to West Wycombe, ostensibly to see the parish church that had been rebuilt by none other than the officiant of the Medmenham Abbey black rites, Sir Francis Dashwood, now Lord le Despenser. The church, located on a hill behind the village of West Wycombe, had fallen into a ruinous condition, and Le Despenser had rescued it but changed it so extensively that many thought he had built a new church. He had heightened the stone tower and placed on top a clever "golden ball," actually a copper ball, inside of which were benches to accommodate four or five people. It was accessible by steep stairs through the old belfry. The ball was an imitation of a similar one in Venice used for optical experiments. What delighted Wilkes were its other purposes: "the best Globe Tavern I was ever in," he said, where were sung "jolly songs very unfit for the profane ears of the world below."

His lordship was hospitable to Wilkes and Churchill, showed them about, and invited them to climb up into the globe with him. Having ordered a servant to bring up some refreshments, le Despenser opened a conversation in which he hinted, or more than hinted, that something might be done for both of them if the new press, etc., etc. What transpired Wilkes obliquely revealed in a piece he called a "tour into Buckinghamshire," which soon appeared in several papers. "It is whispered, that a negotiation was here entamée by the noble lord himself, with Messrs. Wilkes and Churchill. The event will show the amazing power of his lordship's oratory: but if, from perverseness, neither of those gentlemen yielded to his wise reasons, nor to his dazzling offers, they were both delighted with his divine milk-punch."[22]

Le Despenser began to think Jack Wilkes was hopeless. In later years, Wilkes told how he used to meet his lordship at the Medmenham monks, but "he afterwards neglected those meetings, and gave as his reason, that he did not choose to meet Mr. Wilkes who an enemy of Lord Bute. Mr. Wilkes desired their common friends at the Abbey to represent to Sir Francis the nature of such an institution, in which party had not the least concern, that the brotherhood there were us'd to sacrifice to mirth, to friendship and to love, never to fortune, nor ambition."[23]

Churchill went back to Aylesbury, and Wilkes went on to London. He was soon writing back to Churchill, "The plot thickens so fast . . . I have a good deal to say to you about the great business at hand, but [knowing his letter would be opened] I do not choose to say it likewise to the secretaries of state." He and Glynn and other lawyers were planning legal strategies for the trials of the printers' causes: "I am deeply engaged with sergeants, counsellors, attorneys, etc."[24]

Then John Wilkes made the mistake of his life. He had learned that the trials had been put off, unwelcome information, for he had two printers in his house whom he was paying by the week. Could he pay them for another month without their working on the edition? Then he had a thought: he could use the men to complete the project he had begun the previous autumn. He ordered them to print An Essay on Woman.

Curry and Carey were to print parodies of the three poems by Pope that appeared together in Warburton's edition and numerous reissues of the *Essay on Man* — the "Essay on Man" itself and two shorter pieces, the "Universal Prayer" and "The Dying Christian to His Soul." The printers were to use the same type and format as Warburton's edition. The work was to open with that indecent title page, the erect penis beside the ten-inch scale, the bawdy mottos, and the libelous use of the names of clerics. It was to include an "Advertisement" and "Design," both of which Wilkes had written after Potter's death. Warburton's edition of the *Essay on Man* would be disbound and rebound in the Essay on Woman, so that Pope's lines and the corresponding parodic lines of Potter/Wilkes would face each other "in direct contrast." The "Universal Prayer" would be matched line for line with Wilkes's "Universal Prayer," and the "Dying Christian to His Soul" with Wilkes's "Dying Lover to His Prick." To these Wilkes added another poem of his own, written independently of Potter, "The Veni Creator, or the Maid's Prayer," an imitation of the popular hymn the "Veni Creator Spiritus."[25]

The printers were to produce thirteen copies only (some documents say twelve), one for each of the twelve members of the Medmenham hellfire club, and one other, possibly, for its library. When Wilkes delivered the manuscript to the printers, "he enjoined the men in the most solemn manner" to keep the project a deep secret, to print only thirteen copies, and "not to rob him of any sheet of it for he had not the least intention of making it public."[26] Wilkes did not doubt that printing twelve or thirteen copies for the use only of himself and the members of his men's club was a private act and not a publication. A commonsense interpretation of the law had served him very well to this point, but it would not do so here. He would pay for his mistake.

The printing of such a complicated piece was time consuming. Curry could not even begin without borrowing type from Leach that matched the type

Warburton had used for the "Advertisement" and "Design." Curry and Carey managed to work off only two half-sheets before Wilkes stopped them and told them to get ready to do the *North Briton*. They had already printed the "Advertisement" and the "Design" but had completed only 94 of the intended 1,304 lines of the "Essay on Woman." Wilkes stopped the work because he had to be at Aylesbury on 14 July for the quarter sessions. Moreover, he had told Polly he would come to Paris to see her as soon as the quarter sessions were over. Not wanting to leave the *North Briton* project hanging, he decided to complete the edition of those weekly papers before he left. His friends told him it was impossible. He could never print the work the size of the *North Briton* in three weeks. That to Wilkes was a challenge — or a dare. He was certain he could do it and even placed a wager that he could.[27]

Wilkes planned to have men work on two presses day and night. To do that, he would need more printers, so he took on William Huckle, John Bagnall, and Benjamin Burd, all of whom had worked for Leach. Curry would be the foreman. Wilkes ordered Curry and Carey to set up the forms for the *North Briton* and to get the presses ready.

While Curry and Carey were making the preparations for the production of the *North Briton*, Wilkes set the new printers to work on a third half-sheet of the Essay on Woman. Instead of asking them to continue the "Essay" proper, where it had been left off, at line 94, he directed them to turn ahead in the manuscript and to print the smaller poems at the end, "The Universal Prayer," "The Dying Lover to His Prick," and "The Veni Creator." It flattered his vanity to see in print the parodies he himself had written without the help of Potter. When the new printers had run off the thirteen copies of their half-sheet, which was on 1 July, all work on the Essay on Woman was stopped. They never got back to it, and the Essay comes down to us as a fragment.[28]

All attention at Great George Street was now directed toward producing the octavo *North Briton* as fast as possible. The printers worked around the clock in shifts on two presses. A few days later, Curry told Wilkes that if he were to get the work out on schedule, he needed two more men. Wilkes hired Samuel Jennings and a seventh printer named Biggs.

As volumes 1 and 2 were being run off, the printers' trials came on. Leach's cause had been separated from that of the others and put off because it was a more complicated suit involving damage to property as well as false arrest. In the trials of 6 and 7 July 1763, the complainants were journeymen printers and apprentices who were charging false arrest. Four among them were now working for Wilkes, though when arrested they had been working for Leach. William Huckell, one of Wilkes's crew, had a particularly important part to play. The lawyers on both sides had agreed that the first trial should be for the suit of one printer only, and the outcome of that would facilitate the other cases, which then could be tried as a group. Huckell's case was singled out for the trial — trial, so to speak. The case was heard in the Court of Common Pleas by Lord Chief Justice Pratt, who had freed Wilkes from the Tower, and two other judges. Because the alleged crime had taken place in the City of London, the court was obliged to hold the session in the Guildhall instead of Westminster Hall, and in that venue the jury was chosen from City people, not from journeymen and apprentices, but from men of higher status, merchants and traders.

The entire legal community recognized that this would be a precedent-setting case, and Huckell, a simple journeyman printer, found himself represented by Wilkes's lawyer, James Phillips, whose fees were paid by Lord Temple,[29] and counseled pro bono by a battery of five outstanding young lawyers, including Sergeant John Glynn, the youngest sergeant at the bar, and John Dunning, who made a great reputation in this case for his brilliant arguments against general warrants. They were opposed by another battery of formidable men with a great deal of experience, including the attorney general, the solicitor general, and three senior sergeants of the law.

The attorney general opened the defense with a long panegyric on the king — "a very good speech upon the whole," said Thomas Erskine May, the historian, "if addressed to the King himself, but a very injudicious one to a jury of citizens of London." The trial lasted twelve hours. Attorney General Yorke argued that the secretaries of state acted as justices of the peace and the messengers as constables and that their duty was protected by law. Overruled. The lawyers for the messengers "filled two large skins of parchment" with arguments, most of which were more rhetorical than substantive. The lawyers for Huckell demonstrated that the arrests were made on a general warrant in which, to use May's words, "no one was charged, or even suspected; no one named. . . . The offense only pointed at, not the offender; the messengers, responding to rumors, idle tales, and guesses, arrested forty nine persons on suspicion."[30] In a unanimous decision, the justices declared that the general warrant had been illegally executed and awarded Huckell three hundred pounds.

The attorney general immediately protested the size of the award and was told by Chief Justice Pratt that twenty pounds might be fair if only personal injury were considered; but the issues of liberty being considered, three hundred pounds was not at all excessive. He went on with an explanation that delighted Wilkes and the radicals. What the jury saw, said Lord Pratt, was "a magistrate over all the king's subjects exercising arbitrary power, violating Magna Charta, and attempting to destroy the liberty of the kingdom [and] the solicitor of the treasury endeavoring to support and maintain the legality of the warrant in a tyrannical and severe manner. These are the ideas which struck the jury on the trial; and I think they have done right in giving exemplary damages."[31]

The court did not declare general warrants per se illegal, only those "illegally executed," and that was a disappointment for Wilkes. On the other hand, because the court ruled that the authority of the secretaries of state did not derive from their status as justices of the peace, they had been deprived of the right to operate their own police force, a loss which in turn rendered general warrants all but worthless.[32]

The next day, 7 July, the "brother cause" of the other printers was tried by the same court meeting in the same place. The lawyers for the messengers seemed to spend more effort harassing the printers than answering the charge that the arrests were illegal, a tactic which had a negative effect on jury and public. Attorney General Yorke did not hesitate to use the court as a forum from which to attack Wilkes for not responding to the court summons two months before. Personally, off the floor of the court, said Wilkes, he was civil. Michael Curry was awarded £233.6.8, another printer £175, and the rest £120 each. The messengers did not have to pay this money out of their own pockets: it was paid by the Crown out of public funds.[33]

"Mr. Wilkes," reported the newspapers, "appeared at all the trials, and received the repeated congratulations of the public." After the second trial, he made his way through the crowd to the King's Arms tavern in Cornhill, cheered the whole way, while the solicitor general, the near-blind Philip Carteret Webb "was followed by hisses and would probably have been exposed to greater insults, if Attorney-General Yorke had not taken him under his protection and carried him home in his chariot." Wilkes wrote to Temple, "the chief justice was amazingly great." The administration, he said, was "stunned," and poor Webb, whose blindness and weakness had been apparent in the court, was "an object of compassion." A month later, Wilkes received a letter signed by the printers, thanking him for his "spirited endeavors and steady attention to procure us that redress and satisfaction which we have at length obtained by the verdicts of our countrymen."[34]

The public response was so strong that Wilkes began to hope the administration might collapse. It did not, and the battle continued in the courts. Within a space of six years, there were at least forty cases emanating from the general warrant issued against *North Briton* No. 45. Time has proven their importance in the development of democratic government. As Robert Rea, the historian of the press, put it, "The transference of political authority from government and law to the people and law may be dated from the cases revolving about *North Briton* No. 45."[35]

The printing of volumes 1 and 2 of the new edition of the *North Briton* was completed on 9 July 1763, two days after the brothers' trial. They had not yet been sent to the bindery and were stacked in unfolded sheets. These were the volumes as originally conceived, in which No. 45 did not appear. The first forty-four issues had been newly edited with new notes and an index. Wilkes did not have ready the matter he intended to put into the third volume, which included Wilkes's speeches, the warrants for his arrest and confinement, extracts from the House of Commons Journal, the issues of the *Monitor* that Wilkes had written, the letters exchanged with Lord Talbot before and after their duel, and the general warrant for *North Briton* No. 45. These, Wilkes thought, would enhance his image as the champion of Liberty and support the arguments in favor of his cause. This third volume would not be published for another six months.

Wilkes, again in need of money, sat down and wrote a long letter to Lord Temple. Though he had printed two thousand copies, he had only 120 subscribers, few of whom had actually paid. "I am not a little out of pocket by such a bold undertaking, but North Briton and Wilkes will be talked of together by posterity." In short, the books were still unbound and Wilkes could not pay for the binding. But the master of spin was not without an explanation: "I know that I have neither the lust of power nor of money, and if I leave my daughter less dirty coin, I will leave her more honest fame. I trust, next to her own virtue, her greatest honor will be derived from her father. The work is, I believe, the most just and animated account of last year's politics at home." He needed five hundred pounds.[36] Temple sent it.

Wilkes now began to think seriously of adding No. 45 to the book. Since the sheets were not yet folded or bound, it would be easy enough to add another sheet. "If 45 does not appear in the volumes, the idea the public has of my spirit is lost," he wrote to Lord Temple; "I own that I much incline to it. . . . I wait your Lordship's better judgment."

He did not await Temple's better judgment. Leach set up the forms, and Wilkes's men began the printing of No. 45. But the date for the quarter sessions at Aylesbury was upon him, and he rushed off before the work was completed, leaving Leach in charge. The sheets for No. 45 were added to the others on 17 July. They were then sent to a bindery and from there delivered to the publisher, John Williams, on 2 August. Leach, in charge of the shop while Wilkes was absent, was not happy with the work of Michael Curry and some of the others. He called a meeting of the printers who he thought had not done their work well, paid them off, damned them for a lazy lot, and dismissed them. The press would continue, but with a reduced crew.[37]

The quarter session, for which Wilkes had returned to Aylesbury, was a criminal court one step up from the courts of the individual justices of the peace and one step below the assize courts presided over by the king's judges. The chief justice of a quarter session was always the lord lieutenant of the county, and that was Lord le Despenser, who had displaced Lord Temple in that office. "Everything in court passed as usual," Wilkes reported, and then the justices and local gentry repaired to the George Inn for a feast. After the dinner Lord le Despenser rose to thank the justices, but his speech quickly turned political. He praised the peace treaty and then suggested that the gentlemen present should sign an address of congratulation to the king, and, yes, he had prepared such a document. Wilkes leaped up and declared he would sign no such thing, that he trusted that the ministers who had put their signature to the peace treaty would be impeached. Others protested that Lord le Despenser had not given proper notice and had packed the meeting with his allies. The proposed address was read and praised and objected to and le Despenser signed it. His friends came forward and added their signatures, but Wilkes and his supporters sat tight, including the two Aylesbury parsons, Mr. Pugh and Dr. Stephens.[38] Le Despenser went straight to Medmenham and drummed Wilkes out of the hellfire club.

Unbeknown to Wilkes, other scenes that would affect his future were being played out in Great George Street.[39] Samuel Jennings, the last printer hired, knew nothing about the Essay on Woman, for work on the poems had been stopped before he came into the shop, and the printers had told him nothing because they were sworn to secrecy. So he was puzzled one day by a paper he found on the floor, a proof sheet with a few marginal changes in Wilkes's hand. It contained lines from a poem in heroic couplets. "Heroic" may not have been the right word for these couplets, one of which read, "Then in the scale of various pricks, 'tis plain, / Godlike erect, Bute stands the foremost man." Not particularly alarmed that an agitator and playboy like Mr. Wilkes should be printing such stuff, he took it home, read it to his wife, then put it with other papers to be recycled. The next morning, his wife, preparing a lunch for him to take to work, wrapped up a globule of butter in the paper and packed it with the lunch. That day Jennings met another printer, Thomas Farmer, and the two had lunch at the Red Lion in Jerwin Street, their meal consisting of onions, radishes, bread, butter, and beer. The butter-smeared paper catching Farmer's eye, he picked it up and began to read. Interested, he borrowed it and took it to his place of work, the printer's shop of William Faden in Wine Office Court, and showed it to his foreman, Lionel Hassall, who took it at once to Mr. Faden. Faden is remembered today as the publisher of a newspaper, the *Public Ledger*, and of Samuel Johnson's *Idler*. A Scot who had changed his name from McFaden, he detested John Wilkes, but he was nervous about the discovery. A libelous statement about Lord Bute's private parts would be certain to infuriate the king. Not knowing what to do, he contacted an old friend, the Rev. Mr. John Kidgell, the heteroclite morning preacher at the Berkeley Chapel in Westminster and parson of the villages of Godstone and Horne in Surry. The Rev. Mr. Kidgell was the author of a soft-porn piece, *The Card*, for which his bishop had called him on the carpet, and he was the sidekick of the Earl of March, who was lord of the bedchamber to the king and a notorious rake. The parson sometimes accompanied his lordship on nightly prowls about London. Such a man, thought Faden, would surely know what to do with such a paper. Kidgell's first idea was to write a series of essays on the discovery, which Faden could publish in his newspaper; Faden did not take to that plan. So Kidgell copied the pages and took them to Lord March, who took them to the secretaries of state, who directed him to turn them over to Philip Carteret Webb. The next day Lord March informed Mr. Webb that "the government were determined to do their utmost to discover and suppress this abominable work." Webb, who did not fail to understand the code, set in motion a conspiracy to convict Wilkes of libel and blasphemy.

What Faden brought to Webb on 8 July 1763 was the original proof of pages 4–7. No doubt Webb recognized it as part of the "Essay on Woman" that he had seen in manuscript, having found it among Wilkes's papers. What excited him now was that the lines had been printed. There was nothing criminal about having a manuscript of a dirty, satirical poem, but printing it was another matter. He might be able to charge Wilkes with a crime. He would need the full printed text, so he dispatched Faden to get the entire work. The search led back to Farmer, then to Jennings, and then to the other printers who had worked for Wilkes. Webb called them in for an interview and swore them to secrecy. Had anyone saved proof sheets? Carey admitted that he had, but he had burned them as soon as he saw that Wilkes might be in trouble. Their suspicions pointed to Michael Curry. Yes, he had proofs, but they were his, and he would keep them.

Wilkes returned to town on Saturday, 23 July, but hardly paused. He gave orders to the printers to run off some political pamphlets but said nothing about completing the Essay on Woman. Why would he? He was no longer a member of the hellfire club. Six months later, the unfinished work in sheets was still at Great George Street, stored on the top shelf of Wilkes's upstairs library.[40]

Despite Temple's disapproval, Wilkes left for Paris on 26 July. "The voice of nature and miss Wilkes calls me for a few days only to Paris," he told his lordship. I think the earl knew what he meant by "the voice of nature." Along the way, Wilkes was delighted to find himself celebrated at Canterbury by gentlemen of the town, and at Dover cheered by sailors who called out the new popular cry, "Wilkes and Liberty." Before he got into the boat, his servant, Brown, caught up with him. Brown, who had been taking care of Churchill at Prebendal House, had absentmindedly come away with the key to the wine cellar. Wilkes sent it back by express, with a note asking Churchill to drink to his own mistress, Mrs. Johnson, and then to Wilkes's, Mrs. Grosvenor. "What two damned adulterers we are; but so far from the least inclination to repentance, I am now planning a deep scheme for Madame Carpentier to fall into my mouth." Mme Carpentier was the teacher with whom Polly lived.[41]

Meanwhile, in the political underworld of Westminster, Webb was still trying to get Curry to give up his proofs. He told the other printers to talk to him. They did, but Curry refused. Faden's foreman, Hassall, talked to him, but to no effect. Then Faden himself tried to buy the proofs from him but failed to budge him. So Webb turned to Nathan Carrington, the chief of the messengers, whom he continued to trust even after Carrington's blunders during the arrests. Carrington talked to Curry, explaining that he could have the messengers pretend to arrest him and to find the proofs in his pocket: that way he could not be blamed. Curry was not interested in avoiding blame; what he wanted was money. Carrington made an offer of the amount Webb had authorized. It was not enough.[42]

Webb now discarded his guise as a secret agent and put on his legal robes. He had had enough of this troublesome fellow Curry and was thinking of charging him with theft. In the way of eighteenth-century households, Webb's servants overheard the talk, probably because Webb wanted them to hear it, and some of them warned Curry that the administration was thinking of arresting him for a theft. Curry was terrified, as well he might be since a conviction for a felony might result in his being hanged. He was afraid to go home that night; so Webb's servants hid him in Webb's house. Webb discovered him in the morning and forbade the house to him. That afternoon, one of the servants stopped at the tavern called Hercules Pillars, where he found Curry and sat down with him. Curry proceeded to curse Webb as "a damned scoundrel" and Wilkes as "a damned rogue." Convinced that Webb had rather see him arrested than to pay him for his proofs, Curry went to Churchill and told him what he had to offer. Churchill damned him, but said he would write to Wilkes. Curry decided to hang on until Wilkes got back from France.[43]

Wilkes had reached Paris on July thirtieth, left his bags in his usual ground-floor apartment in the Hotel de Saxe, and gone to see Polly, whom he found in perfect health, as he reported to Lord Temple. "She gave me the most sincere testimonies of real affection, many, many tears of joy."[44]

Wilkes met with some surprising good fortune in Paris. For reasons too subtle to trace, Richard Rigby, a stalwart of the Duke of Bedford, recommended Wilkes to the duke. Bedford, a powerful political noble in England, had come to France as the chief negotiator of the peace, the very peace that Wilkes had so vehemently opposed. Bedford received Wilkes "with distinction" and invited him to dine no fewer than three times.[45] Perhaps on one of these occasions Wilkes met the Duke of Richmond, who had recently returned from the the court of Louis XV at Versailles. Richmond told him that the king "asked many questions about me. I find I am not without friends, even among this nation."

Recent events in France were alarming. The parlements of Rouen and other French towns had revolted against the Crown by refusing a new tax. Troops were being dispatched. Wilkes wrote to Churchill, "The most sensible people here think that the French are on the eve of some great revolution," a remark he would repeat in a letter to Lord Temple. But Paris was as gay as ever, he told Churchill: "I have been in clover so long, that I have almost forgot even Mrs. Grosvenor. I am come here to a *carnival* for Pego, and nothing but a very few friends, and the cause I have at heart, should draw me to London before Christmas."[46] *Pego*, you may recall, was an antique word for penis.

On 15 August, Wilkes and a friend, Lord Palmerstone, the member of Parliament for East Looe, were strolling along a Paris street when they were accosted by a young gentleman in the dress of a French officer who asked if he were Mr. Wilkes. Yes, he was. "Mr. Wilkes wrote the *North Briton*, and must fight me." Wilkes answered that it was unbecoming of gentlemen to squabble in the street, and dueling was an affront to the laws of the country in which he was a guest; he would inform him, however, that he was staying in the Hotel de Saxe, and "Good day, Sir." That afternoon, the gentleman left his card at the hotel. He was C. John Forbes, a Scot who had served as captain in a French regiment, now disbanded. They met the next morning at six. Wilkes inquired politely, what was Mr. Forbes complaint? "Mr. Wilkes must fight him because he has wrote against Scotland." Wilkes asked him to show him what it was he objected to. "You have written against my country. Your name is Wilkes. Do you not write?" "Yes," said Wilkes, "I now and then write receipts for tenants." Wilkes then cautioned the captain that he would give no account of his writing to him or anyone else. Forbes wanted to fight that day. Wilkes pulled out his diary, consulted it, and announced that Forbes must wait his turn "for he had nineteen on his list before him."[47] When Forbes insisted, Wilkes became more serious. All right, he would, upon his honor, fight him, but not today for he had a previous account to settle with Lord Egremont, whom he had vowed before Major Rainsford at the Tower that he would challenge the day his lordship left office. If Forbes, understanding this prior commitment of Wilkes's, still wished to fight, he should return at noon with a gentleman who would act as his second, and Wilkes would also have a second. Forbes agreed and left. Wilkes sent a servant to find his friend Pierre Goy, who came at once. At noon Forbes reappeared without a second, made a fuss, and insisted upon fighting then and there. Wilkes refused to talk to him, saying that by the rules of honor only M. Goy would do the negotiating. Forbes huffed, then said he would fetch his second, turned around and left, but soon returned without anyone. He did not need a friend, he said. Mr. Wilkes would soon hear from him. Wilkes observed that such behavior had "more the air of an assassin than of a gentleman." Forbes left.

That afternoon the marshals of France arrested Wilkes. Unable to find Forbes, they brought into court the friend with whom he had been lodged, a notorious Jacobite, Alexander Murray, styled Earl of Westminster in the Jacobite peerage, a peerage that was never recognized in England. The two were questioned and then released on their own recognizances. Outside the court, Wilkes was met by a small group of Scottish soldiers in the French service, who had come, they explained, to try to excuse Forbes's embarrassing behavior, the blusterings of a twenty-three-year-old hothead. But Wilkes thought that a man of twenty-three was responsible for his actions; he had impugned Wilkes's honor, and Wilkes would not drop the matter. As soon as his affair with Lord Egremont was settled, he would indulge Captain Forbes. If Forbes chose at that time not to fight, well and good, but that would be Forbes's choice, "for Mr. Wilkes would meet him for that purpose anywhere in Europe, Asia, Africa, or America, except the dominions of France," where dueling was outlawed.[48] The next day Goy could locate neither Forbes nor Murray, so Wilkes, presuming that the message has reached him, let the matter alone.

In London, Lord Egremont had fallen seriously ill. Three days before the end, he managed to say, "I have but three more turtle dinners to come, and if I survive them I shall be immortal." He died on 21 August, and Wilkes heard the news the following week.[49] "What a scoundrel trick has Lord Egremont played me!" he wrote to Churchill; "I had formed a fond wish to send him to the Devil, but he is gone without my passport. . . . so much for him — I desire you to blot out of your book of maxims, *de mortuis nil nisi bonum* — it is a vile levelling principle . . . I am now at Captain Forbes's service, and will meet him anywhere out of the dominions of France." He intended to suggest the first town one comes to after crossing the border into Austrian Flanders. "Do not think I hold myself obliged to fight every dirty Scot — but I choose to show what I can do with such a fellow as Forbes."[50] Churchill begged him to desist: "You seem rather . . . to live in romance, than under the direction of that well-tempered, cool, distinguishing reason, in which no man is generally more happy than yourself. . . . Your country demands your life; the cause of liberty is in your hands; and that blessing, so much dearer than life, must remain precarious if not fixed by you. No one can try the secretaries of state if you do not, and though there is no doubt but there may be arbitrary ministers in future times, yet it is with me a question whether there may ever be another Wilkes."[51]

On 16 September, Wilkes crossed the border into Austrian Flanders. He had written to Forbes and Murray explaining that since Lord Egremont was dead, he was at Captain Forbes's service and would be outside French borders at Menin. Forbes had answered that he was ready to meet him anywhere Wilkes named. Wilkes waited at Menin, checking the post daily, but, hearing nothing, left on 22 September. "I think Forbes a pitiful fellow," he wrote to Churchill.[52]

Wilkes decided to return via Lille: "I have seen one of the most charming of our countrywomen at Lille, who has made me amends for leaving Paris—I hasten back to her: if honor permits me, love calls. Those stars have been for us the two polars through life, and I am sure will continue so." Then he added, "I found it very pleasant to read an account of my death in the *St. James's Evening Post.*"[53]

The Forbes affair, like that with Lord Talbot, accrued to Wilkes's honor. One day a gentleman appeared at the Hotel de Saxe and introduced himself as the secretary to Senior Grimaldi, the Spanish ambassador to France. He had come to pay the ambassador's compliments and to say that Mr. Wilkes "had acted up even to the ideas of Spanish honor." He begged Mr. Wilkes to be assured of the ambassador's high regard.[54]

Quite aside from the duel, Churchill and Temple had been urging Wilkes to return because the town was abuzz with rumors that Pitt would be brought back into office. On 27 and again on 29 July, Pitt had had long talks with the king. "Changes are much talked of and must soon take place," wrote Churchill, "nor can I think but under such an event, Great George Street will be infinitely more eligible than Paris."[55]

Wilkes arrived in London on 26 September to find rumors flying about that Forbes was in London and looking for him. According to the *Public Advertiser* of 22 September, many Scotsmen are happy in the anticipation that Forbes would find Wilkes and fight him. Wilkes announced that he intended to follow the maxim of a Scots nobleman (that is, Bute) and keep a bruiser beside him. The fact was, Forbes had taken a commission in the Portuguese army and was on his way to Lisbon.[56]

Wilkes had written to Lord Temple as soon as he had gotten home, uneasy because he has heard that Temple disapproved of his conduct in the Forbes business; but Temple was not angry and wrote from Stowe to welcome Wilkes home. "I am very glad you are once again upon English ground, and that your usual spirit and fortitude have extricated you so far from another extraordinary situation." He had indeed disapproved some of Wilkes's conduct but would not talk about it in a letter, for he distrusted the post.[57]

The political news was distressing. Grenville would remain first minister. And who should have been brought in to replace Lord Egremont as secretary of state for the north? Lord Sandwich. Wilkes was disgusted. The despicable Halifax still in power, and Sandwich elevated!

Then there was Wilkes's financial problems. Wilkes had hoped for years that Pitt would be brought back into office and would reward him with a place in a new ministry. Now he would have to take matters in hand without any help. So he offered to sell Temple his holdings in Bucks and Lincolnshire, deducting, of course, what Temple had already advanced. He hoped to raise three thousand pounds.[58] On 20 October, Temple wrote back, sending along five hundred pounds for immediate expenses but saying nothing about buying the estates.

Michael Curry came out of hiding and went to Great George Street and asked to see Mr. Wilkes. He was shown into the room with two pairs of stairs, and Wilkes came down to him. Curry explained that he had a set of proofs, but Mr. Wilkes could have them, for a price. Wilkes did not believe him. He went to a drawer in which he had told Curry to lock up all papers that were to be kept secret. He could not find the key. As Curry later told the story, Wilkes angrily forced the drawer open, but "unfortunately bedaubed his fingers." He found only some half-sheets of the *North Briton*. "What Mr. Wilkes expected to find there besides, he only can tell."[59] Wilkes turned to Curry and pronounced him a thief, a blackmailer, and a son of a bitch, adding that he could go to hell; or, as Curry later put it, Mr. Wilkes "dropped some expressions which affected my private character."

Curry went directly to Faden and gave up the revises, the proof sheets printed in red. It was his revenge, he later said, twisting a point, because Wilkes intended to have him arrested for a felony. What sort of revenge? he was later asked under examination. "To surrender up a copy of a thing I had in my custody." Faden gave him immediately five guineas "security" money, to be sure they were returned, then "by order" gave him for subsistence over some weeks another six pounds, sixteen shillings, and sixpence. Carrington, the chief spy, assured him he would have weekly pay equal to what Wilkes had given him so long as he remained in the service of the government. Carrington later testified in the House of Commons about these payments. Was it customary to pay the government's witnesses? Yes, "indulgence was shown according to the circumstance as they had behaved." But the government was slow in fulfilling its promises, and some of the money was actually paid by Faden, who had considerable difficulty getting it back from the the ministry.[60]

Wilkes now could have no doubt that the government "had no scruples about a robbery of the subject in any way, either by force, under a general warrant; or by fraud in corrupting a domestic." When the story of the government's use of the general warrant and of the buying of Curry arrived in Paris, Wilkes later wrote, "There was not an Englishman who did not blush for the honor of his country except at the hotel de Brancas [where the English ambassador lodged]. Everyone there at that time who was past sixteen was likewise past blushing."[61] Jack Wilkes did have a way with words.

7

Trials and a Trial of Honor

Sandwich, now the newly appointed secretary of state for the north, called on Wilkes the day after he returned and explicitly offered what Yorke had implied: the ministry would drop all legal action against him if Wilkes would drop his actions against the ministers and messengers. Wilkes said no. Two days after Wilkes returned to London, George Onslow contacted him; Wilkes told him about Sandwich's attempt to bribe him and asked Onslow to spread a word to the opposition: "He desires to be understood as being devoted to the service of the opposition, in any plan or writing that may be thought right."[1]

In the ministry, George Grenville did his job and reported Wilkes's refusal to King George and then reminded his majesty of what Lord Chief Justice Mansfield had told him: the courts of law would never do justice to the king's complaints against Wilkes. Somebody, perhaps Yorke, then came up with a new idea, a never-before-tried way for the king to have his justice: his majesty should ask the House of Commons to try "that devil Wilkes" and, what would certainly follow, punish him.

George Onslow, who had spoken with Wilkes just two days after he had arrived from France, was impressed that Wilkes "had knowledge of everything going on better than some people on the spot." True enough, but neither Wilkes nor most people on the spot knew about a secret, illegal conspiracy to vilify Wilkes's name and condemn him in the House of Lords, a conspiracy now being directed by Lord Sandwich, who had been thoroughly briefed by Philip Carteret Webb.[2]

Sandwich and Grenville were meeting with the king's friends to plan simultaneous attacks in both houses of Parliament. A letter from the king to the House of Commons would request that Wilkes be tried for libeling his majesty in *North Briton* No. 45. In the House of Lords, Warburton, now the bishop of Gloucester, would accuse Wilkes of libeling him in An Essay on Woman. Both moves would be kept secret. Wilkes did not learn of the plan to attack him in the House of Commons until days before Parliament opened. He seems to have had no advance knowledge of what was planned for the House of Lords. There was a scurry of activity to gather evidence, for most of which we have no record. But there is a letter from Sandwich to Le Despenser dated 1 November asking Le Despenser to find someone in Bucks who could identify Wilkes's handwriting, or someone who would be willing to testify they had heard Wilkes say he was the author of the *North Briton*.[3]

Webb continued to search secretly for evidence of Wilkes's involvement with the Essay on Woman. In early October, Faden quieted Curry's anxieties about Webb's threat to arrest him for theft and brought him back to Webb's house. Curry, now quite obedient, handed over his revises, that is, the second proofs (printed in red) of all the pages of the Essay on Woman that had been printed. The government also had pages 4–7 in the proof that Jennings's wife had wrapped the butter in, a critical piece of evidence because the corrections written in the margins were in Wilkes's hand. But they had no book because Wilkes had never completed the printing of a book, as the page numbers of the red proofs showed: there was, as Sergeant Glynn put it, a "chasm" between p. 9, ending on line 94 of the "Essay," and p. 119, where Wilkes's "Universal Prayer" began. And they did not have the actual finished pages Wilkes had printed; they had only proofs. The many notes of the ministers and printers, the legal records of the House of Lords, and the judgments of the Court of the King's Bench never use the word *book* and never indicate that these papers were intended to be unified in one work. In a tacit admission on the part of the attorney general that they had not reached a publishable state and were therefore unpublished, that they had been made merely in preparation for publication, the legal documents speak only of "printed papers," "the printed Essay on Woman," "the printed Universal Prayer," and "the printed Veni Creator paraphrased, or the Maids Prayer." The attorney general had no interest in the printed "Dying Christian to His Prick."[4]

Meanwhile, Wilkes, oblivious to the conspiracy, was turning out propaganda for his cause. He wrote squibs, verses, paragraphs, and letters, took them, or most of them, to his friend Bonnell Thornton, who got them inserted in the *Public Advertiser* or the *St. James's Chronicle*, papers in which Thornton had an interest. In September, Wilkes, Thornton, and Churchill went to Aylesbury. From there they made trips to Oxford to gather material for a satire on the Encaenia, a ceremony honoring founders of the university. At least once they stopped at Stowe to see Temple. Two weeks later Wilkes was writing to Temple from London, once again adopting the persona of the philosopher: "As to politics, I have only to say that I have not printed a single line on the subject. I have lived here almost alone, and have even seen very few males." Then he added, "and but two females."[5] It is certain he was not leading a monastic life, as one sees from a surviving report by the government spies, dated 8 November 1763:

> Mr. Wilkes went out the morning at half an hour after eight o'clock, in a hackney coach, to Mr. Beckford's, the present Lord Mayor, in Soho Square, and stayed three quarters of an hour; from thence he went to Mr. Onslow's, in Curzon Street, May Fair, and stayed an hour and a half. Mr. Wilkes brought Mr. Onslow in a hackney coach to Spring Gardens, where Mr. Onslow got out, and said he had some business there but would call on Mr. Wilkes presently; from thence he went home; soon after Mr. Cotes came. At half after two o'clock Mr. Wilkes, Mr. Onslow, and Mr. Cotes came out together, and parted at the top of George Street. Mr. Wilkes then went to Mr. Thornton's, in Chapel Street, but did not stay; from thence went home. A little before seven o'clock he went out in his chair to my Lord Temple's, and left him there at nine o'clock.[6]

There were so many spies about that Wilkes had to take unusual measures to see that he was not overheard. The equivalent of today's electronic surveillance was the listening servant, and gentlemen were seldom out of earshot of servants. On Sunday, 6 November, said a spy report, "Mr. Wilkes got out of the coach the other side of Westminster Bridge, and about the center of the bridge he met Mr. Beardmore, the attorney, and talked with him a quarter of an hour."

In the midst of this scurry of activity, Churchill got into trouble. Never one to keep his sexual impulses under control, he ran off with a fifteen-year-old girl and took her to Wilkes's house in Aylesbury. Her name was Elizabeth Carr. "I own a dread of what is likely to happen," Wilkes wrote to him on 3 November; "I fear much a warrant signed by the pale Mansfield, beginning 'The King against Charles Churchill, Clerk,' then the picture of the said Charles handing into court his Betsy, who will be ordered back to an obliged Papa, locked up, &c., and this you can't prevent . . . you are universally condemned for having made a worthy family unhappy." His friends tolerate the affair, Wilkes continued, but were angry at the manner of it. More important, Churchill's life was in danger. "The father, brother, and a servant went with pistols charged to Kensington Gardens in consequence of an anonymous letter, to have assassinated you." Get out of Aylesbury, Wilkes told him, and stop sending letters addressed in your own hand or the spies will track you down. Churchill replied, "Assassination — a pretty word, fit for boys to use, and men to laugh at. . . . My life I hold for purposes of pleasure; those forbid, it is not worth my care. Mansfield I laugh at and despise . . . to deserve the name of *friend*, which you honor me with, I will rather seek danger than shun it." But he did leave Prebendal House and brought the girl to his lodging in Vauxhall.[7]

The spies reported on 9 November that "the printers are very busy at work in the two-pair-of-stairs room." Wilkes was getting ready to start up the *North Briton* again, and the little press in Great George Street was printing out No. 46. "He is in good spirits," said Onslow, "and intends to begin his 'weekly entertainments' to us . . . about a fortnight before Parliament meets." No. 46 appeared on 12 November.[8] It contained a devastating attack on the ministry, including a vile obituary on Lord Egremont: "His pride and insolence . . . made him as universally odious in private, as he soon became in public life. . . . An ignorance scarcely to be credited, and a mulishness which could never be conquered, rendered him the contempt of all who were so unhappy as to be under a necessity of attending upon him. But he has paid the debt to nature, and is gathered to the dull of ancient days."

Wilkes was not so hard on Lord Halifax but brushed him aside as a nobleman constrained to go along with the ministry out of pecuniary needs. Grenville, he said, was given his position because he was "the dullest and most laborious pack-ass of the state." Sandwich, he flagellated: "He passed his youth in so abandoned and profligate a manner, that when he arrived at the middle age of life, he did not, in the opinion of the world, remain in possession of the smallest degree of virtue or honor. His conduct, with respect to women, was not only loose and barefaced, but perfidious, mean, and tricking. . . . With respect to men, he had early lost every sentiment of honor, and was grown exceedingly necessitous from the variety of his vices, as well as rapacious from the lust of gratifying them."

The paper only spurred on the ministers in their search for the right person to present the charges against Wilkes in the House of Commons. Grenville first approached Lord Strange. Strange was not a nobleman at all but was allowed the honorary title because he was the son of a nobleman. He declined to undertake such an unsavory task. Grenville turned to young Lord North, another member of Parliament with that honorary title. North was also reluctant. The king, urged Grenville, would be obliged. North finally agreed.[9]

Lord George North was short and stout and unattractive. Everyone remarked how much he looked like the king, and it was whispered about that they were half-brothers. North's father, Earl Guilford, had been lord of the bedchamber to Frederick, Prince of Wales, the father of George III. (Frederick never came to the throne, having died before his father.) Frederick was often in the company of Lady Guilford and became godfather to her son. A few years later this Prince of Wales joked to the North family that his son, George, and Guilford's son, Frederick, were so much alike they must have had the same father. Ha Ha. The polemicist called Junius wrote of Lord North, "His tongue is a little too big for his mouth, and his eyes a great deal too big for their sockets. Every part of his person sets natural proportion at defiance. At this present writing, his head is supposed to be much too heavy for his shoulders."[10] For all that, Lord North was a highly intelligent man, well educated (much better educated than the king), and a formidable opponent, as John Wilkes and the American colonies were to discover.

Having settled the leadership in the House of Commons, the ministers turned to the House of Lords. Sandwich, they agreed, should make the case against Wilkes. Though King George privately despised Sandwich, who had been brought into the ministry and cabinet by the powerful Duke of Bedford,[11] the earl's cool temper and total lack of conscience made him the obvious choice to prosecute Wilkes.

The conspiring printers held secret meetings on Friday, the fourth of November, and the following Tuesday to get to know one another and to be introduced to their perverse, nearly blind leader, Philip Carteret Webb. The Rev. Mr. John Kidgell tried to stir up excitement with promises of more dirty evidence.[12] Webb urged them to "concert" their accounts so they would be consistent if they were called before the House of Lords.

Sandwich spoke privately to Earl Henley, who as lord chancellor presided in the House of Lords. Would his lordship allow the matter of the *Essay on Woman* to come before the house as a case of blasphemy? No, he would not, but he would agree to hear Bishop Warburton if he complained that his parliamentary privilege was violated, and then the house could take it where it would. On 5 November, Lord Sandwich showed the *Essay* and title page to Warburton, who was horrified. A "heap of diabolic lewdness and blasphemy," said his grace the bishop. To Sandwich he wrote the next day, "I thank God I can heartily forgive him, but though I forgive Mr. Wilkes, it is no reason the public should, who is the appointed avenger of God's violated Majesty, and of the King's." Sandwich soon was reporting that his grace "comes heartily into the affair, says he will not only authorize me to complain in his name of this outrage, but will take any part in it himself that shall be judged proper by the King's Administration, and he seems much pleased with the scheme in general."[13]

On the evening of Thursday, 10 November, with the opening of Parliament only five days off, Sandwich held a meeting of his majesty's cabinet counsel and showed them for the first time the "printed papers." George Grenville had decided that a few copies of what he called the "briefs" should be printed "to keep it out of the hands of copyists" (as though that made sense), actually to give it to the leaders of the king's friends in the House of Lords. On Saturday, Sandwich ordered Webb to supply briefs to the lord chancellor, himself, Lord Halifax, and four other nobles, Lords Bristol, Marchmont, Egmont, and Hillsborough.[14]

At that point Webb made the kind of mistake that self-righteous conspirators are prone to make. He took a suggestion of Kidgell to forge a new line in the red proofs. It would appear as the last line in the imitation of the hymn "Veni Creator Spiritus," which Wilkes called "The Veni Creator or The Maid's Prayer." In Wilkes's poem, the virgin prays, not for the inspiration of the Holy Spirit, but for the insinuation of the supreme penis. The concluding stanza as Wilkes left it echoes the wording of the hymn:

> Immortal Honour, endless Fame,
> Almighty Pego! to thy Name;
> And equal Adoration be
> Paid to the neighb'ring Pair with Thee.

One might think this was blasphemous enough to satisfy any prosecutor, but no, Webb listened to Kidgell, who despite his wayward ways was in holy orders and knew his hymns. So Webb directed Faden and his foreman Lionel Hassall to impose a new line at the end of the paper, turning the final couplet into a triad in the manner common in eighteenth-century verse:

> Immortal Honour, endless Fame,
> Almighty Pego! to thy Name;
> And equal Adoration be
> Paid to the neighb'ring Pair with Thee.
> Thrice blessed Glorious Trinity!

The "briefs" were then printed off in Faden's shop, producing what has been called the "government edition" of the *Essay on Woman*.[15]

Wednesday, 9 November, the spies reported, "Mr. Wilkes went out this day in his chair at half an hour after twelve, to Sir John Cust's Speaker of the House of Commons, stayed three quarters of an hour; from thence he went to Mr. Thornton's, stayed near an hour; from thence home." He told Cust that he intended to complain of a violation of his parliamentary privilege in his arrest and reminded him that by the rules of the House, a point of privilege took precedence over any other business. Cust replied that in his interpretation of the rules, a letter from the king should take precedence over a point of privilege.[16] Now Wilkes understood how threatened he was. The king would ask the house to condemn him for *North Briton* No. 45, and Cust would violate the rules of the House in setting that before a point of privilege. It promised to be a hard fight.

The next day Wilkes received a distressing letter from Polly. She had left Mme Carpentier's and was staying in the hôtel de la Force, where she had been taken by Pierre Goy after a quarrel with her teacher. Wilkes had failed in a payment to his banker, Foley, and Foley would not advance what was owed to Mme Carpentier. She had seized Polly's clothes and jewelry to cover her costs, not without saying nasty things about her father. So "vastly agitated" was this plucky thirteen-year-old girl, she refused to stay under Mme Carpentier's roof and sent for M. Goy. Goy notified the Baron and Madam d'Holbach, who joined him in looking after Polly. But, oh, she was "impatient to hear from my dearest Papa."[17] So long as Polly was safe, Wilkes decided he would not rush to Paris, not when three days hence he would be complained of by the king in the House of Commons.

The next morning, as the spies reported, Wilkes went to services at St. Margaret's, and from there to the French ambassador's. Polly would have some powerful friends. Wilkes was soon reconciled to Foley, the bill to Mme Carpentier was paid, the clothes and jewelry were reclaimed — but Polly refused to return to madame's house.

The day before Parliament was to open, Sandwich discovered there were not enough briefs, "which is a great distress."[18] There was panic. Webb hastened to Faden, who called the printers, and all day and night Monday they worked at the press to print two more copies. These were badly printed, unproofed, replete with errors, but they would serve in a pinch. Only three eighteenth-century copies of the *Essay* survive, all pirated from this corrupt second government edition. How ironic that the ministry that said it was determined to suppress this blasphemous work and to keep it out of the hands of copyists should have provided the channel through which it was passed to the twenty-first century.[19]

There had been meetings of the printers and conspirators on Sunday and Monday at the Swan at Knightsbridge "to concert matters." On the morning of Tuesday, 15 November, the day Parliament was to open, Webb, Kidgell, Faden, and all of the printers were brought by carriage to the Horn Tavern in Westminster to wait to be called as witnesses.[20]

The king held no levée that day. After his breakfast, he read the *North Briton* No. 46 and a note from Grenville. At 11:12 he wrote to Grenville, "Your account of the meeting last night gives me well-grounded hopes that everything in Parliament will go well; the continuation of Wilkes's impudence is amazing, when his ruin is so near."[21] He then stepped into his splendid gold coach, was taken to the House of Lords, with due ceremony read the address to the two assembled houses, and returned to St. James's palace.

The speech over, the members of the House of Commons left the hall and walked next door to St. Steven's chapel to begin their work. The minutes of the previous meeting were read; then the speaker opened proceedings, at which point Wilkes leapt to his feet to make his complaint of a breach of privilege, but Grenville was also on his feet crying that he had a letter for the House from the king. Cust ruled both out of order, asserting that no business could be conducted until a bill was before the House. Pitt, so badly crippled by gout that he had to be carried in, his legs hugely wrapped in flannel, managed to make a motion to the effect that the speaker was logic-chopping and that preference should be given to Wilkes on the grounds of ancient house rules.[22] A vote was taken, and Pitt's motion was defeated. An ancient bill on outlaw-ries that had nothing to do with the business at hand was read, and a bill to amend it was proposed. The speaker, now satisfied that everything was legal, allowed a vote on a motion to recognize Grenville and not Wilkes. Carried.

Grenville proceeded to read the king's extraordinary letter. Mr. Wilkes had been apprehended for a "most seditious and dangerous libel," wrote the king, but he had been released on privilege; subsequently, Mr. Wilkes had failed to appear at the Court of the King's Bench to answer an information against him by the attorney general. Consequently, his majesty, not willing to suffer a miscarriage of justice, has directed that the libel, *North Briton* No. 45, and the attorney general's information be laid before the House of Commons. In ef-fect, the king's letter asked the House of Commons to act as an appeals court. The House of Lords had been for centuries the highest appeals court of the land, but the House of Commons had never so acted. The complacency with which the House received this extraordinary commission bespeaks both the moral power of the throne and the spinelessness of the majority members who had sold their loyalty. They agreed to hear the case.[23]

Lord North now took over as a sort of government prosecutor. He called for the examinations of John Kearsley and Richard Balfe to be read, purportedly as evidence that Wilkes was the author of *North Briton* No. 45. Kearsley had never claimed absolute knowledge of this fact; Balfe had said it was so, but not while he was under oath. Lord North cleverly guided the argument away from this weak evidence before it was challenged and steered it toward the question of whether or not No. 45 was a libel of the crown and Parliament. A long debate followed. Finally, as George Dempster wrote to James Boswell, "Three hundred of the members voted it all the hard names which Lord North, Norborne Berkeley, Chace Price, or Bamber Gascoyne could bestow upon it," false, scandalous, and seditious, libelous, insolent, "tending to alienate the affections of the people . . . and to excite them to traitorous insurrections." Wilkes rose and, objecting to the word "false," challenged Lord North to find anything false in the essay. North sputtered and choked but did not answer. Pitt moved to delete the words "to excite them to traitorous insurrections," which started a long debate that ended in a "division" — a method of counting votes when a voice vote was questioned: the members voting against the motion left the floor and gathered in the lobby, where they were counted; those in favor of the motion kept their seats and were counted there. The motion was defeated, 273 to 111. The motion condemning Wilkes for libeling the king and Parliament was then read: "That the Paper entitled 'The North Briton, No. 45' is a false, scandalous, and seditious libel, containing expressions of the most unexampled insolence and contumacy towards His Majesty, the grossest aspersions upon both house of Parliament, and most audacious defiance of the authority of the whole legislature, and most manifestly tending to alienate the affections of his people from his majesty, to withdraw from their obedience to the laws of the realm, and to excite them to traitorous insurrections against his majesty's government." Wilkes and Pitt, seeing that further opposition was hopeless, said nothing, and the motion was carried by voice. Another motion was now made and carried without debate, an order to the common hangman to publicly burn *North Briton* No. 45. But the business of the day was not over, for Wilkes's complaint of a breach of privilege was still to be heard.[24]

The House of Lords meanwhile was meeting in the ancient hall next door. The lord high chancellor in black robes and long white wig, sitting upon the traditional sack of wool, called the lords and bishops to order and recognized the bishop of Gloucester upon a point of privilege. Bishop Warburton lifted his tall bony self and turned to the House: his privilege had been violated and his person libeled in an obscene poem called an "Essay on Woman." Lord Sandwich rose to make the case, which he did by reading the poem aloud:

> Awake, my Fanny, leave all meaner things,
> This morn shall prove what raptures swiving* brings.
> Let us (since life can little more supply
> Than just a few good Fucks and then we die)
> Expatiate free o'er that lov'd scene of Man;
> A mighty Maze! for mighty Pricks to scan.
>   [*Anglo-Saxon for *fucking*]

There was pandemonium. Some roared with laughter; some sat in shock. Lord Lyttelton, a slight man, nearly fainted, and "groaning in spirit . . . begged they might hear no more," but there were cries of "Go on." Lord Sandwich explained that these papers were "so infamous, so full of filthy language as well as the most horrid blasphemies that he was ashamed to read the whole to their lordships." He would read only those portions that reviled the bishop of Gloucester and scorned and ridiculed religion:

> Thy lust the virgin dooms to bleed to-day;
> Had she thy reason, would she laugh and play?
> Pleas'd to the last, she likes the luscious food,
> And grasps the prick just rais'd to shed her blood.
> Oh! blindness to the future, kindly given,
> That each m'enjoy what fucks are mark'd by Heav'n.

The bench of bishops sat stonyfaced, but the nobles were buzzing among themselves. The charge of obscenity was being made by Lord Sandwich, the most notorious foulmouthed rake of the day! The Fanny to whom the "Essay" was addressed was Frances Rudman, a famous courtesan who had once been Sandwich's mistress! The irony was not lost on Lord le Despenser, who commented to the nobleman next to him, "Never before heard the devil preach a sermon against sin."[25]

Lord Temple, who had known nothing of the Essay on Woman, was so taken aback that he had to leave the hall in order to collect himself. The title page with its image of an erect penis next to a ten-inch scale was passed around, displaying the name of Warburton as author of the footnotes, or some of them, for he shared the honor with two other commentators, Rogerus Cunaeus (meaning something like "cunt fucker") and Vigerus Mutoniatus ("big strong penis"). Bishop Warburton rose and solemnly declared he had written not a single one of those notes. In response to the laughter, he began to rage. "Foaming with the violence of a Saint Dominic," said Horace Walpole, he managed to spit out that "the blackest fiends in hell would not keep company with Wilkes, and then begged Satan's pardon for comparing them together." The ridiculousness of the bishop's behavior, Walpole went on, was heightened by the widespread rumor that the principal author of the verses themselves was not Wilkes, but his friend the late Thomas Potter, and that Potter had been the lover of Bishop Warburton's wife.[26]

Lord Temple, who had returned to the floor, demanded to know how the ministry had obtained such papers? if they had been gotten by violence or illegal means? But Lord Mansfield assured the House that a paper of this wicked nature could and ought to be censored no matter how the government had obtained it. With hardly any debate, it was resolved that "An Essay on Woman with Notes . . . and another printed paper entitled The Veni Creator paraphrased" was "a manifold breach" of the bishop's privilege and "a most scandalous, obscene, and impious libel, a gross profanation of many parts of the Holy Scriptures, and a most wicked and blasphemous attempt to ridicule and vilify the person of our most blessed Savior."

Sandwich's next task was to prove Wilkes to be the author, and for that purpose he called a dozen witnesses. Lovel Stanhope and the messengers testified that the letters they were presenting to the House were taken from Kearsley's shop. Samuel Jennings, the printer, testified about finding the proofs on the floor. Michael Curry testified at length about the manuscript and printing of the parodies. As Grenville reported to the king, "Lord Sandwich went through the charge and the examination of witnesses with great spirit and ability."[27]

Though no evidence had been presented that would have held up in a court of law, the House was on the verge of declaring Wilkes the author when Lord Mansfield, of all people, pointed out that the criminal should be heard in his defense before being found guilty, so they were obliged to call in Mr. Wilkes. The session was adjourned.[28]

"The plot so hopefully laid to blow up Wilkes," said Walpole, "was so gross and scandalous, so revengeful, and so totally unconnected with the political conduct of Wilkes, and the instruments so despicable, odious, or in whom any pretensions to decency, sanctimony, or faith were so preposterous that, losing all sight of the scandal contained in the poem, the whole world almost united in crying out against the informers." That evening, when Lord Sandwich left the hall, he was booed and hissed by the crowd. The next day he was drummed out of the Beef Steaks, of which he had been president, and that evening, when he attended a production of John Gay's highly popular *Beggars' Opera* at Covent Garden Theatre, when Macheath, the highwayman, said the line, "That Jemmy Twitcher should peach me, I own surprises me," the audience "burst out in an applause of application." For the rest of his days, Lord Sandwich would be called Jemmy Twitcher.[29]

In the House of Commons, as the case against Wilkes continued to unfold, someone whispered the news about the House of Lords in Wilkes's ear, but he kept cool. At one point Samuel Martin, the erstwhile secretary to the treasury, whom Wilkes had described in the *North Briton* of 5 March as "the most treacherous, base, selfish, mean, abject, low-lived and dirty fellow that ever *wriggled* himself into a secretaryship," rose and cried in a passion, "A man capable of writing in that manner without putting his name to it and thereby stabbing another in the dark, is a cowardly rascal, a villain, and a scoundrel." Such words were not to be tolerated by an English gentleman of honor; the spectators in the gallery expected Wilkes to challenge the man but, seeing him sitting unperturbed, concluded he was afraid. They did not understand that the House always intervened to settle personal quarrels that arose during the session. Wilkes kept still because he did not intend the House to intervene.[30]

Not until one o'clock in the morning was Wilkes allowed to make his complaint about the violation of privilege. He quickly reviewed the events of his arrest in April, then startled everyone by offering that, if the House would agree that his arrest has been a violation of his privilege, he would waive that right of privilege and submit himself to a trial by jury. His enemies, reflecting that it probably would be impossible to convene a jury of London citizens who would convict John Wilkes, decided they would not let the suggestion come to a vote. Then they decided they had had enough for one day: their consideration of Wilkes's complaint would have to wait until the next day. The meeting was adjourned at two in the morning.[31]

Wilkes went home, sat down, wrote a message, and sent a servant hurrying through the night to rap at Samuel Martin's door. "You complained yesterday before five hundred gentlemen that you had been *stabbed in the dark* . . . but I have reason to believe you was not so much *in the dark*, as you affected." He was alluding to the custom of the House to interfere in quarrels: "Was the complaint made before so many gentlemen on purpose that they might interpose? To cut off every pretense of your ignorance as to the author, I whisper in your ear, that every passage of the North Briton in which you have been named, or even alluded to, was written by your humble servant, John Wilkes." Furious at having been accused obliquely of cowardice, Martin scribbled a reply and then took the time to write it again neatly: "I must take the liberty to repeat, that you are a malignant and infamous scoundrel, and that I desire to give you an opportunity of showing me whether the epithet of *cowardly* was rightly applied or not." He would walk to the circle in Hyde Park, where he would wait for Mr. Wilkes. Each should bring a brace of pistols.[32] There was light in the east when he went to bed.

At ten o'clock Martin was up and walking to Wilkes's house. Being told that Wilkes was abroad, he delivered the letter to a servant and proceeded to Hyde Park and the circle. The circle or ring was a carriage path around which ladies and gentlemen would take the air, walking or riding or being driven in their carriages, a place to see and be seen by "the world." Wilkes arrived at one o'clock, apologizing for being late: he had been in conference with his lawyer.

We know details about the duel between Martin and Wilkes and what they said to each other because Martin, worried about how it would be seen, went home afterward and wrote a careful account of the affair now at the British Library.[33]

The two men left the circle searching for a low place where they would not be seen. As they walked, Wilkes pointed out that they had come without seconds and without any agreed-upon rules. Martin suggested that they stand back to back, take half a dozen paces, turn, and fire. Are we to fire immediately? asked Wilkes. "Together, if we can," answered Martin, "or in what other manner each of us shall think fit." Suppose one of us is wounded and begs for his life? "Let that be left to chance," answered Martin, "and the occasion when it happens." A couple came toward them, and Wilkes took Martin's arm as they walked, pretending to be in close conversation. Wilkes thought they should exchange one of their two pistols, but Martin would not agree. They came to a rail fence and stepped under the rails. Probably they were on the far side of Constitution Hill, which at that time rose on the west side of the park. Being out of sight, they stopped. Wilkes again declared that pistols should be exchanged, and this time Martin agreed. Wilkes drew his two pistols from the inside pockets of his coat, threw them on the grass and invited Martin to take his pick, which Martin did. Then Martin laid down one pistol. No, no, said Wilkes, you must put down both; so Martin threw down the second. Wilkes chose that one. Perhaps he had been tricked. They placed themselves back to back, a pistol in each hand, and at a signal stepped off six paces. Martin whirled about ready to fire, but Wilkes was stooping over examining one of the pistols. He held up one hand: "Stay a little," he said, "I am not ready." Martin waited. Wilkes then "presented" his pistol at Martin, and Martin said, "Now, Sir." They fired, but both missed. Each threw down the spent pistol and took the other in his right hand; as they did so Wilkes stepped forward, Martin backward so as to keep the distance between them. Seeing that Wilkes presented his second pistol, Martin fired; as he did so, Wilkes pulled the trigger, but the pistol did not fire. It was the one belonging to Martin. Martin ran up to him: "Did it fire?" "No, damn it, and I am wounded." He was still standing when a spot of blood began to show on the front of his clothes. Wilkes unbuttoned his surtout, his coat, his waistcoat, and his shirt, exposing a wound on his abdomen. Martin said, "I have killed you, I am afraid," but Wilkes, grimacing from the pain, said not another word. He buttoned up, turned, stepped to the rail fence, stooped under it, and staggered toward the top of the hill. Martin gathered the four pistols, put them into the long pockets in the lining of his coat, and followed. At the top of the rising ground Wilkes was met by a person Martin did not know who began helping Wilkes to walk. It was his servant Matthew Brown, whom Wilkes had told to follow at a distance. Martin caught up and asked if he could help, but Wilkes replied, "No, no, you have behaved as a man of honor. Take care of yourself and I will say nothing of you." Martin continued to follow at a distance, as the two made their way out of the Park. At Pall Mall, Brown hailed two chairmen, who carried his master the rest of the way home.[34]

From that point Martin's memorandum continues in ink of another color. "The second pistol which Mr Wilkes presented against Mr Martin, and which snapped in Mr Wilkes's hand, was the property of Mr Martin." He had loaded and primed both his pistols before leaving his house, yet when he got home after the duel, he discovered there was no powder in the pan. "He thinks that when he saw Mr Wilkes stooping down, he was employed in opening the pan of Mr Martin's pistol to see whether it was primed, and supposes that by some accident Mr Wilkes did then spill the powder." The next day Martin sent a government scribe, one Bradshaw, to Wilkes's house to return Wilkes's pistols and to assess Wilkes's danger. Bradshaw spoke to Wilkes's servants, returned, made his report, and Martin hastily left for France, not, as he later said, to avoid taking part in the House debates on Wilkes, but to avoid arrest should Wilkes die.

That morning George Grenville was reporting to the king about what had happened in Parliament when "somebody scratched at the closet door." Lord Halifax and Lord Sandwich came in and told his highness about the duel. At St. Stephen's Chapel, Walpole arrived to find "all the members standing on the floor in great hubbub, questioning, hearing, and eagerly discussing." Because the speaker was ill that day, the session was suspended, and Wilkes's friends hurried to Great George Street and crowded into the house. Wilkes was being looked at by his old friend Dr. Richard Brocklesby, who protested that such attention was no good for his patient. But Wilkes, a gregarious man, was much cheered by the visitors. His mother and brother and sister all came to see him that day or the next.[35]

Walpole wrote to his friend George Montagu, "Your cousin Sandwich . . . has outwitched himself. He has impeached Wilkes for a blasphemous poem, and has been expelled for blasphemy himself by the beefstake-club at Covent Garden. Wilkes has been shot by Martin, and instead of being burned at an *auto dafé*, as the Bishop of Gloucester intended, is reverenced as a saint by the mob, and if he dies, I suppose people will squint themselves into convulsions at his tomb, in honor of his memory. Now is not this better than feedings one's birds and one's bantams, poring one's eyes out over old histories, not half so extraordinary as the present?"[36] To another friend, Sir Horace Mann, Walpole wrote, "The Bishop of Gloucester has been measuring out ground in Smith-field for his [Wilkes's] execution; and in his speech begged the devil's pardon for comparing him to Wilkes. . . . We are poor pigmy short-lived animals, but we are comical."[37]

Wilkes did not die, saved by the buttons on his clothes. The ball striking first a coat button and then a waistcoat button, by these was deflected downward, under the skin but not breaking the peritoneum. It came to rest in Wilkes's groin.[38] The next day it was extracted from behind by a surgeon named Graves, Dr. Brocklesby in attendance. Wilkes was said to have born the pain stoically, for of course there were no anesthetics or painkillers in those days. And no antibiotics: so the wound got infected, and when it failed to drain well, the infection grew serious. Two weeks after the duel, on 30 November, the *Public Advertiser* carried a story about the surgeon's removing a bit of Wilkes's coat from the wound. Wilkes would suffer considerable discomfort and handicap in his movements for two months or more, but he had survived the surgery.

The day after the ball was removed, Wilkes wrote to Polly, his hand steady as ever: "I thought it would give you most satisfaction to have a line from my own hand relating to the duel between Mr. Martin and me. . . . The pains I have suffered are beyond what I can describe, but both physician and surgeon declare me out of all danger." He will surely be with her before Christmas. "It was an affair of honor, and my antagonist behaved very well. We are both perfectly satisfied with each other on this occasion."[39]

Wilkes improved, attended by his faithful Matthew Brown and other servants. His friends visited in droves and found him "all spirits and riot." A story went around that the morning after the surgery he sat up in his bed and corrected the press for the next *North Briton.* The story was wrong, for Wilkes was done with work on No. 46 of the *North Briton,* though he might have been reading proof on his new octavo edition. "His bon mots are all over the town," reported Walpole, "but too gross, I think, to repeat."[40] Almost every day the newspapers carried a statement about his health. Mr. Wilkes is recovering. He has relapsed. The wound heals.

The House of Commons sent a summons; Dr. Brocklesby and Mr. Graves answered with letters saying Wilkes was too ill to attend. The House would not honor their report but sent its own physician and surgeon to Wilkes's house; when they arrived, each was handed a note from Wilkes expressing with ironic politeness his pleasure at the concern of the House of Commons for his health, declining to see them, and then, as though they were servants, inviting them to have a bit of mutton in the kitchen before they left.[41]

Next, a bizarre and silly pamphlet game broke out, which brought a festival air to all the angry proceedings in Parliament. Since the Essay on Woman was exposed in the House of Lords, the Rev. Mr. Kidgell was free to publish his exposé, which he proudly did: *A Genuine and Succinct Narrative of a Scandalous, Obscene, and Exceedingly Profane Libel, Entitled, An Essay on Woman,* on the title page of which appeared all of the author's titles, including his chaplaincy to the Earl of March. He told about how he had received a proof and taken it to the earl, etc., etc. Then he described the engraved title page, "to which is affixed the name of a personage . . . eminent for learning and character" but larded with remarks in which "every degree of decency is renounced . . . shameful and obscene, without any manner of concealment or reserve." And so the Rev. Mr. Kidgell continued, condemning the contents with adjectives but never quoting a word. "Many of the most serious and interesting passages of the gospel are dishonored to serve the low lascivious purpose of an impure DOUBLE ENTENDRE which I am persuaded the reader will excuse me if I do not defile my pen with." Kidgell became the laughingstock of the town. First there appeared the anonymous *Full and Candid Answer to a Pamphlet called A Genuine and Succinct Narrative of a Scandalous, Obscene, and Exceedingly Profane Libel, entitled An Essay on Woman*, By a Friend of Truth. Then there was *A Letter to J. Kidgell, Containing a Full Answer to His Narrative*, anonymous but actually by Almon; *An Expostulatory Letter to the Reverend Mr. Kidgell . . .* , By a Layman; and finally, *The Priest in Rhyme: "A Doggrell Versification of Kidgell's Narrative Relative to the Essay on Woman*," by a member of Parliament. Thomas Farmer, the man who had recognized the significance of Samuel Jennings's butter-smeared proof, published *The Plain Truth: Being a Genuine Narrative of the Methods made use of to Procure a Copy of the Essay on Woman*, but he did not come into much teasing, for his book was largely defensive, and he had the sense to quote a few lines. By now, everyone in England knew about the Essay on Woman, but no one had actually seen or heard it except the ministers and printers and members of the House of Lords.

Then Wilkes received a blow more hurtful than that delivered by the pistol, for it shattered the hope he had carried throughout his political and journalistic career. On 23 November, the House of Commons was debating a resolution that "privilege of Parliament does not extend to the case of writing and publishing seditious libels" when Pitt, leaning on his canes, his legs in bandages, speaking in eloquent opposition to the motion, suddenly released a blast against Wilkes. He opposed the motion upon principle, he said, but the *North Briton* was "illiberal, unmanly, and detestable," and the author "did not deserve to be ranked among the human species — he was the blasphemer of his God, and libeller of his King. He had no connection with him."[42] It seems likely that someone had shown him the Essay on Woman, and he had decided Wilkes had become a liability. Thus was Wilkes repaid for having given William Pitt his unbroken loyalty for six years at the risk of his fortune and even his life.

On 25 November, the House of Lords notified the House of Commons that it agreed in the decision that *North Briton* No. 45 was a libel and should be burned by the common hangman. On 29 November the House of Lords moved to agree with the House of Commons that privilege does not extend to the writing of libels, Lords Temple, Grafton, Portland, and fourteen other noblemen entering into the record a lengthy and learned "dissentient."[43]

Both houses were growing impatient to settle the question about whether Wilkes was or was not the author of No. 45 and the Essay on Woman. Wilkes, warned that they might do so without hearing him, sent the House of Commons a petition, a serious one, nothing playful about it except his calling himself both defendant and plaintiff.

> To the Honourable the Commons of Great Britain in Parliament assembled:
> The Humble Petition of John Wilkes Esqr.
>   Showeth
>   That your Petitioner burns with infinite Anxiety Concern, and Surprise that the House is going to proceed upon a business in the event of which he is deeply interested as the consideration of it arises immediately in consequence of complaints now before you wherein he is both Defendant and Plaintiff and this at a time when he lies dangerously wounded and utterly incapable of attending his Duty in Parliament.
>   That your Petitioner has matter of the highest moment upon these subjects to lay before you to which he desires and implores he may be heard in his Place.
>   That it appears to your Petitioner to be the very Essence of Justice that were he but remotely concerned in your Decision upon his case it should not be agitated and decided upon in his Absence.[44]

The House of Lords, meanwhile, had lost patience and forwarded the "printed papers" to Webb, recommending that the king's attorney general commence a prosecution. Only a few days before, Fletcher Norton had replaced Charles Yorke as attorney general. A large man nicknamed "Peter Bullcalf," Norton owed his rise to Lord Bute. He had not Yorke's tendency to waffle on decisions affecting Wilkes. The House of Lords, having listened to their judiciary committee, made up of the lawyers and judges among them, had decided upon ancient precedent that handing a printer a paper with directions to print it constituted publication. On 26 November, Norton filed at the Court of the King's Bench an information (accusation) of libel against Wilkes for publishing the Essay on Woman.[45]

On 3 December, the hangman attempted to burn *North Briton* No. 45 before the Royal Exchange, but a "tumultuous" crowd chanting "Wilkes and Liberty" took the fagots off the pile and seized the paper from the hangman. The constables who tried to intervene were beaten. Alderman Thomas Harley, a sheriff of the City of London and the County of Middlesex who had come to do his duty to supervise the burning, was afraid to get out of his carriage. The mob pelted the carriage with mud, and when one of the windows broke Harley sustained a cut on his forehead. They let him be driven off and proceeded with mock ceremony to burn a petticoat and jackboot, symbols of the princess mother and Lord Bute. His lordship's name was pronounced "boot."[46]

The excitement had hardly died down when, on 6 December, Wilkes's suit for trespassing against Robert Wood, the undersecretary, came to trial before Lord Chief Justice Charles Pratt in the Court of Common Pleas. The testimonies uncovered vivid details about the great noise and disturbance made by the messengers working under Wood's direction, how they had stayed in Wilkes's house for twelve hours, had broken the locks and hinges of twenty doors, pried open cabinets, chests, and drawers, and carried off maps, charts, prints, and printed papers. Webb swore under oath that he had not participated, but Arthur Beardmore swore he had seen Webb with the key to Wilkes's study in his hand. For this, Webb would later be tried for perjury, though in such a feeble, near-blind condition that the jury could not bring themselves to convict him. As the trial of Wilkes's cause against Wood continued, Wilkes made a move that would be illegal today but seemed to cause no concern at that time: he distributed to the jury a pamphlet written by Lord Temple and printed on Wilkes's press, *On the Seizure of Papers*.[47]

Finally, Judge Pratt pronounced the decision that the use of general warrants to search private property was illegal: "The defendant claims a right, under precedent, to force persons' houses, break open escritoires, seize their papers, upon a general warrant . . . where no offenders' names are specified in the warrant, and therefore a discretionary power given to messengers to search wherever their suspicions may chance to fall. If such a power is truly vested in a secretary of state, and he can delegate this power, it certainly may affect . . . every man in this kingdom and is totally subversive of the liberty of the subject." It was this decision that established in law the right of privacy, a right that, as the newspapers put it, "rendered a man's house his castle."[48]

Wilkes was granted one thousand pounds in damages. And there was an unexpected benefit: he was acquitted in court of the charge of being the author and publisher of the original folio issue of No. 45. Thereafter, neither in a court of law nor in the House of Commons could Wilkes be accused of those charges. To allow such an accusation in the House would be a crime on the part of the speaker. From that point on, Wilkes could not be accused of writing No. 45, but he could still be accused of printing and publishing it in the edition produced on his own press.[49]

Wilkes supporters who had packed the spectators' benches and the gallery of the Court of Common Pleas now rushed to Great George Street and stood cheering outside the house, playing French horns, and crying, "Pratt, Wilkes, and liberty for ever!" Inside, many bumpers were drunk to liberty, presumably around the bed of the hero. Wilkes had cause to celebrate, not only his liberty, but the money. He was in need of that one-thousand-pound award. But a mean-spirited ministry found ways to delay the payment, which would not be made for nine months. Wilkes had some hope he might be awarded similar damages for his suit against Webb, but the cause never came to trial because Webb successfully pleaded privilege. Wilkes wrote to Polly, "You may now give me joy of my having carried one of my causes against the tools of the administration." He sent his daughter a print of himself, his crossed eyes peering out from under a wreath of laurel. Polly replied on the fifteenth, "A crown of laurel is not half enough for my dear papa's merit, goodness, and amiable qualities."[50]

At midnight that night, there was a violent pounding on Wilkes's door. The servants opened and found themselves in a struggle to hold back a Scottish soldier who had grown furious at Wilkes's treatment of the Scots in the *North Briton* and was now bent upon killing him. They finally quieted the man, and he left. The next day Wilkes received a note from a local printer saying that the soldier, a Scotsman named Alexander Dun, had been in the taverns swearing he would murder Mr. Wilkes. A warrant was issued for Dun's arrest. Wilkes, cooperating with the constable, sent Dun an invitation to visit, and when he arrived, the constable arrested him. The House of Commons was concerned but upon hearing testimony that the man was mad dropped the matter. Dun was held for a time in the King's Bench prison, from which he made daily attempts to escape. He wrote to Wilkes sending a proposal for a book he was planning to publish by subscription, which would include his comments on Wilkes. Wilkes sent him the subscription money, for which Dun thanked him. Dun's friends finally arrived at the prison and took him off to a lunatic asylum.[51]

A few days later, in the Court of Common Pleas, Dryden Leach won his suit against the messenger John Money and was awarded four hundred pounds and costs. Leach was joined in the suit by some of the printer's devils who had been working in his shop. Printers' devils were the lowest-level workers in a print shop, the men who actually inked the type and pulled the lever of the press machine. At the time the suit had been brought in, there were several more devils as complainants, but the government approached them and offered each one hundred pounds to withdraw. Only five continued to the end, humble heroes in the cause of liberty, forgoing a one-hundred-pound bribe to be awarded only five pounds by the court. Unfortunately for Leach and his five men, though fortunately for the world at large, the government lawyers successfully appealed the case, and they would be tried again the next year in the Court of the King's Bench. There, Lord Chief Justice Mansfield was faced with the necessity of rendering a judgment that pained him, benefiting as it did

Wilkes's side of a controversy. But his lordship did at last pronounce general warrants illegal as instruments of arrest despite the precedents the government had presented. Mansfield broke new ground when he pronounced, "No degree of antiquity can give sanction to an usage bad in itself." His ruling, prohibiting arrests of suspects under general warrants, complemented that of Pratt in Wilkes's case, which prohibited their use for search and seizure. General warrants were dead, and the unsung heroes were Dryden Leach and his five inky devils.[52]

Attempts were made in 1765 and 1766 to abolish general warrants by statute, a measure more symbolic than practical and for that reason fought over bitterly. In the end, it failed. Nevertheless, the decisions in the courts had ended the use of this dread instrument and brought the English constitution to a threshold of liberty. The secretaries of state, who acted for the Crown, were deprived of a police force and prohibited from making arbitrary arrests, arbitrary seizures of private property, or arbitrary invasions of privacy. Thus the court erased the last vestige of absolute monarchical power, the last loophole in the constitution wherein the will of the monarch constituted the law. The ruling did not, of course, put an end to the tyranny of the state over individual citizens, but it ended the easiest tyranny.

Where the monarch lost power, the people gained it. In the juries of middle-class men, the people had discovered a new power to check government. Wilkes wrote to Temple: the strength of their cause lay with the jury of merchants "firm to the cause of liberty."[53] These trials began what would prove to be a momentous shift in the locus of power in government. Since the time of Charles II, the whole of political activity had been the contest for control of the state between the king and his ministers on one side and the privileged gentlemen of Parliament on the other. Now the common folk had entered into the play.

The popularity of the king had sunk so low that his public appearances were accompanied by silence. He went one day to the Drury Lane Theatre, and when an announcement was made that the play the next night would be Arthur Murphy's *All in the Wrong*, the galleries cried out, "Let *us* be all in the right! Wilkes and Liberty!" And not only the common folk of England: those of America thought themselves liberated by the abolition of general warrants, and "Wilkes and Liberty" was the toast from New England to South Carolina.[54]

Popular as he was, Wilkes was not out of danger from the law. Parliament had ruled that privilege did not extend to cases of seditious libel, a ruling that came close to rendering parliamentary privilege meaningless. Now, no one could criticize the government. Even lawmakers were silenced, except in the

Houses of Parliament, where the lawmakers were still protected from prosecution for what they said on the floor. Wilkes began secretly to prepare for an escape to France.

Wilkes handed the printers the letters and documents and articles for the third volume of the *North Briton* and turned the supervision of the printing over to Leach. Volume 3 would be printed in February, Leach would dismiss the printers, John Yallowby would dismantle the press machines, and the Great George Street print shop would come to an end. Because the house itself would soon be sold, the copies of volume 3, still in sheets, were carted off to Humphrey Cotes's London house, though eventually they would be taken to a bindery and from there to J. Williams's shop near the Mitre Tavern in Fleet-street to be sold with the first two volumes.[55]

Wilkes told his friends and servants to spread the word that he was going to spend Christmas at Humphrey Cotes's house in Pittfield, Surrey. On Friday the twenty-third at two o'clock in the morning, one of Webb's spies watched Brown and a coachman strapping two trunks to the top of a large coach to which were hitched four horses. In his pocket, the servant had a letter from Polly written in Paris:

> Brown,
>
> Knowing your zeal and attachment for the best of papas, I beg of you as a great favor to leave him as little as you can, especially in the journey and if it is possible not to leave him at night. At the same time, I am vastly obliged to you for the zeal you have had for him in his last affairs.
>
> Mary Wilkes
>
> My woman languishes to see you.[56]

At three o'clock, Brown and another servant were seen helping Wilkes into the carriage. Brown climbed in after him and a few minutes later the horses, hoofs clanging noisily on the cobbles, drew the carriage down and out of Great George Street. They did not go to Cotes's, but straight to Dover. Wilkes wrote to Cotes from the Silver Lion in Dover on Christmas morning. He had been two days on the road, his wound "fretted by the vile jolts. . . . I think Friday and yesterday were the two most unhappy days I have known." But he had had a good sleep at the inn before being awakened to meet a dozen or fourteen gentlemen of the town who were celebrating Christmas morning by calling on Mr. Wilkes and drinking his health in good claret "with the most flattering testimonies in his favor." It was now eleven o'clock, he wrote, the wind was fair, and he was preparing to embark.

The crossing took less than three hours. He wrote Cotes again at three in the afternoon from Calais: "The wind was so high that I was dreadfully sick and most violently strained with it. I am now recovering every hour, but it has made my wound very painful, and very much inflamed, so that instead of going on, I am going to bed, and so fatigued that I believe it is with purer, less carnal ideas than I fancy you have gone to bed with for many a night."[57]

8

Exile

John Wilkes, his open wound acerbated by a jostling carriage, arrived at
the Hôtel de Saxe in Paris on the night of 28 December 1763. His servant,
Matthew Brown, helped him into the ground-floor apartment waiting for him
and into bed, exhausted. Up early the next morning, ignoring his pain, he went
to the Hôtel de la Force to see his beloved daughter. Polly had been living there
with a motherly servant, La Vallerie, since the argument with Madame Carpentier. Pierre Goy, who had initially looked after them, was no longer in
Paris, having fled to England to escape his gaming debts, but Polly had been
watched and attended to by Madam the Baronness d'Holbach and her next
door neighbor, Madam Helvétius, the wife of d'Holbach's friend and fellow,
the philosopher Claude Adrien Helvétius.[1]

The following day Wilkes was driven to d'Holbach's. Now a naturalized
citizen of France, made rich by the will of his uncle, possessed of a profitable
sinecure, and happily married to his second cousin, d'Holbach had made his
five-story house at the corner of the rue des Moulins and the rue Royale the
center of Parisian intellectual life. He provided his friends with books from his
large library and with dinners every Sunday and Thursday. There sat the
philosophes, whose philosophical materialism and enlightened political theo-
ries have so greatly influenced the thinking, the institutions, and the political
practices of the Western world—Denis Diderot, d'Alembert, Georges-Louis

Leclerc de Buffon, Jean-François Marmontel, Charles-Pinot Duclos, Friedrich Melchior von Grimm, and Helvétius. These regular guests were joined almost every week by visiting philosophers, scientists, historians, and even a few men of the church such as Laurence Sterne who were broad-minded enough to remain cheerful in the company of a dozen atheists. Usually ten or fifteen sat down to table at 2:00 and seldom left before 7:00. "Now, there was the place," said André Morellet, "to hear the freest, most animated and most instructive conversation that ever was. . . . There was no moot point, political or religious, that was not advanced there and discussed pro and con, almost always with great subtlety and profundity."[2] To the baron's right sat Diderot, his close friend and fellow editor and writer for the great *Encyclopédie*, which they were publishing underground. Most of the table had contributed articles to this work, which continues to serve as the very epitome of eighteenth-century Enlightenment thought. D'Holbach himself had written four hundred entries. "They have the art," reported Sterne, "notwithstanding their wits, of living together without biting or scratching — an infinitude of gaiety and civility reigns among them."

David Hume and Wilkes were a case in point. After the *North Briton*, the friendship the two had promised each other in Scotland had died. Now Hume was serving as secretary to the English ambassador, Earl Hertford, representing that Scottish intrusion into ministry that Wilkes had so often deplored. All of Paris seemed to have fallen in love with "le bon David," his polished manners, his portly figure, round face, and amusing, intelligent conversation, while the agile, ugly Wilkes was a nonperson at the embassy and a questionable asset as a friend. Nevertheless, when they met at d'Holbach's, all animosity was left behind, and "we laughed much."[3]

The model for this gathering was not the famous Parisian salons, but the circle of brilliant young Englishmen that d'Holbach had known at Leiden, the students who had gathered three times a week at the boardinghouse of Madam Van der Tasse to drink coffee and smoke tobacco, and sup on red herrings, and chat about politics and life. Wilkes hobbled into d'Holbach's dining room on 29 December, an honored man. He had been d'Holbach's friend longer than any of them. He and d'Holbach had spent many a night at Leiden walking and talking along the the banks of the Rhine. In the years since then, Wilkes had not become anything like the creative philosopher d'Holbach had become, but with courage and at great cost, he had put into practice those enlightenment ideals the philosophes talked about but never suffered for. They called him Gracchus, after two brothers of classical Rome who had united the plebs and equites against the senate.[4]

One of the younger members of the "joyous set," as Sterne called them, had a particular interest in English poetry and fiction: Jean-Baptiste Suard, who, when Wilkes arrived, was preparing to launch a review, the *Gazette Littéraire de l'Europe*, which would turn out to be of considerable importance in the exchange and interinfluence of national literatures. Wilkes suggested articles, and Suard invited him to write others. Wilkes gave him a review of Charles Churchill's poems written by his printer friend Dryden Leach; it was duly published but considerably altered. Wilkes himself did not have the knack for literary criticism, and the tasks he undertook ended up heavily edited by Suard. He once had the temerity to suggest a review of the fateful *North Briton* in volumes, a work in which Wilkes had violently opposed the peace with France. Suard demurred. Although it had nothing to do with the *Gazette*, Wilkes showed Suard the manuscript of the Essay on Woman, which Suard returned with compliments that rose to the level of lukewarm. Though their sensibilities were of differing orders, Suard and Wilkes were genuinely fond of one another, and their correspondence would continue for many years.[5]

Three days after Wilkes arrived, a letter from Samuel Martin was handed in at the Hôtel de Saxe. Martin complimented Wilkes on his recovery and said he would like to see him. Lord Hertford, the English ambassador to France, reported on 6 January, "Wilkes went to see Martin here and talked to him with his usual gay freedom for an hour, as if their acquaintance had never been interrupted by any quarrel." The next day Martin, satisfied that Wilkes was well on his way to recovery, set off for London.[6]

But Wilkes was bothered by Martin's awkward explanation of why he had been so long returning the note in which Wilkes had provoked the duel. Though Martin had fled London after the duel, he could easily have left orders with a servant to return it. Wilkes himself had been prompt in returning Martin's written challenge; he had done so on the very day the ball was removed from his body and he was in great pain. Wilkes's friends in London were hinting in their letters that Martin was not to be believed. He had not challenged Wilkes at the time those insulting lines had appeared in the *North Briton* but had remained silent for eight months. Why had he chosen to instigate the duel by insulting Wilkes in a public setting? Why had he made the choice of pistols when in the laws of dueling the choice of weapons had belonged to Wilkes? A rumor was circulating that Martin had spent the intervening months doing daily target practice with his pistols and had transferred all of the commercial stock he owned to someone the day before he created the fuss that led to the duel. And there was the pistol with the empty pan. It began to look as though the duel had been a cover for an assassination attempt set up by the ministry.

Wilkes, clinging to his notion of gentlemanly behavior and reluctant to relinquish his faith in the code of honor, refused to take such warnings seriously. Before the year was up, he would change his mind and decide that Martin and certain ministers had indeed planned an assassination. Fourteen years later, in 1777, going over the records of secret government expenditure that had been demanded by the House of Commons, Wilkes would discover that between October 1762 and October 1763, the government had paid Martin forty-one thousand pounds for "secret and special service."[7] But at Paris in 1764 the two men parted amicably.

English visitors to Paris usually called at the embassy, left their cards, and hoped for an invitation to dine. Wilkes did that. In his earlier trips to Paris, he had often been the guest of the Duke of Bedford, then the ambassador; but his situation had changed, and the new ambassador, the Earl of Hertford, was uncomfortable about his presence in Paris. Hertford was tempted, for he knew Wilkes's reputation as an entertaining guest and had been told that despite his still-open wound, Wilkes "has the spirits which usually attend him." In the end, he dutifully gave the slightest polite response he could: he sent a servant to leave his card at Wilkes's door. "I shall think it my duty," he reported to George Grenville, "not to show this gentleman any further countenance."[8]

Though the ambassador had not made Wilkes welcome at the embassy, as a British citizen Wilkes could not be excluded from the ambassador's chapel. Polly had been a regular attendant, and now Wilkes began to go with her. In London, the *Public Advertiser* of 1 June 1764 reported, "It is with pleasure we hear, that the two most constant attendants upon divine service in our ambassador's chapel at Paris are David Hume and John Wilkes, Esqrs." Hume's atheism was as well known as Wilkes's libertinism. The services were held in a hall within the Hôtel de Grimbergh, for "the ambassador's chapel" was not a consecrated building or even a particular room, but a movable institution that met wherever it was convenient. The Hôtel de Grimbergh was too small to accommodate the large numbers of English who had rushed to Paris after the peace treaty, and Hertford was making preparations to relocate the embassy.[9]

Two or three times a week Wilkes received letters from the lawyer Alexander Phillips urging him to return and face the House of Commons. The House of Lords, he said, would hold off until Wilkes was tried at the King's Bench (which they did not). He need not fear a trial, for the jury would be on his side. His friends believed, said Phillips, if he did not return now he would never be able to return. Hertford was soon reporting to his government that Wilkes would be in England for the opening of Parliament on 18 January 1764.[10]

Though Wilkes wrote to his supporter George Onslow, "I burn with impatience for the 19th because I shall then have an opportunity of vindicating myself," he was not prepared to make any promises about returning. He had not yet recovered from the channel crossing, he said, and the jolts of the "cursed pavé." On 11 January he wrote to the speaker of the House of Commons, Sir John Cust, explaining that he was not well enough to travel and enclosing a "certificate" of his condition from a French surgeon and physician. But he was faking. As he explained to Humphrey Cotes, his plea of ill health had been made according to the plan that Wilkes, Cotes, and Onslow had concerted before Wilkes left England. He had been able to obtain the certificate because the surgeon and physician were friends of Pierre Goy. Having sent the document to Cust, he was now saddled with the necessity of acting ill: "I have, to keep up appearances, been in my room sick and complaining ever since."[11]

Wilkes had cogent reasons for making this decision, which he was at pains to explain to Cotes. He would certainly be expelled from the House, an act that would render him worthless as a political force. He would be found guilty at King's Bench and would have to flee to France anyway. He could expect no justice from an administration that had bribed his servants to steal out of his house, and neither the king nor the dowager princess would ever forgive *North Briton* No. 5. If he were mistaken and the ministers wanted to make peace, they could send him as ambassador to Constantinople, which would suit him very well, for in that pagan country his "jokes against Christianity" would mean nothing. But he knew it would never happen. Finally, there was no "call of honor" to return. His erstwhile friends had repudiated him, and he was obliged to no one but Lord Temple. He had not deserted the cause, and it was his fight that had expanded the liberties of the public; but he was no longer under any obligation to that public, and he did not trust that they would stand by him. "What then am I to expect, if I return to England? Persecution from my enemies, coldness and neglect from friends, except such noble ones as you and a few more." But here in France he had a chance to do something. The king had sent word that he could stay as long as he liked and had given him permission to publish what he chose. To top it all, he could live on half what it would cost in London.[12]

On the second day of Parliament, 19 January 1764, Wilkes was expelled from the House of Commons. Speaker Mr. Cust began proceedings by reading a letter from Wilkes explaining why he could not appear. He had sent along the French doctor's report, which was then read aloud to the House, in French, a language most of the members did not understand. Pitt was purposely absent. Almost to a man, Wilkes's erstwhile friends repudiated him personally, George Onslow being the only exception. Finally, Lord North moved that Wilkes was guilty of writing and publishing *North Briton* No. 45. Witnesses were heard, mostly printers. The only evidence that Wilkes was the writer of No. 45 was the testimony of Michael Curry, who had never laid eyes on Wilkes until long after the original publication of No. 45. Moreover, Curry had to admit he was a thief: Onslow asked him from the floor if he had received money for furnishing the ministry with a copy of the papers, that is, the Essay on Woman, he had taken from Wilkes's house, and Curry, being under oath, reluctantly said yes. On the basis of this reliable witness, Lord North's motion was carried, and Wilkes was declared the writer as well as the printer of No. 45. North then made a motion to expel him, which was carried by a voice vote, with only one nay, voiced by Onslow.[13]

John Debrett, who wrote his great history of Parliament thirty years after this event, declared unconditionally that the House was in violation of common law to have declared No. 45 a libel without hearing the complaint about privilege which Wilkes had been made on 15 November. Moreover, the House was ethically bound to delay debate until after Wilkes's trial at the King's Bench, whereas they ended up prejudicing the trial. "The justice of the nation and the privilege of Parliament were solemnly mocked and violated to gratify the malice of the court and to obviate a motion of expulsion."

A month later, the House of Commons got around to debating Wilkes's charges that his privilege had been violated. On 13 February, they heard the testimony of Wilkes's servant, Matthew Brown, who had come from Paris at Wilkes's expense to describe the rape of Wilkes's house and the pillage of his papers. Then the chief messenger, Nathan Carrington, gave his version. The next day, the House of Commons systematically, one at a time, absolved of the offense of violating Mr. Wilkes's privilege the three messengers, Blackmore, Money, and Watson, then Robert Wood, undersecretary of state, and finally Philip Carteret Webb. The House did so in blatant defiance of the ruling by the Court of Common Pleas at the time Wilkes was released from the Tower.[14]

The House of Lords, out of patience that Wilkes had not appeared, resolved that he be arrested. Lord Sandwich tried to give the resolution teeth by amending it to include a statement that Wilkes was the author of the Essay on Woman, but Temple and Newcastle opposed on the grounds that authorship had not been proved. Finally on 24 January, the House passed a watered down, unclear resolution: "It appearing to this house, that John Wilkes, Esquire, of Great George Street, Westminster, is the author and publisher of 'The Essay on Woman with Notes' and another paper entitled 'The Veni Creator paraphrased,' he be, for the said offense, taken into custody of the Gentleman Usher of the Black Rod."[15]

The heaviest blow came from the Court of the King's Bench, where Wilkes was tried in absentia on 21 February 1764, Lord Chief Justice Mansfield presiding. The day before the trials, at eight o'clock in the morning, Lord Mansfield summoned to his house in Bloomsbury Square the clerks of the court and the lawyers for the defense and announced that he intended to alter the informations (indictments), changing the phrase "purport and effect" to "tenor and effect." Francis Barlow and William Hughes of the Crown Office said they "could not consent," but Mansfield replied that he did not ask for consent, but for objections. He then cited a long list of precedents and proceeded to change the words. The idea of "purport" had included the idea of the writer's intention, whereas "tenor" meant only what he had actually written. In the judgment of the legal experts of the day, if the question had been Wilkes's intentions, no jury would have convicted him. It would appear that Lord Mansfield had also figured that out.[16]

The two trials for the two crimes Wilkes was accused of were held the next day at Westminster Hall, one for his libeling Crown and Parliament by publishing No. 45, the other for his libeling Bishop Warburton by publishing the Essay on Woman. Both trials were concluded in one day, which was not surprising in a world where trials for capital offenses were usually concluded in half an hour.[17] The prosecution was pursued by Fletcher Norton, the solicitor general, the very "Peter Bullcalf" who had tried to keep Wilkes in the Tower. Sergeants Glynn and Dunning and a lawyer named Stowe, who was recorder of the city, served as pro bono counsel to Wilkes's lawyer, Alexander Phillips.

Lord Chief Justice Mansfield instructed the jury for the first trial that if they found Wilkes had published *North Briton* No. 45 in his second edition printed on the Great George Street press, they must return a judgment of guilty. They were not to judge whether the Essay was or was not a libel, and the truth or lack of truth in the writing was irrelevant. Mansfield was ignoring a precedent established in an American court in the case of John Peter Zenger, a figure strikingly similar to Wilkes. In 1734, Zenger had been charged with libel against the royal governor of New York but had been acquitted on the grounds that the facts in the writing were not untrue.[18] But this precedent having been set in far-off America, Mansfield, if he knew of it, could afford to ignore it. The jury for Wilkes's trial was unhappy about Mansfield's instructions and did not want to convict: they deliberated two hours when the fact supposedly under deliberation, that Wilkes had published No. 45 on his own press, was obviously true. In the end, they were unwilling to contradict Mansfield and so returned a verdict of guilty.

The court then proceeded to the second trial, and a new jury was sworn. At this point, Lord Mansfield stopped the taking of minutes, "deeming the expressions in the 'Essay on Woman' improper to be made public." The Rev. Mr.

John Kidgell was called as witness. He was mocked by Sergeant Glynn as the real publisher of an Essay on Woman in his ridiculous book. As Kidgell left the building, he was pelted and cursed by the crowd as a thief and informer. But the clever defense that Glynn had planned came to nothing. Norton, who was prosecuting this case, too, evoked the obscure precedent that had been cited in the House of Lords: "delivering a paper to a printer to be printed is a legal publication." Mansfield instructed the jury that, according to the definition of publication in this precedent, they were to determine only whether or not Wilkes had published the poems. By obvious implication, the content of the poems was not to be taken into account, yet a copy of the *Essay on Woman* was handed to the jury before they began their deliberations. It took them only half an hour to find Wilkes guilty.[19]

Wilkes wrote to Lord Temple when he received word of the verdicts: "I am not disposed to lose myself in womanish complaints on the hardness of my fate, and the variety of persecutions I have suffered even from those I had most obliged. . . . I will only say in the anguish of my heart, that I owe what I suffer to the neglect of your Lordship's advice."[20] He was as close to despair as John Wilkes ever was known to be.

It was worse than Wilkes knew: his lawyer, Alexander Phillips, had betrayed him. Phillips had asked through Cotes for a copy of the Essay on Woman, and on 29 January, Wilkes, supposing it was needed for the defense, had written to Cotes, telling him to give Phillips a copy and where they could be found in his upper library. When Phillips got the copy, he handed it to Peter Bullcalf, and it was this copy that was given to the jury when they began their deliberations.[21]

Two weeks after the trials, Wilkes began to suspect his lawyer. Wilkes's friends in England began to tell him of *their* suspicions, which rose higher as March and April passed without Phillips's telling him anything about the trials. A letter finally arrived in mid-May, urging Wilkes to return. Wilkes wrote to Cotes, "I must suspect his having been bribed to give such advice." After some hesitation, Wilkes wrote to tell Phillips of his suspicions; Phillips made excuses, but never again would he represent Wilkes.[22]

Wilkes's finances were in a dreadful mess, which is no wonder since most of his life he had freely spent money in excess of his income. Wilkes had never been gainfully employed except in the ill-managed venture of the Great George Street press. Until now he had not gotten in trouble because members of Parliament could not be arrested for debt, but since his exclusion, the creditors had been clambering. Bateman, the master of Will's coffeehouse, famous as the gathering place of the Restoration wits, had gotten around the problem of privilege by taking into hock Wilkes's table silver, which he would gladly return when paid the £320 he was owed.[23]

Wilkes had assigned to Cotes the power to handle his finances while he was abroad, and Wilkes's brother, Heaton, helped. They ran an advertisement calling for all debtors to make their claims and got an unfortunately large response. To meet the claims, they talked Wilkes into selling his impressive library of some seventeen hundred volumes. In May 1764, it was sold in an auction of five days' length.[24] With that money Cotes and Heaton paid off many of the smaller debts, but the debts to money lenders still hung over Wilkes's head.

Over and over Wilkes assured Cotes and his brother that he was living frugally. He had left the expensive Hôtel de Saxe in February and taken Polly from the rooms in which she had been living at Madame de Rolinde's, and the two of them had moved into less expensive rooms in a house on the rue St. Nicaise. The owner was a friend of Wilkes, a disreputable Dutchman named Hope.[25]

Wilkes was now so famous that his company was much sought after by both English and French. Once when he was invited to a card party, he replied, "Dear Madam, do not ask me, for I am so ignorant that I cannot tell the difference between a king and a knave." Horace Walpole met him frequently at dinners given by wealthy Frenchmen, and English visitors were constantly knocking at his door. Walpole himself called upon him, and Wilkes returned the call in the company of Sterne's friend John Craufurd. These two could be pretty raucous when they were together, and they did not much entertain Walpole: "His conversation shows how little he had lived in good company." But he did admire one thing in Wilkes: "He has certainly one merit, notwithstanding the bitterness of his pen, that is, he has no rancor — not even against Sandwich, of whom he talked with the utmost temper."[26]

Wilkes's forbearance of Sandwich's betrayal soon became legend and was memorialized in a song about the Beef Steak Club, the historicity of which may be doubted, though the point is well taken:

> Lord Sandwich and Wilkes when met at this place,
> Ne'er speak of search-warrants as any disgrace;
> The Peer sings his catch, and Wilkes cracks his joke,
> While the steak piping hot on the table does smoke.[27]

The new lodgings were less expensive, but Polly's art instructor and dancing master and language tutors came regularly and had to be paid. She had to be well dressed in expensive Parisian clothes when they were entertained by the dashing Comte de Lauraguais or the Anglophile Comte de Bissy. Wilkes began to ponder purchasing a coach for his daughter because she "dines out frequently." It would cost only eighty or ninety pounds, he told Cotes. Cotes sent back a firm no, and Wilkes gave up the idea. Parisian debts began to accumu-

10. Horatio Walpole, earl of Orford, by T. Evans after Thomas Lawrence. Courtesy of the Lewis Walpole Library, Yale University.

late, including his medical expenses and the furniture he had bought for his and Polly's rooms. Some hint of Wilkes's financial straits may have reached the ears of Madame Geoffrin, the brilliant hostess to politicians and artists, who commented to Wilkes, "A person without a shirt, should not have pride," to which Wilkes responded, "On the contrary, he should have pride, so as to have something."[28]

At least once Wilkes and Polly were entertained by the duc d'Orléans, in the magnificent Palais Royal. The duc's late father, an uncle to the king, had been regent during the king's minority. The son, after an honorable military career, had settled into a life of pleasure with his mistress, Mlle le Marquis, an actress. He had grown fat. A permanent member of the duc's household was Louis Carogis, remembered today by his stage name, Carmontelle. Though he had come originally as tutor to the duc's son, he had acquired the responsibility of drawing and painting portraits of the guests. He worked with pencil and watercolors. Carmontelle's talent was great, but it had a curious limit: he could paint his subjects only in profile. Carmontelle's portrait of Polly and her father is charming. Polly is seated, looking indeed like an alert fourteen-year-old. Her father behind her is leaning over her chair, one hand pointing to a manuscript or perhaps a musical score propped up on a table. Polly's brown eyes are intent upon the paper. They are elegantly dressed: lace trimmings, Polly with an elaborate hairdo, Wilkes with a queue tied with a ribbon hanging between his shoulders. Their faces are very alike, and both have long, pointed chins. There is a suggestion of Wilkes's cast eye, though in a profile the affliction cannot be made specific. No doubt like most portraitists, Carmontelle made them better looking than they appeared in life, painting them with closed mouths to hide the defects of their teeth and slightly modifying their long jaws.[29]

By March 1764, Lord Hertford had moved the English embassy and its chapel into the beautiful Hôtel Brancas, located in a park that ran down to the left bank of the Seine. Today that magnificent house serves as the residence of the president of the Chamber of Deputies. The Rev. Mr. Laurence Sterne was in town. Having established his wife and daughter in the south of France, Sterne was on his way to Shandy Hall in Coxwold, Yorkshire, to finish his great comic novel, *Tristram Shandy*. Lord Hertford paid him the signal compliment of asking him to preach the sermon at the opening service of the Ambassador's Chapel to be held on Sunday, 25 March. Wilkes brought Suard to the service, and Hume brought d'Holbach and Diderot, "a concourse of all nations and religions too," Sterne said. Sterne began the sermon in the usual way by reading out the biblical text upon which he intended to comment, but what he read was not really 2 Kings 20:12–18, but his travesty of the passage, altered to suit the occasion: "And Hezekiah said unto the prophet, I have shown them my vessels of gold, and my vessels of silver, and my wives and my concubines, and my boxes of ointment, and whatever I have in my house, have I shown them; and the prophet said unto Hezekiah, thou has done very foolishly." It was difficult to distinguish the gasps from the laughs.[30]

Wilkes did not want to miss even a minute of the company of the wittiest and most audacious fiction writer in England, and Sterne, despite his clerical bands and sincere devotion to God, loved to spend his time with wits and libertines. Weeks before, he and his wife had agreed on a separation, and he was enjoying his newfound freedom as a single man. Wilkes wrote to Churchill on 10 April, "Sterne and I often meet, and talk of you— We have an odd party for to-night at Hope's, two lively, young, handsome actresses, Hope and his mistress— Ah! poor Mrs. Wilkes!!!"[31]

One of these "actresses," Gertrude Corradini, was an exquisite Italian beauty, eighteen years old, and Wilkes fell head over heels in love with her. She was from Bologna, but she had been, as Wilkes said, educated in the skills of the courtesan at Venice, where she had been the mistress to the British consul, John Udney. When Udney declared bankruptcy, she left him and came to Paris, "on the pretext of perfecting herself in dancing."[32] Wilkes paid her a visit and discovered she lived with her mother. Although his initial importunities were rejected, "he approached the shrine of this modern divinity in the same manner the ancient deities were worshipped," that is, with an offering. The daughter haughtily refused the coin, but "the generosity of his nature won upon the mother, and he was allowed from time to time to leave in her lap a few louis in silver." Then Corradini found a way to break the stalemate without losing face: she one day bemoaned the loss of a beautiful silver crucifix, which she described in detail. Wilkes went the next morning to the Quai des Orfevres and searched the jewelers' stalls until he found a crucifix "exactly answering the description," which he purchased and presented to Carrodini. "That same afternoon she ceased to be cruel. The three following weeks he passed in her arms." In his brief autobiography Wilkes consistently spoke of himself in the third person.

In the autobiography, Wilkes delighted to describe Corradini: she had "a perfect Grecian figure cast in the mold of the Florentine Venus, excepting that she was rather taller, and more flat about the breasts." One of the great thrills for Wilkes was that he and Corradini got naked together. English and French women almost never disrobed to make love, and in London people were sometimes arrested for having intercourse in the nude.[33] Corradini "possessed the divine gift of lewdness," a remark that recalls the "Essay on Woman" and the letters of Thomas Potter. For Potter and Wilkes, lust had been the feminine ideal they most admired. Corradini may have been vain and jealous and had a violent temper, but never mind: "All her sensibility seemed to have a reference to one favorite spot." In Wilkes's view, she also had a moral virtue: she "sacrificed herself to the interests of others."

Wilkes soon moved Corradini and her mother into "elegant lodgings" in the rue Neuve commanding a view of the garden of the Palais Royal, furnished it "in the gayest taste of the Parisians," and hired for them "a ragged footboy brought from Italy" and a "spruce" French footman. "Mr Wilkes generally dined at home with his daughter," he wrote in the autobiography, "or at some friends, and in the evening supped with the fair Italian. Nothing could be more luxurious than this life was to him. He had the happiness of remarking all day the openings of a sensible and elegant mind in his daughter and of experiencing every agreeable return of tenderness for all his parental fondness. In the evening other passions were gratified."

But the perfect life was costly. Wilkes began to think of selling Prebendal House and its estate. For a brief time he entertained a hope that his mother-in-law would buy it and keep it for Polly, only to discover that Mrs. Mead had purchased a country estate at Clapham. On 18 July 1764, Prebendal House and Wilkes's freeholds and leaseholds were sold by the auctioneers Langford and Son in the Great Piazza, Covent Garden. Prebendal House was bought by Sir Wm Lee of Hartwell for forty-one hundred pounds, the properties in Berkshire and Bucks by a Mr. Kent.[34] Cotes began to send Wilkes money, though it was not enough to pay the debts he had accrued in Paris. He wrote back to Cotes, "I begin to think that I am doomed to an eternal exile."[35]

He made a halfhearted attempt to get into the publishing business but letting out the printing part of the job. He would be willing, he said, to have printed whatever was needed by the opposition and send it to England, so long as it said not a word about the French court. He sent Cotes three hundred copies of some letter, warning him to be very careful how he distributed them. But he soon saw he was setting himself the same trap he had fashioned at Great George Street: "My literary projects will in the end be lucrative, at present they too are expensive."[36] It is hard to imagine a worse businessman than Wilkes, not in day-to-day management, at which he was good, but in major decisions, which he made with the recklessness that characterized his public life.

On 4 June, the king's birthday, Lord Hertford threw a grand dinner at the embassy to which were invited David Hume, Adam Smith, Isaac Barré, David Garrick, Horace Walpole, and all the English in Paris except John Wilkes and his daughter. Wilkes was disgruntled but tried to compensate by giving a dinner of his own for some Swedish friends of Cotes who had stopped in Paris. "I passed the day very happily," he wrote, but when it fell his turn to toast the king, "I could not help lamenting my hard and unmerited lot of being forced to give such a toast out of my own dear country, and in a land where the standard of liberty is not yet erected." Only when Polly came to his assistance and held up her glass could he say it with her: "God save great George our King."[37]

Wilkes, who had not heretofore spoken publicly about the reasons for his banishment, now set to work on *A Letter to the Worthy Electors of the Borough of Aylesbury*, a sizable pamphlet in which he defended himself from the charges that had led to his removal as the Aylesbury representative. Step by step he went through the accusation by the House of Commons, contending that nothing in No. 45 was shown to be false, nothing shown to be disrespectful of the Crown or the Parliament. As to the Essay on Woman, the real publisher was not himself but the House of Lords. The poem "contained nothing but fair ridicule of some doctrines I could not believe . . . a few portraits drawn from warm life, with the too high colouring of a youthful fancy, and two or three descriptions, perhaps too luscious, which though *nature* and *woman* might pardon, a Kidgell and a Mansfield could not fail to condemn." His brother was upset when he read this, for he said it virtually admitted that Wilkes was the author. One suspects Wilkes had decided that the danger had passed with his trial at the King's Bench and claiming the authorship obliquely would enhance his image as the cavalier. But he was cautious enough not to have the letter printed until the following winter, when it could be vetted by his advisers. When it finally appeared, it failed of the impact he had expected. Out of sight, he must have thought, out of mind.

In August, Wilkes heard that the undersheriff of Middlesex had placed himself with solemn ceremony in the door of St. Margaret's church and in a loud voice had "exacted" Wilkes's return to the Court of the King's Bench to be sentenced. "Assure him upon my honor," Wilkes wrote to Cotes, "that I was not in my pew, No. 70, on Wednesday last when he made that noise at the great door." Despite the bravado, Wilkes was worried. If he did not appear to be sentenced, he would be outlawed. What did it mean to be an outlaw? No one he or his friends knew had been in such a quandary. He decided to do nothing.[38]

The news from England that John Williams had been pilloried for publishing No. 45 in his new edition of the *North Briton* was oddly reassuring. Williams had served as the publisher of the second edition of the *North Briton* that Wilkes had printed at Great George Street. After Wilkes was incapacitated by his duel with Samuel Martin, Williams, on his own hook, had published a third edition and defiantly included No. 45. He was arrested for seditious libel and sentenced to six months in prison, a fine of one hundred pounds, and the pillory. On 14 February 1765, Williams was pilloried in the New Palace Yard, but his suffering demonstrated that liberty of the press was an issue for which the common folk of London were ready to riot if other options were closed to them. A mob of ten thousand men and women gathered at the pillory and cheered Williams without cessation for the hour he was exposed. They put into his hand a nosegay of laurel and myrtle. They shouted, "Truth in the pillory," "Number 45 forever!" "Wilkes and Liberty!" Passing about hats, they collected two hundred guineas, which they put at his feet. They erected four ladders from which they hung a jackboot and a scotch bonnet, symbolizing Lord Bute, a petticoat, symbolizing the princess mother, and an axe. As a climax to this drama, they put the bonnet on the jackboot and beheaded it.[39]

Having failed to come in for sentencing, Wilkes was pronounced an outlaw at the Court of the King's Bench on 1 November 1764. Outlawed, he had no rights and no protection under British law, but the condition was not as dire as it had been a hundred years before when anyone could have killed him in the open street with impunity. The laws now in effect gave him the comforting right to be killed only by the sheriff.[40] Since he did not have any other rights under law, he could not sue under law, and his case against Lord Halifax was muted. "I am outlawed, not for smuggling, nor for any crime, but that I may not have it in my power to continue my suits in the cause of liberty against a Secretary of State. . . . In such a cause have I any reason to be ashamed of my outlawry?" But cheerful as he remained to the world, he was beginning to think he might be banished for the rest of his life.

Wilkes solaced himself with Corradini, "lost in the gratification of those pleasures which they gave each other, and love alone could furnish out in such a soul-thrilling rapture to either."

Corradini dreaded the approach of the "churlish winter" of Paris. The poor woman was consumptive. The doctor ordered her to her bed and Wilkes out of it. No sooner was this prohibition on love declared than Corradini began to spy upon Wilkes, following him or sending her servant after him. She accused him in a violent rage of being unfaithful. Wilkes protested innocence, and Corradini dissolved into tears, then convulsions, then quiet.[41] The physician advised that Corradini would never regain her health in France and must return to Italy. She begged Wilkes to come with her, but he said no: he had promised Churchill he would meet him at Boulogne. He would follow her in a month or so.

Wilkes had been urging Churchill and Cotes and Heaton to come to Paris, but if they did not want to go that far, he would meet them at Boulogne.[42] In late October, Wilkes set off to meet his friends, and about the same time Corradini and her mother, well supplied with Wilkes's money, left for Italy escorted by a man whom she had introduced as her uncle.

On 28 October, Wilkes and Cotes and Churchill and Elizabeth Carr, the girl

Churchill had eloped with, had a joyful reunion. Though Boulogne was a sinister coastal town, a port of smugglers, they were put up comfortably in the house of a friend of Cotes, a merchant named Walsh. Wilkes could not wait to tell Churchill about Corradini, and the two "fired their imaginations" with the idea of traveling through Italy with Elizabeth Carr and Gertrude Corradini. There was also business to be done: papers Cotes had brought for Wilkes to sign, accounts to go over, and Wilkes's essay addressed to the electors of Aylesbury to be vetted.

On the third day of their reunion, Churchill fell ill. A physician was called and pronounced that he suffered from "a putrid fever," the disease we call dysentery. It is a terrible disease in which the victim is desiccated by unceasing diarrhea. His friends and the servants in the house nursed him, and Wilkes never left his side, but he sank rapidly. On Saturday, in agony but in full command of his mind, he drew up a will. On Sunday morning, 4 November 1764, Churchill's heart ceased to beat. He released his last breath and died in Wilkes's arms.[43]

Wilkes "passed the day and night alone in tears and agonies of despair."[44]

Churchill had bequeathed an annuity of *sixty pounds per annum* to his wife, another annuity of *fifty pounds per annum* to Elizabeth Carr, and the rest of his estate to his two sons. He had named Wilkes his literary executor, desiring him to collect and publish his works with any remarks and explanations he thought fit. Wilkes, Cotes, and Miss Carr took the corpse to Calais, and Cotes and Miss Carr crossed to Dover with it, but not Wilkes, who feared he would be arrested on the other side. Cotes and Carr interred the body in an ancient burying ground near the Dover marketplace that received the bodies of travelers. It belonged to no church, and many thought it fit for a misbehaving parson to lie in unhallowed ground.[45]

Robert Lloyd, Churchill's dear friend from Westminster School days, the poet who had contributed to the *North Briton*, was languishing in Fleet debtors' prison, barely surviving on hackwork that Churchill had gotten for him and on money Churchill had sent. On hearing of his friend's death, Lloyd said, "I shall follow poor Charles," and on 15 December, he too died. He had been nursed by Churchill's sister, who was engaged to him. She died shortly after. For weeks, Wilkes was sunk in a deep melancholy.

Then Wilkes began to make plans to go to Italy. Cotes had convinced him he could no longer afford to maintain a residence in Paris. Wilkes did not tell him he had been maintaining two. Polly was to return to England under Heaton's care, Wilkes was to go to Italy, where he could live cheaply. He would write a book he had been talking about, a history of England, and he would edit Churchill's poems.[46]

Wilkes wrote to Heaton, asking if he would take Polly into his family, insisting forcefully that she not stay with her mother and grandmother. Polly had reached the age of fifteen. "She has prudence infinitely beyond her years," Wilkes wrote to his brother, "and I can safely trust her anywhere she wishes to go. . . . As to Miss Wilkes's mother, I have settled it, that my daughter may visit her whenever she chooses, either to breakfast, dine, or sup, but on no consideration to lie under the same roof. If this condition is broke through, I will never forgive any person concerned, for I know to what consequence it draws. I know the demerit of the Mead family, and I am implacable as to my injuries."[47]

Telling his brother nothing about Corradini, Wilkes promised that when he got to Italy he would find an inexpensive place to board with a decent family. To Cotes, he was more candid. He promised to be prudent about money, but, "as to the Italian girl . . . that amusement I must have." Cotes argued that Corradini might hurt his reputation. Not at all, said Wilkes, "the world shall look after me not with pity, but with envy and admiration."[48]

On 4 December, Polly and La Vallerie, escorted by Brown, sailed from Calais on a little packet boat. Wilkes waited at Calais to hear that they had arrived safely and then returned to Paris. On 9 December, he was handed letters from Polly and another from Heaton. "By God, Heaton is a barbarian," he wrote to Cotes; "he has done the most cruel thing in the world by Miss Wilkes, and has held a language to her about me, which is false, insolent, and infamous. What? To set a daughter against her father! . . . I have cried ever since I read her letter." Heaton had no intention of alienating Polly's affection from her Papa, but he was stuck with the problems Wilkes had created, and when he heard stories about Wilkes in Paris, he had dismissed La Vallerie and sent her back with Brown. The next morning Polly wrote in her journal, "I dressed myself, which I found very awkward, especially as I am used to a handy person."[49] The tight gowns of that time with their hooped skirts were not easy to get into.

Wilkes in his impotence could not afford to alienate the man upon whom he depended to protect his daughter, and so sent Heaton a letter that was stiff but polite. He was to send a monthly account of the expenses for Polly's care. And he reiterated, "I trust to your honor that Miss Wilkes never lies at her mother's." But his trust was not honored. Both Heaton and Cotes were under financial stress, and they could not see the necessity of supporting Polly when her wealthy mother and grandmother would be only too glad to have her with them. They reached an agreement with Mrs. Mead to take Polly in. Mrs. Mead told her daughter that Polly was to stay with them, but nothing else. So when Polly arrived for the first time at the old house in Red Lyon Court behind St. Sepulcher's church, her mother presumed she was there to stay. Polly told the story to her father in a letter. After the greetings all around, her mother asked Polly when her trunks would arrive? "I said I did not know why they should come there at all, and that they were at my uncle's. She asked me if I did not know I was to be at her house. I said I believed not and that I had never heard any thing about it. She said now I was there I should not come away. I then told her that I could not lie there on any account."[50] Faced with stubborn resistance, Heaton took Polly back to St. John's Square. The Meads, angry, summoned their lawyer, who told them that the legal right to custody was invested in the mother when the father was outlawed. There was no helping it now: Polly was forced to move her trunks and her young self to the house behind St. Sepulchur's.

On 2 May 1765, Wilkes received a letter from his cousin John Nesbitt, the friend of Smollett. He had seen Polly at the Mead-Sherbrooke house twice. She was in good health, and though being with her mother and grandmother "was extremely disagreeable to her at first, yet she seems perfectly reconciled." Surprisingly, they had arranged for friends to escort Polly to Ranelagh, to the assemblies at Carlyle House, the "City Ball," and to the theater. They did not interfere with her correspondence with her father. "Her affection for you is the strongest instance of paternal affection I ever saw," said Nesbitt. And he added a final point: when Polly at first refused to come to them, the grandmother was on the verge of changing her will. By mid-June, Polly, cheerful girl that she was, had adjusted to her new life, and Jack and Heaton Wilkes seemed to be getting along again.[51]

Wilkes began to ready himself for the journey to Italy. His Paris lodgings he turned over to David Garrick, who was picking up the lease. On 25 December, 1764, a year after he had left London for Paris, he left Paris for Italy.[52] His man Brown went with him. The traveling went well, and nothing of significance happened until they reached Milan. There Wilkes found himself treated as an honored guest by Prince Trivulzio, who took him to the countess Simonetta, "the first woman of Milan," then to the regent, the Duke of Modena.

Wilkes arrived at Bologna on 18 January, welcomed by Corradini's family and rewarded by Corradini with the "tributes" due to the "true votaries" of pleasure. To Polly he wrote that he dined every day with Mademoiselle Corradini, but "I took private lodgings, where I lay every night," but he was lying. He stayed with Corradini and her family. During the two weeks he lingered at Bologna, Wilkes looked at church art and looked at his mistress. Corradini "still preserved that *air de vierge*, which is found above all so captivating." Wilkes loved the lofty rooms of the house, with little ornament or furniture. In England the beds of gentlepeople were hung on four sides with curtains. Here the only curtain in the room was the one Corradini drew across the picture of the Madonna so as not to offend the spotless Lady. That tiny curtain drawn, Corradini was willing to "yield those matchless charms, those heavenly beauties, to the view, to the touch, to the embrace of a mortal lover." Wilkes was delighted with the way the open bed stood out from the wall so that in the morning he could contemplate at once "the two noblest objects of the creation, the glory of the rising sun, and the perfect form of naked beauty."

Wilkes's plan was to take Corradini to Naples, where they could live at little expense while he worked on his history of England and his edition of Churchill's works. Corradini was willing but suggested that Wilkes make her a settlement of two thousand pounds, for she had heard that such was the customary way Englishmen treated their mistresses. Wilkes had to tell her it was customary for a mistress of years, but not of months.

Wilkes, Corradini, Corradini's mother, and their servants left Bologna on 28 January. They spent ten days in Florence, where Wilkes found himself "caressed," as he told Polly, by his countrymen who were there. But he did not call upon Sir Horace Mann, the friend of Walpole, the famous minister plenipotentiary to the court of Florence, "to save him the *embarras* of returning a visit to a man so very obnoxious to the English (or rather Scottish) ministry." Perhaps also to save himself the *embarras* of having to introduce Corradini, for he had determined not to hide her during this journey.

The party arrived at Rome on 14 February and took rooms at the Piazza di Spagna. John Holroyd, meeting Wilkes for the first time, found him "a charming, wicked, honest, jolly, candid sort of fellow" who had with him "a most exquisite female, an Italian that he collected at Paris."[53]

The exciting person in Rome was the Abbé Johann Joachim Winckelmann, secretary to the Vatican and superintendent of the antiquities, whose authority on classical art was unexceled. Wilkes was more than delighted to be sought out by such a brilliant and distinguished man. Winckelmann, Wilkes told Polly, had "a heart glowing with the love of liberty, and sentiments worthy the freest republics of antiquity." Wilkes spent eight days in his company, often with Corradini and sometimes her mother. The abbé, being a man of "good breeding with a sufficient knowledge of the world," paid no attention to Corradini's faux pas and tolerated with good cheer the inanities of her mother.[54] Such was the party that walked among "the wonders of *Roma antica et moderna*." Wilkes was especially taken with St. Peter's, "the magnitude of the building" and the wondrous painting and sculpture within it. He summed up his impression with a phrase that might serve as a key to neoclassical aesthetics: "The whole is plain, modest, and sublime." Plain? Modest? Today, the most ardent admirer of St. Peter's would hesitate to call it plain or modest. The abbé took them to see an astonishing horse race run "on a pavement, without riders, and between thousands of people," and to the opera, where the women's parts were taken by castrati.

Winckelmann was fascinated by the brilliant, ugly Englishman who had sacrificed so much for his and Winckelmann's political ideals. His affection for Wilkes brings to mind the love of another gentleman of religion and learning twenty years before, Immateriality Baxter. When it was time for Wilkes to leave, Winckelmann presented him with a medal he had had struck as a memorial of their friendship: on one side, Wilkes's head; on the other words from Virgil, "pulchra pro libertate." He also presented Wilkes with an antique sepulcher urn of alabaster, which Wilkes said he would have inscribed to the memory of Churchill. In Winkelmann's letter to Wilkes after they had parted, he did not forget to say with graceful metaphor, "I kiss the lovely hands of Mademoiselle Corradini." Three years in the future, Winckelmann would be murdered by a thief intent upon stealing from his collection. In his will, he had bequeathed to Wilkes his collection of Roman coins.[55]

Wilkes and his party left Rome on 18 February 1765. They followed the famous Roman road, the Appian Way, traveling for many miles between blossoming orange groves. "It was . . . February, yet the air was silky soft, the genial zephyrs of May wantoned among the orange groves of Mola, and the whole face of the country had the gaiety of an Italian spring. . . . All this is indeed necessary for the comfort of a traveller under the dreadful jolting of the Appian way, which you must necessarily traverse to Capua, and the badness of the inns, in which you are almost devoured by vermin." By this time Wilkes had decided he liked the Italians as little as he liked their roads and inns.

The "family" arrived at Naples in the third week of February and, as usual for Wilkes, moved into the most expensive hotel catering to English travelers, which at Naples was Stephano's, by the sea. Wilkes found the situation of Naples breathtakingly beautiful, but the city itself packed and stifling. At the cathedral, he attended the annual ritual of the feast of St. Januarius, in which the blood of the saint was miraculously liquified, or, in Wilkes's opinion, liquified by a hoax. The only English at Naples that he wanted to spend time with were Major Richard Ridley, whom he liked despite his Jacobite past, and Sir William Stanhope, his old Bucks neighbor and fellow of the Medmenham hellfire club, a man in his sixties with "a crazy, battered constitution, and deaf into the bargain" who kept a gaming table in his house at which most of the young English visitors took their turns.[56] But not Wilkes, who was never known to gamble.

James Boswell arrived on 2 March and plucked up the courage to write a letter to Wilkes in Latin, a way to get Wilkes's attention, but risky for Boswell's reputation as a scholar since Wilkes was known to be a master of the language.

They had met in England but did not know each other well. Wilkes was thirty-eight years old and considered an enemy by the Scots; Boswell was a twenty-four-year-old Scot who looked eighteen.[57] He was on the grand tour that young men took to complete their education.

No two men of that period had greater social skills than pudgy Boswell and ugly Wilkes, and they quickly charmed one another. Both had the gift of easy intimacy, and within days they had made a friendship that, with one or two bumps along the way, would last their lifetimes. Boswell lent Wilkes the journal he was keeping. Wilkes confessed to "my old Lord of Scotland," as he affectionately called Boswell, that he hated his wife, though he had been a civil husband. He did not care about Corradini's follies and stupidities because he was in love with her; but he did not trust her relatives. Boswell confessed that he was in love with a brilliant young woman he had met in Holland, Zélide, and read a letter he was sending her. Wilkes advised him, "Go home by Holland and roger [fuck] her." But Boswell, despite his numerous sexual capers, had a Puritan guilt about sex: "A Presbyterian kirk makes me tremble," to which Wilkes replied, "That's the strength of your imagination." Boswell wanted to know why Wilkes spent time with him when in matters of politics and religion they were opposites. Wilkes had been reading the journal, and his answer was ready: "Because you are an original genius." He must continue his journal, Wilkes told him, and then publish it. According to Boswell's great biographer, Frederick Pottle, Wilkes was "the first person who ever assessed Boswell's peculiar gift correctly and encouraged him to exploit it. Everybody else wanted to make Boswell over; Wilkes saw that he was *sui generis.*"[58]

Friday the 15th of March found Wilkes and Boswell riding asses up a mountain, sometimes pushed by porters, toward the village of Vromero to look at the Villa Pietracatella, which Wilkes was thinking of renting. As they walked through the empty house, Wilkes said, "I'm always happy. I thank God for good health, good spirits, and the love of books. I'll live here retired and not go down to Naples; 'tis hell: 'He descended into hell' shall not be said of me." Two days later they went by boat and then climbed up the side of Vesuvius, each pulled by two men and pushed by three. The sun and the hot mountain burned their skin. They lay on their bellies and peered into the opening, about a mile in circumference, and when the smoke was blown aside they could see mountains of a yellow substance they took to be sulphur. They were finally forced away by the smoke and made their way down through ash up to the knees.

Many of Wilkes's remarks that Boswell recorded at Naples have already found a place in this narrative: "Always among women at Leyden. My father gave me as much money as I pleased. Three or four whores and drunk every night." "Thank heaven for having given me the love of women. To many she gives not the noble passion of lust." "I make it a rule to abuse him who is against me or any of my friends point-blank. . . . I abuse Johnson as an impudent pretender to literature, which I don't think, but 'tis all one." After the duel with Lord Talbot, Wilkes's mother: " 'Why rush into the presence of your maker?' 'I've been always in it.' 'And into eternity?' 'Where have I been all this time?' " "Dissipation and profligacy . . . renew the mind. I wrote my best *North Briton* in bed with Betsy Green." One is grateful that Boswell left a record of them.

Getting ready to depart, Boswell sent Wilkes a note: "I would *carpe diem* [seize the day] as much as I can while you and I are near each other. I go for certain on Wednesday. Pray don't grudge a little paper and ink and wax upon an *old* Scotsman who loves you as much as any Englishman whatever." At their parting, Wilkes said, "I shall never forget your civilities to me. You are engraven upon my heart," words that Boswell ever treasured.

Boswell left on 20 March and traveled to Rome, whence he wrote to Wilkes, "I do in my conscience believe you to be an enemy to the true old British Constitution, and to the order and happiness of society. That is to say, I believe you to be a very Whig and a very libertine. But philosophy can analyse human nature, and from every man of parts can extract a certain quantity of good. Dare I affirm that I have found cheerfulness, knowledge, wit, and generosity even in Mr. Wilkes?" Wilkes replied, "You have made me know halcyon days in my exile, and you ought not to be surprised at my cheerfulness and gaiety, for you inspired them." He then set Boswell right about the epithet the Italian newspapers had attached to his name, *Il Bruto Inglese*: it did not mean "the English Brutus"; it meant "the ugly Englishman."

From Lucca that autumn, Boswell wrote to Rousseau,

> I found [at Naples] the famous Mr. Wilkes in his exile, and despite his sharp attacks on the Scots, we got along very well together. All theories of human nature are confounded by the resilient spirit of that singular functionary, who has experienced all the vicissitudes of pleasure and politics without ever having suffered a moment of uneasiness. He is a man who has thought much without being gloomy, a man who has done much evil without being a scoundrel. His lively and energetic sallies on moral questions gave to my spirit a not unpleasant agitation, and enlarged the scope of my views by convincing me that God could create a soul completely serene and gay notwithstanding the alarming reflection that we all must die.

To Wilkes he wrote,

> I look upon you as one of the vigorous few who keep up the true manly character in this effeminate age. . . . Oh John Wilkes, thou gay, learned, and ingenious private gentleman, thou passionate politician, thou thoughtless in-

fidel, good without principle and wicked without malevolence, let Johnson teach thee the road to rational virtue and noble felicity!

Wilkes decided to rent the house on the mountain, and on 3 April moved his little family into the Villa Pietracatella on the mount Vomero, about a mile south of Naples. From the house he could see over a garden, a vineyard, an orchard, and beyond that the town and bay of Naples, the Island of Capri, and Vesuvius. "I took possession of this old crazy castle on the 3rd," he wrote to Boswell; "I am in the bosom of philosophy and Corradini, calm and pensive," working on the Churchill edition and his history. The house was unfurnished, so he had furniture hauled up from Naples. He was delighted with the mosquito nets thrown over the bed, "that give the appearance of two lovers being caught, like Mars and Venus, in the network of the jealous blacksmith." "So sweet a situation, and so beautiful a woman, engrossed the mind of a man naturally too susceptible of pleasure, and though his faculties were not enervated, yet his schemes of ambition and public life were as much neglected as his own private concerns."

In fact, Wilkes never did complete the history of England or the edition of Churchill's poems. Over the next few years, he made a handful of notes on the poems, of minimal editorial value, for they did little but add his own satirical remarks to those of Churchill.

One of these remarks has been used to blacken Wilkes's character, a commentary upon a passage in Churchill's poem "The Duellist." In an attack upon Bishop Warburton, Churchill had alluded to Gertrude Warburton's affair with Thomas Potter, saying openly that Warburton was impotent, and his wife's child was not his:

> No Husband, tho' he's truly wed;
>   Tho' on his knees a child is bred,
>   No father. (lines 788–91)

It is likely Churchill was right about the child's parentage, for the boy was Gertrude Warburton's only child, and he was born nine months after her affair with Potter. But that is not the point: it was slanderous to say that the legal husband was not the actual father. Warburton had begun a suit against Churchill for libel, but the suit was muted by the poet's death. One might excuse Churchill's attacking so prominent a writer as Bishop Warburton, but one can hardly excuse his cruelty to Gertrude and her son. Wilkes now added to this unhappy satire his own witticisms on the subject, which he planned to use as a note in the projected edition of Churchill's poems. The boy he described as "adopted"; "It is generally allowed," he wrote, "that the boy does not in the least resemble him [Warburton]; but seems to be of quite another mould, or *potter's* earth."

These notes eventually found their way into the press, but not through any action of Wilkes. Though he wrote them for an edition he intended to publish, he never got around to editing them for the public because he never completed the edition. Some two years after Churchill's death, he had lost all interest in that project.[59] He did, however, show the notes to friends and acquaintances, including Walpole. Someone betrayed his trust and copied them, perhaps his printer friend, John Almon. In any event, they came into Almon's hands, and he pirated them for a catchpenny collection of supposedly amusing pieces called *The Humours of the Times*, which went through several versions, eventually changing its name to *The New Foundling Hospital for Wit*. Though Almon did not name the author, Wilkes's authorship was apparent to the polite world of London and Bath. Gertrude Warburton, her son, and her husband were all alive when the comments appeared. Wilkes and Churchill have been equally blamed for this cruelty to Gertrude and her son. Churchill must be adjudged guilty; the case against Wilkes is not proven, for it was not he who published the notes.[60]

Wilkes's affair with Corradini came to an end at the Villa Pietracatella. Their disagreements began when she again pressed Wilkes to give her the settlement of two thousand pounds of which she dreamed. Her importunities were unfortunately timed, for she could no longer hide her pregnancy. Wilkes did a little calculating and realized that the child-to-be was not his but had been conceived during the two months they had been separated. Suspicion falls upon the man Wilkes referred to as "a pretended uncle," who had escorted Corradini and her mother from Paris to Bologna and was now living in Wilkes's house.[61]

Corradini made no fuss over Wilkes's refusal of the settlement but asked him to send her home to Bologna to have the child. He said no, there was no reason she could not do her lying-in at Naples. She finally agreed, said Wilkes, but "resolving in her mind, with true Italian artifice, the future plan of her conduct." Wilkes's new friend, the erstwhile Jacobite Major Ridley, had fallen ill, and Wilkes, taking his man Brown, went to visit him on the island of Ischia, intending to stay the night. In the evening, a servant of a neighbor arrived and told him that Corradini and her family were packing up her things and stealing his, but officials at Naples knew what was happening and were ready to act on his complaint. He answered that "Corradini had always been perfectly free . . . that she was incapable of stealing anything but hearts." He thus forestalled the arrest. When he got back to the house, Corradini, her mother, and her alleged uncle were indeed gone, as were his silver and other portable objects of value. Wilkes wrote to tell Boswell what had happened. He put up a brave front as "a laughing philosopher," but how often could a man with a face like his have a lover that looked like Corradini? His heart was broken—as broken as the heart of a libertine can be.

Then, unexpectedly, Wilkes's attention was drawn toward political events in England. He heard that the king was negotiating with Pitt to form a new government. Lord Temple wrote, addressing him as "Most celebrated exile": "I congratulate you on the hopes which you entertain of an approaching pardon, in this world at least." Wilkes decided to return to Paris to be closer to the scene of action. On 27 June 1765, old Stanhope brought his ear trumpets down to the Naples harbor to hear the farewells. Wilkes, Major Ridley, now recovered, and Brown sailed for Marseilles on a "wretched French Tartan, loaded with laths."[62]

Wilkes found an excellent companion in Major Ridley, who like Wilkes had been ejected from a military life he had enjoyed. With such a man Wilkes could talk easily about disappointed love. Weather kept the boat from making Marseilles, and it landed at Toulon. The two old soldiers made their way through a "wild and savage country" to Marseilles, which they reached on 8 July. There Wilkes tried to heal his heart with "a life of dissipation" among the women of Marseilles, who he found were "not to be reproached with cruelty."

Wilkes and the major continued together as far as Grenoble, where they parted company. From Grenoble, Wilkes took a brief trip to the Monastery of the Grande Chartreux, where he made the following entry in the monks' album: "I was charmed with the hospitality and politeness I met with, and edified by the conversation of the *père général* and the *père coadjuteur*. The savageness of the woods, the gloom of the rocks, and the perfect solitude, conspire to make the mind pensive, and to lull to rest all the turbulent guilty passions of the soul. I felt much regret at leaving the place and the good fathers, but I carry with me the liveliest sense of their goodness. John Wilkes, *Anglois*."

On 29 July 1765, Wilkes arrived at Geneva. Although, as he told Polly, he found the mountainous environs beautiful, he thought Geneva "the most melancholy and disagreeable city in the world. . . . But what adorns the neighborhood of Geneva beyond the rest of the world is that it possesses a divine old man, born for the advancement of true philosophy and the polite arts. I mean Voltaire, who has done more to free mankind from the gloomy terrors of superstition and to persuade the practice of humanity and benevolence, than all the philosophers of antiquity. He possesses a fund of gaiety and humor which would be remarked in a young man, and he joins to it such immense stores of literature as age only can acquire." Wilkes said, perhaps exaggerating, that he "passed some weeks" in Voltaire's company. He told Voltaire he was "the first genius of the age," and Voltaire told Wilkes, "You set me in flames with your courage, and you charm me with your wit." "He put me to the blush," Wilkes told Polly, "by the many compliments he paid me. . . . I do not know when I have been so highly entertained."[63]

Wilkes received letters from Corradini at Geneva, but "the laugh of Voltaire banished all the serious ideas [he] nourished of love and the fair Italian," and he declined to answer her.

On 21 September, Wilkes, packed and ready to depart from Geneva, went to say farewell to Voltaire. Voltaire told him, "Sir, you must either live in London, or Paris, or Heaven, or Hell. You must be in one of these four places, no matter which." Wilkes replied he was going to choose Hell because Voltaire, in his ribald poem about Joan of Arc, the *Pucelle d'Orléans*, "puts there the very best company, most of the popes, many cardinals, almost all kings."[64]

Wilkes arrived in Paris on 29 September 1765, "happy in the thought that I am once more near my native London," and his head full of possibilities: "I cannot tell what the womb of fate is big with." Like the gentleman he conceived himself to be, he once more put up in the expensive Hôtel de Saxe. The next day, "I dined at the good baron's," he wrote to Polly, "and there were a thousand inquiries after you. . . . The baron and I are more intimate than ever." But he was homesick for his daughter and told her he was pondering how to get her back to Paris. Polly replied sweetly, "Let us wait patiently for the great events of time."[65] She was at ease with her mother and grandmother, though she did not trust them. Worried that they were nosing about her letters, she told her father to write her in care of Uncle Heaton.

That Parisian autumn Wilkes was called upon by a young man who was destined to play a large role in his life. This was John Horne, remembered today as John Horne-Tooke because he later took the name of an admirer who left him his fortune. Horne was a brilliant man, a political theorist, a legalist, and some think the founder of modern English philology. But Boswell, no slouch of a judge of character, found him vulgar and supercilious, unused to polite company, and offensive in his opinions. He had a blind eye and was dressed in an elegant suit. Because Horne was so well dressed, Wilkes did not learn until a few weeks later that he was in holy orders, the parson of Brentford, the county town of Middlesex. It turned out that Horne kept a stock of stylish suits in Paris, and whenever he went abroad, he traded his clerical black for silk brocade. Wilkes was Horne's idol, and he was eager to help in any way he could. Wilkes, delighted to make an ally of such an intelligent man, was soon calling him "a gentlemen whose friendship he [Wilkes] ranks among the honors and blessings of his life." Alas, they would in time become bitter enemies.[66]

In January 1766, Boswell, passing through Paris on his way home, sought out Wilkes and for the first time saw a Wilkes who was less than cheerful, "a little sunk by distress," Boswell wrote. Wilkes was trying to cheer himself up by rereading Catullus and Voltaire's *Pucelle d'Orléans*. Boswell too was melancholy, for the news from Italy of the death of James Francis Edward Stuart, the Old Pretender, saddened him. It meant the end of all hope for the Jacobites. Then, on the 27 January, in Wilkes's parlor, Boswell picked up a copy of the *St James's Chronicle* and learned that his mother had died. "Quite stunned," he wrote in his journal. Contrary to his expectations, his religion gave him little consolation. Wilkes offered the traditional secular masculine comfort, a stiff drink, followed by what he hoped would be common sense balm: "Consider how you have avoided the pain of seeing your mother dying, and how you'll go back and comfort your father, and amuse him by telling of all you've seen." Boswell, not much comforted, went on about the shortcomings of his religion: "The Christian religion gives you nothing new but the resurrection of the body," he grumbled, to which Wilkes replied, "I care no more to be raised in the same body than in the same coat, waistcoat, and breeches." "You'll think as I do one day," returned Boswell. "Certainly," said Wilkes, "when you think as I do about government, I'll think as you about religion." But when Boswell got home to Scotland, he found that Wilkes's advice had been helpful. "I shall never forget your humane and kind behavior to me at Paris," he wrote. He had found Wilkes to be right about how to comfort his father, "and for once in my life have been of considerable use. . . . I never admired you more than when you tried to alleviate my affliction."[67]

Though Wilkes was much occupied with thoughts about politics, he was not going to deny Pego his carnival, as he had once told Churchill. *Pego,* as you may recall, was an antique word for penis. On 11 October 1765, the scandal sheet, "Anecdotes Gallantes," reported that Wilkes, despite his ugly face, had a very pretty mistress, La Damselle Crecy, who lodged in the rue des Boucheries St. Germain at the hotel Hambourg, whose faithfulness Wilkes had purchased with two elegant dresses, furniture for her apartment, and maintenance of 25 louis a month. In the spring, he was reported to be in love with a certain beautiful Mlle Chassagne, who had moved into Wilkes's lodgings in rue des Saints Pères as his housekeeper, and then absconded with his valuables. Shortly thereafter, there was talk of a mènage in the Faubourg St. Germain with a pretty Mlle Dufort.[68] But none of these accounts came from a reliable source, and little stock can be put in them, though who could doubt that Pego had his carnival?

In England, the negotiations with Pitt to form a new government had fallen through, and the king turned for help to his uncle, the Duke of Cumberland. As first lord of the treasury, Cumberland placed one of his horse-racing friends, the

Marquess of Rockingham, a decent man but inexperienced in government and not too bright. First lord of the treasury was the position usually held by the first minister, but Rockingham was little more than a figurehead for Cumberland, who presided at cabinet meetings and was the actual head. It was an unusual arrangement, and Wilkes, supposing that Rockingham really was the first minister, was excited and hopeful, for Rockingham had been on his side in 1763/64. Both new secretaries of state, the Duke of Grafton and General Henry Seymour Conway, had supported Wilkes in the past. Rockingham's new personal secretary, a brilliant young Irish author named Edmund Burke, was enthusiastic about Wilkes's program. Burke, who would soon enter the House of Commons and become the de facto leader of Rockingham's party, would move gradually into fame as one of the great men of the period. Though these men were well disposed toward Wilkes, they were wary of him.

His friends were excited by the thought that Wilkes might be given a diplomatic post, the traditional service for people heavily in debt. In August, Heaton Wilkes pressed his brother to tell him what diplomatic post would best suit him, to which Wilkes answered, Constantinople, a choice he repeated in August and October of the next year. Once he said in an offhand way he would be happy to serve as governor of Jamaica or, if that did not suit, the Leeward Islands would do, but he put little stock in the idea.[69]

Wilkes seems to have made plans for a secret trip to London in September, stopping for a night with a farmer in Teddington.[70] But it is doubtful he carried the plan through.

The Duke of Cumberland died unexpectedly on 31 October 1765, leaving Lord Rockingham fully vested as first minister. Rockingham spoke to William Fitzherbert, member for Derby, and asked him to serve as his minister in negotiations with Wilkes. Fitzherbert, a calm, reasonable man in his fifties, had gotten to know Wilkes at the Beef Steak Club, and in the ensuing months Wilkes, who considered Fitzherbert "the most benevolent of men," had written affectionate letters to him. Fitzherbert set off for Paris with an offer of an annual payment of one thousand pounds, which the ministers calculated would allow Wilkes to live comfortably in Paris and to pay off his debts there. Wilkes demurred: "The idea of an annual sum of one thousand pounds to be paid to me does not captivate my imagination." Besides, he had not been told where the money was to come from, and Fitzherbert had not been authorized to tell him. A government pension Wilkes could not accept, not after his satires of pensioners in the *North Briton*. A second negotiator was dispatched, Lauchlin Macleane, a highly intelligent Irish adventurer and libertine and an unabashed admirer of Wilkes. Macleane came to Paris, talked with Wilkes, and went back to London with a letter from Wilkes rejecting the offer. Wilkes suspected what neither of these gentlemen would say, that the ministers did not want him in England. Nothing had been said about seeking a pardon, which is what Wilkes thought he deserved. Knowing the ministry had the power to negotiate a pardon with the king, he wrote to Fitzherbert on 4 December, "I ought at the entrance into power of the present gentlemen to have had a pardon under the Great Seal without my asking it, and to have been indemnified as far as it could be for two years' sufferings. . . . I love and honor many of the present ministers, and would serve the cause of liberty in conjunction with them as well as my poor faculties permitted me." And then with a bluster unusual for him, he warned them that if they could not find employment for him, he might find employment for them: "One set of ministers I occupied a year and a half."[71]

Finally, Fitzherbert wrote to explain where the money would come from. The ministers were wealthy men who had no need of the emoluments that went with their offices; so from those emoluments they would make up a fund for Wilkes of one thousand pounds per annum. No one would be able to call it a pension or to say that Wilkes was being paid by public monies, but to receive this money, he would have to agree to stay abroad. Wilkes was furious: "I have rejected this proposal as clandestine, eleemosynary, and precarious. I demand from the justice of my friends a full pardon under the great seal for having successfully served my country. . . . I ask not the grace of a pension or of an employment. I ask justice, and from gentlemen who declare that I have been extremely useful and ill used, and that they are my friends."[72]

Wilkes's financial position was desperate. Cotes had sent no money for a year, and his brother was telling him not to return to England because he would be taken up for debt. The only reason he was not arrested for debt in Paris was a temporary respite given him by an English banker named Thomas Walpole.[73] He decided to take his chances and go to England. He longed to be with Polly again. In terms of politics, the time seemed right because opposition members of the House of Commons were preparing to present a bill to outlaw general warrants. With general warrants being talked about in the papers, it might be the time for the man primarily responsible for their abolition to seek a pardon. And it seemed like the right moment to ask help from Lord Temple. True, Temple had been reconciled with his brother, George Grenville, who for so long had been Wilkes's enemy. But it seemed that Temple had given up none of his political principles and had brought his brother back to the liberal political views they had originally shared. The two were making common cause against an even greater enemy of Wilkes, their brother-in-law, Pitt.[74]

In the company of a Captain Ross of the Forty-fifth Regiment, Wilkes landed at Dover on 12 May 1766. As soon as he was recognized, the townspeople set the church bells a-ringing, and the local dignitaries hustled together a delegation to pay their respects.[75] He hurried to London and into hiding at the house of a Mr. Stewart, a friend of Burke's, in Hollis St., Cavendish Square.

Wilkes was full of unrealistic ideas about what the ministry might do for him. Wanting to keep straight with Lord Temple, he asked Almon to go to Temple and to tell him that "nothing under Heaven should induce him to do any thing that would give that noble Lord a moment's uneasiness." Temple returned a message: he was pleased with Wilkes's conduct and wished him well, but he feared the Rockingham ministers were deceiving him. The bishop of Carlisle summed up the situation in a letter to Grenville: "The ministry are embarrassed to the last degree how to act with regard to Wilkes. It seems they are afraid to press the king for his pardon, as that is a subject His Majesty will not easily hear the least mention of; and they are apprehensive, if he has it not, that the mob of London will rise in his favour, which God forbid."[76]

Burke, being asked to help, joined Fitzherbert in negotiations that went on for three weeks, telling him "your matters will be made very easy in a few days" and urging him to return to Paris. But Wilkes was firm, demanding an unconditional pardon, a pension of fifteen hundred pounds per annum on the Irish establishment, and a grant of five thousand pounds to compensate him for his sufferings.[77] They regretted that the ministers could not agree to that and pressed him to accept a payment of one thousand pounds and to return to France.

Then Wilkes received an unexpected financial blow: Cotes had lost the money he had been holding for Wilkes. He had used it to try to forestall a bankruptcy, but he was doubtful he could succeed. All he could give Wilkes at the moment was £20, when in fact he owed him £487.[78]

Wilkes left London on 31 May 1766. Polly went with him. They did not ask permission of her mother or grandmother. Polly did not say goodby. She and her father just left. Polly, of course, was more than willing to abscond with the person she admired and loved more than any other in the world.

As soon as they reached Paris, Wilkes went to his old banker, Thomas Foley, and without giving any notice to Fitzherbert, drew two bills for five hundred pounds on him. We would say that he wrote two checks on Fitzherbert's account with Foley, a device that was legal and would be honored if Fitzgerald did not object. When questioned by his brother, Wilkes insisted that the transaction was that of gentlemen, he acting on a promise of Fitzherbert, but that the banker had turned it into a harsh transaction by giving Wilkes the money and then making a legal claim against Fitzherbert. The act surprised and confused the ministers since Wilkes had not accepted the terms of their offer, but they were so glad to be rid of him that they made good on the bills. Later, when he was quarreling with Horne, he asserted, "I never did receive from them either pension, gratuity, or reward," but it was a lie.[79]

Mrs. Mead, alarmed at Polly's escape to her father, sent for her lawyer and told him Wilkes had kidnapped her granddaughter. The lawyer wrote to Polly and Wilkes, explaining that the father had no right over the daughter because as an outlaw, he was "dead"; the right was in the mother. Wilkes laughed and told his friends, the lawyer said the right was in the mother, "but nature told her the contrary." In a kinder mood, he admitted that the Mead-Sherbrook family "dote upon her," yet "I do not choose she should, on the verge of seventeen, be with them, because I would not have them choose a husband for her instead of her father."[80]

Polly was glad to be in Paris again and to see the baron and baronness, M. and Mme Helvétius and their daughter, her good friend. But she did not forget her duty to her mother, to whom she wrote regularly. Polly was now an accomplished young lady. She spoke impeccable French and was able to read Latin, German, Spanish, and Italian.[81] She was widely read in French and English literature and knew many of the great authors in the other languages. A talented artist, she often sent her father drawings, which he framed and hung. Her manner and dress were refined, and she was well trained in the ballroom dances of the day. But she had her father's prognathous jaw, and she was beginning a growth spurt that would leave her exceptionally tall.

Wilkes's debts began to grow at a faster rate now that he was supporting Polly. Wilkes wrote Burke, thanking him for his efforts to work out a treaty with the ministry and making mention of the drafts for the money he had drawn. He was in Paris, he said, "feeding among the lilies, in a state of trifling amusement, but casting my longing eyes towards England. . . . The great object of my hopes is a pardon, which I wish to owe to his Majesty's goodness, and to the favour of our friends." Burke replied on 4 July, "Your offers of service are most obliging; and they are understood as they ought to be. But hitherto the system of the next winter is not so clear as to point out any regular digested plan of measures either in the offensive or the defensive." The message was oblique but unmistakable: the Rockingham administration was going to let him rot. "Am I to be left in perpetual exile?" he wrote to ask Fitzherbert; "am I to continue out-lawed?"[82]

Then another change in administration stirred Wilkes's hopes. In July of 1766, Rockingham was dismissed, and August Henry Fitzroy, third duke of Grafton, was brought in as first lord of the treasury. Wilkes presumed, as did most people, that Grafton was now first minister, but he was mistaken. Pitt had been made first minister, but he was so afflicted with gout he could not attend to the daily administration and declined the traditional office. Instead, he took the position of privy seal (the place Temple had once held), which brought him into the cabinet, where he would preside as first minister. The day-by-day management he delegated to Grafton, who was moved to first lord of the treasury. As might be expected, the king now elevated Pitt to an earl-dom, and we must hereafter refer to him as Lord Chatham.

It was an odd arrangement, and Wilkes, like many others, did not fully understand it. Grafton was a man of Wilkes's age, exceedingly handsome, of no great ambition, more interested in horse racing than in governing but with an interest in religion. He was incorruptible, wanting to gain nothing for himself or friends; but as time would prove, he did his job in a desultory manner, giving too much time to sports. He needed a guide, but Chatham was suffering from depression and provided all too little leadership. But in July of 1766, Wilkes was excited that a man with a temperament like that of Grafton should be coming into what he presumed was the highest office. He had spent more than one afternoon dining with Wilkes's circle of friends and had been especially close to Churchill, who on his deathbed had willed a memorial ring to Grafton. Though he did not know Wilkes well, they had dined together several times, he had taken part in the protest against Wilkes's confinement in the Tower of London, and he had stood up for Wilkes when the House of Lords debated the Essay on Woman.

Another member of the new ministry was Charles Pratt, who as chief justice of the Court of Common Pleas had released Wilkes from the Tower and presided over the printers' suits: Pratt, now made Lord Camden, would be lord chancellor. Wilkes wrote to Cotes, "I am sure I shall now have justice done to myself as well as to the great cause, in which I have been so deeply embarked, and for which I have been so long and so deep a sufferer. I hope a full and free pardon will immediately be granted me, and I should have leave to return to England by the first post."[83] But the real power here was not Grafton, but Lord Chatham, and Chatham had declared he had nothing to do with so scandalous a person as Jack Wilkes.

Grafton's brother, Colonel Charles Fitzroy, member for Bury St. Edmunds, came to Paris and met Wilkes at the Hotel d'Espaigne: "He did me the honor of assuring me, that I should find his brother my real and sincere friend, extremely desirous to concur in doing me justice, that he was to tell me this from [Grafton], but that many interesting particulars relative to me could not be communicated by letter."[84]

Wilkes hurried to Calais, but he had misgivings about crossing. "I have no joy in the near prospect of being in my capital," he wrote to Suard. "I have the spleen. I am every hour going farther from my daughter and drawing nearer to my wife." He landed at Dover on 28 October 1766 and arrived in London the next day. Heaton invited his brother to stay with him, but Wilkes preferred to stay in Wigmore Street, briefly with a John Tharpells and then with William Wildman, Parson Horne's brother-in-law, who was proprietor of the Opposition Club.[85]

Wilkes, in the expectation that this ministry would seek a royal pardon for him, asked Fitzherbert what steps toward that end he should take. He was told to write to Grafton, which he did. Waiting for a reply, he wrote to his daughter, "I beg you not to restrain yourself in any pleasure or convenience. I will ever contrive for you as nobly as I can. . . . Always keep a corner in your heart for your affectionate father."[86]

Then the reply came. Although Grafton did not say so, he had taken the letter to the king, who looked at it, returned it, and said nothing. Grafton had then showed it to Chatham, who advised him to ignore it. He could not ignore it entirely, for the government had been negotiating and Wilkes was pressing for a reply. So Grafton sent an oral message by Fitzherbert: "Mr. Wilkes must apply to Lord Chatham; the Duke of Grafton did nothing without the concurrence of lord Chatham." Chatham! Apply to Chatham, Wilkes could not do. Chatham had cast him off and reviled him on the floor of the House of Commons. Moreover at that very moment Chatham had broken "violently" from Lord Temple.[87]

That same day Wilkes left London. On 11 November he wrote to Heaton from Calais, "I arrived here yesterday after a bad passage of twenty hours, buffeted by Boreas, drenched by Neptune, and in some danger of paying a visit to Pluto by water. . . . like a true philosopher, I will endeavor to make the best of untoward events, and draw good out of evil."[88]

Wilkes would, in fact, draw considerable good out of this evil. Within three weeks he had published *A Letter to His Grace the Duke of Grafton*. He impugned Grafton for misleading him but reserved his battery of cannon for Chatham. As William Pitt, this man had been "the favorite character of his countrymen," but now as Chatham, his "flinty heart" is revealed, "his glorious sun is set, I believe never to rise again." Pitt, he revealed, had once declared to Thomas Potter how charmed he was by the bawdy poems Wilkes had written, and then called Wilkes a blasphemer when it suited his politics. Wilkes reviewed Pitt/Chatham's career from the time they had together exposed the treachery of Spain in 1761, to the time Pitt had viciously turned on him when Wilkes was expelled from Parliament in 1764. He wrote with the passion that had once electrified his essays in the *North Briton* and, throwing caution to the winds, sent it to the press without having it vetted by a lawyer. He dated the letter 12 December 1766 and published it in Paris within days of the writing. Less than a week later it appeared in England. Newspapers all over England began to print excerpts, and the *Public Advertiser* printed the entire piece. According to Heaton, the *Letter* destroyed what little reputation Chatham still had: "I hear he is so provoked and storms so much his friends talk of its having had the effect on him of driving him mad."[89] As to Wilkes, the *Letter* so vastly increased his popularity that it provided, said Peter D. G. Thomas, "the springboard for his future career."

But Wilkes was not cautious. At the very time his star was rising, he managed to offend Lord Temple again. Wanting to take advantage of the situation to enhance his image in England, Wilkes sent to the press a long letter he had written to Temple in October 1762 after the duel with Lord Talbot on Bagshot Heath. Now, four years later, it appeared in the *Political Register* and the *St. James's Chronicle*. It did wonders for Wilkes's public image, evoking notions of courage and manliness, suggesting his status as a gentleman of the old school who lived by a code of honor. But Talbot, who came off so badly in the letter, was furious to have it made public and accused Temple of sending it to the papers. The confrontation took place in the lobby of the House of Lords, and Talbot was so insulting that Temple had actually drawn his sword when others stepped in and forced a peace treaty. Temple was furious with Wilkes. Wilkes tried to weasel out of the situation by giving his lordship a trumped-up story of how he had printed a few copies for friends in Geneva that got out of hand, but that was certainly a lie, as everyone saw. If the letter did worlds for his image, it came close to depriving him of a patron.[90]

In February Wilkes learned that Cotes had indeed gone bankrupt. "I cannot express to you," he wrote Heaton, "the anguish of my heart on Mr. Cotes's account, and I am the more miserable because I cannot in any way alleviate his misfortunes." Cotes had asked Wilkes to forget all financial transactions, as he could offer no payments. Wilkes had lost over five hundred pounds. Wilkes took the precaution of removing from Cotes the powers of attorney he had given him; but he did not desert his friend.[91]

Wilkes's finances were now desperate. He had no money whatsoever, and no more was forthcoming from the ministers. Lord Temple had sent him nothing, and the news of Cotes's bankruptcy had brought out Wilkes's creditors crying to be paid. So Wilkes turned his attention to selling his history of England, on the idea of the history, which his brother had told him had generated a great deal of interest. On 13 July 1767, he signed a contract with Almon that would pay him two hundred pounds at once and another three hundred when he would turn in the manuscript of the first volume in January of 1768. But the deal was a scam. When January arrived, Wilkes turned in an introduction of thirty-nine pages that was little more than a political polemic on the Stuart monarchs that he could have written in a day or two. Almon, seeing he had been gulled, pulled his own scam on the public. Hoping people would buy the introduction in expectation of what was to come, he published the thirty-nine pages under the title *The History of England from the Revolution to the Accession of the Brunswick Line*, volume 1. Impecunious though he was, Wilkes without a blush indulged himself in hiring "a little country house in the Bois de Boulogne," where he could retire to write.[92]

By 1768, when Wilkes emerged from his banishment, the world understood that if one wanted the friendship or the services of John Wilkes, one must accept that he was completely irresponsible about money and would tell a bald lie to put off a creditor or to make a new one. About this, Wilkes never felt guilty: he was a gentleman, and gentlemen had a right to live as such. No doubt he found in the concept of gentleman an entitlement that others could not discover. On the other hand, when it came to his political ideals, he never compromised, and he never sold himself to his enemies. No one else on the political scene, his supporters believed, had the hardihood to stand up to ministers and judges, and if they made it possible for him to enter the political arena again, he would again prove their champion. They would not be disappointed.

The day Wilkes arrived to take possession of his cottage in the Bois de Boulogne, he found it "filled with flowers from the number of nosegays our friends sent us in the style of this country." He sat down and wrote a poem to Polly for her seventeenth birthday. He called her Maria, but at that time anyone named Mary, which was Polly's given name, was entitled to the name Maria.

> Again I tune the vocal lay
> On dear Maria's natal day.
> This happy day I'll not deplore
> My exile from my native shore:
> No tear of mine today shall flow
> For injur'd England's cruel woe;
> For impious wounds to Freedom given,
> The first most sacred gift of Heaven.
> The Muse with joy shall prune her wing,
> Maria's ripen'd graces sing,
> And at seventeen, with truth shal own
> The bud of beauty's fairly blown:
> Softness and sweetest Innocence
> Here shed their gentle influence;
> Fair Modesty comes in their train
> To grace her sister Virtue's reign;
> Then to give spirit, taste, and ease,

The sov'reign art, the art to please,
Good humored wit, and fancy gay,
Tomorrow cheerful as today,
The sunshine of a mind serene,
Where all is peace within, are seen,
What can the grateful Muse ask more?
The gods have lavish'd all their store . . .

Sitting in that cottage, he began to write a memoir of his political experiences, but, as he told his brother, it was to be published only after his death.[93]

By the end of 1767 Wilkes had decided on an incredibly bold and unusual step that would address both his weakness and his strength. He would go to England and offer himself as a candidate for a seat in Parliament in the general elections scheduled for March 1768. He had asked John Dunning and John Glynn about the legalities, and they had been sifting the laws. They had concluded that an outlaw could be elected to Parliament legally, though "it would not go smoothly." He was determined not to represent a rotten borough, even if some wealthy person were to offer him one; he would be chosen by *voters*.[94]

If Wilkes won, parliamentary privilege would protect him from his English creditors. His Parisian creditors he just abandoned. It seems likely, however, that they were paid off by Polly when she was grown and had come into her fortune. She made many trips to Paris in those years, and it is doubtful she could have been comfortable knowing her father owed money to many merchants there.

The City of London sent four members to Parliament. To qualify as a candidate, one had to be a member in one of the City companies, as the remnants of the medieval guilds were called. Wilkes would get himself admitted to a company and offer as a candidate for the City. Pleased with the plan, he set to work. He wrote to Sir William Baker, a London alderman of great influence who was retiring as member for the City, sent him a draft of an election speech, and asked his support. His plan got leaked to the *Public Advertiser*, which ran an anonymous letter saying it was known "from good authority" that Mr. Wilkes was planning to stand for City of London even though he was an outlaw. Wilkes had not sent the letter, but he heard that the effect of it was advantageous.[95] Such striking news was picked up and repeated by newspapers all over England, and John Wilkes was back in the political picture even before he had reentered the country.

Wilkes's friends were astonished. His old fellow writer for the *Monitor*, Arthur Beardmore, who had closely watched past London elections, wrote to discourage him. The ministry, Beardmore explained, would use their large block of City votes to put in their two candidates; the remaining four candi-

dates had been campaigning vigorously; and there were not enough uncommitted voters to elect Wilkes. "I fear you are only amusing yourself." Others of
his friends cautioned him to be prudent. "What the devil have I to do with
prudence?" Wilkes answered. "I owe money in France, am an outlaw in England, hated by the King, the Parliament, and the bench of bishops, pursued by
the courts of law, the ministers, &c, &c. What do you talk to me of prudence
for? I must raise a dust or starve in a jail."[96]

Though he was not about to say so, Wilkes did not *expect* to be elected, but
he was not just amusing himself. If, without an organization, without a canvas, without a patron, he could run in the election, speak from the hustings,
shake hands with the voters, he would show the world that the ministry was
afraid to stop him and that he was a viable political force. That would open
possibilities.

Wilkes was so sorely pressed by creditors in Paris that he would have to get
out of France soon. His friends in London were planning to solicit subscriptions to a trust fund to pay off his English debts. Sir William Baker thought
that his London creditors would let him alone for now so that he could establish himself and gain some income. The king's ministers would turn a blind eye
to his political activities, knowing that if they were to persecute him, he could
get himself elected, said Baker, "in half the constituencies of England." But the
House of Commons might raise a rumpus: so he should not come before
Parliament was dissolved.[97] Wilkes could no longer hold himself back. He
would take Polly to her mother, make plans with his friends about the election,
and then go to Holland, where he would wait for Parliament to be dismissed.

Wilkes and Polly left Paris in the middle of the night on 30 November 1767
and three days later crossed the Channel. Wilkes was never to set foot in
France again. A year later, the trying days in Paris blocked from memory, he
sent a nostalgic letter to Suard: "By God, I will write a treatise to prove against
Seneca and Bolingbroke the advantages of exile, for I was never so happy,
neither before nor since, as during the time of my exile and outlawry."[98] The
Icaruses of this world are adept at deceiving themselves.

On 1 December, Wilkes and Polly arrived at Wilkes's mother's house. There
they held secret meetings of advisers and lawyers. His mother drafted a petition to the king from a "widowed mother" asking a pardon for her son,
though it was never used. There being no point in continuing the fight with the
Mead-Sherbrookes, he sent Polly directly to her mother and grandmother
Mead, who received her "with great kindness," Polly wrote.[99] Their legal hold
over her was drawing to an end: in August she would reach the age of eighteen
and no longer be a minor.

Unwilling to appear in public, Wilkes did not go to the opera to see Corradini dance in the corps de ballet, though he knew she was there. He asked Heaton to deliver ten guineas to her "and to let me know how the young one is."[100]

On 6 December, three weeks after he had arrived, he embarked for Holland, arriving in Harwich the next day. "We will have no retrospects," he wrote to Heaton; "we start from this point, our laurels our own and fairly won, and posterity ours." Three days later he took a boat down the coast to The Hague and in a precautionary move set off for Leyden. Because university students could not be arrested for debt, on 23 December 1767 he enrolled as a student of law. The rector magnificus, delighted that the famous John Wilkes had returned, wanted to confer upon him a law degree, but Wilkes, thinking he did not really deserve a law degree, declined: "Am I not, dear Heaton, a singularly modest young man?" He returned to The Hague. "The Dutch torment me with compliments," he wrote to Polly, "they are thronging around me to see if I am like my print, which they have." "I skate almost every day, and amuse myself much with so noble an exercise."[101]

Late in December, Wilkes was approached by the unsavory, now-defrocked John Kidgell, who in 1762 had delivered the proofs of the Essay on Woman to Lord March. When the truth had come to light in the House of Lords, Kidgell had been attacked in the press and abused to his face as an informer and eventually ousted from his parishes. Seeing that the great lords whom he had served had no intention of protecting him, he had fled to Holland. He was in a poor state of health and was eking out a living in Utrecht as a tutor and translator. He had been trying to blackmail Lord March and Lord Halifax by threatening to give Lord Chief Justice Mansfield or Wilkes the information that there had been a forgery in the government edition of the Essay on Woman. March and Halifax had ignored him, of course. Kidgell now approached Wilkes, but not to make good on his threat by giving Wilkes the information: that was not Kidgell's style. He had come rather to sell the information to Wilkes. Wilkes just laughed and made fun of him.[102] Kidgell went back to Utrecht, where his life petered out in abject poverty.

By 8 January, Wilkes was in Rotterdam. "The Maese is the great river which comes to Rotterdam," he wrote to Polly. "You cannot imagine how gay a scene it is at present from the number of *traineaux* of one and two horses, with ladies covered with furs of all the dyes of the rainbow; ice-boats sailing up and down, the skaters, the booths, &c. All Holland is now alive."[103]

Four days later he received a letter from Polly: "I wish I had your happy talent of writing. My letters might then be entertaining, but when there is one in a family like you, it may be compared to the moon and the stars, which latter are not worthy of being looked at or taken notice of, were it not for their accompanying so glorious an object as the former."[104]

Impatient and restless, Wilkes did not wait for Parliament to be dismissed, as Sir William Baker had advised, but on 7 February secretly crossed the Channel. "Remember always," he wrote to Heaton, "in politics, as in war, great and bold actions succeed, when more cautious fail."[105]

9

The Middlesex Election Controversy

On 8 February 1768, John Wilkes, an outlaw, penniless and in debt over head and ears, surreptitiously entered the City of London and went to the house of his sister, Mary Hayley, to embrace his daughter, his mother, his brother Heaton, and others of the family. A few days later, assuming the name of Osborn, he moved to the house of a Mr. Thompson in Masham Street near Dean's Yard. For reasons unknown, Matthew Brown, the faithful servant, had disappeared from Wilkes's life, but he had a new man, Samuel Dyer, hired for him by John Lee, a zealous follower. Dyer waited until dark to bring him his linens.[1] Friends came to him cautiously — George Onslow, William Fitzherbert, Sergeants Glynn and Dunning, Dryden Leach the printer, and Parson John Horne.

On 11 March, when Parliament was dismissed, he came out of hiding, confident the ministry had no desire to arrest him. He hired rooms in a house belonging to a Mrs. Henley in Prince's Court. Wilkes would spend many years in Prince's Court, though not always in the same house. The court was a small square with a central garden enclosed by an iron fence. It bordered on St. James's Park at the place where Bird Cage Walk comes to an end. The space is now occupied by the Institute of Mechanical Engineers. As a residence, Wilkes's rooms were nothing like the fine, large house around the corner on Great George Street from which he had once operated his printing press; but the rooms cost him only two and a half guineas a week.[2] No doubt his admirers paid the rent.

Wilkes made few appearances in public, but he stirred the pot, sending off to the newspapers paragraphs about himself and the injustices done him. Andrew Miller, the printer of the *London Evening Post*, wrote, promising to print accurately any papers Wilkes wished to send him and to keep their origins secret. Printers from the *St. James's Chronicle* began to pick up papers from him three times a week. Most of his creditors left him alone, but not all. His mother wrote to an old acquaintance, a Mr. Lainthill, asking him not to press her son for payment of his debt just now.[3]

On 4 March, Wilkes addressed a "submission" to the king asking for pardon. He was criticized for sending this petition by his man to be delivered to a servant at the palace door, instead of following the tradition for individual petitions, which was to have them carried to a levée by some highly placed person. Wilkes's petition was returned unopened. Perhaps Wilkes sent it in this casual way to make sure it would not be opened, for its value to him was the opportunity for publicity. The petition soon appeared in the press. He had heard that Lord Temple was "much out of humor" with him, but he wrote to him anyway, telling him he was prepared "to take a decided part with respect to the next Parliament," asking his advice, asking permission to see him. Temple, who was angry about the letter describing the duel with Talbot, did not answer.[4]

In early March, Wilkes released an address to the City electors. His outlawry notwithstanding, he would offer himself for one of the City seats in Parliament, qualified as the fighter for liberty, the man who had set the people free from general warrants. He would submit himself to "the good nature of my fellow citizens." In the next few days, he sent to the papers a battery of letters addressed "to the printer" as well as select items that would enhance his image, such as the speeches he had made before the Court of Common Pleas in 1763. A debate broke out in the newspapers whether an outlaw could legally stand for Parliament. The betting odds that he would lose were ten to one until it became known that he was backed by Sir William Baker, when the odds rose five to one for a win.[5] At Aylesbury, there was a joyous celebration when the people learned that their old squire was determined to reenter Parliament.

In the City of London, on 13 March 1768, the Company of Joiners and Ceilers admitted Wilkes to membership. At the climax of the ceremony, they presented him with a box "of the heart of true English oak, like his own" that contained a certificate of his freedom of the City of London.[6] The purpose of the Joiners and Ceilers on this particular day was to qualify Mr. Wilkes to stand for Parliament, and the freedom gave him the right to vote and to stand for office. Most other cities granted freedoms to men not associated with a company, but in London the freedom was given only to livery or in rare cases as an honor.

The Company of Joiners and Ceilers was one of some sixty "livery companies" of the City of London that had evolved from medieval guilds. The members were called "the livery" for the traditional costumes they wore on ceremonial occasions. In the far past, the official status of a guild member was that of a servant to the nobleman who sponsored the guild: so they wore the particular uniform, or livery, of that particular nobleman. Shakespeare and his company at the Globe, you recall, wore the livery of the Lord Chamberlain and then of King James I. The Joiners differed from the Company of Carpenters in that carpenters used nails whereas joiners used wood pins, glue, and mortises and tenons. The ceilers were wood-carvers. It was typical of the City to include not only craftsmen, but men of the middle class, even the elite of the middle classes, such as bankers, traders, and owners of factories. Eight thousand liverymen pretty much ran the City of London.

Wilkes was admitted "by redemption," paying fees of two pounds for the freedom and twenty pounds to become a member. After the ceremony, the company moved to the King's Arms Tavern in Cornhill for a banquet. The King's Arms became that night Wilkes's election headquarters, if a man who had no party can be said to have a headquarters. The ministry let him alone, for as Lord Camden explained to the Duke of Grafton, an imprisoned Wilkes would win any election, and the ministry would bear the blame.[7] He began to refer to himself in his propaganda pieces as "John Wilkes, joiner."

The City of London was the most politically advanced and dynamic constituency in Great Britain, and it had a strong influence upon neighboring constituencies.[8] Kings and their ministers had long competed with great nobles and their factions for control of it. In the coming election, seven candidates would vie for the four City of London seats in the House of Commons. Two were called ministerial or court candidates, or just courtiers. One was backed by Lord Rockingham, two by Lord Bute, and one by Pitt. Then there was Wilkes. The others had good financial support and had been campaigning for weeks. Wilkes had no money, no patron, and no party.

Wilkes was nominated at a pro forma meeting of livery at Bow Street Church, and voting commenced in the Guildhall on 16 March. In those days the Guildhall was crowded in by old timber buildings. A mass of people packed the narrow streets and squeezed into the hall. James Boswell, good journalist as he was, though never called such, had come to observe: "Went to Guildhall to see the poll for members. It was really grand. Harley (Lord Mayor), Beckford, Trecothick, Sir Richard Glyn, Mr. Deputy Paterson, [he failed to mention Sir Robert Ladbroke] and Mr. Wilkes all stood upon the hustings, that is to say, a place raised by some steps at one end of the room. They had true London countenances. I cannot describe them. . . . The confusion and noise of the mob roaring 'Wilkes and Liberty' were prodigious." The candidates made speeches from the hustings, Wilkes dressed in "dark blue with metal buttons." No doubt he used the trick he had mastered by which he could gain the attention of a mob when greater orators could not. He would shout, "Independence! — Property! — Liberty!" and when the voters grew silent to hear more, he would commence his address: "I stand here, gentlemen, a private man, unconnected with the great and unsupported by any party. I have no support but you: I wish no other support: I can have none more certain, none more honorable." Though Wilkes could write an appealing speech, his delivery was poor. One wonders if he did not try to fend off criticism by releasing the news story that appeared about his mediocre speaking abilities. Lord Mayor Harley, himself one of the candidates, spotted a tall young woman in the gallery who was attracting the attention of the voters, who kept cheering and clapping for her. It was Polly. Harley ordered the chamberlain to clear the gallery, but he was refused.[9]

Following custom, the first vote was taken by a show of hands. Up went the hands, the largest number by far for Wilkes. But someone protested that half the people in the hall were not qualified to vote, which no doubt was true; so a poll was begun.[10] Nearly twenty thousand liverymen would cast their votes during the next seven days, each having his name checked against a list, each sworn on the Bible, each signing a poll book to indicate his choice. The only poll in the British Isles that could count more voters was Westminster.

Wilkes appeared on the hustings every day, talking to the voters, answering questions. It was noticeable how those who chose him tended to be the poor liverymen. At one point someone told him that one of his followers had voted for him twice, having disguised himself the second time by turning his coat inside out. "Impossible," said Wilkes; "none of my people has a coat to his back." This lumpen proletariat, delighted finally to have a candidate who promised to stand up for them, paraded about blowing horns and waving banners. At the end of the first day, as Wilkes was entering his coach, they unhitched the horses and pulled the coach themselves to the King's Arms. Unfortunately, they then used the horses to pull down the house of one of their enemies, an act for which Wilkes was blamed in the House of Lords. On the second day, he scribbled a note to Jean-Baptiste Suard, "I am now in the midst of my brother joiners, carpenters, soap-boilers, distillers, &c, &c, and we are polling away at a great rate. My troops are high spirited and think it good generalship to keep back their fire. . . . In racing you walk, then gallop, then urge all the fury of the course. It remains to see if we can come in first, or even second, which I wish for the point of honor. . . . I have gained fresh laurels and at St. James's Palace the character of firmness, temper, calm dignity and conduct." When the polls were stopped for the night, the mob seized Wilkes, seated him in a sedan chair, and hoisted it onto their shoulders. There was a tradition of chairing the winner of an election, but when Wilkes protested that he had not won, they cried, "By God, Master Wilkes, we'll carry you whether you carry your election or not."[11] From then until the polls closed on 23 March, Wilkes was transported to and from the Guildhall and his headquarters in Cornhill in a sedan chair carried above their heads by the mob.

Only a few of those who could be called gentlemen supported Wilkes, but those few worked hard for him. During the week of voting, they opened in a Lombard Street bank a fund for the payment of Wilkes's personal debts and ran advertisements soliciting subscriptions. A few subscribed for £100 and £150, but the fund did not go far toward liquidating Wilkes's mountain of debts. A second fund was opened to pay his election expenses, and that one attracted more subscribers: it rose to £1,227.[12]

Wilkes lost the election. Of the seven candidates, he came in last. The two ministerial candidates were elected, as was Pitt's man, Beckford. Rockingham's candidate, an American named Barlow Trecothick, came in fourth. The two followers of Lord Bute lost out. A great many votes for these candidates had been promised before Wilkes entered the contest.

The results were announced at the Guildhall late in the afternoon of 23 March. The candidates spoke to the crowd from the hustings, the last one being Wilkes, who railed against the ministerial party for chicanery and attributed his losing to his late entry. "I am not in the least dispirited," he cried. When the shouting died down, he announced that he would stand for the county of Middlesex. The great cheer was followed by sounds of fighting, for a mob was struggling to get into the Guildhall. Wilkes wound up his speech with a plea to keep the peace. When he finally emerged from the hall and climbed into a coach, a cheering throng took off the horses and drew the coach through the City.[13]

Even before the City poll had closed, Wilkes had sent a note to the *Public Advertiser* announcing his intention to stand for the County of Middlesex. Middlesex, no longer found on the map because in 1965 taken into the Greater London administrative area, was then the county on the north shore of the Thames that included Westminster and London. Wilkes intended to stand for one of the two Middlesex Knights of the Shire. Counties, as distinct from the boroughs within them, were represented by knights of the shire, two for most counties. These were the most prestigious seats, and Middlesex being such a powerful county, its two seats were generally reckoned the most prestigious of all. The electorate, as in all counties, was defined by a statute of 1430 that gave the vote to freeholders whose properties and tenements were assessed for the land tax at the annual value of forty shillings. To stand for knight of the shire, a candidate was supposed to be possessed of properties that returned an income of *six hundred pounds per annum*. Wilkes still had some Middlesex property he had inherited (land could not be claimed to pay off debts), but it is questionable whether he had enough. The requirement was so often violated that proof was seldom demanded.[14]

Two candidates had already been nominated, William Beauchamp Proctor, a barrister and the squire of the village of Tottenham, and George Cooke, a ministerial candidate who held the lucrative post of joint-paymaster of the armed forces. During the election, a crowd displayed a banner reading, "More meat and fewer Cooks." Until his defeat in London, Wilkes had kept his plans for Middlesex a secret. Proctor and Cooke, expecting to be elected without opposition, had not organized a campaign, while Wilkes's friends were geared up and ready.[15] The nomination by a group of gentlemen and clergy was quickly done.

Polling was to take place in the town of Brentford, west of Westminster, at the Butts, a square beside the magistrate's court on the bank of the River Brent. The Butts can still be found, a charming square with Georgian houses on two sides, though now cut off from the river by a boathouse and from the court building by row houses. Being larger in those days, it could accommodate the hustings and a sizable crowd of voters. Though voters were to come in from all over the county, most would come from the residential and industrial suburbs of Westminster and the City of London. The sheriffs, who were required to serve as polling officers, had seen to it that hustings had been set up and had readied fifteen poll books, five for each candidate.

The Wilkites, as some began to call them, had two election centers, the one Wilkes had already established at the King's Arms in Cornwall, the other east of the City at the Assembly Rooms in Newtown Mile End. Mile End, familiar to us as a rundown area into which have crowded waves of immigrants, was then a village in which middle- and upper-class Londoners had their suburban houses. In the City, Wilkes had many friends among the printers, and it was easy to get the twelve thousand handbills that would be distributed. On the 26 March, the towns were "festooned in blue, the Wilkite color."[16] John Horne, being the parson of Brentford, had booked in advance the best inns and taverns, where the voters could be entertained and in whose stables and pens their horses could be recruited. Horne provided much of the brains of this organization and a great deal of the labor, for he was a man of great energy as well as intelligence.

The number 45 as a symbol of liberty had its beginning in 1763, when Wilkes was arrested for *North Briton* No. 45, but it was in this brief election campaign that it shot up like a rocket which then burst in air. Overnight all England and the American colonies as well became aware of "45," symbolizing simultaneously the abstract idea of liberty and the most concrete of persons, a cross-eyed outlaw who was its champion. Both meanings were readily grasped by illiterate masses who understood numbers and images better than letters. Moreover, it suggested an animus against the Scots, for it recalled the defeat of the Scottish army in the Rebellion of 1745–46, popularly called the '45.[17]

By five o'clock on the morning of election day, the Wilkites had taken control of the Great West Road, which led to Brentford, which was located thirteen miles west of Hyde Park Corners. Boswell, setting out for Oxford that morning, recorded, "All the road was roaring with 'Wilkes and liberty,' which, with 'No. 45,' was chalked on every coach and chaise."[18]

Colors too had their symbolic value, and the mob forced everyone who was walking or riding to put a blue cockade on his hat, that is, a blue knotted ribbon. Candidates were expected to provide transportation for folk who needed it and would promise their votes. The *Public Advertiser* and other papers ran announcements telling the Wilkite voters where they might get carriage rides. Some cabbies volunteered their services and vehicles, but John Almon, who planted himself at Hyde Park Corner, loaded up carriages with people who promised to vote for Wilkes, gave each a handbill, and then paid for the coaches himself. The handbills contained an appeal for order. Most of the morning passed peacefully, but when some of the opposition hoisted banners reading "No Blasphemer" and "No French Renegade," the Wilkite voters attacked them. The skirmish quickly ended, but the Wilkites began smashing the windows of the carriages of the Proctor and Cooke people and then painting "Wilkes and Liberty" on them. A few people in high station called this intimidation, but elections were often rowdy, and no official complaints were lodged.[19] At Brentford Butts itself, the crowd was quiet and orderly.

Wilkes arrived at eight o'clock in a coach in which several ladies and children were riding. He took his place on the hustings and chatted with the people while waiting for Proctor and Cooke, for it was customary to begin the voting only when all the candidates were present. According to one newspaper, "The freeholders were frequently impatient, calling out for the poll, and Mr. Wilkes as often addressed himself to the public, requesting their patience."[20] Proctor finally appeared; and a relative of Cooke's showed up to represent him, for he himself was at home in bed with the gout.

There were brief speeches from the candidates. Wilkes reiterated a promise he had made in the newspapers, that if he were elected, he would turn himself in to the attorney general.[21] The world would see that he was obedient to law. But of course he was hoping that the ministry would give up the pursuit of a member of Parliament-elect or that, if they did send him to prison, he would be released on parliamentary privilege. But Sergeant Glynn must have advised him of the frightening risk. Outlaws had no rights, and an outlaw in prison was a prisoner for life and could be hanged by the sheriff at the whim of the monarch.

It had been agreed in advance there would be no voting by show of hands, so the polling began, the candidates talking to the voters as they approached the hustings. The voting was quiet and orderly, and it was remarked that none of the voters seemed to be intoxicated. One man spat out at Wilkes, "I would rather vote for the Devil than for you," to which Wilkes replied, "And if your friend is not standing?" Fewer than three thousand freemen voted. By four o'clock in the afternoon, anyone who had watched the hustings and the poll books knew that Wilkes was so far ahead that his victory was inevitable. Elated, he scribbled a note to his mother, "Tomorrow morning the numbers are to be declared. I am the first on the poll." He then asked those of his supporters who had not yet polled to cast their votes for Cooke. As Horace Walpole put it, "Wilkes was too triumphant to be resisted; and, master to act as he pleased, he threw his supernumerary votes to Cooke, who was elected with him." Many voters did not wait for the announcement of the results but, certain that Wilkes had won, hurried toward London with the news. As Walpole reported, "Wilkes spread the word that he wanted the peace preserved and ordered the returning procession not to pass St. James's Palace so as not to offend the king."[22]

At seven o'clock, the sheriffs made a proclamation for all freeholders who had not done so to come forward to cast their votes. None appearing, they closed the polls. At nine, just as night was closing in, they announced the results. Proctor had lost, with 807 votes; Cooke was elected with 827; and Wilkes was at the top with 1,292 votes. Wilkes at once mounted the hustings and in the light of many torches, forgetting his speech impediment, he shouted a victory speech: "Let the sons of venality bow the knee to the idol of sordid interest. Let them call their pusillanimity prudence, while they ignominiously kiss the rod of power, and tamely stoop to the yoke. . . . You, gentlemen, have shown, that you are neither to be deceived nor enslaved. . . . The eyes of the whole kingdom, of the whole world, are upon you, as the first and firmest defenders of public liberty."[23] He refused to be chaired but hurried off toward London to try to keep order among the freemen that were surging toward the metropolis.

Wilkes had been elected not by squires and clergy, but by shopkeepers, artisans, and journeymen; and they, having found at last a leader and a voice, went wild with joy.[24] All Brentford was "illuminated" on Monday night, candles in every window, and every door and shutter along the roads marked with the number 45. Knots of Wilkes's people marched joyfully along the Great West Road by torchlight, each mysteriously supplied with chalk or whitewash to mark No. 45 on every door and carriage. Most of the crowd moved toward London, but some headed west. Benjamin Franklin, who traveled the next day from London to Winchester, found No. 45 marked on doors with hardly an exception for fifteen miles, and intermittently for the remaining fifty miles to Winchester.[25]

At London the voters were joined by a mob of the disfranchised poor, crying "Wilkes and Liberty," and "45 forever." Houses were illuminated all along the Strand and Fleet Street. A mob grown to several thousand stopped coaches and forced the passengers to huzzah for Mr. Wilkes, threw dirt and stones at those who resisted, forcing them to cheer for Wilkes and liberty. They stopped Walpole's carriage, and when he did not lower the glass window fast enough, they smashed it. They arrested the coach of the French ambassador and, handing him a glass of wine, ordered him to toast "Wilkes and Liberty," which he did most cheerfully standing on the steps of the coach. They asked the same of the Austrian ambassador, Count de Seilern, "the most stately and ceremonious of men," and when he refused, they lifted him out of his carriage, turned him upside down, painted the number four on the sole of one shoe and number five on the sole of the other. The next morning, said Walpole, he stormed into Whitehall complaining bitterly, but "it was as difficult for the Ministers to help laughing as to give him redress."[26]

Here and there, celebration turned into riot: the mob smashed the windows of Lord Bute's palatial house. Marking Lord Mayor Harley as the enemy because he had beaten Wilkes in the City election, they attacked the Mansion House, smashing the windows with rocks. It was rumored that the government had started to call out the troops but thought better of it when they discovered that some of the regimental drummers were beating the drums for Wilkes. Things quieted down during the night, but the next day the mob rose again and that night demanded every house in London to be lighted up. Despite the damage to houses, Walpole had to admit that the tumult had "ended like other election riots, and with not a quarter of the mischief that has been done in some other towns."[27]

"It is remarkable," said a letter in the *Public Advertiser* of 1 April, "that on no occasion was there ever before seen such universal rejoicing amongst all rank of people, not even excepting the Peers of the blood." It is difficult to credit this last point unless the writer meant the six-year-old Prince of Wales, who, when he was angry with his father, ran into the king's dressing room and shouted, "Wilkes and Liberty!"[28]

The rejoicing was not confined to London and Middlesex. At Aylesbury the bells began ringing at noon on 30 March and had not stopped twenty-four hours later; there was dancing, drinking, singing, and bonfires all night; the windows of houses were either lit up or smashed.[29]

Rejoicing, of course, was not universal. The pious Alexander Cruden, who had just published his great concordance to the King James Bible, began taking a bucket of water and a sponge on his daily walks and whenever he saw "45" on a door, tried to wipe it out. William Rough told a story about those signs showing Wilkes's face and cast eye that were hung out by taverns and inns. "He was accustomed himself to tell with much glee of a monarchical old lady, behind whom he accidentally walked: looking up, she murmured within his hearing, in much spleen, 'He swings everywhere but where he ought'; he passed her, and, turning around, politely bowed." Alexander Wedderburn, the solicitor general, who was on his way up the ministerial ladder toward the lord chancellorship of England, damned Wilkes's followers as "a beggarly, idle, and intoxicated mob without keepers, actuated solely by the word *Wilkes*, which they use as better savages do a walrus, to incite them in their attempts to insult Government and trample upon law."[30] A walrus?

Wilkes's opponents would have been astonished had they been able to see how future historians would mark the Middlesex election: "If a date is to be found for the beginning of the democratic movement," wrote Josef Redlich and Francis Hirst, "the historian will choose the years of Wilkes's election and rejection, 1768–69."[31]

As soon as he could get away, Wilkes went to Bath. He may have enjoyed taking the waters once more in the place he had so often visited as squire of Aylesbury, but his appearance was in part political. The ministry, he now knew, would not arrest him when he was among the mob. Would they arrest him when he was among the mighty? They did not. He was snubbed, of course, but he expected that. Charles Pratt, who in the Court of Common Pleas had freed Wilkes from the Tower, was there, though he was now Lord Camden and lord chancellor of Great Britain. He and Wilkes caught sight of one another in the Pump Room. "Neither of them spoke or bowed to the other," said Thomas Wheately, "but both stopped and stared in such a manner as to set the whole room in a titter."[32] Wilkes could hardly address so great a personage as the lord chancellor, and his feelings were mixed: he admired Camden and was grateful to him, but he resented his joining the ministry. Camden's feelings were ambiguous because he had to be true to the ministry, but his sympathy for Wilkes's cause was not dead, as later events would show.

Letters for Wilkes began to arrive from France. D'Holbach and Crébillon and others of that table sent congratulations and encouragement. Chastellux wrote, "The baron d'Holbach and his entire society were strongly concerned with your affairs. . . . I have a thousand compliments to give to you on their behalf." Diderot wrote, "Your quiet and peaceable demeanor does you infinite honor; and your generous and patriotic principles will render your name immortal." But from their position of comfortable subversion, few of the philosophes could grasp what Wilkes was up to. Most of them advised moderation, something Wilkes knew would accomplish nothing. Friedrich Grimm was the most enthusiastic, Suard reported: "What he hates the most after God is the Kings, and he regards you as a hero of political atheism."[33] This was far from the mark, for Wilkes was loyal to both king and church.

In keeping with his promise, Wilkes wrote to Thomas Nuttall, solicitor for the Treasury, informing him that he would give himself up to the King's Bench on the first day of the next session, which would fall on 20 April. It was time to test the law of parliamentary privilege. The ministers were not happy to have Wilkes at the center of another public event. They were faced with "a hydra," Lord Camden wrote to the Duke of Grafton that morning, "multiplying by resistance and gathering strength by every attempt to subdue it. As the times are, I had rather pardon Wilkes than punish him." Grafton did not agree. Fearful of rioting when Wilkes was brought to the court, Grafton had seen to it that soldiers were in readiness in four stations about the town, while justices of the peace with their constables were waiting at Westminster guildhall, St. James's Coffee House, and the Church of St. Clement Dane in the Strand. A rumor went around that the soldiers had been supplied with sixteen rounds of ammunition. Wilkes had sworn "he would be carried down to the court on the shoulders of the City of London,"[34] but he thought better of it. A cheering throng ran beside his coach and greeted him as he approached Westminster Hall, but they kept the peace.

The Court of the King's Bench met in its accustomed venue, the medieval Westminster Hall, on that portion of the floor reserved for it and set off by removable screens. Lord Chief Justice Mansfield and two other judges, in black robes and white wigs that dangled to their waists, sat elevated on a dais, the clerks at tables before them, the spectators before the clerks or above them in the part of the gallery that offered a view. One of the judges was an old acquaintance, Edward Willes, formerly a member of Parliament for Aylesbury, the younger brother of Wilkes's friend John Willes.

Wilkes was escorted into the court by his brother Heaton, several friends, and four lawyers, including John Glynn, hobbling on a gouty, bandaged leg. Lord Mansfield, as was his custom, began by inviting Wilkes to make a statement. Wilkes took out the speech he had prepared. He had been arrested, he said, for libel in the *North Britain,* written by "he did not know whom," and containing not one false word but expressing "duty and affection to the king." He was accused of publishing a "ludicrous" thing called An Essay on Woman, of which only twelve copies had been printed off on his own press "for the sake of merry laughing friends," but before it was given them, it was "stole." "He hoped God would forgive the jury who had found him guilty of publishing what had never been out of his possession." He then protested Lord Mansfield's changing the record of his indictment on the day before the trial by striking out the word *purport* and substituting the word *tenor*, thereby prejudicing the jury. This shocked William Strahan, the celebrated printer, who was among the spectators: "The criminal, even there, at the tribunal of justice itself, becomes the accuser; and in an insolent speech, which to the amazement of all who heard it, he was permitted to make, he charges the Chief Justice himself, to his face, of having illegally and unconstitutionally altered the record!" King George, when he was told of the speech, was furious. What Wilkes had said in court, he told Lord North, was "reason enough" for the House of Commons to expel him without delay. The public was delighted with the show. The next issue of the *Gentleman's Magazine* featured a foldout engraving of a cocky Wilkes standing before three sober judges (illustration 11).[35]

What followed astonished the entire assembly. Lord Chief Justice Mansfield pronounced that there was no accused person before the court! Someone stood there who, he had been told, was an outlaw, but to the bench he was a nonperson. He did not know him. This nonperson was free to leave. Lord Mansfield then turned to William De Grey, the new attorney general, and berated him for failing to make a legal arrest under a warrant of *capias ut legatum* and failing to bring the person named in the capias to the court so he could be recognized. Mansfield's purpose in this nonsense was political. He was casting the blame upon De Grey for allowing Wilkes to run about free and get himself elected to Parliament. The spectators, however, assumed the court had been afraid to arrest Wilkes, and a jubilant mob took possession of him as soon as he stepped out the door. He managed to get into a nearby coffeehouse and out the back window, and he and some friends sneaked off to Vauxhall Gardens for a quieter celebration.[36]

The capias ut legatum, usually called the wolf's head warrant, was issued the next day. The name was an anomalous holdover from the Middle Ages, when it had been a warrant to kill the outlaw. Fortunately for Wilkes, the law had changed, and he was in no danger of the dagger. Lady Mary Coke went to the opera, where she was told, "Mr Wilkes has been arrested for a thousand pounds, but that the debt had been immediately paid. He seems to have some very good friends." Days passed and no one else arrested Wilkes. The king

Gen.^t Mag. May 17 68.

John Wilkes Esq; before the Court of King's Bench.

11. "John Wilkes Esq, before the Court of King's Bench," *Gentleman's Magazine*, 17 May 1768. Courtesy of Gerald M. Goldberg.

wanted to know why. He was told, lamely, that the capias was good only in Middlesex, and Mr. Wilkes had gone to visit his friend Sir Joseph Mawbey in Surrey.[37]

Wilkes was never arrested on the capias. Instead he himself sent notice to the attorney general that he intended to come into court again, on 27 April. He duly appeared with his entourage, was arrested by a messenger, and taken to the room of the court chamberlain. After a short while Attorney General De Grey came in and asked, "Are you really in custody?" Wilkes assured him he was. So De Grey brought him before the judges, and at last he was recognized as someone before the court who could be sentenced for the crimes of libeling Parliament and Crown in *North Briton* No. 45 and libeling Bishop Warburton in the Essay on Woman, crimes he had been found guilty of four years before when he had been tried in absentia. On this day, 27 April 1768, the court decided it needed more time to consider. Sentences would be pronounced on 18 June.[38]

Lord Mansfield then remanded Wilkes to the King's Bench Prison. Parliamentary privilege was out of the question because, though elected, Wilkes had not been sworn in. Sergeant Glynn pulled himself up on his gouty legs and said that Wilkes was prepared to meet bail. Attorney General De Grey rose to say he was evoking his right under the law to veto the application for bail. Wilkes jumped to his feet and said he did not want to be bailed. As he later told Lord Temple, he would continue to refuse bail because he wanted to be obliged to no one except Lord Temple. Some doubted that Wilkes had decided to refuse bail before the attorney general vetoed it, but Lord Temple believed him. Wilkes probably had heard that Temple was no longer angry with him. Three days before this court scene, Lord Temple had said about him, "His persecutions had been great, and though his faults were enormous, he had suffered abundantly, and his lordship will continue to defend the laws and rights of this country against any attack whatever."[39]

Wilkes was taken prisoner by three tipstaves who bustled him into a hackney coach and set out for the prison. On Westminster Bridge, they were stopped by a mob. Wilkes pleaded with the people not to unhitch the horses, but one of them cried, "I tell you, Master Wilkes, horses often draw asses, but as you are a man, you shall be drawn by men." As they were unhitching, Wilkes advised the tipstaves to make a getaway while they could and promised he would show up at the prison as soon as possible. They took the advice. "Mr. Wilkes," he later wrote, "had that day the happiness of preserving three lives, although perhaps not the three he would have chosen from the whole species." The people turned the coach around and pulled it back into Westminster. A number of constables and justices of the peace were waiting at Westminster Hall but declined to interfere because, they said, there was no violence. The crowd pulled the coach past St. James's Palace, through the Strand, through Temple Bar into Fleet Street and finally to the Three Tuns Tavern in Spitalfields, where they commenced a noisy celebration. Wilkes patiently calmed them down and asked them to disperse, but to no avail. When night fell and the crowd thinned, Wilkes managed to slip out a back door in disguise and went straight to the King's Bench Prison. Wilkes had begged to be arrested, begged to be judged, and then, abandoned by his guards, had disguised himself so that he could surrender himself to the turnkey.[40] He had made a laughingstock of the Court of the King's Bench.

A week later he wrote to Suard from prison, "I have saved three lives last Wednesday, which I hold to be the most glorious day of my life. Such a rescue, such a triumphant entry from Westminster to Spitalfields. . . . I am king of this great people, and will reign for their good. I am you know a mad-man for liberty, and I have glorious schemes to be adored by more than this age."[41]

The King's Bench Prison, which had been moved to its location in St. George's Fields only a decade before, was a dreary place in 1768, not yet the colorful and notorious little town within walls that it would become. Most of the inhabitants were imprisoned for debt, though Wilkes belonged to a sort of elite group who had been prosecuted by the Crown. Those without money lived in miserable conditions, taking turns begging at the gate. But those who could afford them had comfortable rooms. Someone provided the money, and Wilkes was put up in a ground-floor suite in the State House, which formed part of the outer wall close to the gate. His windows were barred but looked out upon St. George's Fields, a broad expanse of open land between South-wark and Lambeth used for large gatherings of all sorts, sometimes for military drill, sometimes for ceremonial greeting of arriving dignitaries, sometimes for family picnics. To the south he could see the corner where the road to Westminster Bridge met the road to London Bridge. The two bridges were roughly equidistant from the prison. Samuel Dyer, his manservant, lived with him and ran his errands outside the walls. Inside, two canaries sang from cages that Polly had hung up for him.[42]

On the first morning, Wilkes awoke to the sound of people milling about outside the prison. When he looked out, a large crowd sent up a great cheer. A letter was brought to him from Lord Temple:

> I little thought that I should ever pay a visit to the King's Bench Prison; but the same opinions which carried me to see you in the Tower now incite me to take an opportunity . . . of returning my thanks to you in person for your sober and discreet conduct of yesterday, manifested in a dutiful submission to the law, though carried on against you with the most unnecessary rigor. . . . Though I have not seen you for many years, yet I shall bring with me the same heart, warm for the support of the just rights and dignity of the crown and for the defence of the constitutional privileges of Englishmen, violated in so many instances in your person. What will be the most convenient and quiet time for you to receive me?[43]

Wilkes's friends began to arrive at the prison in numbers, there being no restriction on visits. He had "an infinite crowd of visitors," he told Suard, and some of them enjoyed the first of several sea turtles that would be sent him in prison: "Yesterday I gave a great dinner of a turtle to several ladies and gentlemen here, with burgundy, claret, Madeira, etc., and was as gay as you ever saw me. I have my choice of all the dear girls of this country . . . but great plans of ambition fill my soul, and the rest is only my whisk or picquet, or what you please."[44] Dear girls mean nothing to Jack Wilkes? The great plans of ambition, however, were no delusion.

Wilkes's visitors brought him the papers and kept him informed about politics. There was nothing to hinder him from continuing his propaganda, and he lost no time in turning out new polemics. He released an open letter "To the Gentlemen, Clergy, and Freeholders of the County of Middlesex": "In this prison, in any other, in every place, my ruling passion will be the love of England and our free constitution. For these objects, I will make every sacrifice."[45]

Wilkes's popularity rose higher and higher. Except for the minor squires and clergy, virtually all of the "middling sort" thought of him as their hero. His every move had been reported in newspapers, not only in London, but in dozens of cities and in the American colonies. According to the historian Stella Duff, "Wilkes was discussed and quoted in the *Virginia Gazette* more than any other single man." A day or two after his imprisonment, his fans at Newcastle in the north of England made a festival in his honor:

> The company consisted of 45 gentlemen. At 45 minutes past one, there were drank 45 gills of wine, with 45 new laid eggs in them. Precisely at 45 minutes past two a very genteel dinner was served up, being five courses, nine dishes each, which made the number 45. In the middle of the table the figures of 45 were inlaid with mother of pearl, on which was placed a noble sirloin of beef weighing 45 lbs. The tablecloth and plates were marked 45. On the back of every chair these figures were carved, and exactly 25 gilt nails on a chair, which with the 20 on each chair, 45. The whole concluded with a ball in the evening, when 45 ladies entered the room; then the dances immediately began; and each lady was saluted at the end of every dance, which were nine minuets, with nine quadrills, and nine cotillions, and 18 country dances, being in the whole 45. After the ladies had been kissed round that number of times, and 45 couple of jellies were eaten, the company retired with great mirth and festivity at 45 minutes past three o'clock.

"In china, in bronze, or in marble, he stood upon the chimney-piece of half the houses of the metropolis," said William Rough, writing in 1803; "he swung upon the sign-posts of every village, of every great road throughout the country." According to a modern historian, sleeve buttons and breast buckles showing No. 45 appeared in the markets. Coins and medals, ceramic punchbowls, snuffboxes, mugs, brooches carried number 45. A wigmaker of Romsey in Hampshire advertised "my new-invented Cork Peruke of 45 curls," and a Worcester staymaker presented Polly with a corset of stays "of 45 pieces or quarters, 45 holes and the no. 45 beautifully marked on the stomacher."[46] Although few of the "meaner sort," as the gentry called the working class, could afford such items, they too adored Wilkes. Most of the crowd that stood cheering by his prison window were of this meaner sort, honest laboring men and women.[47]

Wilkes was never cozy with his constituents or fans, and the middle and lower classes never thought of him as their own. He was a gentleman of a higher class who was willing to stand up for the rights of those below him in rank. They had not forgotten the stories about his libertinism, the Essay on Woman, and the hellfire club, but most of them just did not care. Thomas Hollis, the Puritan book collector and benefactor of Harvard College, wrote, "I am sorry for the irregularities of Wilkes; they are, however, but spots in the sun." Wilkes's public understood, as John Almon put it, that "the foibles of his private life affected no public interest."[48]

Among the journeymen and apprentices and coal heavers who stood cheering outside the prison were ill-fed, ragged people who cheered as loudly as any, the impoverished poor. Not knowing where else to direct their anger, they directed it against Lord Bute, and not knowing whom else to look to for help, they looked to Mr. Wilkes. Even robbers and pirates wore Wilkite cockades of blue in their hats as they were carried in black carts to the gallows.[49]

"The crowd always want to draw themselves from abstract principle to personal attachments," wrote Burke, "and since the fall of Lord Chatham, there has been no hero of the mob but Wilkes." As to Bute, the people were actually misled. George Grenville and the Duke of Bedford had elicited a promise from the king to have no more political dealings with Bute, and the king, punctilious man that he was, was keeping his word.[50] But the public, including many highly placed persons, knew nothing about such a promise. What they saw was Bute still dabbling in City politics. How were they to know that it was on his own hook? They were convinced he was still directing from behind the curtain.

The only power the poor possessed was the threat of riot. The imprisonment of Wilkes brought that power to a head such as England had not experienced since the peasant riots of the fourteenth century. Walpole called the mob "the third House of Parliament."[51]

In 1768, Wilkes's power base was this frightening mob. Wilkes has often been called a demagogue, but he was never the sort that would harangue the crowd, work them up to a pitch, and then lead them to riot. On the contrary, he had done his best to hold down the election riots. He sometimes exercised a peaceful control that would have been completely ineffectual were not the people already keyed up in the cause of liberty and waiting for directions: he would call them by means of handbills passed out in the streets, asking them to escort him to the court the next morning, or some such request. He seldom, if ever, made speeches to the mob other than from the hustings, and when he did speak from a window or carriage, he always accompanied his words with a plea to hold down their violence. For all that, the ministers knew that if John Wilkes wanted to do so, he could spark a riot any time he chose. And experience had shown how mob violence could spread from town to town. The government, said David Hume, was more fearful of Wilkes than of the Catholic powers of Europe.[52]

On the first of May, Lord North held a meeting of the most influential of the king's party to decide what to do about Wilkes, but the only thing they could agree on was to exclude him from the House of Commons. The cabinet told the king they concurred. The king was pleased and wanted to put the plan into effect. He urged them all to agree in advance upon the "exact mode of obtaining the expulsion." Excluding Wilkes, said his majesty, would "curb that levelling principle that has been of late years gaining ground and restore that due obedience to law and government which this constitution has so wisely formed as the sole means of preventing liberty from degenerating into licentiousness."[53] In this belief, the isolation of George III from his people was all too apparent. Neither the king nor his ministers could see what a legal and political morass they were stepping into, and excluding Wilkes from Parliament would only anger the mob.

The mob was especially dangerous at this juncture, but for reasons that had nothing to do with Wilkes. England was entering an economic depression, and that in a time of harsh weather conditions. In the winter of 1768 the Thames froze over. The price of bread had risen steeply. The Spitalfields weavers and coal heavers of Shadwell and Wapping were disputing over wages and work conditions. The sailors, on strike for higher wages, prevented ships from sailing, a situation that threw the coal heavers out of work. The two were soon battling each other. A succession of labor disputes followed, including the watermen who took fares up and down the river. Many highly placed persons attributed these difficulties to Wilkes, but as historians today understand, they had economic and meteorological origins unconnected to the popular prisoner.[54]

The king and ministers were nervous about the suffering of the poor but did nothing to relieve it. No one thought government was obliged to settle labor disputes or relieve hunger. All they could understand was the possibility of riot and the necessity of suppressing it. Parish constables could not contain riots, and the Crown did not command enough soldiery to meet multiple crises.

The ministers watched nervously the people gathered outside the King's Bench Prison that morning. The shouts of "Wilkes and liberty" mingled with shouts about the cost of bread and beer. Some were heard to cry, "It's as well to be hanged as to starve." On Friday, 6 May, the crowd outside the prison was so large and noisy the ministry decided to call in troops. Soldiers arrived, but nothing happened except that the people obliged one soldier to take off his boot, and this symbol of Lord Bute they gleefully burned. William Penrice, the turnkey of the prison, reported that the mob was having a good time: "humorous, mountebank performances . . . diversions and amusements . . . their fun, as they termed it."[55]

The next day Wilkes was to be taken to Westminster Hall to be present when his lawyers would plead for a reversal of his outlawry, but because all the marshals had been called out to control the crowds there was no one to escort him to the Hall! Lord Chief Justice Mansfield ordered a delay until 8 June. The disappointed mob outside the prison began to clamor for Wilkes's release. They "repeatedly called out to come to them and no one should hurt him . . . they would fetch him out if he would come." He told them through the window that he really could not do that, but, unsatisfied, they broke down the outer door of the prison. Wilkes pleaded from the window, finally persuading them to leave; but they came back in the evening and demolished the prison lobby.[56] The next morning, which was Sunday, the crowd arrived to find soldiers on guard.

Mrs. Wilkes went to see her son that day. This intrepid woman made her way though "a prodigious number of people assembled about the prison," some seven thousand she was told, all cheering loudly whenever her son came to the window. "They hung a boot on a long pole," she reported, "and wrote on it, 'No Boots,' and paraded about with it." There were two lines of soldiers with bayonets fixed, "but no outrages at all were committed." At one point, the crowd discovered that a man cursing her son was a Scotsman, said Mrs. Wilkes, so they "forced him to kneel and holloo Wilkes and liberty."[57]

In the early morning of Tuesday, 10 May 1768, the day set for the opening of Parliament, an even larger crowd gathered, expecting Wilkes to be fetched out and taken to the House of Commons. The guard was changed at ten in the morning, and the third regiment of foot guards came on duty, unfortunately a Scottish regiment. The hours passed, and when no one came to fetch Mr. Wilkes, the crowd grew restless and surged around the entrance. The warders, fearing the walls might be breached and prisoners might escape, encouraged the soldiers to push the people back. The officers ordered the guard to fix bayonets. A troop of horse guards arrived but stopped on the edge of St. George's Fields. The crowd began to insult the soldiers, which only caused the foot guard to advance, beating the people with the butts of their guns.

A man in a red coat being particularly offensive, a detachment was sent in pursuit of him. The soldiers chased him into a cow barn, and, seeing a man in a red coat, they shot him dead. They had killed the wrong man. The dead man was William Allen, the son of the innkeeper of the Horse Shoe, who had been working in his father's barn.[58] Word of Allen's murder, as it was called, spread among the people, who began to throw stones at the soldiers.

Two courageous justices of the peace, Daniel Ponton and Samuel Guillam, made their way through the crowd and stationed themselves close to the prison gates. Guillam read the riot act, which announced that anyone continuing to disturb the peace would be subdued or arrested. The crowd responded by hissing and throwing more stones. Guillam cried, "Don't you know the riot act has been read? For God's sake, good people, go away; if I see any more stones thrown, I will order the guards to fire." The crowd grew more angry and violent. Guillam read the riot act a second time. A stone hit his chest. The crowd pasted up a paper on the wall of the prison. Guillam ordered the soldiers to take it down. People began yelling, "Damn the king, damn the Parliament, damn the justices!" A stone hit Guillam on the head; he staggered back, turned to the troops: "Fire!" The soldiers broke into quickstep and arranged themselves in three ranks; the first rank knelt and fired; the second fired standing. The horse galloped in firing pistols. Five or six people fell dead, some of them passersby who had stopped at some distance to watch what was going on. Most of the soldiers had fired over the heads of the crowd, and their balls arcing over the people came down at the distant road and killed some of those who stood watching.[59]

When the firing ceased, a silent crowd moved away from the prison to the barn. William Allen's body was brought out on a board slab and carried off by the crowd. They walked to London Bridge, crossed into the City, and bore the body about the streets "with signal lamentation," said Walpole. Unhappy crowds gathered at the Mansion House and Parliament buildings and along the docks and at industrial centers. Riots broke out and quickly spread. Five hundred sawyers tore down a new wind-driven sawmill in Limehouse belonging to Charles Dingley. The coal heavers began to riot; the Spitalfield weavers rioted. Two days after the shootings at St. George's Fields, London was in a state of virtual civil war. Benjamin Franklin was there, and on 14 May he wrote,

> This capital . . . is now a daily scene of lawless riot and confusion. Mobs patrolling the streets at noonday, some knocking all down that will not roar for Wilkes and Liberty; courts of justice afraid to give judgment against him; coal-heavers and porters pulling down the houses of coal merchants that refuse to give them more wages; sawyers destroying saw-mills; sailors unrigging all the outward bound ships, and suffering none to sail till merchants agree to raise their pay; watermen destroying private boats and threatening bridges; soldiers firing among the mobs and killing men, women, and children. . . . While I am writing, a great mob of coal porters fills the street, carrying a wretch of their business upon poles to be ducked . . . for working at the old wages.

George III threatened to abdicate.[60]

After a few frightening days, the crowds dispersed of their own accord. Though the industrial protests and violence had nothing to do with Wilkes, the mobs of these troubled day were collected in the minds of his enemies as "Wilkes's mob." Dr. Johnson, said Boswell, looked upon the riots with "a sovereign contempt." " 'Sir,' said he, 'had Wilkes's mob prevailed against government, this nation had died of phthiriasis.' " The word means an infestation of head lice.[61]

Wilkes's popularity took a quantum leap after the massacre of St. George's Fields, as the papers called it. A face with an in-turned eye appeared in a hundred papers and broadsides. Taverns changed their names to The Wilkes. In eighteenth-century England, honor was often conferred by invitations from clubs. Wilkes, though confined in the King's Bench Prison, was so honored by the Brotherhood of All Souls and the Society of Hiccobites. The Ancient Society of Leeches not only made him a member, but voted him a "Chief Counsellor." The Order of Bucks, a club of propertied gentlemen of Buckinghamshire, found a way to include their landless hero by voting him an "honorary brother." On 3 March 1769, he was initiated into the Freemason lodge of the Jerusalem Tavern, Clerkenwell.[62]

In America, Wilkes's trial and imprisonment were front-page news. At this juncture, Americans were groping for a way to live peacefully with their king and his ministers, and they held up Wilkes as an example of a manly, civil, rational person who stood for freedom, but abided by the law. The stories were told over and over of his calming the mob, his escaping from them to turn himself in at the King's Bench Prison, and his pleading with them not to break down the prison doors to rescue him.[63]

Even his enemies were impressed by the way Wilkes had tried to hold down the rioters and by the way he had obeyed the law, giving himself up to the court and refusing to allow the mob to free him. Lord Lyttelton, who had been so shocked by the "Essay on Woman," now expressed a high admiration for its reputed author. Benjamin Franklin wrote, "I believe that had the King had a bad character and Wilkes a good one, the latter might have turned the former out of his kingdom."[64]

On both sides of the Atlantic, ordinary people were growing more and more disgruntled with ministers and courts of law. The ministry may have been trying clumsily to keep the peace, but the time was passing when the public would be grateful for protection such as this. Keeping the peace at St. George's Fields looked a lot like tyranny.

In July, one soldier and Justice Guillam were acquitted of the charge of willful murder at St. George's Fields. The trial of two other soldiers accused of killings would not be held until August. The day after the "massacre," Lord

Barrington, a navy man serving as secretary of war, had written to the troops that had been on duty: "I have the great pleasure of informing you that his majesty highly approves of the conduct of both the officers and men; and means that his majesty's approbation should be communicated to them." Some weeks later the letter came into the hands of Wilkes, who sent it to the newspapers with an anonymous preface: the troops were thanked, he wrote, "for the rank and foul murders committed in these fields on the 10th of that month. My hand trembled while I copied it." Walpole commented, "The officious folly of Lord Barrington . . . shocked even those who were not factious."[65] Perhaps for this reason, no action was brought against the papers that published the letter.

On 16 May 1768, six days after the dreadful scene on St. George's Fields, Wilkes was again before the King's Bench for a hearing, not on the charge of libel, but on Wilkes's outlawry. The outlawry, his lawyers argued, was erroneous and his jailing unlawful because it was based upon an erroneous writ, dated from "the county court," when it should have said "the county court of the county of Middlesex." The judges needed time to consider the problem. A week later, on 8 June 1768, Wilkes was brought through ranks of footguards and horseguards to Westminster Hall to hear the outlawry reversed by a unanimous decision of the court. The decision benefited both sides. Wilkes was free of serious danger, and the court had cleared the way to sentence him for libel. To do so the court had to bring him back from the legal vacuum of outlawry and make him a citizen again subject to law. So the outlawry was outed and the way cleared for the court to sentence Mr. Wilkes. The judges chose to postpone that event until 14 June. Wilkes was put into a carriage; the crowd closed in and took possession of the vehicle and drew it to the prison.[66]

Wilkes at once sat down and wrote and sent off a letter to the Middlesex voters describing the outlawry as "an act of equal injustice and cruelty, from the very beginning erroneous and illegal. . . . My enemies have trampled on laws and been actuated by the spirit of tyranny and arbitrary power." When the lawyer for the government, Sergeant Nares, read this, he was so infuriated he came into the King's Bench to seek a warrant to arrest the printer, but Lord Mansfield, determined to keep the ship of state on steady keel, found nothing in the letter "that deserves censure."[67]

As soon as Wilkes was free of the outlawry, his lawyers restarted the suit against Lord Halifax that the outlawry had so long delayed. The government lawyers, however, were clever in putting off the case, which would not come to trial for another seventeen months.[68]

On 18 June 1768, John Wilkes was brought before the King's Bench to be sentenced for the crimes he had been convicted of when he was tried in absentia on 21 February 1764. Invited by the court to make a statement, he made a speech. He pointed out, quite correctly, that the authorship of *North Briton* No. 45 had never been established. He did not contest the accusation that he had written the Essay on Woman but insisted he had not *published* it. "Twelve copies of a small part of it had been printed in my house at my own private press. I had carefully locked them up, and I never gave one to the most intimate friend. . . . The government . . . bribed one of my servants to rob me of the copy, which was produced in the House of Peers, and afterwards before this honorable court." Sergeant Glynn produced a sworn affidavit from George Kearsley, the publisher of the *North Briton*, that all the evidence obtained from his house and used against Wilkes was obtained under an illegal general warrant and argued that the evidence against Wilkes was therefore invalid. But the argument fell on deaf ears since Lord Mansfield, as he had told the House of Lords, thought that illegally obtained evidence could indeed be used to convict a criminal.[69]

Then the two sentences were pronounced, not by Lord Mansfield, but by his associate, Justice Sir Joseph Yates. It was the practice at that time for a judge to accompany the pronouncement of sentences for capital or other heinous crimes with a sort of sermon, designed not only to shame the convicted, but to assure the public that the legal power of the state was being exercised morally for the benefit of the people. Justice Yates opened with a speech designed to justify the punishment for publishing the *North Briton* No. 45. Before the appearance of this paper, he said, the people of Great Britain were united and satisfied: "They saw and loved and admired their sovereign"; but "when this paper was published, what did it serve to produce but that spirit of riot which has gone through the whole land." (Wilkes, it became apparent, would be punished for causing all the troubles of the past five years.) Justice Yates continued: Because *North Briton* No. 45 encourages the people to redress their grievances, the essay "leaves it to the people to determine what is oppressive or not. . . . If we are taught that resistance is a spirit of liberty, instead of submitting to the law, every attempt to overturn it will be called justifiable." At this point, Wilkes took a large toothpick from his pocket and began to pick his teeth.[70]

Justice Yates then began his disquisition on the conviction for the Essay on Woman. He described the papers as a blasphemous strike at the heart of religion, "the precepts and terrors of which, overawing the consciences of men, are the ground on which every human government places its first hopes . . . never was there ever a purer system of morality than that which this poem traduces; it is disgusting to every virtuous ear. . . . Those friends for whose use it was designed are little obliged to you." (In the view of Justice Yates, the poems had been designed not for delight, pleasure, or amusement, but for "use," a word that could only suggest masturbation — a preposterous idea, for the Essay is not pornographic, but bawdy.)[71]

For libeling the king in No. 45, Wilkes was fined five hundred pounds and sentenced to a year in prison; the time was reduced to ten months because he had already served two. For libeling Bishop Warburton in the Essay on Woman, five hundred pounds and an additional prison term of twelve months. He also was required to post sureties for good behavior for another seven years, one thousand pounds from himself and five hundred pounds each from two people standing surety, the identities of whom were not recorded. "The severity of the sentence," said Almon, "was universally condemned . . . as cruel, malignant, and indefensible." Yet Wilkes had not been sentenced to stand in the pillory, ordinarily a part of the punishment for printing a libel. The attorney general did not ask it, though Lord Mansfield much favored it. No doubt the attorney general was thinking of what happened when John Williams had been pilloried for republishing No. 45 and had no intention of giving the public another image of Wilkes as martyr. Wilkes's lawyers did their best and appealed the sentences to the House of Lords, but on 16 January 1769 that august body rejected the appeals.[72]

On 8 August 1768, two soldiers were brought before a grand jury at the Surrey assizes at Guildford, charged with the death of William Allen in the barn next to St. George's Fields. Wilkes, summoned as a possible witness, arrived at nine in the morning in a post-coach, accompanied by a marshall and two tipstaves and followed by a train of coaches of his friends. The bells began to ring as the cavalcade approached, and people ran into the streets to cheer their hero. He was held in the cobbler's house, opposite the court, where the townspeople came bowing before him to present gifts of grapes, melons, plums, and one pineapple, which he saved for Polly. The court sent an order to silence the bells, but the bellringers held a meeting among themselves and decided that because the bells did not speak the words, "Wilkes and liberty," they could not be arrested for libel; so they returned to their ropes and began ringing peals. Or perhaps they did: the story is attributable only to Wilkes. Wilkes testified, but briefly. The grand jury was still sitting at ten o'clock in the evening when he was put into the coach to be taken back to the prison. He learned the next day that the two guards were not indicted because the soldier who actually shot young Allen had escaped. Many suspected the ministry had whisked him off. The other deaths at St. George's Fields, the grand jury decided, were caused by "chance medley."[73]

In a period when food was dear, it is touching that so many gifts of food should be given or sent to Wilkes in prison: a firkin of rock oysters, a Cheshire cheese, a loaf of sugar, a brace of fat ducks, turkeys, geese, fowls, fish, and fruits in season, etc. etc. Friends at Aylesbury sent him a cask of beer. A gathering of gentlemen in Maiden Lane sent a hamper of liquor and twenty guineas. William Hanzelle of Newcastle upon Tyne sent a whole salmon. In April, someone shipped him a 145–pound turtle. Sea turtles were much prized at the time, not only for their taste but because, in an era before refrigeration, they could be kept alive until they were to be cooked. A 145–pound turtle yields only 15 pounds of meat, but that much demanded a feast. Another turtle was sent in May, which resulted, the papers reported, in "a turtle feast for several persons of distinction." Wilkes soon became the most popular man in the prison, not for political reasons but because he gave the other prisoners what he and his friends could not consume. Much food and little exercise took its toll, and he put on weight.[74]

In June of 1768, Wilkes received a letter from Charlotte Forman, a Grub Street writer, as the age tended to call freelance journalists. A highly educated woman in her fifties but unmarried and without the protection of family, Mrs. Forman was struggling to make a living as a political essayist and translator. Her circumstance was desperate, and she was in imminent danger of arrest for debt. The brother who had helped to support her had died, and his employer, the Earl of Hillsborough, had refused to help. Quite aside from the plight of this admirable woman, Wilkes was particularly interested in her story because Lord Hillsborough had recently been made secretary of state for the colonies, that is, the king's administrator for America. Wilkes invited her to come to see him. After the visit, Mrs. Forman wrote to his lordship, "Mr. Wilkes . . . received me with the utmost politeness and affability. He passed a compliment on my letter, and desired me to name the sum required. I did so, and I had it. I went, I spoke, I had. Oh, my Lord, what shall I say to this? Has benevolence then forsaken the gilded mansion to take up her abode in a prison? Is it credible, my Lord, that a private gentleman laboring under the pressure of heavy prosecutions should display more greatness of soul than the mighty and the affluent?" Charlotte Forman subsequently wrote at least ten letters to Wilkes, never again asking for money but always making a strong feminist statement: "Woman, wretched woman! born to be a slave to that lord of the creation called man!" John Wilkes was the only man she admired. Quoting from the agglomeration of broadside poems and newspaper squibs, she wrote, "The father of his country; the English David; the beloved Patriot; the heroic champion; the martyr of Liberty, are, sir, the glorious titles so justly bestowed on you by your grateful countrymen, titles far more honorable than those enjoyed by Venal courtiers."[75]

To his joy, Wilkes was often visited by Polly and her grandmother Wilkes. Polly was still living with her mother and grandmother Mead, but she would frequently go with a groom in the family's small "chariot" to pick up her Wilkes grandmother and take her to the prison. She took the small chariot because, as she explained, Mrs. Mead "does not choose her coach should be seen there." On 5 August 1768, Polly would reach the age of eighteen, the legal age of adulthood. She was planning to leave her grandmother's house and move to her father's, and she was making arrangements to bring over from France the motherly servant whom she loved, La Vallerie. Wilkes wrote, "Mrs. Mead will of course understand that as you no longer make any part of her family after Mademoiselle La Vallerie's arrival; you will take all your things to Prince's Court." Polly did not see her father on her eighteenth birthday, choosing instead to spend the day with her mother, but she came to the prison the following day.[76] Wilkes presented her with a poem:

> How shall the Muse in prison sing!
> How prune her drooping ruff'd wing!
> Maria is the potent spell
> Ev'n in these walls all grief to quell,
> To cheer the heart, rapture inspire,
> And wake to notes of joy the lyre;
>
> . . . .
>
> Let lovers every charm admire,
> The easy shape, the heav'nly fire
> That, from those modest-beaming eyes,
> The captive heart at once surprise:
> A father's is another part,
> I praise the virtues of the heart;
> And wit so elegant and free,
> Attemper'd sweet with modesty.
> Yet may kind Heaven a lover send,
> Of sense, of honor, and a friend;
> Those virtues always to protect,
> Those beauties, never to neglect.[77]

Almost on cue, Grandmother Mead died five months after Polly's birthday. Though Wilkes had hated his mother-in-law, many people had a high regard for this stalwart of the Carter Lane Presbyterian chapel. Her corpse was borne to the burying ground in a grand procession with "116 men carrying lights." How unhappy Mrs. Mead would have been if she had known that the *Gentleman's Magazine* notice of this fine funeral identified her only as "mother to the lady of John Wilkes, Esq."[78] Mrs. Mead left Polly an estate worth one hundred thousand pounds. The interest of this would go to Polly's mother for her lifetime, and the entire fortune would be out of the reach of her father, who, the will stated, was to have "no benefit whatsoever." Just how this was effected is unclear, but it was done. Wilkes continued the compulsive spendthrift running up debts, but his adoring and now wealthy daughter was prevented from discharging them.

Friends in Paris wrote often, Suard, Pelletier, Jean-François, chevallier de Chastallux. D'Holbach himself wrote warm encouragement. Baron Sieten, imperial minister at the Court of Poland, came to the King's Bench Prison to pay his respects. The French ambassador, the Comte du Châtelet, was in communication with Wilkes, though the comte denied it. Wilkes was being talked about even in far-off China. Boswell, traveling in a coach, got to chatting with the captain of a ship who had made the journey to Beijing. There a Chinese merchant had showed the captain a porcelain bust of an Englishman with a prominent jaw and a cast eye. "He knockifar your king," said the Chinese merchant. "Your king fooly king. Do so here, cutty head. Inglis no love your king; [S]cots love your king." It is curious, said a pleased Boswell, "that people at such a distance can understand so much of the minutiae of Britain."[79]

The Chevalier d'Eon sent a dozen bottles of wine and a dozen smoked tongues, with a note expressing his wish that "the tongues might have the eloquence of Cicero and the nicety of the speech of Voltaire." Some months later, Humphrey Cotes brought d'Eon to meet Wilkes. The chevalier, whose full name was Charles-Geneviève-Louis-August-André-Timothée d'Eon de Beaumont, was a diplomat who became one of the most famous cross-dressers in history. Sent to England by Louis XVI as a diplomat, he was currently in open defiance of his king, refusing to give up his embassy in London to the new ambassador, Châtelet. He was blackmailing his government, for he possessed certain diplomatic papers that would be embarrassing to France were he to release them in England. In this circumstance, he had sought the friendship of opposition members who admired his courage, closest among them Humphrey Cotes. The meeting with Wilkes would be the start of a long friendship between two men whose names had often been linked because of their resistance to authority. A handsome, athletic man, d'Eon had the bearing of the soldier and diplomat. He had not yet begun the cross-dressing that would make him famous, or notorious, depending upon one's point of view.[80]

Late in 1768, Wilkes had a visit from Arthur Lee, the youngest son of the neoaristocratic Lee family of Virginia. A lawyer, physician, and firebrand polemicist, Lee would engage Wilkes in the American struggle. He had been educated at Eton, had a medical degree from Edinburgh and another from Leiden. While practicing medicine in Virginia, he had been caught up in the protests against the Townshend Duties, that odd assortment of taxes on glass,

paper, tea, and a variety of items of daily use. "No taxation without representation," the cry at the time of the Stamp Act, in 1765, had been revived in 1767
when Parliament, after repealing the Stamp Act, imposed the Townshend
Duties. Then, adding insult to injury, Parliament had passed a Quartering Act,
requiring American citizens to provide housing for the very soldiers who en-
forced the tax.

The duties were the idea of Charles Townshend, Wilkes's friend at Leiden
and his spy for the *North Briton*, with whom Wilkes had had a falling out in
1762. "Champagne Charlie," as he came to be called for his expensive drinking
and frequent public appearances in a drunken condition, had risen through the
ranks of ministers to become chancellor of the exchequer and in that capacity
had proposed the duties upon the American colonies. Here he drops out of
Wilkes's story, for, having secured for himself an unenviable place in history, he
died.

Lee's letters protesting the Townshend Duties, which appeared in the Virginia *Gazette*, were so well received that Lee decided to devote his life to the
cause of liberty. He had recently returned to England and was preparing himself for his new career by the study of law. His idealism, however, did not stop
him from lobbying for the grant of lands in the undeveloped western Virginia
that his family was seeking.

While an exile in France, Wilkes had voiced doubts about the troublesome
Americans. On 17 November 1765, he had written from Paris to his brother,
"You are much mistaken as to my ideas of America. I am too well informed of
what passes there by some gentlemen I have seen, and there is a spirit little
short of rebellion in several of the colonies. If I am to be an exile from my
native London, it shall not be in the new world."[81] Fundamentally loyal to the
Crown, if not to the person of King George III, Wilkes did not approve of
rebellion.

Lee, however, would show Wilkes how to see America in a new light. An
intense, irascible man with few social skills but a great gift for polemics, Lee
quickly won Wilkes's friendship. They were both shameless propagandists for
liberty; they both had attacked the Scots' encroachment upon England; they
both were members of the Royal Society; they both had studied at Leiden. And
Wilkes was flattered because Lee looked upon him as a hero.

Americans had not forgotten Wilkes. In Boston "Wilkes and Liberty" was as
much a rallying cry as in London, and the number 45 was inscribed on doors
and windows all over the town. John Hancock, the great Boston trader and
patriot, named a ship *The Liberty* in honor of Wilkes. In the South Carolina
elections of 1768, the workingmen of the community, the so-called mechanics,
shook off the domineering gentry by holding a nomination meeting of their

own. They then "consecrated" a Tree of Liberty (a ship mast planted as a pole from which were hung symbols and slogans) and decorated it that night with forty-five lights while firing forty-five rockets. The parade that left the scene included forty-five men carrying candles. Alexander McDougall, a New York City pamphlet writer arrested and charged with libel, chose jail rather than bail so that his case would be compared to that of Wilkes. Forty-five of his friends came to a feast at McDougall's jail, consumed forty-five pounds of beef cut from steers forty-five months old and offered forty-five toasts. "By the end of 1768," wrote the historian Merrill Jensen, " 'Wilkes and Liberty' was a toast from one end of the colonies to the other, and '45' was almost a sacred number." Bostonians had a particular fondness for Wilkes, and some of them invited him to migrate; but others thought he could best serve America from within England.[82]

In late June, Wilkes was handed a beautifully scripted letter from a committee of the Sons of Liberty of Boston. It was signed by the great movers and shakers of revolution in New England, John Adams, Samuel Adams, James Otis, John Hancock, Richard Dana, Joseph Warren, Benjamin Kent, Thomas Young, and Josiah Quincy Jr. Among these signatures was that of the most infamous of Americans, Benjamin Church, who would at a later date be found guilty of treason for spying for the British. The letter opened in a light tone: the signers represented an assembly of forty-five men at the Whig Tavern. They were sending Mr. Wilkes two turtles, one weighing the symbolic forty-five pounds, the other weighing forty-seven, which brought the combined weight to ninety-two. The number ninety-two had become a symbol of liberty when the Massacusetts legislature defied the royal governor by voting ninety-two to seventeen to stand by their circular letter to the other colonies. The tone of the rest of the letter was more serious. They said nothing of the St. George's Fields massacre because they had not yet received the news of it. After congratulating Wilkes on his return to England and election to Middlesex, they began a eulogy of their hero: "May you convince Great Britain and Ireland in Europe, the British Colonies, islands and plantations in America, that you are one of those incorruptibly honest men reserved by heaven to bless and perhaps save a tottering Empire, that Majesty can never be secure but in the arms of a brave, a virtuous, and united people. . . . That the British constitution still exists is our glory; feeble and infirm as it is, we cannot, we will not despair of it. To a Wilkes much is already due for his strenuous efforts to preserve it. . . . Your perseverance in the good old cause may still prevent the great system from dashing to pieces."[83] For Wilkes's information, they were sending along the first installments of John Dickinson's now-famous *Letters from a Farmer in Pennsylvania to the Inhabitants of the English Colonies*. They asked nothing of Wilkes but dared to wish he might write to them. He did so on 19 July 1768 after the ruckus over the St. George's Fields massacre had died down: "I hope freedom will ever flourish under your hemisphere as well as ours, and I doubt not from your spirit and firmness that you will be careful to transmit to your posterity the invaluable rights and franchises which you received from your ancestors. Liberty I consider as the birthright of every subject of the British empire, and I hold Magna Charta to be in as full force in America as in Europe. . . . The favorable opinion which you are pleased to express of me is a great encouragement and a noble reward of my efforts in the service of his Kingdom."[84]

By the time the same group of Bostonians wrote again, on 5 October 1768, a regiment had been brought from Halifax, and their city was under military rule. Their Parliament House had been turned into a "mainguard," and their province factory into a barracks for British soldiers. "Can Britons wish to see us abandon our lives and properties to such rapine and plunder?" they wrote. Their hope lay in leadership in Parliament: "Europe, in a ferment, America, on the point of bursting into flame, more pressingly require the patriot senator, the wise and honest counsellor, than the desolating conqueror." Wilkes was their man.[85]

Wilkes replied, "I have read with grief and indignation the proceeding of the ministry with regard to the troops ordered to Boston, as if it were the capital of a province belonging to our enemies, or in the possession of rebels. Asiatic despotism does not present a picture more odious. . . . Your moderation prevented the effusion of blood which we have seen by the military on St. George's Fields." He gave them permission to reprint his letters but suggested they be discreet: "While I am doomed to this prison, unfair advantages might be taken against me."[86] The Boston Sons of Liberty finally decided not to take the chance and did not publish them.

Individual members of the group began to write to Wilkes, among them Benjamin Kent, Joseph Warren, Thomas Young, Benjamin Church, and Samuel Adams. William Palfrey, the secretary to the Boston Sons, wrote almost every month. Palfrey, friend and chief clerk for the many enterprises of John Hancock, had become a friend of Wilkes's brother-in-law, George Hayley, a London merchant who traded with America and recently had formed a partnership with Hancock in one of his many enterprises. Palfrey yearned not for independence, which hardly anyone was thinking of in 1768, but for ministers of the king who were "reverenced and loved by the people" and for enlightened members of the British Parliament. Wilkes, he hoped, would play that role when he took his seat in the House. "Our eyes," wrote Church, "are at present fixed on the county of Middlesex."[87]

As to Wilkes's personal faults, to most Americans they were irrelevant. "Whatever his fate may be," went a Rhode Island almanac, "and however severely his enemies may arraign his private failings, it will never, can never be denied, that his steady opposition to illegal general warrants has been, and ever will be, of lasting benefit to the subjects of Great Britain; that, if he is not virtuous, he is a lover of virtue; and a friend to the civil and religious liberties of mankind; which we have no doubt of his displaying upon all future occasions, if he should sit in the House of Commons." Benjamin Kent, who was an unfrocked minister, wrote to assure Wilkes that his reputation as a blasphemer carried no weight in America. He had not seen the Essay on Woman, of course, but if he should read it and if he "should find anything too luscious, I assure you I am well fortified by the revolution of sixty cold North American winters."[88]

In January of 1769, Lee, now serving as one of the three agents for Massachusetts, brought to the prison Dr. Benjamin Rush, the physician who would one day sign the Declaration of Independence, though in 1769 he was yet an ardent royalist. As Rush recorded the meeting, some fifteen agreeable gentlemen came to dinner in the prison. "Mr. Wilkes abounded in anecdotes and sallies of wit. He was perfectly well bred. Not an unchaste word or oath escaped his lips. I was the more surprised at this, as he had been represented a monster of immorality." Wilkes had a small adjoining room which contained his library, but Rush was not impressed with the collection—"chiefly . . . histories and common place literature."[89]

It may have been Arthur Lee who put Wilkes in contact with the Real Whigs, a group of philosophical writers who articulated the concepts of liberty and were staunch friends of America. Some of them met in a club they called the Honest Whigs, to which belonged Benjamin Franklin, Richard Price, Joseph Priestly, Stephen Sayre, Arthur Lee, and his brother William. Then there was a larger, amorphous group that included Wilkes's friends Thomas Hollis and Mrs. Catharine Macaulay, whose polemical *History of England* Wilkes much admired. The Real Whigs wrote numerous pamphlets and letters supporting American protests. Many of them met in the house of William Petty, Earl of Shelburne, later Marquess of Lansdowne, the most intellectual of the great politicians of the day, who had gathered a salon of liberal thinkers in the magnificent house at Curzon Street and Berkeley Square. There they discussed the principles of liberty in the writings of Locke and Voltaire, the scientific experiments of Priestley, and the news from America. Shelburne had resigned a cabinet position in protest over the treatment of the colonies. Priestly, who was serving as Shelburne's librarian and tutor to his children, had a laboratory in the house and made his celebrated discovery of oxygen there. The house is now occupied by the Lansdowne Club.[90]

Though Shelburne himself waffled on American questions, that cannot be said of his chief lieutenant in the House of Commons, Isaac Barré, a former soldier who had fought with James Wolfe at Quebec. Possessed of a stentorian voice and the rhetorical skills that could stop the House, Barré had become the most vocal champion of America in Parliament. He was a fierce-looking one-eyed creature, the ball that had shot out the eye still lodged in his cheek. He and Wilkes had known each other as officers at the Winchester camp, but their political paths had not yet crossed. It would not be long before the two most ugly men in England would have their names fused into the name of an American town, Wilkes-Barre, Pennsylvania.[91] They never much liked each other.

The Real Whigs flooded the newspapers with letters and the print shops with pamphlets protesting the treatment of America.[92] They saw Americans as victims of a corrupt English system, and they were fixated upon the image of Lord Bute, who they believed was still directing the ministers from behind the curtain.

Wilkes probably learned a good deal from the English Real Whigs, but he was of a different cut. He was closer to the Americans, who not only talked, but acted upon their ideals. Franklin did not like him, but Wilkes would work with the three Americans who got into politics in the City of London, the Lee brothers and Stephen Sayre. When the conflicts with America would turn into war, the Lees and Sayre would become secret agents for the American Continental Congress and, after the Declaration of Independence, diplomats for their country. To be sure, the English Real Whigs were important to the American independence movement because they provided theory and sometimes inspiration. Wilkes's role was different. Unhappy, middle-class America did not think of him as an apostle of liberty or a philosopher, but as an activist who at great risk and cost repeatedly challenged an oppressive government. He was their model of devotion to liberty. The Real Whigs to Americans were thinkers and writers; Wilkes was a figure of myth. "The fate of Wilkes and America," wrote Palfrey, "must stand or fall together."[93]

In November 1768, the Wilkite party reentered elective politics. The occasion was the death of George Cooke, the knight of the shire for Middlesex, who had been elected along with Wilkes. The livery nominated Wilkes's lawyer, the brilliant John Glynn. The conservatives again put up Sir William Proctor, who had lost the election to Cooke and Wilkes. Proctor had the full support of a ministry determined to defeat anyone in Wilkes's camp, but they were outdone by the Wilkites, who campaigned energetically and cleverly. Polling began on 8 December 1768 at Brentford. Proctor, sensing he was going to lose, showed the true color of a ministerial candidate: he purchased the services of a notorious organizer of mobs-for-hire, Edward MacQuirk, called "the Infant" because of

12. The MacQuirk mob-for-hire attacks the supporters of Glynn during the election for member of Parliament for the Shire of Middlesex. Courtesy of Gerald M. Goldberg.

his enormous size. At the head of a crowd of Irish chairmen armed with clubs, MacQuirk made a vicious attack upon the voters and even mounted the hustings wielding his club. A lawyer named George Clarke was clubbed to death. The sheriffs closed the polls and declared the election void. Some weeks later, MacQuirk and another man were tried for murder and sentenced to transportation; but before they were put on board a ship, they received a royal pardon. An angry House of Commons ordered the polls to be opened again, and on 14 December Glynn won by a large margin.[94]

On Wilkes's forty-second birthday, 28 October 1768, two hundred merry partisans gathered at the 45 Tavern in Gray's Inn Passage, Holborn, waving flags with "45" on them and playing French horns until two in the morning. Other crowds roamed the streets, forcing the houses to illuminate. In Boston, New York, and Williamsburg, Virginia, men gathered to celebrate the birthday with forty-five toasts to Mr. Wilkes. There were also toasts to Sergeant Glynn, who would take his seat as the second knight of the shire for Middlesex.[95] But the hero of the people, in their minds always the number one knight, was a prisoner of the king, and the ministry was at sixes and sevens over him.

IO

Incapacitation

A few days before Wilkes's birthday, in October of 1768, Lord Chatham, crippled with gout and immobilized with depression, resigned as privy seal, leaving the government of Great Britain in the hands of Lord Grafton, who was totally unsuited to run it. Grafton now had the problem of his old acquaintance, Jack Wilkes, a man elected to Parliament but not sworn in, freed of his outlawry but a prisoner. He felt as though he had been tossed a hot potato but could not find anyone else to toss it to. If he mishandled the situation, the mob, he feared, would again turn violent.[1] Grafton's fear of mob violence was extreme.

Shortly before the opening of Parliament, Wilkes published *An Address to the Gentlemen, Clergy, and Freeholders of the County of Middlesex,* reviewing all of his past grievances and then announcing what made Grafton's heart sink: he would present a petition for redress of these grievances to the House of Commons. The last thing Grafton wanted was to have all the sins against Wilkes presented to the House to be judged, the crimes to be acknowledged, the blame to be cast on courts and administrations, or the accusations to be denied by the denial of common sense.

Grafton decided to try bribing this agitator into silence. If Wilkes would withhold his petition, Grafton would withhold all opposition to his being seated as knight of the shire for Middlesex. This would amount to handing

Wilkes the seat, for the ministry controlled the swing votes. The ministers probably congratulated themselves upon their choice of a person to carry the offer to Wilkes, John Almon. During Wilkes's exile, Lord Temple had set up Almon in a printing/bookselling shop in Piccadilly, and he was now a respected member of the business community who printed most of the leftist publications. But Wilkes could see that the ministry was condescending to him. He told Almon he was not highly enough placed to be an ambassador to him, and he would not reply. Grafton then turned to William Fitzherbert, who had been Rockingham's negotiator with Wilkes the year before. Fitzherbert was a member of the administration, one of the lords of trade, and a member of Parliament. Yes, Wilkes would receive him. Taking along as witness the actor David Garrick, whom Wilkes had known in Paris, Fitzherbert went to the prison.[2]

The three men talked for awhile about Wilkes's planned petition, and then Fitzherbert came to the point. To his certain knowledge, if Mr. Wilkes would send another "submission" to the king and would be quiet about his grievances, he might keep the Middlesex seat and receive a royal pardon, but if he insisted upon petitioning the House for redress, he would lose his seat and remain in prison. Wilkes did not at once reply. So little publicity had been given to Chatham's recent resignation, he was uncertain of it. He asked upon whose authority Fitzherbert spoke? Fitzherbert replied that he came in the name of "the minister," but would not be specific about whether he meant Chatham or Grafton. Wilkes was willing, he said, to throw himself upon the mercy of the king, but not upon an unnamed minister.[3] The king, Fitzherbert replied, would not grant a pardon unless it were recommended by the minister.

It was a critical moment in the life of John Wilkes. If he took his seat, he would be released from prison. He would enjoy privilege and be immune to arrest for debt, and who knows what a change of administrations might bring? Perhaps the ambassadorship he dreamed of. He could take the leadership of the fierce little Wilkite party, and real political power would be in his hands. But, no, accepting the offer would be a sellout and seen as such. It would cost him the leadership of the party. Worse, it would cost the popular support without which his cause would be dead. No, everything he really valued lay on the other side. If he went ahead with his petition to the House of Commons, the turmoil he would create would vastly extend the awareness of his cause and firmly fix him in the role he loved, the champion of liberty. His mind made up, he addressed Fitzherbert. He would indeed petition the king, whom he never had intended to offend. As to the House of Commons, he would submit his petition there because he thought it his duty.[4]

On 14 November, Sir Joseph Mawbey, member for Southwark, made a motion in the House of Commons to accept the petition. Wilkes's choice of Mawbey as presenter signified the support of "the middling sort," for Sir Joseph was the very distiller and pig farmer "Hog-sty" Mawbey, who had prevailed upon Wilkes to print his silly ballad *The Battle of Epsom*. The seconder of the motion, John Sawbridge, Mrs. Catharine Macaulay's brother, spoke for the City, where he had great popularity. William Dowdeswell was also on his feet in support of the motion. Dowdeswell, Wilkes's friend from Leiden days, spoke for the Rockingham party and uncommitted Whigs from rural areas. So broadly backed, the petition could not be turned down. It was read to the House and accepted. The petition mentioned briefly Wilkes's arrest and the seizure of his papers under a general warrant, his being held a close prisoner, Lord Mansfield's alteration of the indictment by changing the word *purport* to *tenor*, and Wilkes's being convicted upon evidence obtained by bribing the printer, Michael Curry, who had since forsworn himself. The House then ordered the clerk to fetch the records of Wilkes's conviction from the King's Bench, and the petition "to lie upon the table," "a mark of dislike," said Walpole. In fact, because the information (the charge against Wilkes) contained the offensive passages in the Essay on Woman, it was ordered to be locked up to all except members of the House. Eight weeks later, on 3 February 1769, they bethought themselves of the damage these passages from the Essay might cause if the public were to read them; and so to protect their constituents, they ordered the information destroyed. Consequently, this dangerous document was not transcribed into the journals of the House of Commons.[5]

Wilkes's submission to the king was presented to his majesty at a levée on 28 November: "Showeth: That your petitioner, having stood forth in support of the constitutional rights of this kingdom in opposition to a late violent administration, hath been severely prosecuted at law, and sentenced to pay a heavy fine and to suffer an imprisonment of twenty-two months, that the unfair methods employed to convict your petitioner have been palpable and manifest; that the petitioner has always been your Majesty's loyal subject . . . and humbly supplicates your royal clemency."[6] His Royal Highness did nothing.

Then Wilkes kindled a fire in the House of Lords. On 10 December he sent to the *St. James's Chronicle* a letter which had come into his hands from Secretary of State Lord Weymouth and accompanied it with his own anonymous preface. Weymouth's letter was addressed to Daniel Ponton, chairman of the Quarter Sessions at Lambeth. Before the riots at St. George's Fields, when the mob was appearing daily outside Wilkes's window at the King's Bench Prison, Weymouth had advised Ponton to call for additional troops to be stationed close to the prison. Ponton had taken the advice, and as things turned out it was these soldiers who had fired on the people in St. George's

Fields. The "massacre" had taken place on 10 May. Weymouth's letter was dated 17 April. Wilkes in his preface asserted that the letter showed "how long the horrid massacre in St. George's Fields had been planned . . . and how long a hellish project can be brooded over by some infernal spirits without one moment's remorse." The inevitable happened, and Lord Weymouth complained in the House of Lords of a breach of privilege. Baldwin the printer was arrested and testified at the bar that he had received the letter and preface from another printer named Swan. Swan was brought before the lords and astonished them with his story. Because he admired Mr. Wilkes, from whom he used to pick up papers for the newspaper three times a week, he had asked him what he should say if he were arrested. "You may say at the bar of the House of Lords," Wilkes had replied, that "you received all those papers from me." The reaction of the House of Lords was prompt. On 19 December 1768, they passed a resolution making another condemnation of Wilkes: in writing the preface to the letter, Wilkes had committed "an insolent, scandalous, and seditious libel," the words chosen to match those that had been used in the House of Commons to describe the libel for printing *North Briton* No. 45. They notified the House of Commons of what they had done and recessed for the holidays. The House of Commons did likewise, and further action on Wilkes's petition was put off until the new year. "We are as much occupied as we were four years ago with Wilkes," wrote Horace Walpole to Horace Mann. "His spirit, which the Scotch call impudence, and the gods confidence, rises every day." The House of Lords was resolved to hear him at their bar, "there still being blindness enough not to perceive that the oftener this incendiary is touched, the more he gains ground."[7]

Not long after the holidays, Wilkes received a visit from John Barnard, the son of the late Sir John Barnard, a famous lord mayor and member for the City. The younger Barnard, an ardent admirer of Wilkes, had brought his wife and his daughter by a previous marriage to meet his hero. Wilkes at once recognized the wife as his mistress of five years earlier, the woman whose maiden name is lost to us whom he had met at Blackheath in the house of Grace Ozier. He and Mrs. Barnard managed to cover up their surprise, thinking it would be unwise to reveal their past. But Wilkes, pleased that the lady had lost none of her charms, contrived to pass her a billet doux. Days later, Mrs. Barnard slipped away from her husband and came alone. Thus began a clandestine affair, joyful to them both. Mrs. Barnard was sexy and witty. She sent him sweets. She passed on political gossip. She sang the praises of "Wilkes and Liberty" to the outside world. Once she went to Christies for a show of paintings, and who should be there but "the High Priest of the renowned abbey," Sir Francis Dashwood, now Lord le Despenser, and, placing herself as close to him as she could, she declared loudly, "What a pity it is that such old goats should be suffered to corrupt the morals of younger fellows."[8]

This spirited woman was chaffing under the bonds of marriage to an unattractive, dull husband who slept in a separate room and when he went out preferred the company of his daughter to that of his wife. In her present circumstances Mrs. Barnard had no need for Wilkes's money, as in the past. What she needed was affection and sex, and in both she was satisfied. "I dined very near you and thought of nothing else," she wrote. One day, having left Wilkes, she returned to Berkeley Square in a melancholy mood for having to abandon "what my heart wished most to possess." When her husband and his daughter came in from the opera, "they asked me to partake of their insipid meal, but I despise their proffered fare, having still the flavor of a far more delicious repast." In another letter she wrote, "I admire your——; pray fill up the space yourself." She persisted in writing to him, even though she was constantly interrupted by the family: "In the space of twenty lines your letter is ten times under the bed or drawers or books. But your good nature forgives all faults . . . my joy exceeded those of paradise."

On 30 December 1768, Wilkes took communion in the prison chapel. Alderman Francis Gosling had died, leaving a vacancy in the ward of Farringdon Without in the City of London, and Wilkes had asked for the rite so as to qualify as a candidate to replace him. The City was divided into twenty-six wards, each headed by an alderman who was chief administrator of the ward, judge of the ward's law court, and, when his turn came up, judge of the City court of pleas. Aldermen also took turns on the panel of judges in the Criminal Court of the City of London, popularly called the Old Bailey. The ward in question, Farringdon Without, one of the two largest, had its odd name because it had stood outside the City walls when they were still intact. Wilkes had been pondering the possibility of this move. Before he had been committed to the King's Bench Prison, at least one newspaper had talked about the possibility of his seeking an aldermanship if one became available. Never mind that he was now a prisoner; his popularity had never been so high and now was the time to move. Learning that Alderman Gosling was seriously ill, he had prepared himself. Within hours of the man's death, handbills appeared in the streets all over the City asking for the support of the livery. "He abhors the idea of an aristocracy," said the handbill. "He will assert the conscience of every individual and the interest and freedom of the whole."[9]

The election was made by a cheering throng of liverymen at St Bride's Church on 2 January 1769. There was only one competitor, and he withdrew when it became apparent Wilkes would have twice as many votes. That evening Wilkes wrote an open letter of thanks "To the Worthy Inhabitants of the

Ward of Farringdon Without" and hosted a feast for officials of the City. The meal was made from gifts received in congratulation, perhaps the collar of brawn sent by an admirer. After dinner, Wilkes was presented with the gift of an alderman's gown trimmed in fur, the traditional costume of the office. It was valued, the newspapers said, at forty guineas. A few days later, the election was declared illegal; then it was held again, and Wilkes was again elected; then it was challenged by the court of aldermen; then the challenge was dropped. When Wilkes would be released two years later, he would be sworn in without any problem.[10]

Parliament reassembled in January 1769, aware that the eyes of more than one nation were upon them. Walpole wrote to his friend Horace Mann, "I am grieved to see that the whole nation is still occupied with Wilkes, and that there is no method of suppressing his seditious impudence. You cannot conceive what an impression this makes abroad, where it is trumpeted by all the foreign gazettes. The court French *Gazette*, to which all their ministers have particular orders to furnish materials, is most minutely eloquent on this subject. But surely it is, was, very imprudent to produce that incendiary to his partisans, the mob, to whom alone he owes his reputation and strength."[11]

On the twenty-seventh, the House of Commons took the first step toward hearing Wilkes's petition for redress of grievances. Wilkes was brought from the prison, a cheering mob running beside the coach and crowding into the lobby of the House so that the speaker was forced to order the tipstaves to clear it of all persons except Wilkes and his guard.

Wilkes had arrived well prepared to carry on a lengthy debate, for he had in hand a thirty-page brief made for him, one supposes, by Sergeant John Glynn, containing every argument one could think of about the illegality of Wilkes's arrest and conviction. But it did little good, for Lord North opened debate by moving that Wilkes and his lawyers could argue only two points in the petition, Lord Mansfield's alteration of the record and the subornation of Curry. The motion was opposed and debated all day. Glynn spoke for Wilkes so eloquently that he was applauded by both sides. Burke ridiculed the ministers so effectively that he too was applauded. At ten in the evening, the motion limiting the arguable points was voted by division and carried 278 to 131. Wilkes then was brought to the bar. Though his demeanor was respectful, he asked if it were legal for him to be at the bar without being allowed to deliver in his credentials as elected knight of the shire for Middlesex and to take the oaths. The question was debated briefly, and it was resolved on a voice vote that his being at the bar was legal. He was sent back to prison.[12]

The next day, the business of the House was to establish who could or could not testify as witnesses in the hearing on Wilkes's petition. Again Wilkes was brought to Saint Stephen's Chapel by two marshals in a coach, escorted by a cheering mob. Again the speaker had to order the lobby and galleries cleared. The petition was read. Mawbey rose to ask permission for Lord Temple to be allowed to testify at the bar, which was readily granted. The precedent having been set, Mawbey asked that Lords Sandwich and March be permitted to testify. Many did not want these gentlemen to appear but could not very well say no. Then, having obtained his goal, Mawbey withdrew the request for Temple's appearance.[13] In proceedings that went on until one in the morning, a list of other witnesses was established. Wilkes himself was not called but spent the day holding court in the sergeant's room, to which his friends and followers came to congratulate him on his election as alderman.

"Sandwich is frightened out of his senses," said Walpole, "and March does not like it. Well! This will cure ministers and great lords of being so flippant in dire tyranny, when they see they may be worried for it four years afterwards."[14] *Worried* was a hunting term: when the dogs have cornered an animal they cannot kill, they worry it by barking and biting at it.

Two days later, Wilkes received a letter from John Hatselle, clerk of the House of Commons. Hatselle had brought to the House a copy of the record from the King's Bench, and one of the junior clerks had written on it, "Copy of Information against Wilkes for blasphemy in his 'Essay on Woman.'" Wilkes's lawyers had challenged the word *blasphemy*, and Hatselle had written Wilkes a gruff apology because "blasphemy is not the crime charged in the information." He noted the use of the adjective *blasphemous* but admitted that using the adjectival form of the word did not amount to a charge of blasphemy. Hatselle had provided Wilkes with a new weapon, and the next morning, at the bar, Wilkes made a strong objection. Not only had the court record been given a misleading label, but it had been copied (maliciously, said Walpole) into the voting record of the House. Bullcalf Norton, this "worthless man," as Walpole called him, tried to prove that Wilkes had actually been convicted of blasphemy, but he was argued to a standstill by Glynn. The House finally voted to expunge the word *blasphemy* from the document in question. The error of Hatselle's clerk had turned out to be a boon for Wilkes because the vote to expunge effectively swept away the accusations of blasphemy which had alienated many potential followers.[15]

That business concluded, the event that everyone had been waiting for commenced, the hearing on Wilkes's petition. The first witness brought to the bar was Wilkes's erstwhile foreman who had betrayed him, Michael Curry. Tormented with guilt, Curry had recently made a trip to London from Bristol, where he had been living, so that he could make amends to Wilkes. He had sworn an affidavit before the lord mayor telling how he had stolen the proof sheets of the Essay and sold them to the ministry. He now repeated the story for the House and, as Walpole put it, "owned himself an infamous rogue." Many members of the House were shocked to hear for the first time about the treachery that had been used to convict Wilkes. But Curry's sense of guilt was not relieved: he returned to Bristol and committed suicide. The *Gentleman's Magazine* ran an obituary on Michael Curry, "well known for the information he gave against Mr. Wilkes. . . . His treachery was deemed so ignominious that no person in the metropolis would ever afterwards give him employment, considering the offense of the greatest magnitude to a profession in which secrecy is so essentially requisite, the freedom of the press having always been deemed one of the greatest privileges of an Englishman."[16]

The next witness was Nathan Carrington, the chief of the crown messengers, who had all of the appearance of a gentleman and all of the language of a porter and who had directed the monstrous arrests of 1762. Carrington told about the various sums he had given Curry for the proof sheets and for Curry's testimony before the House of Lords about Wilkes's writing and printing of the Essay on Woman. Some members of the House, their eyes opened, asked if it were customary to pay the king's witnesses. "It was always the custom." And witnesses were paid *after* they testified? Yes, "indulgence was shown according to the circumstance as they had behaved."[17] Wilkes could hardly have planned a better exposé.

The most colorful events of the day were the testimonies of Lord Sandwich and Lord March. These two, perhaps the most notorious libertines of the day, had insisted upon ceremonies of respect that the lowly House of Commons ought to pay to noblemen who deigned to come to their hall, and for days committees from both houses had met to determine the appropriate ceremony. Finally, "Lord Sandwich being brought in by the sergeants and mace, sat in the chair with his hat on, inside the bar." Wilkes, who obviously was more interested in the show than in the testimony, asked only one question: Did his lordship know of Curry's being bribed? No, he had promised Curry protection, "but had nothing to do with the disposition of public money." Lord March was ushered in with like ceremony. He told how Kidgell had brought him the fragment of the Essay on Woman and how he had given it to the ministry but had never connived with Philip Carteret Webb to obtain more of the Essay, and, in fact, had never laid eyes on Mr. Webb until today. Wilkes then asked what had passed between him and Kidgell? March replied that he would answer the question only if the House proposed it, "but the House not thinking it material," said Wilkes, "his Lordship withdrew."[18]

Philip Carteret Webb, the solicitor to the treasury who had directed the conspiracy to convict Wilkes for the Essay on Woman, was now guided to the

13. Hieroglyphics. Attorney General Norton and First Minister Grafton as hounds attack Wilkes. Courtesy of Farley Library, Wilkes University.

bar. No longer a member of the House or the ministry, grown old and feeble and almost completely blind, Webb sat in a chair at the bar and heard himself "grievously abused," said Walpole, by Sergeant Thomas Davenport, Wilkes's counsel. A letter from Webb to Curry and three other printers was put into evidence. In it Webb told the printers to take care that their stories agreed with each other before they testified in the House of Lords. Webb's lawyer explained that Webb could remember little of those days and then pleaded before Webb's face for compassion because his client was "decayed both in eyesight and understanding."[19] The House dismissed Webb and put off proceedings until the next day.

Wednesday, 1 February, the House debated how to respond to Wilkes's petition. Wilkes's lawyers argued that Mansfield's changing of the record in February 1764 had invalidated his conviction, for Wilkes had been indicted on one document and sentenced on another. This was too nice for William Blackstone, the Oxford law professor and author of the widely read *Commentaries on the Law*, who pointed out that the House of Lords, the highest appeals court of the land, had already heard Wilkes's complaint about Lord Mansfield's changing of the record and had declared that the chief justice had acted legally. He moved that Wilkes's complaint against Mansfield was "frivolous, trifling, and scandalous." Glynn opposed. "Norton and the Crown lawyers were warm on the other side," said Walpole, but their forces, said Barré, "resembled the elephants in Eastern armies, which fall back upon and put their own troops in confusion." General Henry Seymour Conway finally moved to amend the motion to read that the charge against Mansfield was groundless and that Lord Mansfield's alteration of the record was "according to law and justice." Carried. So ended the first of the two matters in the petition Wilkes was allowed to argue, that Mansfield's changing the word had invalidated his conviction.[20]

The second, that Curry's subornation invalidated Wilkes's conviction, was dispatched handily. Edward Thurlow, flying in the face of the evidence, moved that Wilkes had not made good his charge against Webb. Thomas Townshend Jr. spoke up: "I pitied Mr. Carteret Webb when he appeared at your bar; and indeed it might have gone hard with him. . . . It is evident that Curry received five guineas as a security for the copy being returned to him: the word 'security' does not wipe off the imputation of a bribe." But no one wanted to condemn a pitiful old blind man, so they decided to declare that Wilkes had not shown him to have committed any wrongdoing. Ergo, Curry was honest and Wilkes justly convicted.[21]

So ended the hearing on Wilkes's petition for redress of grievances. Wilkes was not in the least surprised, but he had had his day. If he had lost in law, he had been morally vindicated and, more important still, had gained a critically important body of allies. Many highly placed gentlemen who had been loath to involve themselves in a cause championed by a scandalous man backed by riffraff and the middling sort now began quietly to support it.

What remained for the House of Commons was to get rid of this man. The next morning he was again brought to the bar. Mr. Speaker Cust solemnly announced that the House of Commons had been informed by the House of Lords that John Wilkes had been charged with libel as the author and publisher of the preface to the published letter of Lord Weymouth in the *St. James's Chronicle*. A hush fell on the assembly, for they understood that the ministerial party was moving toward the expulsion of Wilkes. How would he defend himself? Then Wilkes, at the bar, spoke so that all could hear: "Mr. Speaker, I acknowledge that I transmitted to the press a copy of the Secretary of State's letter, and that I wrote the prefatory remarks upon it; and I will, whenever a secretary of state shall write so bloody a scroll, write some prefatory remarks upon it. I beg pardon that I use so mild and gentle an expression, when I speak of that inhuman 10th of May. . . . I doubt not from the justice of the House but you will immediately order an impeachment against the secretary who wrote that letter."[22] The gasps were audible. Wilkes was dismissed, but as he was being led away, the speaker called him back. He had been charged on the testimony of Baldwin and Swan. Would he like to question them? "No," came the answer, "I desire to examine no witnesses at all. I avow it. I think it a meritorious act." Told to withdraw, he asked permission to sit in the gallery. Granted. Burke spoke brilliantly about the letters of Lord Weymouth and Lord Barrington, showing that they had indeed keyed up the soldiers for violence, and after the violence, he had thanked them for it; he moved to establish a committee to inquire into the St. George's Fields disaster, but the motion was defeated.

It was after midnight when Attorney General Norton moved that the preface to the Weymouth letter was an "insolent, scandalous, and seditious libel," using the wording that had been used in House of Lords. The opposition raised protests. Blackstone himself opposed, arguing that the matter of libel should be tried in the law courts, not the House of Commons. Nevertheless, at two in the morning the motion was passed 239 to 136.[23]

The ground had been cleared for expulsion. Most of the next day, 3 February 1769, the House was concerned with other matters, but in the early evening they were ready to take up the case of Mr. Wilkes. Barrington moved to expel him on the grounds that he had published three libels, *North Briton* No. 45, the Essay on Woman, and the paragraph introducing Weymouth's letter. Burke opposed, arguing that the House had already punished Wilkes for the first two libels. George Grenville, who was chiefly responsible for Wilkes's expulsion in 1763, had changed his view. Old and ill as he was, Grenville made the best speech of his career in opposing the motion.[24]

At three in the morning, the motion to expel was carried. Wilkes was brought to the bar and asked to be allowed to address the House. He was refused. Never mind, the speech he had prepared was published the next day by William Bingley in a *North Britain Extraordinary*. He bore himself with dignity, said the *Public Advertiser*, "firm, manly, decent, revering, but not crouching." Walpole confirmed the confidence but found nothing else to admire. The expulsion was, as he explained to Mann, "passed on Friday night, or rather at three on Saturday morning, by a majority of 219 against 137, after four days of such fatigue and long sittings as never were known together. His behavior in every respect but confidence, was so poor. . . . He has so little quickness or talent for public speaking." A writ was issued for a new election. The clerk of the House was ordered to expunge from its record the mistaken reference of a conviction for blasphemy. The marshals were ordered to return Wilkes to the prison. The meeting was adjourned.[25]

Lord Temple, who had been in the balcony, wrote to his sister, Countess Chatham, "The accumulated crimes of No. 45, the impious and obscene libel, and that against Lord Weymouth, are the foundation of this expulsion; so that in the debate every man dwelt upon the crime he most detested, and disapproved of the punishment for the rest. The various flowers of their eloquence composed a most delightful nosegay." Burke went home and wrote, "The state of the night, the candles, put me in mind of the representation of the last act of a tragic-comedy, acted by his Majesty's servants, by desire of several persons of distinction, for the benefit of Mr. Wilkes, at the expense of the constitution." Heaton Wilkes, who had watched from the gallery, wrote sadly, "Liberty is expiring."[26]

Wilkes did not go to bed until he had written a letter "To the Gentlemen, Clergy, and Freeholders of the County of Middlesex." His spirit, he assured the voters, was not in the least abated. He appealed to them to assert their right of naming their own representatives by electing him again. "If ministers can once usurp the power of declaring who *shall not* be your representative, the next step is very easy, and will follow speedily. It is that of telling you whom you *shall* send to Parliament, and then the boasted Constitution of England will be entirely torn up by the roots."[27] The remark was portentous and would be frequently repeated.

The by-election to fill the now-vacant seat for knight of the shire for Middlesex was held on 16 February 1769. A few days before, gentlemen voters had met at the Assembly Rooms in Newtown Mile End and nominated Wilkes again. On election day, a crowd gathered at Brentford Butts though it was pelting rain. Wilkes was not there, the ministers having found no reason he should be allowed to attend. John Sawbridge, currently a member for Hythe, and James Townsend, member for West Looe, both rising stars in City politics, spoke on Wilkes's behalf. No other candidate appearing, a voice vote was called for at noon, and Wilkes was elected unanimously. The more hearty among the drenched freemen paraded back to Westminster, trying to fly wet colors, blowing French horns, and drumming. Over Westminster Bridge they marched and stood cheering outside Wilkes's prison window. Late that afternoon, a celebratory dinner was held in the prison, the pièce de résistance, a large roasted swan. Before he went to bed, Wilkes wrote an open letter thanking the Middlesex voters. The King's Bench marshals, delighted with the election, illuminated the prison all that night.[28]

The next day in the House of Commons, at the behest of the administration, James Smith Stanley, usually called Lord Strange, moved a resolution that John Wilkes, Esq., was "incapable of being elected a member to serve in the present Parliament." Opposition argued that a constituency can elect whom they please. The ministerial side argued that no one can be elected once he has been excluded. Burke doubted that incapacity could be justified even if Parliament were to pass a law allowing it. North answered it was justified already, by the laws of reason and common sense. There was a division and the motion was passed 235 to 89.[29]

Many opposition members, thinking the important matter was expulsion, had not bothered to appear for what they supposed would be a simple rejection of Wilkes's second election. As it turned out, the poorly attended House went far beyond rejection and passed the motion of incapacitation. Although few realized it immediately, Strange's resolution challenged the very basis of the electoral process. Expulsion was legal but declaring a member "incapable" of election was outside the rules of Parliament. Burke had recognized immediately that the House of Commons was making law without the concurrence of the House of Lords and the king, but it would take many years for the people to grasp that idea. Even more important, this so-called law would open the possibility of a House electing itself. The majority party could block from candidacy all members of the opposition. Thirteen years hence, it would be John Wilkes who would remove this illegal law from the British Constitution, and eighteen years hence James Madison would follow his lead and write into the American Constitution measures to protect against such abuse by the legislature. But in the House of Commons on 17 February 1769, the momentous day that hardly anyone recognized as momentous, ended quietly with an order to issue a writ for a new by-election.

While all of this was going on, Wilkes was being rescued from debt by gentlemen followers, many of them recently won to the cause by the hearing on Wilkes's petition. On 20 February 1769, some four hundred gentlemen gathered at the London Tavern in Bishopgate Street and formed the Society of the Supporters of the Bill of Rights. Sergeant Glynn was elected as chair. The association took its name from the British bill of rights, enacted in 1689, a set of protections against tyranny of the Crown agreed to by William and Mary before they took the throne in 1688. Because it destroyed the doctrine of the divine right of monarchs and virtually ended the unchecked royal prerogative, it had great symbolic value for Whigs and especially for Wilkes's allies. George III was once again claiming the royal prerogative and was encroaching upon the rights of voters through his powerful influence in Parliament. The gentlemen of the Society of Supporters of the Bill of Rights had been brought together because they thought Wilkes was the only politician capable of leading a fight against the king's claims and his ministers' growing power. To keep the fight going, they set about paying his debts. The preamble of the Society's charter began, "Whereas John Wilkes, Esq., has suffered very greatly in his private fortune, from the severe and repeated persecutions he has undergone in behalf of the public, and as it seems reasonable to us, that the man who suffers for the public good, should be supported by the public. . . ."[30]

Many members of this new society, not knowing Wilkes well, assumed, as the historian John Sainsbury said, that "his indebtedness was part of the legacy of his unjust persecution by a vengeful administration." Wilkes's indebtedness seemed like a badge of honor. They would discover before long that his private debts were far from honorable. Walpole was amused that the Society would not give Wilkes what they had collected so he could pay off the creditors but negotiated with the creditors themselves: "They will not trust his divinity with his own offerings," said Walpole, "but are paying his debts and thefts. Is not there a sobriety in our madness that stamps it for our own?"[31]

It was not unheard of for supporters of a politician to pay off his debts. Lord North ran up twenty-nine thousand pounds in personal debts while serving as first minister, an accumulation far greater than Wilkes's, but North's debts were liquidated by George III out of public monies granted to him as the Secret Fund.[32]

Wilkes, his candidacy now assured, released a letter to the gentlemen, clergy, and freeholders of Middlesex on 20 February 1769, asking them to give him their votes for the third time.[33] It was a thoughtful letter in which Wilkes laid out the essentials of an argument that his incapacitation had been illegal because it was offered as a law even though it had been promulgated by one house of Parliament only, as Burke had recognized in the parliamentary debate. Wilkes was not an original philosopher, but he may have been the first person to make this argument in print. He was to refine and expand it in his *Letter to Samuel Johnson, LLD,* discussed below.

Another hurried nomination followed, and then the election on 16 March. That morning, a crowd of freeholders gathered at the Hoop and Falcon in St. Martins le Grand, proceeded with a band playing and colors flying over London Bridge to the King's Bench Prison, saluted Wilkes, marched on to Westminster Bridge, paused before St. James's Palace to sing "God Save the King," gave three cheers, and set out on the thirteen-mile walk to Brentford. Another group, this one of two hundred mounted gentlemen, began their process, as parades were called, at the prison. Having saluted Wilkes, they rode with flying colors over London Bridge to the Mansion House, gave three huzzahs to the lord mayor, on to the London Tavern, where they were joined by many coaches and post-chaises, on to St. James's Palace, sang "God Save the King," and on to Brentford.[34]

This time there might be competition. The day before, Charles Dingley had informed the sheriffs he would stand if nominated while on the hustings. Dingley was the man who had owned the wind-machine-driven sawmill that the sawyers had pulled down during the recent riots, and the grant of two thousand pounds' compensation from the Grafton ministry might have had something to do with his appearance at the election. A former soldier and prone to violence, he had been trying to muscle his way into politics. A few days before he had disrupted a meeting of gentlemen at the King's Arms who were drawing up an address to be presented to the king, got into a fight with Wilkes's new lawyer, John Reynolds, injured his hand on Reynolds's teeth, and got knocked flat for his pains. On this election morning, he came to Brentford, mounted the hustings, and announced he had four hundred supporters in the crowd who would put his name in nomination. No one spoke up. When the crowd began to boo, he left the hustings and withdrew his name. Half an hour later, the sheriffs announced that Wilkes had won unopposed. Again there was a triumphant parade to the prison, again a celebratory dinner, and again Wilkes wrote to thank the Middlesex voters.[35]

The next morning, 17 March, the sheriffs, as the law required, appeared at the House of Commons and handed in the election writ showing Wilkes the winner. The House was in confusion, for they had no precedent to go on. They could not legally refuse the writ. They could not expel the winner because they did not recognize him as elected. They summoned the deputy sheriff, who testified that "no other candidate was proposed but John Wilkes, Esquire, and that no elector gave or tendered his vote for any other person than the said John Wilkes." Finally, in blatant violation of law, they declared the election void and ordered a writ for another.[36]

The ministers were particularly angered that the election writ had been signed by fifteen gentlemen, an unprecedented number of witnesses. Suspicion fell upon James Townsend and John Sawbridge, and that evening the king's cabinet seriously discussed whether they could get them expelled also, though nothing was done. These two troublemakers were regarded as the intellectuals of the radical group. Townsend, the thirty-one-year-old squire of Tottenham, was Oxford-educated and a close friend of Lord Shelburne. He had been protesting the failure of Parliament to seat Wilkes in a way later used by Henry David Thoreau to protest slavery: he refused to pay his land tax. But he was less harshly treated by government than was Thoreau: he was fined but never jailed. Sawbridge, the brother of the radical historian Catharine Macaulay, was scrupulously honest, dreadfully ugly, and the best whist player in London. He was the son of a republican father, the squire of Olantigh, who brought up him and his sister on Roman history. His idealism was deep, but he had no charisma.[37] In the next few years he would follow the lead of Townsend and Wilkes and then waver confusedly when these two broke up.

The king's faction still had many followers in the old City, especially among the wealthy merchants and bankers. A group of these decided they could not just stand by while Wilkes made a mockery of the election. They drafted an address decrying Wilkes's winning of the by-elections and praising the king and managed to get the signatures of 600 liverymen. On 22 March, some 130 of them, including many gentlemen in their finery, set out in a long procession of coaches and horsemen to carry the letter to St. James's Palace. They got to Temple Bar, which at that time was still a medieval stone gate that could be shut by lowering the iron bars. The cavalcade found the Bar shut against them. A mob began to pelt them with mud — with urban mud, largely made up of horse and human feces.[38] They tried to leave the City by Grey's Inn Lane, but it was blocked by a mob. They wound through the narrow streets trying to find a way out, carriages dropping out at each turn. A handful got to St. James's Palace but found it surrounded by a sea of protestors, in the midst of whom was a hearse with pictures painted on the sides representing the shooting of Allen in St. George's Field and the bludgeoning of Clerke at Brentford Butts during Glynn's election. Soldiers were called, but the crowd pushed up to the muzzles of their firelocks. "Everyone was covered with dirt," wrote the Duke of Chandos, "and several gentlemen were pulled out of their carriages by neck and heels at the palace gate." Earl Talbot, Wilkes's opponent in his first duel, who still was serving as steward to the royal household, took his white staff and courageously confronted the mob, who promptly took away the staff and broke it. Talbot, an athlete, seized one man, and the soldiers a few more. The crowd responded by forcing their way into the courtyard of the palace, where they performed a pantomime of beheading the king.[39]

Meanwhile Wilkes kept the election and its suppression before the public. On 23 March, he released a thoughtful letter to the voters: "The question is, whether the people have an inherent right to be represented in Parliament by the man of their free choice, not disqualified by the law of the land? . . . It is part of the original compact between the sovereign of this nation and the subject." Although he called the right to legal representation "inherent," he based his argument on the authority of English law, not Natural Law. And he saw rightly that the case was neither petty nor local: "The cause is national and of the first magnitude. On this public ground I will stand firm. No danger shall deter me from my duty."[40] The cause, in fact, was becoming international.

By now the ministry had decided that the way to stop Wilkes was to find a candidate of their own who would be courageous enough to remain at the hustings. On March 24, there appeared in the papers an open letter to the voters of Middlesex from Colonel Henry Lawes Luttrell, announcing that he would stand for knight of the shire and asking their support. Luttrell, a small man but strong in body, if not in mind, had distinguished himself for courage in the Portugal campaign during the Seven Years War. He was a member of Parliament for Bossiney but had promised to resign that seat to stand for

Middlesex. Luttrell was, said Walpole, "a hotheaded and an interested man, and hitherto had always made the rashness of his head subservient to the lucre that reigned in his heart." He was the eldest son of Simon Luttrell, Baron Irnham, of Four Oaks, Warwickshire, and Luttrellstown, County Dublin. Both father and son were notorious womanizers, and they hated each other. The father once challenged the son to a duel, but the son declined because, he said, his father was not a gentleman.[41]

The recruiting of Luttrell brought a letter from Wilkes warning the voters that the method of the ministry was to divide and conquer. Not wanting his point to be lost, he held off publishing the letter until 7 April, less than a week before the next election.[42]

Polling again was to take place at Brentford, on 13 April 1769. Walpole described the election as more like a martial than an electoral campaign. Besides Luttrell, who was a colonel with a record of courage, and Wilkes, who was a former militia colonel and duelist, there was a late entry into the lists, a dueling Irish adventurer named Captain David Roach. One contestant only had no military credentials, a lawyer, William Whitaker, who entered the lists seemingly in the hope he would be elected should the mob kill Luttrell. Great bets were made on Luttrell's life, especially after it was discovered his life had been insured for a month at Lloyd's coffeehouse.[43]

The poll was prepared for at Brentford. Once again, many voters were brought to the town in prearranged carriages. Again there were cavalcades of horsemen parading to the prison, to the palace, to Brentford. There were constables stationed along the route, horse guards on patrol, justices of peace assembled here and there. The mobs broke no windows and damaged no property, but they were active. Luttrell opened his door that morning to find his way blocked by a crowd of people. He had to leave by breaking down a wall in the back garden and missed the planned breakfast at Lord Holland's. He had expected to ride to Brentford escorted by a hundred or so gentlemen on horseback, but only about twenty hearty souls appeared. At Hyde Park Corner they were met by a crowd who shouted insults, and a sharp-eyed mudslinger knocked off Luttrell's hat. The cavalcade broke into a gallop, and the crowd made way before them. They reached Brentford to find a mass of voters who would not let Luttrell get to the hustings. Wilkes's friends Townsend, Beckford, and Parson Horne pushed their way to Luttrell and took him through the crowd. There were brief speeches, Sawbridge speaking for Wilkes, and there were many pleas for order. Roach the adventurer now showed his colors by trying to pick a fight with Luttrell. Luttrell told him he would give him satisfaction, but not until after the poll. The sheriffs then asked Roach to show them his credentials, but he had none to show. He was eliminated before the polls were opened and left the scene promptly. Whitaker the lawyer stuck it out. The polling itself was peaceful, closing at five o'clock. Wilkes had 1,143 votes, Luttrell 296, and Whitaker 5. Bells were set ringing at Brentford and picked up from church to church until London's hundred bell towers set up a din. Houses on the principal streets were lit up. There was no rioting, but several thousand gay people marched along the Great West Road and met with crowds from the metropolis to throng over London and Westminster Bridges to shout their congratulations at Wilkes in his barred window. Wilkes wrote yet another letter of thanks to the voters.[44]

Two days later, on 15 April, the House of Commons was called to order, although half the members were absent. Those who owed their seats to the administration but were fearful of displeasing their constituents by voting against Wilkes just stayed home. George Onslow, who for so long had been Wilkes's friend and supporter, surprised everyone by moving "That Henry Lawes Luttrell Esq. ought to have been returned a member for Middlesex to serve in this present Parliament for the county of Middlesex." Onslow had become obsessed with the authority of the House and turned against Wilkes because he challenged it. The motion was debated until two in the morning, when it was carried by 197 to 143, and the clerk was directed to amend the election return to show Luttrell as the winner.[45]

Thus a new dimension was added to incapacitation. The seat held empty by an illegal incapacitation was to be filled by appointment. "Tyranny of the majority" was not yet a phrase, for the majority were not yet franchised. But people were coming to realize that the seating of Luttrell was, as John Brooke put it, "an act of aggression against the people — but by the House of Commons, not the Crown." The House of Commons, the people's safeguard against the tyranny of the Crown, had turned against them. Americans were filled with despair, for they too saw in incapacitation a clear sign that Parliament had become the antagonist of the people.[46]

All London was on edge. The streets were full of soldiers, and people hesitated to go out unless they had footmen to protect them. Luttrell was assaulted as he left St. Stephen's Chapel and began to go about armed. Mrs. Barnard, Wilkes's lady friend, saw him at an art show at Christies, "armed cap-a-pie, in boots, spurs, hanger, regimental hat . . . such a pigmy." She gave him her best withering stare and declared loudly to everyone nearby that he would soon lose his "Quixotic war." He tried going to the theater but found himself hissed by the audience. Newspapers abused him. Pamphlets told scandalous stories about him. "The pretender to the County of Middlesex," as Mrs. Barnard called him, hardly dared to leave his house.[47]

There was a wave of pamphlets and public letters. The gentlemen of the

Society of the Supporters of the Bill of Rights and others of their class and sympathy argued that the incapacitation was nothing but a political move: by waiting ten months before expelling him, the House had tacitly admitted that Wilkes was legally elected; when they excluded him the first time, Wilkes had been neither a prisoner nor legally an outlaw. The most effective essay was that of Sir William Meredith, *The Question Stated, whether the Freeholders of Middlesex Lost Their Right by Voting for Mr. Wilkes at the Last Election?*, for he took care to lay the foundation of the argument in common law. He vindicated Wilkes's preface to the letter of Lord Weymouth, who had told the local justices that troops were needed at St. George's Fields whenever civil authority "is trifled and insulted." "For God's sake," cried Meredith, what do these words "trifled and insulted" mean? "Are we doomed to instant death by orders we can neither define nor know the extent of?"

Of the many pamphlets that supported the incapacitation, the only one still being read is Dr. Samuel Johnson's *The False Alarm*. It is read today largely for its witty diatribes against the public clamor, sarcastic attacks upon petitions, and mocking descriptions of election hoopla. But the fundamental argument is a legal one. Johnson's position was that the House of Commons had a right to expel Wilkes because the House was the only judge of its own rights. When Wilkes was unseated, reelected, and reseated again and again, the House had a right to put a stop to the nonsense by declaring him incapable of election. When Wilkes ignored them and offered himself for reelection, the votes for him, being votes for an illegal candidate, were "thrown away." The greatest number of votes for a *legal* candidate was decisive: therefore, Luttrell was elected.[48]

Wilkes answered in a pamphlet published anonymously, though his authorship was an open secret, *A Letter to Samuel Johnson, L.L.D.*, that appeared on 19 February 1770. He began by teasing the great man for his language: "Believe me, Sir, the intellectual sight of ordinary freeholders is liable to be offusqued by a superfluous glare of erudition . . . you must sink into a language of a lower stature than bendecasyllables." Speaking seriously, Wilkes agreed with Johnson that the House had the right to eject a member. But that was not the issue. An ejected member becomes "another man," independent of the rules of the House, which are internal rules. The voters, who can put up whomever they wish for election, can nominate this independent man if they wish. The House makes rules for itself alone, not for anyone outside the membership. In declaring an incapacity, which was a rule affecting people outside, the House of Commons was making law by itself. It would be possible to legalize incapacity, but only by statute, that is, by agreement of both houses of Parliament with royal assent. But if incapacity can be declared on an ad hoc basis by the House of Commons alone, and candidates who have the highest number of votes replaced by others who do not, it is possible for the House to choose itself. The majority party could unseat anyone they disliked and put in the empty place anyone they liked. By ancient common law, constituents have the right, said Wilkes, to elect whom they please. He accused Johnson of speaking treason "when he said that rights were given to the people by the Parliament. "Do you conceive the full force of the word CONSTITUENT?" he asked Johnson. "It has the same relation to the House of Commons as Creator to creature. The RIGHTS OF THE PEOPLE are not what the Commons have ceded to them, but what they have reserved to themselves." For Wilkes, said the historian John Brewer, legitimate political power "was to emanate from below, not percolate down from above."[49]

In the fall of 1769, Wilkes gained some unexpected and unwelcome support from certain aristocrats. George Grenville, who had been first minister when Wilkes was arrested for *North Briton* No. 45 and conspired against him for the Essay on Woman, had been reconciled to his brother, Wilkes's old patron, Lord Temple. For a time the brothers had opposed their brother-in-law, Lord Chatham, but in November of 1769, Chatham came out of seclusion and was reunited with them. These three old-timers now let it be known they would oppose any measure to expel Wilkes. Wilkes was not at all certain he wanted the support of Chatham, who had publicly reviled him as one who "did not deserve to be ranked among the human species." His distrust and dislike of Grenville had turned to fury when Grenville published the speech he had made in the House of Commons opposing the exclusion of Wilkes. Grenville had tried to excuse his own part in the arrest of Wilkes in 1763 and his conviction in 1764 by casting the blame for those events on Wilkes. Wilkes, who found these remarks egregiously misleading and hypocritical, had let them pass when made on the floor of the House, but when Grenville printed them, he was furious. Risking Temple's anger, he attacked the printed speech in *A Letter to the Right Hon. George Grenville*. The pamphlet is sarcastic, even acrimonious, but it seems not to have angered Lord Temple, who continued to give his old protégé moral, if not financial support.[50]

On 8 May, the House of Commons, having listened to a complaint by Luttrell about the uncertainty of his position, by a vote of 221 to 152 declared that Luttrell had been "duly elected."[51] There was no chance now that Wilkes could take his seat during this parliament, but parliaments had a seven-year lifespan, and when this one would expire five years in the future, the incapacity would expire with it.

Disgruntled Middlesex freeholders began to hold meetings in taverns to protest the seating of Luttrell. The king was worried and sent spies to watch them. On 17 April, a vast crowd showed up at the Mile End Assembly Rooms for a meeting called by Sawbridge and Townsend. Most were not qualified to vote, but the radicals respected their wishes and tried to act in their interest. Some fifteen hundred managed to pack themselves into the rooms, and another five or six thousand stood in the road outside. Parson Horne made a fiery speech, after which the crowd accepted his proposal for a committee to prepare a "Bill of Grievances and Apprehensions" for presentation to the House of Commons. Other meetings followed, the content was worked out, the signatures were gathered, and the petition was presented to the House by Sir George Savile on 29 April. The House put off consideration of it. Not in the least defeated, Sawbridge and Townsend called another meeting at Mile End and drafted a second document, this one a petition to the king. They and Glynn and other members of the House presented it to his highness at his levée of 24 May.[52] The king did not respond.

The long-term effects of these meetings were momentous. Fired by the enthusiasm of the populace, the leaders of the Society of Supporters of the Bill of Rights decided to launch a campaign to raise petitions and remonstrances from all over England. At a dinner at the Thatched House Tavern, they convinced Dowdeswell and Burke and others of the Rockingham Whigs to join in. They then divided the tasks: those who had property or interest in a county were assigned that area. In the autumn of 1769 and winter of 1770 they carried out the plan. Individual members undertook long, often arduous journeys in order to organize meetings of local folk, showing them how to do petitions and urging them on. The petitions were not uniform, but two demands appeared in all of them: that voters be guaranteed those rights that had been denied in the seating of Luttrell and that ministerial influence over the House of Commons be reduced or abolished. Beyond these cardinal points, a variety of demands appeared in one or another petition— demands for a "place law" that would prohibit those who have government position from serving in the House of Commons, for tighter control of public monies, for shorter parliaments, for members of Parliament to take an oath forswearing bribery in elections, for the abolition of rotten boroughs, for the right of printers to a jury trial when accused of libel, and for a secret ballot.[53] No attempt was made in Scotland or Wales, where most of the voters were dead set against Wilkes.

Many of the gentlemen taking part in this campaign did not much like John Wilkes personally, but they could not do without him because his distorted face, his No. 45, his cry of "Wilkes and Liberty" had become the symbols that converted public discontent into public action. Sergeant Glynn, despite his gout, traveled through the southwest, speaking at Cornwall, Devonshire, and

Exeter. Mawbey did Essex. Parson Horne and George Bellas, an attorney, concentrated on Surrey. Lord Temple took a particular interest in the Aylesbury petition and authored that of Buckinghamshire. There were petitions from Wiltshire, Worcestershire, Hertfordshire, Wells, Derbyshire, Northumberland, Durham, Carnarvon, seventeen counties in all. There was even a petition from Boston, presented by Colonel Barré. The most spectacular success was the Yorkshire petition urged by Lord Rockingham, Sir George Savile, and John Fountayne, the dean of York Minster. By posting the petition here and there in the market squares of towns, they secured eleven thousand signatures.[54] Not every attempt was successful. At the request of the ministry, the lord lieutenants of some counties organized counter meetings and petitions. But the petitions on that side had far fewer signatures. In the end, the petitions of protests had been signed by sixty thousand people, more than a quarter of the voters in England.

None of the petitions did George III deign to answer. His majesty, said an anonymous writer, must be of the opinion "that the inferior freeholders were not capable of understanding what they signed, that the farmers and weavers of Yorkshire and Cumberland could neither know nor take any interest in what befell the freeholders of Middlesex," that their petitions would be regarded as the work of "a rabble . . . an ignorant multitude, incapable of judging."[55]

The House of Commons now entered the petition movement by debating the question of how the king ought to respond to remonstrances. The debate was so acrimonious that Walpole thought it dangerous: "Such was the dangerous and disgraceful situation into which the unconstitutional intrusion of Luttrell had drawn the Court . . . one of the humiliating effects that had flowed from their original illegality in the prosecution of Wilkes, — a speaking lesson to Princes and Ministers to stretch the strings of prerogative! The whole reign of George the Third was a standing sermon of the same king; and the mortifications I have been recounting were but slight bruises compared to the wounds he afterwards received by not contenting himself with temperate power and established obedience."[56]

The livery of London were particularly indignant that the king had not responded to their petition. To jump ahead in our story, because the event did not happen until the next year, the livery drew up a "remonstrance" on the Middlesex election, declaring that "the majority of the House of Commons had done a deed more ruinous in its consequences than the levying of ship-money by Charles the First, and the dispensing power of James the Second." It was to be presented by Lord Mayor Beckford, the unchallenged leader of the City radicals, but a laughable public speaker. Wilkes had made fun of him in the *North Briton* for declaring he was going to argue "*à priori* from facts." On this occasion, the presenters of the petition, a group of liverymen and City officials, including Wilkes's friends the Rev. Dr. Thomas Wilson and John Sawbridge, paraded to St. James's Palace, where with all due ceremony the lord mayor presented the remonstrance to his majesty, who read it and then nodded to his chamberlain, Lord Hertford, who read aloud the prepared response. The king then addressed Lord Hertford and informed him that if the delegation desired, they might kiss his hand. They did so desire and did so kiss, except that when Dr. Wilson and John Sawbridge came forward to kneel, his majesty withdrew his hand. The ceremony finished, the king "instantly turned round to his courtiers and burst out laughing." Abashed, the City people retired. A report of this event got the dander up of Lord Chatham, and he moved in the House of Lords an angry resolution that the king's response to the City remonstrance was "disrespectful to his Majesty, injurious to his Parliament, and irreconcilable to the Principles of the Constitution." It failed to carry. But Chatham's old friends in the City did not fail. They prepared another remonstrance, and a determined Mayor Beckford and the livery again marched to St. James's and presented it to his highness. The king replied curtly. The lord mayor, instead of backing away bowing, as was the custom, stood his ground and addressed his sovereign: "Permit me, Sire, farther to observe that whosoever has already dared or shall hereafter endeavor . . . to alienate your Majesty's affections from your loyal subjects in general, and from the City of London in particular . . . is an enemy to your Majesty' s person and family, a violator of the public peace, and a betrayer of our happy Constitution, as it was established at the Glorious Revolution." The company was shocked and amazed, as was Beckford himself. There is a story that as soon as he left the palace, Parson Horne rushed up to him and asked what he had said. The lord mayor, according to this story, replied that he was so confused he could not remember. Horne then said they had to have something to give the newspapers and rushed off and wrote the speech. Beckford died shortly thereafter, still the hero. A statue of him was raised in the Guildhall, and the words of the speech placed below it.[57]

The Society of Supporters of the Bill of Rights had been wonderfully successful in raising money. Among the contributors was the Commons House of South Carolina, which paid Wilkes the great compliment of sending the society fifteen hundred pounds. Wilkes was not named in their letter. The money was sent "for the support of the just and constitutional rights and liberties of the people of Great Britain and America," but the delegates knew it would be used to support Wilkes. Someone reported what had happened to the ministry, and on 14 April 1770, Lord Weymouth sent a letter to the royal governor of

South Carolina ordering him to stop the payment. Commons House refused, asserting they were within their rights. The governor suspended all payments of allocated money until the grant to the Society was recalled. The stubborn resistance of the Commons House brought to a halt all normal government in the colony. There were no annual tax bills, no payments of claims. A virtual anarchy continued in South Carolina for five years! all over a dispute about the right of the legislature to send money to support John Wilkes. The dispute never was resolved: it was muted when the revolutionary provincial congress of South Carolina took over legislative authority in 1775.[58]

In the summer of 1769, the Boston Sons of Liberty sent Wilkes two more turtles. He wrote to thank them, assuring them "of all the services in my power for the common cause we have at heart." Friends of America, he told them, were trying to find ways to bring Governor Sir Francis Barnard to England and to trial in Westminster Hall, "for having dared to quarter troops contrary to an express act of Parliament." Sergeant Glynn was advising them gratis: "Petitions to the King and Parliament are useless, although necessary, forms. They are both determined against you. . . . You have many warm friends here who will never give up your cause, nor rest till the declaratory bill, as well as all the late duties are absolutely repealed. I am proud to be one of the foremost in that cause."[59]

Late in 1769, Wilkes received another letter from the Boston Sons of Liberty, bearing the same impressive list of signatures: "Our city is yet a garrison filled with armed men, as our harbor is with cruzers, cutters, and other armed vessels. A main guard is yet placed at the door of our Statehouse." The soldiers are brutal, the streets unsafe, the criminal courts interested only in crimes by Americans. The Sons of Liberty fear another "family compact" between France and Spain, who with their Indian allies are making sounds of war in the Mississippi valley and western Canada. If the Spanish or French forces gathered in the Caribbean should attack America, the British navy cannot defend them, attenuated as they are down the whole coast in support of customs officers who are bent upon destroying American commerce: "We flatter ourselves you will be so kind as yet to accept of our most sincere thanks for all your noble and generous expressions of regard for the colonies. We yet so sensibly feel the loss of every right, liberty, and privilege that can distinguish a freeman from a slave not to sympathize in the most tender manner with you in the conflicts you have been so long engaged in, and in the sufferings you now severely labor under, so far as we can judge, only for a firm and intrepid opposition to ministerial despotism."[60]

The protests at Boston only caused the king to send another troop of soldiers. On 5 March 1770, a street crowd jeered at them and threw stones. The soldiers fired, killing several. American newspapers called it the Boston Massacre and likened it to the Massacre of St. George's Fields. The reaction in the colonies, not only in Massachusetts but in all the colonies, was to harden their resolve to resist. "The colonists," wrote the American historian Pauline Maier, "had begun to advance along the road from resistance to revolution." On 20 March 1770, James Bowdoin, Samuel Pemberton, and Joseph Warren, at the behest of the Town of Boston, wrote to Wilkes to inform him of the facts of the Boston Massacre. Because accounts they considered false had been sent to England, they were distributing the "true" account to "persons of character." The pamphlet they sent, written by the three, was "an emotionally charged and highly inaccurate rendering that presented the soldiers as bloodthirsty miscreants and murderers."[61] Another copy reached Thomas Hollis, who started up his propaganda machine again, scattering over England this account of the Boston Massacre.

The Society of Supporters of the Bill of Rights, meanwhile, was collecting money and satisfying creditors. When Wilkes would be released from prison, the Society would have liquidated virtually all of his debts. They paid one thousand pounds in fines. They satisfied twelve thousand pounds of personal debts and gave Wilkes one thousand pounds for his personal use. They paid off three thousand pounds of election debts. Wilkes had borrowed five hundred pounds on a bond to bribe his election to Aylesbury. The original bond had later been bought by an eccentric London banker, Isaac Ferdinand Silva, well known for transacting his business at the exchange, buying and selling bonds and stocks, from the back of a magnificent stallion held by a servant. Silva, who had a reputation for generosity, agreed to settle for five hundred fifty pounds, though the value of the bond, through compounded interest over a dozen years, had grown to two thousand pounds.[62]

The Society was hesitant to return the money owed to the Foundling Hospital, for they had been told it was acquired through "a breach of trust." It was returned by three unidentified members who, as Almon reported, went to Aylesbury and "compounded this remnant."[63]

On 21 April, Wilkes was brought by habeas corpus to Lord Mansfield's rooms in Sergeants Inn, located at Fetter Lane and Fleet Street. The Society posted bail against various charges for unpaid debts. Some days before, they had given notice to Wilkes's creditors that he would be there, and they might appear and charge him if they thought fit. None were willing to risk public displeasure, and none showed up. Wilkes was put into a coach to be returned to the prison, but a crowd chased after it and at St. Clement Danes stopped it, took off the horses, and pulled it toward City. Wilkes escaped into the Crown and Anchor Tavern and then sneaked into another coach to get back to the prison.[64]

At long last, on 10 November 1769, Wilkes, represented by his lawyers, won the suit against Lord Halifax which he had initiated six years before. Lord Temple testified as a witness. Wilkes had asked for twenty thousand pounds in damages but was awarded four thousand. Halifax had expected to pay nothing out of his own pocket, for he had an agreement with the Treasury that his expenses in prosecuting Wilkes would be reimbursed; but Wilkes, as he told his old friend Jean-Baptiste Suard, "forced Halifax's agent to pay them to my solicitor without any intervention of the Treasury, for I would not touch their money." It was some months before the money was actually given up, but when he had it in hand, he paid off his legal fees and the old militia debt, which the Society had been reluctant to pay. He was left with some two thousand pounds, which he offered to the Society; they declined to accept it.[65]

In the spring of 1769, the daughter of Laurence Sterne came to the prison to see Wilkes. The novelist had died two years before, leaving a widow and daughter without fortune enough to maintain their way of life, and Lydia, the daughter, was trying to make as much money as she could out of her father's letters and sermons. She proved herself an unscrupulous editor, bowdlerizing letters that were unflattering to her mother and forging others. This ridiculous woman came to Wilkes to ask him to collaborate with John Hall-Stevenson, a friend to both Sterne and Wilkes, on a life of Sterne. No doubt Hall-Stevenson had the information needed, but Wilkes, whose personal knowledge of Sterne was limited to their visits in Paris, could contribute little more than his name. Unwisely, both he and Hall-Stevenson promised. Lydia and her mother went to France, where they would live out the rest of their lives, and Hall-Stevenson and Wilkes would never fulfill their obligation.[66]

In the autumn, Wilkes made arrangements for Jackie Smith to go to Paris to study. He would stay with M. Cauchoix, *maitre de pension*, à la Barrière de Trone, Fauxbourg St Antoine, Paris, and he would study to become a soldier. A friend, Stratford Canning, would handle the money Wilkes sent, and Suard would from time to time evaluate his progress.[67] The boy would take to this sort of education, and Wilkes, who loved the soldier life himself, would in time find him a delightful companion.

Polly continued to visit the King's Bench Prison and to represent her father outside it. At an elaborate dinner and ball given by Lord Mayor Beckford, she had been "prodigiously huzzahed," said Wilkes. In November 1769, we find Wilkes inviting Polly to join him and John Reynolds for dinner.[68] Reynolds had replaced Glynn as Wilkes's lawyer. Glynn continued as a major voice in arguing Wilkes's side, but now spoke from the floor of the House of Commons. Wilkes had never been personally close to Glynn, a refined gentleman. But he enjoyed the company of the rough-mannered Reynolds, who laughed heartily at his dirty jokes.

It was gratifying to Wilkes to learn he had never been removed from his position as one of the governors of the Aylesbury grammar school, and pleasant to hear how his forty-fourth (perhaps) birthday was celebrated noisily but peacefully all over England. In London, forty-five tradesmen dined on forty-five pounds of beef in a room lighted by forty-five candles.[69]

Mrs. Barnard ceased coming to the prison late in 1769, but Wilkes soon was making advances toward another woman, a Mrs. Otto, the mistress of another Wilkite supporter. Her protector did not object to her coming to see Wilkes alone, she said, but she wanted nothing more than Wilkes's friendship. When he persisted, she was peeved: "I have not observed your injunctions as far as relates to my male friend. He is thoroughly satisfied I shall act perfectly consistent with my feelings for him, and I am sure when you have considered the matter you will be convinced your request is an improper one."[70] Wilkes stopped insisting, and Mrs. Otto lost her place in history.

Parliament opened on 9 January 1770 with the king's traditional address to both houses written by his ministers. Having returned to their separate halls, both houses began discussing the address each would return to his majesty. In the House of Lords, Chatham moved an amendment to the address, begging the House to "take into consideration the causes of the discontent which prevails . . . and particularly the late proceedings of the House of Commons touching the incapacity of John Wilkes." The electors of Middlesex are deprived of their free choice of a representative, said Chatham, and a man's rights are taken from him, not by a law of the land, but by the resolution of one house of Parliament only. Lord Chancellor Camden surprised everyone by rising in the House to support Chatham and to deplore the illegal and unconstitutional action of the House of Commons in declaring Luttrell elected. The amendment was voted down. The next day Camden resigned as lord chancellor. Grafton's ministry was tottering.[71]

In the House of Commons, Sir George Savile, whose moral authority was preeminent in Parliament, rose to say about the incapacity, "I look on this House as sitting illegally after their illegal act. They have betrayed their trust. I will not add epithets, because epithets only weaken; therefore I will not say that they have betrayed their country corruptly, flagitiously, and scandalously, but I do say they have betrayed their country; and I stand here to receive the punishment for having said so." General Conway suggested they send Savile to the Tower, but no one would take him up.[72]

Then a member of the ministry unexpectedly rose to support Savile. John Manners, usually called the Marquis of Granby, was one of those noblemen who could sit in the House of Commons because his father, the third duke of Rutland, sat in the House of Lords. Granby was commander-in-chief of the army and the idol of the soldiers and the populace. He raised his portly self, his bald head conspicuous among the powdered wigs, and abandoned the ministry by repenting of his vote on the seating of Luttrell. "I am not content with the vote I gave on the Middlesex election," he told the House. "I see it now in a different light. Had I seen it in that light before, I should have voted otherwise." Walpole might sneer that Granby "recanted a vote he had not understood, for reasons he understood as little,"[73] but his speech wounded the ministry badly. Granby and Camden were in violation of a time-honored tradition. When a cabinet member feels he must vote against his own ministry, the honorable thing is to resign *before* he speaks his opinion, for if he speaks out before resigning, he is repudiating the ministry and giving strong support to the opposition. Granby and Camden spoke out and then resigned. Their resignations constituted a revolt.

Other resignations followed. The king, desperate to keep Grafton's cabinet going, asked Charles Yorke to replace Camden as lord chancellor. The son of the late, universally admired Lord Chancellor Hardwicke, Yorke was a distinguished lawyer in his own right, and his lifelong ambition had been to follow his father as lord chancellor. As attorney general, he had more than once pursued or prosecuted Wilkes. But his sense of law told him that in the incapacitation of Wilkes, the king's friends had gone too far. Some of the people whom he most admired were disgusted with the government and going into opposition. He declined the chancellorship, but then, when urged by the king, accepted in an agony of doubt, kissed the king's hand, and three days after, cut his throat. Some believed he died of natural causes (as do some historians today), but most of the opposition agreed with the anonymous writer Junius: Yorke had died, "unable to survive the disgraceful honors which his gracious Sovereign had compelled him to accept. He was a man of spirit, for he had a quick sense of shame, and death has redeemed his character."[74]

The following day, 21 January 1770, Grafton resigned.

Lord North took over as first minister. This pudgy little man who looked so much like the king had a genius for manipulating Parliament. Unlike other first ministers, he did not relinquish the trust of manager of the king's interest in the House of Commons. He lost no time repairing the damage done to the king's ministry. Within a week, he had induced the House to pass a resolution declaring Wilkes's incapacity "agreeable to the law of the land and custom of Parliament." Chatham kept up the agitation from the House of Lords, and on 7 February, Chatham strongly argued that his House should interfere with the House of Commons for their resolutions incapacitating Wilkes. The lords voted that they had no right to interfere, but a dissentient was read into the record signed by forty-one nobles, including Temple and Rockingham, saying that the precedent in Wilkes's case opened the possibility of a House electing itself. Lord North was determined to admit no weakness, and on 16 February 1770, he led the House of Commons to pass a resolution declaring Wilkes's incapacity to be legal.[75]

The resolution sent John Hope, member for Linlithgow, into a state of despair. Those in power, he wrote, still "look down upon the lower class of people . . . as a distinct race of beings, despicable and worthless . . . the scum of the earth . . . not born to the common rights of humanity."[76] Hope was right about the ministry, but his despair was unwarranted. Wilkes, the champion of the middle and lower classes, had for the second time brought down a ministry that would not recognize the rights of voters. He had challenged the House of Commons and exposed its corruption and its failure to represent the people. "Wilkes and Liberty" had come to mean liberty from elected representatives as well as from the Crown and had become a battle cry in America. Wilkes's example had given courage to America, and his defeat in the Middlesex election controversy and before the King's Bench had taught them to distrust the justice of Great Britain.

Shortly before Wilkes was released from the King's Bench Prison, he received a letter from Mrs. Barnard apologizing for staying away for so long. He would understand that she was putting her hopes in the eighteenth of April, when she would be "a *freed-man*." Then she adds, "A *free-man* you know I have ever been, and will remain." Probably the eighteenth was the day she ran off to Paris with her stepdaughter's music master. But music masters being notoriously poor and unstable, she returned before long and was received by her husband into the old bondage. Wilkes dined with them at Berkeley Square during the Christmas holidays, but he passed no *billet doux* to Mrs. Barnard.[77]

On the day of his release, two open letters from Wilkes appeared in the newspapers, one addressed to the freeholders of Middlesex, the other to the inhabitants of the ward of Farringdon Without. They said nothing Wilkes had not said before and exaggerated the pains of his imprisonment, but they were much admired. Wilkes thought of them as his manifesto and wondered if the ministry would try to suppress them; but, as he wrote to Suard, "I rather suspect that Wilkes is too troublesome a fellow for any of them to choose to meddle with again."[78] He was right about that.

Wilkes was released from the King's Bench Prison at six in the afternoon on 17 April 1770. The ministry had put the Guards and Light Horse in readiness in case there was rioting, but the small crowd that had gathered outside the prison kept the peace.[79]

Wilkes waved to the crowd as he stepped from the prison gate to a post-chaise in which Polly was waiting; John Churchill, John Reynolds, and a young lawyer named John Trevanion followed in another, and off they went to

Reynolds's house at South Barrow, near Bromley, Kent. They were greeted by Mrs. Reynolds, who proudly brought downstairs her five-year-old son, Frederick, and told the story about how as a baby his first words had been "Wilkes and Liberty." The boy took one look at Wilkes, as he later wrote: "His forehead was low and short, his nose shorter, and lower, an upper lip long and projecting, and sunken eyes, squinting to a degree that their lines of vision must have crossed each other within two inches of the nose." The boy burst into tears. Wilkes only laughed and soon had the party relaxed and enjoying themselves.[80] The little boy also noticed Miss Wilkes and how her father doted upon her. Trevanion would write a letter to Wilkes saying he and his wife hoped some day to have a daughter and consider Wilkes the "best example" of fatherhood they had ever seen.[81]

The next day Wilkes called on Lord Chatham at his country house, Hayes. Now that Wilkes had been cleared of the charge of blasphemy, one suspects, Chatham wanted to make peace with him. Lord Temple was there and other political gentlemen, but not George Grenville, whose friendship Wilkes would never have accepted. Then it was back to Reynolds's, where his sister, Mrs. Hayley, and her daughter had arrived. In the next two days, he had numerous visitors, including Humphrey Cotes, James Townsend, William Sawbridge, Parson Horne, and Heaton Wilkes. On Sunday, friends took him home. He had not been at Prince's Court since Polly, with the help of her woman, La Vallerie, had taken charge. He wrote in his diary simply, "Lay there."[82]

Annual Register reported for the month of April 1770, "it has been remarked with astonishment, that there never was perhaps so general and voluntary illuminations and rejoicings on any occasion, as on the event of Mr. Wilkes's release; not in London only, but in every part of England." Cheering prisoners at Newgate illuminated their own windows. A table forty-five feet long was laid in a London street. In Sunderland, forty-five skyrockets were fired at forty-five-second intervals. At Greenwich, an inn used three hundred wax tapers to fashion the words "Wilkes and Liberty," skyrockets were set off every forty-five seconds, and there was a salute by forty-five cannons fired in sequence. In Northampton, forty-five couples did a country dance called the Wilkes's wriggle. "Illuminated," said Walpole sourly, were "many houses of the lower rank."[83]

II

The City of London

A saying went around London that "if Jack Wilkes were stripped naked and thrown over Westminster Bridge on one day, you would meet him the next day in Pall Mall, dressed in the height of fashion, and with money in his pocket." By the time he walked out of the King's Bench Prison, the Bill of Rights Society had cleared his debts. The next day, on 14 April 1770, the aldermen and other City officers gathered at the Guildhall to invest him as the alderman of the Ward of Farringdon Without. He arrived in a carriage with cheering people running beside. After informal greetings, he donned the traditional fur-trimmed robes that an admirer had presented to him. He then mounted the dais and was sworn in by the recorder. He turned to Lord Mayor Beckford, who with all due ceremony placed over his head a chain bearing the seal of his office. The lord mayor then ceremoniously escorted the new alderman to the door of the Guildhall and, with trumpeters blasting on either side, to the gilded coach of the lord mayors. With four footmen clinging to the rear, they were drawn slowly through cheering throngs to the Mansion House for a banquet.[1]

Wilkes was the least wealthy alderman in memory. His income amounted to something like four hundred fifty pounds a year, whereas Beckford had thirty-five thousand a year, most of it from vast plantations in Jamaica. The great wealth of Richard Oliver, another rising star in City radical politics, came

JOHN WILKES, Esq.

Elected Alderman of London Jan. 2. 1769

14. Wilkes as alderman of Farringdon Without. Courtesy of Gerald M. Goldberg.

from plantations in Antigua. Dr. Johnson famously asked, "How is it that we hear the loudest yelps for liberty among the drivers of negroes?"[2]

The next day, Alderman Wilkes, dressed in somber black robes with a long white wig upon his head, took his seat on the judges' bench at the Old Bailey. Most of the sessions of the Criminal Court of the City of London were held at the Old Bailey, an ancient sessions hall named for the road upon which it fronted. The court still sits in that place, but in a modern building. Newgate prison, to which the court then was attached institutionally and physically, is now gone, but at that time rose ominously above and behind the sessions hall. A panel of five judges sat, two of them full-time judges with primary duties elsewhere, perhaps in the Court of King's Bench or Common Pleas or one of the assize circuits. The remaining three were City officers, usually aldermen. Sessions often lasted until ten o'clock in the evening.[3]

Contemporary prints show the judges sitting elevated behind a high table, scribes below, large boxes containing the jury for London on one side, the jury for Middlesex on the other, with the accused standing in his own small box. The only participants not boxed are the lawyers, who speak from the floor. Spectators are crowded into the galleries above.[4]

A man could be called to jury duty if he owned a little property, enought to return ten pounds a year. Most jurymen were successful craftsmen or small businessmen, shoe menders, or fishmongers, a class often victimized by thieves and pickpockets but low enough on the social scale to be able to understand the impoverished poor who committed most of the crimes. The fate of most criminals rested upon the sympathy or lack thereof that they could elicit from the jury.[5]

The duties of the judges and juries were not light. Most of the men, or occasionally women, before the court were accused of theft. The prosecutor would make his case in five or ten minutes. The jury would deliberate. If they found the person guilty, they would set a monetary value on the stolen goods, and the prosecutor would do likewise. The judges would consider these estimates and mete out punishment accordingly. On a typical day, one man among the forty or so tried was sentenced to whipping for stealing two holland shirts evaluated at eight shillings by the prosecutor, but ten pence by the jury. Another was burned in the hand for stealing a gold ring. A print at the Guildhall Library, dated 1770, shows a man being branded on the palm of his hand at the Old Bailey, while a group of people, including women and children, are watching, perhaps the criminal's family. One child buries his face in the arm of the man who is holding him.[6] A third man, convicted of stealing a bed, two blankets, and a rug, was sentenced to be hanged.[7]

Other offenses were defined in law as capital crimes, punishable by death or

15. A panel of judges at the Old Bailey. Wilkes, second from the left, Lord Mansfield in the center, and various aldermen and City officers sit in judgment of a prisoner in the foreground. The jury for the City of London sits on the left, that for the County of Middlesex on the right. Courtesy of Gerald M. Goldberg.

transportation. Men were hanged for murder and rape, but also, by law, for poaching a hare, for refusing to pay taxes, or for planting a tree in Downing Street. Fortunately, juries had a more nuanced sense of justice than the law-makers and often acquitted those who they knew were guilty only because they thought the law unjust. Nevertheless, in the year Wilkes began to take turns on the bench, sixty-one times one judge or another at the Old Bailey put the black handkerchief upon his wigged head and pronounced, "To be hanged until dead."[8]

The hangings took place at Tyburn, on the edge of the Mayfair, close to Marble Arch, and hanging day was always a celebration, with vast numbers of people showing up to watch. In 1788, the hangings were moved to Old Bailey Street, outside the court, where temporary gallows were erected for the purpose of killing five or six at a time. "We hang at eight, now," said George Selwyn, "and breakfast at nine."[9]

Following the sessions, there was always a dinner for the judges in a dining hall at the Old Bailey court. In fact, there were two dinners, one at three o'clock and another at five for those who had been on duty at the earlier hour.

(Nothing was served at the second meal but beefsteaks.) One or another of the sheriffs presided, for it was they who provided these feasts. One finds from Wilkes's diary that the judge with whom he most often dined was Edward Willes, who had been one of the members of Parliament for Aylesbury when Wilkes arrived in that town, the brother of Wilkes's friend John Willes. Edward Willes was on loan, so to speak, from the King's Bench. Since his days representing Aylesbury, he had risen to associate justice of the Court of the King's Bench and had been one of the panel of judges that sent Wilkes to jail. But the meals passed amicably, for Wilkes never thought public enmity should stand in the way of private comradery.

Only days after Wilkes's release from prison, one of the members of Parliament for Westminster had a carriage accident and fractured his skull. A by-election was immediately called for. John Churchill, brother of the late poet, an apothecary who was a prominent political figure in Westminster, offered the support of his friends if Wilkes would run for the seat. Wilkes declined the offer, for he was at the moment, he said, "as much a legal member of the House of Commons as our Speaker himself. The only difference I can find out is, I represent the first county in England, he a small borough in Lincolnshire. I am a Knight of the Shire, he is a simple Burgess." Having no intention of vacating his Middlesex seat, he could not stand for Westminster. "I have taken my resolution, which you know is always very decided." Horace Walpole saw that, if Wilkes declined standing for Westminster, he could "name whom he pleases" to stand for that city.[10] Behaving like those great lords who dealt in parliamentary seats, Wilkes named Robert Bernard, one of the stalwarts of the Bill of Rights Society (they had recently simplified their name). The society promised to pay Bernard's election expenses, but they came to nothing for he was elected without opposition.

Wilkes's position as alderman was demanding. He now began "drudging," as he put it, "through the vast arrear of City business."[11] We find him "haranguing" the liverymen of his ward on political matters, substituting for the lord mayor in the mayor's court, and meeting the commissioners for new paving. The wardmen for Farringdon Without usually met in the vestry room of St. Sepulchre's Church, next to which stood the house of Mrs. Mead, where Wilkes's wife lived. He often had to attend great dinners in the Guildhall or Mansion House. "I fear I grow dull in this thick aldermanic air." In May, Walpole remarked, "I don't know whether Wilkes is subdued by his imprisonment . . . or whether his dignity of alderman has dulled him into prudence and the love of feasting, but hitherto he has done nothing but go to City banquets and sermons and sit at Guildhall as a sober magistrate."[12]

Polly and La Vallerie were off to Paris for a visit with her friend Madame

Chantereine, so they could see and help celebrate the spectacular wedding of the Dauphin. Wilkes often visited his mother in Hart St. Bloomsbury and others of his family, the Hayleys, his brothers, Heaton and Israel, and once Molly Nesbitt, Polly's cousin on her mother's side. He went to a ball at Mrs. Corneley's in Soho Square, but he declined to dance, having "scarcely yet learned to walk after so long a confinement," but stayed until two in the morning, "which you know," he wrote to Polly, "was a scene of great rakery for me." In June, he went for a few days to the country as guest of Squire William Tooke, and the two rambled about the countryside on horseback so that Wilkes could regain what he had lost in prison, the horseman's legs.[13] Horsemanship was as much a part of an eighteenth-century gentleman's equipment as the sword at his side.

Wilkes gave up his lodgings that spring and moved to the other side of Prince's Court, to a house that stood at the northeast corner, with windows opening onto Bird-cage Walk and the park. He had purchased the lease from a cousin. One wonders where he found the money to buy the lease of so valuable a property, but he had a genius for debt. No doubt Polly's expectations helped. Polly was still abroad. Wilkes would have an admired neighbor, Mrs. Catharine Macaulay, who had recently purchased another house in the Court. Mrs. Macaulay had published four volumes of her polemical history of seventeenth-century England and was hailed by liberals as a truth-sayer. She and her brother, John Sawbridge, member of Parliament for Hythe, were important in the circle of Wilkes supporters. Sawbridge, an unswerving advocate of liberty, had recently purchased the freedom of the City of London and was ambitious to give up Hythe and represent the City. Wilkes called Mrs. Macaulay "a noble English historian, who does so great honor to her sex, and ought to cover ours with blushes."[14]

Wilkes's new house needed renovation, so he leased a furnished house in Fulham, about four miles south of London, to wait for the work to be completed. He took with him Polly's cat, who had adopted him, he said, as well as her pet bullfinch, her canary, her linnet, her two parakeets, and her goldfish.[15]

On 15 May, he went to Mrs. Corneleys' "grand masquerade." The notorious masked balls offered by Theresa Corneleys in Carlisle House, Soho, were the nightclub life of the time. Wilkes wore his "new blue silk domino." He was amused to see one gentleman with a squinting mask carrying a cap of liberty on a pole in imitation of Hogarth's satire, and another as a squinting alderman. Ladies fussed over him, he told Polly, especially a charmer dressed as "the celebrated peasant with eggs," that is, Marie Antoinette. A few days later he went to another ball at Vauxhall with Sir Joseph Mawbey and after that another at Ranelagh. And there were gentlemen's clubs. A week after his release, he had been made president of the Antigallacians, a City club for the encouragement of manufacture, a group he continued to meet regularly at Mile End. As his diary reveals, he was often at the Beef Steak Club. On 1 February 1771, he dined at the Devil Tavern with the Retribution Club.[16]

The Dauphin's wedding took place in May, but Polly lingered in Paris for two months. She did not fail to make several visits to her young "cousin," Jack Smith, now in his teens, to see that he was properly cared for. "I am sure," Wilkes wrote to his daughter, "he will be disposed to look up to you with gratitude, as his second best friend. Have you seen him dance? Pray, desire Monsieur Cauchoix to do every thing in a handsome manner for him, and to let him enjoy all reasonable pleasures."[17] Wilkes sent Madam de Chantereine a token of gratitude for her hospitality to Polly, that prized delicacy, a pineapple from the West Indies, and made sure that Polly would present her with more appropriate gifts of thanks when she departed.

In August, Wilkes and his servant set off on horseback to meet Polly and La Vallerie in Dover. The churchbells were rung for him at every town, and he was fussed over at every stop. In Lewes, which lay on his route, he was entertained at a local club, the one occasion when John Wilkes might have shaken the hand of Thomas Paine, who five years in the future would shake the earth of America with his rousing *Rights of Man*. There is no documentary evidence of a meeting. Paine, as yet neither an American nor a republican, was living in Lewes, serving as an excise officer.[18] If Wilkes had any influence upon him, it would have been smothered by the greater influence of Benjamin Franklin, who loved liberty but not Wilkes. Paine would move to London in 1774, where he would meet Franklin, who would send him off to America to join the cause.

Polly and La Vallerie duly arrived, and Wilkes and the two women set off on a leisurely journey through Sandwich, Margate, Canterbury, Olantigh, Ashford, Maidstone, bells ringing, wined and dined at every stop. Renovations were not yet completed at Prince's Court, so Wilkes brought his little family to the house he had rented in Fulham, which they would occupy through the autumn of 1770. On 20 December, they moved to Prince's Court. Though the house was new to Polly, the household was not. La Vallerie had served Polly when she was a girl. Charles, the footman, had traveled with Wilkes in France during his exile. The valet, Samuel Dryer, had served Wilkes in the King's Bench Prison. Finally, there was a "bonne," a cook whom Polly had brought from France. His enemies found it a fault that so many of his servants were French.[19]

Late in the summer, between court terms, Wilkes and Polly made another trip through the southeast, but this was a political trip for Wilkes, who was assessing his support in rural areas. Again he and Polly were feted and fussed over. "The people here in the West," said Thomas Hollis, the radical writer, who had moved to Devonshire, "do not talk much concerning politics." But as to Wilkes, "they perceive no other person who stands forth with any tolerability to combat ministries, and uphold their rights." Soon after Wilkes and Polly got back, on 8 September 1770, Wilkes was given the freedom of the city for King's Lynn. But his head was not turned, and he had made his assessment: he was honored in those towns and counties as the hero of the Middlesex election controversy, but the people had little interest in the causes he looked toward in the future, freedom of the press, parliamentary reform, the rights of Americans. He decided he could best effect these programs in the old City of London. He could also serve himself best there, for election to some lucrative City office on top of his aldermanship was a possibility. He would concentrate upon City politics.[20]

Wilkes, who had grown up on the edge of the City, knew very well it was vulnerable to control from outside. Monarchs and great nobles from time immemorial had meddled in City politics, trying to control the councils and to put their own people into City offices by buying votes, purchasing the freedom of the City for their supporters, and granting favors. Lord Bute was still trying to exercise this sort of control. But Pitt, now Lord Chatham, had found a better way. Without a single bribe, he had won the votes and the hearts of the livery, by stimulating trade and commerce and manufacture. He brought wealth to the bankers and traders and work to the working forces. Lord Rockingham's faction tried to follow the Chatham model and assigned Edmund Burke to keep his influence alive in the City.[21]

Wilkes was not worried. Rockingham would never abandon the Whig oligarchy, and Chatham's hold had weakened when he accepted a peerage and when he had temporarily withdrawn from politics because of his breakdown. After Chatham returned from this period of illness, he repeatedly urged the House of Lords to reverse the Middlesex election decision, but, as Walpole said unkindly, "Like an old beauty in an unfashinable dress which became her in her youth, he found that his charms are no longer killing."[22]

Wilkes would have to work with Lord Mayor Beckford, who for many years had been Chatham's lieutenant in the City. He had no objection to Beckford's "platform of reform," except that his program was standing still. He had long advocated shorter parliaments, to break the king's hold on the House of Commons; a place-and-pension bill to keep out of the House those whose incomes depended upon their support of the government in the legislature; and more equitable representation of the people. By "equitable representation," Beckford meant doing away with pocket boroughs and giving the populous towns of the north a representation that reflected their numbers, but he never doubted that the franchise should be limited to people of property. His program had the virtue of simplicity and could be carried in every voter's head. Or *on* their heads. Many people could be seen walking the streets of the City with tickets in their hats on which was printed, "Annual Parliaments. Equal Representation. Place and Pension Bill."[23]

On 21 June 1770, while Wilkes was waiting for the right moment to challenge Beckford, the man died. City politicians began scrambling for position, but Wilkes stood aside, waiting to see what would happen. There was a by-election to choose a mayor to fill out the remaining months of Beckford's term. The winner was Barlow Trecothick, an American.

Trecothick was not very bright, and within weeks of taking office he blundered and thereby gave Wilkes a chance to step forward. Trecothick signed a warrant that recognized the right of press gangs to operate in the City.[24] Press gangs were navy seamen or soldiers who, under orders from their superiors, kidnapped men of a serviceable age and "pressed" them, that is, forced them into the navy and less often the army. The navy was especially dependent upon press gangs when they needed to build up their ranks rapidly, and that was the case in the autumn of 1770, the time of the first Falkland Islands crisis, when Spain tried to seize islands that Great Britain considered hers.

It was John Wilkes, in his black robes and wig, who reversed Trecothick's ruling and banished press gangs from the City. He was presiding at the Guild-hall when a young barber named John Shine brought before the court an appeal for release from a naval press. With the temerity born of years of opposition to government, Wilkes ruled that press warrants were illegal within the City and ordered the press officers to discharge young Shine. The ruling caused a hubbub in the newspapers, and Wilkes was accused of making new law, which probably was the case. But other aldermen, seeing how popular the ruling had made Wilkes, followed suit in their courts and began releasing those who contested the impressment. Wilkes welcomed their backing, but the attorney general objected. Eventually the City solicited a legal opinion from the highly respected Sergeants Dunning and Glynn, who advised that press warrants were of doubtful validity and magistrates were not required to sign them. Thereafter press gangs had to look elsewhere. Wilkes's popularity with the working-class livery shot up.[25]

Wilkes was now moving, slowly but deliberately, toward the leadership of London politics. According to Louis Namier and John Brooke, among the greatest historians of eighteenth-century England, in the two or three years after his release from prison, Wilkes's case "turned a mass of inchoate, deeply-felt discontent into political channels," and a "new political force" came into being, urban radicalism. "It is one of Wilkes's main titles to fame," wrote George Rudé, "that he drew into political activity many thousands who had previously been considered to lie beyond the pale of the 'political nation' and gave them in 'Wilkes and Liberty' a cause which, however vaguely and incoherently, they believed to be their own."[26]

Wilkes's political strength lay with the City voters, the livery, particularly the livery of the "lesser companies," in which many members still practiced the traditional crafts of their companies. Wilkes had an easy rapport with these men of humble origins. He seldom took a chair or a hackney coach but chose to walk through the streets of the City, unabashed by the filthy gutters and beggars and drunks, but greeting folk as he strode briskly along. Junius, the unidentified polemicist, admired Wilkes but faulted him for walking through the streets, something that gentlemen did not do. Wilkes paid no attention. The carpenters and weavers who doffed their caps to him trusted him because he had been born a Cockney. *Cockney*, a word falling rapidly out of use, meant someone born and reared in the City of London. It was said that one was a Cockney if he or she was born within the sound of Bow bells, the bells of Bow Church on Fleet Street. But the working livery admired Mr. Wilkes because he had risen above his Cockney origins to become a fine gentleman. Said one liveryman to another after listening to Wilkes speak, "Tom, what a damned fine, handsome fellow, Master Wilkes is!" to which Tom replied, "Handsome! Nay, not so much of that, for he squints most horribly." "Why yes, to be sure, he squints a little, but, damn my eyes, not more than a gentleman should do." When Wilkes was among men of his own class, he had a way of poking fun at these men who so admired him. Burke told about sitting next to him at a feast and hearing him ridicule his own people; Burke suggested he should treat his friends with more decorum. "Oh, says he, I never laugh at my friends, but these are my *followers*." To his followers, he represented success. He dressed elegantly, his bearing was manly, he carried a sword, and he fought duels. Everyone talked about how perfect were his manners, his heterosexuality was beyond question, and his libertinism well known. "Free from cock to wig," said an admiring drayman.[27]

Taking Wilkes's victory in the press gang case as a mark of how he would protect them, the liveried weavers and carpenters went to work for him in earnest. They formed a network of interconnected political clubs that met in inns and taverns, acted as his intelligence service, and kept wayward liverymen in line.[28]

But it was a small world, and Wilkes had to attend every meeting so as to assert his preeminence. At least once he failed. He and Sawbridge, with whom he was vying for the leadership, called a meeting to convince the livery to send a remonstrance to the king protesting the bumbling of the Falkland Islands affair. Wilkes began by reading aloud his draft of the remonstrance, but a workingman in the audience called out that he could not hear. Since this man was possessed of a strong voice, the crowd cried out for him to read the paper. The man marched to the dais, took the paper, began reading it but kept stopping to dispute points raised in it. Some protested, others shouted, read on. Sawbridge, seeing that the meeting was in confusion and Wilkes unable to control it, stepped in with a loud voice and took command. Let us settle this matter, he cried. Forget that remonstrance. Let us write another, protesting the Middlesex election. Yes! that made the livery happy. A remonstrance on Middlesex was not what Wilkes was after at all, but seeing that he was defeated, he gave in and signed the substitute remonstrance.

The loss of leadership to someone else in such a meeting was no small matter, but the next day Wilkes deftly took it back. He wrote a letter for the newspapers praising the meeting as one in which "the people" had taken charge. "I firmly and sincerely believe the voice of the people to be the voice of God," he wrote; "I wish always to hear it clear and distinct. When I do I will obey it as a divine call."[29] It was an arresting bit of grandiloquence, but Wilkes got away with it because his public had come to associate him with the principle he had often articulated, that the ultimate authority in government lay with the voters, not with the elected.

In the law courts, Wilkes's lawyer friends were having some success in defending the press. Occasionally the judges were on their side, but more often it was the juries who stood up for freedom of the press. In recent weeks, five printer-publishers of newspapers had undergone trials for libel: John Miller of the *London Evening Post*, Henry Baldwin of the *St. James's Chronicle*, Henry Samson Woodfall of the *Public Advertiser*, Charles Say of the *Gazetteer*, and George Robinson of the *Independent Chronicle*. All were acquitted. Even Lord Mansfield could not control the juries, who repeatedly ignored his instructions and found the printers innocent. The Rev. Mr. John Horne was tried for a letter he had published, but he gained his freedom. John Almon was convicted of libel only because he sold a book in his shop that contained Junius's insulting letter to the king. But Almon had powerful friends, and he managed to avoid prison by furnishing securities. He promptly published *The Trial of John Almon*, which gave him an excuse to republish the Junius letter under the guise of governmental evidence.[30]

In the last weeks of 1770, there arose an unexpected opportunity to win a battle in this war between the press and the establishment. Since the fifteenth century, when the printing press was introduced into England, printers had been forbidden to report in print what was said on the floor of the Houses of

Parliament. No doubt in the past, when opposition to a monarch might cost a member his life, there had been good reason to keep parliamentary debates secret, but in 1770 there could be no secret from a king who controlled a third of the members. The secret was being kept, not from the Crown, but from the people. The king and the House of Lords approved the practice because they thought government should be *for* the people, not *from* them. It was countenanced by the House of Commons because many members, perhaps most, did not think they had any responsibility to the people who had elected them other than to provide all the liquor the voters wanted on election day. True, if the candidate were the twenty-one-year-old son of a nobleman, he had a particular obligation to the people: he had to stand in the hustings bowing to the voters as they threw rotten vegetables and eggs at him. That done, his obligation to the voters was complete.

In the early months of 1771, John Wilkes and his friends tore down this ancient barrier between the people and their representatives by freeing the press to report the speeches and debates in the House of Commons.[31] The stage for this drama was set by Almon, who for two years had been publishing accounts of the House of Commons debates in his newspaper, the *Political Register*, and had gotten away with it. His reporter, a man named Augustine Wall, could station himself in the gallery of the House but could take no notes, for note taking was forbidden. All he could do was to watch and listen. Wall, however, was a man of genius with a phenomenally capacious and acute memory. Consequently, the *Political Register* reports were fairly accurate and did not draw the ire of the speakers. Then other publishers of newspapers, seeing that Almon had not been arrested, began doing the same, but, not having such a talented reporter, their accounts were inaccurate. Members of Parliament grumbled, and the king asked the ministers to look into the matter. In December 1770, the House of Lords solved the problem by shutting their galleries. In the House of Commons, on 5 February 1771, Colonel George Onslow moved that an old resolution in the House Journal of 1728 forbidding the publication of proceedings be read to the House.[32] This George Onslow was popularly called "little cocking George," to distinguish him from his cousin, also George Onslow, Wilkes's erstwhile supporter, now turned against him.

The Bill of Rights Society decided they would not be passive in the face of this hardened resolve. They talked to Roger Thompson, a printer who had recently bought the *Gazetteer*, and John Wheble, printer of the *Middlesex Journal or Chronicle of Liberty*, suggesting they "refuse obedience" to the House and "trust to the laws of the land." Wheble replied he would "suffer any extremity" rather than obey any power except the law. The two printers then put together a news story calculated to anger Cocking George, implying he was colluding with the ministry to suppress the press. They ran it in both their papers, and Cocking George bit. On 8 February 1771, he complained to the House of Commons of a breach of privilege. A summons was issued for Thompson and Wheble to appear at the bar,[33] but they had gone into hiding. They were summoned again, and yet again. The House ordered the sergeant at arms to arrest them, but he could not find them. A motion was passed asking the king to take action, and on 9 March there was a royal proclamation of a reward of fifty pounds for the arrest of each.

While this was going on, Wilkes, Almon, John Miller the printer, and Robert Morris, a Welsh lawyer and secretary to the Bill of Rights Society, hit upon a way for the City of London to challenge the House of Commons' prohibition of reporting debates. No doubt they laughed about their crazy plan, but at bottom it was no joke: they would use the City law courts to trap the messengers of the House of Commons when they tried to arrest the printers. For centuries the City had operated under a charter that gave their courts jurisdiction over all cases of crimes committed in their territory. As a magistrate, Wilkes would construe these legal rights to mean that an officer of an outside jurisdiction would be in violation of the law if he tried to function within the City. Printers would be encouraged to report on the debates, messengers would be sent to arrest the printers, and, as Morris said, "messengers may yet be sent to Newgate Prison."[34] Wilkes had little difficulty getting a promise of help from Richard Oliver, an alderman who was also a member of Parliament for the City, and Brass Crosby, who was at once alderman, lord mayor, and a member of the House. They would have to proceed without the help of the great. Chatham was reluctant to help anyone to challenge an ancient custom of Parliament, and Rockingham had cooled to radicalism. Even some of the younger politicians who had come to power as supporters of Wilkes stood back from this dangerous move, James Townsend and William Sawbridge, though Sawbridge belatedly joined the effort.

The four men presented the plan to the Society of Supporters of the Bill of Rights in a secret meeting, and the Society approved. They now approached half a dozen prominent printers, all of whom agreed to abide by the directives of the Society. They would report on the House of Commons debates; the messengers would come to arrest them, but they must not allow themselves to be arrested until the situation was such that they would be brought into a court presided over by a member of the Society.

Then John Horne spoke up: if they were apprehended, they would be free to say that he, the Rev. Mr. Horne, had written the paragraphs that Cocking George Onslow complained of. This was not exactly true, though he might have reworked the story that Wheble and Thompson had written. Whatever the case, Wilkes resented Horne's trying to worm his way into the action. He took the printers aside and told them that Horne was a tricky man, and they should ignore him. Horne was resentful but said nothing.

The *Gazetteer* and *Middlesex Journal* commenced publishing reports on the House, and other newspapers began to follow their lead. Colonel Onslow on 12 March made complaints against six newspaper publishers, contemptuously speaking of the printers in the way sportsmen number dead ducks, "three brace." Opposition members were angry, but they had too few votes to stop the action. They resorted to harassment. One of them moved to have the newspapers read aloud, which caused a squabble. They made motion after motion, forcing each to a division, until the "nays" had marched into the lobby to be counted twenty-three times! Nevertheless, the motion to call in the six printers was finally passed.[35] Four of the printers appeared at the bar on 14 March. Henry Samson Woodfall of the *Morning Chronicle* and the *Public Advertiser*, Wilkes's staunch supporter, was not there, but he was reported to be in the custody of Black Rod, the chief security officer of the House of Commons. The whereabouts of John Miller, printer and publisher of the *London Evening Post*, were not known. Two of the four standing at the bar made a submission deemed adequate and were released, but the statements of Henry Baldwin of *St. James's Chronicle* and Thomas Wright of the *Whitehall Evening Post* were thought not good enough, and they were reprimanded on their knees before they were released.[36] The country as a whole was beginning to awaken to the printers' cause. The justices of the peace of the nearby County of Hertford called a meeting and unanimously agreed they would release the printers should they be brought into their courts.

Three printers were still at large, Miller, Thompson, and Wheble. Wheble was a good friend of Morris, the Welsh lawyer, and had retained him as his counsel. The two of them in a state of amused excitement sent an open letter to the speaker, in which Wheble protested, tongue in cheek, that he had just returned from the country, and being told he was sought after had asked for a legal opinion from Morris, which opinion he was attaching to his letter. The opinion was a sarcastic, mocking disquisition arguing that the summons was not legal.[37] This evoked another order for the miscreant printers to come to the bar.

Finally, on 15 March 1771, the printers and the Society had an opportunity to carry out their plan. Wilkes was presiding over a session of the City Court being held at the Guildhall. Wheble talked one of his own printer's devils, Edward Twine Carpenter, into arresting him, pointing out that he could claim the reward. The ink-covered Carpenter marched his captive to the Guildhall and before Alderman Wilkes. Wilkes asked Wheble if he were a freeman of the City; Whebel swore he was. Then, declaring that under the laws of the City, Wheble was guilty of no offense, Wilkes set him free. He then had the printer's devil arrested for assault, but this being part of the plan, the devil found sureties at hand and was released. Since the man had brought in Mr. Wheble upon the royal proclamation, could he have a certificate of that fact so he could claim the fifty-pound reward? Wilkes complied.[38]

Wilkes then indulged himself in the pleasure of reporting what he had done to the secretary of state for the north, none other than George Dunk, Lord Halifax, who in 1763 had sent Wilkes to the Tower. "My Lord," Wilkes wrote, "as I found there was no legal cause of complaint against Wheble, I thought it clearly my duty to adjudge that he had been apprehended in the City illegally, in direct violation of the rights of an Englishman, and of the chartered privilege of a citizen of the Metropolis, and to discharge him."[39]

At the very moment Wilkes was writing this letter, William Whittam, a messenger with a warrant from the speaker of the House of Commons, arrested John Miller at his house. Miller had hung himself out as bait and seen to it that a City constable was standing by. The constable, observing that the messenger had arrested Miller, stepped in, arrested the messenger, and charged him with assault and false arrest. Both of them called upon the bystanders to assist them, but this being the City of London, no one came to the aid of the messenger. Miller, the constable, and the constable's prisoner, with an assortments of witnesses, marched to the Guildhall. Wilkes had dismissed the court and gone to the Mansion House. The party followed and soon found Mr. Wilkes, who explained that in this venue the president of the court was Lord Mayor Crosby. His lordship was in bed suffering from the gout, but he sent down word that he would hold court despite his pain. Whittam asked if they could put off the hearing until six in the evening so he could get word to his superiors. Granted. Before long the deputy solicitor of the treasury arrived. He was told that having no right to take part in a trial in a City of London court, he would serve only as "behind the scenes" advisor. Next, the House of Commons deputy sergeant at arms, one Clementson, arrived and demanded the messenger. He was invited to wait with the others. Morris, Wilkes's ally in all this, arrived, officially to act as Miller's counsel, unofficially to make as much trouble for the deputy sergeant at arms as he could. Finally, Alderman Oliver joined them. He and Wilkes donned their black robes and white wigs and waited for the court to open, when they would share the bench with Lord Mayor Crosby.

But there was no bench. At six, the hearing was convened in the lord mayor's bedroom. Lord Mayor Crosby, a man of coarse appearance and manner with a rich vocabulary of oaths, ran a no-nonsense court.[40] With his white wig dangling down to his nightclothes, he called the court to order. He quickly ascertained that Climentson was not a City officer, and the warrant he carried had no signature of a City magistrate. He then made his first ruling: Climentson could not have the prisoner. Crosby then turned his attention to the messenger, Whattam. Did he have a certificate from a City magistrate ordering any City officer to assist him when he arrested Miller? No, came the answer, whereupon the lord mayor proclaimed, "No power on earth should seize a citizen of London without authority from him or some other magistrate of the franchise."[41] Or so it was reported; he just might have made the point in more vulgar terms. Climentson spoke up, ordering the messenger not to let the warrant out of his hands, though he could read it aloud. The lord mayor demanded to see it, otherwise "no notice would be taken of it." Once in his hands, he gave the warrant to a scribe with orders to copy it. That done, he gave his second ruling: since the arrest was illegal, Miller was free. Miller himself then turned the tables and made a complaint of assault against the messenger. The lord mayor made out a warrant for Whittam's arrest. Climentson could do nothing to help his ally but to post bail. Done. Crosby ordered Whittam to appear at the next quarter session, told the deputy sergeant at arms to take him away, and dismissed the court.

To this scene there was added an after-act. Thompson seems to have persuaded Wilkes that, though he wanted to cooperate in completing the plan, he did not want to invite further anger from the House of Commons by being too conspicuous. As soon as all the strangers had left the Mansion House, Thompson was brought in as the prisoner of a neighbor who had made a citizen's arrest. In an unusually brief, quiet trial, the lord mayor released Thompson and gave a certificate to the man who had arrested him so that he could claim the reward. Alas, when this man and Carpenter, the printer's devil who had arrested Wheble, tried to claim their rewards, the ministry refused to pay on suspicion that the lord mayor had colluded with the printers.[42] No one seems to have challenged their ruling.

That weekend, the king sent a message to Lord North: "The authority of the House of Commons is totally annihilated if it is not in an exemplary manner supported tomorrow, by instantly committing the Lord Mayor and Alderman Oliver to the Tower. But fearful of apprehending his old enemy, he added, "as to Wilkes he is below the notice of the House."[43]

On Monday, 18 March, the members had to make their way through a mob surrounding St. Stephen's Chapel. The session was opened, but there was such a clamor outside it was difficult to hear the proceedings. The speaker, in an unusually detailed narrative, told the House what had happened the night before at the Mansion House. Oliver was present, but Lord Mayor Crosby had been so ill after the court sessions in his bedroom that he had not left the Mansion House. Welbore Ellis, Wilkes's old enemy in Aylesbury politics, who was handling the case for the ministry, moved that the lord mayor be required to attend the next day. This was protested because the man was ill. There was a division, and the motion was carried, 267 to 80.[44] Lord Mayor Crosby, when informed of this order, said he would rise from his sickbed the next morning to attend the House. Word of what he had said got around, and that afternoon handbills were distributed around the City asking for an escort.

The next morning a huge crowd, not a rabble, but a crowd of livery and shopkeepers and gentlemen, many of them mounted, brought the lord mayor through the streets to St. Stephen's Chapel. When the session opened, Ellis began by questioning him. Crosby maintained stoutly that in freeing the print-ers and having the messenger arrested, he was only doing his duty; had he acted otherwise, he would have been subject to a charge at the King's Bench for failing of his obligations as mayor. But the poor man was too ill to bear much questioning, and so was excused and escorted back to the Mansion House in a long parade. Lord North, furious at what he conceived to be an insult to the House, moved that the clerk of the mayor's court should come to the bar the next day bringing the records of the sessions held in Crosby's bedroom. The motion was carried.[45]

Mawbey, at Wilkes's request, of course, moved that Wilkes also attend the following day, and for some reason the guard of the ministerial party was down and the motion was carried by a voice vote. This gave Wilkes the oppor-tunity to write in response to the summons, explaining to the speaker he could not legally appear *at* the bar of the House of Commons, but only *beyond* the bar to be sworn in and take his seat as knight of the shire for Middlesex. The next day, Wednesday, 20 March, Mawbey, when recognized by the speaker, waved a copy of Mr. Wilkes's letter and offered to read it aloud. The speaker would not allow it, and another order was passed for Wilkes to appear on the twenty-fifth. Then the lord mayor's clerk, standing before the House, was forced to expunge from the book of recognizances the entry on the arrest of Whittam, the messenger.[46] Many opposition members, protesting this order as an illegal "act of violence," left the house in protest. The walkout backfired, for it only made it easier for Lord North to obtain a pass for a resolution that no one could sue Whittam for this "pretended assault."

Wilkes, seeing how little respect the House of Commons showed to law, left Polly in charge of Prince's Court and moved to temporary lodgings within the City, where he would be safer.[47] The entire City had risen in support of Oliver and Crosby. For the first time in years, the differences between the radicals and the court party were forgotten, and a noisy Court of Common Council unanimously moved a thanks to Crosby, Oliver, and Wilkes for having upheld the privileges of the City. They appointed a committee to find the best counsel for the prisoners and allocated a sum of money to pay for it.

At the March 25 session of the House, St. Stephen's Chapel was again surrounded by a mob. Again a large crowd brought Oliver and Crosby from the Mansion House and pushed into the lobby of the House, and again the speaker called upon the high constable and sheriffs to do their duty and disperse the crowd. It soon became apparent that Crosby was too ill to testify, and he was ordered home. Attention was then turned to Richard Oliver. Oliver had a prestigious seat in the House of Commons, for he had been elected as a representative of the City, filling the vacancy left by the death of Beckford. He was a handsome man and, though born in Antigua, had the impeccable manners of an English gentleman. Did he care to explain his action? No, he replied, "I know the punishment I am to receive is determined upon. I have nothing to say. . . . I defy you." He was told that if he would say he was sorry for what he had done, the House would be satisfied. He replied, "he had done what he thought right, and would do it again." Ellis moved that he be sent to the Tower of London. The vote was 170 to 38. When the results were announced, most of those thirty-eight opposers left the floor in protest, including Barré, Savile, Glynn, Meredith, Townsend, and Sawbridge. The sergeant at arms took Oliver prisoner and, braving the mob, took him to the Tower.[48]

The order was then given for Wilkes to be brought back on 27 March, but the ministerial members, fearful of confronting him, moved to put the date off. "Lord North," said Walpole, "shuffled it off by saying Wilkes was so desperate that what would be punishment to others would be an advantage to him."[49] So the House ordered Wilkes to attend on 8 April,[50] an order that was moot as soon as made, for 8 April fell within the Easter recess when Parliament would not meet. John Calcraft wrote that evening to Lord Chatham, "The ministers avow Wilkes too dangerous to meddle with. He is to do what he pleases; we are to submit." Whether the House saved face by avoiding a confrontation is questionable, but they had conformed to the wishes of their king, who had told his ministers, "We will have nothing more to do with that devil Wilkes."[51]

Now it was Lord Mayor Crosby's turn to be condemned. On 27 March he was brought by a parade of carriages and horse reaching from St. Paul's to Charing Cross. The mob attacked Lord North and tried "to tear him out of his chariot, which they entirely demolished." He was rescued by his opponent Sir William Meredith, but the mob cut up North's hat and sold the pieces as "relics of their fury." The mob quieted down, and the business of the day commenced. Crosby was found guilty of violating privilege and ordered to the

Tower by a vote of 202 to 39. But because of his weak condition he was turned over to the sergeant at arms to be taken home. He protested: he would ask no favor! He had done his duty and would make no apology; he should be given the same punishment as Oliver. Upon that, the speaker ordered the sergeant at arms to take him to the Tower.[52] Climentson, the deputy sergeant at arms who had been so humiliated by the lord mayor at the trial in the Mansion House, now took charge of the lord mayor and set off toward the Tower. At Fleet Street, he found Temple Bar shut against him. A mob seized the carriage and began debating whether to hang poor Climentson from a signpost; but the feeble lord mayor pleaded with them that the man was only doing his duty. They tried to coax the lord mayor out of the carriage, but he refused, and they finally let it go. Climentson, worried that his prisoner seemed so weak, took him to the Mansion House against his will, where he was put to bed. Early in the morning Crosby sneaked out and took himself to the Tower.

Without exception, every ward of the City of London sent their thanks to the lord mayor and Alderman Oliver. Letters poured in from all over the country. The next day some 150 coaches came to the Tower, among them that of Lord Temple. Crosby and Oliver were flattered by addresses from voters, honored with the freedom of cities, and showered with presents. The "inferior sort" expressed their collective opinion in another way: they brought stuffed figures into the square before St. James's Palace, the identity of the king's ministers being revealed by initials on the cards pinned to them: Lord Barrington, Lord Halifax, Alderman Harley, Colonel Luttrell, Attorney General De Grey. One was identified by full words, "Jemmy Twitcher." One at a time, the crowd held solemn mock trials and then beheaded each.[53]

Crosby and Oliver remained in the Tower for over a month, until the close of the session on 8 May 1771, when the order of the House lapsed. It was the expectation that Parliament would be prorogued on 9 May, but the king, fearing a mob would gather at the Tower on that day, appeared unannounced in the House of Lords a day early and prorogued Parliament. The ploy may well have prevented a riot. Nevertheless, word spread quickly, and the next morning two heroes walked across the drawbridge to the sound of a twenty-one-cannon salute from the soldiers stationed there and the sight of fifty carriages and a crowd of cheering people on horse and foot. Wilkes was among the guests at a celebratory feast at the Mansion House. The town was bright with illuminations that night.[54]

The Court of Common Council voted large, elaborately worked silver cups to Crosby, Oliver, and Wilkes. The Constitutional Society of Dublin presented Wilkes with a formal certificate of thanks for his "steady perseverance in the cause of public liberty and in particular for the spirited conduct in refusing to

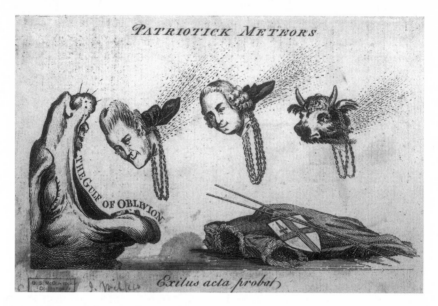

16. Aldermen Wilkes, Crosby, and Bull hurtle toward the mouth of Oblivion. Courtesy of Farley Library, Wilkes University.

comply with the illegal mandates of the House of Commons in the case of the printers." Wilkes's high popularity in America rose even higher. The Sons of St. Patrick, meeting in New York in March 1769, toasted him as a champion of the freedom of the press, adding, "May all authors who by their writings support the cause of liberty be introduced into Heaven by St. Patrick!"[55]

Wheble and Thompson had continued to publish debates throughout these events, and the other papers had taken up the practice before Oliver and Crosby were released. The House of Commons continued for a short while to hold the door partly closed. Note taking in the galleries was still prohibited and continued to be prohibited into the twentieth century. A few newspapers got into trouble for inaccurate reporting. But finally, seeing that any attempt to return to the old position would be doomed, the House gave in, though they meanly revenged themselves by imposing heavy duties on newspapers.[56]

There was one more skirmish. Late in 1774, the House of Lords opened their galleries to the public, and Wilkes lost no time setting a trap for them along the lines of that which had succeeded so well for the House of Commons. Shortly after the papers began publishing accounts of their debates, they took umbrage at an article in the *Public Ledger* and ordered the arrest of its printer. Wilkes told the man not to leave the City but to inform the lords of his whereabouts. Wilkes then let it be known that Black Rod himself would be imprisoned if he tried to arrest the man. Having no desire to send John Wilkes to the Tower, the lords gave up. "From that time," wrote Almon, "the debates in both houses have been constantly printed in all the London newspapers, and copied into all the provincial ones."[57] Freedom of the press, as we understand it in the twenty-first century, was thus established. In 1788, the *Times* began printing daily reports on the debates, and the *Morning Post* took up the practice in 1795. The modern newspaper had come into being.

For the first time since Wilkes had returned from exile, the City had heroes other than Wilkes. Lord Mayor Brass Crosby did not desire the honor. A man who was often drunk at public occasions, he was not a figure to inspire the intelligentsia or to excite the mob. He was happy to follow Wilkes's lead, which he did for many years. But Richard Oliver, the perfect gentleman at every point, was ambitious and did not like sharing the limelight with Wilkes. The Society had a plan to run Oliver and Wilkes together for the office of sheriff, but Oliver declined to form a team with Wilkes.[58] Then Oliver's close ally, the Rev. Mr. John Horne, stinging from Wilkes's treatment of him in the printers' affair, sent a letter to the newspapers that was harshly critical of Wilkes. The result was a rancorous paper war.

For the next few weeks the newspapers were full of letters in which Horne vilified Wilkes as the ungrateful benefiter of Horne's own efforts to raise Wilkes from penniless outlaw to debt-free alderman. Dragging out charges that had been laid to rest, Horne asserted that Wilkes had embezzled the funds of the Foundling Hospital and the militia. Wilkes, he said, had cheated Isaac Silva, the banker who held the note for the money Wilkes had borrowed to buy votes at Aylesbury. He rifled the papers of the Society so he could list Wilkes's debts and divulge the amount of his rent and the number of his servants. Wilkes was defended in letters to the newspapers by someone who signed himself "Scourge," probably Wilkes himself. Scourge was answered by "A Freeholder of Middlesex," thought to be Horne. "Cat O'Nine Tails," supported Scourge. Oliver and others wrote letters saying that the charges against Horne by Scourge and Cat were false. They in turn were attacked. "Jairus" even accused Horne of being a spy for the ministry.[59]

Horne was one of those people whose nature it is to enjoy making trouble for others. Although the coolness he tried to create between Wilkes and Humphrey Cotes might have had some political purpose, it is hard to imagine what advantage he could have had in attempting to sew seeds of distrust between Wilkes and Laurence Sterne. He had a knack for taking a damaging detail from Wilkes's history and blowing it up. A story had been going around that Wilkes had been sued by a French jeweler to recover the cost of jewels he had purchased in Paris but never paid for. Horne asserted it was not one, but three

suits by French jewelers. Other charges were Machiavellian: Wilkes was plot-
ting to take control of the City by placing his friends in key positions, his
lawyer Reynolds for city clerk, his brother Heaton for chamberlain. Both men
denied they had been approached with such a plan. Most of the charges were
petty and vitriolic. Not wanting to admit he had helped Wilkes when he came
secretly to London in 1767, Horne asserted he had not been "protected" by
William Wildman, Horne's brother-in-law, but had paid for the rooms. There
were more serious charges: Wilkes had cheated Wildman by asking him to
send various items to France, including a little Welsh horse Wilkes sent to
Madam d'Holbach but never paid for. Early in this paper war, Horne acquired
the sobriquet of Malagrida, the name of a Spanish Jesuit notorious for meanly
fomenting enmities.[60]

When Wilkes spoke up to defend himself, he seems to have told the truth for
the most part. There are a few blatant lies, such as his denying that in his exile
he had ever received from the Rockingham administration "pension, gratuity,
or reward."[61] More often he was, as Louis Armstrong would have put it, "just
careless of the truth." When he was criticized for employing French servants,
he said he had only one, when he probably had three or four. But Wilkes was
not embarrassed by the charges. It is to his credit that he, not Horne, collected
the items from the newspapers and published them under the title *The Controversial Letters of John Wilkes, Esq., the Rev. John Horne, and their Principal
Adherents*. It would not be unlike him to bias the edition; but if he did so it is
not apparent, for this curious book exposes many of his own faults.[62]

Wilkes won the paper war. "The popular sympathies went in favour of the
lay combatant," wrote the Earl of Albemarle. "All the abuse that his reverend
rival could heap upon him seemed only the more strongly to cement the attachment of his partisans. It was in vain that his profligacy, his habits of
begging, and his shabbiness in money-matters, were set forth; even his hideous
aspect found admirers in men who could perceive no defect in the obliquity of
his conduct." Horne only succeeded in making enemies. "Although Mr. Horne
had most, if not all, the respectable men on his side," wrote his early biographer, "yet the public . . . at length declared fully and unequivocally in behalf of
Mr. Wilkes." Horne's effigy, in full canonicals, was consumed in a bonfire
before the Mansion House.[63]

One careless letter in this controversy almost involved Wilkes in a duel.
Lauchlin Macleane, the Irish friend of Burke who had acted as intermediary
between Wilkes and Rockingham at the time Wilkes was claiming his right to
return to England and to be given a pardon, had at that time lent Wilkes
£1,350. Now, in 1771, he was a member of Parliament for Arundel but financially ruined by a fall in the price of East India stock. Enormously in debt, he

had pressed the Bill of Rights Society to discharge Wilkes's debt, which he had agreed to settle for £650. Before the society got around to paying the money, there was a letter about the demand in the *Public Advertiser* to which Macleane took offense. He asked Henry Samson Woodfall, the printer, to show him the manuscript. Woodfall declined. Macleane told him he was certain Wilkes had written it. Woodfall would not confirm that but did say that the manuscript had been given to him, not by Wilkes, but by a friend of Wilkes. Macleane said he was certain Wilkes had written it and sent Wilkes a letter in which he challenged him. His brother would be his second and would negotiate time, place, and weapons, all of which were in Wilkes's choice. When he did not get an answer fast enough to satisfy him, he published the letter, but he made the mistake of saying in it that Woodfall had confirmed his suspicions about Wilkes. Woodfall was constrained to publish a letter to clear himself, but it was a tactful letter, assuring the reader that Mr. Macleane had misunderstood him. Macleane backed down, and Wilkes was spared the necessity of once again fighting a duel to defend the right of a paper to publish anonymous letters. The society was not impressed by Macleane's quick temper and did not revise its priorities. Not until a year later did they get around to paying him the £650.[64]

To his family, Wilkes showed no sign that he was disturbed by any of this. "Indeed, my dear Papa," Polly wrote from the house of a friend she was visiting, "I cannot express how much I am obliged by your kind attention, nor how highly delighted with your letter. It plainly shows the serenity and cheerfulness of mind that have always distinguished you, and which your *now* possessing so eminently, evinces a greatness of mind truly astonishing."

But the controversy fractured the Bill of Rights Society. Things came to a head when Horne moved that the Society should send money to printers who had been jailed for standing up for liberty. Wilkes, seeing his income in danger, packed the next meeting with friends, who passed a resolution that limited the purpose of the Society: because the subscriptions had been raised in support of Wilkes alone, went the resolution, the money could be used for no other purpose until all of Wilkes's debts were discharged. Anonymous letters appeared in the newspapers accusing Horne of embezzlement. Sergeant Glynn, who had for so long been Wilkes's partner in political endeavors, though never his personal friend, now wrote in defense of Horne.

Finally, on 9 April 1771, the Bill of Rights Society divided. Horne, Oliver, Townsend, Sawbridge, Glynn, and a considerable number of others, openly encouraged by Lord Shelburne, resigned and formed the Constitutional Society. The break damaged the radical movement by dividing loyalties and exposing the jealousies and pettiness of the leaders, but the programs of the

17. A satire of the quarrel in the Bill of Rights Society. Parson Horne and Alderman Wilkes throw books at each other. Courtesy of Farley Library, Wilkes University.

two societies differed little. Men on opposing sides, such as Glynn and Wilkes, continued to work together in the cause of liberty. History has judged the Constitutional Society meritorious. Several societies active in reform movements at the end of the century were direct heirs, including the influential London Corresponding Society.[65]

The Bill of Rights Society, now numbering sixty-three members, continued under Wilkes's leadership. Wilkes soon mollified the critics by moving to rescind the resolution that had set off the quarrel, that which prohibited subscriptions for anyone's benefit other than Wilkes's.[66] So subscriptions continued to come in, most of the money going to support Wilkes. A few wealthy members, Rev. Dr. Thomas Wilson, Sir Joseph Mawbey, the brewer and pig farmer, and Wilkes's brother-in-law George Hayley, contributed large sums. A handful of wealthy noblemen made annual contributions but never joined. So for a brief time the Society supplied Wilkes with a reasonable annual income. But, of course, his income was never enough, and he continued to run up debts.

Cotes was an enthusiastic participant in the Society. He had lost a wife, had married again, and with the fortune of his new wife had been able to recover from his bankruptcy and start up again as a wine merchant. It seems probable he made up to Wilkes the money he had lost when he went bankrupt.

The Society met regularly at the London Tavern.[67] Brass Crosby and Sir Watkin Lewes, also an alderman, traded off as chair. Frederick Bull, an alderman and tea merchant, served as treasurer. These successful men of the middling sort, tired of the patrician power of nobles, had found in the Society a voice such as they had never had before. Over the next months the Society changed. It no long made the support of Wilkes its sole purpose; it became a center for radical propaganda and agitation.

One of Horne's charges against Wilkes had been that he hated America, but nothing could have been further from the truth. The previous December, Wilkes had received a letter from Samuel Adams: "No character," wrote Adams, "appears with a stronger luster in my mind that that of a man who nobly perseveres in the cause of public liberty and virtue through the rage of persecution: of this, you have had a large portion." In April 1771, the Society gave a strong signal of support for America by making the American Arthur Lee their secretary. Lee's first innovation was to attempt to organize corresponding societies among the radical groups scattered through Great Britain and abroad. At the time, nothing much came of this in England, but Lee's idea had profound effects in America. He wrote of his plan to Samuel Adams. Adams dawdled for a year, but when sorely vexed by the royal governor in September 1772, he led the Sons of Liberty to form the Boston Committee of

Correspondence, "to state the rights of the colonists and . . . to publish the same to the several Towns in this Province and to the World." Within months, correspondence societies sprang up in New York, Philadelphia, and all the major American cities. In a letter to the Bill of Rights Society, Adams acknowledged that the Society had inspired his work, and the Society responded by making him a member. General Thomas Gage, commander of the British forces in America, the archenemy of the Sons of Liberty, and Thomas Hutchinson, the royal governor of Massachusetts, were soon saying the Boston Sons of Liberty were being tutored by London radicals.[68]

In the colonies, people who had remained loyal to the Crown through thick and thin were now beginning to despair and to listen to those who argued that revolution was inevitable. Samuel Adams had said to Wilkes, "In this little part of the world, a land till of late happy in its obscurity . . . even here the stern tyrant has lifted up his iron rod. . . . But I have a firm persuasion in my mind that . . . this country will approve herself as glorious in defending and maintaining her freedom as she has heretofore been happy in enjoying it."[69] He would soon be acting upon this conviction, for Samuel Adams would become, in the words of the historian Pauline Maier, "the architect of the final stages of the revolution."[70]

In July 1771, Wilkes was elected one of the two high sheriffs of London and Middlesex. The Bill of Rights Society, determined to seize control of the City, had rather easily manipulated the election of Wilkes and Frederick Bull. Walpole wrote to Horace Mann, "Wilkes is another phoenix revived from his own ashes. . . . His colleagues betray him, desert him, expose him, and he becomes sheriff of London. I believe if he was to be hanged, he would be made King of England."[71]

In the distant past, there had been a sheriff for London and another for the county, but these had long been combined. The term was for one year, and the duties not unlike those of the high sheriff of Buckinghamshire, a position Wilkes had filled honorably almost thirty years before, though the duties in London were much more onerous. Moreover, there were considerable expenses which had to be borne by the sheriffs themselves. We can be sure that in this particular partnership, Bull paid most of the bills. Other than the honor, only one reward was given the sheriffs: the service qualified them to stand for lord mayor. Most past sheriffs were senior aldermen of a conservative cut, men who had stepped easily into the mayorality. The penniless, radical Wilkes was an interloper. "I am," he wrote, "the poorest sheriff, I believe, in Europe."[72]

Wilkes and Bull served admirably, though Mrs. Thrale remarked it was like "the Consulate of Caesar and Bibulus, as poor Bibulus like Bull had no Share in the management of public Affairs." They had many duties. They supervised elections. They were masters of Old Bailey court and Newgate prison. They honored ancient ceremony by escorting the lord mayor to official functions, and when it was Lord Chief Justice Mansfield's time to serve on the bench of Old Bailey, they met him at Temple Bar and escorted him ceremoniously to the court. They presided at dinners for the judges and lawyers at the Old Bailey. To fend off Horne's sinister insinuations about his connections with France and to counter a reputation as a Francophile, Wilkes announced that he and Bull would serve no French wines at those meals, but when he asked the lord mayor to do the same when it came his turn to treat the table, the mayor refused.[73]

Many of the sheriff's duties had to do with crime and criminals, and here they tried to make reforms. They discovered one of the sheriff's officers extorting money from prisoners and successfully prosecuted him. To prevent judges from packing juries, they ordered a "Freeholders book" to be drawn up, listing all who were eligible to serve on juries so they could be called in rotation, though the project was never quite completed. To correct a "glaring abuse" at the Old Bailey, they ordered the keeper of Newgate to desist from bringing prisoners into court in chains: "This we conceive to be equally repugnant to the laws of England and of humanity; every person at so critical a moment ought to be without any bodily pain or restraint, that the mind may be perfectly free to deliberate on its most interesting and awful concerns in so alarming a situation." The difficulty was that leg irons had to be knocked off and put back on by a blacksmith in a rough operation that few prisoners suffered without some bodily pain. The prisoners objected, and that reform was given up. Wilkes and Bull also ordered the keeper of Newgate to stop his servants from taking money for admission to Old Bailey court: "It is one of the most glorious privileges of this nation that our courts of justice must always be open and free." The result was that a noisy mob took over and made the business of the court almost impossible. The sheriffs had to backtrack.[74] To refurbish his image, Wilkes joined a fireman's company.

One or the other of the sheriffs was required to attend the hangings of those condemned to death at the Old Bailey. It was not an obligation Wilkes relished: "The very worst use to which you can put a man," he said, "is to hang him." Nevertheless, he did his duty and saw that the executions were carried out. One particular hanging day was given considerable coverage in the newspapers. A beautiful young matron, Mary Jones, was condemned for stealing twelve yards of lace. The open cart in which this poor creature and two condemned men were being drawn toward the gallows at Tyburn was followed by a handsome coach in which sat Sheriff John Wilkes, dressed all in black with a black-handled sword in a black sheath at his side. Mary Jones took the privilege of the condemned and made a speech from the gallows, telling how her husband had been pressed into the navy and she had been driven to steal in order to feed her two babies. Then she was hanged.[75]

On 21 August 1771, a porter knocked on Wilkes's door and handed in a letter that a gentleman in the Strand had paid him to deliver. It was signed Junius. The writer was at this point the leading political polemicist in England. Not so vigorous and vulgar as Wilkes had been in the *North Briton*, Junius was more of an Augustan satirist, smooth and bitingly ironic. His earliest letters, in January 1769, had taken the government to task for its treatment of Wilkes.[76] After Wilkes's release from prison, the chief targets of his satire had been the Dukes of Grafton and Bedford and Lord Chief Justice Mansfield.

Junius's fame had been made by his audacious letter of 19 December 1769 addressed to King George III himself. In it he had talked about the hounding of Wilkes and the foolishness of ministers who had "transferred the question from the rights and interests of one man to the most important rights and interests of the people." But the real shock came when Junius put the blame for the troubles of his realm upon the king himself. The Wilkes fiasco had begun in the king's "personal resentment" of the man, he said; and in the aftermath, the monarch had brought upon himself the hatred of the Irish and the resentment of America. Finally, Junius blatantly warned his king that the people had a right to rebel if driven to extremes. The letter, said Walpole, was "the most daring insult ever offered to a prince, but in times of open rebellion."[77]

The king sent his spies scurrying about trying to identify the writer, but no one could. The combination of mystery, daring, and skillful satire was irresistible, and Junius became the rage of England. In the two centuries that have passed, the game of identifying him (or her) has never quite died. At least sixty-one persons have been suggested as the author, including Wilkes, though Wilkes's candidacy was soon discarded when it was noticed how harshly Junius had criticized him. Though no direct evidence has been found, today there seems to be a consensus among scholars that the Junius letters were written by Philip Francis the younger, a functionary in the war office, a man who was close to Chatham and the chameleonlike John Calcraft. Francis was in a position to gather inside information, though most of Junius's writings made use of what was already known. Junius was not a spy, but a brilliant observer, interpreter, and critic of the political scene.[78]

By sending messages to each other in obscure newspaper advertisements, Junius and Wilkes were able to strike up a correspondence. Wilkes supplied Junius with information about the arrest and trial of a law student, one John Eyre, for stealing writing paper from the Guildhall. Junius used the information to blast Lord Mansfield, who had granted bail to Eyre, a fellow Scots, though bail had been denied by City judges.[79] In most points, Junius supported Wilkes, but he was the more conservative man. He had no interest in giving equitable representation to towns like Birmingham and Manchester, and on the matter of the navy press gangs, he and Wilkes agreed to disagree. His friendship turned out to be a burden for Wilkes. Though Junius knew far less about City than national politics, he did not hesitate to tell Wilkes exactly what he was to do to seize control of the City. Wilkes agreed with almost none of this gratuitous advice, but he could not afford to make an enemy of Junius. His answers were polite and slippery, and he managed to get on with his own program without a conflict.

Wilkes, Arthur Lee, and the Bill of Rights Society now took a step to the left of Junius, to the left of Beckford's program, to the left of anyone else actually engaged in the political game. On 23 July 1771, the Society issued a manifesto and announced that any candidate for Parliament who hoped to have their endorsement must swear to abide by this manifesto. The document incorporated some of Beckford's old program, calling for annual parliaments and the exclusion of placemen and pensioners from the House of Commons, but it extended the program into matters of practical government, controls over the expenditure of public money, and the prohibition of bribery in elections. It spoke to the right of privacy by calling for the abolition of excise taxes. And, urged by Lee, it extended the sphere of concern to America, calling for the restoration to America of the right not to be taxed without representation.[80]

The most radical article of the manifesto was the one that called for "full and equal representation of the people." Exactly what was meant by "full and equal representation" was unclear, and whom they meant by "the people" was vague. Never mind, the words were caught up and reiterated by the livery, delighted they could take effective political action without relying upon nobles or ministers or wealthy conservative aldermen.[81]

The manifesto was too extreme for the great ones who had so long dominated City politics from afar, and they began to withdraw. Chatham said the program was impractical.[82] Rockingham, believing that any reduction in the benevolent influence of the aristocracy would be a loss to the people, pulled out of City politics, taking with him Wilkes's old allies William Dowdeswell and Edmund Burke. Of the more liberal lords, only Shelburne retained an interest, his chief agents being James Townsend, Richard Oliver, and the Constitution Society. But the ministerial, court party remained active in City politics, thinking to take advantage of the split in the radicals.

The influence of the court was apparent in the election for mayor in the autumn of 1771. John Sawbridge, who had inherited much of the following of the late Lord Mayor Beckford, had the highest number of votes, and William Nash, a courtier, came in second. But the aldermen, exercising their right to choose between the two top candidates, chose Nash.[83]

The two high sheriffs, their duty to supervise the election over, set off together for a Christmas holiday at Bath. Polly stayed behind in order to be with her mother. Wilkes and Bull lodged with a Mrs. Harford in the last house toward the river on the South Parade and plunged into the ever-lively social life, breakfast parties, informal gatherings in the orangerie-style Pump Room next to the King's Bath, afternoon assemblies, evenings of backgammon or billiards or cards. Then it was off Bristol to dine with the "friends of freedom."[84]

Though scrupulous in his duties, Wilkes took as many holidays as he could. He loved the windy, nautical world of the Isle of Wight and had begun going there in summer as early as 1762. The natives have preserved a story of Wilkes's crossing from the mainland when the wind failed, and his saying, "Nothing has been so obnoxious to me through life as a dead calm." Once he spent the morning riding horse along the strand, "conversing with old ocean . . . enjoying the boundless view of such an amazing expanse of waters, the most sublime of all ideas." But, he added, "I long for the company I like best, without which all other pleasures are incomplete."[85] Polly often went with him to the island.

In September, Wilkes always returned to his regular duties in the ward of Farringdon Without and the Old Bailey with its "tedious and melancholy sessions."[86] On days when he was not required, he had a life out-of-doors such as would make one's head spin. Not that he was unusual in this. In a world in which every practical need of a gentleman was looked after by a servant, he could afford to write propaganda while breakfasting, call on a friend or political associate in the late morning, dine at an alderman's house in the early afternoon, make a call on a politician about six, go drinking in a tavern with one's club at seven, return home for a light supper at nine, and write letters before retiring.

From the time of his release from the King's Bench Prison, Wilkes kept a diary of visits and dinners. The City being dominated by successful people of the middle class, it is no surprise that one finds few names of people of high station or extreme wealth. An exception was Lord Bathurst, the friend of Jonathan Swift and Alexander Pope, who,"despairing ever to find their equals," had "closed his accounts" but opened them again to entertain the Rev. Mr. Laurence Sterne and now to entertain the less reverend John Wilkes. Wilkes was much impressed that this cheerful ninety-year-old man "rides, walks, eats and drinks well," and though he tells many tales, he "is not got into his *anecdotage*." He dined at The Grove in Muswell Hill, the country house of the bibliophile and friend of Johnson, Topham Beauclerk, and his wife, Lady Diana Spencer, not a direct but a collateral ancestor of the twentieth-century Princess of Wales. This Diana was the great-granddaughter of the celebrated General Marlborough, and Beauclerk was the great-grandson of Charles II and Nell Gwyn. Wilkes more often moved among theatrical people. Several afternoons he spent with George Coleman, the elder, lawyer, journalist, playwright, manager of the Covent Garden Theatre, and founder of the Beef Steak Club, which met above the theater. On 12 March, Wilkes was at Le Tellier's Coffee House in Half Moon Street with a company that included a rising young star in theater, Richard Brinsley Sheridan. In May, the great actor David Garrick and wife entertained Wilkes and Polly at their house in the Adelphi. Perhaps the visit had something to do with the new play about Wilkes that had just appeared, *The Association, A Comic Tragedy*.[87]

The morning after a meeting of political folk at Cricklade, Wilkes was taken on a hunt. He was not used to jumping walls and chasing wild red canines, but he found the exercise beneficial to his health and vowed to do more of it.[88]

Wilkes often saw the Chevalier d'Eon, the disobedient French diplomat who had left Humphrey Cotes's house and moved into the *école d'escrime*, the schoool for fencing and horsemanship of Dominico Angelo in Soho. Frequently Wilkes, who was reputed to be the ugliest man in England and had once fallen from a French post-horse, went to the *école* to enjoy the companionship of the two men reputed to be the best-looking men and best horsemen and best swordsmen in the country. But the coterie of these three men of genius was soon interrupted when one of them announced he was not a man. D'Eon took up women's dress and, to the astonishment of friends and associates, presented himself as Mademoiselle d'Eon. He let his hair grow long and began to do it up in elaborate coiffeurs. He explained to everyone that he was a woman who had loved the life of the diplomat and soldier (he wore the Croix de Guerre) and so passed herself off as a man. Actually d'Eon had sometimes dressed as a woman when he served as a spy in the court of Catherine in Russia, but few knew about that. A gullible public, perhaps influenced by the romances of Jeanne d'Arc, accepted his explanation and began to treat him as a woman. Walpole was not so sure. He once met d'Eon at Lord Ossory's house in Berkeley Square and was fascinated by the change in him, or her: "The night was hot, she had no muff or glove, and her hands and arms seem not to have participated of the change of sexes, but are fitter to carry a chair than a fan." At the equestrian arena of Angelo's establishment, d'Eon began to put on demonstrations of how a woman can use a sword, fencing while wearing a long dress. At least once Wilkes took Polly to watch this entertaining spectacle. Several times he brought d'Eon to his house for dinner, Polly serving as hostess, and sometimes Jack Smith at the table. But he was not taken in by the hairdo and the dresses. When d'Eon returned to France in 1777, Wilkes wrote Suard, tongue in cheek, "I lamented her departure in elegiac verse, which would beguile you of too many tears or I should send it to you. When will you restore her to my longing arms?"[89]

Wilkes and Polly were frequently in the company of the radical historian

Mrs. Catharine Macaulay and her daughter, usually at the house of the radical member of Parliament for King's Lynn, Crisp Molineux, and his wife. The young women were perhaps Polly's closest friends, and the adults were bound together by their passionate political views. Through Mrs. Macaulay, Wilkes met Thomas Hollis, the polemical advocate of liberty and benefactor of Harvard College.

Not infrequently, Wilkes dined with sea captains and officers aboard their boats, Captain Barnwell on the *Anchorwick* at Depford, Captain Chambers on the *London* at Horsley Down. He went to them, not only to enjoy their imported wines and genial companionship, but to hear news from abroad. Newspapers might have friends in the capitals of Europe who wrote letters about what was happening (giving rise to the newspaper term *correspondent*), but conditions and events in far-off countries were known through the oral reports of travelers. Nicholas Antoine Boulanger's groundbreaking work, *The Origin and Progress of Despotism in the Oriental and other Empires, of Africa, Europe, and America*, which Wilkes had printed in the original French at the Great George Street press and had subsequently translated, had been compiled largely from interviews with sailors and other travelers.[90] Wilkes dined on board the *Queen*, an East Indiaman anchored at Depford, with Captain Stainforth, and came away sickened by the accounts of "monstrous cruelty and wickedness of many of those tyrants of the East."[91]

The names of a few clergy appear in the address book, notably that of the Rev. Dr. William Dodd, the popular preacher and chaplain in ordinary to the king who in 1777 was hanged for forging the signature of the Earl of Chesterfield on a check.

One of the persons who watched the trial of Dr. Dodd was Wilkes's younger sister, Mary, who had become Wilkes's valuable ally. Mary had the Wilkes jaw, but that did not stop her from getting married three times. She had married first a successful London merchant, Samuel Storke, and when he died she married his manager, George Hayley, who ran the business. She was an enthusiastic partisan of her brother. In the Pump Room at Bath, she overheard someone behind her speaking: "That Wilkes is a very troublesome fellow; I wish the King has his head." Mrs. Hayley turned about: "I wish, he had half his Head." Mary Hayley would rather spend her time with men than with women, liked to be driven in her carriage at breakneck speeds, and liked to watch the trials at the Old Bailey, which she did so frequently that a place was always held for her. Ignoring the judges' request for women to withdraw, she sat in the gallery popping gingerbread nuts and drinking ale while she listened to the judge pronounce the death sentence upon Dr. Dodd.[92]

Mary brought her second husband into Wilkes's political circle. George Hayley had risen from rags to riches. He had begun as an apprentice in Storke's trading firm, risen to manager, and, when the owner died, married the widow. Though he was aggressive in business, at home he was the docile husband to his energetic wife, and in Parliament the docile follower of Wilkes. A silent man for the most part, he once spoke on the floor of the House of Commons on a question of trade with America, after which Frederick Bull commented to Wilkes, "Brother Hayley's speech was short. I hope he did not stop in the middle. I think he told the House that if it had not been for his instructions, he would not have troubled himself about the Americans."[93]

The rest of Wilkes's family was flourishing. Wilkes's mother moved to a house with a view of Palace Yard from the front and of Westminster Bridge and the river from the back. Polly was most admiring. Heaton moved to a house in the trendy neighborhood of Twickenham. He suffered a carriage accident and broke a rib, but Jack Smith, who had been with him, escaped injury. Jack had returned from France, embarrassingly Francophied in speech and manner, and Wilkes had placed him with Dominico Angelo at the *école d'escrime* to learn the manly arts of swordsmanship and horsemanship. Jack had decided he would become a soldier. On 16 August 1771, Wilkes gave a large dinner party at Prince's Court in honor of Polly's twenty-first birthday. Polly's great uncle, Richard Sherbrooke, died in 1772, leaving his fortune to Polly's mother for her lifetime, and afterward to Polly.[94] Mary Mead Wilkes would not die for another twelve years, but one supposes Polly now had an allowance.

In polite company, Wilkes was at every point a gentleman. He dressed in the latest fashion. He never took snuff. Once when offered a pinch, he declined, explaining, "I never deal in little vices." To men Wilkes made no bones about his great vice, but never in the company of ladies. According to Henry Angelo, Dominico Angelo's son, "Mr. Wilkes, being most courteous in his attentions to the ladies, was a welcome guest at many a family table. He was considered to be one of the most polite gentlemen of his day." After he had attended a service at Trinity Chapel, Cambridge, some undergraduates presented him with a book of anthems, for which he thanked them and, turning, bowed to a pretty woman who was standing by and presented it to her. People enjoyed seeing courteous manners in this man with the famously ugly face. Wilkes himself liked to tell the story of his saying, "give me twenty minutes to talk away my face" (sometimes he reduced the minutes to ten), but what was being talked away was not his face, but his heartache. His face was growing more and more grotesque as he lost teeth, and his protruding jaw began to collapse into his nose. He had what Burke called a "pursed mouth." His breath was bad, and his speech was so badly affected, said Henry Angelo, that "it required particular attention to understand him, so imperfect was his articulation."[95]

Wilkes had to look outside the polite world for his sexual gratifications. In the past he had taken his women servants to bed. From one such liaison was born his "nephew," Jack Smith. But he could not behave that way in a house under the care of his daughter. Since his student years at Leiden, he had stayed away from streetwalkers. But prostitutes came in many forms, and some of them were genteel in their manner and relatively free of disease. Two letters survive from the madam of a high-class brothel to Wilkes. One wonders whether Lucy Ballards, whom Wilkes met at Miles Andrews, might not have been a decorous prostitute. She lived always in Soho but she frequently changed her address. Or Kitty Towlers, to whom he had been introduced by Mrs. Ballards. There was also Wilkes's visit to his friend Samuel Petrie at Lothbury, when he declined an invitation to sleep at the house but went instead to the inn called the Barrow Hedges. "I dedicate to Petrie and pleasure the day," he wrote; "to Venus and Neptune the night at Barrow Hedges, where I mean to be the Hedge's sparrow."[96]

The women who made love to Wilkes were in some degree professionals. His affairs that continued for months or even longer, were with the professionals that were called courtesans, women who offered not their bodies for a night, but their whole lives to the gentleman who would support them — Corradini, Mrs. Barnard, and Jenny Wade of Prince's Court, with whom he began an affair in the spring of 1779 that lasted a year. The women in Paris, Crecy and Dufort, whom according to rumor he set up in their own rooms, and Chassagne, who, according to the gossips of Paris, moved into Wilkes's house and then stole his furniture, were living by their wits. Most of the letters of Mrs. Gardiner, who lived in Charlotte Street, Bloomsbury, are arrangements for meetings, but Wilkes's mother, unhappy with the gossip about her son, asked him not to leave his carriage before the house of so notorious a courtesan as Gardiner.[97]

The arrangements that gentlemen made with courtesans had a sanction, of a sort, by the so-called sentimental moral philosophers of the time, Shaftesbury, Hutcheson, and Hume. Why, the philosophers asked, do men go to the great trouble and expense of setting up mistresses in lodgings? It cannot be for sex because they could have had sex inexpensively from any prostitute. They do so because they find in a mistress gratifying moral qualities, loyalty, understanding, and the desire to please.[98]

Wilkes was often foolish in his haste to find such mistresses, but to his credit, once he found them he gave them the ultimate respect one can give to a courtesan: he fell in love with them. We know about his passion for Gertrude Corradini because he wrote about it in his brief autobiography. We know about his affection for the others, or most of them, because he treated their letters as treasures, collecting, organizing, and labeling them, as though he wanted to preserve their memory.[99] But courtesans, almost by definition, seek financial security, and Wilkes, being a man of limited means, could not provide that. Even if he had wanted to do so, he could not give the settlement that Corradini and Mrs. Barnard had asked for.

Wilkes had an unusually long-lasting affair with Marianne Geneviève de Charpillon, a Swiss-born woman of a family of charlatans and mountebanks who had come to London when she was a child. She was thirty-three years old when Wilkes met her on 24 September 1773 at a dinner party at the Old Swan Inn in Chelsea given by Chase Price, member for Radnorshire. A beautiful woman, she was not put off by Wilkes's ugliness, for she was used to that sort of thing: she had been the mistress of another ugly man, an Italian diplomat, Count Morosini. At the age of seventeen or eighteen, Charpillon had collided with the famous lover Giovanni Casanova, who immortalized her in his *Memoirs* as the conniving "mistress of deceit," whose family, a mother and two haglike aunts always accompanied by one or two thugs, constituted a gang that specialized in the swindling of amorous gentlemen. Charpillon, who had fallen on hard times, was delighted to be discovered by a gentleman such as Wilkes. He soon set her up in a house at No. 30, Great Titchfield Street, though in order to do so he had to borrow from Chase Price. Into the house in Titchfield Street she moved herself, her mother, her aunt, her grandmother, and her young son, Tommy. From there she sent numerous letters with greetings from the family. Grandmama made Wilkes jelly and sugar candy, and Tommy sent his wishes, sometimes accompanied with a kiss. Her numerous letters are written in an unembarrassed, flowing street French, phonetically spelled and strikingly similar to Quebecois. For example, she uses the word *jusquasteur* rather than *maintenant*. Master Jack Smith came sometimes to dine at Great Titchfield Street, but Polly never. When Wilkes was away, he often sent the family there game or chickens, and once he wrote his daughter from Portsmouth to ask her to have some hams delivered to Mme Charpillon, for which attention Charpillon expressed deep gratitude. Wilkes and his mistress quarreled from time to time, but most often her letters were playful. She sometimes addressed him as "Mr Wilkes and Liberty." She laughed him out of an ill humor by describing it as "son humeur +." She wished him a good night full of rose-colored dreams. If ever he began to scold her, she would place her hand over his lips and coax him not to make "the mouth of an elephant," implying that at other times he had a normal mouth.[100]

Charpillon would be his mistress for the next four years, during some of his greatest triumphs, but Wilkes learned it was a mistake to appear in public with her. A broadside letter addressed to the livery took him to task for taking "his French whore" to a ball at the Guildhall given by Lord Mayor Bull.[101] Thereafter, he would send her tickets to the theater but would not accompany her.

He once gave her two tickets to a ball, but she sent them back, haughtily declaring she would not go without a proper escort. In 1777, they had a violent quarrel, and the affair came to an end.

In April of 1772, Wilkes saw Boswell for the first time since they had been together in Paris in 1766. The occasion was a feast given by Lord Mayor Nash at the Mansion House. Boswell told about watching the prodigious dinner being carried into the Egyptian Hall. Officers with long staves guarded the door. The lord mayor and his lady went in, followed by the aldermen and their ladies, including Wilkes and Polly, and then visiting foreigners of distinction. A struggle at the door ensued because more invitations had been sent out than there were places. Boswell managed to get in, and the recorder of the City, James Eyre, gave up his seat so that Boswell could sit next to Wilkes. Meat, drink, fruit, confections, ices, a bottle of Burgundy and another of Champagne were set before each guest. "Boswell," said Wilkes, addressing his old friend, "you was a pleasant fellow when I knew you. But now you're grown the gravest of grave mortals. You should have come and seen a friend in jail." "I do assure you I am glad to meet with you," replied Boswell, "but I could not come to see you. I am a Scotch laird and a Scotch lawyer and a Scotch married man. It would not be decent." "Do you remember," said Wilkes, "how melancholy you was at Paris when the news came of the Old Pretender's death? I kept your secret." Fearing his Jacobitism would be exposed to the table, Boswell changed the subject: "Upon my word, you had a grand entertainment here today." Ah, said Wilkes, alluding to Scottish dietary crudities, "you did not see the sheep's-head. You did not see the haggis."[102]

In the summer of 1772, Wilkes decided to become himself lord mayor. It was an audacious ambition, for the lord mayor rode in one of the three gilded coaches of England, the others belonging to the speaker of the House of Commons and the king. In a great procession the lord mayor's coach went before that of the speaker. The king could not enter the City of London without the permission of the lord mayor. Though the lord mayor was administrator of the City, it was for one year only. During that year, he occupied the palace called the Mansion House, where in the great Egyptian Room he entertained ministers and monarchs in feasts like that at which he had sat with Boswell. Of course he had to pay for the food and the Burgundy and the Champagne himself as well as for the household expenses and the services of a battery of footmen, butlers, waiting ladies, maids, and cooks. It was thought disgraceful for a mayor to keep any part of the salary. No one in memory who was not wealthy had stood for the office until John Wilkes, who was notoriously in chronic debt.

Wilkes was nominated for mayor in the autumn of 1772, and he would have been elected except that he was tricked by Richard Oliver, that prominent member of the Constitutional Society who in his capacity as one of the sheriffs of London and Middlesex was supervising the polls. When the polls closed on 6 October 1772, the two court candidates were far behind the two radicals. Wilkes had the highest number of votes. Second was James Townsend, another one of the group that had left the Bill of Rights Society and followed Horne into the Constitution Society. "The King trembled," wrote Walpole, "for Wilkes had evidently the voice of the City; Townsend, without his assistance, would have had scarce any votes; and the majority of aldermen were supposed to favor Wilkes."[103]

The names of the two with the highest number of votes were to be presented the next day to the Court of Aldermen, who would exercise their ancient right to choose between the two top candidates by "scratching." No one knows the origin of this verb, used nowhere in politics except in the aldermen's choosing of a mayor. The practice itself had been instituted in the far past to keep the mob from electing a mayor, but by the eighteenth century, the aldermen usually bowed to the popular choice and selected the candidate with the highest number of votes. Sheriff Oliver, however, was determined that Wilkes would not be chosen. In the evening of the day when the polls closed, Oliver sent his servants scurrying to the houses of the aldermen with letters calling the meeting early the next morning. Most of them were too sleepy to make it, and only fourteen appeared. One at a time they retired to the lobby and scratched by whispering their choices to the City recorder. Wilkes abstained, feeling he should not vote for himself. Townsend was chosen, eight to seven.[104]

Wilkes was "thunderstruck" and angry, but his enemies were delighted. A print appeared in which Wilkes was teased as a Macaroni, a slang term for a man who dresses in high French style. He is shown tumbling to the floor when the "City Chair" and "Liberty" stools are pulled away by devils, one of which is labeled "Oliver." The jingle under it does not jingle well: "There's many a slip 'twixt the Cup and the Lip, / We often have found. / And the Proverb's as clear 'twixt the stool and the Chair / The Breach falls to the Ground" (illustration 18). But the figure of Wilkes is amusing. As in many satiric prints of him in this period, he is represented as fat. His feasting in the King's Bench Prison had had its effect.

The next day was Lord Mayor's Day, traditionally a great festival during which the newly elected mayor is invested with his office. The three thousand people who filled the streets before the Guildhall were not celebrating, but shouting, "It's Wilkes's turn!" The celebration limped along, and that evening at the ball in the Guildhall ladies and gentlemen tried to dance with the sounds outside of breaking glass and shouted curses. "The real damage," commented

Walpole, "was to the nation, which saw those who would have gone farthest to stem the encroachments of the Crown divided and warring on each other."[105]

Some time later a Court of Common Council of the City passed a resolution that the riots had been prompted by "false and inflammatory" paragraphs and that the authors "merit the severest censure of this court as enemies to peace and good order, and as indulging themselves in licentiousness, which has a direct tendency to destroy the glorious and invaluable liberty of the press." Wilkes jumped to his feet and declared that he agreed with the resolution, that though he was the author of many paragraphs and letters, he always made it a principle to write nothing but truth, that no one had yet proved otherwise. But Townsend proceeded to read several inflammatory pieces written by Wilkes, who, defeated, left the meeting. A motion was made to deprive him of his freedom of the City, but Townsend opposed it, saying he did not "desire to see Mr. Wilkes lower than he then was."[106]

Wilkes, who did not usually hold a grudge, held one this time. A year later, as Townsend's mayoralty was drawing to a close, Wilkes sent a signed letter to the newspapers: "All parties in the City look forward with pleasure to the conclusion of a mayoralty in which violence, tyranny, neglect of public business, a contempt of all order and decorum, with the most sordid parsimony have prevailed."[107]

In the spring of 1773, Wilkes took advantage of a "call" that Lord North had ordered for the House of Commons, summoning all members to appear. The high sheriffs of London and Middlesex did their duty, as they saw it, by giving the notice to Wilkes instead of Luttrell. Wilkes presented himself at the Crown Office asking for his certificate of membership, and when he was refused, appeared at the House on the opening day and demanded that the clerk administer the oaths. He was refused. He made a complaint, and Sergeant Glynn moved that it be heard. It was voted down. A year later, on 15 February 1774, with the assistance of two new sheriffs, Wilkes repeated the entire act. Luttrell, fed up with this nonsense, moved to summon the London and Middlesex sheriffs to the bar, but nobody wanted another contest with Wilkes, and the motion was voted down.[108]

That spring Wilkes's old friend, Dr. John Armstrong, quarreled with him. Armstrong had recently returned from Germany, where he had been serving since 1760 as an army physician, an appointment Wilkes had gotten for him. Before Armstrong departed for service, Wilkes had asked if he could publish the long poem Armstrong had written about Wilkes's life at Aylesbury. Armstrong had agreed and had given Wilkes permission to make alterations in the piece as he saw fit. Wilkes did so but, being Wilkes, slanted certain lines so as to flatter himself. The doctor did not see the published version until his return, and the changes angered him. Wilkes's treatment of the Scots in the *North Briton* also angered him. Words were exchanged. Wilkes pointed out that he had the doctor's permission to make changes. Armstrong maintained that he had not given permission for that sort of change. Then a series of anonymous letters about the quarrel appeared in the *Public Advertiser*, from 23 March to 1 April 1773. Armstrong, raging, appeared at Prince's Court on 7 April and accused Wilkes of writing the letters and insulting him in them. The quarrel rose to a pitch, and they came close to challenging one another to a duel but stopped short. Nothing more was heard of the matter, but the friendship was over, and Dr. Armstrong drops out of the story of Wilkes's life.[109]

One wonders what had put Wilkes in so bellicose a mood. No sooner had Armstrong departed for Scotland than Wilkes quarreled with a "tricking attorney" named Lane. Wilkes called him about something Lane had said when discussing a subscription raised by the society. Their brief exchange ended with Wilkes's challenging Lane to a duel. Edward Thompson, acting as Wilkes's second, tried to talk him out of fighting; but he was saved the trouble by Lane, who on the grounds that he had just been doing his job representing his client, declined to fight.[110]

When autumn came, Wilkes again stood for mayor. It had become clear, however, that many of the wealthy but liberal aldermen had followed Horne into the Constitution Society. Wilkes was confident he would be elected with the highest number of votes, yet he predicted the aldermen would not scratch for him but would put in the other winner, the candidate with the next highest number. Wilkes decided to keep the Constitutional Society from putting in one of their own even if it meant sacrificing his own mayoralty. He asked Frederick Bull if he would run as his partner in the election, which was tantmount to handing Bull the mayoralty. If Wilkes did not have the support of the majority of aldermen, he had the support of the majority of liverymen. He knew that his tapping Bull would result in their both being elected. They won handily, but with Wilkes ahead of Bull at the polls. The election had put the Constitution Society out of the picture. Then, as expected, the aldermen, rather than put Wilkes in office, scratched for Bull. According to Walpole, "This proscription of Wilkes, though for two years together he was first on the poll, did but serve to revive his popularity from the injustice done him, and in this instance did not hurt his power, Bull being entirely his creature, and the odium on Townshend, Horne, Oliver and Sawbridge increasing. The two first were knaves, and the latter weak men. Wilkes was the only man . . . who preserved credit in spite of character." "It is wonderful to think," commented Dr. Johnson, "that all the force of government was required to prevent Wilkes from being chosen the chief magistrate of London, though the liverymen knew he would rob their shops, — knew he would debauch their daughters." But Johnson had not been watching the election closely: the court had given up trying to beat Wilkes and had not put up a candidate that year.[111] Wilkes bided his time, having worked out a plan whereby he was sure he would win in the following year.

In 29 January 1774, Wilkes was substituting for Lord Mayor Bull in the mayor's court when an event occurred that would have pleased Dr. Johnson. It was written up in the *Gentleman's Magazine*:

> A young woman with a child in her arms, and big with another, applied to Alderman Wilkes, who sat at the Mansion-house for the Lord-Mayor, for a pass to the parish to which she belonged, saying that she was married to a Black, who was a slave to a merchant in Lothbury, but that having no wages he was not able to support her . The Alderman granted a warrant to bring her husband before the Lord-Mayor; accordingly he was brought, when the poor fellow declared, that he was born in Guadaloupe, of Negro parents, that he had served his master in England fourteen years, but was never allowed any wages; that when his wife lay in, he applied to his master for a little money for her support, but without success; and in the course of his examination he expressed such tender feelings for the distress of his wife and child, that it drew compassion from all present. Upon which his Lordship discharged him from his master, telling him that he was not a slave, according to the laws of this free country, and that if he should be molested in getting bread for himself and family, on applying to him, he would see justice done. His Lordship then gave him a guinea, and the gentlemen present subscribed another towards his support, till he could get employ, and recommended him to an attorney in the mayor's court, to bring an action against the master for the recovery of his wages for the fourteen years he had served him in England.[112]

During 1773, the newspapers were full of stories about American intransigence and the colonies' boycott of British goods. In December 1773 occurred "the Boston tea party," when the Sons of Liberty and other Bostonians, protesting taxation without representation in general and the tea tax in particular, had disguised themselves as Indians and surreptitiously boarded a British ship and dumped her cargo of tea into the sea. Though it was a peaceful protest in which no one was hurt, the tea party was treated in England as an act of violence. In rapid succession Parliament passed the Boston Port Act, closing the port; the Massachusetts Government Act, making the governing council appointees of the Crown and forbidding town meetings more than once a year; the Administration of Justice Act, giving the governor the right to remand accused persons, including accused soldiers, to English courts for trial in England; and a new Quartering Act, requiring householders to give up their houses on command to be used for barracks. No one but the radical members from London spoke in opposition to these Coercive Acts, as they were called in both England and America. Sawbridge's speech in the House of Commons protesting them was interrupted by constant coughing.[113] A fleet of warships now enclosed Boston harbor, their guns at the ready, and the entire colony was under military control. A new military governor was installed, General Thomas Gage.

Then came the Quebec Act, establishing in that province a government controlled from Westminster but allowing the continuation of the Catholic Church. The act was especially alarming to the thirteen American colonies, who feared that Britain was now using Quebec as a staging area from which to control them. In London there was an uproar of opposition because the act legalized Catholicism in a British colony. The London radicals as a whole were as alarmed as anyone else and launched a petition to the king asking him not to sign the act.

A notable exception to this anti-Catholic movement was Jack Wilkes, who now showed a side of himself heretofore little noticed, his religious tolerance. He did not protest the petition, for that would not have been politic, but he absented himself from the meetings at which the petition was drawn up and signed. He would have more to say on this matter in the not-distant future.

That autumn, as he had planned, Wilkes was elected lord mayor. Nominations were opened on 29 September. Sawbridge made a speech from the hustings, pleading for unity among the radicals and announcing that he would not himself stand. Wilkes had quietly drawn him away from the Constitutional Society by a bargain: if he would help Wilkes in the contest for mayor, Wilkes would support him to represent the City in Parliament. Wilkes's strategy in the mayoral election was to run with a partner, for both to win, and then for the partner to step aside. Who was to be the candidate who would sacrifice his election to throw the contest to Wilkes? Humphrey Cotes offered himself, but there being no encouraging response from the livery, he withdrew. Then Lord Mayor Frederic Bull came forward and was nominated to serve a second term. Bull was particularly indebted to Wilkes because Wilkes had not only handed him the mayoralty the year before, but in a by-election had put him into Parliament. The Constitution Society had had enough and put up no candidate. So the ministry decided to reenter the fray and put up two men of the court party. "The phoenix will rise from its ashes," predicted Walpole, "with most of its old plumes, or as bright."[114]

On 3 October 1774, the polls closed, and the sheriffs announced that Wilkes had come in first and Bull second. The aldermen were convened immediately to scratch, to whisper their choices to the new recorder, who was John

Glynn. Glynn's gout had become crippling and his purse near empty. So the livery had made him their recorder, a post that gave him prestige and income and allowed him to continue in Parliament.[115] Before the scratching began, Wilkes explained to the aldermen that he would abstain because he could not in conscience vote for himself. Then Bull asked them not to scratch for him because, he candidly told them, he had allowed himself to be nominated only to assist Wilkes. All but two aldermen were willing to cooperate, but the implacable Oliver and Townsend scratched for Bull despite his request.[116]

A large crowd had gathered at the Guildhall to hear the result. Sergeant Glynn, as the recorder, was to announce it from the hustings, but his legs were so weak he could not rise. Finally, held up by two men, he declared in a tremulous voice the next lord mayor would be John Wilkes. There was an enormous cheer and the bells of Bow Church began to peal. One after another, the bells of the City took up the ringing so that a hundred could be heard as Lord Mayor Bull lifted the chain of office to place it over Wilkes's head. Oops. The chain came unlinked and fell to the floor. Nonplused, Wilkes strode to the rail of the hustings: "As you have chosen me to be the guardian of your rights and liberties," he cried, "I shall always be ready to defend the franchise of this city and the liberties of the people!"[117] A great cheer arose.

"Thus, after so much persecution of the Court," wrote Walpole,

> after so many attempts on his life, after a long imprisonment in a jail, after all his own crimes and indiscretions, did this extraordinary man, of more extraordinary fortune, attain the highest office in so grave and important a city as the capital of England, always reviving, the more opposed and oppressed, and unable to shock Fortune, or make her laugh at *him*, who laughed at everybody and everything. The duration of his influence was the most wonderful part of his history. . . . Wilkes was seen through, detected, yet gained ground: and all the power of the Crown, all the malice of the Scots, all the abilities of Lord Mansfield, all the violence of Alderman Townsend, all the want of policy and parts of the Opposition, all the treachery of his friends, could not demolish him. He equally baffled the King and Parson Horne, though both neglected no latitude to compass his ruin. It is in the tenth year of his war on the Court that he gained so signal a victory!

Wilkes's comment was candid: "If the king had sent me a pardon and a thousand pounds to Paris, I should have accepted them, but I am obliged to him for not having ruined me."[118]

There was no time to celebrate, for the king had dismissed Parliament on 30 September, and a general election was upon them. King George had dismissed Parliament in advance of the mandated seven-year termination and forced an early election to assure himself that his people approved of his handling of the

American problem. If the court party could maintain its majority in the House of Commons and the opposition show no significant growth, the king would be assured he had not gone too far in the Coercive Acts and other demands upon the unruly colonies. Election day was set for 20 October.

Wilkes offered himself as a candidate for one of the two knights of the shire for Middlesex. The incapacity that had been imposed upon him had dissolved with the dismissal of the Parliament that had established it. At the nomination meeting at Miles End, Wilkes and Glynn were nominated.[119] On 20 October, the two, riding in the lord mayor's "gingerbread coach," as Wilkes called it, were escorted to Brentford Butts by a great crowd of horsemen with colors flying and horns blaring. No opposition appearing, Wilkes and Glynn were elected by a show of hands and a great huzzah. In two months, Jack Wilkes would again take the seat for Middlesex from which he had been excluded almost six years before.

George III kept his control over Parliament in this election, but the radicals emerged a tightly knit party with a strong hold over the metropolis of London. In the contest for the four City representatives, a full slate of radicals came in. Bull, Sawbridge, and Wilkes's brother-in-law George Hayley, all belonging to the Bill of Rights Society, were elected. The odd man out was Wilkes's enemy, Richard Oliver, a member of the Constitutional Society, but no less a radical because of that. They had not only the parliamentary seats, but also their great lawyer as City recorder and their political leader as lord mayor. But the triumph was confined to London and Middlesex. In the rural areas and small buroughs, the radical opposition to the war did not go down well, and the people voted overwhelmingly for the court candidates. Sir Joseph Mawbey lost at Southwark, just across the river, and Humphrey Cotes came in at the bottom of the poll for Westminster.[120] (Alas, Wilkes's old friend died soon after.) Those who recalled Wilkes's election to Middlesex in 1768 might have expected another riot of celebration with the number forty-five painted everywhere, but nothing like that happened. Most of the common folk of London saved their energies for the "Lord Mayor's Show," which had been put off until 5 November.

For Wilkes, Lord Mayor's Day opened as he was getting dressed in the morning. He was presented with a letter containing a banknote of one thousand pounds from his wife![121] Then the ceremonies began. A new lord mayor was not considered fully vested until he had taken the required oath before the barons of the exchequer and received the approval of the king through the lord chancellor. The cabinet had actually considered asking the king to refuse the approval but decided otherwise on the argument of an unidentified minister, "Better to permit him to be Lord Mayor for one year than King of the City for life." The trip from the City to Westminster to fulfill these obligations had become the traditional Lord Mayor's Show. According to a writer for the *London Magazine*, "a greater concourse of people never appeared in the streets and houses" than in the show this year; "and, what is more rare, none were drunk, riotous, or indecent." The trip to Westminster was made by boat, the lord mayor's barge followed by those of the city companies, newly painted and gilded, and a crowd of festooned smaller boats. Cheering mobs crowded at the windows and along the banks: "The silver Thames was so covered with boats that you could hardly tell on what the vessels moved; they formed one surface of wood and looked like a temporary bridge for the sudden convenience of giving passage to an army. The northern parts of the town were abandoned, and people of every denomination crowded the banks of the river to testify their joy and approbation of his election, for the city of London and the county of Middlesex." The lord mayor's party landed on the steps at Westminster and proceeded to Westminster Hall. "Having walked around the Hall," said the *Gentleman's Magazine*, "and solemnly saluted all the courts, they went to the Exchequer bar, and the new Lord Mayor did there take the oaths." Through crowds of cheering people they made their way to the house of the chancellor, who declared "his majesty approved of him." These ceremonies over, the boats returned and landed at Blackfriar's bridge. Wilkes addressed the crowd, thanking them and asking for "decorum." Then it was on to the Guildhall for a feast at which Polly, stole the show: "Harmony and good nature kept pace with festivity, and the amiable daughter of the patriot did honor to the occasion, whose purity of mind, elegance of manners, sweetness of disposition, and accomplished and refined education, with the most lively natural good sense, did so ornament the jubilee of the sons of freedom that the first courts in Europe might allow themselves outdone with her graces, wit, and distinguished sense." Jack Smith had come wearing a new pair of pumps that were uncomfortably tight. During dinner, he slipped them off under the table, but when the dancing began he found his feet had swollen and he could not get them on again. His "uncle" had looked forward to seeing him dance and was puzzled that he just sat there.[122]

Outside, the common people were running through the streets in a riot of joy. They had triumphed, for they had supplied the power that made possible the rise of their leader; they were joyful, for he had given them a new voice in the councils of their City and in the forum of Great Britain. But a pall hung over the minuet in the hall and the riot in the streets. A war in America loomed, a war with France was certain to follow, and their leader was getting older and uglier and more needful of rest. This would be the last time the "inferior sort" of London would riot in support or celebration of Mr. Wilkes.[123]

12

My Lord Mayor

Wilkes was now a celebrity, and he did not hesitate to act the part, giving dinner after dinner in the Mansion House, ball after ball. The honorary title of lady mayoress, heretofore given to wives, was now bestowed upon Polly. One newspaper described the opening ritual of the "brilliant Lady Mayoress's Rout."

> Yesterday the Lord Mayor, aldermen, etc, went from the Mansion House to St. Bride's Church in the following order. 1. The Head Marshal. 2. The Bridewell boys. 3. The surgeons and apothecaries. 5. The governors. 6. The deputy city marshal, the under marshal, and six footmen in rich liveries. 7. The state coach with the Lord Mayor and Miss Wilkes, as Lady Mayoress. 8. His lordship's private coach, with three ladies and a gentleman, and three footmen behind. 9. Aldermen Bull, Sawbridge, Thomas and lady, Hayley and lady, in their respective carriages. 10. The Town Clerk. 11. The two sheriffs and their ladies. The procession was closed with the two city counsels. The Lady Mayoress was dressed in rich silk, a maiden's blush, trimmed with a bouquet of diamonds in her bosom.

The service over, the entire procession returned to the Mansion House. Those who were not gentlemen scattered to their various posts, and the gentlemen with their ladies at their sides entered the great Egyptian Hall. There they met a company that included the Duke of Leinster, Lord Mahon, Prince Pallavicini ("the late Pope's nephew"), Sir George Savile, Edmund Burke, John Trevanion, George Colman, James Boswell, Arthur Lee, John Sawbridge, and sundry other aldermen and dignitaries. Some two hundred sat down to dine. On the wall behind the high table "was a beautiful piece, painted in an inimitable taste, which, it is said, represented the triumph of Bacchus and Ariadne, or love united with wine. Besides the usual profusion of wines and eatables, which were remarkably good in their kind, and set off in the greatest elegance, as well as much warmer than commonly is the case at those great dinners: the guests were here presented with another novelty, which had a most pleasing effect: many of Mr. Cox's pieces of mechanism from the Museum, all in full tune . . . continued their musical movements during the greatest part of the dinner. Coffee, tea, negus, ices, etc., were handed by female servants in a room below." Coffee over, the lord mayor and lady mayoress led the way to the ballroom, where they met another thousand guests. The Duke of Leinster opened the dancing by taking Polly on a whirl about the floor to the applause of the company, after which Lord Mahon danced a minuet with "the accomplished daughter of the host." "The dancing of minuets, cotillons, allemands, and country dances continued till three yesterday morning, and about half an hour after the whole company departed, greatly pleased with the elegance of the entertainment, etc." Her years of education showed clearly in the lady mayoress, "who for affability, ease, attention, and politeness perhaps is superior to most of her sex." Able to read six languages and converse in three or four of them, she also liked to laugh. "Much vivacity and wit passed amongst the company, and some humorous strokes were produced by the ladies' feathers." D'Holbach sent his and his wife's "very best compliments to your very amiable lady-mayoress, who acted so well her part lately in the Egyptian Hall, to the satisfaction of that prodigious crowd." But from those crowds emerged no suitor for the hand of the tall, accomplished lady mayoress with the long jaw. Tiger Roach sent a challenge to a fellow officer who had spoken slightingly of her looks, but gallantry went no further.[1]

Wilkes, whose polished manners were everywhere acknowledged, was the perfect host, amusing and cordial to the ladies, and reputed to be one of the most hospitable mayors in memory. Word got around he was hoping to have Dr. Johnson himself to the Mansion House, "to eat turtle with him, forsooth," said Mrs. Thrale to the doctor; but she added, " 'tis a liberal fellow in spite of his principles, and a genteel fellow in spite of his mean birth." "He *is* a fine fellow," replied Johnson, "but let us remember that it would be a triumph to Wilkes, to show me that he is just where King, Lords, and Commons, and myself, forsooth, have all endeavored to prevent him from being."[2]

Wilkes's allowance as lord mayor covered only part of the cost of these entertainments, but Wilkes did not hesitate to pay with promises. The debts would hang over his head for the next four or five years.

Wilkes took up his duties as administrator of the old City against a somber background of news from America. The colonies seemed to be moving toward war, not a war they wanted, but one they now believed they could not escape if they were to preserve their liberties. But Wilkes's attention was on local problems, which he addressed like the militia colonel he had once been, demanding strict discipline and subordination among the City officers and servants. He got surprising results in an office limited to one year. He reformed the way the drovers treated the cattle brought daily into Smithfield markets and set standards for more humane butchering. He instituted a campaign against merchants' cheating with weights. For the greater convenience of the aldermen, he changed the venue of the court sessions from the Guildhall to the Mansion House. He oversaw the completion of Blackfriars Bridge and arranged charities for prisoners at Newgate. He regulated prices so that the poor could eat and was thanked for so doing by his pastor, the Rev. Dr. Thomas Wilson, who had himself instituted more than one humanitarian effort to relieve poverty. "As a lover of the poor and distressed," he wrote, "I must thank you for the tender care you have taken of them, in reducing the price of bread and provisions, &c . . . you will receive the honest applauses of thousands."[3]

But the laughing, convivial Wilkes was not lost. Boswell, no longer worried that his image might suffer from association with a scandalous anti-Scot, reentered Wilkes's life with éclat. He and Charles Dilly, the printer, called at Mansion House and were shown to a parlor. When Wilkes appeared, Boswell jumped to his feet, made a low bow, and, addressing him as "My Lord," made "a mock formal introductory speech." They drank "chocolade" and were then taken to Miss Wilkes's dressing room, where after the curtseys and bows and chatter, she gave them tickets to the next ball at Mansion House. In April, Boswell came again to dinner: Wilkes "classical and gay," he said, "as when at Rome and Naples."[4] There would never again be a break in this friendship.

It is odd that Wilkes was so easy with Boswell, who called himself a Tory. Actually, Boswell's politics was a crazy mixture of conservative and liberal. He was England's most vocal advocate of liberty for the Corsicans, and in 1768 had written *An Account of Corsica*, which resulted in the sobriquet Corsica Boswell. He steadily supported the Americans. Yet he considered himself a Tory and was forever warning Wilkes of that. "Though we differ widely in religion and politics," he once told Wilkes, "il y a des points où nos ames sont unies [there are points at which our souls are one], as Rousseau said to me in his wild retreat." In one argument over a meeting of some sort, when Boswell stubbornly insisted he was right, Wilkes put his arm about him, so to speak, for he

actually wrote the words in a letter: "Indeed, my dear Boswell, political phle-
botomy [bloodletting] is sometimes necessary — but come to Prince's Court,
and we will discuss this, and other grave subjects, with the good humor, which
never forsakes either of us."[5]

Did Polly accompany her father in the gingerbread coach as he rode to the
House of Lords on the morning of 2 December 1774 for the opening of Parliament? Did the lord mayor show her up to the gallery before he joined the
assembled members of both houses to hear the king's address? After the speech,
the elected representatives crossed to St. Stephen's Chapel, where Wilkes was
sworn in and took his seat as knight of the shire of Middlesex, the seat that he
had claimed for six years. The significance of the act was not lost upon the other
members as they filed past him, nodding to acknowledge his victory. He sat in
the front row to the left of the speaker. He would always sit on the left, the side
of the opposition, and usually would vote with them, but, being attached to no
faction, he was not, properly speaking, a "member of the opposition" but
rather an "independent." The most prestigious seats in the House were those of
the knights of the shires, and none more prestigious than knight of the shire for
Middlesex, the most powerful and respected county in England. The man who
had outwitted the speaker from behind the bar and tweaked the conscience of
the assembly now would address them from from what a colleague called, "a
great Parliamentary eminence."[6]

On his way to this eminent seat, Wilkes paused to twist the arm of the king.
He let it be known that his first motion would be to unseat the speaker of the
House, Wilkes's old enemy, Sir Fletcher Norton, and replace him with Robert
Mackreth, the member for Castle Rising. Mackreth's election had been a
shock to the nation because only a few years before he had worked in a
coffeehouse as a waiter! King George, when told what Wilkes was up to, was
horrified and called in his first minister. "Mackreth for Speaker! This would
appear impossible to be true if the author's character was not known to be so
void of decency." Lord North was authorized to carry to Mackreth his majesty's request to resign. Mackreth refused. Lord North tried a bribe. Also
refused. On the afternoon of 18 February 1775, the member for Middlesex
dined with the speaker, Bullcalf Norton himself, who had attempted to keep
him in the Tower in 1763 and prosecuted him at his trial in absentia in 1764.
How Wilkes must have gloried in Speaker Norton's asking a favor — if he did,
which is more than we know. However, the rumors died, and Norton's chair
was not challenged.[7]

Wilkes's first speech was just as audacious. Parliament had a century-old
custom of attending church on the anniversary of the beheading of Charles I in
1649, to hear a memorial service for that unfortunate king and a sermon on

his beheading. Two days before this scheduled event, Wilkes rose in the House to protest the tradition. The thirtieth of January, he declared, should be not a day of mourning, but a day of festival for the execution of "a determined enemy of the liberties of his country." The London radicals, the Real Whigs, and even Dr. Johnson believed that in the extremes of abuse a people could legitimately rise against a government, but they were shocked at the idea of king-killing. In what they thought of as their own "glorious Revolution" of 1688, James II had been driven from the country but not executed! The speech did not go unnoticed by dissenters, whose traditions came down from the Presbyterians who had executed the king. Wilkes would enjoy the support of dissenters for years to come.[8]

Thus the House was reminded that the lofty seat of the knight of the shire for Middlesex was occupied by a man who, his imprisonment notwithstanding, had won his battles with king, ministers, and Parliament. He certainly was a comedian, but he was not to be fooled with.

On forty-two recorded occasions and doubtless many unrecorded, Wilkes made, or mangled, speeches in the House. As his teeth loosened and fell out, his diction went from bad to worse, yet no one except the prime minister and the opposition leaders spoke more often. At that time speech handicaps were more tolerated than in our age of good dentistry and speech therapy. Nathaniel Wraxall, who sat opposite Wilkes in the House, much admired Wilkes's speeches, "full of wit, pleasantry, and point," though always prepared in advance and always sent to Woodfall of the *Public Advertiser* before he pronounced them.[9] He once asked the House to delay its adjournment so that he could make his speech: it would be ridiculous, he explained, for it to appear in the newspapers before it had been delivered.

In mid-February, Wilkes let it be known he would offer a motion in the House of Commons to remove from the House record the motions by which he had been incapacitated. The ministry, said Walpole, was in a panic. Lord North declared he would resign if such a motion were to carry.[10] On 22 February 1775, Wilkes moved to expunge from the Journals of the House of Commons the resolution of 17 February 1769 by which he had been incapacitated. "The motion which I shall have the honor of submitting to the House affects, in my opinion, the very vitals of this constitution, the great primary source of the power of the people whom we represent and by whose authority only, delegated to us for a time, we are a part of the legislative body of this kingdom." He reminded the House that "all the great powers of the state at one time appeared combined to pour their vengeance on me," but he had forgiven all of that. "The broad shield of the law protected me." His purpose now was to remove a dangerous precedent subversive of the rights of electors.

"While these resolutions, Sir, remain among our records, I consider a precedent established under the sanction of this House to rob not only a whole county, but the entire collective body of electors of this kingdom of their birthright and most valuable inheritance." The question was moved and the debate began. The discussion of election law reminded the house that Mr. Wilkes had been trained in law and associated with the best British lawyers of the day. Historians have said he took his arguments here from James Burgh's *Political Disquisitions*, 1774–75, but it is more likely that Burgh, who did not begin writing his great book until 1771, took the arguments from Wilkes, who had made them at the time of the incapacitation in 1768. His fundamental tenet, that Parliament derived its authority from the electors, he had held for years. That authority was denied, he now said, in the precedent of incapacitation. The majority party in the House, he warned, could trump up accusations against any member who opposed them and have him summarily removed: "If you can expel whom you please, and reject those disagreeable to you, the House will be self-created and self-existing. The original idea of your representing the people will be lost."[11]

Lord North's tactic of opposition was to be facetious. As reported in the *Parliamentary Register*, North "entered into a physical, surgical, and political disquisition on the nature and effects of amputations in general as operating on the body natural and body politic." His ally, Speaker Norton, thinking it safe to do so, recognized John Luttrell, the brother of the man who had usurped the Middlesex seat in the previous parliament. To Norton's surprise, Luttrell spoke in support of Wilkes: "I have no knowledge of him in his private capacity, but in his public one I have ever held him respectable; he has exercised the great office of magistracy in this metropolis, with an assiduity and firmness that is scarce to be paralleled; he has ever displayed that consistency and uprightness in all his public actions, that in these times of supineness and ductility, claim peculiar admiration." Then there was the opposite *ad hominem* argument by Charles Van, member for Brecon, who asserted that Wilkes had been excluded from the previous Parliament because he was guilty of blasphemy. Wilkes jumped to his feet and demanded that the exclusion motion be read. It was, and the word *blasphemy*'s not appearing "occasioned much laughter." Wilkes, as he was sitting down, muttered under his breath, "A Puppy! Does he think I don't know what is blasphemy better than he does!" The debate on Wilkes's motion continued for eight hours, Sergeant John Glynn admirably laying out the legal argument; but it was finally defeated, 239 to 171. The king was pleased: "I flatter myself we shall in the future not hear the old bone of contention brought into agitation." He was wrong. Wilkes offered the resolution a second time on 30 April 1776 and made another memorable speech.[12] He would repeat the motion every year for the next seven years. The third or fourth year, the newspapers began to use the reductionist term, "Mr. Wilkes's annual motion." If they could have taken, as Wilkes liked to call it, "a peep into futurity," how astonished these printers and lawmakers would have been to discover that Wilkes's motion would provide one foundation stone of the American Constitution and open the door to British election reform.

Wilkes's life outside St. Stephen's Chapel was crowded with aldermanic demands, mayoral management, and court sessions. He continued to write Wilkite propaganda, turning out a pamphlet called "A Dialogue between a Liveryman and a Placeman."[13] But his social life continued as busy as ever. He often saw the Chevalier d'Eon, but in 1777, she/he negotiated a pension from Louis XVI and returned to Paris, where she was immediately recruited into the service of Queen Marie Antoinette and would serve for four years as one of her ladies in waiting.

The twenty-third of June 1775 was a memorable festival day. The first regatta in English history was held on the Thames, and a vast crowd of gentry who had agreed to dress in white waved from the gardens and windows of the great houses along the river or from hundreds of small boats crowding the water, leaving a sort of street down which the sculls were rowed. Wilkes and Polly and what Wilkes described ironically as the entire *corps diplomatique*, nibbled at ices and watched from beneath the canvas awnings of the lord mayor's barge.[14]

The news from America was sobering. On 7 September 1774, the first Continental Congress assembled in Philadelphia. Though united in their opposition to the British siege of Massachusetts, they still acknowledged George III as their king. They sent his majesty a petition protesting their loyalty but asking for the removal of standing armies and juggernaut navies and admiralty courts used to enforce tax laws. They asked for reform of the common law courts, to which judges were appointed in England and from which offenders could be sent to England to be tried for crimes committed in America. They asked for relief from customs officers who broke and entered houses at will, and they asked for recognition of the right to recall their own assemblies, now "injuriously dissolved" "To a sovereign who 'glories in the name of Briton,' the bare recital of these acts must, we presume, justify the loyal subjects who fly to the foot of his throne and implore his clemency for protection against them."[15] Here for the first time, America spoke with one voice.

The British public was torn with agony over the situation. Many looked upon the Americans as rebels against law and Crown. Others feared the king's refusal of liberties to the colonies was the thin edge of the wedge between themselves and their own liberties. America, they feared, was the testing ground for the "personal government" of George III. The king received in equal numbers addresses supporting his Draconian measures and petitions begging for relief for Americans and the return of their rights.[16]

Josiah Quincy Jr. and William Palfrey were both in London preparing reports, talking with Arthur Lee and his brother William, with Wilkes, Priestly, Price, Hollis, and having conferences with Lord North and other ministers. They found little they could hope for. American newspaper articles and letters, pointing out that the colonies had received no reassurances, began to shift the blame from the ministers to the king himself. Some were saying the king was trying to reduce them to slavery.[17]

On 3 February 1775, Wilkes made his first speech on America. His purpose was to amend the "address" the House was sending to the king. The king, in his speech to the Parliament, had put the label of "rebellion" on the heretofore peaceful resistance of Massachusetts. The address, said Wilkes, should object to such wording, for it amounted to a declaration of war. The word *rebellion* "appears to me unfounded, rash and sanguinary, and most unjustly to draw the sword against America; but before administration are suffered to plunge this nation into the horrors of civil war, before they are permitted to force Englishmen to sheathe their swords in the bowels of their fellow-subjects, I hope this House will seriously weigh the original ground and cause of this unhappy dispute. . . . Who can tell, Sir, whether in consequence of this very day's violent and mad address to his Majesty, the scabbard may not be thrown away by them as well as by us, and should success attend them, whether in a few years the Americans may not celebrate the glorious era of the revolution of 1775 as we do that of 1688." Britain cannot win a war, he warned, not in the vast spaces of America, not against a hearty, courageous people. Do not deceive yourselves: "The whole continent will be dismembered from Great Britain, and the wide arch of the raised empire fall."[18] His attempts to help the Americans were not lost on the colony of North Carolina, whose new revolutionary legislature in 1777 created a new county and voted to call it Wilkes County.[19]

The speech was published in the *Boston Gazette* and copied into other papers.[20] In England, it was largely overshadowed by a stirring speech from Charles James Fox, a speech that started this remarkable man toward a takeover of the opposition in the House of Commons. Fox was the son of the old scamp who in 1762 had purchased the House of Commons for Lord Bute in such a shocking manner. The son had turned out quite different from his father, candid, honest, hardworking, and a forceful speaker. Wilkes never joined the opposition, though he usually voted with them.

And there were others who spoke for America. Six weeks later, on 22 March, Edmund Burke, who was serving as the agent for New York, made a motion setting out the Rockingham party's plan of reconciliation with America and then spoke eloquently for two and a half hours, undoubtedly the most famous of all parliamentary speeches in support of America. Isaac Barré, spokesman for Earl Shelburne, Joseph Dunning, the great lawyer, Chatham in the House of Lords, and others eloquently opposed the Coercive Acts and suggested programs for bringing harmony between colonies and king. But none were so harshly critical of the British ministers as Wilkes.

In the City, Wilkes and his party kept up the agitation. Wilkes presented a petition to the House of Commons from American traders in London.[21] The livery defied the government by electing an American as alderman of Aldgate Ward, William Lee, the brother of Arthur, who with two American partners was trading in Virginia tobacco.

In April, Wilkes chaired a meeting of two thousand livery in Common Hall and obtained signatures on an audacious petition to the king, stating bluntly that the ministers were trying "to establish arbitrary power over all America" and praying for the removal of Lord North and the cabinet. George III haughtily refused to accept a petition from the livery. There followed a battle over protocol, with Wilkes and livery marching back and forth between Guildhall and St. James's Palace, and city sheriffs confronting the lord chamberlain with resolutions, one of which stated that the king's refusal was "evasive, nugatory, and insulting." His highness thought it unsuitable for the low-class livery to present a petition, but he accepted Wilkes's compromise: the petition would be from the entire corporate body of the City of London. Also at issue was the right of the City to have its petition received "from the throne." Wilkes wrote a long, scholarly argument about the ancient rights of the City. A petition presented at a levée by some nobleman acting for the City, he pointed out, might never be read; but a petition received from the throne was promptly read aloud by the king or one of his courtiers, thus assuring the petitioners that they had been heard. His majesty withdrew his condition but insisted that if Lord Mayor Wilkes were to appear with the delegation, he would not speak to him, to which Wilkes responded he had not expected the honor.[22]

The petition was presented on 7 April 1775. In what Walpole called Wilkes's "ne plus ultra," he knelt before the throne of King George III and humbly offered the scroll. For the first time he was face to face with his monarch. For the first time George III looked into the eyes, or at least one eye, of the man whom he hated and feared, "that devil Wilkes." Little or nothing was spoken between them, but as soon as the entourage had departed, the king remarked, he "had never seen so well-bred a Lord Mayor."[23] The next day the king sent a letter to the City, his response to the petition. His majesty was astonished that the petitioners should encourage "the rebellious disposition" of his colonies.

By this time most American leaders had come to the conclusion they would have to separate themselves from this unjust king. Convinced there was no other way to obtain their rights, a little group of armed farmers confronted a British regiment at Lexington and were mowed down. The Battle of Concord followed, after which the "minute-men" inflicted much damage upon the British troops retreating to Boston. On 28 May 1775, John Derby, a member of the Boston Sons of Liberty assigned the task of bringing accounts of these events to England, hid his ship in a stream in the Isle of Wight, was rowed to the mainland, rode to London in the night, and handed the papers to Arthur Lee the next day. Lee had them copied, gave the originals to Lord Mayor Wilkes for safekeeping, and set about distributing the American account of the fighting. A day later it appeared in numerous papers.[24] Then came the news that a second Continental Congress had met in Philadelphia and decided to merge their various colonial militias into a national army. General George Washington, ordered to take command, had been dispatched to Cambridge, Massachusetts, on the Charles River, upstream from Boston.

On 23 June 1775, Lord Mayor Wilkes laid before the City Court of Common Council a letter from the correspondence committee of New York saying they are resolved to fight if the king and Parliament do not rescind the recent repressive laws.[25] In London, the Rev. Mr. Horne's Constitutional Society advertised an appeal for funds for "the relief of the widows, orphans and aged parents" of Americans "inhumanely murdered" by the king's troops at Lexington and Concord. Five publishers of newspapers that carried the appeal were arrested and tried for seditious libel. Horne himself was arrested and eventually convicted by Lord Mansfield.[26]

In late June 1775, the shocking news of the Battle of Bunker Hill arrived in London. Close to Charlestown, Massachusetts, an American militia held the heights of a hill against a British army of twenty-two hundred soldiers, whose officers foolishly sent them upward into the unrelenting fire of the Americans. The Americans fled when their ammunition ran out, but left behind half the British soldiers dead or wounded on Bunker Hill. Now there could be no turning back.

Britons began to rally behind their leader, as people are wont to do in time of war. Addresses supporting the king flowed into St. James's. Petitions for peace dwindled to a few, and the tone of them was less strident. The king thought a peace petition which Wilkes and the City presented on 14 July was "the most decent and moderate in words that has been for some time fabricated on that side Temple bar." This was too much success for Wilkes's taste. He "hoped the king would not smile upon him, for that would ruin him for ever."[27]

Within weeks, Lord George Germaine was made secretary of state for the colonies and commenced the direction of the new war. In Wilkes's naughty projected book An Essay on Woman, Wilkes had satirized Germaine under the name he was then using, George Sackville. In a subscription on the title page, he had accused Sackville of sodomizing his friend the archbishop of Ireland. Germaine was a tolerant man. Some years later, at a meeting of commissioners for a new paving of streets in Westminster, he deigned to shake hands with Wilkes. He was "cold and formal," Wilkes wrote to Polly, and "looked very stately."[28]

On 22 August 1775, heralds proclaimed from the steps of the Royal Exchange that his royal majesty would on the next day make a proclamation. Knowing what was coming, Lord Mayor Wilkes forbade the attendance of any City official except the town crier and, in defiance of custom, would not lend horses to the heralds. As expected, George III proclaimed the colonists to be "in open and avowed rebellion." He demanded full information about "all persons who shall be found carrying on correspondence with, or in any manner or degree aiding or abetting the persons now in open arms and rebellion against our government." The habeas corpus was suspended, and Mrs. Macaulay, who was in Paris, was fearful of entering the American embassy there for fear she would be arrested when she returned to England.[29]

Open exchanges of letters with the colonies came to a halt. Secret exchanges of letters were made, but it became increasingly difficult for Englishmen to hear the American side of the story, to express a sense of solidarity with Americans, or to offer concrete support. Wilkes tested the waters in a meeting of the Common Council on 29 September 1775. He read them a letter from John Hancock, who spoke for the American Congress, of which Hancock was president. He urged the City of London, which he called "the patron of liberty," to work for peace. But the livery were afraid to reply, though they sent Hancock's letter to the newspapers. Wilkes grew more and more disgusted with the livery, "no longer worthy the name of freemen . . . mean vassals, ignominiously courting and bowing their necks to the ministerial yoke. . . . If we are saved, it will be almost solely by the courage and noble spirit of our American brethren, whom neither the luxuries of a court, nor the sordid lust of avarice in a rapacious and venal metropolis have hitherto corrupted." This was sour grapes, for Wilkes was losing control of the livery. In fact, the Common Council proved itself much more courageous than Wilkes would allow: it awarded the freedom of the City to Richard Price for his daring *Observations on the Nature of Civil Liberty*. Price and others of the Real Whigs courageously continued to write essays, letters, and sermons criticizing the ministry and opposing the war.[30]

The Bill of Rights Society, their passion for American liberty squelched, ceased most activities and gradually disappeared. Wilkes was left with no command staff and, having lost control of the livery, no soldiers. The Wilkite party consisted of little more than twelve members of Parliament whom Wilkes called his apostles. Press gangs returned to the City and were supported in the courts.[31]

Collaboration with America went underground. The crown messengers, who had begun to spy on radical London, reported that George Hayley was sending military supplies to America under the pretense of selling them to Spain. William Lee was fingered as leader of a scheme to transport disgruntled shipwrights from the navy yards to America, where men of their skill were needed. Probably both were true, but the messengers were inept and the solicitor general, Alexander Wedderburn, was confused. Wedderburn began drafting an indictment of William Lee, but he never completed it. In October, Stephen Sayre, an American who had established a City banking firm and who, with Wilkes's backing, had served as sheriff in 1773, was arrested and charged with conspiring to kidnap the king on his way to the House of Lords. The case was flimsy, the evidence false, and the witnesses corrupt. Most of the ministers themselves thought it laughable. Wilkes was present at the King's Bench when Sayre was brought before Lord Mansfield. Sayre was freed on bail, and soon thereafter the charges were dropped. Taking a cue from his friend, Sayre sued the secretary of state for false arrest, and the jury awarded him a considerable sum; the secretary, evoking a technicality of law, never paid it.[32]

Wilkes himself was drawn into a subversive scheme to aid America. He was not exactly a spy, but he could have been hanged for treason if caught. At this point, France was sympathetic to America but careful not to give material support openly for fear England would declare war on her. Nevertheless, a small group of Frenchmen, encouraged by Louis XVI, were planning to send arms to America secretly. Wilkes's involvement with this group began at the dining table of Mansion House. In the autumn of 1775, a number of Americans and sympathizers were guests, among them Arthur Lee, William Lee, and Richard Penn, grandson of the founder of Pennsylvania. On 11 September, there appeared at the lord mayor's table the famous Frenchman Pierre-Augustin Caron de Beaumarchais, courtier, musician, inventor, publisher, playwright, and author of the *Barber of Seville* and the *Marriage of Figaro*. Beaumarchais was a secret agent for France, and he had come to England to induce the Chevalier d'Eon to give up the papers he was holding that could be so embarrassing to the king of France. He had succeeded in his mission. How he met Wilkes is unknown, but they became, wrote George Otto Trevelyan, "sworn brothers," who resembled each other "as nearly as an Englishman can resemble a Frenchman, in defects and qualities of his character." At this gathering in Lord Mayor Wilkes's house, Beaumarchais met Arthur Lee for the first time. Beaumarchais was a passionate supporter of America. His meeting with Lee came at a propitious time, for the Continental Congress had appointed Lee as their "confidential correspondent" in London, which was a way of saying their London spymaster. That winter, after his term as mayor had ended, Wilkes and Polly hosted three suspicious dinners at Prince's Court to which came Beaumarchais, Arthur Lee, Captain Robert Orme, an American adventurer and erstwhile aide de camp to General Edward Braddock in the French and Indian wars, and Louis-Léon-Felicité de Brancas, Comte de Lauraguais, a French playboy whom Wilkes and Polly had known in Paris and entertained in London. Lauraguais, under orders from the French ministry to watch Beaumarchais, was spying on the spy. At one such dinner, John Hatselle, clerk of the House of Commons, was present, though what this scholarly lawyer was doing in this den of conspirators is hard to imagine.[33]

Within months, Beaumarchais and Lee had set up a false commercial company in Paris designed to sell arms to America. During the summer of 1776, Wilkes carried on a weekly correspondence with Beaumarchais in Paris, their letters and packages carried back and forth by one Charles Jean Garnier, secretary to the French embassy. Though evidence is circumstantial, Wilkes was surely collecting money from a network of American sympathizers and sending it to Beaumarchais by Monsieur Garnier. Beaumarchais, with money from England, Spain, and his own king, purchased arms from French arsenals and prepared to ship them to America. But Dr. Edward Bancroft, one of the conspirators, was a double agent and among other things reported Wilkes's activities to Lord Stormont, the British ambassador to France. Lord Stormont protested to the French ministry, but they did nothing because the king was backing the project. Bancroft next reported Wilkes's activities to the English ministry, but to no avail. In the summer of 1777 Beaumarchais dispatched three ships to America. Seven or eight more were to follow. In America's first major victory, the battle of Saratoga in October 1777, most of the American arms were French. Washington's raggle-taggle army on the west bank of the Delaware had many French muskets.[34]

Although Wilkes's involvement was known, there was no raid upon his house and no charge leveled against him. Perhaps the ministers were afraid to move against him without an airtight case, which they did not have. Or they may have feared the mob would rise again. After Beaumarchais's three ships were on the ocean, Wilkes stopped his subversive activities and never took them up again. But Lord Orford spread a rumor that someone had seen a pension list of a French minister on which Wilkes's name appeared, and that was proof enough for Orford that Wilkes had been a French agent.[35]

Wilkes did not accept the ridiculous proposal to become a spy for America that he received in 1779, which offered to pay him two hundred pounds per quarter and asked him for information he could not possibly have, "earliest advice of all the determinations and designs of the British Secret Cabinet, of every plan of operation against America or her allies as soon as it is concerted or even proposed . . . the secret instructions given to the commanders by sea and land," and so forth. Who would have thought that Wilkes had access to such information? The letter is signed "W. L.," probably William Lee, who had closed up his business in London in 1776 and was serving as the American ambassador to Austria and Prussia. If "W. L." was indeed William Lee, he must be put down as mad.[36]

As Wilkes was approaching the end of his one-year term as lord mayor, he could look back on the year with some satisfaction, confident that his practical accomplishments as mayor had benefited the City, content that he had stood by his political principles in Parliament and been faithful in his support of America.

But the end of his mayoralty was unexpectedly marred by a disturbed confession from his old lover Mrs. Barnard, the same Mrs. Barnard who had had an affair with Wilkes when he was writing the *North Briton* and a second time in the King's Bench Prison. On 25 September 1775, Mrs. Barnard and her husband were included in a large gathering at the Mansion House. Barnard, a great admirer of his host, had never told Wilkes or Mrs. Barnard that he had rewritten his will, leaving eight thousand pounds and a valuable collection of prints and books to Wilkes. The afternoon passed without event, though Mrs. Barnard was in low spirits. Four or five days later, quite without warning, Mrs. Barnard blurted out to her husband a confession of her past sins with the lord mayor. On or about the 10 October, Wilkes received a letter from a distraught John Barnard, who told him his wife had been seized with remorse, and in a state that "savored of madness" had confessed her sins with Wilkes. Barnard could forgive what had gone on between the two of them before he knew them, "but if you have so cruelly injured me, as she says you have since done . . . for God's sake give me some satisfaction." Not, he hastened to add, by sword or pistol, for he was too infirm for such an encounter.[37]

Was the woman mad? wondered Wilkes. If not mad, what was she up to? He was not going to confirm her accusation until he better understood the situation. Hoping he could be vague enough, he wrote to Barnard: "Conscious innocence, Mr. Wilkes has always found the firmest shield against the envenomed shafts of malice and falsehood." There could be no malice or false-hood in such a confession, responded Barnard, for she has accused herself "to her own certain ruin."[38]

Wilkes reluctantly took himself to Barnard's house in Berkeley Square. Though weak and ill, Barnard received him in the downstairs parlor. His wife was upstairs, dreadfully distracted, he said. She had been wandering about the house at night, and by day shut herself in her room, constantly weeping. She was being haunted, said Barnard, by his daughter, the child of his first mar-riage, who had died two years ago. This apparition had appeared several times and had bid Mrs. Barnard to tell her husband how Wilkes "had frequently lain with her, both before and since her marriage." Her father, said the ghost, deserved to know about these crimes "so that he might not leave his fortune to a man who had so cruelly injured him." If Mrs. Barnard failed to make a confession, the ghost would return to haunt her.[39] This was the first time Wilkes had heard about Barnard's leaving him anything. In the days that followed, said Barnard, his wife had told him many details about her affairs with Wilkes. She had told about that day at the prison when Wilkes had passed her the billet-doux. She had told about the role played by Parson Horne, whom she described as Wilkes's "pimp general." Barnard seemed to relish these stories, especially that of his wife's accidentally meeting Wilkes in the shop of a cabinetmaker. Wilkes had hailed a hackney coach, Barnard said, taken his wife home, behaved rudely to her, threw her on the sofa, "and enjoyed her on the spot where you are now sitting."[40] Wilkes protested that it was all imagination or fiction, except that he had indeed once met Mrs. Bar-nard in a cabinetmaker's shop and carried her home in a hackney coach. But that was all. He pooh-poohed the ghost, the product of "a distempered brain, and real, or feigned, sickness." All right, said Barnard, if you will give me permission, I will call her downstairs so she can tell you about the ghost herself. Wilkes declined, not being of a mind, he said, to deal with anyone so wild and mad.[41]

Wilkes went home and without much scrupulousness asked a friend to try to soften Barnard's demands. Samuel Petrie, who had known Mrs. Barnard at the time Wilkes was seeing her, was to write to Barnard expressing a hope that two people who were his friends should be reconciled. Wilkes suggested that Petrie write from Scarborough, speaking of his ill health and his desire to help his friends while he was still able. He might remind Barnard of incidents of Mrs. Barnard's behavior that suggested she was not always in her right mind.[42]

Then Wilkes wrote to Barnard, asking him to "weigh and examine" all the particulars of a woman's behavior that "savored of madness," as Barnard had said, or of deceit, as Wilkes thought.[43] Barnard would reconsider nothing, so angry was he over Wilkes's "wanton and deliberate cruelty."

Then Barnard began to add to his list of Wilkes's crimes items that did not seem criminal to Wilkes. Mrs. Barnard had told her husband how in 1762, when she was Wilkes's mistress, she had asked for a "settlement" (a permanent income). Wilkes's refusal Barnard considered a base act. Even more base was his refusal to pay the bill of the lawyer whom she had consulted to learn how to obtain such a settlement. Obviously Barnard had no understanding of the world of courtesans and protectors.

Nor had he any understanding of simple lust. How could Wilkes have wanted to sleep with his wife, he asked, "after your lust had been long sated, several years had elapsed, and there were neither the charms of novelty or youth to excite you?" He could think of only one explanation: Wilkes had acted out of cruelty; he had found "a new relish" for his "decayed appetite" in cuckolding a friend. It seems obvious that Mr. Barnard had never known strong sexual passion.[44]

Wilkes thought the man a fool, but it interested him that Barnard knew his wife had once been a courtesan. Something of an expert on courtesan behavior, Wilkes might be able to convince the husband of his wife's courtesan syndrome, so to speak. The motive for her confession, he told Barnard, was money. His wife, believing most of her husband's fortune had been willed to Wilkes, had risked her husband's anger in order to turn him against Wilkes. It was simple: she wanted him to change the will and to leave the money to her. Barnard rejected the analysis, maintaining that his wife had not known about the will until the ghost told her.[45]

Alas for Mrs. Barnard, no matter whether Wilkes's accusation of her was true or not, her husband was now planning to write a new will, leaving almost nothing of his affluent fortune to his wife. He would give her, he said, an annuity that would "keep her from want," but no more. We hear no more of this unfortunate lady who had once been for Wilkes so gay and affectionate a lover. When John Barnard died in 1785, he left his fortune to his nephew.[46]

Wilkes vacated the office of lord mayor on 17 November 1775, a month after his last correspondence with Barnard. The Common Council thanked him for "his diligent and unwearied attendance in the administration of justice," and the Court of Aldermen thanked him for "his unblemished conduct and exemplary behavior during the whole course of his mayoralty."[47]

13

Poverty, Paternity, and Parliamentary Reform

Wilkes was now broke and enormously in debt. The collapse of the Bill of Rights Society had left him with no income but the rents from his small estates and the modest income from fees and allotments due him as alderman of Farringdon Without. For sitting in the Old Bailey and in Parliament, he was paid nothing. His mayoral expenses, including those lavish entertainments, had come to £8,226, which was £3,337 above his allowance. He was not arrested because members of Parliament could not be seized for debt, yet creditors were knocking at his door. A certain Thomas Skinner, determined to collect what he was owed, sent his servant to Prince's Court to make an assessment of Wilkes's "effects." He was denied admittance. A group of creditors petitioned the Court of Common Council to make good on the debts Wilkes had run up as mayor, and a motion was made to grant Wilkes £500 out of the City cash. But many members were fearful of setting a precedent, and it was voted down.[1]

Did Wilkes feel guilty? No. His sense of entitlement was such that off he went to Bath for his annual Christmas holiday. To the numerous attacks of him in the newspapers, he was indifferent. When an alarmed friend pointed out an "infamous libel" against him in one paper, Wilkes replied, yes, he had seen it, and he was writing to some other papers to suggest they copy it. On another occasion, when one of his enemies accused him to his face of numerous failures to pay his debts, he listened and then bent forward and said quietly, "You have a wretched memory: you have forgotten all about the Foundling Hospital."[2]

Nevertheless, Wilkes was laying plans to get out from under this giant debt. The day after he quit the office of mayor, he wrote to the City chamberlain, Sir Stephen Rheodore Janssen, inquiring tactfully if it were true, as he had heard, that Janssen intended to resign his office? and if so, would he assist Mr. Wilkes to "the honor of succeeding a gentleman whom I highly venerate and wish to imitate"? Since Janssen himself had been in enormous debt when he was elected and had used the chamberlainship to extricate himself, Wilkes thought the man would understand his own embarrassment: "After being harassed for so many years, I cannot but earnestly desire to arrive in a safe port."[3]

The chamberlain of the City of London was the treasurer for the City, and the office was thought to be the most lucrative of all City offices. It was not a sinecure. A chamberlain had dealings with many people and supervised a staff of four. Legally, the office was for a year only; but the results of annual elections were usually foregone conclusions, for there was a strong tradition that the chamberlain could remain in office for life if he so desired.[4]

In February 1776, Sir Stephen did retire. Wilkes at once offered himself for election but found he was opposed by Benjamin Hopkins, also an alderman and a member of Parliament, but a director of the Bank of England and a member of the court party. Boswell was excited about the election and wrote a campaign song that Wilkes did not much like, though he allowed it to be printed as a broadside with a woodcut portrait of the cross-eyed candidate at the top: "The Patriotic Chamberlain, an excellent New Song for Midsummer's Day, 1776 in eight thumping stanzas." But Wilkes's hold over the livery had been broken, and Hopkins won the election, 2,868 votes over Wilkes's 1,673. Wilkes refused to honor the tradition that a chamberlain was elected for life, and the next year he challenged Hopkins, charging him with corruption. The livery, anxious about the wars with America and France, still preferred Hopkins, who seemed to promise safety, over Wilkes, the celebrated daredevil. Wilkes lost the election again, and yet again in 1778.[5]

Surprisingly, Dr. Samuel Johnson thought Wilkes would make a good chamberlain.[6] In the five years since Johnson's and Wilkes's pamphlet controversy over the Middlesex election, Boswell had often argued Wilkes's side to the Great Cham. Though he had not won Johnson over in the legal argument, Johnson's attitude toward Wilkes seemed to be softening. Perhaps it was the right time to find out how the doctor would react to his old enemy. Boswell had a mischievous streak, and not infrequently he manipulated Johnson into compromising situations to see how he would act. He asked Edward and

Hopkins triumphant, or Wilkes in the dumps.

19. Hopkins is chaired after defeating Wilkes in the election for chamberlain. Wilkes, comforted by Alderman Bull and Lady Liberty, holds a scroll, "Alas, how unstable the affections of a mob." Courtesy of Gerald M. Goldberg.

Charles Dilly, the convivial bookseller brothers, to invite the two to dinner at their house, which was located in the street called The Poultry. The day was set for 15 May 1776. Boswell decided to prepare Johnson in advance. He hinted that the doctor might not like the company. Johnson huffed a bit about not prescribing what company his host could invite. Suppose Dilly's radical friends were there? "Poh." "And if Jack Wilkes should be there? What is that to me, Sir?." On the appointed day, Boswell called for Dr. Johnson, took him in a hackney coach to The Poultry, and brought him into the house. Wilkes had not before seen the great lexicographer up close. There he stood, his frame huge, his jowls hanging, his skin scrofulous. Johnson, squinting with his weak eyes, became aware that strangers were in the room. To Boswell: " 'Who is that gentleman, Sir?' — 'Mr. Arthur Lee.' — . . . 'Too, too, too,' (under his breath)." Then Johnson caught a glimpse of a tall man dressed in the latest fashion, but with such a face! " 'And who is the gentleman in lace?' — 'Mr. Wilkes, Sir.' "

> This information confounded him still more; he had some difficulty to restrain himself, and taking up a book, sat down upon a window-seat and read. . . . The cheering sound of "Dinner is upon the table," dissolved his reverie, and we *all* sat down without any symptom of ill humour. . . . Mr. Wilkes placed himself next to Dr. Johnson, and behaved to him with so much attention and politeness, that he gained upon him sensibly. No man eat more heartily than Johnson, or loved better what was nice and delicate. Mr. Wilkes was very assiduous in helping him to some fine veal. "Pray give me leave, Sir: — It is better here — A little of the brown — Some fat, Sir — A little of the stuffing — Some gravy — Let me have the pleasure of giving you some butter — Allow me to recommend a squeeze of this orange; — or the lemon, perhaps, may have more zest." — "Sir, Sir, I am obliged to you, Sir," cried Johnson, bowing, and turning his head to him with a look for some time of "surly virtue," but in a short while, of complacency.

When the subject of Shakespeare's *Macbeth* came up, Wilkes remarked that the boldest stroke was "making Birnam-wood march to Dunsinane; creating a wood where there never was a shrub; a wood in Scotland, ha! ha! ha!" They talked about Horace and Homer and Restoration poets and returned always to joking about Scotland. "Upon this topic he and Mr. Wilkes could perfectly assimilate," wrote Boswell; "here was a bond of union between them." At one point, Johnson, speaking of Boswell, said, " 'I turned him loose at Lichfield, my native city, that he might see for once real civility: for you know he lives among savages in Scotland, and among rakes in London.' Wilkes: 'Except when he is with grave, sober, decent people like you and me.' Johnson: (smiling) 'And we ashamed of him.' "[7] The next day Johnson wrote to Mrs. Thrale, "I dined yesterday in the Poultry with Mr. Alderman Wilkes, and Mr. Alderman Lee, and counsellor Lee, his brother . . . breaking jokes with Jack Wilkes upon the Scots. Such, Madam, are the vicissitudes of things."

Not long after this, John Coakley Lettson sat at a dinner table with Johnson, Wilkes, Boswell, and William Lee. "What a group!" he wrote. They spent much of the afternoon teasing Boswell about the Scots, all in play, but Johnson's play "was as rough as that of a bear, and you felt fearful of coming within the embraces of so fierce an animal."[8]

Johnson was reluctant to admit that Wilkes had charmed him. On one occasion he reacted when someone spoke of Wilkes as a celebrated wit: "One may say of him as was said of a French wit, *Il n'a de l'esprit que contre Dieu* [He has no wit except against God]. I have been several times in company with him, but never perceived any strong power of wit. He produces a general effect by various means; he has a cheerful countenance and a gay voice. Besides his trade is wit. It would be as wild in him to come into company without merriment, as for a highwayman to take the road without his pistols." At another time he told Boswell, "Did we not hear so much said of Jack Wilkes, we should think more highly of his conversation. Jack has great variety of talk, Jack is a scholar, and Jack has the manners of a gentleman. But after hearing his name sounded from pole to pole, as the phoenix of convivial felicity, we are disappointed in his company. He has always been *at me*: but I would do Jack a kindness, rather than not. The contest is now over."[9]

Wilkes's poverty did not interrupt his annual visits to Brighthelmstone or the Isle of Wight in the summers when the Trinity term of the courts ended, or to Bath at Christmas. Wilkes had a sick spell in the late spring of 1776 but managed to get away to Brighthelmstone. He had hoped he might be joined by Polly and Mrs. Molineaux, the wife of Wilkes's supporter, the member for King's Lynn, and the Molineaux daughters, who were Polly's close friends. He was disappointed to learn that none of them could come. Polly wrote to apologize: "As to myself, it is a constant satisfaction to me to flatter my mind that you are well acquainted with all the feelings of my heart towards you. . . . My dear papa's kind offer is engraven on my mind, with all his other goodness, never to be obliterated." Feeling a little lonesome, Wilkes took "my old little cabin at Garringe's on the cliff," where he set about recuperating, bathing, riding, and taking the widely used nostrum James's powder.[10]

In 1776, Polly did not spend Christmas with her mother as usual but came to Bath with her father for the holiday. They set off on Saturday, 7 December, stopping for the night at Salt Hill. Wilkes, up early in the morning, bought a nosegay and presented it to his daughter at breakfast. They stopped at Marlborough the second night and arrived at Bath the next day. Polly took her things to rooms at No. 3, North Parade; Wilkes stayed at Henry Philpot's at the Bear, where very likely he had feminine companionship. They joined one another in the morning to take in the diversions of that holiday city and went together to dine with the Molineaux family.[11]

On Christmas day, Polly and her father had dinner at Alfred House, the large, handsome residence of Rev. Dr. Thomas Wilson, a founding member of the Bill of Rights Society and a major financial contributor. Wilkes wanted to make a personal friend of this rare bird, a prominent parson (once a chaplain to George II) who had turned radical. Dr. Wilson admired Wilkes and had told him so, yet he had not asked Wilkes to dine. So Wilkes and Polly were pleased to be invited for Christmas dinner, especially because the guests included his admired friend and neighbor, Mrs. Catharine Macaulay, the historian, and her daughter, Catharine Sophia. Dr. Wilson was pastor of this company, for he was rector of their church, St. Margaret's, which stands next to Westminster Abbey. He was also a prebendary (we would say a canon) of Westminster Abbey, rector of St. Stephens, Walbrook, in the City of London, and master of Wilkes's company, the Joiners and Ceilers, a position more of honor than of use.[12] But Dr. Wilson was old and in poor health, and in recent years had allowed his curates to run his churches while he lived at Bath. He had no family of his own, and he loved company, especially that of women. He delighted in Polly and Catharine Sophia, but he was in love with Mrs. Macaulay.

The following spring, Dr. Wilson invited Mrs. Macaulay and her daughter to live with him in Alfred House.[13] She, being in some financial difficulties, accepted. Some eyebrows went up, but the arrangement gave rise to no vicious scandal. Both were widowed, and Dr. Wilson, who was seventy-three years old, a very great age in the eighteenth century, was hardly a threat to Mrs. Macaulay's virtue. She, on the other hand, was forty-five and still interested.

Mrs. Macaulay was an exceptionally tall and stately woman, but she had been in poor health and had come to Bath to take the waters. Scrupulous about her diet, she believed implicitly that ice cream "strengthens and braces the stomach."[14] Dr. Johnson disapproved of Mrs. Macaulay's republicanism. "One day when I was at her house," he told Boswell, "I put on a very grave countenance and said to her, 'Madam, I am now become a convert to your way of thinking. I am convinced that all mankind are upon an equal footing; and to give you an unquestionable proof, Madam, that I am in earnest, here is a very sensible, civil, well-behaved fellow-citizen, your footman; I desire that he may be allowed to sit down and dine with us.' I thus, Sir, showed her the absurdity of the levelling doctrine. She has never liked me since."[15]

Mrs. Macaulay's presence transformed Alfred House into the Bath center for radicalism, where, said Wilkes, "nothing is talked of but America."[16] At the moment Mrs. Macaulay was the toast of radicals everywhere, for she had completed the fifth volume of her polemical history of seventeenth-century England, and the left-leaning political world found her interpretations of history compatible and her prose inspiring. Her book was often contrasted with David Hume's history of the same period, to which the king and ministry turned for justification of their projects.

Though Dr. Wilson was in love with Mrs. Macaulay, "the world" still believed theirs was a Platonic relationship. He gave a spectacular party for her birthday in which she was celebrated as the high priestess of liberty — a title she certainly deserved, for her ideas were inspiring republicans in England and America. Next, Dr. Wilson employed a well-known sculptor, J. F. Moore, to make a statue of her as the Muse of History, standing attentively but with a pencil in her hand. He mounted this handsome, but by no means small, work of art in the chancery of St. Stephen's Walbroke. The congregation were not so enchanted with Mrs. Macaulay as Dr. Wilson, and the vestry asked him to remove it. He declined to do so, and they charged him in the spiritual courts with desecrating St. Stephen's. The spiritual courts had never met such a problem, and they were confused. No one had the heart to take it down, for the rector was growing older and weaker. Wilkes wrote to Polly, "Dr. Wilson is half gone, and it would scarcely be a sin to bury him as he is."[17]

The next year, during the time France was giving covert military support to America but had not declared war on Britain, Mrs. Macaulay made another visit to Paris, in part to listen to the rumblings of republicanism. Indeed, she did hear rumblings and eventually would write about France. More immediately, she had learned a new skill in Paris. She had learned how to "paint." The ladies of Paris were adept at facial makeup. She was feeling her age, and her stately beauty was suffering from her illnesses. After he had dined with her and Dr. Wilson on 3 January 1778, Wilkes wrote to Polly telling how Mrs. Macaulay punctuated almost every sentence with, "Lord Jesus Christ," and "was painted up to the eyes, and looks quite ghastly and ghostly." A few days later, Wilkes and Lord Irnham called on Kitty, as Wilkes liked to call her, and found her looking "as rotten as an old catharine-pear." Lord Irnham, he added, was "disgusted with her manner."[18] Lord Irnham was hardly one to find fault with so accomplished a woman as Mrs. Macaulay, being himself a worthless old libertine. Besides, he did not know this lady.

In December of 1778, Mrs. Macaulay, now forty-seven years old, astonished the polite world of Bath and London by eloping with William Graham, a twenty-one-year-old surgeon's mate, a Scotsman without family or fortune. Dr. Wilson learned of her desertion when he received a letter from her written hours before the ceremony. He was furious! He tore down the statue, rewrote his will, and fired all of Mrs. Macaulay's servants that were still at Alfred

House. Wilkes hurried over and found the doctor "outrageous . . . he thinks her a monster." "His love seems turned to rage and hatred." Dr. Wilson showed Wilkes her letter. Wilkes was appalled by what he read, for it contained, as he told Polly, "every variety of style: it is indecent, incoherent, mean, fawning, threatening, coaxing, menacing, and declamatory. Such words I believe never escaped a female pen." He also was shown the doctor's "short and pithy" answer, declaring "that her character is gone, and that she shall never again come to Alfred House." Mrs. Macaulay's letter, or possibly a later letter from her, appeared in the papers a few days later, and the doctor was thinking about answering it. Wilkes advised him not to do so and suggested, "as she complains loudly of the Doctor as having treated her unkindly, he might let her tell her own story to the world, which would be his full justification."[19]

The newspapers in Bath and London were delighted to hear such a story about two celebrities, and every day there appeared squibs or satirical letters or comic ballads about the quarrel. Nine months later, Dr. Wilson, still raging, was preparing to publish a collection of her letters, not only those addressed to him but others sent to the man with whom she was thought to have had an affair.[20] But Wilkes advised against publishing them. The old man had already had his vindication, and some of these letters were "too grose for the public eye." Dr. Wilson threw them into the fire, but Betty, the serving maid, snatched them from the flames, and they ended up in Wilkes's hands. Mrs. Macaulay's own words in these letters, he told Polly, showed her to be "a most abandoned prostitute and a swindler." It seems they confirmed the rumors that she had had an affair while living with Dr. Wilson and had drawn considerable sums of money from his bank accounts. Wilson's anger did not abate, and a year later he wrote another accusing letter, which Polly hoped he would withhold from the press. Wilkes tried, without success: "I have endeavored to get the letter about Mrs. M. suppressed, but the Doctor is violent . . . and I have no chance of succeeding. I read him on Sunday night chosen parts of the Memoirs of my Life, with which he appeared to be much charmed." One can imagine which parts he skipped.[21]

Wilkes now found himself treated at Alfred House as "the declared favorite." On 27 December 1778, he wrote to Polly from Bath telling how he and several gentlemen dined at Alfred House: "The doctor insisted on my being at his right hand, and told the company, *that* should always be my place, that I should be his right hand, as I was in his heart. He treated me with a kind distinction the whole day." Wilkes began to hope that he might leave his fortune to Polly. On 7 January 1779, he wrote, "I am still the favorite. If it holds, *tant mieux pour une certaine demoiselle.*"[22] The doctor confounded all expectation and lived on another three years.

During those three years, when Wilkes came to Bath for his semiannual holiday, he called on Dr. Wilson every day. If the old man had had his way, Wilkes would have taken every dinner with him, but Wilkes managed to get out of some of them. As he told Polly, "His appetite seems to fail him, and the *frequent and powerful* eructations from his holy entrails render assisting at his dinner rather disagreeable."²³

One might think that Wilkes's alliance with Dr. Wilson might have alienated Wilkes's political ally, Mrs. Macaulay's brother, John Sawbridge, but Sawbridge was almost as furious with his sister as was Dr. Wilson and considered her, as he himself told the doctor, "in the last degree infamous."²⁴

Wilkes did not really break from Mrs. Macaulay, though he saw little or nothing of her for the next three years while she and her husband were living in Leicestershire. They finally moved to Chelsea, and Wilkes met her from time to time. In March of 1783 at Bath she dined with Wilkes, and he found her "tolerably cheerful" and in good health. She had reason to be cheerful. Her marriage had turned out a happy one and would remain so. Though she lost most of her following in England, in 1784 she sailed to America, where she was greeted with great enthusiasm by the American founding fathers. She was the guest of the Washingtons at Mount Vernon and became the correspondent and advisor to that great man. She would exercise a strong influence on Mercy Warren, encouraging her to write her history of the Revolution. On her return to England, Catharine Macaulay Graham and her husband took up residence at Binfield near Reading, and here she drops out of Wilkes's story. When she died at Binfield in 1791, she had completed eight volumes of her history and numerous pamphlets, including one of the major answers to Edmund Burke's well-known *Observations on the Reflections on the Revolution in France*.²⁵

Wilkes liked to keep up his reputation as a libertine, and the attention of one of the most notorious of rakehells was welcome even if a little embarrassing to Polly. "Lord Irnham tells everybody," he wrote to her, "that he comes to Bath to see Wilkes, and so I engross him." He enjoyed organizing rakish parties for middle-aged gentlemen. In October 1777 at Brighthelmstone, Arthur Murphy introduced Hester Lynch Thrale to Wilkes. Mrs. Thrale, with whom Johnson was in love, was married to Johnson's friend Henry Thrale, member for Southwark. Mrs. Thrale did not like Wilkes when she met him, and even less the next day when he invited Thrale to a dinner of rakes—Beauclerk, Lord Kelly, other "men of worth and honor," as she ironically put it. She was present when Wilkes extended the invitation to her husband, and, as she told Dr. Johnson, she put on a scowl. "Says Murphy looking at me, 'He dares not go.' 'I would not have him go,' said I gravely. I am not fond of trying my power over my husband . . . but if I keep him out of such company, I should think I did him an act of real friendship. . . . I got severely rallied for my prudery, and at last lost my labor, for he does go, but I know I did right."[26]

Wilkes did not have to dig very deeply into his pocket to throw a bachelor party at Brighthelmstone, but keeping a mistress and her entire family in their own house was another matter. He was strapped for money, and probably it was for that reason, and not their quarrel, that he broke up with Marianne de Charpillon. In any event, he gave up the house in which he had installed her, at No. 30, Great Titchfield Street.

Wilkes's condition of genteel poverty lasted for four years. Well into 1778, he wrote to Samuel Petrie, "I am well; no fever, no stranguary; but 'steeped in poverty to the very lips'; yet far from poor in spirit; on the contrary, as determined and inflexible, and more high-spirited than when you saw me." His brothers could not help. The distillery, so profitable to their father, failed under the management of Heaton, though perhaps not for any fault of his. In 1760, a new and heavy duty was imposed on mineral spirits. Heaton then bought into a coal-transporting business, but that too failed. Israel's father-in-law had gone bankrupt, and Israel's money seems to have been tied up in various schemes in Martinique, the seat of the eccentric family of Ponthieu, into which he had married. It was another story with Wilkes's brother-in-law, George Hayley, whose business flourished, who was grateful to Wilkes for his seat in the House, and who provided a good deal of his income in these lean years.[27]

There were a few other windfalls: Wilkes was left a legacy of five hundred pounds by William Temple, a radical lawyer who had written one *North Briton*, No. 19, but the money did not go very far. Some of the members of the defunct Bill of Rights Society sent around letters explaining they could no longer take subscriptions, but those who wished to support Mr. Wilkes could send their contributions directly to Prince's Court. Rockingham and the Dukes of Devonshire and Portland paid regular gratuities to Wilkes through their mutual friend and colleague in the House, Chase Price. Samuel Cutler, an eccentric gentleman who corresponded under the name of Philo-Wilkes, gave his hero much and lent him more. For Philo-Wilkes's support Wilkes paid interest, not in money, but in time and attention to Philo-Wilkes's inane talk and gratuitous advice.[28]

In a parliamentary debate over government spending, someone threw a question at Wilkes: "What did the representative for Middlesex think of using public money to pay the king's debts?" Wilkes jumped to his feet: "I shall never be against helping anyone to pay his debts." The timing was skillful and a good laugh followed. In the spring of 1778, Lord Granby, the old soldier who had resigned from the ministry to support Wilkes, sent him £300. A surprising contribution came from Sir James Lowther, the richest commoner of England, who controlled eight seats in the House of Commons and is known to have spent £25,000 for votes in a single election. Lowther was a son-in-law of Lord Bute and had never supported Wilkes, but he sent him banknotes "and other notes," amounting to £202.10.0. The contribution raises the question of possible bribery. In his letter thanking him, Wilkes says he and Mr. Adair, the city recorder, had joined forces in the House of Commons. Probably Wilkes was referring to a bill that City members had brought in to permit the City to underwrite a loan to two contractors who would build "a commodious street for carriages" through part of the City. It is not unlikely Lowther wanted the street widened so as to have easier access to his Westminster residence and sent the money as a gentle nudge in that direction. But Wilkes surely did not see Lowther's gift as a bribe since Lowther would have known that, with or without his support, Wilkes would favor the improvement.[29]

Usually Wilkes avoided the subject of his debts, but when it came up anyway, he tended to break into hyperbolic expressions of courage in the face of threatened indigence. When friends asked what he was going to do without an income, "Nothing," he replied; he "had his own good spirits to feed and clothe him." In writing to Adair, he allowed himself a metaphor as lengthy as any one in a Shakespearean sonnet: "You find me at my lowest water mark. The rivers that ran in and raised my fortunes are all dried up or take another course. What I have left is from my native spring. I have still a heart that swells in scorn of fate, and lifts me to my banks." And he never hesitated to mix his metaphors: "I must still hang upon the chapter of accidents and wait to drive the first nail that offers."[30] His witticisms were better. When pressed by one creditor, he wrote in reply, "I take the liberty to inform you that at present it is not my interest to pay the principal, neither is it my principle to pay the interest."[31]

Wilkes wrote to his solicitor, Peter Fountain, "Mr. Wilkes . . . will not involve his daughter in any personal and pecuniary transactions of his." He had to keep Polly clear of his financial affairs so as not to violate the terms of her grandmother Mead's will. But Polly, whether legally or not, found her own way to help. In 1776, Wilkes could not even afford his heretofore annual Christmas holiday at Bath. In 1777, he had scraped enough money together to go, but on a tight budget. When he was seated in the carriage, Polly handed him a package. As the carriage rattled out of town, he opened it to find a purse filled with money. At Speen Hill, where he stopped for the night, he wrote to her, "I have a daughter, the sweetest-tempered girl in the world, generous and noble minded. She gives me both a purse and money, and writes me at the same time the prettiest, most elegant compliments possible, of more value than all the purses and money in the world. . . . The purse I shall keep as long as I live; the money I shall lay out at Bath as a souvenir for her of one of the politest and most obliging actions I ever knew. I must always add, happy, happy father in such a daughter." Polly replied from her mother's house on Christmas Day: "Christmas and New Year's Day are dear when they allow the expression of wishes such as a parent like you inspires. None can be more tender and fervent, dear Papa, for your long enjoyment of every happiness. You inspire in me all the best possible friend, and most agreeable companion, combine to claim from me the tenderest solicitude."[32]

Polly's letters had the formality that went with the careful training of a lady. Wilkes's were more candid and spirited. "Adieu, my dearest girl, I am just going to dine in Garrard Street; but before that, a thing worth all the dinners in the world, to kiss the honeydew off the lips of sweet Judy Brereton." Judy Brereton was a young lady of good family, well known to Polly. Because nothing could come of his infatuation, Wilkes did not hide it from his daughter: "The sweet Judy Brereton I saw and saluted yesterday. I hope so beauteous a flower will not wither on the stalk from whence it grew, and die uncropped." And about a certain Miss Linley, he waxed poetic:

ON MISS LINLEY'S RETIRING TO RICHMOND
Ah! fatal groves, sad Echo cries,
You're fair Eliza's choice:
The dying swains accuse her eyes,
The nightengales her voice.

Polly was tolerant. One Saturday evening she wrote about her plan to go to church: "I shall attend tomorrow the summons of the neighboring bell. If I was Mr. Churchill, I would say it was the only *belle* to which you could be indifferent." But Wilkes's sexual interests never stood in the way of their devotion to each other. Not many daughters have received from their fathers verses such as Wilkes sent her on her birthday:

TO MISS WILKES ON HER BIRTHDAY, AUGUST 16, 1777
The noblest gift you could receive,
The noblest gift *today* I'd give.
A father's heart I would bestow,
But that you stole it long ago.

Sometimes a note of sadness creeps into Wilkes's letters to his daughter. He wrote to her from Bath on New Year's Day 1778: his first wish was for her happiness in the new year; "My second wish only is for myself to see you happy, which will be the truest felicity to me." Polly had reached the age of twenty-seven still unmarried. The following spring, Wilkes wrote, "The greatest blessing which Heaven can bestow on any man is a daughter like you — unless, indeed, it be the favored mortal who can call you his by a still closer connection, and be perpetuated by another resemblance of yourself and him, which could complete my happiness as a father."[33] Polly would never find a husband.

In 1779, John Zoffany, a portrait painter much in demand, did a painting of Wilkes and Polly, not on commission but at the request of the painter. Before photography entered the Western world, people were anxious to be painted, even if they could not afford to buy the work themselves. Zoffany kept the painting and exhibited it at the Royal Academy exhibition in 1782. It is now at the National Portrait Gallery. Like most portraits, the painting is flattering, but Zoffany so posed his subjects as to make believable its untruth. Wilkes is seated, looking upward and to the side at his standing daughter, a situation that brings his two eyes into the same focus and disguises the cast of one. The artist must have retracted their chins as far as he thought he could get away with, but he could not completely obscure the jut without losing the likeness. Their closed lips hide the lost teeth. Still, Walpole commented when he saw it, "Horridly like." One thing that does not lie is the love in Wilkes's face as he looks at his daughter, or as Walpole saw it, "squints tenderly at his daughter" (illustration 20). Wilkes is dressed in his militia uniform, and Polly, according to a curator at the National Portrait Gallery, is overdressed by the standards of the day.[34]

In 1775, Wilkes had sent Jack Smith to a tutor in Germany to add the mastery of German to his accomplishments. Though he was not the best behaved of the students, he did well enough. Arthur Lee, who was abroad in 1777, saw him in Berlin. "He is well educated," he wrote to Wilkes.[35] Polly suggested he might get a commission in the cavalry, for "it would be a great pity for Mr. Smith to lose the advantage of the proficiency he made in riding under so good a master." She meant Dominico Angelo. Wilkes enquired about buying a commission in the Prussian cavalry,[36] but it was such a distinguished service that the price of a commission was beyond his reach. He brought the young man back to London and entered him once more into Angelo's *école d'escrime* in Soho Square.[37]

On a Saturday morning — it was 21 March 1778 — Boswell, who had recently returned from Scotland, called at Prince's Court. He found Wilkes "the same cheerful, gay, polite, classical man as when he and I were happy together at Naples in 1765. I really felt some kindness for him, and he seemed to feel some for me." They drank chocolade, and Wilkes showed him the newly published volume of his speeches in Parliament. He would not give him a copy but told him he might steal one. Would Wilkes inscribe them? No, because that would indicate he had been the editor, which of course he was.

20. Wilkes and Polly, by Johan Zoffany. National Portrait Gallery, London. The dog belonged to Zoffany.

Wilkes then read Boswell a poem he had written to a lady with whom he said he was in love. It was called "Four in the Morning: Maria Hath Murdered Sleep." He called them "gentlemen's verses," which Boswell thought a good name for a certain type of love poetry. The poem was about "his waking pain" and "the pleasing delusions" he might have if he could fall asleep. A copy of these gentlemen's verses addressed to the god of sleep is among Wilkes's letters to Mrs. Maria Stafford.

> . . . When no foul crimes disturb my peace within,
> No quiet, no sin, unless to love's a sin,
> Then, sleep, oh gentle sleep, grant me repose,
> Vouchsafe a wretch's weary eyes to close,
> Thy balmy rest this languid frame o'erspread.
> Come peaceful power, to calm my troubled breast,
> Oh! come and give me something more than rest.
> In all her charms Maria make appear,
> And let her seem as kind as she is fair.
> Thus let me dream, and may the vision prove
> An happy omen of my future love . . .[38]

Wilkes had gone to Bath for the Christmas holidays in 1777, staying in rooms he had engaged for the season from a Mrs. Temple, who was very fat. When she greeted him, he wrote, she "dropped me such a broadwheel curtsey that I trembled for the floor, and floor trembled likewise."[39]

Wilkes met Maria Alethea Ellis Stafford on 10 January 1778 at a dinner party at Bath when the two of them spent the afternoon in conversation. She was the estranged wife of William Stafford of Holt, near the town of Workingham. Wilkes was smitten, and when a day or two later he was setting off for London, he stopped by her rooms in Russell Street and left his card. A few minutes before he rapped at Maria Stafford's door, he had taken leave of the youthful mistress he kept at Bath, Amelia Arnold. This simple county girl was destined to play a more important role in the drama of Wilkes's life than the fine lady, Mrs. Stafford. Milly, as she was familiarly called, was known to John Almon, who described her as "a woman of some education, and not of very humble origin, being the daughter of George and Christian Arnold, of Sutton Veny, in Wiltshire." Her father was a yeoman farmer, that is, he owned the land, or some of it, that he farmed. Milly was a pretty woman of twenty-five when Wilkes met her, three years younger than Polly. But she was not much in his heart that morning when he said good-bye to her, for he was thinking of Maria Stafford, with whom he felt himself falling in love. Cupid does have his tricks. Wilkes and perhaps even Milly did not know it, but Milly was a few weeks pregnant.[40]

A day or two after his return to London, Wilkes was delighted to receive a note from Maria in response to the card he had left. When he returned to Bath, she wrote, she would be "truly glad to see him." Wilkes responded at once, sending her a print of a Cipriani painting that they had talked about the night they met. "You are formed to taste and admire all the fine arts, as well as to give the artists the most perfect model of whatever excels in more ways than I will enumerate." Could he present his daughter to her?[41] When she did not reply, he wrote again, asking to be forgiven for his forwardness: "If you will only say that I may come to Bath in April and ask forgiveness at your feet, you will restore the tranquility of a man who finds his boasted liberty exchanged for your soft bondage." At last she replied, rather stiffly, thanking him for the print and saying, yes, she would be glad to meet Miss Wilkes when she comes to Bath. She went on to talk about discretion and asked him to write no more letters.[42]

Wilkes wrote anyway: "I approve of discretion, but would not let it run away with my happiness. . . . After all human evils had issued from Pandora's box, Hope was seen at the bottom to cheer wretched mortals on their way. Could I see that one word written by you, it would pour balm into a wounded heart."[43] She replied that she would welcome a friendship, but they must not exchange letters. "Death has deprived me of my natural protectors and advisors, infidelity of my legal one; therefore, the smallest deviation from prudence must inevitably ruin me, unsupported, unprotected, as my wayward fate has left me." She could not write "hope" until they had determined its limits. What she hoped for was his good opinion.[44] Wilkes, now knowing that her separation from her husband was caused by his infidelity, wrote again, on 7 February: "Mention not limits when you are the subject." He was displeased with her for holding up Jonathan Swift and his Stella as examples of friendship between people of the opposite sex. Reiterating a popular myth about the marriage of Swift and Esther Johnson, his Stella, Wilkes wrote, "He never was one moment alone with her. Is this an object to be held up for imitation?" Wilkes was right that Swift never slept with Stella, but scholars today say that Swift was never married to her.[45]

Maria Stafford was not a very original person, and despite Wilkes's admiration, he was sometimes annoyed. "I cannot bear your expressions of 'good wishes,' " he wrote, "and 'returning them' and 'acquaintance.' I soar infinitely beyond those limits. I beg to be called even now friend, and I will fully merit the title, protector, guardian, on any occasion in which you will distinguish me."[46]

Wilkes, who was a friend of Laurence Sterne and had read *A Sentimental Journey*, knew that "l'amour n'est rien san sentiment, et le sentiment est encore moins sans amour." In his feelings for Maria, sexual desire and sentimental affections enhanced one another: "A beautiful Ionic column is in no small danger single and unconnected, but forms the best part of an elegant building. I am sure that I mean your lasting happiness. A deserted state is unnatural to a woman formed by all the virtues and graces to enjoy life, and inspire the most exquisite happiness." It lacked the Sternean touch, but it was sweeter and more gentle than anything Stafford had ever heard. She replied with musings upon what their relationship might hold for the future. Matrimony was out of the question, and a Platonic relationship ridiculous: "The metamorphosis of Mr. Wilkes into a Platonist would perhaps undo any of Ovid's in strangeness." What then was possible? Oh, "the bare idea of any connection less durable and innocent" would be "too horrible even to be hinted at." The only thing to do was to cease corresponding. "Your little note, which I received this afternoon," he replied, "has the beauty of a very fine pearl, and in my eye is more precious for it comes from you." He drew a far-fetched analogy between her husband's desertion of her and James II's desertion of the throne; William came to fill the empty throne, and Wilkes would play a similar role. He told her about the North Carolina Assembly's voting to name a county after him, but he would exchange the whole county and all of America for "a small, but paradisiacal spot" that her husband had abandoned. She reminded him that she was a Tory, and he reminded her that "the first article of the Tory creed is passive obedience and non-resistance." She asked him, "Are we not both the property of others?" Wilkes was not so sure of that and went on to tell her what his marriage had meant to him:

> In my non-age, to please an indulgent father, I married a woman half as old again as myself, of a very large fortune, my own that of a gentleman. It was a sacrifice to Plutus, not to Venus. I never lived with her in the strict sense of the word, nor have I seen her near 20 years. I stumbled at the very threshold of the temple of Hymen.
>   The God of love was not a bidden guest,
>   Nor present at his own mysterious feast.
> Are such ties at such a time of life binding , and are school boys to be dragged to the altar? I have since often sacrificed to beauty, but I never gave my heart, except to you.

What Wilkes wanted was not an affair, but a permanent relationship, perhaps, if he could bring it about, a marriage. When Maria accidentally forgot to sign a card she had sent, he wrote, "The blank, a happy future day may fill with a more fortunate name than the present." And shortly thereafter, "At your shrine I would make the dearest offering, and wear your chains, for they would be light, and the flowers twined round them would make them easy and gay . . . you mention a 'sentimental unimpassioned friendship.' A 'sentimental friendship' undoubtedly it will be, but never 'unimpassioned.' It is impossible to esteem, or to love you by halves. . . . You are the only person of your sex, either at home or abroad, who has inspired me with the wish even of an honorable and indissoluble union for life."[47]

Wilkes announced he was coming to Bath to see her in the Easter holidays. She protested, but he came anyway. After holding him off for a day or two, she finally told her servant to open her door. He waited in a small anteroom. He would treasure the memory of "that moment when . . . you entered the room with 'grace in all your steps, heaven in your eye.' " He bowed and presented a bouquet of roses. Servants were bustling about, and their tête-à-tête was well within the bounds of the etiquette of the time. He hoped they would meet at the concert, but as for the music, "hearing you is the most pleasing melody to me." She had forbade him to send a corsage of lillies of the valley, but he begged her to wear at the concert one of the roses he had brought, "Sweet, envy'd rose, beyond all roses blest / To live and die on dear Maria's breast."[48]

There was a drama out of a Sheridan play when an older woman friend of Maria spotted on the hall table the roses and ticket to the concert and scolded the younger woman into a confession and then a promise to break off the engagement.[49] Maria did not go to the concert, but she continued the correspondence.

There was a dark side to the relationship, and that was Maria Stafford's health. Wilkes made repeated inquiries, but she was reluctant to tell all, though she confessed she had been unhealthy for many years. "Heaven save the amiable Maria from all pain, all uneasiness of body or mind!" She was prevented from coming to Bath for Easter holiday, 1778, "by a cough attended with spitting of blood to which I am subject." Wilkes replied, that he feared for her health and even her life but despite that longed for "an honorable and indissoluble union for life." Neither of them said the words "tisick" or "consumption," but clearly she suffered from the disease we call pulmonary tuberculosis.[50] It was a fashionable disease of the day, in part because Sterne had made it central to his novels. It was a requirement of Sternean sentimental lovemaking to show a tender concern for the health of the beloved, but the concern for the beloved expressed by Sterne and Wilkes was no less real for that, and the disease no less deadly than romantic. Sterne himself died of it, as did his beloved Eliza Draper. Maria Stafford's illness lingered throughout the Easter season, and he had to leave Bath without seeing her. He heard nothing for the rest of the year.

When Wilkes arrived at Bath for the Christmas holiday in 1778, Maria was not there. She had returned to her husband. He at once sat down and wrote her at Holt. She replied with a brief note, followed by other brief communications in which she asked him to return her letters. Wilkes proved himself something less than a faithful lover, for he did not return all of her letters, and those he did send back he copied first. They were for him tokens of immense value and he would set them apart in the letters he would gather when he was an old man.

Seeing in the Bath newspaper that her furniture was for sale, Wilkes went to look at it. "I sat half an hour in your chair. I had a group of ideas I dare not express. I was even in your bed-chamber, but hurried away from a scene too luxurious for a warm imagination." He especially liked the two chairs in the little parlor: "It was in that room I had the bewitching conversation with you, every word of which I could whisper in your private ear." He bought the chairs. "Adieu, belle Marie, la plus amiable et la plus aimée des femmes."[51]

For Wilkes, Maria was a treasure just out of reach, a woman of class who was not revolted by his face. She was indiscreet, poor woman, in encouraging the courtship, but because of her separation she felt rejected from polite society and unloved in her family. In a manner not at all uncommon, she compensated by allowing herself the fantasy of love. Wilkes too was playing a fantasy role, in part, giving himself permission to be the lover he had always wanted to be even though little encouraged.

When Maria returned to her husband, Wilkes's heart might have been broken. But perhaps not. When he arrived at Bath he found pretty Milly Arnold with the prettiest two-month-old baby he had ever seen. Born on 20 October 1778, eight days before her father's fifty-second birthday, she was enjoying the privilege of infants born into the lower social orders: she was being nursed by her own mother. They named her Harriet.[52] So far as the record shows, Wilkes never told anyone that he loved Amelia Arnold. But as they say in the Caribbean, a man has three tongues, one in his head and two in his feet. Milly was to become his common-law wife. He could not legally marry her, for his wife was still alive, and to our knowledge he did not go through a marriage ceremony with her after his wife died. But he would soon establish a home for Milly, and for the rest of his life he would treat her with affection and respect. The child would eventually make her debut with the name of Harriet Wilkes.

Since Maria would not leave her husband for Wilkes, he decided to keep her as a friend. On his next trip to Bath, he turned aside from his usual route to call at Holt. That evening he wrote to Polly, unable to refrain from speaking of William Stafford as "her puppy of a husband." Nevertheless, Wilkes persisted, sending to William Stafford, in December 1779, some "witty" (read "bawdy") verses "just arrived from France," that, he forewarned the husband, were "too gay" for his wife's eyes. In the end, Wilkes made a friend of the man. For the next four years he continued to see the couple, calling at Holt when traveling to and from Bath, inviting them to dine at Prince's Court. Once they wrote to

21. Mildred Arnold, around 1790, artist unknown. In a private collection.

Wilkes as a couple, asking to be excused for their tardiness in thanking him for a gift of "french paper" and speaking of Maria's "very indifferent state of health and long and dangerous illness." Unable to resist showing his admiration, Wilkes bombarded Maria with presents — books, china, an "elegant almanack," other "costly presents," and once a pie. The gifts embarrassed her, for she thought her servants would read in them a mistaken meaning, but her protests seemed never to stop him. She knitted him a purse.[53]

Wilkes could see the irony in the contrast between Jack Wilkes, the Bath lover, and Alderman John Wilkes, the member for Middlesex. In a letter to Maria of March 1778, he included some verses:

> Oh, that I had been born some happy swain
> In humble life, far from ambition's train . . .

> Are not these pretty ideas to occupy a man who is going to a Committee of the House of Commons where a dozen peers of the realm are to solicit our votes for a damned Basingstoke navigation bill of which I am as ignorant as my Lord Mayor — for an example of all ignorance?"

The mayor so roughly treated was Sir James Esdaile.[54]

The record does not show why the friendship between Wilkes and Mrs. Stafford ended, but there can be little doubt that consumption finally took the life of Wilkes's beloved Maria.

Wilkes would have won a place in history had he done no more than to stand up in the House of Commons and propose a reform bill that would give the vote to all adult males. He was the first to do so. The word *reform,* when used in conjunction with representative government in Great Britain, means any attempt to make representation of the people more equitable. The program of Pitt and Beckford to shorten parliaments and reorder constituencies so that members were elected by roughly equal numbers of voters was a reform. The Bill of Rights Society had moved reform further along by demanding that political aspirants put their signatures to the manifesto of the Society, thereby giving their promise to work for "full and equal representation of the people." Yet Wilkes's proposal startled the House, for no one before him, at least in the eighteenth century, had proposed universal suffrage. He would give the vote to every farmer and laborer, even to the poor! Of course *universal* was a misleading adjective, for Wilkes intended only men to vote. As an idea, universal male suffrage was not new. It had been advocated by the Levelers of the seventeenth century and talked about by Locke and Rousseau and Mrs. Macaulay among others. Irving Brant has pointed out that the fundamental principle can be traced as far back as Nicholas of Cusa in the fifteenth century, who had said, "Since all men are by nature free, government rests on the consent of the governed." But until Wilkes's motion, no parliamentary action had been made toward effecting this ideal.[55]

It was on 21 March 1776 that Wilkes rose in the House of Commons to propose bringing this momentous idea into law. He asked permission of the House to introduce a bill for "a just and equal representation of the people" as part of a detailed plan of reform, the first ever offered in Parliament. It included the old radical plan to abolish "rotten boroughs," where a member was elected by a handful of voters, and he got a laugh from the House when he admitted that the rotten borough of Banbury had the "merit" of sending Lord North to the House.[56] He deplored the situation in the northern counties of England, where one member represented many thousands of voters. The Scots were poorly represented, he said, and the Americans have harsh laws passed against them without any representation at all. "In my opinion, Sir, the American war is in this truly critical era one of the strongest arguments for the regulation of our representation, which I now submit to the House. During the rest of our lives, likewise, I may venture to prophesy, America will be the leading feature of this age."

The shock came when Wilkes decried the English system of basing the franchise on private property, a "monstrous absurdity in a free state as well as an insult on common sense":

> I wish, Sir, an English Parliament to speak the free, unbiased sense of the body of the English people and of every man among us, of each individual, who may justly be supposed to be comprehended in a fair majority. The meanest mechanic, the poorest peasant and day laborer has important rights respecting his personal liberty, that of his wife and children, his property, however inconsiderable, his wages, his earnings, the very price and value of each day's hard labor, which are in many trades and manufactures regulated by the power of Parliament. . . . We ought always to remember this important truth, acknowledged by every free state, that all government is instituted for the good of the mass of people to be governed; that they are the original fountain of power.[57]

Frederick Bull seconded the motion, but no one spoke in support of it. Seeing that his proposal had no support, Wilkes did not ask for a division, and the motion was negated by voice vote.

Wilkes had given, however, a new impetus to reform. In 1780, the Duke of Richmond would move in the House of Lords for universal suffrage. Neither was his motion carried, but it was noted by the public. In 1783, William Pitt the younger offered a plan even more detailed than that of Wilkes. This too failed, but the proportion of votes supporting reform increased with every effort. At long last, in 1832 a major reform bill was passed, abolishing the rotten boroughs and equalizing representation. But Great Britain would have to wait until 1884 for a bill that established the universal male suffrage that Wilkes had moved in Parliament in 1776. British women would not attain the vote until 1928.[58]

Today in London, if one walks up Fetter Lane from Fleet Street, one finds in the fork where New Fetter Lane branches off, a bronze statue of John Wilkes. His vigorous figure and handsome clothing are wonderfully rendered, but his face is too young and strong to represent well the damaged countenance of

Wilkes at the age of forty-nine. The statue, unveiled in 1988, is by the well-known sculptor James Butler, and the funds to make and place it were raised by the London physician and Wilkite, Dr. James Cope. Dr. Cope's activities in the government of the City had opened up to him Wilkes's history, and, conceiving a great admiration for Wilkes, he determinedly set out to establish a memorial that would honor his hero. Following Dr. Cope's instructions, Mr. Butler designed a statue of Wilkes addressing Parliament on 21 March 1776. The figure makes a sweeping gesture with his arm, and in his hand is a paper bearing the words, "A bill for a just and equal representation of the people of England in Parliament."

I4

Chamberlain

Benjamin Hopkins, the city chamberlain who had thrice defeated Wilkes in elections, died in November 1779, and Wilkes at once announced his candidacy for the office. There was a nomination meeting, and on the hustings Wilkes promised to devote half the profits of the office to paying off the debts he had run up as lord mayor. Yes, his intention was to hold the office, if he could, for the rest of his life. Two other candidates withdrew, but William James, a court candidate, stayed in. All the old radical group, including those with whom he had been quarreling, came to Wilkes's assistance. Townsend canvased for him. Bull, Crosby, and Sawbridge pitched in. They raised twenty-four hundred pounds for a campaign fund. Sawbridge, Hayley, and two others put up four thousand pounds' surety to guarantee the Court of Aldermen that Wilkes would not neglect his duties.[1]

James's people sent to the papers a squib about Wilkes's profligacy and predicted poor management of City money. The *London Evening Post* responded on 11 November: "He has been an active friend of the public for these sixteen years past, during which he has never, in any one action of his life, deserted for a moment the popular cause."[2]

On 22 November 1779, the election commenced with fifteen hundred livery crowding into the Guildhall. The recorder tried to open with a speech but could not be heard. Wilkes then spoke, no doubt beginning with his old cry of

"Independence! — Property! — Liberty!" and then waiting for the crowd to quiet down. When they did, Wilkes talked about his "superabundant gratitude to the livery" and repeated his promise to devote half the profits of the office to the discharging of his mayoral debts. Then James spoke, but according to the *Lady's Magazine*, "seemed to be oppressed with the weight of his own diffidence." The sheriffs then called for a vote by show of hands, but James demanded a poll, and, that being his right, the sheriffs set one in motion. Wilkes scribbled a note to Polly, "Everything succeeds to my utmost wishes. An infinite number of people at the common hall, and almost unanimous in my favor." The final vote was 2,343 for Wilkes, 371 for James.[3]

On 2 December 1779, Wilkes was sworn into office. The next day he walked to work, as he would do for many years. The chamberlains of the City of London had their own building, an old timber house at the back of the Guildhall, with a walled garden connecting it to the larger building. There Wilkes had his own office, opening to a larger room where his assistants worked, and he had a separate reading room. He soon had the city carpenter in and instructed him to reface the chimney in the reading room with Bath stone, to build bookcases on the wall opposite the window, but to leave room for a sofa.[4]

Wilkes's duties were a sort of combination of banker, stockbroker, and ombudsman for the City. The chamberlain received all the money from leases, lease-renewal fines, duties on coal, and numerous other sources, but not from property taxes. He had the management of various accounts and of the sizable Orphan Fund, a stock fund from which many of the City debts were paid. He settled all disputes between masters and apprentices. He authorized the granting of freedoms of the City and presided in ceremonies in which the freedom was granted as an honor.

The chamberlain had the right to invest the unused balances of money entrusted to him and to keep the profits. Though the public scorned ministers of the Crown who used government money in this way, the practice by the chamberlain of the City was accepted. Wilkes had no hesitancy about claiming it, for it was known to provide the bulk of the chamberlain's income.[5] He also received various fees and grants. In most years during the third quarter of the century, the chamberlains had an income of something like *fifteen hundred pounds per annum*. In a letter to a friend, Wilkes wrote, "It is a post adequate, after the payment of my debts, to every wish I can form at fifty-three: profit, patronage, and extensive usefulness, with rank and dignity." Happy for Wilkes that he could continue to serve the livery that had well served him and yet, as John Almon put it, be "raised above want, and made easy and independent."[6]

It has been said that in accepting the chamberlainship, Wilkes violated his often repeated promise never to accept "either place, pension, gratuity, or emolument of any kind."[7] His long advocacy of a "place bill" would not have been convincing had he said otherwise. But his promise was not to accept a place under the Crown and ministers, the point being that a member of Parliament who was being paid by the ministry was not independent and could easily be corrupted. But a dependency upon the livery of London was not slavish, but honorable.

Three years later Wilkes would indeed break his promise, at least by a strict construction of his words. When Lord Rockingham was in the process of establishing a new ministry, Wilkes asked him for the office of receiver of the land tax for Middlesex and London. There was a certain logic to the request, for the only income for the City that did not pass through the chamberlain's office was the land tax. It would be efficient to allow those funds to be handled by an office well prepared for such a service, and in the past the receivership had often been held by the chamberlain. For all that, Wilkes had broken his promise, for the receivership was a ministerial post. Then on 12 April he withdrew the request because he had discovered that the office was incompatible with a seat in the House of Commons. Giving up his seat as knight of the shire for Middlesex, he told Rockingham, would be unthinkable.[8]

During the years since Wilkes had left the mayor's office, he had continued to stand by America. After the Declaration of Independence, when many Englishmen withdrew their support of the colonies, Wilkes had stayed in, advocating the recall of armies and fleets and the repeal of the Coercive Acts and telling the House repeatedly, you cannot win a war with America.

In 1776, the adventurous Scottish seaman turned American admiral, John Paul Jones, was raiding ports on the Irish Sea in both Scotland and England. On the night of Christmas day, 1776, Washington crossed the Delaware River with his tattered army and captured New Jersey. In October of 1777, General John Burgoyne, having complacently moved his clumsy army down from Canada, was defeated at Saratoga. In the House of Commons, Wilkes repeatedly pointed out that these setbacks for England would draw support for America from the Continent. He warned that France was secretly aiding America and that Portugal had joined France in this support.

As Wilkes had predicted, early in 1778, Louis XVI, impressed with the American victories, decided to send assistance openly and, what naturally followed, declared war on England. King George, his eyes suddenly opened, asked Lord North to propose a peace in which the Coercive Acts would be revoked, taxation without representation would cease, Congress would be recognized, and negotiations would commence on the question of how to elect Americans to Parliament. Had he offered this two years before, there would have been no war. Now it was too late.[9] North duly brought a motion for peace before the House of Commons, but the loss of British lives in America and the entrance of France into the war had hardened the members' resolve, and they rejected North's peace plan. In the House of Lords, Chatham, no longer able to reconcile his advocacy of civil and political liberties for America with the loss of the empire he had built, came down hard on a similar peace proposal. He thundered for more troops, more war! Then he collapsed. He was taken home, and a month later, on 11 May 1778, he died as his son was reading to him from the *Iliad* the story of the death of Hector.[10]

On 26 May 1778, the House of Commons resolved itself into a committee of the whole to consider whether to launch an inquiry into General Burgoyne's campaign and his surrender at Saratoga. Only months before, Wilkes had attacked Burgoyne's ordering of his Indian allies to attack the colonists. "Merciful Heaven! Thousands of Indian savages let loose. . . . Has the feeble old man, the helpless infant, the defenseless female ever experienced the tender mercies of an Indian savage?" So when the general himself returned to be questioned by the House, of which he was a member, Wilkes rose, not, he said, to make any charges, but only to ask for information from "an intelligent officer of high rank just returned from the great scene of action." Thereupon he proceeded to excoriate the man: "Every Gazette of Europe and America has published the disgrace of our arms at Saratoga, the ignominious terms of the convention, the charges of frequent murders and massacres of the defenseless inhabitants, and the wanton devastation and burning of the country by British troops. I am entitled to the General's thanks for assisting in giving him this long-wished opportunity of clearing up many particulars confessedly perplexed and intricate, of justifying himself and others under the charges which have been exhibited at the bar of public." Sir William Meredith, no longer a radical but a placeman in the royal household, accused Wilkes of insulting the general. Wilkes replied, he was "merely the echo of the public voice," and, by the bye, he had with him all the letters and papers he had spoken about and would like to present them to the House. He then produced page after page of accounts, documents, letters, and congressional records as evidence of Burgoyne's mismanagement of the march down from Canada, his disastrous misuse of his Hessian mercenaries, many of whom had been killed, his use of the Indians to attack villages and farms, his paying them for scalps, and his manipulating the ministers at Whitehall. But the knight of the shire for Middlesex wanted no more than to give the general an opportunity to answer such criticism. Burgoyne replied by accusing Wilkes of having damaged his reputation during his absence in America. Wilkes retorted by asking about the burning of houses and villages and "the wanton destruction and devastation of property."

Burgoyne said he did not know of any. In the end, he suggested Wilkes owed him an apology. Wilkes made none and the general won the battle anyway. The papers that Wilkes had offered as evidence were not ordered to lie upon the table for examination, and the motion to make a formal inquiry was defeated.[11]

In July of 1778, the French foreign minister, Charles Gravier Comte de Vergennes, wrote a justification for the declaration of war with England which he sent to diplomats of other nations, the *Exposé des motifs de la conduite du Rois de France relativement à l'Angleterre.* The English ministers then called upon Edward Gibbon, now a member of the Board of Trade and much celebrated for his first volume of the *Decline and Fall of the Roman Empire,* to write a *Mémoire Justificatif* to be circulated in the diplomatic community explaining the British position. Wilkes thought Gibbon's paper stupid and dishonest and attacked it in a bitter pamphlet at first called *The Observer,* later renamed satirically, *A Supplement to the Miscellaneous Works of Mr. Gibbon.* He opened by making fun of the vulgarity of Gibbon's peccable French, which in diplomacy should be impeccable. A more serious purpose was to expose the differences between the ministers' declarations to Parliament in the last few years and their diplomatic letters to Louis XVI. The *Mémoire* spoke of Lord Stormont, the English ambassador to France in 1773, and his knowledge that ships had been sent to America carrying ammunition and arms, including nine vessels sent by Beaumarchais. "Are the English people and Parliament to learn all these important circumstances first from a state paper in French, delivered by order of their own sovereign to all foreign courts? . . . How carefully was the truth concealed from them!" He said nothing, of course, about his own part in helping Beaumarchais to stock those ships.[12] Then he attacked Lord Sandwich, not grudgingly, though he had cause enough for personal grudges; rather, he blamed him as first lord of the admiralty for doing nothing to develop a navy that could match that of France. English harbors were unsafe, and only one battalion had been left at home to protect the British Isles. "Every lover of his country must look with horror on the treachery of ministers in thus leaving us an easy prey to our ancient enemies while the great force of the nation was employed in the mad scheme of establishing arbitrary power in America."

Wilkes's indictments of his own people grew more and more violent as the war progressed. After the ceremonies opening Parliament in November 1778, Lord North presented the House of Commons with a draft of "the address," and in the traditional manner modifications were offered from the floor and debated. About the passage on America Wilkes was indignant: "Americans avoid us as a tyrannical, unprincipled, rapacious, and ruined nation. Their only fear is that the luxury and profligacy of this country should gain their people . . . I rejoice that liberty will have a resting place, a sure asylum in America."[13] One would think that he would have been arrested for such a speech, but by law members of the House of Commons could not be impugned for speeches made from the floor.

Whether it was true or not, many people believed that Wilkes still had contacts with America, and in at least one instance that proved to be a burden. In the fall of 1779, he received a letter from a family relative, a teenaged boy, Richard Booth, who with his cousin, John Brevitt, had run away from home, gone to France, and was trying to get to America to join Washington's army. Arthur Lee, whom they approached in Paris, told them they needed a letter of recommendation from their relative, John Wilkes. Richard was the son of John Booth and Elizabeth, née Wilkes, probably the cousin to Wilkes's father, who had married first one Hughes, and after his death, John Booth. Booth was a prosperous silversmith, and the couple lived in St. John's square and were considered family by the Wilkeses. When Wilkes received the boys' letter, he immediately wrote to the father. Booth managed to have his son and nephew arrested in France and brought home. John Brevitt eventually got to America, fought in the army, rose to the rank of captain, and settled at Baltimore. Richard never made the escape but grew up to be a London lawyer. He remained an ardent admirer of Washington and had a picture of him hanging in his parlor to which everyone entering his house had to bow. He married Elizabeth Game, and they named their two sons for radical heroes, Algernon Sydney Booth and Lucius Junius Brutus Booth. Junius Booth became a tragic actor, second in popularity only to Edmund Kean. When he fell out of favor in London, he abandoned his wife and ran off to America with Mary Ann Holmes, a flower girl. In America he had a second highly successful career as a tragedian and ten children by Mary Ann, most of whom became actors. One son, Edwin Booth, had a remarkable career and is credited with inventing the style of contemplative acting that still dominates the stage. His brother, John Wilkes Booth, a somewhat less successful actor, was proud to have been named for his collateral ancestor (as they say in England) and always insisted that he be called Wilkes Booth, instead of John Booth. His passion for rebellion, which he traced to the Wilkes line, had, as you know, tragic consequences.[14]

On the northern side during the Civil War was John Wilkes Booth's distant relative, Rear Admiral Charles Wilkes, the grandson of Wilkes's brother Israel. Charles Wilkes, born and reared in New York, became a great naval explorer, commander of the naval expedition of 1838–42 that surveyed and mapped the South Pacific islands and Australia, discovered the land mass under the south polar ice, and surveyed the California coast northward to Alaska. During the Civil War, he commanded the James River Flotilla, which took part in the attack on Richmond. In his memoir, he felt compelled to mention his collateral ancestor but, not being proud of the connection, said no more.[15]

One of the attractions of the American leaders with whom Wilkes had so often corresponded was their religious tolerance, or perhaps the other way around. His statements in Parliament about religious freedom preceded by several years the debates in the American Congress on the amendments that Americans call the Bill of Rights. Wilkes's sentiments were, for that time, extreme. James Harris reported, "John Wilkes, in describing to me his ideas of toleration, said they were so general and unlimited that he wished to see a mosque on one side of [St.] Paul's and a synagogue on the other."[16]

Some thought Wilkes could be liberal because he himself had no religion. It is true that among his friends Wilkes often affected a lack of faith. Once Boswell mentioned that Dr. Johnson had spoken about liberty, whereupon Wilkes exclaimed, "What! does *he* talk of liberty? *Liberty* is as ridiculous in *his* mouth as *Religion* in *mine*." Boswell also had a story about Wilkes's taking him to see a curious, melancholy procession passing up Parliament Street, the funeral of a lamplighter "attended by some hundreds of his fraternity with torches": "Wilkes, who either is, or affects to be, an infidel, was rattling away, 'I think there's an end of that fellow. I think he won't rise again.' I very calmly said to him 'You bring into my mind the strongest argument that ever I heard against a future state'; and then told him David Hume's objection [to the doctrine of immortality: if the doctrine were true,] Wilkes and his Mob must be immortal. It seemed to make proper impression, for he grinned abashment." But Boswell knew that Wilkes's irreligion was only an affectation. At a later time, he called at Prince's Court: "He was so gay and pleasant," Bowell wrote, "I said, 'Your soul must be immortal.' 'I hope so,'" Wilkes replied.[17]

Wilkes's father had brought him up in the Church of England, from which Jack Wilkes had never turned. Once he was overheard disputing theology with a Catholic priest, who asked, "Where was your religion before Luther?" to which Wilkes replied, "Where was your face before you washed it this morning?" On the record, the only religion he disliked was the newfangled movement within the Church of England called Methodism. The fishermen at Brighthelmstone, he told Polly, were "infected" with the "heresy of Methodism." One would like to have been present when the elegantly dressed man with the ugly face met these fishermen on the docks of Brighthelmstone. No doubt they thought they were meeting the devil incarnate, and probably they did what Methodists did at that time, fell on their knees and prayed God to convert the sinner. "I remain however sound in faith," Wilkes wrote to Polly, "and will keep to my good orthodox mother, the Church of England"[18]

Painted by Sir Joshua Reynolds   Engraved by John Jones

JAMES BOSWELL OF AUCHINLECK, ESQ.ᴿ

London, Pub.ᵈ as the Act directs Jan. 17, 1786 by I. Jones, N.º 63 Great Portland Street, Mary-le-bone.

22. James Boswell of Auchinleck, Esqr, engraved by John Jones after a painting by Sir Joshua Reynolds, 1786. Courtesy of Gerald M. Goldberg.

Wilkes urged what we Americans call the separation of church and state. The position was not new: it had been advanced a century before by Anne Hutchinson in Massachusetts and Roger Williams in Rhode Island. At the time it was being advocated in Virginia by James Madison, who believed that liberty of conscience was fundamental to all law. In England, the most famous statement was that of Milton in his *Treatise of Civil Power in Ecclesiastical Causes: Shewing that It is not Lawfull for Any Power on Earth to Compell in Matters of Religion*, 1659. But Hutchinson, Williams, and Milton were passionately religious and wanted the government to leave them alone. Wilkes's position on the separation of church and state was more like that of Madison, who was another lukewarm member of the Anglican commuion, the position of a man of the Enlightenment.[19]

Religious tolerance was not to be attained easily. The Church of England was a state religion that had survived two centuries of struggle against Catholics and bloody warfare between Anglicans and Presbyterians. Legally, at the Restoration of 1660, England had been returned to the position given it by Henry VIII: the monarch was the head not only of the state, but also of the church. The Act of Toleration of 1689 had guaranteed to all Protestants the right to practice their religions, but the "dissenters," the Protestant sects outside the Church of England, did not have full legal rights. Presbyterianism was the established religion in Scotland, but a dissenting religion in England. The licences granted to dissenting ministers and churches in England could be revoked at any time by the bishops of the established church. The Jews had no religious rights at all. It was specifically against the law to hold a Roman Catholic mass, and a Catholic who took in pupils or opened a school could be imprisoned for life. But in the middle years of the century, these harsh punishments were seldom, if ever, exacted. The establishment, that is, the lawmakers, the ministers, and the judiciary, had become tolerant of English Catholics because they had remained loyal to the Crown during the Jacobite Rebellion of 1745. The attitude of the common man was something else, as would soon become apparent.

The first step in the eighteenth century toward full acceptance of religions other than the established church was made by Sir George Savile on 14 May 1778. Sir George, mindful of the loyalty to the Crown of the numerous Catholic families of Yorkshire, moved the Catholic Relief Act, designed to return to English Catholics full rights of inheriting and purchasing land and to return to priests the right to conduct private masses. The most risky part of the bill was its allowing Catholics to serve in the military by taking an oath of loyalty to the Crown. Government had no objection, and the bill quickly passed both houses and received royal assent.[20]

The second step was attempted by Sir Henry Hoghton, the chief spokesman in Parliament for dissenters. He proposed a bill to relieve dissenting clergy of the requirement of subscribing to the Anglican "thirty-nine articles of religion." The thirty-nine articles had been drawn up in the sixteenth century as the doctrines of the Church of England; two centuries later, almost all officials were required to subscribe to them, aldermen, sheriffs, bailiffs, parish officers —and also (and this was the point of the bill) dissenting ministers. The London radicals strongly supported Sir Henry's bill, in large part because many of the prominent Real Whig leaders were dissenting ministers, including Richard Price and Joseph Priestley.

If Wilkes spoke in support of Sir George Savile's bill for the relief of Catholics, the record does not show. But his speech in support of Hoghton's bill is known:

> I deny that the civil magistrate has the least concern with the salvation of souls, or that a power of that nature is delegated to him. Men assemble in society only for the security of their civil rights, for the preservation and possession of life, liberty, houses, goods, effects, all kinds of property. The magistrate is therefore armed with the whole force of the state to assist the weak against the violence of the strong. Here his power ends.
>
> I would not, Sir, persecute even the atheist. . . . I wish to see rising in the neighborhood of a Christian cathedral, near its Gothic towers, the minaret of a Turkish mosque, a Chinese pagoda, and a Jewish synagogue, with a temple of the sun, if any Persians could be found to inhabit this island and worship in this gloomy climate the God of their idolatry.

Then, showing himself aware of the textual criticism of the Bible, he asked,

> Is the text [of the Bible] in so pure a state that I am certain it was dictated by the wisest and best of being, that it is truly the word of God? We all know of the thirty thousand various readings in the New Testament, some of them confessedly important; and most of the Bishops have encouraged a learned divine of our Church, Dr. Kennicott, to examine the various manuscripts of the Old Testament. . . . The indefatigable doctor has already discovered many thousand various readings in the Hebrew, and will be lucky if he does not double the number of the Greek.

Hoghton's bill did not cause much of a stir among the people, but the House of Commons did not pass it. A few days later, the "Order of the General Body of Protestant Dissenting Ministers" sent unanimous thanks to Wilkes for his "kind attention to their bill, and his generous and active zeal in support of the cause of religious liberty." Joseph Priestley spent an evening with him and gave him a copy of his *View of the Principles and Conduct of the Protestant Dissenters.*"[21]

In the midst of these quiet developments, violent riots against Roman Catholics exploded in Scotland. The discontent rapidly spread to England. After England and Scotland had struggled so many centuries to keep their nations Protestant, the thought that Catholics were now being recruited for the army was frightening. Stories were circulated that the pope had sent instructions to Catholic youths to lie when they enlisted so that they could gain the opportunity to kill Protestants in America. For every one killed, they would receive an indulgence of twenty days.[22]

In November 1779, Lord George Gordon, the half-mad member for Ludgersall, was elected to be president of the Protestant Association, the primary goal of which was the repeal of Savile's Catholic Relief Act. For months the Association gathered signatures on a petition, said to have finally attained 120,000 signatures. On 2 June 1780, Gordon gathered a huge crowd on St. George's Fields for the purpose of presenting the petition to the House of Commons. The plan was for this vast crowd to meet Lord George on the Lambeth road and to hand him the petition. He would then cross Westminster Bridge, walk to St. Stephen's Chapel, and present it to the House. The people were to stay south of the Thames. But they had no intention of doing that. They formed two parades. One marched over London Bridge and through the City and the Strand into Parliament Street. As they approached the Houses of Parliament, they received a great cheer from the other group that had paraded across Westminster Bridge. By the time Lord George got the floor and moved the acceptance of the petition, fifty thousand people were crowded around the buildings of Parliament. Lord George's motion was seconded by Wilkes's colleague and friend Frederick Bull, who was a member of the Association. A motion was made to delay the hearing on the petition. Lord George believed that any delay would kill the movement, for Parliament was due to dissolve early the next week. As the point was debated, Lord George kept leaving the floor and going outside to inform the mob of what was happening: "Lord North calls you a mob." "The Member for Bristol [Burke] is now speaking. He is no friend to your petition." Finally, as he was reentering the hall, General Conway grabbed him by the collar and told him in a growl that if a single one of that mob dared to enter the House, "I shall protect the freedom of debate with my sword." The question was called on the motion to delay consideration of the petition, but it could not be voted on because the lobby, to which the negative voters always retired to be counted, was packed with protestors. Not until eight in the evening could the House vote by division, which they did, overwhelmingly voting to delay consideration. Meanwhile troops had been called, and in the next two hours by clever diplomacy managed to disperse the mob.

At eleven o'clock that night, a mob had reassembled. They broke into the Catholic chapel of the Sardinian ambassador in Duke Street, smashed everything they could smash, and set fire to the structure. Then the chapel of the Bavarian embassy in Warwick Street, Golden Square, was gutted, but not burned. In the week of riot that followed, other Catholic chapels, schools, houses, and even pubs where Catholics gathered were attacked. There were certainly vagrants and criminals in these mobs, but most were established citizens of the lower orders, laborers, apprentices, journeymen, waiters, domestic servants, and a few craftsmen or small tradesmen. Though their cries of protest were directed against Catholics, the violence released their resentments of the upper classes. A hundred houses were pulled down and their contents burned in the streets. Sir George Savile's house was gutted; Lord Mansfield's utterly destroyed.[23]

Henry Angelo watched on 7 June as rioters broke down the gates of Newgate prison with pickaxes and sledgehammers, released the prisoners, and set the prison afire. He left the scene walking through streets crowded with felons and hearing in the houses the clink of hammers as they knocked off their fetters. When Wilkes learned about Newgate, he rushed to Lord Mayor Kennett and urged him to raise the *posse comitatus,* but the mayor would not. Because several City aldermen, like Bull, were sympathetic, the Court of Aldermen did nothing. The next morning Dr. Johnson and a friend watched as rioters calmly plundered the Sessions House at the Old Bailey. Brideswell prison and other prisons were broken into, the convicts released, and the buildings set afire. There was vast looting. Parliament did not meet for a week. The king, exasperated, authorized the army to act without permission of magistrates.[24]

Wilkes again became the soldier. Angelo was watching the mob attack London Bridge, setting it afire in several places, when a party of soldiers rushed upon the scene, led by Alderman Wilkes. In the struggle, "many were thrown over into the Thames," but Wilkes's soldiers managed to put out the fires. Later that same day, the mob attacked the Bank of England, and Wilkes, the old radical, led his soldiers to the rescue of the very institution that was central to right-wing monied interests. Several rioters were killed in the fray. Dr. Johnson thought the action was justified because the destruction of the bank would have caused irrevocable damage to the nation. "Jack Wilkes headed the party that drove them away," he wrote to Mrs. Thrale; "Jack, who was always zealous for order and decency, declared that if he be trusted with power he 'will not leave one rioter alive.' "[25]

Johnson's irony was not far from the truth. Wilkes had put his ward under military control. He requested a detachment of twenty men, went to the barracks on Ludgate Hill, and marched out at the head of them. He ordered all taverns in the ward closed at ten. He organized patrols of the ward at night. He issued a warrant on 10 June "for searching for and securing all idle and disorderly persons, and all concealed arms, in the ward of Farringdon Without." He seized the sixty Spanish muskets he had been told of. By nightfall of 8 June, things were quiet enough that he found a moment to write a note to Polly from St. Sepulchre's churchyard (next to the house where his wife dwelt). He was in charge of "a good party of horse and foot" and had armed the neighbors. He had heard that the riot was subsiding, but he would continue the patrols all night. On 10 June, he wrote Polly from the Globe Tavern, Fleet Street, where he was examining prisoners, telling her not to wait up for him. He has been "on hard duty for some days." On 16 June he issued a warrant "to search for rogues and vagabonds" in the ward. Ironically, on 13 June, Alderman Wilkes committed one William Moore "for being the printer and publisher of two seditious and treasonable papers, entitled *England in Blood* and *The Thunderer*." One hopes the order was an early application of the clear-and-present-danger criterion.[26]

Nathaniel Wraxall was of the opinion that had Wilkes been mayor at the time, many of the "disgraceful scenes" would not have taken place. Wilkes, he said, gave "indelible proofs" of his loyalty to the Crown during the riots, "when Bull . . . crouched under Lord George Gordon's mob, while Kennett, the Lord Mayor, exhibited equal incapacity and pusillanimity." Lord Clarendon wrote to James Harris, "Wilkes was *the* heroic justice." Old Dr. Wilson wrote from Bath congratulating Wilkes for his "late noble behavior, which I have from all hands. . . . I may not, but you may live to see better times."[27]

On 19 June 1780, John Sawbridge presented to the House of Commons a petition asking for repeal of the Catholic Relief Act, and the House dissolved into a committee of the whole, to debate the act and the riots. Wilkes attacked Bull for taking no action in his ward during the riots and permitting his constables to wear the blue cockades of the rioters. Bull, proud of his hatred of papism, admitted both. Nevertheless, the Catholic Relief Act was retained. A month later, Lord George Gordon was tried for high treason, a ridiculous charge; he was a demagogue, but hardly a traitor. He was acquitted, but twenty-five of those who had followed his lead were hanged.[28]

Wilkes, now seen as a defender of Catholicism, lost the leadership of what remained of the Wilkite party, the public cooled toward him, and his support of America suffered. Weeks after the riots, when his first year as chamberlain was drawing to a close, he faced reelection. He himself had broken the tradition of offering no challenge to the annual reelection of a chamberlain, and he was worried that the precedent he had set would be used against him by the very liverymen whom he had offended by voting for the Catholic Relief Act and angered by his military leadership during the riots. The meeting was held on 24 June 1780. Wilkes was hissed as he entered the Guildhall. He mounted the hustings to explain his actions, but the hooting was so loud he could not be heard. Nevertheless, when the sheriffs announced that the election would commence with a show of hands and the recorder called out Wilkes's name, a resounding cheer went up, so great that the recorder entered into the record, "re-elected by acclamation."[29] The livery seem to have discovered that, as Almon put it, "a more punctual, patient, penetrating, and discriminating chamberlain had not filled the office during the . . . century." He would be chamberlain for the rest of his life.

Wilkes usually eschewed the coaches, horses, and sedan chairs used by most gentlemen, preferring to walk to his office in the City. Henry Angelo remembered how, when Angelo was a boy, he used to walk with him: "His dress, for he was a celebrated beau, was usually either a scarlet or green suit, edged with gold. His town house was in Princes Court, near the Park gate, George Street, Westminster. He had a good library there and the parlor, looking into the Birdcage Walk, was hung with Hogarth's prints."[30]

Outside London, Wilkes was still the hero of the Middlesex election rumpus, the man who had courageously defied the government. In May of 1778, he wrote to Polly from Stourton, where he had gone when a rainstorm drove him out of his usual route back from Bath. "The bells rung here two hours for me. . . . At Frome, the whole town was in an uproar. I think I am a public nuisance." He remained the most popular figure in Aylesbury, and in February 1780 returned to that town "to attend the great meeting called by the yeomanry of Bucks."[31] The bells began ringing as he approached, and the common folk turned out in droves to welcome him. But in the City, he was tolerated, appreciated, loved, at least by some, but not followed.

Wilkes's personal life was not markedly different from what it had been, though now he had money for clothes and books. He continued to go to Bath, but he often spent the summer holidays on the Isle of Wight. Sometimes he combined politics and pleasure. At the close of the season of 1779, Wilkes left the island and crossed over to Lime: "I found Mr. Thomas Hollis, and other true friends of liberty, with whom I passed the remainder of the day." Hollis had been keeping up a barrage of essays in support of America. A few days later Wilkes was dining with Catharine Macaulay and congratulating her upon the completion of the sixth volume of her *History of England*.[32]

When he returned to London, Wilkes resumed his old social position as the delight of every table at which he dined. We find him taking Boswell to dinner with the judges at the Old Bailey, and constantly teasing him about Scotland

and its lack of trees: "There Judas might have survived his desperate intention." Inevitably he saw Lord Mansfield at the Old Bailey, for Mansfield was on the rota of judges. No doubt Wilkes and the man who had sent him to prison occasionally served on the same judges' panel and sat down to dinner together afterward. "Mr. Wilkes," Lord Mansfield told his friend Andrew Strahan, "was the pleasantest companion, the politest gentleman, and the best scholar he ever knew."[33]

Lord Temple died at Stowe early in 1780.[34] The previous autumn, he had been badly injured in a carriage accident, and in his last months he was terribly crippled and bent double when he walked. His lordship had cooled toward Wilkes, in part because he did not agree with Wilkes's position on America but believed that England had the right to subdue the colonies.[35] Perhaps his brush with death caused him to rethink his relationship with Wilkes and to reach out to an old friend whom he had not seen for a long time. He broke the silence on 15 December 1779, writing to congratulate Wilkes on his election to the chamberlainship and inviting him to stay with him at his house in Bath when Wilkes came there at Christmas. "The dining room apartment which you used to have is now empty and at your service. It will give me great pleasure to see you." No doubt Wilkes wrote to thank his lordship, but he did not take up the offer.

Wilkes was still the family man, devoted to Polly, who was his hostess and the mistress of his household. In 1780, she attained the age of thirty. When Polly was away, he took care of her menagerie. He wrote about her cat, Mademoiselle Suzette, who spilled the milk and stole the bread. "I expect you soon to rescue an aged father from this CATilinarian tumult." Acceding to Polly's wishes, he once supped with her Mead cousins. When Polly could not come to Bath with him, he arranged for regular deliveries from Calais of a hamper basket of hares, partridges, and chickens so that she would have enough supplies to do her entertaining. Were these animals alive? He himself went to the fish market in Bath and bought "a pair of soles" and "a fine piper," not alive, which he sent to her. One cannot but wonder how many days they had been dead when the *bonne* prepared them for dinner.[36]

Wilkes continued to act the part of the soldier. A fire broke out in the house of a neighbor at Prince's Court. "Guards, mob, firemen, engines, buckets, pails filled the court," he wrote to Polly. When they had the blaze under control, Wilkes took the two pistols he kept by his bed and posted himself as guard at the door of the damaged house to prevent looting. Finally a detachment of soldiers arrived and took charge.[37]

In 1780, Wilkes decided he should again take up the writing of the memoir we call his "Autobiography." The manuscript which comes down to us opens with a few pages containing a story of Wilkes's birth and family and early childhood. This is followed by a hundred or so pages that are perfectly blank, after which it takes up the description in luscious detail of Wilkes's affair with Gertrude Corradini. The memoir is of great value to a biographer and has been quoted frequently in these pages, but it is a deep disappointment to political historians, who would have liked those blank pages to be filled with the story of Wilkes's political secrets, his views upon his struggles for a free press, the inside story of his imprisonment in the Tower, and the politics of his return from exile. Sad to say, the evidence suggests that Wilkes had indeed written down his recollections of the political story some years before, but they are lost to us. In May 1767, Wilkes had written to his brother from France, "I have very carefully drawn up my own Memoirs, though . . . it shall be posthumous, and if I die tomorrow, it shall be printed by a friend here [Diderot?] the month after with all names at length." In 1780, when he again went to work on his autobiography, he may have intended to copy the manuscript of 1767 onto those blank pages. In 1779, he had read from his memoirs to cheer up old Dr. Wilson, but we do not know from which manuscript.[38]

During the time when Charpillon was out of his life and Amelia Arnold and her baby still at Bath, he turned his attention to a neighbor, Jenny Wade, who lived at 8 Prince's Court. Jenny seems to have been another country girl living by her wits. Because their houses were so close, they took special precautions to keep their affair secret from Polly, meeting in a carriage with the blinds drawn, carrying on in the house of a certain Mrs. Elvington, using chairmen rather than servants to carry their letters. Mrs. Wade was constantly fearful of arrest for debts and at one point had to escape into the country. The poor woman badly wanted Wilkes to become her "protector," but he declined to take that step. The affair seems to have ceased early in 1780.[39]

Wilkes was still the scholar. He wrote articles on Churchill and Baxter for *Biographia Britannia*. He and Joseph Wharton, the poet and scholar, talked about doing an edition of Pope, and Wilkes made many notes for it, though the edition never materialized.[40] He became a champion of the British Museum. The Museum had been established by a statute of 1753 and set up at Montagu House, Great Russell Street, where were brought together the great collections of books, manuscripts, and artifacts of Sir Hans Sloane, Robert Harley, Earl of Oxford, and Sir Robert Cotton. In April 1777, Wilkes spoke eloquently in favor of a motion to increase the funding of the museum: "I wish their plan much enlarged, especially on two important objects, Books and Paintings. . . . London has no large public library. . . . The British Museum, Sir, is rich in manuscripts . . . but it is wretchedly poor in printed books. I wish, sir, a sum was allowed by Parliament for the purchase of the most valuable editions of the best authors, and an Act passed to oblige every printer, under a certain penalty, to send a copy of every publication he made to the British Museum." Another sixty-five years would pass before a new copyright law would accomplish this goal. He advocated the purchase of paintings for the Museum so as to recognize an English school. Tactfully, he concluded his speech with a compliment to Lord North, a man of "wit, genius, a great deal of true taste, and a very cultivated understanding," and asked him to be a protector of English art.[41]

Unbeknown to Wilkes, Boswell had been trying to convince Dr. Johnson that he had been wrong in his essay about the Middlesex controversy, *The False Alarm*, but his arguments had fallen on deaf ears. Lord Newhaven, however, seems to have succeeded in this attempt. This was William Mayne, a Scotsman who represented Canterbury and had voted with Wilkes in the motion to expunge. He had since that time, and for other reasons, been created Baron Newhaven. One evening in October of 1779 Lord Newhaven and Johnson had a long discussion of the expulsion and incapacitation of Wilkes: " 'As it is clear [said Johnson] that the House of Commons may expel, and expel again and again, why not allow of the power to incapacitate for that parliament, rather than have a perpetual contest kept up between parliament and the people?' Lord Newhaven took the opposite side; but respectfully said, 'I speak with great deference to you, Dr. Johnson; I speak to be instructed.' This had its full effect on my friend. He bowed his head almost as low as the table, to a complimenting nobleman; and called out, 'My Lord, my Lord, I do not desire all this ceremony; let us tell our minds to one another quietly.' After the debate was over, he said, 'I have got lights on the subject to-day, which I had not before.' "[42]

A year later, on 8 May 1781, Boswell, Johnson, and Wilkes again sat down at Dilly's table. Johnson, Boswell tells us, was "very glad to meet Wilkes again." In the course of the evening, they talked about the odd problem of how to pay the English soldiers in America; the ministry could not pay them in British currency because there was a law against exporting it. Wilkes suggested, "Might not the House of Commons, in case of real evident necessity, order our own current coin to be sent into our own colonies?" Johnson came back quickly, "Sure, Sir, *you* don't think a *resolution of the House of Commons* equal to the law of the land?" Wilkes, at once perceiving the application, replied, "God forbid, Sir." Obviously, Johnson had understood Lord Newhaven's argument and probably had accepted it. Boswell was delighted with the evening: "The company gradually dropped away." Happening into the room where he had left Wilkes and Johnson, "I was struck with observing Dr. Samuel Johnson and John Wilkes, Esq. literally *tête-à-tête*; for they were reclined upon their chairs, with their heads leaning almost close to each other, and talking earnestly, in a kind of confidential whisper, of the personal quarrel between George the Second and the King of Prussia. Such a scene of perfectly easy sociality between two such opponents in the war of political controversy, as that which I now beheld, would have been an excellent subject for a picture. It presented to my mind the happy days which are foretold in Scripture, when the lion shall lie down with the kid."[43]

Wilkes and Polly tried three times, that we know of, to bring Johnson to their house for dinner, but one thing and another seemed to have stood in the way. Dr. Johnson had friendships with so very many people, including most of the best artists and most accomplished intellectuals of the day, that his friendship with Wilkes would not have ranked among those he valued the most. But then, as Boswell pointed out, Johnson enormously enjoyed "the marks of respect and benignity which he had received from those whom he had made by his own behavior his enemies." When speaking of this penchant, Johnson used Wilkes as his example: "Mr. Wilkes (with whom I had a very rough bout) called upon me soon after my recovery and sat with me some time. He asked me to give him my books which he said he should be glad to have but was too poor to buy them; as you may be sure, he had them." It was the last time Wilkes saw the old man. He died on 13 December 1784.[44]

In September 1780, there had been a general election for the House of Commons. Wilkes was reelected unopposed, as was his running mate, George Byng, the popular choice to replace Sergeant John Glynn, who had died.

In the American war, the southern colonies had suffered an ignominious defeat. The British had taken Charleston, captured the American southern army, and seized control of Georgia and South Carolina. Washington sent General Nathaniel Green to take command of such forces as the colonies had in the South. Green brilliantly turned the tables, enticing General Charles Cornwallis into chasing his little army deep into the country, then doubling back to cut the drawn-out, ill-defended British supply lines. Cornwallis's men, reduced to near starvation, began raiding farms and succeeded in making the populace detest them.

On 27 November 1780, a motion was made in the House of Commons to thank Generals Sir Henry Clinton and Cornwallis and Admiral Marriott Arbuthnot for their campaign in the Carolinas. According to Wraxall, "Wilkes, rising in his place, pronounced a speech of great length, and of still greater severity . . . spirited, classic, and stamped with the characteristic energy of his fearless mind." He would oppose any motion that implied approbation of the war. He admitted the "heroic courage and superior military virtues" of the three men, but "Lord Cornwallis, Sir Henry Clinton, and Admiral Arbuthnot I will not consent to thank, for I consider them as having drawn their swords against their innocent American fellow subjects and without provocation bathed them in their blood." For all that, the motion to thank the three was carried. The Westminster Committee of Correspondence sent Wilkes a letter of thanks for his courageous stand. America still had friends in England.[45]

In the summer of 1781, Cornwallis pushed his exhausted army to York-town, Virginia, on the Chesapeake Bay, rounded up the local slaves, and set them to work building fortifications. But a French army under General Jean-Baptiste-Donatien de Vimeur, Comte de Rochambeau had arrived, and Washington had moved his refreshed and resupplied army south. Seventeen thousand allied troops laid siege to the fortifications at Yorktown, manned by nine thousand dispirited British soldiers. On 17 October, Cornwallis surrendered. Shortly thereafter, the French army sailed for home, leaving the Americans in charge of all their colonial territory except the coastal towns of Charleston and Savannah.

The House of Commons in effect ended the war on 27 February 1782. The ordinary business of that day was interrupted when the high sheriffs of London and Middlesex appeared and presented a petition from the lord mayor, aldermen, and Commons in Common Council of the City of London imploring the House of Commons to intervene with matters of state to prevent the continuance of the American war. As soon as he could get the floor, General Conway moved the cessation of hostilities. There was a division, and the motion was carried, 234 to 215, a margin of victory of only nineteen votes. On 1 March a motion was passed "that his Majesty will consider as enemies to his Majesty and the country all those who shall endeavor to frustrate his Majesty's paternal care . . . by advising or by any means attempting the further prosecution of offensive war on the continent of North America." King George thought seriously of abdicating. Nevertheless, on 6 March he sent word to the House that he did graciously receive their advice.[46]

On 20 March, Lord North resigned. It was the end, not only of the American Revolution, but of the attempt to establish "personal government" by the king, an attempt that George III and Lord Bute had initiated twenty years before.[47] A few days later, the despondent king called in Lord Rockingham, who agreed to form a new government, the second Rockingham ministry. Peace negotiations were commenced.

It was a propitious time for Wilkes to offer again his motion to remove from the records of the House the resolutions that had incapacitated him. A house free of Lord North and for a short time of virtually all royal influence would receive the motions with an open mind. On 3 May 1782, Wilkes moved to expunge the resolution of 17 February 1769, "That John Wilkes, Esquire, having been in this session of Parliament expelled from this house, was and is incapable of being elected a member to serve in this present Parliament"; also to be expunged were "all the declarations, orders, and resolution of this House respecting the election of John Wilkes, Esquire, for the County of Middlesex, as a void election, [and] the due and legal election of Henry Lawes Luttrell, Esquire, into Parliament for the said county, and the incapacity of John Wilkes, Esquire, to be elected a member to serve in the said Parliament." Wilkes then spoke to his motion:

> It is scarcely possible, Sir, to state a question in which the people of this free country are more materially interested than in the right of election, for it is the share which they have reserved to themselves in the legislature. When it was wrested from them by violence, the constitution was torn up by the roots. I have now the happiness of seeing the Treasury Bench filled with the friends of the Constitution, the guardians and lovers of liberty, who have been unwearied and uniform in the defense of all our rights, and in particular of this invaluable franchise. I hail the present auspicious moment, and with impatience expect the completion of what I have long and fervently desired for my friends and country, for the present age, and a free posterity.

The motion passed without a division, that is, by a voice vote. One of the most satisfying sights of Wilkes's life was that of the clerk of the House standing at the table and inking out the passages in the Journals.[48]

Three days later, Wilkes published an address to the gentlemen, clergy, and freeholders of Middlesex, explaining how this remarkable vote had come about. "No unfair method was taken to secure a majority, nor ministerial maneuver practiced. No letter from the Treasury, no mandate from any secretary issued to enforce attendance. The slightest solicitation was not urged by any man in power, nor a single emissary sent on the wing to collect scattered mercenaries. . . . Every man was left to follow the dictates of his conscience, which insured our success." All of this was true, but Wilkes's statement ignored the fact that only 162 members were present that day, and 47 of them had voted against the motion. One might compare these numbers to the session called to vote money for the military, when 442 members showed up.[49] The "dear lady mayoress" gave a celebratory dinner for her father's victory that evening, to which came Sir George Savile, Alderman and Mrs. Sawbridge, and other friends of liberty.[50]

By the fall of 1782, Wilkes's great work was done. General warrants were a thing of the past, and the right to privacy had been recognized as common law. He had established a principle within the House of Commons that the monarch's speech at the opening of a Parliament could be treated as a speech written by the ministers. He had succeeded in removing the dangerous precedent that the House could make law without the participation of the House of Lords or of the king. He had established the right of electors to elect whomever they please and the principle that no constituency could be represented by anyone they had not elected. He had brought before the British public the injustices of the electoral system and the need for further reform, including the need for universal male suffrage. Because of his efforts, the press was enjoying a freedom that before 1760 they could hardly have dreamed of, reporting freely on the debates and speeches in Parliament, in consequence of which, as Wilkes wrote, "the people are now made the judges of the conduct of their representatives."[51]

Wilkes had helped to inspire a love of liberty in America, and his accomplishments for English law would have a profound influence upon the laws of America. The Constitutional Convention of 1787 broke radically from the Anglo-American tradition by abolishing what Wilkes had once called the "monstrous absurdity" of election law, the ownership of property as a qualification to stand for election. But the draft before the convention left to the legislature unlimited freedom to make its own rules about who could be elected. James Madison, pointing to the Middlesex election crisis, argued that they were about to vest in the legislature "an improper and dangerous power." He then repeated Wilkes's argument: if the legislature is to be free to set its own rules about who can be elected, "it can by degrees subvert the constitution . . . by limiting the number capable of being elected. . . . Qualifications founded on artificial distinctions may be devised by the stronger, in order to keep out partisans of a weaker faction." Madison proposed to avoid the danger by fixing three simple legal qualifications, age, American citizenship, and residence in the area represented — Article I, Section 2, no. 2, and Section 3, no. 3 of the Constitution.

A similar situation obtained with the prohibition of general warrants of arrest. Under British rule, Americans had suffered the use of pernicious "general writs of assistance" issued by British-appointed judges to help in the collection of the Townshend and other duties, virtually the same thing as general warrants. In 1776, when independence had been declared and the war had begun, the Virginia House of Burgesses drew up a new state constitution. One article, written by Madison, proscribed "general Warrants . . . to search suspected places without evidence of a fact committed, or to seize any person or persons not named, or whose offence is not particularly described and supported by evidence." A decade later Madison's article became the foundation of the fourth article of the Bill of Rights. As the legal historian Jeffrey Rosen put it, when the founding fathers drafted the fourth amendment, banning unreasonable searches and seizures of persons, houses, papers, and effects, "it was Wilkes's house and Wilkes's papers that they had in mind."[52]

In 1969, U.S. Supreme Court Chief Justice Earl Warren, in setting out the majority opinion in favor of Adam Clayton Powell in his suit against the House of Representatives for excluding him illegally, cited Wilkes's success in expunging the records of his own exclusion as the precedent upon which the Court made its decision. The Court's decision was a landmark in American law and the culmination of Chief Justice Warren's lifework, for it reaffirmed the responsibility of the Supreme Court to act as the ultimate interpreter of the Constitution, and it reestablished the duty of the Court to intervene when the executive or legislative branches of the government transgressed the limits of their constitutional power.[53]

Wilkes, living in a world which had neither a supreme court nor a constitution (as Americans understand these terms), provided the stuff by which James Madison, Earl Warren, and the many others who were engaged in the process, fashioned and strengthened the American Constitution.

In 1782 Jack Wilkes attained the age of fifty-six and the appearance of a man much older. To be sure, it is difficult to reconcile the difference in his appearance in the Zoffany portrait of him sitting next to Polly, made in 1779 when he was fifty-three (illustration 20), and the sketch portrait of him by J. Sayers, done in 1782 when he was fifty-six (illustration 23). Wilkes may have been ill or may have aged rapidly, though he had not let up on his physical activities. Probably the difference is more political than physical. Probably Zoffany was a Wilkite who wanted to flatter his leader, while Sayers was a courtier who wanted to disparage him. In any event, in Sayers's portrait of 1782, he is exceedingly ugly.

One spring day, Boswell, anxious to tell something to Wilkes, hurried to the Guildhall and mischievously called him out a meeting of aldermen. Wilkes, laughing, scolded him for interrupting the gods, who always listen to their deliberations: when the Council of Aldermen meets, said Wilkes, "Jupiter bends an ear." Boswell would not tell his news until he had been fed; so they took a hackney coach to Prince's Court and sat down to dine with Polly.

That morning, explained Boswell, he had called upon his fellow Scot, the most ancient of Wilkes's enemies, Lord Bute. "All the Scotch world and half the English," he had told Lord Bute, believed that John Wilkes had offered to sell himself to Bute during the period when Wilkes was lambasting him in the *North Briton*. "His Lordship candidly told me, not so." Boswell that night wrote in his diary, "Wilkes was much pleased, and when after dinner I toasted John, Earl of Bute, he drank it, seemingly *de son coeur*, and said, 'You may tell Lord Bute I was in two mistakes. I mistook Lord Temple, and I mistook Lord

23. Wilkes at the age of fifty-six. Engraving by J. Sayers, published 17 June 1782 by C. Bretherton. Courtesy of Gerald M. Goldberg.

Bute.'" They toasted Dr. Johnson. Boswell then offered a toast to General Pasquale Paoli, the Corsican who had liberated his country from Genoa, only to have it overrun by France. Wilkes and Paoli had never gotten along, and Wilkes was reluctant. Boswell insisted: "I told him," Boswell recorded, "that the General had said, 'I forgive the father for the sake of the daughter.' 'You never told me that before,'" said Wilkes, and he and Polly raised their glasses to General Paoli. "Miss Wilkes," wrote Boswell, "was very polite and agreeable, but spoke indistinctly."[54]

Epilogue

The last fifteen years of Wilkes's life passed pleasantly. He was to die in 1797 at what was then the great age of seventy-one, but until his final illness, he continued to walk the two and a half miles to the chamberlain's house. As a servant to the City that had so long served him, he had repaid the debts he had so rashly accrued as her chief magistrate. Polly was wealthy, the entire Mead-Sherbrooke fortune having fallen to her when her mother died in April of 1784. (For six months Wilkes dutifully wore the black suits required of mourning husbands.) Jackie was in training for a military career, Harriet was bright and full of promise. He was lucky that John Barnard had not raised a stink about his cuckolding him, but Barnard had not, and Wilkes's libertinism was accepted by the public as one of the features one puts up with in a great politician.

In 1791, Polly and her father left Prince's Court, turning the house over to Wilkes's brother Heaton, and moved into a new house in Grosvenor Square at the corner of South Audley Street. Polly had reached the age of thirty-eight unmarried, elegant in her dress and manner, kind to everyone about her, and devoted to her father. Mrs. Marion Hastings wrote to her after she had chatted with Wilkes, "I had the satisfaction and the pleasure to see today the person whom you love above all others the best in this world (and I believe you will in the next)." Polly managed the household, was hostess to numerous guests, and presided at the table. She made frequent visits to France during which she and her father exchanged numerous letters, Wilkes always concerned that she have

the right clothes for her appearances, sending her tea and chocolate; she buying china and prints and sometimes clothing to send him. She read a great deal,
sometimes in French or German or Latin. She pursued her hobby of drawing
and etching, and etched the front windows of the new house in designs of
"eastern subjects in the most beautiful taste," said Henry Angelo.[1] More believing than her father, she regularly worshiped at the lovely little Grosvenor
Chapel that still stands in South Audley Street. Wilkes, still the skeptic but
never willing to deny faith, cheerfully accompanied his daughter.

Wilkes worked much harder than most men of his class, to say nothing of
his age. He took his turns on the bench at the Old Bailey, presided over the
aldermanic courts, administered his ward, and managed the finances of the
City. Inevitably, there were complaints about his management of the chamberlain's office, usually for failing to open his books for inspection; but they
were few, and those few, being investigated, were dismissed. John Almon's
assessment stands: "In these capacities he has not left a rival."[2]

When Boswell was admitted to the English bar and appeared for the first
time before Lord Mansfield and the Court of the King's Bench, he celebrated
by giving a dinner to which Wilkes came. Boswell had long practiced law in
Scotland, but like many another Scottish lawyer, he had looked upon admission to the English bar as the epitome of professional success. He was proud of
the inauguration dinner, which was served in the Inner Temple to men of
distinction, Boswell and Wilkes; Sir Joshua Reynolds, the painter; Edmond
Malone, the Shakespeare scholar; John Courtney, a poet and member for
Tamworth; William Windham, member for Norwich, who was a prizefighter,
a balloonist, and a mathematician; Dr. Richard Brocklesby, Wilkes's friend
from Leiden days who had looked after him when he had been wounded in the
duel and now looked after the king; William Dowdeswell, another Leiden
friend, once the chief strategist for Rockingham; Charles Dilly, the printer and
brother to Edward, at whose house Wilkes and Johnson had met; and Daines
Barrington, master of the bench at the Inner Temple, a naturalist and the first
person to propose a voyage to the North Pole. These ten men of genius consumed that evening twenty-six bottles of claret, eight of port, and four of
Madeira. One can only point out that bottles in that day were smaller than
today's.[3]

Boswell not only admired Wilkes, but made of him a father figure, looking
to him for comfort in adversity. On 15 February 1791, he wrote in his diary, "I
was still sadly ill. I went between three and four and called on Wilkes, who was
not yet come from the City. I said I would look for him, and I luckily spied him
in the Park, walking home. When I joined him . . . he kindly said, 'come along,'
and asked me where I dined today. 'With you,' said I, 'if you'll give me leave.'

He made me very welcome. I told him and Miss Wilkes of my being in bad spirits, and that I wished to try if he could animate me. I soon felt some relief. . . . The perpetual gaiety of Wilkes amazed me. But the inarticulation both of him and his daughter strained my ears."[4]

In 1784, after Wilkes had discharged the debts accrued during his mayoralty, he brought Mildred Arnold and little Harriet from Bath and set them up in a small house in Kensington Gore, a country road west of Westminster running along the south edge of Hyde Park. Though close to the metropolis, it was a healthy place for a child, free of the smog which hung over Westminster and London from thousands of coal fires. Wilkes furnished the house attractively, hanging many prints from his collection and many mirrors, making the small rooms unusually light. There he regularly visited his "dear saucy females." He found nurses and tutors and dancing and drawing masters, determined that Harriet would enter the world as a gentlewoman.

To this cheerful house Wilkes brought his more intimate friends to dine, Milly sitting at table as hostess and pretty little Harriet always putting in a brief appearance. The first time Boswell went there, he recorded in his diary, "His house was all elegance: an exquisite collection both of prints and china, and an extraordinary number of large mirrors. The woman seemed decent enough. A maidservant attended us, and we had a very pretty dinner, with Madeira, mountain, port, and afterwards coffee and gunpowder tea [a green tea]. It was a gay, social scene, but I drank rather too much, and when I got to town, wandered about in the mob . . . and had my pocket picked."[5]

Wilkes and Harriet delighted in each other. The child loved animals, and within the compass of the Kensington Gore house were a dog named Brush, a cat, and numerous birds, including an owl named Peter. When Peter died, Wilkes wrote an epitaph:

> Minerva's bird, poor Peter's dead;
> The gravest form, the gravest head;
> From glare and noise he chose to go
> To quiet in the realms below.

Once Wilkes received a letter from Punch and Judy, the parakeets, who presented their compliments to their Grosvenor Square master and hoped his cold was better; as to their mistress in Kensington Gore, "she is as pert as ever." Harriet, being a normal, lively child, sometimes displeased her father. He once wrote to her mother about her contradicting him before a gathering of Wilkes relatives. "I really thought it the height of insolence from a daughter to a father," but he had to add, "in justice to the mother," that usually Harriet's conduct was "unexceptionable." He thought it might do the child some good to read his letter "more than once." Wilkes took a keen interest in Harriet's education, correcting the errors in her spelling, teaching her grammar, and encouraging her in the study of languages: "Pray send me a fable of Aesop both in English and in French." At fifteen she was fluent in French and on her way toward mastering Italian. There is some indication she had made a visit to France. Wilkes was proud of her and would send her into the world with his own surname. She always called him Papa.[6]

Polly is never known to have expressed disapproval of her father's second family, but she chose to keep apart from them. They sometimes communicated by letter, and once Polly received a present of an engraving of Hygeia made by little Harriet.[7] But not for a minute did the child stand in the way of Wilkes's affection for Polly. Grosvenor Square was home to Wilkes, and its mistress the companion of his life, the person in whom he confided, to whom he turned when ill, whom he loved above any other.

As Polly advanced into middle age, her face grew more and more like that of her father's, and her speech was more and more affected. Boswell spoke of Polly's speech defect in 1786, writing, "I dined with Wilkes and his daughter very pleasantly, only their imperfect articulation made them not easily understood." Polly was no longer the toast of the town, as she had been when lady mayoress. On one occasion, Horace Walpole caught sight of Wilkes and his daughter entering an assembly and with cruel irony parodied St. Paul, "There goes Sin with his daughter Death."[8]

It was different in Paris, where Polly had highly placed friends who valued her for her good mind, her extensive education, and her perfect social manners. Early in 1791, in Paris visiting her friend the Duchess of Châtillon, she saw a copy of Edmund Burke's *Reflections on the Revolution in France* and was touched by a sentimental passage on Queen Marie Antoinette, mortified and threatened by the revolutionaries. The age of chivalry, Burke wrote, was dead. Polly immediately translated the passage into French and gave it to ladies in waiting, who took it to the queen, "who when she had read half the lines, she burst into a flood of tears." This was told to Burke in a letter from Edward Jerningham. As Burke wrote, replying to his friend, he did not think he had done justice to the sad spectacle of greatness oppressed, but one paragraph "had merit when it passed through the hands of so perfect a judge both of French and of English as Miss Wilkes. If what that lady has done should afford a moment's melancholy consolation to illustrious persons sinking under unmerited calamities, I should think myself happy in furnishing the crude materials to her skill."[9]

In 1792, Polly made the acquaintance of Elizabeth Montagu, the celebrated, wealthy bluestocking, who brought her into her London literary salon. The bluestockings were the intellectual and literary women of the time, and Polly, with her excellent education in the classics, her wide reading, her travels, and her mastery of languages, fit in easily.[10]

Jack Smith was ensconced at Dominico Angelo's equestrian academy while Wilkes negotiated a commission for him as a cadet in the East India Company's army. Employees of the company were allowed to engage in business on the side, and everybody knew of vast fortunes made in that way. So off went Jackie to Bengal, certain he too would make a fortune. The last we hear of him are letters complaining of the dreary life of a soldier without a war.[11] Jack is not mentioned in Polly's will of 1802, which suggests he had succumbed to the diseases that killed nearly half the English who went to India.

Catherine Smith, in the far past Wilkes's servant upon whom he had begot Jack Smith, was in London, desperately poor and in failing health. In 1793, she plucked up the courage to write to her old lover to tell him she was ready to "doe my selfe that Secret Pleasure of Weighting on you . . . I hope, Sir, you are well, I am exceeding Poorly My Selfe." Wilkes went to see her, and a certain goodhearted Benjamin Parrin began to call on him every three months to receive a half guinea that he took to Catherine and in turn carried back to Wilkes the letters of thanks to "the only friend I have in the world." In one letter she mentioned a daughter, whom she had not seen in years. Never did she mention her son. The quarterly allowance grew to two guineas, always delivered, as she wrote, "boy Mr. Perren." Once she ventured to say, "That day I had the honor of meeting you I often dremt of you and wist my self young againe." In the summer of 1795, Parrin wrote to tell Wilkes he was no longer in touch with Catherine Smith and supposed she had died during the very severe winter.[12]

Wilkes's mother died in 1781, leaving him her farms at Enfield, Middlesex. Attached to her will was a memorandum of a conversation in which Wilkes had promised his mother to give the revenue of the estates to his brother Heaton since he himself was financially secure through the chamberlainship. Heaton had failed in one business after another. An "unaccountable animal," Wilkes called him. He had not Wilkes's genius for manipulating debt and not infrequently had to leave town to avoid arrest. But ultimately Wilkes stood behind him, and Heaton never went to debtor's prison. Their older brother, Israel, had settled in New York with his son, Charles, an officer of a New York bank.[13]

George Hayley died in 1781, and his wife, Wilkes's eccentric sister Mary, took over the running of his American trade. Never one to turn down an adventure, she did not hesitate, when in doubt about her affairs there, to sail to Boston. In 1786, at the age of fifty-eight and as ugly as her brother (she had but one tooth showing, very brown), she married at Trinity Church in Boston one Captain Patrick Jeffery, a man twenty years her junior. In her passion, she refused to put her wealth in a trust; consequently, all of it passed to her young husband. When she grew unhappy, he put her on an allowance and allowed her to return to England, where she passed the last two decades of her life playing cards at Bath while he purchased the mansion of the last royal governor of Massachusetts, Thomas Hutchinson, and lived there like a king.[14]

In Parliament, Wilkes moved further and further toward the right. Lord Rockingham died in office on 1 July 1782, and the king brought in Lord Shelburne as his first minister. Shelburne, that nobleman whose house was the center for London intellectuals, was a moderate in politics, open to reform, but a meliorist rather than a radical. He disliked the idea of American independence but conceded it could no longer be avoided. Most of the old radicals went into the camp of Charles James Fox and into opposition. Wilkes, though always declaring himself an independent, stayed with Shelburne, a position which put him for the first time on the side of the king's ministers. With Shelburne he began to attend the king's levée and found himself well received. Once the king spoke to him, mentioning Wilkes's friend the late Sergeant Glynn. "My friend, Sir!" Wilkes replied, "He was my counsel (one must have a counsel), but he was no friend; he loved sedition and licentiousness, which I never delighted in. In fact, Sir, he was a Wilkite, which I never was."[15] George III never sat down at his levées because there were so many people at them of whom he disapproved, and the only way to avoid speaking to them was to pass by. His speaking to Wilkes, especially in a light tone, implied that he valued him as a companion or political supporter or, more likely, both.

A few months later, the king summoned Wilkes for a private interview. One would like to know what was said between the monarch, whose health Wilkes at one time could not drink without the help of his daughter, and the man whom the king had once hated more than any other of his subjects. We know nothing, but we may be reminded that Wilkes, the master of polite formal behavior, had once before dazzled the king with his urbanity. No doubt his majesty was pleased. From that point, King George could have had no objection to the way Wilkes voted in the House of Commons. Of course, eyebrows went up among the London livery. When one of them asked Wilkes if he were ever going to return to his old radical politics, he replied, "Not at all. Adversity may be a good thing to breakfast on; nay, a man may dine upon it; but, my good friend, believe me, it makes a confounded bad supper."[16]

Shelburne resigned in 1783, unable to reach an agreement with Parliament about the peace terms with America. The king could not form a government to his liking and reluctantly accepted a coalition ministry of Charles James Fox and, of all people, Lord North. Wilkes, disgusted that a government should be formed by two men who had been such enemies to each other, followed Shelburne into opposition. He made one speech during this period, on 8 December 1783, and that was against Fox's East India Bill. Fox wanted to abolish the semi-independent East India Company and give control of India to a ministerial body of commissioners. Wilkes opposed on the grounds that the vast patronage, amounting to two million pounds, would fall into the hands of ministers and threaten the balance of power between Crown and Parliament.[17] The speech was admired, but primarily in print, for not only did Wilkes slur the words, but his voice had grown weak.

The Fox-North government lasted only a year, and the king brought in as first minister the brilliant, twenty-four-year-old William Pitt, son of Wilkes's old leader. Like his father, young Pitt was an excellent speaker, but he was a loner who would not play factional politics. He kept control of the House of Commons by force of his clear reasoning and keen debating skills, and his ministry was to last seventeen years. Pitt was a reformer of government and thus a natural leader for Wilkes the reformer. But the French Revolution and the resulting wars turned Pitt into a conservative, and this too suited Wilkes's changing temperament. For the remainder of his parliamentary career, Wilkes voted with Pitt.

There was a general election in 1784, and Wilkes barely squeaked in. He went to the Guildhall to hear the sheriffs announce his victory, then to a hurried dinner of celebration at the White Hart in Holborn, and finally to the Cockpit to hear the preliminary reading of the king's speech.

The speech Wilkes thought remarkable, for King George III was vowing he would rule by the Constitution. He was giving up his claim of a right to "prerogative," a right to demand anything from his subjects on the sole ground that he was king, a claim he had struggled to establish from the day he had inherited the crown. Aside from electoral reform, which proposed changes in the law, Wilkes the reformer had asked little in his entire career but that the king, the ministers, the courts of law, and the Parliament exercise the functions of government according to the Constitution, that is, according to law. To be sure, his majesty had not agreed to accept the radicals' interpretation of law, and innumerable contests over law lay ahead.[18] But at long last the "Tory" doctrine of prerogative was dead, and Wilkes could adhere to the Crown with a clear conscience.

But few politicians would allow Wilkes such an easy out. One newspaper ran the following:

What! Liberty-Wilkes, of oppression the hater,
Call'd a turncoat, a Judas, a rogue, and a traitor!
What has made all our patriots so angry and sore?
Has Wilkes done that now which he ne'er did before?

Consistent was John all the days of his life;
For he loved his best friends as he loved his own wife;
In his actions he always kept self in his view,
Though false to the world to John Wilkes he was true![19]

In this Parliament, too, Wilkes made only one speech, and that was in support of Warren Hastings, the governor-general of India, whom Edmund Burke had impeached on grounds of "maladministration, corruption in office, and cruelty towards the people of India." Wilkes lisped out a speech, arguing that Hastings had saved India for Britain during the American war and asserting that he had "laid the foundation for the present prosperous state of India." Wraxall admired this performance: "Wilkes . . . though he already began to feel the infirmities of approaching age, came forward on this occasion. The same unconquered spirit, wit, and classic fire which he displayed on the 30th April 1763 when brought before the Earls of Egremont and Halifax by virtue of a general warrant pervaded every sentence that he uttered. But his articulation, which never had been perfectly distinct even in youth, grew annually more embarrassed from the inroads of time on his organs of speech." Wilkes's motives for supporting Hastings were largely personal. He had no particular love for the man himself, but Hastings's wife and daughters were among Polly's closest friends. The impeachment was to drag on for seven years and terminate in the acquittal of Hastings.[20]

As the general election of 1790 approached, Wilkes announced in the newspapers that he would not campaign, but he would be open for nomination. Alas, it had become all too apparent he was neglecting his obligations in the House of Commons. On 19 March 1790, he had presented a Middlesex petition against Pitt's Tobacco Act; but when the petition came up for debate the next day, he was absent. At the meeting to nominate candidates for knight of the shire for Middlesex, when Wilkes was named, only forty-five hands were raised. He at once withdrew his name and left the hustings without a parting speech. He did, however, take himself to Westminster, where he gave a rousing speech in support of his old enemy, John Horne, who, in defiance of a tradition that clergy could not serve, was standing for that city. Horne lost the election, but he wrote to thank Wilkes: "It was judicious and handsome." Others of the radical element were less kind. The *Gazetteer* of 29 June 1790 ran this letter: "To Mr. Wilkes. You are not compelled to retire into that obscurity to which your subservience to a court which you rose in to notice by insulting, your dereliction of those principles by which you became popular, ought long since to have consigned you. . . . For you, Mr. Wilkes, the language of patriotism and unmeaning promise will no longer pass. . . . We have found your promises to be, as you once were in our esteem, great; and your performance, as you now are, nothing." When friends at the Beef Steaks Club joked about his withdrawal from the election, Wilkes spoke up: "Once I emitted as much flame and fire as the best of you; now you must look upon me as a burnt-out volcano."[21]

Wilkes watched unhappily the events in France following the taking of the Bastille on 14 July 1789. His old friend, the great Baron d'Holbach, had died in January of that very year, and both Voltaire and Diderot were dead. But many others whom he had known in Paris were in danger. As violence escalated, he grew more and more passionate in his disapproval.[22] In August of 1792, Louis XVI was imprisoned. This was followed by a shocking massacre of prisoners, and on 22 September the monarchy was abolished and a republic declared. On 14 December, Wilkes called a meeting of the Ward of Farringdon Without to explain to the livery his position on these developments. His conservatism was transparent in a declaration that might have been made by Samuel Johnson: "Our persons are safe, our property secure, and our commerce most extensively flourishing, especially during the reign of his present Majesty." But Wilkes's concern for people of all classes was also there: "We are governed by wise and equal laws, the same laws for the poor as for the rich, for every subject of the state." Finally, he explained why, throughout his career, he had resisted republicanism and remained a monarchist: "I have spent no small part of my life abroad; in countries where the government depended on the caprice of an individual . . . in a republican government there is a continued struggle who shall be the greatest . . . But here the line is clearly chalked out by law, no subject can with us be so ambitious, or so mad, as to contend for the sovereign power. We are preserved from all those evils which necessarily attend a republican government."[23]

In February 1793, France again declared war on England. The following April, a London mob, attacking what they supposed were the houses of sympathizers with France, mistook Wilkes's house and smashed the beautiful windows upon which Polly had etched her designs. The *Morning Post* reported, "Mr. Wilkes bears the loss of his fine windows with that pleasant humor so peculiar to him, and absolutely refuses to prosecute any of the mob. 'They are only,' he said, 'some of my pupils now set up for themselves.' "[24]

Having retired from the political scene, Wilkes more and more often turned his attention to scholarship. "I have not seen a daily paper since I left the capital," he wrote to Polly, and had instead "confined myself to the ninety-two

volumes of Voltaire, that great store of science, genius, learning, and gaiety."
His commonplace book from this period reveals his wide reading in English,
French, and classical authors. In 1788 appeared an edition of the works of the
racy Roman poet *Caius Valerius Catullus*, edited by John Wilkes. This was not
a translation, but an edition of the original Latin. There was no scholarly
paraphernalia. The book offered nothing but a meticulously rendered Latin
text, not a single misspelled word nor a single misplaced or omitted period.
Only a hundred or so copies were printed, in a small quarto, most of which
Wilkes gave away. It was reviewed favorably in the *Gentleman's Magazine*
and soon gained the reputation of being the most accurate text available. In
1790 appeared his edition of the *Characters* of Theophrastus. Again, this was
not a translation but an immaculate edition of the original Greek. The favorable review in the *Gentleman's Magazine* mentioned that some critics found
fault because there were no accents in the text, but other experts approved
because accents were missing from the most ancient manuscripts. The book
was printed as a small quarto and matched the Catullus. Of the 124 copies,
most were given away.[25] The great care showed by John Nichols in the printing of these books might have had something to do with Wilkes's appointment
of him as deputy alderman for the south half of the Ward of Farringdon
Without.[26]

Wilkes kept up a lively social life in these years. His more intimate friends,
such as Bonell Thornton and Bennet Langton, usually were invited to Kensington Gore, but he entertained his political guests and persons of rank at
Grosvenor Square, with Polly presiding. One finds among his guests colleagues from the House of Commons such as Isaac Barré and Joseph Jekyll; old
friends such as Crisp Molineaux and his family; writers such as Henry Swin-
burne, the traveler; and occasionally a nobleman, Lord Shelburne. As frequently, Wilkes dined out, at least once at Elizabeth Montagu's. He went
regularly to the dinners at the Royal Society, and always to the Beef Steaks
Club.[27]

Mademoiselle d'Eon had returned from France in 1786, and Wilkes was
often in her company. By this time, d'Eon, her pension from Louis XVI cut off,
was making a living by charging admission to the demonstration duels at
Angelo's academy, which she did in a long dress. English high society now
accepted that d'Eon was a woman who had passed as a man in her years as
soldier and diplomat. D'Eon would spend the rest of her life in England, but
not until her death in 1810 was it discovered that she was a man.

More than once Wilkes found himself dining in the company of the young
Prince of Wales. On one such occasion, when it came Wilkes's turn to propose
a toast that everyone supposed would be a lady, he surprised the table by

24. The Assault or Fencing Match . . . on the 9th of April 1787, between Madamoiselle le Chevelier D'Eon de Beaumont and Monsieur de Saint George, in the presence of His Royal Highness the Prince of Wales. V. M. Picot after C. J. Robineau. Courtesy of the Lewis Walpole Library, Yale University.

toasting, "The King, and long may he live." "When did you become so loyal?" exclaimed the heir to the throne, to which Wilkes replied, "Ever since I had the honor of knowing your Royal Highness." King George really liked this story and laughingly told it to Lord Chancellor Eldon.[28]

Wilkes was always a favorite of "the gang," as Boswell called the five brilliant friends who often dined or drank together, Boswell himself, Sir Joshua Reynolds, Edmund Malone, John Courtney, and William Windham. The gang often dined at Kensington Gore, and often they pulled Wilkes out of his evening chair to go drinking with them. Wilkes was so gay and talkative in this company that he sometimes annoyed Malone for keeping him from displaying his own well-known wit. "Mr. Wilkes," said William Rough, "was often too prodigal of wit, and upon all occasions would lose a friend, rather than a jest."

Wilkes did not necessarily need a large company to show off his conversational skills. At the London Tavern, said Boswell, "when Wilkes and I sat together, each glass of wine produced a flash of wit, like gunpowder thrown into the fire. Puff! puff!"[29]

When the first edition of Boswell's *Life of Johnson* came out, a small octavo edition, he presented a copy to Wilkes. Wilkes, not liking it, did not spare his friend: "What a horrid deal of trash you have made the press groan under. If it were possible, you would kill his [Johnson's] reputation. The pocket pistol of your octavo has sorely wounded him. Your blunderbus quarto will be his coup de grace."[30]

As Wilkes got older, many stories grew up about him, most of them alluding to his notorious libertinism. It was said that he was hurrying through the streets toward Kensington when a friend tried to speak to him: "Don't stop me," Wilkes exclaimed; "I have an erection now. Did it go down, I don't know when I shall have another." On another day he told his apothecary, "My sins of omission are daily increasing, and my sins of commission daily diminishing." Yet in 1788, he had an affair of gallantry with a naïve woman, obviously much younger than he, who in her one surviving letter confesses her love for Mr. Wilkes and and asks him to meet her out of town. We know no more. In 1793, when he was sixty-six, he often visited "a juvenile Dulcinea" who lived in Dean Street, named Sally Barry. One newspaper reported, "Alderman Wilkes is finishing his Essay on Woman in the neighborhood of Soho; but it is a weak and miserable performance." Once Wilkes visited the classy brothel of Madame Watson at No. 2, George Street in the Adelphi, though Mrs. Watson was disappointed he did not return for a second visit. Then there was the young woman who wrote to arrange meetings in 1781, who signed herself, "FP," but whose full name, if you can believe it, was Fanny Perfect.[31] Such amours, of course, counted for nothing at Grosvenor Square or Kensington Gore, where Alderman and Chamberlain John Wilkes continued the devoted *paterfamilias*.

Wilkes took as many holidays as his duties permitted. During the period when Milly and Harriet were at Bath, he usually went to that city. There he continued to see Dr. Wilson almost daily. When the old man died without family in 1784, Wilkes and Polly donned mourning black for six months. But the legacies they expected turned out to be worthless. Dr. Wilson had spent or given away the considerable wealth he once had, but in his senility had imagined himself still rich when he really was poor. Wilkes wrote to his daughter, "The doctor left in legacies many thousands more than he was worth." There was not even money to pay the servants their wages, let alone the thousands of pounds he had willed to one friend or another. The will was in Chancery, but

EUROPEAN MAGAZINE.

The COTTAGE of the late JOHN WILKES Esq.*in the* ISLE of WIGHT.

Published by J.Sewell.Cornhill.April 1.st 1798

25. Wilkes's cottage on the Isle of Wight. The Print Collection, Miriam and Ira D. Wallach Division of Art, Prints and Photographs, New York Public Library, Astor, Lenox and Tilden Foundations.

there was no point in trying to sue for what was due them. "You and I shall scarcely seek a remedy by throwing our own guineas after the Doctor's."[32]

After Milly and Harriet were established in Kensington Gore, Wilkes returned to his habit of vacations on the Isle of Wight. He and Polly rented various houses over several years, but in 1788 he found his dream house and promptly purchased the lease. Sandown Cottage stood above the east shore cliffs, close to Sandown Castle but isolated from other houses. On the sea were the white sails of ships out of Portsmouth, and on a clear day one could see Normandy on the horizon. Wilkes thought it the most beautiful vista on the island. The cottage was a small, ivy-covered, two-story house on a four-acre plot, with stables and outbuildings. To reach it, Wilkes would take a sailboat from Portsmouth to Ride, or if there was no wind, he would be rowed across. Two men at the oars could bring a skiff across in an hour. Then Wilkes would mount a Welsh pony and ride some four miles to the cottage. Dalman, the gardener, and his wife, the cook, lived year-round in one of the outbuildings and took care of the place. They kept the dog, Trusty, and looked after the poultry and a small herd of pigs.[33]

Wilkes had been a keen gardener at Prebendal House, and he delighted to use his gardening skills once more. At Sandown Cottage, he did not revert to the squire who simply told the servants what to do, but, donning old clothes, he spread the manure himself. Frederick Reynolds, arriving for a visit, found Wilkes in "Arcadian" dress, hoe in hand, "raking up weeds and destroying vipers." He soon could furnish his table from a kitchen garden and a fishpond. At the center of the garden he set up a shrine to Churchill, an imitation of Petrarch's tomb. He had a Doric column made that seemed to be broken off at a height of nine feet.[34] In the cracks and crevices of the column he induced laurels to grow, and before it he placed the antique urn given him by the Abbé Winckelmann, now inscribed to the memory of Churchill.

In their years of coming to the island, Wilkes and Polly had gotten to know many local gentry, and London friends came there regularly. To prepare for a lively social life, Wilkes erected in front of the cottage, a short way down the hill, two permanent tents of heavy canvas in which he entertained. In the larger, some twenty-five feet long and beautifully furnished, he set up a plaque, "To Filial Piety / and / Mary Wilkes / erected by John Wilkes / MDCCLXXXIX." The smaller tent, which he called his Tuscan Room, was painted white on the inside, and on the heavy canvas walls he hung many prints from his collection.[35]

Polly came often to the cottage but never stayed there without her father. Refined lady that she was, she enjoyed the garden enormously but never touched a trowel. It was about the garden that Wilkes usually wrote when she was away: "We have violets, primroses, and cowslips in great abundance, and our peach, apple, and apricot trees are in full bloom and perfume the air."[36]

It was a different story with Milly, who had grown up on a farm and had, said Wilkes, "more taste and understanding in gardening" than Dalman, the gardener. Milly entered wholeheartedly into the maintenance and management of Sandown Cottage, and Wilkes often left her and Harriet there for months at a time. "I hope my dear females," he wrote, "had a cheerful and gay fair at Shanklin and have got a fairing for the garden. I suspect there is a little gosling who eats ten times more of my strawberries than any six pigeons, but she is heartily welcome. . . . Remember me most tenderly to the sweet little girl, but you cannot tell her how much I love her, although she is almost as saucy as her Mama."

Before many seasons had passed, he could sit on a bench overlooking the bay with Harriet, in her teens, reading beside him. In the last autumn of his life, sitting on that bench, Wilkes composed a birthday ode for his eighteen-year-old daughter:

> Minerva's self at Harriet's birth
> Forsook the skies to visit earth;
> And with the grave and stately dame,

QUONDAM
A FRIEND TO LIBERTYNISM
"So politic as if one Eye
Upon the Other were a Spy

26. Wilkes trudges home from work during the last year of his life. Anonymous etching. The obelisk announces that Blackfriars Bridge was completed during his mayoralty. Whereabouts unknown; formerly in the collection of Horace Bleackley.

The laughter-loving Venus came.
The graces too were in her Train,
Nor did a Muse in Heaven remain.
Cupid, and he alone, still coy,
Appears a pouting, angry boy:
The nymph derides his power supreme,
And darts and arrows calls a dream.
Beware, proud girl — the boy, in rage,
Not all thy magic can assuage;
Vain all thy prayers, vain all thy art —
Then nought can sooth him but thine heart.[37]

Wilkes had enjoyed Sandown Cottage for eleven years when he wrote the poem. He was never to see either of his daughters married.

In London Wilkes continued to walk four or five days a week back and forth between Grosvenor Square and the chamberlain's house, or on some mornings from Kensington Gore to the chamberlain's house, usually arriving before seven. He became a familiar figure to the shopkeepers and street folk, trudging along, tall but agile, said a contemporary, "so very thin . . . that his limbs seemed cadaverous." His face grew more grotesque, with what Burke called his "pursed mouth" tucked between his nose and his collapsing jaw. He liked to tell the story of the keeper of a lottery office in the town of Shanklin on the Isle of Wight who offered him ten guineas not to pass his window while he was selling tickets because the customers thought the evil eye would bring them bad luck.

Toward the end Wilkes grew careless of his dress, appearing on the street in his favorite coat, the red coat of his militia uniform, now faded and threadbare, a white cloth waistcoat, and breeches tucked into military boots. He continued to wear his tricornered, cocked hat, though it had long gone out of fashion.[38] These details show in an unkind print of him trudging home after work, printed during the last year of his life (illustration 26).

By the time Wilkes reached his seventy-first birthday, on 17 October 1797, his frame had begun to waste away at an alarming rate. On the 16 December he managed to get to the meeting of the Scotch Society, where "he bore his part in the pleasantries of the day with his usual wit and good humor." A few days later he was unable to rise from his bed.[39] He lay in the Grosvenor Square house, lovingly nursed by Polly, but he grew weaker and weaker. They managed a feeble celebration of Christmas. On the following day, sensing the approach of death, he called to Polly for something to drink, held up the glass and toasted "My beloved and excellent daughter." He handed her the glass, closed his eyes, and after a short time died.[40]

Only the most intimate friends were invited to the funeral. The procession consisted of the hearse, three mourning coaches, and Polly's carriage. As Wilkes had directed in his will, six of the poorest men of the parish carried the coffin, for which they received a suit of course brown cloth and a guinea. The procession had but a few hundred yards to go, for the Grosvenor Chapel was not far down South Audley Street. There the body was placed in the crypt, which is under the street. A plaque was mounted on the wall at the northeast corner of the gallery, where it still may be seen:

Near this place is interred
The remains
of
John Wilkes
A Friend of Liberty

Obituaries appeared in the papers. That in the *Times* complimented Wilkes's exemplary service as alderman and chamberlain and acknowledged that his "exertions and intrepidity added legal security to the liberties of Englishmen."[41]

The will directed that all accounts with the City of London be adjusted and the money due to the City be paid. All debts were to be discharged. To Mrs. Amelia Arnold, he willed the lease of the house at Kensington Gore No. 2 with all the furnishings, the cash in the house, and one thousand pounds. To Harriet Wilkes went Sandown Cottage, all the furnishings, and two thousand pounds. The lease of the house in Grosvenor Square and all the furnishings and contents were willed to Polly, who was also named as residuary legatee. John Smith, an officer in the service of the East India Company, was to receive one hundred pounds. Various smaller sums were willed to the men with whom he had worked in the chamberlain's office, and five guineas each to the servants.[42]

Most gentlemen in that age who held offices such as the chamberlainship of the City, died wealthy. The most convincing proof of Wilkes's honesty is that he died poor. His executors could not find enough to meet all of the bequests.

Polly died at Grosvenor Square on 12 March 1802, at the age of fifty-one. Feeling unwell, she had excused herself from a large party and gone to her house and to bed at one in the morning. She rang for help five minutes later; the servants called a doctor, but she was dying when he arrived. Six weeks later, on 25 April, Milly Arnold died at the Kensington Gore house.[43] Both women had been looking forward to the wedding of Harriet, which took place two months after her mother's death.

Polly left a will designed in part to carry out those bequests of her father's will that could not be made, in part to pay off her father's remaining debts.

There were legacies for some forty named individuals — her servants and servants of her late parents and grandparents, her father's old assistants at the chamberlain's bureau, her lawyers, her close friends in London and Paris, numerous cousins, with certain sums designated for the support of her aged uncles. She left moderate fortunes to Harriet and her mother and willed to Harriet their father's gold watch. The bulk of her fortune she left to the church to be used for charitable purposes.[44]

While Harriet was yet a girl, she acquired the surname of Wilkes. She married William Rough, a struggling poet who at Cambridge had been in the literary society of Coleridge and Christopher Wordsworth, the poet's brother, and was a particular friend of the poet Walter Savage Landor.[45] Forced by financial considerations to the study of law, he was called to the bar in 1801. The next year he married Harriet, who was twenty-three years old. It was a marriage of love. Harriet was accepted by her husband's friends and was described by Henry Crabb Robinson, the diarist of that circle, as "a woman of some talents and taste, who could make herself attractive." In 1816, Rough published *Poems, Miscellaneous and Fugitive, now first Collected by the Author on His Preparing to Leave England*. In the front flyleaf of the copy at Columbia University is a penned note in Rough's hand:

> W.R.:
>   To his dear wife Harriet, trusting, in spite of Indolence, that, for her sake, he may yet leave behind him something more worthy to be holden in remembrance than these trifles.
>   June, 1818

Rough had accepted an appointment as a judge at Demerara and Essequibo, towns in Guyana.

Harriet died at Demerara in 1820, aged forty-two, the victim of a tropical fever, as was the small girl named Mary, buried with her. She was survived by her husband and four other children.[46] William was recalled to England and after a period of financial struggle obtained a judgeship in Ceylon. In 1836, he was named chief justice of the Supreme Court of Ceylon. He was knighted in 1837 and died the following year.

27. Harriet Wilkes, soon after her marriage to William Rough. In a private collection.

Nathaniel Wraxall, who for ten years sat opposite Wilkes in the House of Commons and whose authority on Parliament and its members is acknowledged by all historians, wrote about his late colleague, the knight of the shire for Middlesex,[47]

> He was an incomparable comedian in all he said or did, and he seemed to consider human life itself as a mere comedy. In the House of Commons he was not less an actor than at the Mansion House or Guildhall. His speeches were full of wit, pleasantry, and point, yet nervous, spirited, and not at all defective in argument. . . . If any man ever was pleasing who squinted, who had lost his teeth, and lisped, Wilkes might be so esteemed. His powers of conversation survived his other bodily faculties. I have dined in company with him not long before his decease, when he was extenuated and enfeebled to a great degree, but his tongue retained all its former activity, and seemed to have outlived his other organs. Even in corporeal ruin , and obviously approaching the termination of his career, he formed the charm of the assembly. His celebrity, his courage, his imprisonment, his outlawry, his duels, his intrepid resistance to ministerial and royal persecution, his writings, his adventures, lastly, his triumphant and serene evening of life, passed in tranquillity amidst all the enjoyments of which his decaying frame was susceptible, for to the last hour of his existence he continued a votary to pleasure, — these circumstances combined in his person rendered him the most interesting individual of the age in which he lived.

An Afterword

I have written this book for a general audience of well-read, intelligent people. I hope scholars will approve of it, but I did not have them in mind as I wrote. I seldom say "it seems" or "the evidence suggests," and I seldom call attention to the quality of the evidence. On the other hand, the notes, which will be of little help to the general reader, are made for the scholar. My view of Wilkes is so different from that usually held by historians, it will certainly be challenged. I want the challengers to have no doubt of the primary evidence I have used, or from what secondary sources I have taken facts.

To students of eighteenth-century literature who are familiar with my work on Laurence Sterne, I have a special word. I wrote the Sterne volumes trying to live up to an ideal expressed by Frederick Pottle: a definitive biography, said Pottle, uses *all* the known primary evidences. No doubt, I failed in the Sterne biography to attain Pottle's ideal. Here, I did not try. I have been tracking John Wilkes for fifteen years, but the volume of material on him is huge, and the number of years left to me are few. Others are welcome to write the definitive biography.

Although most of my story is founded upon primary evidence, I could not have completed it in the year 2004 without consulting the biographies of John Almon, who was a contemporary of Wilkes, William Rough, who never met him but married his daughter Harriet, Percy Fitzgerald, who wrote in the nineteenth century, William Purdie Treloar and Horace Bleackley, who wrote in the first quarter of the twentieth century, Charles Chenevix Trench, who wrote in the third quarter, and Peter D. G. Thomas, who is alive and well and living in Wales. I am grateful to all of them.

I have taken liberties with quotations that I would not have taken in a work written for scholars. I have modernized the spelling, punctuation, and italicization. Pottle-like, I have sometimes turned Boswell's notes into full sentences. In a few cases I have followed the eighteenth-century practice of changing punctuation, articles and the tenses of verbs to make a quotation fit neatly into the narrative, but I have been careful not to change the substance.

I am grateful to the late Sir Francis Dashwood, who kindly allowed me to rifle his study for information about the hellfire club. I am especially grateful for the assistance of Wilkes's descendants, David Alexander, the York art historian, his late uncle, Lieutenant Colonel W. G. Sedgwick-Rough, OBD, and Roger Sedgwick-Rough. I am deeply endebted to Professor Joel Gold, who generously gave me notes, transcripts, and microfilms of Wilkes letters. For reading and commenting upon earlier drafts of this work, I thank my daughter Anna Mirer and my friend Gerald Goldberg. Gerald Goldberg generously allowed me access to his collection of books, letters, and prints, primarily related to Samuel Johnson, but secondarily to Wilkes. I thank John Sainsbury for his help.

I wish to acknowledge the generous support of my colleagues in the Columbia Faculty Seminar in Eighteenth-century European Culture, most especially Professors Betty Rizzo, Randolph Trumbach, Marlies Dansinger, John Middendorf, Dustin Griffin, Richard Quaintance, Elizabeth Denlinger, James Basker, and Paul Korshin. I am grateful for the help given me by Edith Hazen, Dr. W. Otterspeer, Melvyn New, Barbara Schnorrenberg, Kappa Waugh, Donald D'Elia, Antonia Forster, Ruthe Battesten, James Mosley, David Plante, Martha Hamilton-Phillips, and the late Kenneth Monkman. I am grateful for the help I have received from librarians and archivists at Butler Library of Columbia University, the Wollman Library of Barnard College, the Grollier Club, the City of London Guildhall Library, the British Library, the National Portrait Gallery, the Historisch Museum of the University of Leiden, the archives of the Royal Society, the Morris Library of Southern Illinois University at Carbondale, the Farley Library of Wilkes University, the Clement Library at the University of Michigan, and the Houghton Library at Harvard University.

Finally and most importantly, I thank my wife, Mary Gordon, for the generous, unstinting support of my scholarly endeavors throughout the twenty-five years of our marriage.

Notes

Abbreviations

Printed books on the abbreviations list are also listed in Books and Articles Cited, with full bibliographical information.

Add Mss   Additional Manuscripts at the British Library

Autobiography   Wilkes's manuscript autobiography, Add Mss 30,865A. For published editions, see below under Wilkes, *John Wilkes Patriot*

BL   British Library

Bon Mots   "Anecdotes, Bon Mots, &c. &c. of the Late Alderman Wilkes," an obituary in the *European Magazine*, xxxiii (April 1798), pp. 225–30

Controversial Letters   Published letters and papers from the Wilkes-Horne paper war

Diary   Wilkes's manuscript diary, Add Mss 30,866

DNB   Dictionary of National Biography

Guildhall   Manuscript papers at the Library of the City of London, commonly called the Guildhall Library

Letters to His Daughter   William Rough edition of letters to Mary Wilkes, commonly called Polly, 1805

Minority notes   Marginal notes by Wilkes in the BL copy of Almon, *History of the Late Minority*

Namier and Brooke   Sir Lewis Namier and John Brooke, *House of Commons, 1754–1790*

Webb's Calendar   MS calendar by Philip Cartert Webb of events related to Wilkes's trials. Guildhall 214/3. ff. 252–53

Wilkes-Churchill Correspondence   Edward Weatherly edition, 1954
Wilkes Papers   Manuscript letters and papers at the Clements Library, University of Michigan

Prologue

1. *A Letter from Scots Sawney the Barber to Mr. Wilkes, an English Parliamenter,* 1763, as quoted by West, "Wilkes's Squint."
2. Though often repeated or copied, the dictum may not be apocryphal: a writer for the *Edinburgh Review,* 70 (October 1839–January 1840), 106, asserted that he himself heard of the witticism "from one who was present when the dialogue took place."
3. 395 U.S. [1969], 486–574, p. 531.
4. Add Mss 30,877, f. 34; Pitt, *Correspondence,* iv, 122–23.

Chapter 1. The Making of a Gentleman

1. Autobiography. There is nothing certain about the family history; see the discussion in Bleackley, *Life of Wilkes.*
2. Wilkes Papers, i, 25–25a. See also the excerpt from the will of Mary Heaton Wilkes in *Public Advertiser,* 29 January 1781.
3. Autobiography; letters of Israel Wilkes to and from Matthew Leeson, Wilkes Papers i:4–5; AB (probably John Almon) in *Political Register* for 1767, ii, pp. 409–11; Letters to His Daughter, i, 11–12; *Gentleman's Magazine,* lxviii (1798), pt. I, pp. 77, 126; Pinks and Wood. The *Gentleman's Magazine* has a piece signed Philalethes submitted by a Presbyterian minister formerly pastor to the congregation in Southwood Lane, Highgate. He had been told by older parishioners that Israel Wilkes worshiped there regularly, arriving in a coach and six. The story is not unlikely if one is talking about occasional visits, but I am in considerable doubt that his worship there was regular. A few records of the holdings of Israel Wilkes are at the Greater London Record Office, BRA/437/4. At one point, Israel owned a sizable parcel of land on the east side of the City, in Babbleford, which for reasons unknown he deeded to his nephew. It seems unlikely that anyone will ever trace the ins and outs of Israel Wilkes's fortune, but it is certain it was large.
4. Wilkes Papers, i, 2.
5. Sarah and Isreal Wilkes had six children; John was the third child and the second son: Sherston Baker, "Genealogical Table of the Family of Wilkes," appendix to Bleackley, *Life of Wilkes.*
6. No birth record of any Wilkes child can be found in the baptismal records of St. John the Baptist Clerkenwell or nearby St. James's (to which St. John's was a chapel) now housed at the Greater London Record Office. Wilkes's mother is known to have attended Carter Lane Chapel, of which some parish registers are at the Public Record Office, but those for the relevant years have been lost. Librarians use the birthyear 1727 because Wilkes himself gave it in his autobiography. He had originally put another date but rubbed out the last number and substituted "7": Add Mss 30,865A. Wilkes seems to have wanted people to think he was younger than he was, probably because he wanted the world to know he was a minor when he married. Virtually every record that is traceable

to his own word gives the year 1727. The celebrated Abbé Winckelmann, for instance, secretary of the Vatican and superintendent of Roman antiquities, who knew Wilkes in Rome, had a medal struck in his honor, which gives the date of birth as 1727: *Political Register*, iii, 119. The memorial tablet in the Grosvenor Chapel says 1727. John Almon, Wilkes's earliest biographer, at first said he was born in 1727 (Almon, *Correspondence*, i, 8), but later said he was twenty-one at the time of his marriage, which would make the birth year 1725 (i, 19). Horace Bleackley, whose account of the family in *Life of Wilkes* is the most authoritative, includes a genealogical table worked out by Sir George Sherston Baker, which gives the birth as 17 October 1725 and that of Heaton Wilkes, a younger brother, as 9 February 1727. Bleackley also has an excellent appendix on Wilkes's birth-date, in which he points to an account in the *Public Advertiser* of a Wilkes birthday celebration that places Wilkes's birth in 1725. Actually, there are accounts of three such celebrations on 28 October reported in the *Public Advertiser* for 30 October, 3 November, and 7 November. A sketch of Wilkes's life in the *Annual Register*, 1797, pt. 2, pp. 369–78, gives the birth year as 1725. When Wilkes was enrolled at the University of Leiden on 8 September 1744, his age was put down as twenty-two, but this is certainly a clerical error, for it would place Wilkes's birth in 1721, which is quite out of the question: University Library, Leiden, ASF 14, p. 317. Alexander Carlyle, who knew him at Leiden, said he was eighteen, which would place the birth in 1727: Carlyle, *Autobiography*, 87. Bleackley takes as the most authentic document the license of marriage granted at the bishop of London's office, which states that at the time of his marriage on 17 May 1747 he was twenty-one—which would imply a birth year of 1725. But I am not sure that record is more reliable than the announcement of the sale of the Aylesbury estate in 1764, which states that Wilkes was born in 1726, his wife in 1715: Hanley, *Prebendal*, 7. This welter of evidence must leave one in doubt. Nevertheless, I think Wilkes was born in 1726 and was therefore a minor when he married.

7. Finsbury Library: *Clerkenwell Poor Rate Books, 1723–50, f/6, 1750*, ff. 54–55; Cromwell, *Clerkenwell*, 151; Pinks and Wood, *Clerkenwell*, 314 and passim; information supplied by the Museum of the Order of St. John of the Cross at the gatehouse. On Garrick: Clifford, *Young Sam Johnson*, 244. The gatehouse and the church, which was badly damaged by bombs in World War II, are now owned by the charitable Order of St. John of the Cross.

8. Autobiography; Bleackley, *Life of Wilkes*, 8; Worsley to Wilkes, Add Mss 30,867, f. 4; McCracken, "John Wilkes, Humanist."

9. Wilkes Papers, i, 4; Autobiography.

10. Letters from Leeson to Sarah Wilkes bespeak their friendship and her interest in the move to Aylesbury: Wilkes Papers, i, ff. 1, 3, 6; photograph of the house on Parson's Fee in Viney and Nightengale, *Old Aylesbury*.

11. Dated, Aylesbury, 22 January 1744, Columbia University Manuscript Collection, Gen. Ms. Coll/ALS.

12. Hanley, *Prebendal*, 40; Almon, *Correspondence*, i, 11; Wilkes, *Life and Political Writings*, 2.

13. Wilkes Papers i, 2. *Records of the Honorable Society of Lincoln's Inn*, i (1896), 425.

14. University Library, Leiden, ASF 14, p. 317.

15. Wilkes Papers, i, 12.

16. Boswell, *Life,* iii, 183.

17. Carlyle, *Autobiography.* This and subsequent quotations of Carlyle from pp. 136–40.

18. During the early months of the *North Briton,* Townshend was secretary at war in the Bute ministry. This would seem to have made him a target for Wilkes's satire, but no; instead of attacking him, Wilkes praised him in the *North Briton.* I speculate below that Townshend might have been Wilkes's spy in the ministry.

19. Boswell, *Grand Tour,* 53–54.

20. Baxter, *Enquiry,* iii. At the BL there are seventeen letters From Baxter to Wilkes, Add Mss 30,867, ff. 7–40. References to Baxter's letters are to this collection. Only one has been printed, by Wilkes himself, *A Letter from Andrew Baxter,* 1753, discussed below.

21. Sir Leslie Stephens's article in DNB.

22. Republished in *Gentleman's Magazine,* lxviii, 124–26, prefixed by a letter saying that Wilkes had published the letter because it had appeared in a "mutilated" form in a Scottish magazine, and he wanted the correct text to be made public. I am in some doubt, for I suspect the prefatory letter was propaganda aimed against the Scots written by Wilkes.

23. No letters from Wilkes to d'Holbach survive. At least nine autograph letters from d'Holbach to Wilkes at the BL, Add Mss 30,867, ff. 7–40. Eight were published by Sauter and Loos, *D'Holbach.*

24. Boswell, *Grand Tour,* 55; Arthur Wilson, *Diderot,* 176. According to George Rousseau, Wilkes's relationships with Baxter and d'Holbach had a homosexual basis. I have found fault with his use of evidence and his argument, concluding that there are no grounds for holding that Wilkes, Baxter, or d'Holbach were attracted to each other sexually or engaged in homosexual liaisons: Cash, "Wilkes, Baxter, and D'Holbach." Support for my argument has been given by Robin Dix.

25. Add Mss 30,867, ff. 18–19.

26. Broadley, *Brother John Wilkes.*

27. Almon, *Correspondence,* i, 12.

28. Boswell, *Grand Tour,* 55. I have made use of the expansion on Boswell's lines by Pottle, *James Boswell,* 208.

Chapter 2. The Squire of Aylesbury

1. Letters to His Daughter, ii, 42–44.

2. Almon *Correspondence,* i, 19–20.

3. Wilkes Papers, i, 14; parish registers of St. John the Baptist, Clerkenwell, the copy at the Order of St. John Museum at the Gatehouse. They were married by license by Edmund Warnerford, 23 May 1745. Mary is recorded as being of St. Sepulchre's parish and John of St. James's, Clerkenwell. St. John's was no longer parochial, its parish having been absorbed into that of St. James's.

4. Add Mss 30,880B, f. 71; Almon, *Correspondence,* i, 22–23. In the Autobiography, he said that Mary was ten years his elder.

5. Almond's description, Letter signed AB [Almon], *Political Register,* ii, 415–16. The stories about the calf's head and the gossiping women were told by Elizabeth Smart Le Noir, the daughter of Christopher Smart the poet, to Cuthbert Sharp, 22 August 1831, both passed on by a Mrs. Fleming. The letter was edited by Arthur Sherbo for *Durham University Journal,* June 1965. Wilkes's annual income is stated in the advertisement in the *Daily Advertiser,* 30 May 1764, when his lands were put up for sale. For location of the house, Wheatley, *London,* iii, 155. Red Lyon Court is no longer there, but the house may be one of those that border the little garden on the north side of the church.

6. Hanley, *Prebendal,* 41; Dell, "Political Agent." The settlement itself is at the Buckinghamshire Record Office, 3/D/DU, number 138.

7. Birth recorded in the registers of Carter Lane Chapel, Blackfriars, PRO RG.4/4231. Boswell, *English Experiment,* 33–34, alludes to the disfigurement. Her portraits show her with brown eyes.

8. Hanley, *Prebendal,* 41.

9. Trevelyan, *Raleigh.*

10. Keir, *Constitutional History,* 292.

11. Hanley, *Prebendal,* 42; Keir, *Constitutional History,* 31.

12. Wilkes Papers, i, 31–34.

13. Wilkes Papers, vi, 54; Hanley, *Prebendal,* 31–32; Bleackley, *Life of Wilkes,* 20–21; Boswell, *Grand Tour,* 56. I have translated the Latin on the monument, which is, "Illum etiam lauri illum etiam flevere myricae." A sketch of the monument is in Bleackley, opposite p. 20.

14. Brewster to Wilkes: Add Mss 30,867, f. 87. Wilkes's reading habit: Armstrong, "A Day." His libraries: *A Catalogue of the Very Valuable Library of John Wilkes, Esq.,* auctioned by Samuel Baker, 3 May 1764; *Catalogue of the Very Valuable Library of the Late John Wilkes, Esq., M.P., Alderman and Chamberlain of the City of London,* auctioned by Leigh, Sotheby, and Son, 29 November 1802. There is yet a third catalogue, but I have not seen it: noticed in *List of Catalogues of English Book Sales, 1676–1900 now at the British Museum,* 1915; listed under date of 27 May 1799 and called "Part of a Library of John Wilkes," sold by Leigh and Sotheby.

15. Died in January 1755: Wilkes Papers, i, 23v.

16. They never arrived (Edwards to Wilkes, 27 November 1747), but other oyster shipments made it (26 December 1748): Bodleian Library, Mss Bode 1011.

17. Edwards is noticed in the DNB. His letters to Wilkes are badly water damaged: Add Mss 30,867, ff. 16, 25, 28–38, 47, 68.

18. John Willes's letters to Wilkes: Add Mss 30,876, ff. 145–47; 30867, ff. 44, 46, 69, 73, 93.

19. Letters from Brewster, badly water damaged, at Add Mss 30,867, ff. 49–119, passim; *English Liberty,* 353–57; Almon, *Correspondence,* i, 40–45.

20. On the back flyleaf of Wilkes's copy of the first edition of his octavo *North Briton* at the BL, Wilkes has copied a bawdy comic passage from *Tristram Shandy* as a note to vol. i, p. 195: "My sister, mayhap," quoth my uncle Toby, "does not choose to let a man come so near her ****." Make this a dash, —— 'tis an Aposiopesis. —— Take the dash away, and write *Backside,* —— 'tis Bawdy. —— Scratch Backside out, and put Cover'd-way in, —— 'tis a Metaphor; —— and I dare say, as fortification ran so much in my uncle Toby's head, that

if he had been left to have added one word to the sentence, — that word was it" (volume ii, chapter 7). My quotation of Armstrong's opinion of *Tristram Shandy* from Knapp, "Dr. John Armstrong."

21. There are numerous letters of Armstrong to Wilkes in Add Mss 30,867 and 30,875. The best biographical study is Knapp, "Dr. John Armstrong."

22. Smollett, *Letters,* 79. The first meeting of Wilkes and Smollett: Add Mss 30,875, ff. 13, 28–30; the friendship with Nesbitt: Knapp, *Tobias Smollett,* 168.

23. Add Mss 30,867, f. 93.

24. Add Mss 30,875, f. 6.

25. Add Mss 30,867, f. 93; 30,875, f. 6; Wilkes Papers, iv, f. 3.

26. She is mentioned in at least three extant letters: Add Mss 30,867, ff. 111–12, 113–14; 30,875, f. 17. Knapp in "Dr. John Armstrong," p. 1032, speaks of these scraps of evidences around the figure of Peggy.

27. Issue of 18 April 1764; Bredvold, *Contributions to the Gazette.*

28. Boswell, *Life of Johnson,* i, 300. A draft of Wilkes's letter in his mother's hand in Wilkes Papers, i, 32. Wilkes's criticism must have seemed entirely justified to his contemporaries, but it is not acute enough to stand in the light of twentieth-century linguistics. It is clear from Johnson's full remarks that he is thinking in phonetic terms, whereas Wilkes was concerned only with the printed word. His example, for instance of dis-honorable, is not really the sort of word that Johnson had in mind because the "h" is silent. Moreover, Wilkes had not read or perhaps willfully passed over Johnson's more accurate comment upon the uses of "h" in the *Dictionary* entry for the letter: "The h in English is scarcely ever mute at the beginning of the word, or where it immediately precedes a vowel: as house, behavior." *Behavior* was one of the words Wilkes had cited to prove Johnson wrong: Mugglestone, "The Use of /h/. . . ." Wilkes's authorship is attested by Almon, *Correspondence,* i, 47, n. A copy of Wilkes's letter "to the printer" is among the Wilkes Papers, i, 32. It does not name the *Public Advertiser,* but Wilkes's signature is copied at the close; it may, however, have been copied from the broadside described below. Boswell said the piece was published in the *Public Advertiser,* but so far no one has been able to find it there: see Liebert, *Bear and Phoenix.* Perhaps it was another newspaper. In any event, it was reprinted as a broadside, "To the PRINTER," prefaced with the explanation, "We are desired by many of our Readers to re-print the following LETTER" (I use the facsimile in Liebert). In this form it would have gotten a wide circulation, sold out of numerous Fleet-street shops. But it was not usual for newspapers to do such reprinting. One suspects that Wilkes himself arranged it. True, an extant manuscript among the Wilkes Papers is not in Wilkes's hand. See Gold, "John Wilkes and 'Pensioner Johnson."

29. He was elected in April and admitted as a fellow the next month: Royal Society archives, Certificate of Election, I.354, f. 385; Journal Book Copy, vol. xx, 1748/9, 12 January, f. 36, 13 April, f. 96, and 4 May, f. 106. For Dr. Mead's place in the Mead family, see the genealogy in Hanley, *Prebendal,* 39.

30. *Tristram Shandy,* I, vii; Cash, *Sterne: Early and Middle Years,* 295 and n. 2.

31. Arnold, *Beef Steaks;* Boswell, *London Journal,* 51–52. Two lists of members with dates of their induction and a list of club rules among Wilkes's papers suggest he might have served for a time as the club secretary: Add Mss 30,891.

32. Hart, *Wilkes and the Foundling Hospital.*

33. Hart, *Wilkes and the Foundling Hospital.* The author is unknown. I will take up later the vexed history of Wilkes's service as a governor of the Foundling Hospital.

34. Ronald Paulson, *Hogarth,* ii, 318–23, 456, n. 44.

35. Brooke, *George III,* 145; Green, *Visits to Bath,* 4.

36. Wilkes Papers vi, 42.

37. Keir, *Constitutional History,* 302. Hart forgives Wilkes for what he calls embezzlement because he so admires what Wilkes accomplished in the areas of political and civil liberties. See also Nichols and Wray, *Foundling Hospital,* 299–301.

38. Letters to His Daughter, ii, 217, n.

39. Pugh was also absentee vicar of Tattenhoe in Bedfordshire: *Victoria County History of Buckinghamshire,* iii, the article on schools. The petition, ibid., ii, 548–49. The payment of the debt: Wilkes Papers ii, 50; Almon, *Correspondence,* iv, 10–11, and note.

40. Add Mss 30,867, f. 65, 95. Potter is noticed in Namier and Brooke and DNB. His letters may be found in Nichols, *Illustrations,* iii, 687–90, and iv, 333–45; Add Mss 30,867, ff. 50–137 *passim,* and 30,876, 12–14.

41. Almon, *Correspondence,* i, 18; Add Mss 30,867, f. 62; 30,880B, f. 1.

42. Add Mss 30,880B, f. 3.

43. I have told the story in the Historical Introduction to Cash, *Essay on Woman,* and so shall not repeat it here.

44. Dashwood, *Dashwoods of Wycomb,* 225. For information about the club, I am much indebted to the late Sir Francis Dashwood, who was the outstanding authority on the membership, buildings, and activities of the club. Sir Francis kindly shared his information with me in two visits. I am also indebted to several other sources: Geoffrey Ashe, *Do What You Will,* an excellent book, unfortunately not documented, which gives an unusually good explanation of the politics of the club; Almon, *Correspondence,* iii, 6 ff.; Paul Whitehead, *Poems and Miscellaneous Compositions; Nocturnal Revels,* said to have been written by Agnes Perrault; Thomas Langley, *History of Desborough,* 335 ff.; Louis Clark Jones, *Clubs of the Georgian Rakes,* chap. vi; and Trumbach, *Gender Revolution.* Ronald Fuller, *Hell-fire Francis,* 1939, and Donald McCormick, *The Hell-fire Club,* 1958, should be used with caution.

45. Walpole, *Correspondence,* xviii, 211.

46. Robert Darnton, "Sex for Thought." Dr. Armstrong's assessment of hell-fire religion, Add Mss 30,867, f. 165–68. Trumbach, *Gender Revolution,* makes a convincing case that English libertines had a naturalistic philosophy influenced by Lord Shaftesbury.

47. Wraxall, *Posthumous Memoirs,* i, 399. On Sandwich's mismanagement of the navy, see DNB. Rogers, *Insatiable Earl,* calls the DNB article "extremely hostile," but the case he makes for Sandwich is not convincing. According to Albemarle (*Rockingham,* 361–63), who ought to have known, when France went public with its support of the American Revolution and in 1778 declared war on England, it had a fleet of thirty-two ships in the channel and the Atlantic. Sandwich declared he had forty-five ships of the line ready and would have ninety by end of year, but when Admiral Kepple went to Portsmouth on 20 March, he found six ships, too few sailors to sail them, and not enough stores to supply them. See also Walpole, *Last Journals,* ii, 124.

48. One picture was painted by Dance, one by Carpentiers, one by Knapton, and one by Hogarth.

49. As quoted by Dashwood, *Dashwoods,* 36. Hall to Wilkes, 31 August 1761, copy at West Wycombe House.

50. *Town and Country Magazine,* May 1769, pp. 122–23, exemplifies the current rumors. A more critical account in Perrault(?), *Nocturnal Revels,* 1779. The information about Sir Francis's illegitimate children in Dashwood, *Dashwoods.* The most reliable evidence of sexual activity at Medmenham is that of Walpole, *Country Seats,* 50–51. Other evidence is slight. Dr. John Armstrong in one letter speaks of "the sisters" at the club: Add Mss 30,867, f. 165; and Churchill in his poem *The Candidate,* lines 695–98, wrote, "Whilst Womanhood, in habit of a Nun, / At M[edmenham] lies, by backward Monks undone." Betty Kemp, *Dashwood,* 130–36, thinks there was never a hell-fire club: She argues that Medmenham Abbey was a private amusement park or country club, that the reputation for devilish activities and orgies arose from highly unreliable sources, a popular romance by Charles Johnstone called *Chrysal, or the Adventures of a Guinea,* the poems of Churchill, Wilkes's comments thereon, and articles in the *Town and Country Magazine.* She does not deny that there may have been some sort of comic ceremonial involving clerical dress, but that, she says, is a far cry from an orgy. I find her argument unconvincing.

51. This explanation by an anonymous defender of Wilkes (Wilkes himself?) was made in the *Political Register,* 1768, iii, 42–44, . Wilkes's remarks about the garden in Almon, *Correspondence,* iii, 60–84, and *New Foundling,* iii, 89–107.

52. Trumbach, *Gender Revolution.* John Sainsbury's excellent review of Wilkes's libertinism includes a discussion of how it enhanced his appeal as a political figure, his attacks upon sodomy, and his placing himself within the perimeters of a new notion of exclusively heterosexual manhood: Sainsbury, "Wilkes and Libertinism." For an example of Wilkes's antipathy toward homosexuality, see his remarks on the Duke of Villars at Marseilles, Autobiography, f. 87.

53. Boswell, *Grand Tour,* 56.

54. Boswell, *Grand Tour,* 56. Wilkes's poem and the archbishop's replay, dated 13 December 1753, in Wilkes Papers, v, 29 and verso.

Chapter 3. Into Parliament

1. Almon, *Correspondence,* i, 23.

2. Add Mss 30,867, f. 95; *Grenville Papers,* i, 102; Hanley, *Prebendal,* 41.

3. DNB.

4. Add Mss 30,867, f. 103.

5. Albemarle, *Rockingham,* i, 65–66. *Grenville Papers,* iii, xxxvii.

6. Wiggin, *Faction of Cousins.*

7. He once wrote Wilkes to say he would be unable to do a particular favor that Wilkes had asked but added that he would be glad, when he could, "to promote your desires." Then he stopped in the middle of his sentence, went back, drew a caret after the words "promote your desires," and wrote above the line, "always meaning your virtuous ones": Add Mss 30,877, f. 14.

8. Add Mss 30,867, ff. 103. He was also planning to show the poem to Dr. Brewster.

9. Ibid., 30,877, ff; 21–23; Clarke, "Lady with the Squint."

10. Add Mss 30,867, ff. 99–104; Thomas, *Wilkes*, 6.

11. Add Mss 30,867, ff. 99–100; Almon, *Correspondence*, i, 26; Bingley edition, *North Briton*, xcvii–xcviii.

12. *Public Advertiser*, 30 April 1754. I am in doubt of the report that the election cost Wilkes three or four thousand pounds. The information seems to come from Almon, *Correspondence*, i, 27, and though uncorroborated is repeated by Bleackly, *Life of Wilkes*, and Thomas, *Wilkes*. But the idea stands in contrast to what is known about Wilkes's statements that he will not offer a bribe, and it seems unlikely that a man who would charge his opponents with the crime of bribery should himself be guilty of the very crime, especially when it is a crime hard to hide. I think Almon was mistaken. I also distrust the anecdote of Wilkes challenging a Scottish lawyer to a duel because he would not return the money paid by Wilkes even though he had not represented Wilkes's case for corruption. If I am not mistaken, the story is traceable to a newspaper very friendly to Wilkes, *Public Advertiser*, and appeared on 9 July 1768 in the midst of the Middlesex election controversy. It reappeared in *Wilkes's Jest Book*. I believe it was a piece of propaganda, possibly written by Wilkes himself.

13. Add Mss 30,877, ff. 1–3; Hume, *Letters*, i, 194, 205.

14. Excerpt from the *St. James's Chronicle* in *Political Register*, 1767, iii, 42–44.

15. Namier and Brooke, iii, 291; Commons Journals, xxvii, 30–31, 151–52, 250, 302; Bleackley, *Life of Wilkes*, 35.

16. Add Mss 30,867, ff. 103–04.

17. Wilkes Papers, vi, 23v–24; Commons Journals, xxvii, 430.

18. Since the records of the court were destroyed, we do not know why an information was prepared against Wilkes in the King's Bench in 1754. Potter, in a letter of 10 September, speaks of an indictment and asks Wilkes to consider allowing him to add something to the affidavit that Wilkes is preparing in his own defense: Add Mss 30,867, ff. 101–02. The notion that Wilkes's wife separated from him because of the money he had lost at Berwick is traceable to William Rough's introduction to *Letters to His Daughter*. As I explained in a previous note, I am in doubt that Wilkes lost money by bribing voters at Berwick. Almon is the major source of information about the separation, and he does not blame it upon the election, but upon Wilkes's high living and libertinism, naming the leaders of the Medmenham club: Almon, *Correspondence*, i, 28. Almon prints a letter from one of the Mead family solicitors that confirms the major articles of the separation and the amount but does not date the agreement: Almon, *Correspondence*, i, 30–32. I date it from Hanley, whose scholarship I respect: Hanley, *Prebendal*, 43.

19. Add Mss 30,879, ff. 1–7; 30,875, f. 28; Bleackley, *Life of Wilkes*, 41; Knapp, "Elizabeth Smollett."

20. Wilkes Papers, vi, 37–39; Add Mss 30,867, ff. 135–36; 30,875, ff. 30.

21. Wilkes Papers, vi, ff. 11, 15, 33.

22. Hanley, *Prebendal*, 9; Wilkes Papers, vi, ff. 14, 15, 17, 32.

23. Namier and Brooke, i, 10; Potter to Wilkes, 15 March 1753, Add Mss 30,867, f. 75.

24. When Wilkes was living in France, he wrote to Cotes, who was acting as his financial manager, explaining that a Mr. Thomson, no doubt the original lender of the money for the Aylesbury election, had died, and Wilkes had agreed to have the bond

Notes to Pages 46–55

transferred to Isaac Fernandes Silva, a London banker: "Mr. Swale, an attorney whom my brother Heaton knows, can assist you as to my titles, &c. better than any man. He was recommended to me by Potter, who was plunged much deeper than me in annuities, and gave me the worst advice": Almon, *Correspondence,* ii, 55; see also i, 35. By the time the debt was paid off, the worth of the bond had grown to two thousand pounds. It was paid off in 1768 after compounding with Silva to waive most of the interest. See below, chap. 10.

25. Wilkes Papers, vi, ff. 5, 19, 27–28, 61; Richard W. Davis, *Political Change,* 21. Almon, *Correspondence,* i, 34, says that the election cost Wilkes more than £7000, but since there were only about three hundred voters, that can't be right: he would not have paid £25 per vote. The estimate of 300 guineas (£315) made by Davis, a sound local historian, is the more reliable.

26. Wilkes Papers, vi, f. 53; Add Mss 30,867, f. 138; 30,877, f. 5.

27. Burrow's *Reports,* Easter term, 31 Geo 2, p. 542; Almon, *Correspondence,* i, 23, 34–37. Wilkes's statement to Mrs. Stafford in 1778 in Add Mss 30,880B, ff. 71–72.

28. Fritz Lugt, *Repertoire,* i, 1138.

29. Samuel Johnson, *Present State of Affairs.*

30. Commons Journals, xxviii, pp. 28, 31, 32, 34.

31. Wilkes-Churchill Correspondence, 38; Wraxall, *Memoirs,* ii, 49; v, 2–3.

32. Commons Journals, xxix, 115; Wilkes to the Secretary, dated 20 January [1758], facsimile in Brownlow, *Memoranda.* I have not been able to locate the passing of the grant in the Commons Journals, though I do not doubt it is there somewhere.

33. On the use of influence, Keir, *Constitutional History,* 296–97; Brewer, *Sinews of Power,* 74. On Wilkes's uses or attempted uses of influence, Nichols, *Anecdotes,* ii, 311; Smollett, *Letters,* 75, 77, 102–03; Add Mss 30,877, ff. 9–10, 14; Boswell, *Other Papers,* 165 ff.; *English Liberty,* 380–82; Boswell, *Life of Johnson,* i, 348–50; Johnson, *Letters,* nos. 132–34.

34. Smollett, *Letters,* 76–77, 82; *Critical Review,* v, 438–39 (May 1758); Knapp, *Smollett,* 217–18; Robin Fabel, "Patriotic Briton."

35. Wilkes Papers, vi, f. 4.

36. *Letters on Regicide Peace, 1796,* as quoted by Sambrook, 92.

37. Knapp, "Dr. John Armstrong."

38. Wilkes to his brother, 1 October 1758, Wilkes Papers, i, f. 36; Boswell, *Life of Johnson,* iii, 73. The nobleman was Archibald, 3rd duke of Argyll (1682–1761).

39. *Scots Magazine,* xxv, 321, as quoted by Joel Gold, "The Unlikely Visitor"; Wilkes Papers, vi, f. 46; Add Mss 30,867, f. 148.

40. C. J. Smith, *Records,* 196; Thomas Wilson, *Diary,* 1331–37, 1750; *Political Register* for 1767. Wilkes and Samuel Pierson were both elected for 1759, but at the end of the term the vestry thanked Pierson alone.

41. Walpole, *Correspondence,* xxii, 136.

42. Armstrong to Wilkes, 20 December 1760, copy at West Wycombe House. The letter in hexameters, dated 27 July 1761, is also in the collection at West Wycombe House, pasted in the back of a large, black-letter folio entitled *The Goliard Legemont.* See also Dashwood, *The Dashwoods,* 29–30, especially the quotation from a letter by Sir William Stapleton.

43. Temple's letter, Guildhall 214/1, f. 235; Mrs. Cibber's appearance, Add Mss 30,879, f. 86.

44. Temple to Wilkes, 10 June 1760, Add Mss 30,877, f. 16.

45. Hotten, *Essay on Woman,* 127–29.

46. Wilkes Papers, iii, ff. 23a, 24; iv, f. 11; Bleackley, *Life of Wilkes,* 345, 394. Wilkes's statements about when Jackie was born are inconsistent. In this letter to Cotes, Add Mss 30,868, ff. 40–41, he says the child is two years old, which would place his birth in 1762; but years later, in 1769, he told his friend Suard that the boy was born on 10 December 1760: Wilkes Papers, iii, f. 23a. I surmise that the 1762 date is the accurate one.

47. Brooke, *George III,* 64. Brooke, 48–49, makes a strong argument that the rumor about Bute and the Princess Mother was not true. See also the Sedgwick's Introduction to George III, *Letters to Lord Bute.* Sterne, *Letters,* 126.

48. Albermarle, *Rockingham,* ii, 93–95; Almon, *Correspondence,* i, 57–58.

49. Wilkes to Dell, 6 January 1761, Buckinghamshire Archaeological Society; Wilkes Papers, vi, 12–13, 58.

50. Wilkes Papers, i, 5, 37; Namier and Brooke, ii, 398; Israel Wilkes's will as quoted by Nobbe, *North Briton,* 15. On election techniques, Bon Mots. On the death, *Gentleman's Magazine,* xxxi (1761), 44; Wilkes Papers, vi, 5. See Wilkes's discussions of finances with his brother in the letter of 3 September 1760, cited above, and that of 23 July 1762 in Wilkes Papers, i, f. 38.

51. *Political Register,* ii, 413, as cited by Almon, *Correspondence,* i, 59–60. Appendix to the W. Bingley edition of the *North Briton,* 1769, lxxxiv. A false story about a similar application was made by John Courtenay, M.P. for Tamworth, whose political loyalty was to Wilkes's enemy Lord North. According the Courtenay, in September or October of 1762 Wilkes had asked Richard Rigby, the henchman of the Duke of Bedford, to request Bedford to ask Bute to give the governorship of Canada to Wilkes; when Bute refused, Wilkes swore to ruin him in the *North Briton.* The story is obviously apocryphal: Bedford would never have made such a request, and Wilkes's animosity to Bute was established much earlier than these supposed events. See Sir James Prior, *Life of Malone,* 362–63. Years later Bute told Boswell that Wilkes had never asked him for anything: see below, chapter 14.

52. Walpole, *Correspondence,* xxi, 528–29.

53. Wilkes Papers, vi, 72. St. Mary's parish register as cited by Dell, "Political Agent." On Coronation day, front seats in the galleries of the Abbey went for ten guineas. Brooke, *George III,* 85, says that one house along the route of the procession was hired for the day at a thousand guineas.

54. Walpole, *Correspondence,* ix, 388–89, and n. 28; Walpole, *George III,* i, 36.

55. Walpole, *George III,* i, 65.

56. Walpole, *George III,* i, 71–77; Commons Journals, xxix, 133–34.

57. Described at length in Debrett's *History.* See also *Life and Writings of John Wilkes.*

58. Add Mss 30,867, f. 173.

59. BL Egerton MSS 2136, ff. 29–30; Beckett, "Wilkes and the Militia."

60. Gibbon, *Journal,* 145–46.

61. The House of Lords in their hearing of Wilkes's case required the presence of these two engravers: Commons Journals, xxx, 453. David Alexander of York, the expert on

eighteenth-century prints, kindly informed me about these obscure figures. Tringham was an engraver and printseller who engraved satires, trade cards, some book illustrations, and at least one children's fold-up book entitled *Mother Shipton*. Sherwin, known to have done some frontispieces, may have been Tringham's assistant or someone Tringham called in to do the lettering, a specialty of some engravers.

62. Cash, *Essay on Woman*, Historical Introduction and Appendix vi, on the title page.

Chapter 4. *The* North Briton

1. Walpole, *George III*, i, 140–41.

2. Wilkes-Churchill Correspondence, 23, 33, 65; Add Mss 30,88B, f. 12 (the only letter of Wilkes to Churchill not included in Wilkes-Churchill Correspondence). Unless otherwise noted, the historical facts in my account of Churchill are taken from Wilkes-Churchill Correspondence; the DNB article by Sir Leslie Stephens; chapter iv of Nobbe, *North Briton;* and Douglas Grant's introduction to Churchill, *Poetical Works.* For the pamphlet war sparked by the *Rosciad,* see Beatty, "Battle of the Players."

3. *Political Register* for 1767, i, 14. See Halsband, "Poet of *The North Briton.*"

4. Boswell, *London Journal,* 266; Pottle, *Boswell,* 116–17; Rizzo, "Bonnell Thornton."

5. Rae, *English Press,* 28–29. An amusing print at the Guildhall (cat. No. p5383313) shows clients of a coffeehouse absorbed in newspapers. The *London Gazette* can be seen on the floor. The best studies of the common folk who supported Wilkes are to be found in the brilliant books of George Rudé, *Wilkes and Liberty, The Crowd in History,* and *Hanoverian London.* See also Spector, *Political Controversy,* 48–49. An invaluable source of information about Wilkes's followers and how he solicited their support and manipulated their responses can be found in Brewer, *Party Ideology.*

6. Another essay by Wilkes followed on 12 June, No. 360. Nobbe, *North Briton,* assigns Nos. 357 and 360 to Wilkes, pp. 31–34. Peters, "History and Propaganda," says he also wrote 377 and 380.

7. Fabel, "Patriotic Briton"; Schweizer, "Lord Bute and the Press," 83–98. The only reprint of the *Briton* is that edited by O M Brack, Jr., with introduction by Byron Gassman, included in *Poems, Plays, and the Briton: Tobias Smollett* (Athens: University of Georgia Press), 1993.

8. Smollett, *Letters,* 104; *English Liberty,* 382.

9. In fact, the ministry had letters from Wilkes to his publisher, Kearsley, which offered sound evidence of his authorship, but the only evidence presented to the House of Commons was a written "examination" of the printer, Balfe, that had not been taken on oath. Wilkes's marginalia to pp. 58 and 145 of Almon's Minority notes that he publicly admitted to No. 12 (in connection with the duel with Talbot) and Nos. 37 and 40 (in regard to the duel with Martin). Nobbe, *North Briton,* worked out the authorship of individual numbers through such private papers. Wilkes, Nobbe concluded, wrote thirty-six issues; Churchill wrote five (7, 8, 10, 27, 42). No. 19 is devoted to a very interesting letter from William Temple of Trowbridge, seemingly no relation to Lord Temple. Three others are fillers — when the situations did not allow Wilkes or Churchill to write. Nos. 22 and 26 are made up largely of verses by Robert Lloyd, and No. 13 is a pastiche of passages from a

virulent slander of Scottish culture by James Howell, *A Perfect Description of the People and Country of Scotland.*

10. Add Mss 22,131, ff. 118–21.

11. Two copies at the BL, shelf nos. 629.l.6, and P.P.3611.lbb.[1].

12. Only once that we know of was his challenge taken up, and that merely in a friendly way. Henry Bilson Legge wrote, not to protest, but to set the record straight: Wilkes was mistaken in assuming he was in office as chancellor of the exchequer when the scandalous "new loan" was made: *English Liberty*, 383–84.

13. Rea, *English Press*, 5.

14. See especially *North Briton*, No. 33. For the importance of dialect to the Scots and English at this time, see Basker, "Scotticisms."

15. Murdoch, "Lord Bute," 117–46.

16. *North Briton*, 127.

17. Wilkes's marginal Minority notes, 399–409. In a letter to Cotes, 4 December 1764, Wilkes spoke of Pitt as "the best orator and the worst letter-writer of our age": Almon, *Correspondence*, ii, 217. Militia matter: Guildhall 214/1, ff. 226–27; Temple's comment: *Grenville Papers*, i, 456–57.

18. As noted above, Nobbe says he wrote Nos. 7, 8, 10, 27, and 42. Douglas Grant, in the introduction to *Poetical Works of Charles Churchill* (Oxford: Clarendon, 1956), p. xv, n. 4, says he wrote 7, 10, 18, 21, 27, and 42. On the editing and vetting of the paper, Guildhall 214/1 f. 105; Add Mss 22,131, ff. 175–78; Wilkes-Churchill Correspondence, 3. After No. 26, the legal advice was given by Charles Sayer, a lawyer in the Inner Temple.

19. Wilkes identified him in a letter to Temple as "Mr Brookes," author of a *North Briton Extraordinary* with which Wilkes had no connection: Rea, *English Press*, 98 and n. 34; *Grenville Papers*, ii, 137; Add Mss 22,132, ff. 33, 93. John Caesar Wilkes's notes to *Political Controversy*, usually supported the *Monitor/North Briton* position.

20. Smollett, *Letters*, 137. The most authoritative study of the *North Briton* is Nobbe's. That of the entire group of papers, the *Monitor, Auditor, Briton,* and *North Briton* is Spector's.

21. As quoted by Murdoch, "Lord Bute." Wilkes's comment, Minority notes, 399–409.

22. Brooke, *George III*, 145; Boswell, *Letters*, 40–41.

23. Wilkes had originally written this satire for the series on royal favorites in the *Monitor,* suppressed it at Lord Temple's request, and then rewrote it for the *North Briton:* Nobbe, *North Briton*, 44–45.

24. Wilkes, *Letters between Grafton et al.,* 203–04; *English Liberty*, 372–74.

25. Walpole, *George III,* i, 141. Wilkes had taken the precaution of having both the essay and the play vetted by his legal advisor: Guildhall 214/1, ff. 102–03.

26. I take the liberty of quoting this anachronistically, for it was written to Temple on 7 July 1763: *Grenville Papers*, ii, 73.

27. Add Mss 22,132, ff. 91v–92; Walpole, *Correspondence*, x, 52. The only copy of the play at the BL (shelf no. 11777.b.58.) appears to be a pirated Dublin edition of 1766 or 1767: Wilkes's dedication is dated 15 March 1763, no doubt close to the publication date. See Fitzgerald, *Life of Wilkes*, i, 111; *Critical Review* (1763), xv, 234. Wilkes was proud of the dedication and saw to it that it was republished in *Complete Collection* and *English Liberty.* It reappears in Almon, *Correspondence*, i, 70–90, with footnotes.

28. Add Mss 30,867, f. 191; Nobbe, *North Briton*, chap. 9; *North Briton*, No. 21; *Grenville Papers*, ii, 486.

29. *Auditor* of 18 December, quoted by Nobbe, *North Briton*, 162, 164. Wilkes's authorship is attested by the inclusion of the essay in the so-called *Works* of Wilkes, 3 vols., published by John Williams, 1763 (Butler Library, Columbia Univ., call no. 942.073/W65).

30. Smollett letters, 110–11 and n. 4.

31. Assigning the profits to Churchill: Almon, *Correspondence*, i, 99. The quotation from Gibbon, *Journal*, 145–46. On clerical careers, J. H. Plumb wrote, *Walpole*, 71, "The only path to preferment for poor clergy was a well-placed patron and unwavering devotion to his politics."

32. Peters, "History and Propaganda."

33. *North Briton*, No. 33.

34. Minority notes, 399–409.

35. *North Briton*, No. 40, p. 265.

36. Wilkes-Churchill Correspondence, 20–23, 50. On Townshend, see Namier and Brooke, iii, 543. During a period when Townshend was a follower of Lord Temple, Wilkes wrote to his patron, "I do not hold Mr. Charles Townshend a *fixed* star, though he is a very bright one": *Grenville Papers*, ii, 63. The story about the sour grain did not appear in the *North Briton* until 5 March 1763, a month after Townshend had taken up his post on the Board of Trade. But Wilkes may well have obtained the material long before he decided to use it.

37. *Grenville Papers*, i, 471–78; Add Mss 30,867, ff. 186–90; *English Liberty*, 46–53; Almon, *Correspondence*, iii, 41–49.

38. Wilkes to Temple, dated ten p.m. from the Red Lion at Bagshot, in Almon, *Correspondence*, iii, 29; *Public Advertiser*, 16 May 1767; *English Liberty*, 54–59, verified at key points by Edmund Burke in a letter to Charles O'Hara, which adds a few details: Burke, *Correspondence*, i, 149–51. Lord Temple's account in a letter to his sister, Lady Chatham, 10 October 62, is not so helpful because it is mostly taken from Wilkes's letter: Albermarle, *Rockingham*, ii, 192–93. I have based my account upon these sources. Later, when Wilkes was in exile, he had a few copies of his letter to Temple printed. One he sent to the *St. James's Chronicle*, whence it was copied into many other papers: Add Mss 42,084, f. 176. Talbot thought Temple had published it and accused him at the House of Lords in such rude terms that it almost ended in another duel: Almon, *Biographical Anecdotes*, ii, 60.

39. The letter to the earl in *Grenville Papers*, i, 477.

40. Many thought so at the time. At the Guildhall, there is a satirical broadside poem asserting that they fired into the air, with an illustration showing the act: Broadside 20.143. See Rough's comment in his "Life" of Wilkes, in Letters to His Daughter, 21, 26.

41. Wilkes-Churchill Correspondence, 19, 23; Grenville Papers, i, 486, 471, ii, 164–64; Boswell, *Grand Tour*, 13 March 1765; Sainsbury, "Wilkes and Dueling."

42. Wilkes-Churchill Correspondence, 60, 64; Add Mss 30,880B, f.39.

43. I know of no evidence for these events except Wilkes's Minority notes, 387–95.

44. Boswell, *Grand Tour*, 53–54; Wilkes-Churchill *Correspondence*, 4.

45. I take my quotations from *New Foundling Hospital for Wit*, 80–89; a note says

that it was previously published in a newspaper. According to Nichols, *Anecdotes,* 454–55, Wilkes published the satire privately. Either way, it must have appeared before John Caesar Wilkes published it in *Political Controversy,* III, x, 21 March 1763, pp. 351–56.

46. Add Mss 30,867, f. 179.

47. Temple to Wilkes, Guildhall 214/1, ff. 226–27, 232, 234; Beckett, "Wilkes and the Militia."

48. Wilkes-Churchill Correspondence, 28–29.

49. Watson, *Reign of George III,* 56, n. 3; Add Mss 30,867, ff. 201–02.

50. Wilkes-Churchill Correspondence, 39.

51. Ronald Paulson, *Hogarth: His Life, Art, and Times,* 354–99; *English Liberty,* 366–68; John Ireland, *Hogarth Illustrated,* 1804 ed., iii, 212–16, as quoted by Nobbe, *North Briton,* 94; *Grenville Papers,* ii, 4–5; Guildhall 214/1, f. 90, copy in Add Mss 22,132, f. 93; Minority notes, 387–95; Wilkes-Churchill Correspondence, 15.

52. Howell, *State Trials,* xix, 1029–76; Guildhall 214/3, ff. 287–95; *Grenville Papers,* ii, 3. Both warrants at BL, T.1155. 1–17. The *Public Advertiser,* 27 May 1763, printed the warrant for Entick's arrest. Both named Nos. 357 and 380, which, according to Nobbe, *North Briton,* were by Wilkes. Peters, "History and Propaganda," would agree with No. 380, but not No. 357.

53. The case was settled on 27 November 1765: Webb's Calendar. Nobbe, *North Briton,* 133; Howell, *State Trials,* ii, 86; xix, 1029–76.

54. Spying on Wilkes and Temple: *Letters George III to Bute,* 153; Add Mss 22,132, ff. 90v–91; *Grenville Papers,* i, 457, 489. Dryden Leach was also spied upon: Add Mss 22,131, ff. 133–70; Guildhall 214/3, ff. 139–40, 276.

55. Wilkes to Churchill, 15 June: Add Mss 30,878, f. 1; the examination of William Johnston, Add Mss 22,131, ff. 175–78.

56. Wilkes's cover letter when sending this to Balfe, at Guildhall 214/3, f. 221.

57. Add Mss 22,131, ff. 29–32; 22,132, ff. 33–34; Wilkes-Churchill Correspondence, 34–35; *State of Facts.*

58. Bon Mots.

59. Minority notes, 399–409. Print at the BL: see the BM Print Catalogue, no. 4041. Another copy of the print at the Guildhall Library, no. 5437316.

60. Almon, *Anecdotes of Pitt,* i, 438–39; Namier and Brooke, ii, 464–65; Walpole, *George III,* i, 157; Riker, *Henry Fox,* ii, 268–69. For a demurrer on the story of the massive bribery, see Brooke, *George III,* 99.

61. Burke, *Correspondence,* i, 158; [John Almon], *Letter to George Grenville.*

62. Walpole, *George III,* i, 175–76, 184–90. The preliminary treaty may be found in Commons Journals, xxix, 361–67, 395. For a convenient summary of their terms, Nobbe, *North Briton,* 117–18; the definitive treaty in Commons Journals, xxix, 576–80.

63. Rudé, *Hanoverian London,* 211.

64. *Life and Letters of Sir Gilbert Eliot,* iii, 246, as quoted in Nobbe, *North Briton,* 158.

65. Rea, *English Press,* 37–38.

66. Ibid., 38–39.

67. Guildhall 214/1 ff. 195–200.

68. Ibid., 214/3 ff, 87–88.

69. Wilkes Papers, vi, 77. Wilkes's detailed itinerary of this trip, 26–30 March, in Wilkes Papers, i, 40a.

70. Walpole, *Correspondence*, xxii, 137. I have taken the liberty of slightly misquoting. In Walpole the words are "trying to know," which I think would be confusing to a modern reader. Walpole has another version at 38:202. In yet another version, Mme Pompadour puts the question to Wilkes about abusing the royal family: Letters to His Daughter, i, 164, n. In yet another, the question is put by a French nobleman: Bon Mots.

Chapter 5. Number 45

1. Add Mss 30,879, ff. 8–10.

2. The suppressed No. 45: the copy had been prepared with the help of John Walsh, member for Worcester: Nobbe, *North Briton*, 206. It was later printed as a *North Briton Extraordinary*, the copy of which at BL bears a note in Wilkes's hand, "This North Briton was never published": bound with the first edition (shelf mark 629.l.6.). Bute's lame-duck appointments, Guildhall 214/3, f. 271.

3. Harris, *Hardwicke*, 493–94.

4. Also bound with the first edition at the BL. It reappeared as a preface, date unchanged, to the published No. 45 of April 23. Given in Nobbe, *North Briton*, 207. A draft in a hand not Wilkes's is in Wilkes Papers, i, 41.

5. Almon, *Correspondence*, i, 93–95, said that Wilkes wrote his most famous *North Briton* that evening, basing it upon Pitt's and Temple's comments, but that was never the way John Wilkes worked. His patrons would have said little or nothing he did not already understand. See the critical assessment, in Nobbe, *North Briton*, 208.

6. Wilkes on le Despenser, Minority notes, 399–409. Almon has another version in *Correspondence*, i, 75, n.: "From puzzling all his life at tavern bills," said Wilkes, he "was called by Lord Bute to administer the finances of a kingdom above one hundred millions in debt." Le Despenser on himself, Walpole, *George III*, i, 197–98.

7. Walpole on Webb, *George III*, i, 219. Webb and Wilkes meet, brief of one of Wilkes's lawyers, unidentified, at Guildhall 214/3, ff. 45–46.

8. Nobbe, *North Briton*, 213.

9. Add Mss 22,132, ff. 26, 30; 41,355, ff. 199–205; Harris, *Hardwicke*, iii, 342; Cella, "Privilege."

10. Add Mss 32,948, ff. 71–72; copy at f. 194.

11. Howell, *State Trials*, 982. Many criticisms of the warrants were published at the time. I find helpful *Observations upon the Authority, Manner and Circumstances of the Apprehension and Confinement of Mr. Wilkes*, printed for Wilkes's friend John Williams, 1763. I would guess that John Glynn wrote it. See also Philip Carteret Webb's collection of documents to establish legal precedents for general warrants: BL, 518.l.34.

12. Minutes of the Huckle trial at Add Mss 22,131, ff. 133–70; Almon, *Correspondence*, i, 140–42; *State of Facts*; Howell, *State Trials*, 981–1001.

13. Almon, *Correspondence*, i, 98–99; Howell, *State Trials*, 1001–28; testimony of George Bigg in the suit of William Huckle: Add Mss 22,131, ff. 133–70.

14. See Kearsley's affidavit of 16 June 1768, in "A Collection of Fugitive Pieces Printed in the News Papers Relative to the Essay on Woman and the North Briton," in Bingley, ed., *North Briton*, lxxxi.

15. Minority notes, 145, 341.

16. Kearsley's examination before Lord Halifax, Huntington Library, STG Box 18 (36).

17. Add Mss 22,132, f. 45; Almon, *Correspondence* i, 99; *State of Facts*.

18. *State of Facts*; Minority notes, 147–49; Almon, *Correspondence*, i, 100.

19. Minority notes, 345–47; Wood to Webb, Guildhall 214/3, f. 162.

20. Carrington testimony: Add Mss 22,132, ff. 49–51; *State of Facts*.

21. The issue of No. 46 cited here is included in the BL first edition. In Wilkes's version of this story, he himself went up the ladder and printed the proof: Minority notes, 345–47. The testimonies of Williams and Balfe's apprentice Charles Shaw, are more reliable: Add Mss 22,132, ff. 39–42. Both testimonies also appear in *State of Facts*.

22. See Rosen, "Is Nothing Private?"

23. Wilkes, *Letter to Grafton* (cf. Almon, *Correspondence*, i, 100–01); Testimony of Money, Add Mss 22,132, ff. 54–57.

24. Almon, *Correspondence*, i, 103.

25. *Gentleman's Magazine*, xxxvii, 248; Letters to His Daughter, i, 32.

26. Brief for the court by an unidentified lawyer, Add Mss 22,131, ff. 58, 59; deposition of John Gardiner in Almon, *Correspondence*, i, 141–51; Yorke, *Hardwicke*, iii, 492; Add Mss 41,355, ff. 199–205; Howell *State Trials*; *State of Facts*.

27. Testimony of Chisholme, Add Mss 22,132, ff. 47, 48,

28. Wilkes, *Letter to Grafton*; Almon, *Correspondence*, i, 103.

29. *State of Facts*; George III, *Letters to Bute*, 232–33; Wilkes, *Letter to Grafton*. The habeas corpus and the original warrant, dated Saturday 30 April, signed by Rainsford, in Add Mss 22,131, ff. 47, 48; the warrants from the secretaries to Collins and Ardran, and from them to the constable of the Tower, both dated the thirtieth, are given in notes to Almon, *Correspondence*, i, 104–06; that to the Tower is in *State of Facts*. See also Harris, *Hardwicke*, 348. No doubt the news of the habeas hurried the secretaries into sending Wilkes off, and Wilkes's friends were right to make an issue over an attempt to evade the law; but I find their assertions that the ministry was in this case elaborately devious a bit strained, for it was a regular practice. A statement of the position on the Wilkes side as extracted from the St. James's Chronicle may be found in the BL collection of pamphlets related to Wilkes, shelf no. T.1155 (1–7); another in Wilkes Papers i, 47; a response on the government side is in *State of Facts*.

30. Wilkes's suit against Webb as reported in the *Public Advertiser*, 16 December 1763; Almon, *Correspondence*, i, 107–08; Webb, *Records*, 64–66; *State of Facts*; Chisholme's testimony, Add Mss 22,131, ff. 295–96; testimonies of Blackmore, Stanhope, Chisholme, Carrington, Money, Bullock, and Collins, 22,132, ff. 46–59.

31. Walpole, *George III*, i, 219.

32. Walpole, George III, i, 219; Almon, *Correspondence*, i, 111, and note; Add Mss 22,278, f. 1; Howell, *State Trials*, 932; testimony of Thomas Ardran at Guildhall 214/3, f. 52; Hardwicke to Newcastle, Add Mss 32,948, ff. 188–89. Copy of the warrant itself, Add Mss 32,948, f. 194.

33. Beardmore's testimony, Add Mss 22,132, ff. 62–64.

34. Add Mss 30,879, f. 13; Almon, i, 112–13, note.

35. Wilkes, *Letter to Grafton*, 209.

36. *Public Advertiser*, 25 May 1763. Wilkes's holograph copy of the orders, Add Mss 27,278, f. 1.

37. Add Mss 32,948, ff. 201–09.

38. Add Mss 22,132, f. 65; 30,867, f. 204; Grafton, *Autobiography*, 190; copy of the order for incarceration, Add Mss 22,132, f. 65, and in *State of Facts*; a note to the same effect from Webb to Beardmore at Add Mss 30,867, f. 204; letter from Webb to Wilkes in Wilkes Papers, i, 50. Wilkes on his brother Israel, see Wilkes to his brother Heaton, Wilkes Papers, ii, 20a.

39. Harris, *Hardwicke,* 348–49; Albermarle, *Rockingham*, iii, 483. Glynn was interesting himself in Wilkes's legal affairs at least by June 1763: Wilkes-Churchill Correspondence, 56.

40. Wilkes to Temple, Add Mss 30,867, f. 205; Harris, *Hardwicke*, 358; Grafton, *Autobiography*, 192.

41. *Public Advertiser*, 25 May 1763, p. 2. Wilkes's speech is quoted from Howell, *State Trials*, 983.

42. Almon, *Correspondence*, i, 109–11; Add Mss 22,131, ff. 61–104; 32,948, ff. 215–20; Howell, *Hardwicke*, iii, 348–49.

43. Egremont to Temple in Wilkes, *Complete Collection*, 27–28; Add Mss 30,877, f. 20; *Public Advertiser*, 6 May, p. 3; Almon, *Correspondence*, i, 113–16, 130–31; Wilkes Papers i, 49; *Grenville Papers*, ii, 55.

44. For Wilkes's overwritten description of Hogarth in the gallery, *English Liberty*, 367–68. The pen sketch at the British Library, cat. No. 95 (reproduced in A. P. Oppé, *The Drawings of William Hogarth* [New York: Phaidon, 1948], which I think admirably captures Wilkes's face, was probably made when Hogarth got home. What he drew in the gallery of the court is lost.

45. Add Mss 22,131, ff. 105–15. A transcript of the trials, including Wilkes's speech and Chief Justice Pratt's pronouncement, in Howell, *State Trials*, 982–90.

46. Onslow to Newcastle, Add Mss 32,948, ff. 234–36; Almon, *Correspondence*, i: 117–24; Harris, *Hardwicke*, 349–50; Add Mss 22,131, ff. 105–15; *Public Advertiser*, 7 May 1763; Minority notes, 168.

47. Add Mss 30,867, 205–08; Almon, *Correspondence*, i, 126–29. *Public Advertiser*, 9, 25 May 1765. Wilkes, *Complete Collection*, 34; *State of Facts*; "Contributions to the Public Advertiser," at Add Mss 27,777, f. 4. The handbill may be the one reproduced as an "Extraordinary North Briton," dated 12 May 1763, in John Caesar Wilkes's *Political Controversy,* iv, 5, 161.

48. Wilkes to Cotes, 10 December 1764, Add Mss 30,868, ff. 160–62; Minority notes, pp. 379–81. The *Public Advertiser* of 25 May carried a story about how some of Wilkes's "sensible and opulent" friends were shocked by the letters. See also the pamphlet, *An Authentic Account of the Proceedings against John Wilkes*, [1763].

49. Minority notes, 168, 375.

50. *Grenville Papers*, ii, 239.

51. The *Public Advertiser* of 25 May 1763 carried a story of the Minority Club subscribing one thousand pounds per annum to Wilkes during his life. No doubt the account was exaggerated.

52. *Grenville Papers*, ii, 71–76.

53. *State of Facts*, f. 96; a note attached to the papers returned to Wilkes seen by Henry Spencer Albee, *Catena Librorum Tacendorum*, 1885, Appendix "Authorities Consulted." On the asset of libertinism in Wilkes's case, see Sainsbury, "Wilkes and Libertinism."

Chapter 6. The Great George Street Printing Shop

1. Ms of an anonymous historian, Guildhall 214/1, ff. 155–58. Webb to the Secretaries of State, 7 May, in *State of Facts*.

2. Newcastle to Rockingham, 24 May, 1763, at Add Mss 32,948, ff. 371–72.

3. Newcastle to Devonshire, 23 June 1763, Add Mss 32,949, ff. 191–92; *State of Facts*; Webb's Calendar. In a letter to Temple, *Grenville Papers*, ii, 72, Wilkes describes Yorke's attack on him for not responding to the summons made during the printers' trial.

4. *Grenville Papers*, ii, 57.

5. Add Mss 41,355, ff. 173–205; Guildhall 214/3. f.241; Howell, *State Trials*, 1002–27.

6. Brewer, *Party Ideology*, 170–74.

7. Add Mss 22,132, f. 93.

8. *English Liberty*, 367–68, note.

9. *Poetical Works*, 230.

10. Wilkes-Churchill Correspondence, 59–60.

11. West, "Wilkes's Squint."

12. Wilkes to Ashwell, 1 November, Add Mss 30,867, f. 223; *Grenville Papers*, ii, 63 and note. I have not enough evidence to decide whether Wilkes was innocent or not. Henry Allnut, the merchant who sold the uniforms, complained to Dashwood that he had not been paid. On the other hand, Wilkes reported to Dashwood that he was unhappy about Allnut's profit and about the quality of the clothing: Bodleian Mss D.D. Dashwood (Bucks).

13. Add Mss 30,877, f. 21.

14. Draft brief at Guildhall 214/3, f. 240.

15. Printers' testimonies at Add Mss 22,132, ff. 187–88, 283–86.; Guildhall 214/3, ff. 236–39; Wilkes to Polly, 14 June, Add Mss 30,879, ff. 18–19.

16. *Grenville Papers*, ii, 61.

17. Ibid., 57, 59–60.

18. Webb's Calendar; lawyer's brief, Guildhall 214/3, ff. 234–41.

19. Guildhall 214/3, ff. 236, 322–29.

20. On Mawbey, Walpole, *George III*, iii, 174–75; Namier and Brooke. On publications of Wilkes's press: *Annual Register* of 1763, pp. 142–43, as cited in Burke, *Correspondence*, i, 171, n. 1; Guildhall 214/3, ff. 234–41. For Wilkes's purpose in printing the affidavit, see Guildhall 214/1, f. 177. Tear-outs of Wilkes's poems are included in a miscellaneous collection made by Wilkes, now at the BL, shelf number 11601.ccc.33. The Boulanger book was originally published posthumously at Paris, 1761. A translation under the title *The Origin and Progress of Despotism, in the Oriental, and other Empires, of Africa, Europe, and America* (Amsterdam [?], 1764), has frequently been assigned to Wilkes, but MacCracken, 134, n. 77, expresses doubt that Wilkes was the translator. James Mosley, in his yet-to-appear handlist of what Wilkes produced on his press, strongly refutes the attribution; see Wilkes to Cotes, 24 June 1764, Add Mss 30,868, ff. 90–91; and Wilkes to Temple, *Grenville Papers*, ii, 81.

21. Wilkes to Temple, *Grenville Papers*, ii, 59; Wilkes to Cotes, 5 June 1764, in *Complete Collection*, 72.

22. *Public Advertiser*, 2 June 1763; Almon, *Correspondence*, iii, 55–59. Churchill

wrote a few satirical lines about the renovation of the church in *The Ghost*, part IV, which appeared in November 1763, lines 627, *Poetical Works*. A very different description of the church in the *St. James's Chronicle*, 5–7 July 1763. A sound modern description and account in Kemp, *Dashwood*, 119. Wilkes's description of West Wycombe Park and the church were often-enough published and republished that the variations among them could bear close examination for a study of Wilkes as a writer and propagandist: for instance, Almon, cited above, *St. James's Chronical*, 2–4 June, 1763, Wilkes, *Letters between*, 34 ff, and *New Foundling Hospital for Wit*, 75–80.

23. Minority notes, pp. 399–409.

24. Wilkes-Churchill Correspondence, 56; *Grenville Papers*, ii, 62, 64.

25. Wilkes's own account of the Essay is in his speech before the King's Bench on 20 April 1768, reprinted many times: see Add Mss 33,053, ff. 317–22. Because the pages of the Essay that Curry printed are lost, I have been at some pains to reconstruct the printing in detail in my edition, Cash, *Essay on Woman*. I also make the argument there for my assignment of authorship between Potter and Wilkes, for which there is no direct evidence.

26. Sergeant Glynn's brief, "In Behalf of Colonel Wilkes," Add Mss 30,885, f. 155v.

27. Curry's examination, Add Mss 22,132, ff. 283–86.

28. Cash, *Essay on Woman*.

29. Almon, *Correspondence*, i, 135–36.

30. May, *Constitutional History*, iii, 3–6; Almon, *Correspondence*, i, 134–38; *Public Advertiser*, 8 July 1763; Webb's Calendar; minutes of the trial at Add Mss 22,131, ff. 133–70.

31. Howell, *State Trials*, 1405.

32. Rea, *English Press*, 60–61.

33. Albemarle, *Rockingham*, 230–35; extract from the "Treasury Minute Book," Appendix 12 of Wilkes's *Letter to the Right Honourable George Grenville*, printed for Isaac Fell, 1769, BL shelf No. T.1155 (1–7), reprinted in Almon, *Correspondence*, i, 133–34; Treasury memo at Add Mss 22,132, ff. 154–55. A "bill of exceptions," i.e., an appeal, was entered, which if granted would move the case, with disastrous consequences, to the King's Bench, *Grenville Papers*, ii, 78–79; but there was a public outcry and it was never acted upon. Webb's Calendar; Lawyer's note and receipt at Add Mss 22,132, ff. 154–57; *Public Advertiser*, 1 and 6 July 1763. A summary of the trials and their outcomes (in two copies, a fair and a foul) can be found in Add Mss 41,355, ff. 173–205.

34. Yorke *Life of Hardwick*, 109–10; *English Liberty*, 370; Harris, *Hardwick*, 509–10; *Grenville Papers*, ii, 72.

35. Wilkes to Temple, 23 July, *Grenville Papers*, ii, 78; Cuddihy, "Wilkes Cases," 2063–64; Rea, *English Press*, 59.

36. *Grenville Papers*, ii, 71–76.

37. Draft of a lawyer's brief, Guildhall 214/3, ff. 224–40; "In Error"; Add Mss 22,131, ff. 171–72; 22,132, ff. 184.

38. *Grenville Papers*, ii, 76–77.

39. I have pieced together the story of the discovery and subsequent conspiracy from the following sources: Lord's Journals, xxx, 417; Add Mss 22,131, ff. 278–95; 22.132, ff. 185, 271–96; Guildhall 214/1, ff. 82, 145–72, 162–72, 214–19; Guildhall 214/3, ff. 31–

32, 78, 92, 94, 241, 256, 297, 301; Lionel Hassall, "Account of the Discovery of the Black Proof," in Add Mss 22,132, ff. 185, 291–92; Sandwich to Holland, quoted in Nobbe, *North Briton*, 240; "Affidavit of Michael Curry, sworn at the Mansion House, London, before Thomas Harley, Mayor, 3 August 1768," appended to Wilkes, *Letter to Grenville*; Farmer, *The Plain Truth*; Kidgell, *Genuine and Succinct Narrative*; *English Liberty*, 255–66; Gordon Goodman, DNB article on Kidgell; Walpole, *George III*, i, 247; *Grenville Papers*, ii, 153–55; Hotten, *Essay on Women*, Appendix 17; *An Expostulatory Letter to the Reverend Mr. Kidgell . . . By a Layman*, 1763; *Letter to J. Kidgell*, 1763.

40. Wilkes to Cotes from Paris, 29 January 1764, Add Mss 30,868, f. 30v.

41. *Grenville Papers*, ii, 80–83; Add Mss 30,880B, f. 9, a letter missing from the Wilkes-Churchill Correspondence.

42. Webb to Kidgell and Faden, 27 September 1763, Guildhall 214/3, f. 241; Farmer, *The Plain Truth*, 11.

43. William Clark et al., deposition given for the trial of Webb on 9 December 1768, Add Mss 22,132, ff. 295–96. *English Liberty*, 257.

44. *Grenville Papers*, ii, 82–83.

45. Memorandum by ?Grenville at Add Mss 42,083, f. 38.

46. Wilkes-Churchill Correspondence, 63–65. More on French affairs, in Wilkes to Temple, *Grenville Papers*, ii, 98–101.

47. Bon Mots.

48. My account and quotations are from Almon, *Correspondence*, i, 213–18; a similar account in the *London Magazine* (1763), 549–50.

49. Fitzgerald, *Life of Wilkes*, i, 271 n.; Walpole, *George III*, i, 224.

50. Add Mss 30,878, f. 32; Wilkes-Churchill Correspondence, 64; *Grenville Papers*, ii, 98–100; Bon Mots.

51. Wilkes-Churchill Correspondence, 68–69.

52. Ibid., 71–72; Wilkes to the Hon. Alexander Murray, dated 7 September, *London Magazine*, (1763), 550–51; Wilkes to Temple, *Grenville Papers*, ii, 124; spurious letter of Forbes addressed to his father, *London Chronicle*, 15–17 September, the errors pointed out in that paper on 27–29 September and 4–6 October. Also see *London Magazine*, xxxii (October 1763), 516.

53. Wilkes-Churchill Correspondence, 71–72.

54. Wilkes Papers, i, 51; *Grenville Papers*, ii, 131.

55. Wilkes-Churchill Correspondence, 69.

56. Bleackley, *Life of Wilkes*, 125.

57. *Grenville Papers*, ii, 129–30.

58. Ibid., 138–39.

59. Curry's third narrative, Add Mss 22,132, ff. 279–80.

60. Bill for "costs incurred" in getting the "Essay," in Faden's hand, dated July 1763, probably an error for 1764, along with letters asking for payment, Guildhall 214/1, ff. 69–76; Curry's examination 21 February 1764, Add Mss 22,132, ff. 283–86; draft of Webb's defense, Guildhall 214/1, ff. 162–72; Curry's testimony, *English Liberty*, 255–59; Carrington's testimony, *English Liberty*, 261–64.

61. *Political Register*, as cited by Almon, *Correspondence*, i, 152–53.

Chapter 7. *Trials and a Trial of Honor*

1. Onslow to Newcastle, 29 September 1763, at Add Mss 32,951, ff. 220–23.

2. Six letters, Sandwich to Webb, Guildhall 214/1, ff. 202–13.

3. BL Egerton Mss 2136, ff. 85–86.

4. Glynn's brief, Add Mss 30,885, f. 155 ff.; list of papers proved at Wilkes's trial at the King's Bench at Add Mss 22,132, f. 142; Webb's drafts of a defense, at Guildhall, 214/1, ff. 155–58, 162–72. Webb also set Curry on the task of writing his three narratives now at Add Mss 22,132, ff. 271–74, 279–80. Also see Cash, *Essay on Woman.*

5. *Grenville Papers,* ii, 131–32, 140; *Daily Advertiser,* 4 October. My thanks to Professor Betty Rizzo for the information that Thornton was one of the party and a satire of the Encaenia their project.

6. *Grenville Papers,* ii, 155–60.

7. Wilkes-Churchill Correspondence, 73–75. I follow Douglas Grant in his edition of *Poetical Works,* xviii, n. 4, where he rejects Joseph M. Beatty's identification of Miss Carr with Elizabeth Cheere, daughter of Sir Henry Cheere, a well-known sculptor. See Beatty's article, "Mrs. Montagu, Churchill, and Miss Cheere," *Modern Language Notes* xli (1926), 384–86.

8. Add Mss 32,951, ff. 220–23. Almon, *Correspondence,* i, 224–38, gives the entire paper, but I think he was wrong in saying that only a few were printed for friends.

9. Grenville to Strange, *Grenville Papers,* ii, 134–36; North to Halifax, ii, 151–52. In the general election of 1761, twenty-three sons of noblemen entered Commons on the first opportunity that came along after they reached the age of twenty-one: Tuchman, *March of Folly,* 134–35.

10. Valentine, *Lord North,* 10–11; Junius, *Letters,* 189, note.

11. Jensen, *Founding of a Nation,* 158.

12. Guildhall 214/1, f. 81; 214/3, f. 30–33.

13. National Maritime Museum, SAN V/14. No. 69; *Grenville Papers,* ii, 153–54. On the king's eagerness, see Grenville's diary, *Grenville Papers,* ii, 223.

14. Two notes from Richard Phelps to [Webb] from Whitehall, Guildhall 214/1, ff. 214–16; Charles Lloyd, the undersecretary, to Webb, 22 October, Guildhall 214/3, f. 301. Sandwich's notes to Webb urging him to produce the "Essay": 214/1, f. 175; 214/1, ff. 214–16, 218–19. Sandwich refers to "the papers," not to a book. In all legal proceedings against Wilkes, the several parts of what we think of as a book were proof sheets and therefore called papers.

15. The forgery is discussed in detail by Cash, *Essay on Woman.* In "A Goldberg Variation," I correct the identification of the forged lines that I made in appendix 5 of my edition. The printing in Faden's shop is my own speculation based upon a note from Webb at Guildhall 214/1, ff. 155–58, in which Webb said he employed Faden and Hassall "to print a work for him"; Faden's bills for "printing state papers relating to proceedings against the *North Briton*" sent to Webb on 4 December 1763, 12 May, and 20 July [1764]; and his three letters, one from 1765, two from 1767, asking for payment and telling how he has been rebuffed even by Fletcher Norton: Guildhall 214/1, ff. 66–76.

16. Cust to Grenville, Guildhall, 2892, as cited by Thomas, *John Wilkes,* 41, and n. 87.

17. Wilkes Papers, i, 52.

18. Erick R. Watson, "Essay on Woman," 204. Watson did not document the citation, but I have the highest respect for his scholarship and have no doubt he saw this letter.

19. Two of the three copies are out of the same pirated edition. They are housed at the Bibliothèque Nationale and Southern Illinois University at Carbondale. The third, the Dyce copy at the Victoria and Albert Museum, was a botched attempt at a facsimile of the BN/SIU edition: see Cash, *Essay on Woman*, the Textual Introduction.

20. Webb's notes, Guildhall 214/1, f. 174; Farmer, *The Plain Truth*, 12–13. Hassall laid out money for the coach hired to move the conspirators to meetings and had a hard time collecting from the government for whom he had "been made contemptible by the odious name of informer": Guildhall 214/1, ff. 84–86.

21. King to George Grenville, *Grenville Papers*, ii, 161.

22. Almon, *Anecdotes of Pitt*, i, 493 ff.

23. For the extrajudicial manner of proceeding with a charge of libel, see Brewer, "Wilkites and Law," 128–71.

24. Commons Journals, xxix, 667–68; Grenville to the king, Add Mss 42,083, ff. 38–41; Walpole, *Correspondence*, xxii, 181–86; Boswell, *Holland*, 72–73.

25. William Pultney, Earl of Bath, to Elizabeth Montagu, 17 November 1763, Huntington Library MO4452; Wilkes, *Letter to Grenville*, 69. To be quite clear, the passages from the "Essay" quoted here do not appear in the Lords Journals; rather the Journals state, "some passages in the said printed papers being read." Only the "Essay on Woman" proper and the "Veni Creator" were complained of. No interest was taken in the "Universal Prayer" or "The Dying Lover to His Prick."

26. Almon, *Correspondence*, iii, 80–81. Walpole, *George III*, i, 247–48. Warburton's two speeches may be found in the 1871 Hotten edition of the *Essay on Woman*, appendix 17. See also John Selby Watson's *Life of Warburton*, 552; W. A. Evans, *Warburton*, 241–44; Walpole, *Correspondence*, xxxviii, 229–31, for another amusing account.

27. Lords Journals, xxx, 415–17; George III, *Correspondence*, no. 29, misdated as April 63 (pp. 50–51); Walpole, *Correspondence*, xxxviii, 229–31.

28. Lords Journals, xxx, 415 ff. Walpole, *George III*, i, 248. Holograph copy of a letter from Lord Vere to Thomas Rothley, 16 November 1763, at Morris Library, University of Southern Illinois at Carbondale.

29. Walpole, *George III*, i, 249–52.

30. Ibid., i, 252; Walpole, *Correspondence*, xxxviii, 227.

31. Debrett's *History*, iv, 144–45; George III, *Correspondence*, no. 32; collection of Thomas Frye at BL, P.P.3611.lbb. (1), under date of 15 November 1763; Commons Journals, xxix, 668; Lords Journals, xxx, 415 ff.

32. Almon, *Correspondence*, ii, 12–13.

33. Add Mss 41,354, ff. 75–87.

34. That the man who helped Wilkes was Brown is my speculation. Walpole heard that Francis Cotes was waiting close to the park in a carriage, but I am in doubt: Walpole *Correspondence*, xxxviii, 228; Wilkes to Polly, 18 November, Add Mss 30, 879, f. 20; a brief account in Almon, *Correspondence*, ii, 15–16; Bleackley, *Life of Wilkes*, 136, who draws his account of the duel from five newspaper stories.

35. Grenville's memoir, Add Mss 42,083, f. 41; Walpole, *George III*, i, 251–52. Wilkes almost certainly knew Brocklesby when they were students at Leiden: Alexander Dyce

introduction to Akenside, *Poetical Works*, xxv. Brocklesby's obituary appeared in the *Annual Register*, 1797, pt. II, p. 58.

36. Walpole, *Correspondence*, x, 111.

37. Ibid., xxii, 185–86. Warburton's exact wording was, "blasphemies . . . the hardiest inhabitant of hell would blush, as well as tremble, to hear repeated." (Kilvert, *Unpublished Papers of Warburton*, 281).

38. Almon, *Correspondence*, ii, 17; Grenville's account of the wound that he gave to the king, George III, *Correspondence*, nos. 34–35.

39. Add Mss 30,879, f. 20, printed in Almon, *Correspondence*, ii, 27–28.

40. Walpole, *Correspondence*, xxxviii, 232.

41. Commons Journals, xxix, 709; *English Liberty*, 112–13; *Public Advertiser*, 21, 23 December 1763.

42. Debrett's *History of Parliament*, iv, 150.

43. Commons Journals, xxix, 675; Lords Journals, xxx, 425–29; Walpole, *George III*, i, 249–54; Howell, *State Trials*, 994–1000.

44. It was "offered to be presented to the House" on 24 November: Commons Journals, xxix, 675. A draft of the petition in Wilkes Papers, i, 57, dated at Great George Street, 24 November 1763, and signed by Wilkes. A note in his hand is found at the bottom: "Wrote by Humphrey Cotes / signed by John Wilkes." The note and signature are in a shaky hand for Wilkes; he must have made them from his bed. The script is beautiful. Wilkes would not have sent off this copy to the House of Commons since a large portion of it is crossed out. Presumably he signed it as originally written, changed his mind, crossed out what he did not want, and made a fair copy. Then, not troubling to make a second fair copy for his own record, he wrote the note about Cotes so as to explain why his signature should appear on a foul copy and filed it. If this surmise is correct, he must have sent the petition, for otherwise he would not have filed a copy.

45. Lords Journals, xxx, 422; Boswell, *Correspondence with Temple*, 79.

46. *Public Advertiser*, 5–6 December 1763; Lloyd to Webb, Guildhall 214/3, ff. 112–13; *Grenville Papers*, ii, 232; Walpole, *Correspondence*, xxxviii, 256–57.

47. *Grenville Papers*, ii, 137.

48. Pratt's speech quoted from Howell, *State Trials*, where one finds full coverage of the case, pp. 1153–68. The newspapers, *Annual Register*, 1797, pt. ii, 378. I have altered the quotation: the words used were not "a man's," but "an Englishman's." For the import of the decision upon modern American law, see Jeffrey Rosen, "Is Nothing Private?"

49. In Glynn's brief, Add Mss 30,885, ff. 117–18. On the trial: *London Magazine*, xxxii (December 1763), 672; Howell, *State Trials*, 981–1001, 1153–76; Keir, *Constitutional History*, 310–11.

50. Add Mss 30,879, ff. 22–23.

51. Almon, *Correspondence*, i, 168–72; Add Mss 30,867, ff. 231–40; *London Evening Post*, 18 February 1764; *Public Advertiser*, December 1763–February 1764 passim; *London Magazine*, xxxiii, 107; Bleackley, *Life of Wilkes*, 140–41.

52. Guildhall 214/1, f. 62; Howell, *State Trials*, 1001–28; Keir, *Constitutional History*, 310–11.

53. *Grenville Papers*, ii, 71–72.

54. Walpole, *Correspondence*, xxxviii, 276; Maier, *Resistance to Revolution*, 163; Tuchman, *March of Folly*, passim.

55. Spies report: Add Mss 22,131, ff. 234–36; Memorandum from ?Curry, Add Mss 22,132, f. 184; Wilkes to Cotes, 17 February 1764, Add Mss 30,868, f. 40–41; Kidgell to Webb, Guildhall 214/3, f. 30.

56. Add Mss 30,879, f. 25.

57. Add Mss 30,867, f. 245. See the letter written at the same time to Lord Temple in *Grenville Papers* ii, 185–86; and two letters to his brother Heaton, Wilkes Papers, i, 58–59.

Chapter 8. Exile

1. Kors, *D'Holbach's Coterie*, 109.

2. As quoted by Wilson, *Diderot*, 175.

3. Almon, *Correspondence*, ii, 35–37.

4. Wickwar, *D'Holbach*, 21; Kors, *D'Holbach's Coterie*, 11–12.

5. Add Mss 30,876, f. 76; Louis I. Brevold, *Contributions of John Wilkes*; Bono, "Lettres de Suard à Wilkes," 161–280.

6. Add Mss 41,354, ff. 86–87; 30,867, f. 252; *Public Advertiser*, 24 February 1764; Almon, *Correspondence*, ii, 19–21; Walpole, *Correspondence*, xxxviii, 280.

7. Wilkes, *Speeches*, 122; Almon, *Correspondence*, ii, 17, 98–99; Wilkes Papers, i, 55a; Walpole, *George III*, 252–53.

8. *Grenville Papers*, ii, 249–50.

9. Harlan Hamilton, "Sterne's Sermon," 316–25.

10. *Grenville Papers*, ii, 249–59.

11. Add Mss 30,868, ff. 21–24, 67. The doctors' certificate in Almon, *Correspondence*, ii, 43–44.

12. Add Mss 30,868, ff. 24–26, 37–39.

13. Commons Journals, xxx, 722; Debrett's *History*, 1792.

14. Commons Journals, xxix, 838–39, 843.

15. Lords Journals, xxxi, 459.

16. "In Error"; affidavit of Francis Barlow in *Political Register*, iii (July 1768), 38–40; Appendix No. 3 to the BL copy of Wilkes's *Letter to Grenville*, 1769, shelf No. T.1155 (1–7); Howell, *State Trials*, 1075–78.

17. J. M. Beattie, *Crime and the Courts*, 379.

18. See Zechariah Chafee, Jr., *Free Speech*, 499–505.

19. At the Public Record Office, KB 7/6 is an official transcript of Wilkes's trials, outlawry, reversal of outlawry, and sentencing made by scribes of the King's Bench upon the request of the House of Lords (see Cash, *Essay on Woman*, 76–78). The trials are given full coverage by Howell, *State Trials*, 1075–1138. They are described in the *London Evening Post*, 23 February 1764. In Add Mss 22,132, f. 142, the papers proved at both trials are listed; the government lawyers' plans for prosecuting the libel of No. 45 in ff. 103–17; a partial set of minutes of the trial at ff. 120–53. Glynn's brief, entitled "In Behalf of Colonel Wilkes," at 30,885. See also Kidgell to [March], 20 August 1765, Guildhall 214/3, ff. 39–42; Phillips to Wilkes, Add Mss 30,868, f. 80, printed in Almon, *Correspondence*, ii, 70–73.

20. *Grenville Papers*, ii, 267–69.

21. This is my inference. The copies of the *Essay on Woman* in Wilkes's library were in

uncut sheets. If the government had obtained one, they would have taken it to a bindery and had it turned into a book. This could be done (I argue in my edition of the *Essay on Woman,* appendix 4) because the sheets were printed in such a manner as to be used in two ways, either pasted into a copy of Pope's *Essay on Man* or bound by themselves as a book. Of course it remains a possibility that one of the noblemen who had received a copy of the government edition of the "Essay" before Wilkes's trial in the House of Lords may have lent it to Fletcher Norton.

22. Add Mss 30,868, f. 57; *Correspondence,* ii, 64–67, 70–77; Add Mss 30,878, ff. 43–45; Guildhall 214/3, f. 111.

23. Almon, *Correspondence,* ii, 62.

24. *A Catalogue of the Very Valuable Library of John Wilkes, Esq . . . auctioned by Samuel Baker . . . ,* 3 May 1764; Add Mss 30,868, ff. 73–74; McCracken, "John Wilkes, Humanist."

25. Wilkes-Churchill Correspondence, 83.

26. Bleackley, *Life of Wilkes,* 69; Walpole, *Correspondence,* vii, 286, 289, 291; x, 180; xxxviii, 362.

27. Almon, *Asylum for Fugitive Pieces,* i, 282–83.

28. Bleackley, *Life of Wilkes,* 157–58. Garrick, *Private Correspondence,* i, 250–53; Add Mss 30,868, ff. 36, 50–51.

29. The writer for Christie's *Old Master Drawings,* 4 July 1995, identified the woman or girl as Corradini, who was eighteen years old; but John Ingamells, in the National Portrait Gallery's forthcoming catalogue of mid-Georgian portraits, identifies her as Polly. I agree, largely on the grounds of the similarities between the two figures and their jaws, but also because I think it unlikely that Wilkes would have taken Corradini to the Palais Royal.

30. Cash, *Sterne: Later Years,* 184–88.

31. 10 April 1764, Add Mss 30,878, ff. 43–45; Wilkes-Churchill Correspondence, 83; Cash, "Sterne, Hall, Libertinism."

32. Unless otherwise indicated, all of the information on Corradini and all of Wilkes's words about her are taken from the autobiography, Add Mss 30,865, part B. There is no documentary proof that this was the night Wilkes met Corradini, but he does say he met her at Hope's, and the time frame is right. For Hope, Wilkes's landlord in Paris, see his letter to Wilkes from Holland, Add Mss 30,870, f. 235.

33. Randolph Trumbach, *Sex and the Gender Revolution,* i (1998), 107–08, 156–62.

34. Add Mss 30,868, ff, 70–71. Hanley, *Prebendal,* 7; Bleackley, *Life of Wilkes,* 152.

35. Dated 4 December 1765, Almon, *Correspondence,* ii, 216–22.

36. Add Mss 30,868, ff. 37–39, 108–09, 156–57.

37. Wilkes to Cotes, 5 June 1764, *Complete Collection,* 72–78.

38. Wilkes to Churchill, 15 August, Add Mss 30,878, f. 47. The official orders for the exacting, Guildhall KB.33.5/7.

39. *Public Advertiser,* 15 February 1765; *London Magazine,* xxxiii (1764), 595; xxxiv (1765), 54; Carrington to Webb, 27 December 1763, Add Mss 22,131, ff. 234–36, 171–72. Copies of Williams's edition are at the BL, shelf no. P.P.3585.ab., and at Butler Library, Columbia University, 942.073\W.65. A print depicting Williams in the pillory being cheered as a martyr to liberty is at the Morris Library, Southern Illinois University, Carbondale.

40. *Battle of the Quills,* iv.

41. The consumption is my speculation, but her symptoms were much like those of other consumptives, and her doctor's advice was typical for that disease.

42. Add Mss 30,868, ff. 90–91, 99; Wilkes-Churchill Correspondence, 95–96.

43. Wilkes described the death in the Autobiography, 20: "Mr. Wilkes never left him, and he expired in the arms of his friend."

44. Autobiography, f. 20; Almon, *Correspondence,* iii, 67.

45. *Political Register* i, 137–40. An official copy of the will is found among Wilkes's collection of Churchill's individually published poems and proof sheets at the BL, shelf no. C.61.c.3.

46. Add Mss 30,868, ff. 141–42, 144, 165–66; Wilkes Papers, i, 80.

47. Wilkes Papers, i, f. 81.

48. Add Mss 30,868, f. 164.

49. Add Mss, 30,880, f. 164; 30,879, f. 29.

50. Add Mss, 30,879, f. 30.

51. Wilkes Papers, i, f. 84; John Nesbitt to Wilkes, 2 May 1765 at Add Mss 30,868, f. 172.

52. Many details of Wilkes's journey I take from the Autobiography.

53. As quoted by John Ingamells, *Dictionary of Travelers,* 1001.

54. Wilkes to Suard, 16 February 1765, Wilkes Papers, ii, 12–12a.

55. Letter purportedly from Wilkes "to a friend" in the *Public Advertiser,* 7 October 1765, and the *Political Register,* iii, 119 (August 1768); Almon, *Correspondence,* ii, 200; iii, 67. Winckelmann's letters to Wilkes, Add Mss 30,877, ff. 37, 65; 30,869, ff. 146–47. Winckelmann's obituary, *Political Register* iii, July 1768, p. 119.

56. Walpole, *Correspondence,* xxii, 292.

57. The portrait by George Willison painted at Rome only weeks before this meeting, now at the Scottish National Portrait Galley, Edinburgh, shows a boyish young man, seated but looking ill at ease, dressed in a fur-trimmed coat and boots. Reproduced as frontispiece to Pottle, *Boswell Earlier Years.*

58. Ibid., 208–09. All quotations of the Wilkes-Boswell conversations in this chapter are taken from Boswell, *Grand Tour,* 59–73, 96–101.

59. At the BL are evidences of Wilkes's halfhearted attempt to edit the works. Wilkes's copy of *Poems by Charles Churchill,* 3 vols., 1767, printed for J. Wilkes (not the subject of this book, but a known printer of the same name), 1767, with a few marginal notes by Wilkes is at BL, shelf number 11609.aaa.11–13. Also at the BL, C.61.c.3, is a collection of first editions of Churchill's poems printed individually and one or two proofs of such, with marginal notes in Wilkes's hand. It includes a copy of Churchill's will.

60. Wilkes's comments are in Almon, *Correspondence,* iii, 70, 74, 79. Walpole's seeing the notes: *Correspondence,* x, 180. The most authentic accusation of Wilkes and Churchill is that of Benjamin Boyce, *Benevolent Man,* 231–32. In my edition of *Essay on Woman,* 24–25, I also blamed Wilkes for the publication, but upon discovering the following letters to Heaton Wilkes and Maria Stafford, I have changed my mind: Wilkes Papers, ii, 20; Wilkes to Maria Stafford in Green, *Bath Love Letters,* 39. I have not traced what seems to have been a version of *The Humours of the Times* published 1766 or 1767. The earliest version I have seen appeared in 1771. Subsequent versions under the title *The New Foundling Hospital for Wit* appeared in 1784 and 1786. My citations are to the 1786 edition, iii, 89–107.

61. When he moved into the house, Wilkes was still enchanted with her beauty, for example, in the scene with the nets thrown over the bed. If she was carrying Wilkes's child, she would have been over five months pregnant and would show. If this were the child of someone else, she might have been three or four months and not show.

62. Temple's congratulations: Add Mss 30,877, f. 55. Wilkes's decision to return: Wilkes in the Autobiography said that it was news of the Rockingham administration that determined him to return. The Autobiography was not written until 1789 (*Letters to His Daughter*, ii, 200), and it is obvious that Wilkes misremembered. Rockingham's administration began 13 July, and Wilkes sailed from Naples on 27 June. For the presence of Matthew Brown, *Wilkes Papers*, ii, 15.

63. Wilkes arrival in Geneva, Almon, *Correspondence*, ii, 179, 184–85. Friendship with Voltaire: Voltaire's letters to Wilkes, Add Mss 30,877, f. 34, 37; Wilkes to Polly, Almon, *Correspondence*, ii, 184–85; Wilkes to Cotes, Add Mss 30,868, f. 187; Wilkes letter in *Public Advertiser*, 2 September 1765, p. 1.

64. Boswell, *Grand Tour*, 269.

65. Almon, *Correspondence*, ii, 206–07; Add Mss 30,879, ff. 74, 78; 30,868, f. 193.

66. Boswell, *Great Biographer*, 30; Wilkes, *Letter to Grenville*; for the meeting of Wilkes and Horne in Paris and the letters over which they later quarreled, see Stephens, *Horne Tooke*. On Horne's contribution to philology, see Yarborough, *Horne Tooke*.

67. Boswell, *Grand Tour*, 269–76, and *General Correspondence*, i, 25.

68. *Les Rapports de Police de Marais*, BN, 11,359, ff 60, 778–79; BL 11359, ff. 778–79; *European Magazine* xxx, 164, as cited by Bleackley, *Life of Wilkes*, 176, n. 2.

69. Add Mss 30,868, f. 187; Almon, *Correspondence*, i, 58–62; Treloar, *Wilkes and the City*, 43–45.

70. Leslie and Taylor, *Reynolds*, 250 and n. (in chap. 4, for 1765).

71. Add Mss 30,868, f. 209, published in Treloar, *Wilkes and the City*, 43–45. For Macleane, see Namier and Brookes.

72. Add Mss 30,868, ff. 151–52, 201–02; Burke, *Correspondence*, i, 230–31 and nn. 1–3; Almon, *Correspondence*, ii, 211–15. Wilkes's letter to Fitzherbert is in Treloar, *Wilkes and the City*, 47.

73. Wilkes to Cotes, 4 December 1764, in Almon, ii, 216–21; Add Mss 30,869, ff. 1, 14–15, 22–23.

74. Add Mss 30,869, f. 31; Brooke, *George III*, 118; Almon, *Correspondence*, ii, 226. The proposed bill against general warrants, though fiercely contested, was finally voted down after Pitt joined the ministry in opposing it.

75. *Public Advertiser*, 14 May 1766.

76. Grenville Papers, iii, 241. Almon, *Anecdotes of Pitt*, 351; Wilkes to Lord Temple, 15 May 1766, *Grenville Papers*, 233, n. 1.

77. Add Mss 30,869, f. 42; Burke, *Correspondence*, i, 256–57; *Wilkes Papers*, ii, 10.

78. Wilkes to Fitzherbert, 6 August 1766 and 30 March 1767, at the Derbyshire County Record Office; Add Mss 42,085, ff. 3–5; *Grenville Papers*, iv, 1–4, 15–18.

79. Wilkes Papers ii, ff. 2–6; *Controversial Letters*, 199.

80. Wilkes to Lord Temple, 11 May 1767, Add Mss 42,085, ff. 21–22; John Woodhouse to Wilkes, 2 July 1766, 30,869, ff. 47–48; Wilkes to Heaton Wilkes, 6 March 1767, *Wilkes Papers*, ii, 10.

81. Green, *Visits to Bath*, 11.

82. 6 July 1766 at the Derbyshire County Record Office. Burke, *Correspondence*, i, 256–59.

83. Add Mss 30,869, f. 61.

84. *Letter to Grafton;* Wilkes to Temple, Add Mss 42,085, ff. 3–4.

85. Wilkes Papers, iv, 10; Add Mss 30,869, f. 78; Bleackley, *Life of Wilkes,* 178.

86. Add Mss 30,869, ff. 79–80; 30,879, f. 103; 42,085, ff. 3–5; Almon, *Correspondence*, iii, 178–80.

87. The oral message to Wilkes: Fitzherbert said he did not recall using those exact words, though he confirmed the substance of the conversation, Wilkes Papers, ii, 19. Grafton, *Autobiography,* 193; Wilkes, *Letter to Grafton.*

88. Wilkes Papers, i, 96.

89. Add Mss 30,869, ff. 86–87, 121–22; Wilkes Papers ii, 97. For Pitt's response to the bawdy poem, Cash, *Essay on Woman,* Historical Introduction.

90. Add Mss 30,869, f. 139; 42,084, f. 176; 42,085, ff. 176–77; Almon, *Memoirs,* 49–50; *Grenville Papers,* iv, 188–90.

91. Wilkes Papers, ii, 7–9, 22; Add Mss 42,085, ff. 21–22.

92. Wilkes Papers, ii, 15, 25, 28. The contract with Almon can be found at Add Mss 30,869, ff. 136–37, and facsimile in Almon, *Correspondence,* i, 256. See also Nichols, *Anecdotes,* 458.

93. Polly's birthday poem, *New Foundling Hospital for Wit,* iii, 110–11. The memoir, Wilkes Papers, ii, 15–15a. For a discussion of the possible relationship of this work, now lost, with the extant Autobiography, see below, chapter 14.

94. Wilkes Papers, ii, 2.

95. Wilkes Papers, ii, 29a, 30, 36–37.

96. Add Mss 30,869, f. 149; Bon Mots.

97. Add Mss 30,869, ff. 155–56; 30,870, f. 8.

98. Wilkes to Suard, 1 December 1769, Wilkes Papers, iii, 26.

99. Wilkes Papers, ii, 38–39; Add Mss 30,870, f. 2; 30,879, f. 105.

100. Wilkes Papers, ii, f. 28; Add Mss 30,879, ff. 108–09.

101. Add Mss 30,879, ff. 108–11; Wilkes Papers, ii, 38–40, 44; University Library, Leiden, ASF 15 (Matriculations 1755–1808), p. 142; Almon, *Correspondence,* iii, 222–24.

102. Kidgell, two letters to Richard Phelps, 20, 23 December 1763, National Maritime Museum, SAN V/14 Nos. 72–75; Kidgell to ?Halifax, 29 November 1768, Add Mss 22,132, ff. 297–98; Kidgell to [Lord March] from Utrecht, 29 November 1768, Add Mss 22,132, ff. 297–98; Guildhall 214/3, ff. 5–8, 33–34.

103. Add Mss 30,879, ff. 118–19; Almon iii, 228–31.

104. Add Mss 30,879, ff. 116–17.

105. Wilkes Papers, ii, 37v.

Chapter 9. The Middlesex Election Controversy

1. Almon *Correspondence,* iii, 237; Wilkes Papers, ii, 46–47.

2. Wilkes Papers, ii, 46; Add Mss 30,879, f. 126; Stowe and Strype, *Survey of London and Westminster,* 64; Bleackley, *Life of Wilkes,* 195; Almon, *Correspondence,* iii, 239.

3. Add Mss 30,875, f. 215; Lord's Journals, xxxii, 205–09; Wilkes Papers, ii, 51.

4. *Letter to Grenville*; Nichols, *Anecdotes*, ix, 457; Christie, *Wilkes, Wyvell, and Reform*, 26; Wilkes Papers, ii, 31; *Grenville Papers*, iv, 262–63.

5. Bon Mots; Thomas, *Wilkes*, 72.

6. *Public Advertiser*, 14 March.

7. Grafton, *Autobiography*, 199. Admission to the company, Bingley, ed., *North Briton*, xliv; *Public Advertiser*, 15–16 March 68. Treloar, *Wilkes and the City*, 63, gives the papers of admission and other curious documents from the company archives.

8. Namier and Brooke, i, 328.

9. The scene at the Guildhall: *Boswell in Search of a Wife*, 142; Wilkes's dress: *Bristol Journal*, 19 March 1768, as cited by Rudé, *Wilkes and Liberty*, 40; Wilkes's technique of gaining attention: Reynolds, *Life and Times*, ii, 97; Wilkes's speech: *Public Advertiser*, 17 March 1768; *Political Register*, ii, 299–304; the article on Wilkes's poor speaking abilities: *Public Advertiser*, 20 March. Harley's ordering the gallery cleared: *Political Register*, iii, 81–83.

10. *Political Register*, ii, 300–301.

11. Anecdote of the coatless voters: Bleackley, *Life of Wilkes*, 187; Wilkes blamed for mob destruction: Cavendish, *Debates*, i, 141–42; Wilkes to Suard: Wilkes Papers, v, f. 13; Chaired by the mob: *Public Advertiser*, 23 March 1768.

12. *Public Advertiser*, 23 March; Controversial Letters, 145–60.

13. *Political Register*, ii, 299–304; Almon, *Correspondence*, iii, 266–68; Pitt, *Correspondence*, iii, 323–24, n.

14. The qualifications of candidates are stated in Sir William Meredith's *The Question Stated*. Bleackley and Thomas think Temple had already given Wilkes the freehold he needed to qualify, but I am in doubt and have found no evidence on the question. Brooke, *George III*, 152, said that Wilkes "did not possess the necessary property qualification, but then neither did many of those who voted against him."

15. Burke, *Correspondence*, i, 349.

16. Thomas, *Wilkes*, 73.

17. Jensen, *Founding of a Nation*, 156; Brewer, "Number 45."

18. *Boswell in Search of a Wife*, 146; Walpole *Correspondence*, xxiii, 6–8.

19. Almon, *Memoirs*, 51; Grafton, *Autobiography*, 194, said that Wilkes won by intimidation, but his opinion has not been confirmed by historians. Thomas, *Wilkes*, 75, attributes Wilkes's success to "a cocktail of superb organization and popular enthusiasm."

20. Walpole, *George III*, 129; *Public Advertiser*, 30 March 1768.

21. *Political Register*, ii, 369–73; *Public Advertiser*, 23 March; *English Liberty*, 233–34.

22. Wilkes Papers, ii, 52; Walpole, *George III*, iii, 129–31.

23. *Political Register*, 30 March, ii, 304.

24. Rudé, *Wilkes and Liberty*, 89.

25. Franklin, *Papers*, xv, 99.

26. Walpole, *Correspondence*, xxiii, 6, and *George III*, iii, 130–31.

27. *London Magazine*, xxxvii, 224–25; *Gentleman's Magazine* (1768), 140; *Annual Register*, ii, 304; Rudé, *Wilkes and Liberty*, 43–44; Walpole, *George III*, iii, 129; Walpole, *Correspondence*, xxiii, 6–8.

28. James E. Thorold Rogers, *Historical Gleanings*, ii, 165; Letters to His Daughter, i,

65. Other versions in Nesta Pain, *George III at Home,* 68; and Richard Aldington, *Four English Portraits, 1801–1851,* 4.

29. Alexander Coke to Sir William Lee, 31 March 1768, Lee Papers, D2, Letter 98.

30. Bleackley, *Life of Wilkes,* 194; *Grenville Papers,* iv, 264.

31. Redlich and Hirst, *Local Government,* 71.

32. Thomas Whately to Grenville, as cited in *Grenville Papers,* iv, 267, n. 1; John Lord Campbell, *Lives of the Chancellors,* v, 275; *Public Advertiser,* 30 March.

33. Add Mss 30,870, ff. 40–45, 58–63, 79; Almon, *Correspondence,* v, 243–46; Kors, *D'Holbach's Coterie,* 302.

34. Walpole, *Correspondence,* xxiii, 8 (Walpole gave the date as 17 April); *Political Register,* ii, 326–28; *Grenville Papers,* iv, 271.

35. Vol. xxxviii (1768), p. 198. Cochrane, *Johnson's Printer,* 177; Brooke, *George III,* 148.

36. Minutes of the proceedings at Add Mss 33,053, ff. 317–22. Add Mss 32,948, ff. 363–66; 35,887, ff. 97–114; Almon, *Correspondence,* iii, 270; *London Magazine,* xxxvii (1768), 225–26; *Gentleman's Magazine* (1768), 195–96; *Annual Register,* 1768, p. 96; *Grenville Papers,* iv, 270–71; Walpole, *George III,* iii, 134–35; Thomas, *Wilkes,* 80.

37. George III, *Correspondence,* no. 614. Lady Mary Coke's comment is datable only by the year, 1768: Lady Mary Coke, *Letters and Journals,* ii, 213.

38. *Public Advertiser,* 23, 28 March 1768; Wilkes, *Letter to Grenville.*

39. Reported by James West to Newcastle, 24 April: Add Mss 32,989, ff. 377–78. Grafton in *Autobiography,* 201–02, said this was the court session at which the outlawry was lifted, but not so: that session was held on 8 June (see below). He also said the matter of bail was argued for some hours, which if correct would contradict my account. But Grafton's memory served him badly on some details, and he must have been thinking of another court scene.

40. Wilke's mother's account in Wilkes Papers, ii, 63–64v; *Public Advertiser,* 28 April 1768; Wilkes, *Letter to Grafton; London Magazine,* (1768), 228; Almon, *Correspondence,* iii, 270–71; *Political Register,* iii, 268.

41. Wilkes Papers, iii, 18.

42. Bleackley, *Life of Wilkes,* 234–35; Wilkes Papers, iii, 25a. See the map in Gypson, *Triumphant Empire,* 207.

43. *Grenville Papers,* iv, 279; cf. p. 2.

44. Wilkes Papers, iii, 18a.

45. Dated 5 May 1768: *Political Register,* 6 May 1768; printed also in the *Public Advertiser* of 6 May.

46. Rudé, *Wilkes and Liberty,* chap. 5; Brewer, "Wilkites and the Law"; Stella Duff, "The Case against the King"; Letters to His Daughter, i, 112; Brewer, "Number 45." The Newcastle festivities are quoted in Brewer, p. 353, from *Newcastle Journal,* 30 April 1768.

47. Rudé, *Wilkes and Liberty,* passim.

48. On the public tolerance of Wilkes's sexuality, see, for instance, "To the Serious Consideration of the Liverymen of the City of London," signed "Junius Junior," at the Guildhall, City Parliamentary Elections, 1768, Broadside No. 88. Hollis, *Memoirs,* i, 289.

49. Brewer, "Wilkites and Law." See Rudé, *Hanoverian London*, 202, 211–17, for a summary of Wilkes's support from the mob.

50. Burke, *Correspondence*, 1, 349; Taswell-Langmead, *Constitutional History*, 713; Jensen, *Founding of a Nation*, 158; Brooke, *George III*, 120–21.

51. Rea, *English Press*, 4.

52. Cochrane, *Johnson's Printer*, 182, n. 2. William Strahan echoed him in a letter to John Hall: the ministry is "more afraid of the mob of London than of the potent Houses of Bourbon."

53. King to George Grenville, 2 May 1768, Grafton Papers, 423/S14; Brooke, *George III*, 148.

54. Walpole, *George III*, iii, 140; Rudé, *Wilkes and Liberty*, 38–39 and chap. 6; Rudé, *London*, 202; Gipson, *Triumphant Empire*, 196–99.

55. Brewer, "Number 45"; Wilkes Papers, ii, 47.

56. Add Mss 32,990, f. 25; Rudé, *Wilkes and Liberty*, 49.

57. Wilkes Papers, ii, 56.

58. *Political Register*, ii, 417–22; iii, 117–18, 171–79, 179–86; Walpole, *George III*, iii, 141; *English Liberty*, 169–73; Bleackley, *Life of Wilkes*, 197–201.

59. My speculation. *Public Advertiser*, 11, 12 May; *Political Register*, ii, 417–22.

60. Walpole, *George III*, iii, 141; Brooke, *George III*, 149; Walpole, *Last Journals*, ii, 494; Franklin's description, *Writings*, v, 133–34.

61. *Boswelliana*, 274.

62. Broadley, *Brother John Wilkes*; Bleackley, *Life of Wilkes*, 238, and n. 1.

63. Maier, *Resistance to Revolution*, 167–77.

64. As quoted by Treloar, *Wilkes and the City*, 104.

65. George III, *Correspondence*, no. 634; Almon, *Correspondence*, iii, 281–82; Walpole, *George III*, iii, 141; *English Liberty*, 184.

66. Almon, iii, 271–72; Add Mss 35,887, ff. 115–17; 32,990, ff. 77–78, 186–87; Burrow's *Reports*, iv, 2527–78; Walpole, *George III*, iii, 151–52, n. 1; Howell, *State Trials*, xix, 1109–17, 1402–03, *Gentleman's Magazine* (July 1768), 327.

67. *Political Register*, iii, 35–36, 18, 20 June 1768.

68. *Political Register*, ii, 416–17; iii, 32, 56.

69. *London Magazine*, xxxvii (1768), 225–26. Kearsley's affidavit in Complete Collection, 240–42, and in Almon, *Correspondence*, i, 164; *London Magazine*, xxxvii (1768), 225–26; Kilvert, *Selection from Warburton*, 229.

70. George III, *Correspondence*, ii, no. 630. On the oratory of judges, see Linebaugh, *The London Hanged*.

71. Add Mss 35,887, ff. 120–21.

72. Almon, *Correspondence*, iii, 272; Hume *Letters*, ii, 182; "In Error"; Burrow's *Reports*, 2527–78; Lords Journals, xxxii, 200–23 *passim*.

73. Add Mss 30,879, f. 128; 30,884, ff. 65–75; *English Liberty*, 195–202; *London Magazine*, xxxvii (1768), 426–28; *Gentleman's Magazine*, xxxviii, 394–95; *Public Advertiser*, 12 August; Walpole, *George III*, iii, 159.

74. Wilkes to Dell, 9 July 1768, Wilkes Papers, vi, 79; Add Mss 30,870, ff. 81, 90; *Public Advertiser*, 2 May, 16 July 1768; Bleackley, *Life of Wilkes*, 235–36.

75. All quotations and information about Charlotte Forman are taken from Joel Gold, "Charlotte Forman." Many of the poems and eulogies are collected in Add Mss 30,882.

76. Polly to her grandmother Wilkes, Wilkes Papers, ii, 55; Almon, *Correspondence*, iii, 283–86; Add Mss 30,879, ff. 125–27.

77. *New Foundling Hospital for Wit*, iii, 111–12.

78. Vol. xxxix (1769), p. 55.

79. Add Mss 30,870, ff. 27, 40–44, 58–62, 170; Walpole, *George III*, iii, 138; Boswell, *In Search of a Wife*, 285.

80. Morton and Spinelli, *Beaumarchais*, 20; Gary Kates, *Monsieur d'Eon*; Anna Clark, "D'Eon and Wilkes."

81. Wilkes Papers, i, 91.

82. *Public Advertiser*, 7 February 1769; William M. Fowler, Jr., *The Baron of Beacon Hill*, 77; John Cary, *Joseph Warren*, 70; Jensen, *Founding of a Nation*, 260; Barnet Schecter, *The Battle for New York*, 32–33.

83. Add Mss 30,870, f. 46.

84. Ibid.

85. Ibid., ff. 75–76.

86. Ibid., 135–36. Wilkes published this letter in Controversial Letters, pp. 165–67.

87. Add Mss 30,870, ff. 137–39, 160–61, 166, 171–76, and passim; Maier, *Resistance to Revolution*, 144–45.

88. *New England Town and County Almanack for 1768* as quoted by Maier, *Resistance to Revolution*, 168; Kent to Wilkes, Add MSS 30,870, ff. 77–78.

89. *Autobiography*, 62.

90. Sainsbury, *Disaffected Patriots*, 7–13, 48–49, and passim; Tuchman, *March of Folly*, 153–54; Potts, *Arthur Lee*; Richard Henry Lee, *Life of Arthur Lee*.

91. See O. J. Harvey, *History of Wilkes-Barre*.

92. Gipson, *Triumphant Empire*, 192.

93. Add Mss 30,870, f. 114.

94. *Public Advertiser*, 9 December 1768; George Grego, *Parliamentary Elections*, chap. 7; Junius, *Letters*, 54–56; *English Liberty*, 209–29; Namier and Brooke, i, 331–35.

95. *Grenville Papers*, iv, 392–93; Walpole, *George III*, iii, 171; Nichols, *Anecdotes*, ix, 459; Rudé, *Crowd*, 50–65.

Chapter 10. Incapacitation

1. Grafton, *Autobiography*, 195–96.

2. Almon, *Correspondence*, iii, 293–95.

3. Bingley, *North Briton*, xciv–xcv; Wilkes, *Letter to Grenville*; Thomas, *Wilkes*, 90–91.

4. Almon, *Correspondence*, iii, 295–96.

5. Commons Journals, xxxii, 33–34; George III, *Correspondence*, no. 672; Walpole, *George III*, iii, 175; Howell, *State Trials*, 1382–1402; Cavendish, *Debates*, i, 46–49. The petition can be found in Commons Journals, xxxii, 33–34, and Almon, *Correspondence*, iii, 290–92, n.

6. Nichols, *Anecdotes*, xi, 459, dated 10 November 1768; Add Mss 22,132, ff. 299–300; Guildhall 214/1 ff. 145–48; Tracts Related to Wilkes; Wilkes, *Letter to Grenville*; *English Liberty*, 245–46; Polly to her mother, Wilkes Papers, iii, 60.

7. Walpole, *Correspondence*, xxiii, 77–78. George III, *Correspondence*, no. 617;

Lords Journals, xxxii, 205–06, 213–14; Commons Journals, xxxii, 208–09, 113; Walpole, *George III*, iii, 193–94; Gipson, *Triumphant Empire*, 211–12. A bowdlerized version of Weymouth's letter and Wilkes's preface in Almon, *Correspondence*, iii, 273, n.

8. The letters from Mrs. Barnard are at Add Mss 30,880B, ff. 35–57.

9. Thomas, *Wilkes*, 116 and n. 32; Brewer, *Party Ideology*, 165, 191.

10. *English Liberty*, ii, 237–38. The challenge to the election is discussed at length by Treloar, *Wilkes and the City*, 70–76, who reproduces many of the documents. The newspapers gave good coverage of these events: *Public Advertiser*, January 2–29, 1769, passim; *Political Register*, iv, 121; *Town and Country Magazine*, i, 52; *London Magazine*, xxxviii, 52, 109.

11. Walpole, *Correspondence*, xxiii, 80.

12. The brief at Add Mss 30,884, ff. 1–31. The scene in the House of Commons: Commons Journals, xxxii, 156–57; John Hope, *Certain Proceedings*; *Public Advertiser*, 30 January; Walpole, *George III*, iii, 211–12 and n. 1. Wilkes's speech at the bar in *English Liberty*, 234–35.

13. Walpole, *George III*, iii, 185–86; Commons Journals, xxxii, 58–113 passim; Lords Journals, xxxii, 187.

14. Walpole, *Correspondence*, x, 272.

15. Hatsell's letter, Add Mss 30,870, ff. 105–06. Probably the document in question is that at the BL, Add Mss 57,733, described in the Textual Introduction to Cash, *Essay on Woman*, 78. The proceedings: Walpole, *George III*, iii, 212–13; Commons Journals, xxxii, 58, 169–79; *English Liberty*, 249–50.

16. Curry's affidavit was published in *Political Register*, iii, 219–24; it can be found in Wilkes, *Complete Collection*, 240 ff., in Appendix i of Hotten's *Essay on Woman*, and in Guildhall 214/1, f. 151. Curry's career: Plomer, *Printers*. His suicide: A note in Wilkes's edition of the *Speeches of Mr. Wilkes*, 1786, p. 124, says of Curry that after testifying against Wilkes in 1764, he left London because no one would hire him, went to Norwich and then to Bristol, "where he delivered the world from one of the most wretched, as well as wicked, of the human race." I agree with the interpretation of these words advanced by Postgate, *That Devil Wilkes*, 88, that they mean suicide. Rea, *English Press*, 75, n., also believed that Curry committed suicide. However, suicide is not mentioned in the *Gentleman's Magazine* obituary of Curry, lii, pt. 2, p. 752 (August 1788).

17. *English Liberty*, 263–64.

18. Commons Journals, xxxii, 170–71; *English Liberty*, 259–61; Walpole, *George III*, iii, 213–14.

19. Walpole, *George III*, iii, 113–216.

20. *English Liberty*, 250–55; "In Error"; Commons Journals, xxxii, 172. For the Lords decision about the alleged "error," see Lords Journals, xxxii, 221–23. See the "afterword," or caveat, read by Wilkes's lawyer, Davenport, to the House of Lords, 9 December 1768, Add Mss 35,887, ff. 124–27. I do not understand why Wilkes's lawyers made an issue of the change of the record. Blackstone was right. Six weeks before, on 21 December 1768, the House of Lords considered Wilkes's complaint that Lord Mansfield's changing of the information had been illegal. Wilkes's lawyers, Glynn and Davenport, appeared at the bar and argued Wilkes's case. The Lords gave the case to a committee of judges who were members. On 16 January 1769, the House on the recommendation of

the committee rejected Wilkes's complaint and upheld Lord Mansfield's changing of the record. This should have settled the matter, for the House of Lords was the highest law court of Great Britain. "In Error" is a copy of the official record. See also "Appeals to the House of Lords," Add Mss 36,174, ff. 57–62.

21. Commons Journals, xxxii, 172; Walpole, *George III*, iii, 216–17.

22. Commons Journals xxxii, 176; Cavendish, *Debates*, i, 139–40.

23. *English Liberty*, 286. Commons Journals, xxxii, 178; Cavendish, *Debates* i, 151–56; Walpole, *George III*, 218–19; George III, *Correspondence*, nos. 696, 697.

24. Published by Almon as *The Speech of a Right Honorable Gentleman on the Motion for Expelling Mr. Wilkes*, which can be found in "Tracts Related to Wilkes." The publication is datable as mid-October 1769 from *Grenville Papers*, iv, 475.

25. *Public Advertiser*, 4, 8 February 1769; Walpole, *Correspondence*, xxiii, 86; Commons Journals, xxxii, 178–79; in Cavendish, *Debates*, one can find an excellent account of these proceedings, pp. 152–86; Walpole, *George III*, 217–18; Almon, *Correspondence*, iii, 297–300.

26. Temple's comment in Pitt, *Correspondence*, 349–50; Burke, as quoted by Thomas, *Wilkes*, 98; Heaton's remark in Wilkes Papers, ii, 59.

27. Broadside, dated 4 February, in the collection of Gerald M. Goldberg.

28. Bleackley, *Life of Wilkes*, 218; *English Liberty*, 293–98.

29. Commons Journals, xxxii, 228; Thomas, *Wilkes*, 99.

30. Almon, *Correspondence*, iv, 8. On the bill of rights: Keir, *Constitutional History*, 268–72.

31. Sainsbury, "Debt and Patriotism"; Walpole, *Correspondence*, xxiii, 92.

32. Peter Whitely, *Lord North*, 28, 38–39, 169, 210–11.

33. Broadside in the collection of Gerald M. Goldberg.

34. *English Liberty*, 304–06.

35. Pitt, *Correspondence*, iii, 352; Walpole, *George III*, iii, 230–31; Bleackley, *Life of Wilkes*, 218–19; *English Liberty*, 307–08.

36. Commons Journals, xxxii, 324; Hope, *Proceedings in Parliament*; *English Liberty*, 303–04.

37. For a report on the trial of Townsend, Walpole, *Last Journals*, i, 120–23. On Sawbridge, Walpole, *George III*, iii, 192, n., 230–31 and n. 1; obituary in *Gentleman's Magazine*, lvii (1787), 640.

38. Walpole, *Correspondence*, x, 273–74; *Grenville Papers*, iv, 415–17; Rudé, *Wilkes and Liberty*, 62–66. See the print at the Guildhall, "The Battle of Temple Bar," cat. no. 5428441.

39. Walpole, *Correspondence*, x, 273–74; *Grenville Papers*, iv, 415–17; Rudé, *Wilkes and Liberty*, 62–66; Wraxall, *Memoirs*, i, 333–34; Walpole, *George III*, iii, 232; Walpole, *Correspondence*, x, 274. See the print at the Guildhall, "The Battle of Temple Bar," cat. no. 5428441.

40. I quote from the version in *English Liberty*, 309–12.

41. *English Liberty*, 313; Walpole, *Last Journals*, i, 330; Namier and Brooke; Bleackley, *Life of Wilkes*, 219–20.

42. *English Liberty*, 315–17.

43. Walpole, *George III*, iii, 234–35.

44. *English Liberty*, 317–21; Walpole, *George III*, iii, 236; Rudé, *Wilkes and Libery*, 68–70; John Hope, *Certain Proceedings*.

45. Commons Journals, xxxii, 387; Namier and Brooke; Almon *Correspondence*, iv, 5–6; Rudé, *Wilkes and Liberty*, 70; Walpole, *George III*, iii, 237.

46. Brooke, *George III*, 152; Maier, *Resistance to Revolution*, 167–77.

47. Add Mss 30,880B, f. 50; Walpole, *George III*, iii, 239; Almon, *Correspondence*, iv, 5–6; Namier and Brooke.

48. The argument had been made by George Onslow at the time he moved to incapacitate Wilkes. Onslow had cited an obscure precedent: "Votes given to a person incapable of being chosen were looked upon as being thrown away and the person next on the poll was always elected."

49. Brewer, *Party Ideology*, 165, 191.

50. On the united purpose of the Grenville faction, *Political Register*, iii, 331; Add Mss 30,870, 107. Grenville's *Speech of a Right Honourable Gentleman on the Motion for Expelling Mr. Wilkes* (printed in October 1779: *Grenville Papers*, iv, 475, 479) and Wilkes's *Letter* can be found in "Tracts Related to Wilkes." According to Thomas, *Wilkes*, 97, Wilkes showed his *Letter* to Temple, who asked him not to publish it; he did anyhow, and "the two men never spoke again afterwards." I have not been able to corroborate this account. It was rumored that Temple himself had written the *Letter to Grenville*: Rockingham to Burke, 9 December 69, in Burke, *Correspondence*, ii, 116–17. Temple had cooled to Wilkes after his reconciliation with Grenville in November 1768. Walpole reported on 2 December 68, "Lord Temple . . . I hear disclaims having had any connection with Wilkes for some time" (Walpole, *Correspondence*, xxiii, 74). Yet Temple was among those who greeted Wilkes at Chatham's house when he was released from prison, 1770. Wilkes asked Temple's approval of the plan to get the printers to publish parliamentary doings, June 1772 (*Grenville Papers*, iv, 536–37). Temple withdrew from politics in roughly 1772, and it was at this time or later that he rebuilt the west pavilion of Stowe, on the roof of which is his tribute to Wilkes, the statue of Liberty with the cast eye (Clarke, "Lady with the Squint"). Temple gave Wilkes no active support between 1772 and his death in 1780, but shortly before his death he wrote Wilkes with a peace overture. Wilkes finally decided he had been mistaken in trusting Temple (see below, chap. 14).

51. Commons Journals, xxxii, 451; Rudé, *Wilkes and Liberty*, 71–72; Walpole, *George III*, iii, 240–42.

52. The order of king to have the meeting watched: George III, *Correspondence*, no. 709; *London Magazine* (May 1769), 219; Walpole, *George III*, iii, 240–43; Rudé, *Wilkes and Liberty*, 70–72. The petition itself in *English Liberty*, 223–30.

53. Unless otherwise indicated, my information on the petition movement is taken from Rudé, *Wilkes and Liberty*, chaps. 7, 8. For a searching analysis of the appeal of radicalism, see Brewer, "Wilkites and Law."

54. Walpole, *George III*, iii, 243; Christie, *Wilkes, Wyvill, and Reform*, 68–85; *Grenville Papers*, iv, 445–46.

55. *Annual Register*, 1770, p. 60, as quoted by Postgate, *That Devil Wilkes*, 154–55.

56. Walpole, *George III*, iv, 70–71.

57. Wilkes's poking fun at Beckford, *North Briton*, 257–58, 293. The king's mistreatment of the petitioners, Hill, *Republican Virago*, 62; Walpole, *George III*, iv, 64–66;

Albermarle, *Rockingham*, 173–74 (a somewhat different account in *London Magazine*, xxxix (9 April 1770). Beckford's impromptu address to the king is quoted from Valerie Hope, *My Lord Mayor*, 119–23. The story that Horne wrote it: *Table Talk of Samuel Rogers*, 1903, as cited by Treloar, *Wilkes and the City*, 99–100. See also *Grenville Papers*, iv, 520; Namier and Brooke.

58. Add Mss 30,870, f. 237; a version of the letter in Almon, *Correspondence*, v, 42–43; the account sent by an officer of the house at Add Mss 30,871, f. 7; *Annual Register*, 1770, p. 71. The South Carolina story: Jack P. Greene, "Bridge to Revolution." Jensen, *Founding of a Nation*, 377–80.

59. Wilkes to John Palfrey, 27 September 1769, in Norton Autographs, Houghton Library, Harvard University.

60. Dated 4 November 1769: Add Mss 30,870, ff. 222–23.

61. Maier, *Resistance to Revolution*, 145; Fowler, *Hancock*, 128. An account of this pamphlet, *A Short Narrative of the Horrid Massacre in Boston*, is given by John Cary, *Joseph Warren*, 95. The letters to Wilkes at Add Mss 30,871, ff. 18–20 (printed in Almon, *Correspondence*, v, 265–69).

62. According to Horne, Wilkes induced Silva to accept a compound of £550 to settle for the £2000 owed by agreeing to pay him an additional £262 in one year; but he never paid it (Controversial Letters, 207). I am suspicious of Horne's story about the additional payment, but the increase in the value of the bond is confirmed in the obituary of Silva in *Gentleman's Magazine*, lxxx, pt. I, p. 499: "He lent £500 to Mr. Wilkes on his bond, which he afterwards increased to £2000 and the bond was burnt."

63. Almon, *Correspondence*, iv, 8–13; *Annual Register*, 1769, p. 75; *Gentleman's Magazine*, xxxix, 108; Add Mss 30,870, f. 137; Walpole, *George III*, iii, 225; *English Liberty*, 300–301, 317, 333–34; Gipson, *Triumphant Empire*, 192; Treloar, *Wilkes and the City*, 102–04; Controversial Letters, 145–60. Good general accounts of Wilkes's debts in Bleackley, *Life of Wilkes*, 241–44, and Sainsbury, "Debt and Patriotism."

64. *English Liberty*, 331–32.

65. Wilkes Papers, iii, 25v–26; *Grenville Papers*, iv, 481; Wilkes, *Letter to Grenville*; Howell, *State Trials*, xix, 1075–1138, 1153–76, 1406–08, including the government agreement to cover Halifax's expenses; Philip Yorke, *Hardwicke*, iii, 460; Add Mss 41,355, ff. 173–205; Almon, *Correspondence*, iv, 13.

66. Sterne, *Letters*, 10–20, 448–53, and *passim*; Cash, *Sterne: Later Years*, 348–49, 351–52, and *passim*.

67. Letters from Cauchoix, Add Mss 30,870, f. 192; from Canning, Add Mss 30,870, ff. 201, 229–30, and 30,875, f. 76; Wilkes to Suard, at the McClintock Room, Farley Library, Wilkes University.

68. Wilkes Papers, iii, 25; Wilkes to Polly, letter in the McClintock Room, Farley Library, Wilkes University.

69. Add Mss 30,870, f. 8; *Public Advertiser*, 3, 7 November 1769.

70. Add Mss 30,876, ff. 233–34.

71. An account of the debate in Hume, *Letters*, 93–96. See Namier and Brooke article on Charles Pratt, Lord Camden; Bleackley, *Life of Wilkes*, 246.

72. John Hope, *Certain Proceedings*; Albermarle, *Rockingham*, 173; another version in *Grenville Papers*, iv, 502–03.

73. Namier and Brooke, iii, 105.

74. Junius, 176. The method of Yorke's suicide is specified by J. Stephen Watson, *George III*, 146.

75. On the change of ministries, Brooke, *George III*, 156–58; Gipson, *Triumphant Empire*, 217. Chatham's motion: Pitt, *Correspondence*, iii, 449–54; Bingley's *North Briton Extraordinary*, cxlix, 7 February (1770), bound with the Frye pamphlets, BL P.P.3611.lbb. North's motion: Gipson, *Triumphant Empire*, 217–18.

76. Hope, *Certain Proceedings*.

77. Add Mss 30,866, f. 12; 30,871, f. 27; 30,880B, f. 35.

78. Wilkes Papers, iii, 32. Texts of Wilkes's open letters in Almon, *Correspondence*, iv, 14–23.

79. Walpole, *George III*, iv, 78.

80. Reynolds, *Life and Times*, i, 19, 45.

81. Add Mss 30,871, f. 190.

82. Opening entries of Wilkes's diary, Add Mss 30,866; *London Magazine*, xxxix (1770), 17–18 April; the 1769 edition of *English Liberty*, 366–67.

83. Walpole, *George III*, iv, 78. The Wilkes wriggle: Brewer, "Number 45."

Chapter 11. The City of London

1. The anecdote from James E. Thorald Rogers, *Historical Gleanings*, 178. The Bill of Rights Society and the clearing of Wilkes's debts: Gipson, *Triumphant Empire*, 218. A possible exception was a debt to Lauchlin Macleane, the Irish adventurer who had tried to negotiate between Wilkes and the Rockingham ministry. Macleane had lent Wilkes £1350. The society had negotiated, and the debt had been reduced to £650. Before the society got around to paying the money, a letter about the demand appeared in the *Public Advertiser*. Macleane, feeling insulted and thinking that Wilkes was the author (which he was not), challenged Wilkes to a duel. But Woodfall, the publisher of the paper, smoothed things over. The society, however, did not discharge the debt until March 1772. See *London Magazine*, xli (1772), 3 March, 142–43, and Add Mss 30,871, ff. 52–62, passim. The ceremony: Bleackley, *Life of Wilkes*, 249–50; Add Mss 30,879, f. 133; Wilkes Papers, iii, 33.

2. Samuel Johnson, *Taxation No Tyranny*, 454. On Beckford's wealth, Almon, *Correspondence*, iv, 13; Rudé, *London*, 55.

3. Wilkes to Polly, 27 April 1770, Add Mss 30,879, f. 134; Wilkes Papers, ii, 92.

4. Guildhall prints, cat. nos. p5430248, q804110x.

5. Linebaugh, *The London Hanged*, 74–86.

6. Guildhall, cat. no. q8040625.

7. These examples are taken from Linebaugh, *The London Hanged*.

8. Rudé, *London*, 96–98, 255.

9. Treloar, *Wilkes and the City*, 191–92.

10. On the offer to Wilkes, Bingley, ed., *North Briton*, c [i.e., p. 100]. Bingley dated this event 1769, but he must have made a mistake. Walpole spoke of the vacancy as occurring in April 1770: Walpole, *Correspondence*, xxiii, 206; and Namier and Brooke date the beginning of Barnard's tenure in that same April. Walpole, *Correspondence*, xxiii, 206.

11. Wilkes to Suard, 1 May 1770, Wilkes Papers, iii, 34.

12. Walpole, *Correspondence*, xxiii, 208; Almon, *Correspondence*, iv, 32; Wilkes Papers iii, 34; Add Mss 30,879, ff. 142–43 and passim.

13. Add Mss 30,879, ff. 133, 137–38, 144–45, 153–54; Diary.

14. Wilkes Papers, ii, 80; Add Mss 30,879, f. 145; Bleackley, *Life of Wilkes*, 252.

15. Add Mss 30,879, ff. 138–47; Controversial Letters, 191–92.

16. Almon, *Correspondence*, iv, 42; Diary.

17. For Polly's attention to her half-brother, see Almon, *Correspondence*, iv, 38–39, 55, 68; Add Mss 30,879, ff. 148–49, 158–59.

18. Keane, *Tom Paine*, 67.

19. Controversial Letters, 196. Wilkes and Polly's trip recorded in Diary.

20. Hollis, *Memoirs*, i, 464. Wilkes's and Polly's return to London: *Public Advertiser*, 9 September. The King's Lynn honor: Add Mss 30,871, ff. 37–39. The *St. James's Chronicle* of 4 June 1768 carried a story about how Wilkes's popularity in London had begun to fade because people had forgotten what he had accomplished.

21. Porritt, *Unreformed Commons*, i, 80–81. See Add Mss 30,875, ff. 82–83, for a memorandum about Burke's activities in City politics.

22. Walpole, *Correspondence*, xxiii, 167; Pitt, *Correspondence*, 449–54; Albermarle, *Rockingham*, 174.

23. Sutherland, *City and Opposition*, 12; Rudé, *London*, 164. For a brief, useful history of the attempts to broaden the electorate, see John Cannon, *Parliamentary Reform*, chap. 1.

24. Controversial Letters, 219.

25. Walpole, *George III*, iv, 120–21, 130–31; *Public Advertiser*, October 26, 29, November 24, 226; *Gentleman's Magazine* (1770), 484. The issue did not die, and during the American war the press gangs again appeared in the City and were vigorously opposed by Sawbridge as lord mayor and his successor, Sir Thomas Halifax: Rudé, *London*, 174–75.

26. Namier and Brooke, i, 330; Rudé, *London*, 172.

27. As quoted in Sainsbury, "Debt and Patriotism," from Richard Sennett, *The Fall of Public Man* (New York, 1992), p. 103. The anecdote of the admiring liveryman, Bon Mots; also in Reynolds, *Life and Times*, ii, 397; Burke's remark, *Correspondence*, ii, 483.

28. Sutherland, *London and Opposition*, 17–19.

29. Walpole, *George III*, iv, 122; *Public Advertiser*, xxxi, 1–2 October and 10 November, 1770, as cited by Bleackley, *Life of Wilkes*, 257. In the *North Briton*, 127, Wilkes had written, "My only patron is the PUBLIC, to which I will ever make my appeal, and hold it sacred."

30. Baylen and Gossman, *Biographical Dictionary*, 18.

31. My account is based primarily upon Robert L. Haig, *The Gazetteer*. I have also used the excellent account in Thomas, *Wilkes*, chapter 8, much of which is taken from his earlier article, "John Wilkes and the Freedom of the Press, 1771," *Bulletin of the Institute of Historical Research*, 33 (1960), 86–98. Wilkes's account of these events appears in *Speeches* as a long footnote, pp. 155–66, and many of the legal papers are given in appendix 4, pp. 402–17. Good accounts can be found in Treloar, *Wilkes and the City*, 115–25, and Rea, *English Press*, 202–11. Almon, *Correspondence*, v, 51–64, has a brief

account with notes printing some of the documents; and Walpole, *Correspondence*, xxiii, 279–81, an even briefer account. On the place of these events in legal history, see Keir, *Constitutional History*, 342–43.

32. Commons Journals, xxxiii, 142. On Augustine Wall, Almon, *Memoirs*, 1790, 118–21.

33. Commons Journals, xxxiii, 149.

34. Morris to Wilkes, 13 March, as quoted by Thomas, "Wilkes and Freedom of the Press."

35. May, *Constitutional History*, 39; Gipson, *Triumphant Empire*, 219–21; Pitt, *Correspondence*, iv, 115–17.

36. May, *Constitutional History*, 40.

37. Thomas, *Wilkes*, 131.

38. Bleackley, *Life of Wilkes*, 260–62; Crosby, *Memoir*.

39. Almon, *Correspondence*, v, 58–59, n.

40. Albermarle, *Rockingham*, ii, 205.

41. Crosby, *Memoir*, 22.

42. Crosby, *Memoir*, 1–19; Thomas, *Wilkes*, 131, n. 31.

43. George III, *Correspondence*, nos. 933–34. The story of Brass Crosby's commitment by the House of Commons is covered in Howell, *State Trials*, 1138–51.

44. Commons Journals, xxxiii, 264. On the mob: Rudé, *London*, 169.

45. Crosby, *Memoir*, 20–28; Commons Journals, xxxiii, 269.

46. Commons Journals, xxxiii, 269, 275–76; Crosby, *Memoir*, 86.

47. Walpole, *George III*, iv, 195.

48. Commons Journals, xxxiii, 285–86; Albermarle, *Rockingham*, ii, 206; Walpole, *George III*, iv, 199.

49. Walpole, *George III*, iv, 200.

50. Commons Journals, xxxiii, 286.

51. Pitt, *Correspondence*, iv, 122–23; George III, *Correspondence*, nos. 936–41.

52. Walpole, *George III*, iv, 201 and n. 1; Commons Journals, xxxiii, 289.

53. Crosby, *Memoir*, 38, n.; Walpole, *George III*, iv, 203–04; Albemarle, *Rockingham*, 208–09. The nickname "Jemmy Twitcher" was attached to Lord Sandwich after his prosecution of Wilkes for printing the "Essay on Woman": see above, chapter 7.

54. Diary, 8 May 1771; Rudé, *Wilkes and Liberty*, 164.

55. Schlesinger, *Prelude to Independence*, 122, 113. On the silver cup, Treloar, *Wilkes and the City*, 122.

56. Almon, *Memoirs*, 1790, 119–20; also see Almon's *Political Anecdotes*, i, 406–08.

57. Almon, *Correspondence*, v, 62–63. *Grenville Papers*, iv, 536; Walpole, *Last Journals*, i, 432.

58. Oliver's open letter to Wilkes in *London Magazine*, xl (1771), 214, and Wilkes's reply, in Controversial Letters, 273–75; Walpole, *George III*, iv, 210.

59. Controversial Letters, 13–25, 308–11, and passim.

60. On Horne as troublemaker, Controversial Letters, 41–42; Stephens, *Memoir of Horne Tooke*, i, 77; Cash, *Sterne: Later Years*, 232–33. On 5 June [1771], Wilkes wrote his brother, "I have Mr. Garrick's permission to publish a letter of his which proves Horne a liar in another most essential point": Wilkes Papers, ii, 83. On the suit by the

jewler(s): Walpole, *George III*, iv, 138; Controversial Letters, 208. As to Heaton Wilkes and the chamberlainship, Heaton did ponder standing for chamberlain, but Wilkes publicly opposed his doing so: Controversial Letters, 101; copy of a public letter signed by Wilkes on May 28, at Guildhall, City of London Elections, 1768, Broadside No. 13; Almon, *Correspondence*, v, 151. On the pony: Controversial Letters, 41. When Wildman sent the horse to Madam d'Holbach, Wilkes paid five guineas in advance, but whether he paid the balance owed, I do not know: Wilkes Papers, ii, 6. On the sobriquet of Malagrida, *London Magazine*, xl (1771), 212; Controversial Letters, passim. The name was more often given to Horne's patron, Earl Shelburne.

61. Controversial Letters, 199; see above, chapter 8.

62. For Horne's version of events, see Stephens, *Horne Tooke*, i, 168–99, and chapter 6, which contains many of the letters from Controversial Letters.

63. Albemarle, *Rockingham*, ii, 234–35; Stephens, *Horne Tooke*, i, 196, 318–19; Christie, *Wilkes, Wyville, and Reform*, 48–49.

64. *London Magazine*, xli (1772), 3 March, 142–43. The challenge and related correspondence at Add Mss 30,871, ff. 56–62.

65. Almon, *Correspondence*, iv, 85–86.2; Rudé, *London*, xii–xiv, 247–48; Christie, *Wilkes, Wyville and Reform*; Shelburne's involvement: Walpole, *George III*, iv, 200.

66. Thomas, *Wilkes*, 143.

67. Diary.

68. Sainsbury, *Disaffected Patriots*, 49–50; Maier, *Resistance to Revolution*, 161; Jensen, *Founding of a Nation*, 584. Horne's accusation, Controversial Letters, 158; Wilkes's reply, including copies of letters to America, at 161–67. Adams's letter, Add Mss 30,871, f. 51. Forming the Committee of Correspondence, William M. Fowler, Jr., *The Baron of Beacon Hill*, 148.

69. Add Mss 30,871, f. 51.

70. Maier, *Resistance to Revolution*, 226. Adams's letter, Add Mss 30,871, f. 51.

71. Walpole, *Correspondence*, xxiii, 317.

72. To Heaton, 1 December 1771, Wilkes Papers, ii, 98. On aldermen, Rudé, *London*, 125.

73. *Gentleman's Magazine*, ili (1771), 471; Almon, *Correspondence*, iv, 172; Burke, *Correspondence*, ii, 357; Mrs. Thrale's comment, *Thraliana*, 142–43.

74. Treloar, *Wilkes and the City*, 124–25; Walpole, *George III*, iv, 230; Bleackley, *Life of Wilkes*, 269–70; Thomas, *Wilkes*, 147.

75. *Gentleman's Magazine*, xli (1771), 471. In 1783, the hangings were moved from Tyburn to the streets next to the prisons where the condemned were held. Thomas Rolandson made a print of the hangings outside Newgate, reproduced in Burke, *Streets of London*.

76. Earlier, Junius had said unkind things about Wilkes's motives, for which statement he would later, in a fashion, apologize. See Junius, 423.

77. Junius, 159–73; Walpole, *George III*, iii, 266.

78. Junius, appendix 8, "A Note on Authorship," 539–72.

79. Junius, 313–14, 320–42, 433–34. A warrant for the arrest of Eyre for stealing eleven quires of writing paper valued at six shillings is among Wilkes's papers at the BL: Add Mss 30,881, f. 29.

80. For a detailed study of the radicals and law, see Brewer, "Wilkites and Law."

81. *English Chronicle*, as quoted in Namier and Brooke, i, 328. The complete text of the manifesto in Junius, 404.

82. Christie, *Wilkes, Wyvill, and Reform*, 50–51.

83. Ibid., 49; Thomas, *Wilkes*, 146.

84. Add Mss 30,879, f. 184. For Bath recreations, see Graham Davis and Penny Bonsall, *Bath*, and Trevor Fawcett, *Bath Entertain'd*.

85. Add Mss 30,879, f. 208; Wilkes Papers, i, 39; Bleackley, *Life of Wilkes*, 398.

86. Add Mss 30,879, f. 203, printed in Almon, *Correspondence*, iv, 138.

87. Diary, 52v; To Polly from Cricklade, 27 February 1775, Letters to His Daughter, ii, 5–6; *Letters of Sterne*, 304–06; Cash, *Sterne: Later Years*, 27–28. Wilkes dined with Beauclerk and Lady Diana on 13 October 1773: Diary. For this couple, see Carola Hicks, *Improper Pursuits*, 207–08, and Lyle Larsen, "Dr. Johnson's Friend." The Lord Bathurst with whom Wilkes dined was Allen Bathurst (1684–1775), created Baron Bathurst in 1712, elevated as Earl Bathurst 1772, not to be confused with his son, Henry Bathurst (1714–94), the incompetent lord chancellor. "The Association" was advertised in the *Public Advertiser*, 26 June 1771.

88. Letters to His Daughter, ii, 7, 10.

89. Walpole, *Correspondence*, xxxiii, 510–11. Taking Polly to Angelo's: Diary, 17 March 1773. Wilkes to Suard, 19 September [1777], in the collection of Gerald Goldberg. I would certainly like to find this elegy!

90. The translation, probably by Wilkes, was published as *The Origin and Progress of Despotism in the Oriental and other Empires of Africa, Europe, and America*. The title page announced no translator and stated that the book was published in Amsterdam, a not-uncommon device to keep publishers out of trouble: J. M. Riggs article on Wilkes in the DNB attributes the translation to Wilkes; see also McCracken, "John Wilkes Humanist," 134, n. 77.

91. Add Mss 30,879, f. 203.

92. George Lyman Kittridge, *The Old Farmer*, 3–10. The anecdote of Mary Wilkes Hayley in the Pump Room told by Mrs. Thrale, *Thraliana*, 142–43.

93. Namier and Brooke.

94. Family activities: Almon, *Correspondence*, iv, 115, 142–43, 167–69; Diary; Sherbrooke's death: *Daily Advertiser*, 23 June 1772.

95. Bon Mots; letter to Polly, Almon, *Correspondence*, iv, 82; Reynolds, *Life and Times*, i, 20; Burke, *Correspondence*, iv, 206; Angelo, *Reminiscences*, 42, 45–46.

96. Add Mss 27,925, ff. 3–4; 30,880B, ff. 25–26; Diary, 23, 37v, 43, 44v, 45, 66v; 48v; Bleackley, *Life of Wilkes*, 339; Wilkes Papers, iii, 35.

97. Add Mss 30,871, ff. 73, 96–116 passim; 30,875, ff. 130–58; 30,880A, ff. 1–34; Wilkes Papers, ii, 95; Bleackley, *Life of Wilkes*, 355–56, 367–68.

98. Shaftesbury, *Characteristics*, i, 310–11; Hutcheson, *Inquiry*, 250, 258; Hume, *Enquiry*, 300. See Cash, *Sterne's Comedy*, 61–63.

99. Add Mss 30,880A-B.

100. My account of Charpillon's general history is based upon Bleackley's well-researched story, *Life of Wilkes*, 339–46. My description of the contents of her letters is based upon an examination of the originals at the BL, Add Mss 30,880B, ff. 35–173;

cited here are ff. 75, 101, 107, 109. The meeting of Wilkes and Charpillon: two letters of Charpillon's addressed originally to Chase Price but copied by Wilkes at Add Mss 30,880A, ff. 35–37. The borrowing from Price: Wilkes to Price, 6 November 1773, in Albemarle, *Rockingham*, ii, 235–37. Casanova and Charpillon, *Life and Memoirs of Casanova*, chap. 18. On Charpillon and Polly, compare Add Mss 30,880B, f. 74, with *Letters to his Daughter*, ii, 34.

101. See at the Guildhall, City Parliamentary Elections, 1768, Broadside No. 90.

102. *Boswell in Search of a Wife*, 286; *Boswell for the Defence*, entry for Monday, 20 April 1772.

103. Walpole, *Last Journals*, i, 157.

104. Treloar, *Wilkes and the City*, 130–33; George III, *Correspondence*, nos. 1134–37, 1141–44, 1156; Walpole, *Last Journals*, i, 156–57; Bleackley, *Life of Wilkes*, 275–76; Christie, *Wilkes, Wyville, and Reform*, 57.

105. Walpole, *Last Journals*, i, 158; *London Magazine*, xli (1772), 548–49; Rudé, *London*, 125; Treloar, *Wilkes and the City*, 126–27.

106. Broadside "To the Worthy Liverymen of the City of London," signed " a member of the Common Council," in the Guildhall collection of broadsides, City of London Elections.

107. As quoted in William Lee, *Letters*, i, 16.

108. George III, *Correspondence*, no. 1232; Walpole, *Last Journals*, i, 189–96, 130–31; Bleackley, *Life of Wilkes*, 279.

109. Wilkes wrote a memorial of their meeting, which is given in Almon, *Correspondence*, i, 204–11. In telling this story, I depend upon the best account of Armstrong I know of, Knapp, "Dr. John Armstrong."

110. Add Mss 30,871, ff. 174–80. I do not know just what Lane had said or written.

111. Walpole as quoted by Treloar, *Wilkes and the City*, 128. Boswell, *Life*, v, 339, under date of October 1773.

112. *Gentleman's Magazine*, xliv (February 1774), 89, under date of January 29. My thanks to James Basker for calling this to my attention.

113. Sainsbury, *Disaffected Patriots*, 58.

114. Walpole, *Last Journals*, i, 397; George III, *Correspondence*, nos. 1520–32; *London Magazine*, xliii (1774), 506–07; Walpole, *Correspondence*, xxxix, 196.

115. Namier and Brooke; George III, *Correspondence*, nos. 1318, 1324–25; Christie, *Wilkes, Wyville, and Reform*, 59.

116. Thomas, *Wilkes*, 152.

117. *London Magazine*, xliii (1774), 506–07; Bleackley, *Life of Wilkes*, 283; Treloar, *Wilkes and the City*, 137–38.

118. Walpole, *Last Journals*, i, 397–98 and 197, n.2.

119. *Gentleman's Magazine*, ixiv (1774), 444.

120. Christie, *Wilkes, Wyville, and Reform*, 60–61; Walpole, *Correspondence*, xxxix, 196; Thomas, *Wilkes*, 154–55.

121. According to the *London Magazine*, xliii (1774), 560, the gift was from "his lady." Polly would have been called "his daughter" or "the Lady Mayoress."

122. Thomas, *Wilkes*, 155; *London Magazine*, xliii (1774), 515–16; *Gentleman's Magazine*, xliv (1774), 538; Bleackley, *Life of Wilkes*, 283–85. A full account of the

procession in Treloar, *Wilkes and the City*, 144–47. Treloar also describes other ceremonial feasts occasioned by a change of mayors, pp. 152–53 and n, 1; Angelo, *Reminiscences*, 42–43. On Wilkes's interest in Jackie's learning to dance, Wilkes Papers, iii, 25.

123. Rudé, *Crowd*, 57.

Chapter 12. My Lord Mayor

1. Quotations are from press cuttings at the Guildhall as quoted by Treloar, *Wilkes and
the City*, 147–48. See also Guildhall 3332(2) as cited by Thomas, *Wilkes*, 155. For prints
of mayoral banquets, see Guildhall prints, cat. nos. q4921300, q8021361, q8021243.
Polly's linguistic accomplishments, Green, *Visits to Bath*, 11. D'Holbach's compliments,
Almon, *Correspondence*, iv, 176–77. Roach's challenge, Bleackley, *Life of Wilkes*, 292.

2. *Thraliana*, 193.

3. Almon, *Correspondence*, iv, 174; Bleackley, *Life of Wilkes*, 288–89.

4. Boswell, *The Ominous Years*, entry for 24 March 1775; Almon, *Correspondence*, iv,
317.

5. Brady, *Boswell, Later Years*, 93; Almon, *Correspondence*, iv, 319; Wilkes to Boswell, 25 March [1779], in the Yale Boswell archives C3093.

6. Wraxall, *Memoirs*, ii, 48–49.

7. Walpole, *Correspondence*, xxxix, 221; George III, *Correspondence*, no. 1558;
Namier and Brooke; Diary, f. 52.

8. *Parliamentary Register*, i, 116; Speeches, 1–2. Here and in the following quotations,
I use the edition of Speeches of 1786. In September 1777 first appeared the *Speeches of
Mr. Wilkes* (dated from Add Mss 30,872, f. 85). On 25 March 1778 he wrote to Philo-
Wilkes that another volume would appear "in the summer" (Add Mss 30,872, f. 95). In
the preface to the edition of 1786, Wilkes says that the book contains three earlier
volumes: pp. 1–176 make up "the two prior volumes, with the Notes . . . and the third
continues to p. 296. The rest is new matter, and on a great variety of interesting subjects."
On Johnson's position apropos of revolution, Boswell, *Life of Johnson*, i, 424; ii, 170.

9. Wraxall, ii, 48–49. On the number of times Wilkes spoke, Bleackley, *Life of Wilkes*,
301. Speaking at a meeting of shopkeepers in 1787, Wilkes "was not well heard": *Gentleman's Magazine*, lvii, 144–47.

10. Walpole, *Last Journals*, i, 437–38.

11. Wilkes, *Speech of the Lord Mayor*; Speeches, 19–39; *Parliamentary Register*, 214–
22.

12. North's speech, *Parliamentary Register*, ii, 432–41; Luttrell's speech as quoted by
Thomas, *Wilkes*, 178; Van's speech and Wilkes's response, *Parliamentary Register*, i, 230,
and Walpole, *Last Journals*, i, 438; defeat of Glynn's motion, Commons Journals, xxxv,
141; King's comment, George III, *Correspondence*, no. 1603; Wilkes's repetition of the
motion, *Speeches*, 72–82.

13. I have not seen it, but Wilkes said he wrote something with this title: Wilkes to
Suard, 19 September [1777], in the collection of Gerald Goldberg.

14. Walpole, *Correspondence*, xxxii, 237–38; *Last Journals*, i, 466.

15. As quoted in Treloar, *Wilkes and the City*, 166–67.

16. Kathleen Wilson, "Empire, Trade, and Popular Politics"; Bradley, *Popular Politics*

and the American Revolution, 12. The king often urged loyal addresses, paid for the cost of raising them, and rewarded their presenters with knighthood: Porritt, *Unreformed House of Commons*, i, 270.

17. Maier, *Resistance to Revolution*, 237–43. I know of no direct evidence of the meeting of Quincy and Palfrey with Wilkes, but it is suggested in a letter of Samuel Adams to Wilkes of 28 December 1770, which Adams handed to Palfrey asking him to deliver it: Add Mss 30,871, f. 51.

18. *The Speech of the Right Hon. John Wilkes, Esq. Lord Mayor*; Wilkes's version, which differs considerably, in *Speeches*, 7–19; see also *Parliamentary Register*, i, 141–46, where the speech is dated 6 February; Simmons and Thomas, *Proceedings and Debates*, v, 365–68.

19. Add Mss 30,880B, ff. 71–72.

20. Jensen, *Founding of a Nation*, 565.

21. The petition, organized by Wilkes's brother-in-law, George Hayley, was presented to the assembly on 23 January 1776: Commons Journals, xxv, 71.

22. Bleackley, *Life of Wilkes*, 290.

23. *Daily Advertiser*, 11–12 April; the text of the address in *Public Advertiser*, 11 April. See also *London Magazine*, xliv (1775) 208–11; *Gentleman's Magazine*, xlv (1775), 109–10, 203, 220–22, 302, 348; xlvi (1776), 140. The king's comment, Walpole, *Correspondence*, xxiv, 89; Walpole, *Last Journals*, 456.

24. Jensen, *Founding of a Nation*, 589.

25. *Gentleman's Magazine*, xlv (1775), 302.

26. Sainsbury, *Disaffected Patriots*, 89–90; Maier, *Resistance to Revolution*, 256; Thomas, *Tea Party to Independence*, 272 and n. 100.

27. Treloar, *Wilkes and the City*, 167–69; Sainsbury, *Disaffected Patriots*, 93–94.

28. Add Mss 30,874, ff. 142–43; published by Almon, *Correspondence*, iv, 34.

29. Walpole, *Last Journals*, i, 473; Letters to His Daughter, ii, 61–62; Maier, *Resistance to Revolution*, 257; Bradley, *Popular Politics and the American Revolution*, 98–99.

30. Sainsbury, *Disaffected Patriots*, 96, 125–31; Walpole, *Last Journals*, i, 475–76; *Annual Register*, 1776, 154; *London Evening Post*, 4 July 1776. The Common Hall entered Hancock's letter into their records, a document which Sainsbury records as Common Hall Book, 8 [1751–88], 193–94. I have a copy given to me by James Cope.

31. Sainsbury, *Disaffected Patriots*, 136–39.

32. Ibid., 98–106; Maier, *Resistance to Revolution*, 259–63; Walpole, *Correspondence*, xxiv, 138–39; Walpole, *Last Journals*, i, 481–82.

33. Add Mss 30,866, ff. 57–59, the meetings discussed by Morton and Spinelli, *Beaumarchais and the American Revolution*, 18–19; Trevelyan, *The American Revolution*, abridged edition by Richard B. Morris (New York: David McKay, 1964), p. 325. Maier, *Resistance to Revolution*, 256; Sainsbury, *Disaffected Patriots*, 103. Diary, 30 June 1771, 10 February 1776. Lauraguais and Beaumarchais: William Lee, *Letters*, 47–52. Hatselle or Hatsell, clerk of the House of Commons from 1768 to 1797, eventually wrote *Precedents and Proceedings in the House of Commons*, the most authoritative work on procedures during the eighteenth century: see Wilding and Laundy, *Encyclopaedia of Parliament*.

34. Morton and Spinelli, *Beaumarchais and the American Revolution*, 60; Maier, *Resistance to Revolution*, 256–57; Sainsbury, *Disaffected Patriots*, 103. In "The Observer," Wilkes spoke of Beaumarchais's operation, though not his own part in it: Almon, *Correspondence*, v, 207–37. Though they do not mention Wilkes's part, Morton and Spinelli devote their third chapter to the operation, which was intricately complicated by economic and political considerations. In their conclusion, Morton and Spinelli, 327–28, give Wilkes credit as one who inspired Beaumarchais.

35. Letters to His Daughter, i, 175.

36. The letter, at Add Mss 30,872, ff. 101–04, is dated 17 June 1779 and bears a note in Wilkes's hand, "Received from Mr Hayley July 20, 1779, in two covers." The covers still accompany the letter, the outer addressed to Hayley, the inner to "Miss Wilkes" at Prince's Court; but the letter opens, "Dear Sir." It is signed "W. L.," which historians have taken to be William Lee. In a naïve and badly written preamble, Lee, if it is he, blames Bute for the "horrid and savage war" that "must inevitably put an end to the remaining liberties of Englishmen. . . . For these reasons, I presume you can have no objection to undertake to give me regularly the information I want." He offers a compensation of two hundred pounds a quarter. He sends a code so simple it could be cracked by a child. He lines up "a, b, c, d, e," etc., and places under them an offset alphabet, so that "i" falls under and represents "a," "j" represents "b," etc. to the end of the alphabet.

37. Diary, f. 58; Add Mss 30,866, f. 58; 30,880B, f. 40 The Barnard letters: Add Mss 30,880B, ff. 29–43. Barnard is mentioned in the DNB account of his father, Sir John Barnard, 1685–1764.

38. Add Mss 30,880B, ff. 32–35.

39. Ibid., f. 35.

40. Ibid. f. 36.

41. Ibid., ff. 35–37.

42. Almon, *Correspondence*, v, 23–28.

43. Add Mss 30,880B, f. 38.

44. Ibid., ff. 39–40.

45. Ibid., f. 42.

46. Ibid., ff. 40–41. Obituary, *Gentleman's Magazine*, lv (1785), 155.

47. Treloar, *Wilkes and the City*, 173.

Chapter 13. Poverty, Paternity, and Parliamentary Reform

1. *Gentleman's Magazine*, xlvi (1776), 363; Add Mss 30,872, 71–73; *London Magazine*, xlvi (1777), 532; George III, *Correspondence*, no. 773.

2. Paraphrased from Bon Mots.

3. Add Mss 30,871, f. 258v.

4. Betty R. Masters, *Chamberlain*, 53–67.

5. *Boswell in Extremes*, 3; *Gentleman's Magazine*, xlvi (1776), 285, 332; *Gentleman's Magazine*, xlviii (1778), 330. An excellent full discussion of this election in Sainsbury, "Debt and Patriotism."

6. *Johnson Miscellanies*, ii, 373–74.

7. Boswell, *Life of Johnson*, iii, 64–69. A study of Wilkes's allusions to and familiarity with Johnson's writings may be found in Joel Gold, "Wilkes and the Writings of Johnson."

8. Lettsom, *Memorials*, ii, 403. Since William Lee permanently left England in this same year, 1776, this dinner must have followed within months of the meeting at Dilly's.

9. Boswell, *Life of Johnson*, iii, 183, 188–89.

10. Almon, *Correspondence*, iv, 241; Letters to His Daughter, ii, 15–18, 21.

11. Emanuel Green, *Visits to Bath*.

12. Add Mss 30,872, ff. 10–11; Letters to His Daughter, ii, 50. Wilkes wrote to Heaton, 24 August 1771: he is going to the Joiners to swear in Dr. Wilson as master: Wilkes Papers, ii, 89.

13. Wilkes to [Petrie], 1 October 1776, Wilkes Papers, iii, 44.

14. Sylas Neville, as quoted by Hill, *Republican Virago,* 17.

15. Boswell, *Life of Johnson*, i, 447–48.

16. Letters to His Daughter, ii, 69.

17. Ibid., 84. The statue by J. F. Moore that now stands outside the public library at Warrington: DNB; Hill, *Republican Virago*, 99–102, 114.

18. Letters to His Daughter, ii, 62, 93.

19. Ibid., 115–16, 122; Hill, *Republican Virago*, 107–10.

20. Dr. James Graham, a well-known quack who had treated Mrs. Macaulay and exercised considerable influence over her. It was his brother, Dr. William Graham, who married Mrs. Macaulay.

21. Letters to His Daughter, ii, 165–66, 200.

22. Ibid., 116, 126, 173.

23. Ibid., ii, 224–25, 237.

24. Ibid., ii, 127.

25. Ibid, 224, 229 ; Rea, *English Press*, 172. A list of Macaulay's works in Hill, *Republican Virago*, 253. I take my facts about Macaulay's late history from Hill, 123–29. The reader may want to look at Hill's fifth chapter, where she tells a story of "Wilkes's involvement in, and obvious enjoyment of the scandal that was so effectively to destroy Catharine Macaulay's reputation" (Hill, 120). Her interpretation of the evidence is vastly different from mine.

26. Letters to His Daughter, ii, 93. My quotation of Mrs. Thrale is taken from James L. Clifford, *Piozzi*, 156.

27. Wilkes to Petrie, Wilkes Papers, iii, 48; Almon, *Correspondence*, v, 32. I do not know whom Wilkes was quoting. Heaton's distress: Wilkes Papers, vi, 56. Israel: Wilkes Papers, ii, 114–114a; Bleackley, *Life of Wilkes,* 21–22; Almon, *Correspondence*, v, 147–49.

28. William Temple's bequest, Nichols, *Anecdotes*, ix, 463; *Daily Advertiser*, 21 May 1773; Almon, *Correspondence*, v, 40; Add Mss 30,871, f. 184. The gratuities, Albemarle, *Rockingham*, ii, 235–37, 345; Namier and Brooke. Philo-Wilkes, Add Mss 30,872, passim.

29. Wilkes's quip in the Commons, Malmesbury Mss memo, 22 March 1777, as cited by Thomas, *Wilkes*, 267, n. 27. The gifts, Add Mss 30,872, ff. 92–93v. The bill, Commons Journals, xxxvi, 856.

30. Wilkes to Price, in Albemarle, ii, 345; Bon Mots; B. Lambert, *History of London*, iv, 466, as cited by Bleackley, *Life of Wilkes*, 313, n. 2.

31. Told by Wilkes's lawyer W. Peter Fountain, who handled Wilkes's financial affairs, about "a gentleman," but one can hardly doubt the gentleman was Wilkes: Wilkes Papers, v, 12a.7E

32. Wilkes to Fountain, Wilkes Papers, v, 2. Letters to His Daughter, ii, 42–43.

33. I quote the two poems from Wilkes's letter to Suard, 19 September [1777], in the collection of Gerald Goldberg. The second, on Polly's birthday, appeared in *New Foundling Hospital for Wit*, i, 290. The letters: Almon, *Correspondence*, iv, 267–68; Letters to His Daughter, ii, 57, 89.

34. The National Portrait Gallery identification number is 6133. See Mary Webster, "'Horridly Like.'" The picture can be roughly dated from Walpole's remarks on it, *Correspondence*, xxxiii, 138.

35. Almon, *Correspondence*, v, 118–22.

36. Add Mss 30,872, ff. 116–17; Letters to His Daughter, ii, 29.

37. Almon, *Correspondence*, v, 118–22; Add Mss 30,872, ff. 116–17, 220–21; Letters to His Daughter, ii, 29.

38. *Boswell in Extremes, 1776–1778*, 226. I quote the poem from Add Mss 30,880B, f. 73. Green, in *Love Letters*, 23, and *Visits to Bath*, 44, records two other longish poems written by Wilkes for Maria Stafford, dated 21 May and 8 July 1778.

39. Letters to His Daughter, 11, 80.

40. Amelia Arnold was born on 29 May 1753: Almon, *Correspondence*, v, 140.

41. F. 61v. Wilkes's correspondence with Mrs. Stafford cited thus refers to Add Mss 30,880B, ff. 61–114. The correspondence was published (with questionable accuracy) by Emanuel Green, *Some Bath Love Letters of John Wilkes, Esq*. I did not find a copy of Green's little book until I had drafted the story from notes I had taken on the BL manuscripts. Consequently, I sometimes refer to the Add Mss and sometimes to Green.

42. Ff. 61–62.

43. F. 64.

44. F. 65; Green, Letters, 15.

45. Ff. 64–65; Green, *Love Letters*, 15; Ehrenpreis, *Swift*, iii, 405 and n. 1.

46. F. 66v.

47. Ff. 68, 71–72, Green, *Love Letters*, 9, 71–72. Sterne's sentimentalism provided a stone in the foundations of more than one political figure of the day. For his influence upon Jefferson and Burke, see Paul Giles, *Transatlantic Insurrections,* chap. 4.

48. Ff. 75, 79.

49. Ff. 83–90.

50. Ff. 83v–84; Green, *Love Letters*, 15, 29, 31. Maria's illness: Ff. 78, 79v, 84, 85. See also Green, *Love Letters*, 19, "My owner [is] much more likely to live than myself."

51. 18 January 1779, f. 93; Green, *Love Letters*, 45–46.

52. Harriet's birth date given by Almon, *Correspondence*, v, 143.

53. Ff. 97v–98; Letters to His Daughter, ii, 176–77, 222–23, and passim; Green, *Love Letters*, 49–53.

54. Green, *Letters*, 26–27.

55. Irving Brant, *Fourth President*, pp. 33–34; Rudé, *London*, 163; Redlich and Hirst, *Local Government*, 66.

56. Commons Journals, xxxv, 673; Redlich and Hirst, *Local Government*, 78; Walpole, *Correspondence*, xxiv, 187.

57. The version of the speech reported in the newspapers can be found in *Parliamentary Register*, ii, 432–41; Wilkes's final edition, in *Speeches*, 54–71.

58. Redlich and Hirst, *Local Government*, 67 ff.; Christie, *Wilkes, Wyville, and Reform*, 63–67; Bleackley, *Life of Wilkes*, 305–06; Holdsworth, *English Law*, x, 102; Veitch, *Parliamentary Reform*, 144–45.

Chapter 14. Chamberlain

1. Treloar, *Wilkes and the City*, 199–205; Thomas, *Wilkes*, 189–90.

2. As quoted by Thomas, *Wilkes*, 189.

3. *Lady's Magazine*, x (1779), 614–15; Treloar, *Wilkes and the City*, 200–01.

4. *Gentleman's Magazine*, xlix (1779), 610; Almon, *Correspondence*, iv, 200; Treloar, *Wilkes and the City*, 204; Wilkes Papers, iv, 1.

5. Letters to His Daughter, iii, 74–75; iv, 83.

6. Masters, *Chamberlain*, 61–67; Treloar, *Wilkes and the City*, 219–20; Almon, *Correspondence*, v, 37, 86.

7. Wilkes, *Complete Collection*, 230.

8. Add Mss 30,872, ff. 190, 224; Masters, *Chamberlain*, 62–63.

9. Walpole to Mann, 18 February 1778, Walpole, *Correspondence*, xxiv, 354.

10. Almon, *Anecdotes of Pitt*, 514–15; Tuchman, *March of Folly*, 220–21.

11. Wilkes, *Speeches*, 192–212, 267–96; *Parliamentary Register*, viii, 5–14; ix, 216–36.

12. Morton and Spinelli, *Local Government*, 264.

13. *Speeches*, 296–315; *Parliamentary Register*, xi, 18–30.

14. Sherston Baker genealogy appended to Bleackley; Asia Booth Clarke, *Elder and Younger Booth*, 1–8, including the letters from Richard Booth and John Brevitt to Wilkes, and from John Booth, silversmith, to Wilkes, the originals of which are at Add Mss 30,872, ff. 120–21, 126–27.

15. Charles Wilkes, *Autobiography*.

16. Thomas, *Wilkes*, 185, citing Malmesbury Mss memo of 24 March 1779.

17. Boswell, *Life*, iii, 224; *Boswell: The Ominous Years*, 344–45; *Boswell in Extremes*, 233.

18. Bleackley, *Life of Wilkes*, 68; Letters to His Daughter, ii, 19. On Methodism, see Lewis P. Curtis, *Anglican Moods*, 57–58 and passim.

19. Brant, *The Fourth President*, 34–40, 126 ff.

20. Thomas, *Wilkes*, 186–87.

21. Wilkes, *Speeches*, 316–43; *Parliamentary Register*, xii, 309–18. Add Mss 30,872, f. 100; Almon, *Correspondence*, v, 251.

22. Petition of Scottish Catholics, Commons Journals, xxxvii, 263; *London Evening Post*, 23 March 1779, as cited by Sainsbury, *Disaffected Patriots*, 156.

23. Christopher Hibbert, *King Mob*.

24. Angelo, *Reminiscences*, 112–13; Johnson, *Letters*, no. 677; *Gentleman's Magazine*, l (1780), 312–16; Commons Journals, xxxvii, 903; Thomas, *Wilkes*, 187; Treloar, *Wilkes and the City*, 207; Add Mss 30,866, ff. 240–48.

25. Angelo, *Reminiscences*, i, 114; Johnson, *Letters*, no. 679.

26. Treloar, *Wilkes and the City*, 206–07; Letters to his Daughter, ii, 212–14; Johnson, *Letters*, nos. 677–79.

27. Wraxall, *Memoirs*, ii, 50; Thomas, *Wilkes*, 188; Dr. Wilson to Wilkes, Add Mss 30,872, f. 196.

28. Commons Journals, xxxvii, 906; Thomas, *Wilkes*, 188–89; Rudé, *The Crowd in History*, 57–65.

29. Ditchfield, "The Subscription Issue"; Sainsbury, *Disaffected Patriots*, 158–59; *London Evening Post*, 24 June 1780.

30. Angelo, *Reminiscences*, 42.

31. Letters to His Daughter, ii, 100; Wilkes Papers, v, 14.

32. Add Mss 30,879, ff. 200, 203; Diary, where the meeting with Hollis is dated as 17 August. Many letters to Polly from this period can be found in Almon, iv, *Correspondence*, 102–37.

33. Teasing Boswell: Jerningham Papers, i, 285, as quoted by Bleackley, *Life of Wilkes*, 324. Mansfield on Wilkes: Nichols, *Anecdotes*, ix, 479, n.; Letters to His Daughter, i, 163.

34. I am uncertain of the date of Temple's death. The *Gentleman's Magazine*, xlix (1779), 471, reported him dead on 11 September 1779 a few days after the carriage accident in which he fractured his skull; the *London Magazine*, xlviii (1779), 425, gave his death as 12 September. The DNB article on him, viii, 570–72, followed the *London Magazine*. The editor of the Grenville Papers (vol i., p. vii) followed the *Gentleman's Magazine*. But in the Wilkes Papers at the BL is the letter from Temple to Wilkes here cited, which is dated 15 December 1779 (Add Mss 30,872, f. 157). The date cannot be doubted because Temple congratulates Wilkes on the chamberlainship to which he had been elected on 22 November 1779 and sworn into on 2 December. I have compared the handwriting of this letter to others by Temple and am convinced it is his. I conclude that the reports of Temple's death in the papers were based upon mistaken information probably obtained from servants soon after the carriage accident when he was not expected to live. He did live and recovered enough to make a trip to Bath two or three months later. Stross, *Magazines of Mortality*, 105–12 and passim, has demonstrated that eighteenth-century newspaper information about deaths was often incorrect.

35. Lady Chatham to Lord Temple, *Grenville Papers*, iv, 574–76.

36. Letters to His Daughter, ii, 218–19; Add Mss 30,866, f. 64; Almon, *Correspondence*, iv, 259–60.

37. Letters to His Daughter, ii, 161–62; Polly's reply, Almon, *Correspondence*, iv, 288–91.

38. Wilkes's work on the Autobiography in 1769 is established by the letter to Heaton in Wilkes Papers, ii, 15–15a. Work on it in 1780 is established in Letters to His Daughter, ii, 200.

39. Add Mss 30,880A, ff. 1–34; Bleackley, *Life of Wilkes*, 355–56.

40. Add Mss 30,872, f. 76; Almon, *Correspondence*, v, 70–71; Letters to and from Wharton, Almon, *Correspondence*, iv, 328–35; marginal notes in Wilkes's copy of the Warburton edition of Pope's *Works*, 1751, at the BL, shelf number G12850–8.

41. *Speeches*, 140–49.

42. Boswell, *Life of Johnson*, iii, 408.

43. Ibid., iv, 101–07.

44. Johnson, *Letters*, no. 840; Boswell, *Life of Johnson*, iv, 224, n. 2; Boswell, *Correspondence Relating to the Making of the "Life,"* 252.

45. Wraxall, *Memoirs*, i, 265; Commons Journals, xxxviii, 91; Wilkes, *Speeches*, 357–69, 368, n.

46. Commons Journals, xxxviii, 861–66.

47. Keir, *Constitutional History*, 299; Sainsbury, *Disaffected Patriots*, 161.

48. Wilkes, *Speeches*, 373–77; Commons Journals, xxxviii, 977.

49. Commons Journals, xxxviii, 82, 881. To be sure, smaller houses were not infrequent. Only eighty-seven members appeared to vote on a bill to tax fire insurance. But most houses were larger.

50. Letters to His Daughter, ii, 5–6.

51. *Town and Country Magazine*, iv (1772), 220–21, as cited by Rea, *English Press*, 224.

52. Knollenberg, *Origin of the Revolution,* 67–69; Brant, *Fourth President*, i, 39; Jeffrey Rosen, "Is Nothing Private?"

53. Charles Warren, *Making of the Constitution*, 420–21, n.; Brant, *Fourth President*, 182–83; Kinoy, *Rights on Trial*, 309–16.

54. *Boswell, Laird of Auchinleck*, 355.

Epilogue

1. Letters to His Daughter, iii, 10–11, 24, 67, 84, 159, and passim; Almon, *Correspondence*, v, 5; Angelo, *Reminiscences*, 46–47.

2. Almon, *Correspondence*, v, 87; *Gentleman's Magazine*, lviii (1789), 559; Masters, *Chamberlain*, 64.

3. Boswell, *The English Experiment*, 36–37.

4. *Great Biographer*, 124. See also Boswell, *English Experiment*, 201–02.

5. *The Applause of the Jury*, 336.

6. Add Mss 30,874, f. 53. See the letters to her father in Almon, *Correspondence*, v, 140–45. Some of my quotations of the letters of Wilkes and Harriet are taken from Trench, *Portrait of a Patriot*, 365–68. Trench had access to a collection of letters that I have not been able to see.

7. Letters to His Daughter, iv, 140.

8. Boswell, *The English Experiment*, 33–34. Walpole's remark, cf. Romans, 5:12. The remark is recorded by Lady Louisa Stuart, *Letters*, in 1820, 87. Walpole enjoyed his witticism and used it another time when commenting upon Zoffany's painting of Wilkes and Polly: *Correspondence*, xxxiii, 138 and n. 22.

9. *Correspondence*, vi, 203–06.

10. Letters to His Daughter, iv, 107–08; Blunt and Climinson, *Mrs. Montagu*, ii, 114–15, 313.

11. Wilkes's placing of Jack Smith at Angelo's, letter of Wilkes to Angelo, in the possession of Gerald M. Goldberg; Add Mss 30,872, ff. 181; Almon, *Correspondence*, v, 123–39.

12. Add Mss 30,874, ff. 30, 34, 51, 112, 118, 126, 128, 131, 153; 30,876, ff. 38.

13. Will of Sarah Wilkes, Add Mss 30,874, f. 33; 30,894, f. 20; Almon, *Correspondence*, v, 147–55; Letters to His Daughter, iii, 93. There are numerous letters from Heaton Wilkes to his brother in the Wilkes Papers.

14. Kittredge, *The Old Farmer and His Almanac*, 3–10. I take the name of the new

husband from articles at the Buckinghamshire County Record Office, D/DU Bundle 3, no. 145. I take the age difference from Kittredge. The Sherston-Wilkes pedigree appended to Bleackley, *Life of Wilkes*, describes him as "Uncle of Lord Francis Jeffrey."

15. Lord Chancellor Eldon, as reported in Twiss, *Life of Eldon*, ii, 354–57, wrote about the king: "The confidence and humor of the man [Wilkes] made him forget at the moment his impudence." There is something wrong with Eldon's account. Glynn died in 1778, when it is highly unlikely that Wilkes would have been to a levée, yet the story makes it seem that the king was making an inquiry about someone alive. Perhaps the king did not know of Glynn's death. Perhaps Eldon misremembered the king's inquiry, which might well have been about Glynn's and Wilkes's past relationship.

16. Bon Mots. On the king's meeting with Wilkes, *Morning Herald*, 27 February and 15 March 1783, as cited by Thomas, *Wilkes*, 193, and n. 78.

17. *Speeches*, 377–94; Commons Journals, xxxix, 831.

18. Letters to His Daughter, iii, 11–12; Brewer, "Wilkites and the Law."

19. Prior, *Malone*, 363.

20. Wilkes's speech, Almon, *Correspondence*, iv, 180–90; Wraxall, *Memoirs*, v, 2–3; Letters to His Daughter, iii, 148.

21. Commons Journals, xlv, 314, 320; Thomas, *Wilkes*, 197; Horne to Wilkes, Add Mss 30,877, f. 98; *Gazetteer*, 29 June, as cited by Thomas, *Wilkes*, 198; Bon Mots.

22. One can trace Wilkes's growing horror of the Revolution in Letters to His Daughter. On 23 April 1790, he expressed pleasure with the initial stages of the Revolution, praising the revolutionaries for having instituted a jury system in their courts (iv, 18). On 11 July, he was shocked by the barbarities he had heard of (iv, 36). On 31 May 1792, he was aghast at the reports (iv, 120). By 27 July 1793, he was in despair of Liberty in France (iv, 153–54), and by 20 July 1795 was horrified at the murder of "the charming and excellent Duchess de Biron. The cup of iniquity of the bloody savages at Paris seems to run over" (iv, 163).

23. Almon, *Correspondence*, v, 156–59.

24. Angelo, *Reminiscences*, 46–47; *Morning Post*, 24 June 1793, as cited by Thomas, 199.

25. McCracken, "John Wilkes, Humanist"; Nichols, *Anecdotes*, ix, 468–69.

26. Letters to His Daughter, iv, 142. Almon, *Correspondence*, iv, 223–25. *Gentleman's Magazine*, lx (1790), 917, 1013; Treloar, *Wilkes and the City*, 215. The commonplace book, Add Mss 30,888.

27. Letters to His Daughter, iv, 242.

28. Twiss, *Life of Eldon*, ii, 354–57; another version in Bon Mots.

29. Brady, *Boswell*, 293, 481; Letters to His Daughter, i, 142; Boswell, *Boswelliana*, ii, 21, n. 4.

30. As quoted in Gold, "Wilkes and the Writings of Johnson."

31. The anecdotes, Thomas, *Wilkes*, 208, who cites Add Mss 32,566, f. 153, and 32,568, f. 24. The unidentified lover: Add Mss 30,880B, f. 17, dated in Wilkes's hand, 1 March 1786. Sally Barry, Bleackley, *Life of Wilkes*, 396–97. Mrs. Watson, Add Mss 30,880B, ff. 25–26. Fanny Perfect, Add Mss 30,876, ff. 4–5. Although no year appears in the dates of these letters, I place the affair in 1781: the second letter is dated Saturday, 13 October. October thirteenth fell on a Saturday in 1770 (which seems unlikely) and in 1781 (which seems likely).

32. Letters to His Daughter, iii, 59, 97, 125.

33. Letters to His Daughter, iii, 220–21, 300; iv, 1–2, 92–93, 104.

34. Reynolds, *Life and Times*, ii, 105. The columm cost £350: see Add Mss 30,874, f. 26.

35. *Gentleman's Magazine* (September 1794), pt. 2, pp. 779–80; Bleackley, *Life of Wilkes*, 379–82; Treloar, *Wilkes and the City*, 209–15.

36. Letters to His Daughter, iv, 22–23.

37. Letters to His Daughter, iii, i, 205.

38. Burke, *Correspondence*, iv, 206; the lottery office anecdote, Bleackley, *Life of Wilkes*, 396; Wilkes's appearance, *Annual Register*, 1797, pt. II, pp. 369–78.

39. Bon Mots.

40. Bleackley, *Life of Wilkes*, 400–01.

41. Almon, *Correspondence*, v, 88; Colby, *Mayfair*, 76–77; *Annual Register*, 1797, pt. II, p. 58; *Monthly Magazine*, reprinted in the *Annual Register*, ibid., 369–78; *Gentleman's Magazine*, lxvii (January–June 1797), 1077. The *Times* obituary, as quoted by Treloar, *Wilkes and the City*, 216.

42. The will at Buckinghamshire County Record Office, D/DU/5/144, a version of it published in the *Lady's Magazine*, xxix (1798), 93.

43. Treloar, *Wilkes and the City*, 221; Almon, *Correspondence*, v, 140; *Gentleman's Magazine*, lxxii, pt. 1 (January–June 1802), 466–68.

44. A copy of her will in Almon, *Correspondence*, v, 105–16. In the Buckinghamshire County Record Office are a number of papers indicating that the recipients of funds willed them must release any claims of debt: D/DU, Bundle 3, nos. 146–56.

45. DNB; David Alexander. At Cambridge University Library is a letter from Harriet Wilkes to her mother, mentioning her interest in a young William Rough, and an acrostic on Harriet in Rough's hand: Add. 8781/3, 2ii.1

46. Her descendant the late Colonel W. G. Sedgwick-Rough of Queenbury, Reed, Herts, informed me that he had visited her grave in the military cemetery in Georgetown, Guyana, and had taken the information about the child from the monument.

47. Wraxall, *Memoirs*, ii, 48–49.

Sources

Books and Articles Cited

Akenside, Alexander. *Poetical Works,* ed. Alexander Dyce. 1835.

Albemarle, George Thomas [Kepple], Earl of. *Memoirs of Rockingham and his Contemporaries,* 2 vols. London: Richard Bentley, 1852.

Aldington, Richard. *Four English Portraits, 1801–1851.* London: Evans, 1948.

Alexander, David. "William Rough," *Trinity Review,* Michaelmas, 1962, pp. 10–12.

Almon, John. *Anecdotes of the Life of the Right Honourable William Pitt,* 3 vols. 1793.

——. *Correspondence of the late John Wilkes . . . Memoirs of his Life,* 5 vols. 1805.

——, ed. *Biographical, Literary, and Political Anecdotes,* 3 vols. 1797.

——. *History of the late Minority.* 1765, third impression, 1766. The copy with Wilkes's marginal notes in the BL, shelf number G.13453.

——. *Memoirs.* 1790.

Angelo, Henry. *Reminiscences.* New York: B. Blom, 1969.

Armstrong, John. "A Day: An Epistle to John Wilkes of Aylesbury, Esq." *Miscellaneous Works in Prose and Verse.* Dublin, 1767.

Arnold, Walter. *The Life and Death of the Sublime Society of Beef Steaks.* London: Bradbury Evans, 1871.

Ashe, Geoffrey. *Do What You Will: A History of Anti-Morality.* London and New York: W. H. Allen, 1974.

Asylum for Fugitive Pieces, [ed. John Almon], printed for J. Debrett, 1785–98.

Basker, James G. "Scotticisms and the Problem of Cultural Identity in Eighteenth-Century Britain." *Eighteenth Century Life,* xv (February and May 1991), 81–95.

Battle of the Quills: or, Wilkes Attacked and Defended. 1768.

Baxter, Andrew. *Enquiry into the Nature of the Human Soul.* 1750

——. *Letter from Andrew Baxter,* [ed. Wilkes]. 1753.

Baylen, Joseph O., and Norbert J. Gossman, eds. *Biographical Dictionary of Modern British Radicals.* Sussex: Harvester Press; New Jersey: Humanities Press, 1979.

Beattie, J. M. *Crime and the Courts of England, 1660–1800.* Oxford: Clarendon, 1986.

Beatty, Joseph M. "The Battle of the Players and Poets, 1761–1766." *Modern Language Notes,* xxxiv, 1919.

Beckett, Ian. "Wilkes and the Militia 1759–1763." *The Army Quarterly and Defence Journal,* vol. 112 (April 1982).

Bedford, John, fourth duke of. *Correspondence,* iii, ed. Lord John Russell. London: Longman et al., 1846.

Bingley, William, ed. *North Briton.* 1769, BL shelf No.P.P.5640.b.

Bleackley, Horace. *Life of John Wilkes.* London and New York: John Lane; Toronto: Gundy, 1917.

Blunt, Reginald, and Emily Climenson, *Mrs. Montagu, "Queen of the Blues," Her Letters and Friendships from 1762 to 1800,* 2 vols. London: Constable, [1923].

Bono, Gabriel. "Lettres Inédites de Suard à Wilkes." *University of California Publications in Modern Philology,* no. 15 (1932), 161–280.

Boswell, James. *Boswell: The Great Biographer, 1789–1795,* ed. Marlies K. Danziger and Frank Brady. New York: McGraw-Hill, 1989.

——. *General Correspondence of James Boswell, 1766–1769, vol i,* ed. Richard C. Cole. Edinburgh: Edinburgh Univ. Press; New Haven: Yale Univ. Press, 1993.

——. *Boswell for the Defence, 1769–1774,* ed. William K. Wimsatt, Jr. and Frederick A. Pottle. New York: McGraw-Hill, 1959.

——. *Boswelliana: The Commonplace Book of James Boswell,* ed. Charles Rogers. London: Grampion Club, 1874.

——. *Boswell in Extremes, 1776–1778,* ed. Charles McC. Weis and Frederick A. Pottle. New York: McGraw-Hill, 1970.

——. *Boswell in Search of a Wife, 1766–1769,* ed. Frank Brady and Frederick A. Pottle. New York: McGraw-Hill, 1956.

——. *Boswell, Laird of Auchinleck, 1778–1782,* ed. Joseph W. Reed and Frederick A. Pottle. New York, Toronto, London: McGraw-Hill, 1977.

——. *Boswell on the Grand Tour: Italy, Corsica, and France, 1765–1766,* ed. Frank Brady and Frederick A. Pottle. New York: McGraw-Hill, 1955.

——. *Boswell's London Journal, 1762–1763,* ed. Frederick Pottle. New York: McGraw-Hill, 1950.

——. *Boswell: The Applause of the Jury, 1782–1785,* ed. Irma S. Lustig and Frederick A. Pottle. New York: McGraw-Hill, 1981.

——. *Boswell: The Ominous Years, 1774–1776,* ed. Frederick Pottle and Charles Ryskamp. New York: McGraw-Hill, 1963.

——. *Correspondence and Other Papers of James Boswell Relating to the Making of the "Life of Johnson,"* ed. Marshall Waingrow. New York: McGraw-Hill, nd.

——. *Correspondence of James Boswell and William Johnson Temple, 1756–1795, i, 1756–1777.* New Haven: Yale Univ. Press, 1997.

——. *Letters of James Boswell*, 2 vols with continuous pagination, ed. Chauncey Brewster Tinker. Oxford: Clarendon, 1924.

——. *Life of Johnson*, 6 vols., ed. George Birkbeck Hill, revised L. F. Powell. Oxford: Clarendon Press, 1934, 1971.

——. *The English Experiment: 1785–1789*, ed. Irma S. Lustig. New York: McGraw-Hill, 1986.

Boyce, Benjamin. *The Benevolent Man: A Life of Ralph Allen of Bath.* Cambridge: Harvard Univ. Press, 1967.

Bradley, James E. *Popular Politics and the American Revolution in England.* Macon, Georgia: Mercer Univ. Press, 1986.

Brady, Frank. *James Boswell: The Later Years, 1769–1795.* New York, Toronto, London: McGraw-Hill, 1984.

Brant, Irving. *The Fourth President: A Life of James Madison.* 1970.

Bredvold, Louis I. *Contributions of John Wilkes to the "Gazette Littéraire de l'Europe."* Univ. of Michigan Contributions in Modern Philology, no. 1, February, 1950.

Brewer, John. *Party Ideology and Popular Politics at the Accession of George III.* Cambridge: Cambridge Univ. Press, 1976.

——. *Sinews of Power: War, Money, and the English State, 1688–1783.* New York: Knopf, 1989.

——. "The Number 45: A Wilkite Political Symbol." In *England's Rise to Greatness, 1660–1763*, ed. Stephen B. Baxter, 349–80. Berkeley, Los Angeles, London: Univ. of California Press, 1983.

——. "The Wilkites and the Law, 1763–74: A Study of Radical Notions of Governance." In *An Ungovernable People: The English and Their Law in the Seventeenth and Eighteenth Centuries*, ed. John Brewer and John Styles, 128–71. New Brunswick: Rutgers Univ. Press, 1980.

Broadley, A. M. *Brother John Wilkes.* 1914. BL shelf no. 04782.g.11, 1914.

Brooke, John. *King George III.* New York: McGraw-Hill, 1972.

Brownlow, John. *Memoranda; or Chronicles of the Foundling Hospital.* London: Sampson Low, 1847.

Burke, Edmund. *Correspondence*, 10 vols, ed. Thomas W. Copeland et al. Cambridge: Cambridge Univ. Press; Chicago: Univ. of Chicago Press, 1958–78.

Burke, Thomas. *Streets of London.* New York: Scribner's; London: Batsford, 1940.

Cannon, John. *Parliamentary Reform, 1640–1832.* Cambridge: Cambridge Univ. Press, 1973.

——. *Samuel Johnson and the Politics of Hanoverian England.* Oxford: Clarendon, 1994.

Carlyle, Alexander. *Autobiography*, ed. J. H. Burton. Boston: Ticknor and Fields. 1861.

Cary, John. *Joseph Warren: Physician, Politician, Patriot.* Urbana: Univ. of Illinois Press, 1961.

Casanova. *Life and Memoirs*, trans. Arthur Machen, ed. George Dunning Gribble. New York: Da Capo, 1984.

Cash, Arthur H. "A Goldberg Variation." *Age of Johnson*, xiii, 239–54.

——. *Essay on Woman by John Wilkes and Thomas Potter: A Reconstruction of a Lost Book with a Historical Essay on the Writing, Printing, and Suppressing of This "Blasphemous and Obscene" Work.* New York: AMS Press, 2000.

——. *Laurence Sterne: The Early and Middle Years.* London: Methuen, 1975.

——. *Laurence Sterne: The Later Years.* London: Methuen, 1986.

——. "Sterne, Hall, Libertinism, and *A Sentimental Journey.*" *Age of Johnson,* xii, 291–327.

——. *Sterne's Comedy of Moral Sentiments: The Ethical Dimension of the "Journey."* Pittsburgh: Duquesne Univ. Press, 1966.

——. "Wilkes, Baxter, and D'Holbach at Leiden and Utrecht: An Answer to G. S. Rousseau." *Age of Johnson,* vii, 397–436.

Cavendish, Sir Henry, *Debates in the House of Commons,* 2 vols., ed. J. Wright. London: Longmans, 1841–43.

Celle, Alexander J. "The Doctrine of Legislative Privilege." *Suffolk University Law Review,* ii, 1 (Winter 1968), 1–43.

Chafee, Zechariah, Jr. *Free Speech in the United States.* Cambridge: Harvard Univ. Press, 1954.

Christie, Ian R. *Wilkes, Wyvill, and Reform.* London: Macmillan; New York: St. Martin's, 1962.

Churchill, Charles. *Poetical Works,* ed. Douglas Grant. Oxford: Clarendon, 1956.

Churchill, Charles. See Wilkes, *Correspondence.*

Clark, Anna. "The Chevalier d'Eon and Wilkes: Masculinity and Politics in the Eighteenth Century." *Eighteenth Century Studies,* xxxii, 1 (1998), 19–48.

Clarke, Asia Booth. *The Elder and the Younger Booth.* Boston: J. R. Osgood, 1882.

Clarke, George. "Lady with the Squint: An Examination of Revolutionary Iconography at Stowe." In *La Grecia Antica: Mito e Simbolo per L'Eta Della Grande Rivoluzione.* Milano: Guerini, 1991.

Clifford, James L. *Hester Lynch Piozzi (Mrs. Thrale).* Oxford: Clarendon, 1941, 1952.

——. *Young Sam Johnson.* New York: Oxford Univ. Press, 1961.

Cochrane, James Aikman. *Dr. Johnson's Printer: The Life of William Strahan.* Cambridge: Harvard Univ. Press, 1964.

Coke, Lady Mary. *Letters and Journals,* 4 vols. Edinburgh: D. Douglas, 1889–96.

Colby, Reginald, *Mayfair: A Town within London.* London: Country Life Ltd, 1966.

Cromwell, Thomas. *History and Description of the Parish of Clerkenwell.* London: Longman et al., 1828.

Crosby, Brass. *Memoirs of Brass Crosby, Esq.* London: n.p., 1829.

Cuddihy, William. "Wilkes Cases." *Encyclopedia of the American Constitution,* ed. Leonard W. Levy. New York and London: Macmillan, 2001.

Curtis, Lewis P. *Anglican Moods of the Eighteenth Century.* Hamden, Connecticut: Archon, 1966.

Darnton, Robert. "Sex for Thought." *New York Review of Books,* 22 December 1994, 65–74.

Dashwood, Francis. *The Dashwoods of West Wycombe.* London: Aurum, 1987.

Davis, Graham, and Penny Bonsall. *Bath: A New History.* Stratfordshire: Keele Univ. Press, 1996.

Davis, Richard W. *Political Change and Continuity, 1760–1885: A Buckinghamshire Study.* Newton Abbot: David and Charles, 1972

Debrett, J. *History, Debates, and Proceedings of Both Houses of Parliament . . . 1743–74,* 7 vols. London: printed for J. Debrett, 1792.

Dell, John. "A Political Agent at Work in Eighteenth-century Aylesbury." *Records of Buckinghamshire*, xxx, 117–22.

Ditchfield, G. M. "The Subscription Issue in British Parliamentary Politics, 1772–79." *Parliamentary History*, vii, pt. 1 (1988).

Dix, Robin. "The Pleasures of Speculation: Scholarly Methodology in Eighteenth-century Studies." *British Journal for Eighteenth-century Studies*, xxiii (Spring 2000), 85–103.

Duff, Stella. "The Case against the King: The *Virginia Gazettes* Indict George III." *William and Mary Quarterly*, ser. 3, vi (1949), 390.

Ehrenpreis, Irvin. *Swift: The Man, His Works, and the Age*, 3 vols. London: Methuen, 1983.

Evans, W. A. *Warburton and the Warburtonians*. Oxford: Oxford Univ. Press; London: Humphrey Milford, 1932.

Fabel, Robin. "The Patriotic Briton: Tobias Smollett and English Politics, 1756–1771." *Eighteenth Century Studies*, viii (1975), 100–14.

Farmer, Thomas. *The Plain Truth: Being a Genuine Narrative of the Methods made use of to Procure a Copy of the Essay on Woman*. 1763.

Fawcett, Trevor. *Bath Entertain'd: Amusements, Recreations, and Gambling at the 18th-Century Spa*. Bath: Rutton, 1998.

Fitzgerald, Percy. *Life and Times of John Wilkes, M.P.*, 2 vols. London: Ward and Downey, 1888.

Fowler, William M., Jr. *Baron of Beacon Hill: A Biography of John Hancock*. Boston: Houghton Mifflin, 1980.

Franklin, Benjamin. *Papers*, vol. 15, ed. William B. Willcox. New Haven and London: Yale Univ. Press, 1972.

Franklin, Benjamin. *Writings*, vol. 5, ed. A. H. Smyth. New York, 1907.

French, Allen. *General Gage's Informers*. New York: Greenwood, 1968.

Garrick, David. *Private Correspondence*, 2 vols. London: H. Colburn and R. Bentley, 1831–32.

George III. *Correspondence, 1760–1783*, 6 vols., ed. John Forteque. London: Macmillan, 1927.

———. *Letters from George III to Lord Bute, 1756–1766*, ed. Romney Sedgwick. London: Macmillan, 1939, as reissued Westport, Connecticut: Greenwood Press, 1981.

Gibbon, Edward. *Gibbon's Journal: to January 28th, 1763*, ed. D. M. Low. New York: W. W. Norton, 1929.

Giles, Paul. *Transatlantic Insurrections: British Culture and the Formation of American Literature, 1730–1860*. Philadelphia: Univ. of Pennsylvania Press, 2002.

Gipson, Lawrence Henry. *Triumphant Empire: The Rumbling of the Coming Storm, 1766–1770*, vol. xi of *British Empire before the American Revolution*. New York: Knopf, 1967.

Gold, Joel. " 'Buried Alive': Charlotte Forman in Grub Street." *Eighteenth-Century Life*, viii (October 1982), 28–45.

———. "John Wilkes and the Writings of 'Pensioner Johnson.' " *Studies in Burke and His Time*, xviii (1977), 85–98.

———. "The Unlikely Visitor: John Wilkes in the Highlands." *Notes and Queries*, February 1979, 41–44.

Grafton, Augustus Henry, third Duke of. *Autobiography,* ed. Sir William Anson, 1898.

Greene, Jack P. "Bridge to Revolution: The Wilkes Fund Controversy in South Carolina, 1769–1775." *Journal of Southern History,* xxix (1963), 19–52.

Green, Emanuel. *John Wilkes and His Visits to Bath.* Bath: Herald Office, 1905.

——. *Some Bath Love Letters of John Wilkes.* Bath, 1918.

Grego, George. *A History of Parliamentary Elections and Election Engineering in the Old Days.* 1886.

Grenville Papers: being the Correspondence of Richard Grenville Earl Temple, K. G., and the Right Hon: George Grenville, their Friends and Contemporaries, 4 vols., ed. William James Smith. London: John Murray, 1852–53. See John R. G. Tomlison's critique of this edition in the introduction to *Additional Grenville Papers, 1763–1765,* Manchester Univ. Press, 1962.

Haig, Robert L. *The Gazetteer, 1735–1797.* Carbondale: Southern Illinois Univ. Press, 1960.

Halsband, I. R. "The Poet of *The North Briton.*" *Philological Quarterly,* xviii (1938), 389–95.

Hamilton, Harlan. "Sterne's Sermon in Paris and Its Background." *Proceedings of the American Philosophical Society,* cxxviii (1984), 316–25.

Hanley, Hugh. *The Prebendal, Aylesbury: A History.* Aylesbury: Ginn and Co., 1986.

Harris, George. *Life of Lord Chancellor Hardwick,* 3 vols. London: E. Maxon, 1847.

Hart, V. E. Lloyd. *John Wilkes and the Foundling Hospital at Aylesbury, 1759–1768.* Aylesbury: HM+M Pulishers, 1979.

Harvey, O[scar] J[ewell]. *History of Wilkes-Barre.* Wilkes-Barre: Raeder, 1929.

Hibbert, Christopher. *King Mob: The Story of Lord George Gordon and the London Riots of 1780.* Cleveland and New York: World, 1958.

Hicks, Carola. *Improper Pursuits: The Scandalous Life of Lady Di Beauclerk.* London: Macmillan, 2001.

Hill, Bridget. *The Republican Virago: The Life and Times of Catharine Macaulay, Historian.* Oxford: Clarendon, 1992.

History of the Late Minority. See Almon, John.

Holdsworth, William. *History of English Law,* 17 vols. Methuen, 1903–72.

Hollis, Thomas. *Memoirs,* 2 vols. London, 1780.

Hope, John. *Letters on Certain Proceedings in Parliament during the Sessions of the Years 1769 and 1770.* 1772, the copy bound in "Tracts Related to Wilkes."

Hope, Valerie. *My Lord Mayor: Eight Hundred Years of London's Mayoralty.* London: Weidenfeld and Nicolson, 1989.

Horne, John. See Wilkes, *Controversial Letters.*

Hotten, J. C., ed. *Essay on Woman and Other Pieces.* 1871.

Howell, T. B. *State Trials,* 21 vols. 1816. All citations are to vol. 19.

Hume, David. *Enquiry Concerning the Principles of Morals.* In *Enquiries,* ed. L. A. Selby-Bigge, Oxford, 1902.

——. *Letters,* 2 vols. ed. J. Y. T. Greig. Oxford: Clarendon, 1932, 1969.

Hutcheson, Francis. *Inquiry into the Original of Our Ideas of Beauty and Virtue.* 1738.

In Error. "House of Lords between John Wilkes, Esquire, Plaintiff in Error, and Our Sovereign Lord the King, Defendant in Error." Legal document presenting the facts in the matter of Wilkes's complaint against Lord Chief Justice Mansfield. At Morris Library, Southern Illinois Univ., Carbondale.

Ingamells, John. *Dictionary of British and Irish Travelers in Italy, 1701–1800.* New Haven: Yale Univ. Press, 1997.

Jensen, Merrill. *The Founding of a Nation: A History of the American Revolution, 1763–1776.* New York: Oxford Univ. Press, 1968.

Johnson, Samuel. *Johnson Miscellanies,* ed. George Birkbeck Hill. Oxford: Oxford Univ. Press, 1897.

——. *Letters of Samuel Johnson,* 3 vols., ed. R. W. Chapman. Oxford: Clarendon, 1952.

——. *Present State of Affairs.* In *Political Writings,* ed. Donald J. Greene. New Haven: Yale Univ. Press, 1977, Vol. x of the Yale Edition of the *Works of Samuel Johnson.*

——. *Taxation No Tyranny.* In *Political Writings,* ed. Donald Greene. New Haven: Yale Univ. Press, 1977, Vol. x of the Yale Edition of the *Works of Samuel Johnson.*

Jones, Louis Clark. *Clubs of the Georgian Rakes,* Columbia University Studies in English and Comparative Literature, no. 157. New York: Columbia Univ. Press, 1942.

Junius. *Letters of Junius,* ed. John Cannon. Oxford: Clarendon, 1978.

Kates, Gary. *Monsieur d'Eon Is a Woman: A Tale of Political Intrigue and Sexual Masquerade.* New York: Basic Books, 1995.

Keane, John. *Tom Paine: A Political Life.* London: Bloomsbury, 1995, 1996.

Keir, David Lindsay. *Constitutional History of Modern Britain Since 1485,* 7th ed. London: Adam and Charles Black, 1964.

Kemp, Betty. *Sir Francis Dashwood: An Eighteenth-century Independent.* London: Macmillan; New York: St. Martin's, 1967.

Kidgell, John. *Genuine and Succinct Narrative of a Scandalous, Obscene, and Exceedingly Profane Libel, Entitled, An Essay on Woman.* 1763.

Kinoy, Arthur. *Rights on Trial: The Odyssey of a People's Lawyer.* Cambridge: Harvard Univ. Press, 1983.

Kittredge, George Lyman. *The Old Farmer and His Almanac.* Boston: W. Ware; Cambridge: Harvard Univ. Press, 1904, 1920.

Knapp, Lewis Mansfield. *Tobias Smollett: Doctor of Men and Manners.* Princeton: Princeton Univ. Press, 1949.

——. "Dr. John Armstrong, Littérateur, and Associate of Smollett, Thomson, Wilkes, and Other Celebrities." *PMLA,* lix (1944), 1019–58.

——. "Elizabeth Smollett, Daughter of Tobias Smollett." *Review of English Studies,* viii (1932), 312–15.

Knollenberg, Bernhard. *The Origin of the American Revolultion: 1759–1766.* New York: Macmillan, 1960.

Kors, Alan Charles. *D'Holbach's Coterie: An Enlightenment in Paris.* Princeton: Princeton Univ. Press, 1976.

Langley, Thomas. *History and Antiquities of the Hundred of Desborough.* 1797.

Larsen, Lyle. "Dr. Johnson's Friend, The Elegant Topham Beauclerk." *Age of Johnson,* xiv, 221–37.

Lee, Richard Henry. *Life of Arthur Lee, LLD.,* 2 vols. Boston: Well and Lilly, 1829, 1969.

Lee, William. *Letters, 1766–1783,* 3 vols., ed. Worthington Chauncy Ford. New York: Burt Franklin, 1891, 1968.

Leibert, Herman W. *The Bear and the Phoenix: John Wilkes' Letter on Johnson's "Dictionary,"* 1978.

Leslie, Charles Robert, and Tom Taylor. *Life and Times of Sir Joshua Reynolds,* 2 vols. London: J. Murray, 1865.

Lettsom, John Coakley. *Memorials,* 2 vols. 1817.

Life and Memoirs of Casanova, trans. Arthur Machen, ed. George Dunning Cribble, 1929 (reissued, Da Capo), 1984.

Linebaugh, Peter. *London Hanged: Crime and Civil Society in the Eighteenth Century,* 2nd ed. London and New York: Verso, 2003.

Lugt, Fritz. *Repertoire des Catalogues de Ventes Publiques,* 4 vols. LaHaye: Nijhoff, 1938–87.

Maier, Pauline. *From Resistance to Revolution: Colonial Radicals and the Development of American Opposition to Britain, 1765–1776.* New York: Knopf, 1974.

Masters, Betty R. *Chamberlain of the City of London, 1237–1987.* London: Corporation of the City of London, 1988.

May, Thomas Erskine. *Constitutional History of England . . . 1760–1860,* 3 vols., 6th ed. 1878.

McCracken, George. "John Wilkes, Humanist." *Philological Quarterly,* xi (1932), 109–34.

[Meredith, Sir William]. *The Question Stated, whether the Freeholders of Middlesex Lost their Right by Voting for Mr. Wilkes* [1768].

Morton, Brian N., and Donald C. Spinelli. *Beaumarchais and the American Revolution.* Lanham, Boulder, New York, Oxford: Lexington Books, 2003.

Mugglestone, L. C. "Samuel Johnson and the Use of /h/." *Notes and Queries,* 234 (1989), 431–33.

Murdoch, Alexander. "Lord Bute, James Stuart Mackenzie and the Government of Scotland." In *Lord Bute: Essays in Re-interpretation,* ed. Karl W. Schweizer. Leicester Univ. Press, 1988.

Namier, Sir Lewis, and John Brooke. *House of Commons, 1754–1790,* 3 vols. London: Her Majesty's Stationery Office, 1964, reissued Secker and Warburg, 1985.

New Foundling Hospital for Wit, Being a Collection of Fugitive Pieces in Prose and verse, 6 vols. 1786.

Nichols, John, ed. *Illustrations of the Literary History of the Eighteenth Century,* 8 vols. 1817–58.

——. *Literary Anecdotes of the Eighteenth Century,* 9 vols. 1812–15.

Nichols, R. H., and F. A. Wray. *History of the Foundling Hospital.* Oxford and London, 1935.

Nobbe, George. *The North Briton: A Study in Political Propaganda.* New York: Columbia Univ, Press, 1939; reissued AMS Press, 1966.

North Briton. See Wilkes, *North Briton.*

Observations upon the Authority, Manner and Circumstances of the Apprehension and Confinement of Mr. Wilkes, [by John Glynn?] printed for John Williams, 1763.

Pain, Nesta. *George III at Home.* London: Eyre Methuen, 1975.

Paulson, Ronald. *William Hogarth: His Life, Art, and Times,* 2 vols. New Haven and London: Yale Univ. Press, 1971.

Perrault, Agnes[?], *Nocturnal Revels.* 1779.

Peters, Marie. "History and Political Propaganda in Mid-Eighteenth-Century England: The Case of the Essay Papers." *Eighteenth-Century Life* xi (February 1987), 66–79.

Pinks, William J., and Edward J. Wood, *History of Clerkenwell*. London: C. Herbert, 1881.

Pitt, William. *Correspondence of William Pitt, Earl of Chatham*, ed. by the executors of his son, John, Earl of Chatham, 4 vols. London: John Murray, 1838–40.

Plomer, H. R., et al. *Dictionary of the Printers and Booksellers*. Oxford: Bibliographical Society, Oxford Univ. Press, 1932 for 1930.

Plumb, J. H. *Sir Robert Walpole: The Making of a Statesman*. Boston: Houghton Mifflin, 1956.

Porritt, Edward. *Unreformed House of Commons before 1832*, 2 vols. 1998.

Postgate, Raymond. *That Devil Wilkes*. London: Dobson, 1956.

Pottle, Frederick, *James Boswell: The Earlier Years, 1740–1769*. New York: McGraw-Hill, 1966.

Potts, Louis W. *Arthur Lee, Virtuous Revolutionary*. Baton Rouge and London: Louisiana State Univ. Press, 1981.

Prior, Sir James. *Life of Edmond Malone*. London: Smith Elder, 1860.

Rea, Robert R. *The English Press in Politics, 1760–1774*. Lincoln: Univ. of Nebraska Press, 1963.

Redlich, Josef, and Francis W. Hirst. *History of Local Government in England*, 2nd ed. New York: Kelley, 1970.

Reynolds, Frederick. *Life and Times of Frederick Reynolds, Written by Himself*, 2 vols., 2nd ed. London: H. Calburn, 1827.

Robbins, Caroline. "The Strenuous Whig, Thomas Hollis of Lincoln's Inn." *William and Mary Quarterly*, 3rd series, vii, 406–53.

Rogers, James E. Thorold. *Historical Gleanings*, 2 vols. London: Macmillan, 1870.

Rogers, N. A. M. *The Insatiable Earl: A Life of John Montagu, Fourth Earl of Sandwich, 1718–1792*. New York and London: Norton, 1993.

Rogers, Samuel. *Reminiscences and Table Talk*, ed. Alexander Dyce and William Sharp. London: R. B. Johnson, 1903.

Rosen, Jeffrey. "Is Nothing Private?" *New Yorker*, 1 June 1998, 36–41.

Rudé, George. *Crowd in History: A Study of Popular Disturbances in France and England, 1730–1849*. New York: Wiley, 1964.

——. *Hanoverian London, 1714–1808*. Berkeley and Los Angeles: Univ. of California Press, 1971.

——. *Wilkes and Liberty: A Social Study of 1763 to 1774*. Oxford: Clarendon, 1962.

Rush, Benjamin. *Autobiography*, ed. George W. Corner. Princeton: American Philosophical Society, 1948.

Sainsbury, John. "'Cool courage should always mark me': John Wilkes and Duelling." *Journal of the CHA 1996 Revue de La S. H. C.*, New Series, vol. 7, 19–33.

——. *Disaffected Patriots: London Supporters of Revolutionary America, 1769–1782*. Kingston and Montreal: McGill-Queen's Univ. Press, 1987.

——. "John Wilkes, Debt, and Patriotism." *Journal of British Studies*, xxxiv (April 1995), 165–95.

——. "Wilkes and Libertinism." *Studies in Eighteenth-Century Culture*, xxvi (1998), 151–74.

Sambrook, James. *The Eighteenth Century: The Intellectual and Cultural Context of English Literature, 1700–1789,* 2nd ed. London: Longman's 1993.

Sauter, Hermann, and Erick Loos, *Paul Thiry Baron D'Holbach, die Gesamte Erhaltene Korrespondenz.* Stuttgart: Franz Steiner, 1986.

Schecter, Barnet. *The Battle for New York: The City at the Heart of the American Revolution.* New York: Walker, 2002.

Schlesinger, Arthur M. *Prelude to Independence: The Newspaper War on Britain, 1764–1776.* New York: Knopf, 1958

Schweizer, Karl W., ed. *Lord Bute: Essays in Re-interpretation.* Leicester: Leicester Univ. Press, 1988.

———. "Lord Bute and the Press: The Origins of the Press Wars of 1762 Reconsidered." In *Lord Bute: Essays in Re-interpretation,* q. v., pp. 83–98.

Shaftesbury, Anthony, Earl of. *Characteristics of Men, Manners, Opinion, Times,* ed. John M. Robertson. London: G. Richards, 1900.

Simons, R. C., and Peter D. G. Thomas, eds. *Proceedings and Debates of the British Parliaments Respecting North America, 1754–1783,* 6 vols. White Plains, New York: Kraus International, 1982–86.

Smith, C. J. *Catalogue of Westminster Records.* 1900.

Smollett, Tobias. *Letters,* ed. Lewis M. Knapp. Oxford: Clarendon, 1970.

Spector, Robert D. *Political Controversy: A Study in Eighteenth-century Propaganda.* New York: Westport; London: Greenwood, 1992.

"State of Facts: Wilkes against the Earl of Halifax." Printed brief at the Public Record Office, TS.11/1027/4317. A MS of this document is to be found in the BL: Add MS 22,131, ff. 4–25.

Stephens, Alexander. *Memoirs of John Horne Tooke,* 2 vols. London: J. Johnson, 1813.

Sterne, Laurence. *Letters,* ed. Lewis Perry Curtis. Oxford: Clarendon, 1935/1965.

Stowe, John, and John Strype. *Survey of the Cities of London and Westminster,* 2 vols. [c. 1760].

Stross, Wendy Anne. "Magazines of Mortality: A Cultural History of the Obituary in Eighteenth-Century London." Ph. D. diss., University of Toronto, 2004.

Stuart, Louisa. *Letters of Lady Louisa Stuart to Miss Louisa Clinton,* ed. James A. Home. Edinburgh: D. Douglas, 1901.

Sutherland, Dame Lucy S. *The City of London and the Opposition to Government, 1768–1774.* Creighton Lecture in History, 1958. London: Athlone Press, 1959.

Taswell-Langmead, Thomas Pitt. *English Constitutional History.* Boston: Houghton Mifflin; London: Sweet and Maxwell, 1946.

Thomas, Peter D. G. *John Wilkes: A Friend to Liberty.* Oxford: Clarendon, 1996.

———. *Tea Party to Independence: The Third Phase of the American Revolution.* Oxford: Clarendon, 1991.

———. "John Wilkes and the Freedom of the Press (1771)." *Bulletin of the Institute of Historical Research,* xxxiii (1960), 86–98.

Thrale, Hester Lynch, Mrs. Piozzi. *Thraliana: The Diary of Mrs. Hester Lynch Thrale (Later Mrs. Piozzi), 1776–1809,* ed. Katharine C. Balderston, 2 vols. paginated as one. Oxford: Clarendon, 1942.

Tomlison, John R. G. *Additional Grenville Papers, 1763–1765.* Manchester: Manchester Univ. Press, 1962.

Topazio, Virgil W. *D'Holbach's Moral Philosophy: Its Background and Development.* Geneva: Institut et Musée Voltaire, 1956.

"Tracts Related to Wilkes." Bound collection of pamphlets at BL, shelf number T.11551.

Travelyan, Raleigh. *Sir Walter Raleigh.* London: Allen Lane, 2002.

Treloar, William Purdie. *Wilkes and the City.* London: John Murray, 1917.

Trench, Charles Chenevix. *Portrait of a Patriot: A Biography of John Wilkes.* Edinburgh and London: Blackwood and Sons, 1962.

Trevelyan, George Otto. *The American Revolution,* abridged ed. by Richard B. Morris. New York: David McKay, 1964.

Trumbach, Randolph. *Sex and the Gender Revolution,* vol. i of *Heterosexuality and the Third Gender in Enlightenment London.* Chicago: Univ. of Chicago Press, 1998.

Tuchman, Barbara W. *The March of Folly from Troy to Vietnam.* New York: Knopf, 1984.

Twiss, Horace. *Public and Private Life of Lord Chancellor Eldon,* 3 vols. 1844.

Valentine, Alan. *Lord North.* Norman: Univ. of Oklahoma Press, 1967.

Veitch, George Stead. *Genesis of Parliamentary Reform.* London: Constable, 1913.

Viney, Elliott, and Pamela Nightingale. *Old Aylesbury.* Luton: White Crescent, 1976.

Walpole, Horace. *Journals of Visits to Country Seats, Etc.,* Walpole Society, xvi. Oxford: Oxford Univ. Press, 1928.

——. *Last Journals of Horace Walpole during the Reign of George III from 1771–1783,* ed. Francis Steuart. London and New York: John Lane, 1910.

——. *Memoirs of the Reign of King George the Third,* 4 vols., ed. G. F. Russell Barker. London: Lawrence and Bullen; New York: Putnam's Sons, 1894.

——. Yale Edition of *Correspondence,* 48 vols., ed. W. S. Lewis et al. New Haven: Yale Univ. Press, 1937–83.

Warburton, William. *Selections from Unpublished Papers of the Right Reverend William Warburton, DD,* ed. Francis Kilvert, 1841.

Warren, Charles. *Making of the Constitution.* Boston: Little Brown, 1937.

Warren, Earl. "The decision in the Adam Clayton Powell case against the officers of the House of Representatives": 395 U.S. [1969], 486–574.

Watson, John Selby. *Life of William Warburton.* London: Longman Green, 1863.

Watson, J. Steven. *The Reign of George III, 1760–1815.* Oxford: Clarendon, 1960, 1964.

Webb, Philip Carteret. *Copies Taken from Records of the Court of King's Bench at Westminster,* 1763, at BL 518.K.7 (4), pp. 64–66.

Webster, Mary. " 'Horridly Like': Zoffany's Portrait of Wilkes." *Sotheby's Preview,* October/November 1990, pp. 18–19.

West, Shearer. "Wilkes's Squint: Synecdochic Physiognomy and Political Identity in Eighteenth-Century Print Culture." *Eighteenth-Century Studies,* xxxiii (Fall 1999), 65–84.

Wheatley, Henry B. *London Past and Present.* London: J. Murray; New York: Scribner and Welford, 1891.

Whitehead, Paul, *Poems and Miscellaneous Compositions,* ed. Edward Thompson. 1777.

Whitely, Peter. *Lord North: The Prime Minister Who Lost America.* Rio Grande, Ohio: Hambleton, 1996.

Wickwar, W. H. *Baron D'Holbach: A Prelude to the French Revolution*. London: Allen and Unwin, 1935.

Wiggin, Lewis M. *The Faction of Cousins: A Political Account of the Grenvilles, 1733–1763*. New Haven: Yale Univ. Press, 1958.

Wilding, Norman, and Philip Laundy. *Encyclopaedia of Parliament*. New York: St. Martin's, 1968.

Wilkes, Charles. *Autobiography of Rear Admiral Charles Wilkes, U. S. Navy, 1798–1877*, ed. William James Morgan et al. Department of Navy, History Division, 1978.

Wilkes, John. Autobiography. All references are to Wilkes's manuscript in Add Mss 30,865A. Published as *John Wilkes, Patriot, an Unfinished Autobiography* [ed. R. des Habits], 1888; reissued, Lion and Unicorn Press, 1955

——. *Complete Collection of the Genuine Papers, Letters, &c in the Case of John Wilkes, Esq.*, dated March 28, 1768, but published at Berlin (doubtful), 1769, "Avec Aprobation et Privilege." Another edition at Butler Library, Columbia University, which states on the title page, "á Paris. Chez J. W., rue du Colombier, Fauxburgh St. Germain. á l'Hotel de Saxe, 1767, Avec Aprobation et Privilege."

——. *Controversial Letters of John Wilkes, Esq., the Rev. John Horne, and their Principal Adherents*, [ed. John Wilkes]. Printed for J. Williams, 1771.

——. *Correspondence of John Wilkes and Charles Churchill*, ed. Edward H. Weatherly. New York: Columbia Univ. Press, 1954

——. *English Liberty*. 2 vols paginated as one, printed [by Dryden Leach] for T. Baldwin, 1769.

——. *Letters between the Duke of Grafton, Earls of Halifax, Egremont, Chatham, Temple, and Talbot . . . &c. &c. and John Wilkes, Esq.* No bookseller named, 1769.

——. *Letters from the Year 1774 to the Year 1796, of John Wilkes, Esq. Addrssed to His Daughter, the Late Miss Wilkes: with a Collection of His Miscellaneous Poems. To which is prefixed a Memoir of the Life of Mr. Wilkes.*, 4 vols., [ed. William Rough]. London, 1805.

——. *Letter to his Grace the Duke of Grafton.* 1767. As reprinted in Almon, *Correspondence*, iii, 181–218.

——. *Letter to the Right Honorable George Grenville.* London, 1769.

——. *Life and Writings of John Wilkes, Esq.* Birmingham: Printed for J. Sketchley and Co., 1769.

——. *North Briton, from No. I. to No. XLVI. inclusive. With useful and explanatory Notes, Not printed in any former Edition . . . Corrected and Revised by A Friend to Civil and Religious Liberty.* No date, no place, no bookseller; reprinted in facsimile by AMS Press, 1976

——. *Speech of the Lord Mayor upon the Motion on Wednesday the 22nd of February.* BL, shelf number 1850.c.10 [44].

——. *Speech of the Right Hon. John Wilkes, Esq. Lord Mayor . . . in the House of Commons*, a two penny pamphlet published by E. Johnson, 1775, BL shelf number 102.h.32.

——. *Speeches of Mr. Wilkes in the House of Commons.* 1786.

Wilkes's Jest Book, or the Merry Patriot, 1770.

Wilson, Arthur M. *Diderot*. Oxford: Oxford Univ. Press, 1972.

Wilson, Kathleen. "Empire, Trade, and Popular Politics in Mid-Hanoverian Britain: The Case of Admiral Vernon." *Past and Present,* cxxi (Nov. 1988), 74–107.

Wilson, Thomas. *Diary,* ed. C. S. L. Linnell. London: S. + C. K., 1964.

Wraxall, Nathaniel William. *Historical and Posthumous Memoirs,* 5 vols., ed. Henry Wheatley. London: Bickers and Son, 1884.

Yarborough, Minnie Clare. *John Horne Tooke.* New York: Columbia Univ. Press, 1926.

Yorke, Philip C. *Life and Correspondence of Philip Yorke, Earl of Hardwicke,* 3 vols. Cambridge: Cambridge Univ. Press, 1913.

Index

This is a selective index to people, events, and details that figure in the story of John Wilkes. Contemporary broadsides, essays, and books that appear in the story are indexed by author, if named in the text, otherwise by title. The index does not include newspaper stories, correspondents of Wilkes, or persons who told anecdotes about him or commented upon his behavior or his politics. It does not include scholars or source materials whether mentioned in the text or cited in the notes. Under "Wilkes, John" one can find a chronology of key events in his life and an index to certain themes in his story.

Wilkes, Mary (*continued*)
17, 19; declines to attend sick daughter, 44; receives Polly when W. is abroad, 180–81; gift to W upon election as lord mayor, 310; death, 375
Wilkes, Mary, sister of W, 7
Wilkes, Sarah, née Heaton, mother of W: family and character, 5–6; assists W upon return from exile, 201; braves mob to visit W in prison, 222; death, 379
Wilkes, Sarah, sister of W, 7, 21–22
Willes, Edward, brother of John, MP Aylesbury, later a royal judge, 23, 37; contests W in elections, 45–46, 45, 57–58; one of judges for W's trial at King's Bench, 214; colleague of W as judge at Old Bailey, 271
Willes, John, brother of Edward, MP for Aylesbury: friend of W, 23, 37; 45; contests W in election, 57–58
Willes, John, Sir, father of Edward and John, chief justice Court of Common Pleas, 23, 45
William Hughes, lawyer for Crown office, 171
Williams, John, printer and bookseller: propagandist for W, 123; assists W to rescue *North Briton* No. 46, 105; publisher of 2nd edition *North Briton*, 134; printer of 3rd edition, 178; pilloried, 178–79
Wilson, Rev. Dr. Thomas: career, 333; W's pastor, 54; contributes to Bill of Rights Society, 291; praises W for his help of the poor, 314; stormy love for Catharine Macaulay, 333–35; death, 386

Winckelmann, Johann Joachim, Abbé, antiquarian: entertains W in Rome, 183–84; presents antique urn to W, 184; bequeaths W collection of coins, 184
Windham, William, MP for Norwich: celebrates Boswell's admission to English bar, 376; one of "the gang," 385
Woodfall, Henry Samson, printer, owner, and editor *Public Advertiser*: propagandist for W, 123, 277; arrested for helping to free the press, 280
Wood, Robert: undersecretary to Lord Egremont, 109; seizes W's papers, 109; W's suit against, 122, 160; absolved of violating privilege, 170
Worsley, Rev. Mr. John, W's tutor, 8, 43
Wright, Thomas, printer, reprimanded on knees in House of Commons, 280

Yallowby, John, press carpenter, 127–28
Yates, Joseph, Sir, associate justice of King's Bench: pronounces sentence on W, 226–27
Yorke, Charles: attorney general, 101: enters information (indictment) against W then drops charges, 122; represents government in printers' cause, 132; rescues Webb from mob, 133; accepts appointment as Lord Chancellor but commits suicide, 264
Young, Thomas, of Boston Sons of Liberty, 232–34

Zenger, Peter, American printer, 171
Zoffany, John, painter, does portrait of W and Polly, 340–41, 372